'What [Farrell] shows is what so many liberals want to suppress: that just because a dictator is Right-wing does not mean that he is as bad as Hitler, and that no dictator so far, apart from Hitler, was as bad as Stalin, for whom many a liberal was an apologist. Farrell has written much the most plausible biography of Mussolini'
Frank Johnson, *Daily Telegraph*

'Farrell has a fine polemical point ... a nicely written skirmish'
Scotsman

'Here is a deviant and controversial biography that seeks to revise recent history. It pulls Mussolini out of Hitler's shadow, where he long languished as the Fuhrer's semi-comic sidekick, and sets him before us as by far the more interesting, original and gifted of the two dictators ... This interestingly dissenting book explains why he was so popular and why some, perhaps many, Italians still think of *Il Duce* with nostalgia' Peter Lewis, *Daily Mail*

'The author ... has Italianised himself in a way that is certainly helpful for his understanding of Italian points of view and general attitudes and reactions to events ... this book contains masses of interesting detail' John Jolliffe, *Catholic Herald*

'Nicholas Farrell has produced a fascinating biography of Mussolini which is bound to be controversial ... It is inevitable that Farrell will have the adjective "revisionist" attached to his name, although surely the alternative to "revisionist" history is plagiarism? ... Farrell's greatest contribution is to ground [Mussolini] in his context as a very Italian phenomenon ... The questions Mussolini was trying to answer are, Farrell makes clear, as pertinent now as they were then ... this mammoth but highly readable work'
John Charmley, *Spectator*

'Of course, each of Farrell's points will be debated, but the book offers a fresh perspective on an otherwise closed subject. Wonderful'
Good Book Guide

Nicholas Farrell read history at Cambridge University (Gonville and Caius College) and was for many years on the staff of the *Sunday Telegraph*. Since the summer of 1998 he has lived in the Apennine village of Predappio in the Romagna where Mussolini was born and is buried like a saint. He is a contributor to the *Spectator* and writes two weekly columns, *Fumo di Londra*, for *Libero*, and *Zuppa Inglese*, for *La Voce di Romagna*. His daughter, Caterina, was born in 2003.

THE LIBRARY
GUILDFORD COLLEGE
of Further and Higher Education

Mussolini

A NEW LIFE

Nicholas Farrell

PHOENIX

945.091

FAR

151737

A PHOENIX PAPERBACK

First published in Great Britain in 2003
by Weidenfeld & Nicolson
This paperback edition published in 2004
by Phoenix,
an imprint of Orion Books Ltd,
Orion House, 5 Upper St Martin's Lane,
London WC2H 9EA

Copyright © 2003 Nicholas Farrell

3 5 7 9 10 8 6 4

The right of Nicholas Farrell to be identified as the author of
this work has been asserted by him in accordance with the
Copyright, Designs and Patents Act 1988.

All rights reserved. No part of this publication may be
reproduced, stored in a retrieval system, or transmitted, in
any form or by any means, electronic, mechanical,
photocopying, recording or otherwise, without the prior
permission of the copyright owner.

A CIP catalogue record for this book
is available from the British Library.

ISBN 1 84212 123 5

Printed and bound in Great Britain by
Butler & Tanner Ltd, Frome and London

www.orionbooks.co.uk

To my father

CONTENTS

Contents

ACKNOWLEDGEMENTS

I should like to thank the following people for their help: Fabio Andriola, Patrick Bishop, Carla Camerani, Vittorio Celli, Giorgio Frassinetti, Natasha Garnett, Lorenzo Giovene, James Hale, John Hunt, Frank Johnson, Luke John Oxlade, Stuart Reid, John Sartini, Ion Trewin and Victoria Webb. N.F.

ILLUSTRATIONS

Mrs Mussolini, brandishing a shotgun, flanked by friends, as they stroll down the high street in Predappio, during the 1930s.[9]

Mussolini and clergymen doing the Roman Salute.[4]

Mussolini personally battles for wheat.[5]

Mussolini and Vittorio Emanuele III, 'the Little King', on military manoeuvres in the Abruzzi in 1938.[3]

Mussolini listens to Neville Chamberlain, British Prime Minister, at Munich on 30 September 1938.[10]

Hitler, wearing a yellow mackintosh, meets Mussolini for the first time in Venice in June 1934.[3]

Mussolini meets Hitler and Göring at Hitler's advance headquarters in the Ukraine in August 1941, not long after the German invasion of Russia.[3]

Mussolini with Francisco Franco, the Spanish dictator, and Serrano Suner, Spain's Foreign Minister, at Bordeghera on the Italian Riviera in February 1941.[3]

A propaganda newsreel reconstruction of the last successful cavalry charge by the 'Savoia' cavalry regiment near the River Don on 23 August 1942.[1]

Mussolini, his wife (veiled) and daughters Anna Maria (veiled) and Edda (unveiled), at the funeral of Mussolini's second child, Bruno.[1]

Taken in late April 1945 in the courtyard of the Milan Prefettura, this is believed to be the last picture taken of Mussolini before his death.[1]

Milan, 28 April 1945: Mussolini, his mistress Claretta Petacci, and other Fascist leaders, who include Starace and Bombacci the former Communist leader, hanging by their feet from the girders of the petrol station in Piazzale Loreto.[6]

The author and the publishers offer their thanks to the following for their kind permission to reproduce images:

1 Dominique Lormier, Bordeaux
2 Hulton Getty, London
3 AKG, London
4 Publifoto, Milan
5 Alinari, Florence
6 The Imperial War Museum, London
7 Franco Nanni, Predappio
8 Le Donne di Salò, Sperling & Kupfer, Milan
9 Giorgio Moschi, Predappio
10 Mary Evans Picture Library, London

MAPS
(by John Gilkes)

Page xxi   The village of Predappio in the Romagna where Mussolini was born. (inset) The scene of the capture and execution of Mussolini in April 1945.

Page xxii   The Austro-Italian front in the First World War, and the territorial gains made by Italy at the expense of Austria under the 1919 Treaty of Versailles.

Page xxiii   The front lines in the winter of 1943–44 and 1944–45.

FOREWORD

Mussolini was one of the most talked about figures of his age and most of that talk was favourable. Pope Pius XI called him the man 'sent by Providence' to save Italy, the American ambassador in Rome, Washburn Child, 'the greatest figure of his sphere and time' and Churchill 'the Roman genius'. But history is written by the victors and once Mussolini became a loser his place as one of the very bad men of history was guaranteed.

Those victors who believed in free will (western liberals) dismissed him as a grotesque buffoon and those who did not (Marxists), wherever they lived, as a mere tool of the bourgeoisie. Both were wrong because neither view explains how it was that Mussolini was able to get power and hold it, by and large bloodlessly, for two decades until his disastrous alliance with Hitler, or why for so long there was no resistance to him inside Italy and so much praise for him outside. Quite apart from anything else Mussolini began as a left-wing revolutionary and he could not stand the bourgeoisie. He was also a brilliant journalist, and you only have to read an article by him to realise that he was no buffoon.

We live in post-Communist times and there are signs that we are moving into post-democratic times as well. So perhaps the point has been reached at which it is possible to try to set the record straight.

When Mussolini abandoned Socialism to found Fascism as an alternative left-wing revolutionary movement he lived in a time of even greater uncertainty than our own. Fascism – the so-called Third Way – seemed to offer a viable alternative to both democracy and Communism. Mussolini did away with democracy but he did not, like most dictators, use mass murder to retain power. There was no need. He and Fascism had mass appeal because unlike democracy, especially Italian democracy, they got things done and unlike democracy they transformed politics into a form of religion – from an isolated act involving the ballot box to a daily act of religious faith.

Mussolini was as popular with women as men, if not more so. Behind every great man, it is said, there is a woman. Behind this great dictator, who had 169 lovers according to one estimate, stood a nation of women. They were attracted by his masculinity; they were even more attracted by his politics. Such was the magnetism of both Mussolini and Fascism that the only honest verdict must be that he ruled with the consent of the Italian people.

Mussolini's fatal error was his alliance with Hitler, whom he despised, but this alliance was far from inevitable because Fascism and National Socialism were like chalk and cheese as were the Italians and the Germans; Italy and Germany did not even share the same strategic aims. The Pact of Steel resulted more from Mussolini's fear of Hitler than from any wild desire for world domination let alone the extermination of the Jews.

Just as none of the victorious powers went to war with Germany to save the Jews neither did Mussolini go to war with them to exterminate the Jews. Indeed, once the Holocaust was under way he and his Fascists refused to deport Jews to the Nazi death camps thus saving thousands of Jewish lives – far more than Oscar Schindler.

It was only when he started losing battles that any resistance to him from within Italy worthy of the name began to form and despite what the post-war myth would have us believe this resistance was a largely irrelevant factor in the liberation of Italy. Once the liberation had happened, however, its Communist-dominated elements were responsible for the slaughter of 35,000 Italians without trial who joined the 15,000 Italians slaughtered by Tito's Communist partisans in north east Italy – slaughtered not because they were Fascist, but because they were Italian.

One of the aims of this book is to encourage the reader to consider whether Mussolini had better vision than Marx. For whereas Communist ideas appear terminally ill, the Fascist idea of the Third Way lives on and is championed by the standard bearers of the modern Left such as New Labour in Britain. This might surprise some, but to assume that Fascism was a phenomenon of the extreme right is to deny Mussolini's vision: he despised the bourgeois way of life – *la vita comoda* – above all else and remained at heart a Socialist to his dying day.

In Italy, barely a day goes by without discussion of Mussolini in the press or on the television. Since the re-election of the media tycoon Silvio Berlusconi as Prime Minister in 2001 such talk has increased as its focus has moved out of the realm of national soul-searching and into the political arena with the left shouting Fascism at Berlusconi's every move. But if dictatorship is to replace democracy in Italy, or anywhere else in the west, it will be something quite different from the government of Berlusconi, a mild Thatcherite, let alone Fascism – though it will undoubtedly contain a potent religious cocktail as a core attraction.

Most people, presumably, would agree that democracy, despite its faults, is the best political system on offer. But I have lived in Predappio for five years, where Mussolini was born, and is buried like a minor deity. And when I see a beautiful young woman doing the Roman salute in front of Mussolini's tomb I realise that she is yearning for something. And I know that whatever it is, it is not democracy.

This book, I hope, will above all make the reader wonder about the nature of good and evil – and how difficult it is to tell them apart. Mussolini was a great man who failed because, as he himself was only too aware, of the nature of dictatorship. For as he said just before his death, 'Have you ever seen a prudent, calculating dictator? They all become mad, they lose their equilibrium in the clouds, in quivering ambitions and obsessions. And it is actually that mad passion which brought them to where they are.' Mussolini was not a good man but nor was he half as bad a man as he has been portrayed. And he certainly was not an evil man.

Nicholas Farrell
Predappio, 2003

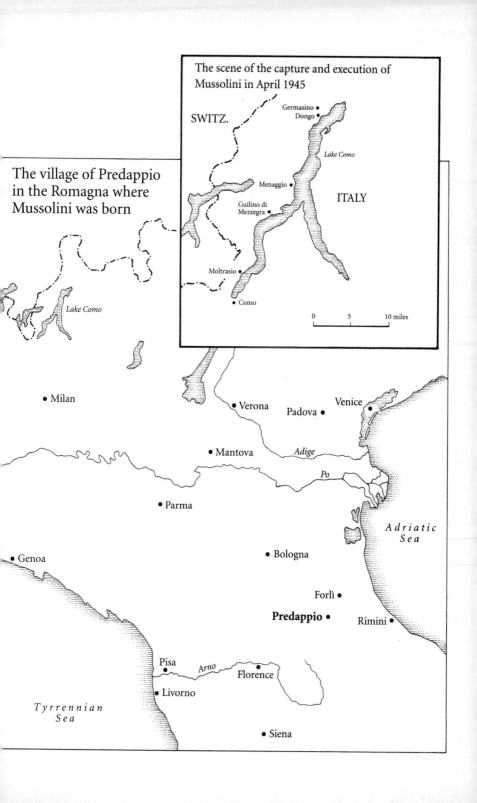

The scene of the capture and execution of
Mussolini in April 1945

SWITZ.

Germasino •
Dongo •

Lake Como

Menaggio •

Guilino di
Mezzegra •

ITALY

Moltrasio •

• Como

0   5   10 miles

The village of Predappio
in the Romagna where
Mussolini was born

Lake Como

• Milan

• Verona   Padova •   Venice •

• Mantova   *Adige*

Po

• Parma

• Genoa

*A d r i a t i c
S e a*

• Bologna

Forlì •

Predappio •   Rimini •

Pisa
•   *Arno*   Florence •

• Livorno

*T y r r e n n i a n
S e a*

• Siena

The Austro–Italian front in the First World War and the territorial gains made by Italy at the expense of Austria under the 1919 Treaty of Versailles

The front lines in the winter of 1943-44 (The Gustav Line) and 1944-45 (The Gothic Line)

1

THE LAND OF THE DUCE

Each day, Luigi Pompignoli and Alfredo Ferrini take up opposing positions in the car park at the cemetery just outside Predappio where Benito Mussolini is buried like a saint in the Mussolini family crypt. The two old men sell fascist souvenirs and are bitter rivals, and the car park is their battlefield were they have been known to attack each other with wine bottles, which once contained the local Sangiovese red.

The cemetery antics of Pompignoli and Ferrini are not the image of Predappio which the post-Communist councillors who control Predappio wish to project. 'We want to be normal', they say. But Predappio can never be normal because it is where Benito Mussolini was born on Sunday, 29 July 1883 just after lunch. Ominously, the boy did not speak for three years.[1]

There are, it is true, three Mussolinis (distant relations) in the local telephone book, many old men called Benito, and the shaved head is once again in vogue. There are also black eyes like Mussolini's everywhere. He was famous for his black blow-torch eyes.

Predappio, in the Romagna, thirty-five miles south-east of Bologna and twenty miles west of Rimini, looks normal enough. It sits in a narrow valley, through which flows a thin river, the Rabbi, a series of green pools. Hemmed in on either side by the jagged foothills of the Apennine mountains, it is a small, sleepy place with a population of about 6000 where a significant event is the appearance of a nun in white, a summer storm, or a coachload of Fascists. Out of the mountainous earth, rich in sulphur, calcium and clay, grow woods in which there are wild boar, red squirrels, green woodpeckers, white and black truffles, roe deer, porcupines and pheasants; and in between the woods, on the steep slopes, small wheat fields and vineyards that produce the very small, bitter-sweet, black Sangiovese grape. Still, local people who are superstitious will not bottle their Sangiovese when there is wind or a full moon because inevitably, they explain, it will go sour. The Romagnol Apennines are one of the few places in western Europe where wild wolves live. There is also a vicious giant wasp, with a murderous sting, known in dialect as a *bombo*. The big hum of its wings is like that of a high-voltage electricity cable.

The inhabitants of the Romagna, for centuries a Papal state until Italian reunification in 1861, especially the men, are deeply superstitious but they have always had a reputation for a scornful attitude to the Catholic Church, if not God Himself. In accordance with that tradition, a local pasta dish is called *'strozzapreti'* ('priest-strangler') and one of the most famous Romagnoli is *Il Passatore*, a nineteenth-century brigand who died in a shoot-out with papal gendarmes in 1851. The head of this Robin Hood of the Romagna appears on the bottles of Sangiovese like a badge of honour.

Mussolini is the cause of the trouble between Pompignoli and Ferrini at the cemetery and much other trouble besides. But in the case of the old men it is not a question of politics. It is a question of money. They own the two biggest shops in Predappio which sell Mussolini memorabilia. Mussolini, unlike Hitler, is in big demand. According to the council, 50,000 tourists of Fascism visit his tomb each year – 150,000 say the souvenir shop owners – which makes it more visited, they say, than even the tomb of Dante in nearby Ravenna.

At the cemetery where Pompignoli and Ferrini hover, Mussolini's stone tomb lies as if in state in the crypt the Fascists built during the years of the regime for the Mussolini family. On top of the tomb is a large marble bust of his head and behind it on the wall several glass cases containing the black riding boots he was executed in, his black shirt – and a brown flask. The flask contains a piece of his brain. The Americans ordered the Italian pathologists who did the autopsy on Mussolini to remove and hand over a piece of his brain so that American scientists could study it in an attempt to unravel the mysteries of the dictator and his Fascism. It was not until 1957 – twelve years after his death – that the Italian government handed over the dictator's remains to his widow Rachele for burial in the family crypt. And it was not until 1965 that the Americans sent the piece of brain back to her – none the wiser.[2]

In front of the stone tomb is a visitors' book on a lectern. The messages are of the kind reserved for the greatest of heroes. 'Fascism is the only medicine for the ills of Italy.' 'Communists – Cowards, Bastards, Children of Whores!' And so on – the book fills up so rapidly it has to be changed once a month. Elsewhere in the crypt are the stone tombs of Mussolini's immediate family. There are candles and flowers in permanent abundance. The air is thick with the sugary smell of candle wax and white lilies. On important days in the year, the anniversaries of Mussolini's birth and death, for example, or the March on Rome, special masses are held in the cemetery church. These memorial masses attract thousands of Fascists, young and old, many wearing black shirts, who, after the mass file down into the crypt, where they do a Roman salute in front of Mussolini's tomb and deliver the Fascist greeting: *'A Noi!'* ('To Us!').

Elsewhere dotted about the Romagna, for example at Forlì, the provincial capital ten miles away, are the graves of Allied soldiers – the young men who came to fight the Duce in the Second World War and the Germans who had by then become his masters. Each grave contains about 1000 dead Allied soldiers. Forlì was twenty-five miles behind the German side of the Gothic Line – the front line in the summer of 1944, which ran across Italy from Pesaro on the east coast to just north of Pisa on the west. The Allies attacked the line on 25 August 1944. The battle lasted 135 days, ending on 6 January 1945. The terrain comprising mountains and rivers was very difficult and got worse with winter. The Allied forces were bloated and bogged down with excessive supply units and their generals lacked audace. By the end of the battle the Allies had advanced north just fifty miles. The human cost was about 200,000 military and civilian casualties (killed or wounded) on both sides.

Some of the fiercest fighting was in Forlì as Hitler ordered his generals to hold the city of Mussolini's youth at all costs. The Allies attacked Forlì on 21 October. It took them until 9 November to capture it. The Reuters news agency journalist wrote, 'In no other city in Italy ... was there a less enthusiastic welcome for the Allied forces than in Forlì. There was no applause ... only cold and hostile stares and in many cases the repugnance of the populace was hardly concealed at all.' There are few visitors to the Allied war graves in Forlì, where neat lines of little white rectangular gravestones stand like a battalion at attention. Only the names of those 738 dead young men, chiselled into those white stones, made by Italian stone masons, and the messages underneath, distinguish one stone from another – nearly all in their twenties such as Corporal W. H. Tuck, Somerset Light Infantry, died 15.11.1944, aged twenty-eight, or Lieutenant A. W. I. Brooker, the Queen's Bays Royal Armoured Corps, died 25.11.1944, aged twenty-one. The visitors' book records only about a dozen messages a month such as ' "Hello", at last Dad' or 'Take care, mate'. There are no souvenir shops to keep the memory of these dead young men alive.

With all these visitors to the tomb of the Duce, Mussolini is a major industry in Predappio along with the Sangiovese and the chicken farms which, especially in summer, fill the outskirts of the town with the pungent smell of feet. In the souvenir shops, which are festooned with Italian flags, you can buy replicas of the accoutrements of Mussolini and his Fascism: all that you need to be the complete Fascist.

Romano Mussolini, youngest of Mussolini's five children and the only one still alive, professional jazz musician, ex-husband of Sophia Loren's sister and father of Alessandra Mussolini, the post-Fascist MP, cashes in too. His paintings are on sale in one of the souvenir shops. They look like the chocolate box offerings along the railings of London's Green Park or in Montmartre in Paris. In pride of place, in the shop window, is a garish painting of a clown's face. The face resembles that of Romano's father.

It is not just the coachloads of Fascist visitors. Another odd thing about Predappio is that although the council has been 'red' since the war, a majority of people you meet, certainly of older people, seem to be, if not Fascist, then very keen indeed on Mussolini. Many carry photographs of him in their wallets with his sayings printed on the back – as if they are the ten commandments or the words of the rosary. The cult of *Il Duce*, it is clear from a study of Predappio, lives on.

Under the Italian constitution it is against the law in Italy to do or say anything which is an apology for Fascism or to abuse the Italian flag. Similar shops devoted to Hitler and the Nazis in Germany, for example, would be unthinkable. Is selling a bust of Mussolini an apology for Fascism? What of the labels on bottles of wine depicting him in one of his many uniforms doing the Roman salute? Is this blatant association of the Italian flag with Mussolini an abuse of the flag? Presumably the shops are guilty on both counts. But money talks and times change.

Ferrini's bear of a son, Benizzi, mans the Ferrini shop and answers the telephone by shouting 'Jawohl'. 'You're writing a book on Mussolini you say?' he asked me in his big booming voice on my first visit. 'Just tell me this: will you be "pro" or "contro"?' There is a famous Fascist slogan which says, '*O con noi o contro di noi*' ('Either with us or against us'). 'The truth,' I replied. He laughed.

Back in 1883, in this valley where modern Predappio now stands and through which runs the Rabbi, there was only a small hamlet, Dovia, either side of the road which connected the two nearest big towns – Forlì ten miles east and Premilcuore fifteen miles west. The road was little more than a rock-strewn dirt track that became a quagmire as soon as heavy rain fell – which it always does outside summer – made worse by the abundance of clay in the soil. Old Predappio, now called Predappio Alta, was one mile away on top of a nearby hill. It was in Dovia, not Predappio, that Mussolini was born. His father, Alessandro Mussolini, a devout Socialist, was the local blacksmith. His mother, Rosa Maltoni, a devout Catholic, was the local primary-school teacher. The Mussolinis lived in two rooms on the first floor of a small three-storey house in Dovia called Varano de' Costa. A third room on the first floor served as the school. Alessandro Mussolini's forge was on the ground floor. The Mussolinis were poor. But they did not live in poverty.

This is how one writer, Skem Gremigni, described the situation at Varano de' Costa in *Duce d'Italia*, a book published in 1927 about Mussolini's family tree and targeted at schoolchildren: '... Just think, dear children, how clearly destiny prepares the way for great men! The school, where the horizons of the history of the world are opened up, was above the noisy forge, where the fire tamed and dominated by that man transformed coarse metals into gleaming tools with which to enrich this "*terra natale*"

4

and strong weapons with which to defend it against the greedy foreigner.'

The Fascists began to build new Predappio within a year of Mussolini's seizure of power in 1922 and it soon consumed Dovia. Today it remains more or less as they built it – a museum of Fascist civic architecture in red brick and white marble that climaxes in a large square through which runs the main road. People often deride Fascist architecture as grotesque, usually, if they are honest, on political rather than aesthetic grounds. But it is much more impressive than most other 20th-century architecture such as that, say, of consumer capitalism. New Predappio was the Fascist Bethlehem – being the place where the infant Mussolini was born, a place to idolise him – and *La Casa Natale*, the house where the birth took place, the equivalent of the stable where Jesus was born: the Fascist crib.

The focal point of the town was not the *Casa Natale*, however, but the straight main road and the big bleak square – the road a place to march along, the square a place to hold a rally. Around the square itself stand the buildings of the regime – the headquarters of the *carabinieri* and those of the Fascist party the *Casa del Fascio*. From the *Casa del Fascio* rises a tall, thin, square-shaped bell tower. On the far side is the church of Sant' Antonio. This was built later, between 1932 and 1934 – after the 1929 Lateran Accords by which Pope Pius XI became the first Pope to recognise the Kingdom of Italy and its sovereignty over the city of Rome and by which Mussolini recognised the Vatican as a separate state. Above the entrance of the church, just below the verdigris cupola, there is a large stone *fasces* embedded in the façade. Initially, Fascism was fiercely anti-Catholic. Catholicism was a serious rival in the battle for dictatorship of the hearts and minds of the Italian people, if not their souls. But the church and the party headquarters – the one whose bell still rings, the other whose bell is silent – stand opposite each other as they always stood: uneasily.

To the right of the square, perched on a grassy hillock in front of a wooded public park, is the imposing three-storey Palazzo Varano to which the village school was transferred in 1884 less than a year after Mussolini's birth. In consequence the Mussolinis also moved there. At that time the Palazzo Varano was a large dilapidated three-storey farmhouse – much bigger than *La Casa Natale* but still very much a *casa rustica*. It was in Palazzo Varano that Mussolini's brother, Arnaldo, was born on 11 January 1885 and sister, Edvige, on 10 November 1888. The school was on the third floor. Mussolini and his brother shared a bed, a sack filled with corn. Edvige slept with her parents in the only other room. Other families lived in the building on the two floors below.

The Palazzo Varano became new Predappio's town hall in 1925 as the seat of local power was bundled down the hill and Predappio renamed Predappio Alta, a mere suburb of new model Predappio. On the lawn in front of the new town hall the Fascists grew municipal flowers in the shape of an enormous *fasces*. The primary school where Mussolini's mother had taught was moved to a new Fascist-built convent, on the main road near the market, named Santa Rosa di Predappio in her honour. On the wall of the main corridor of the convent is a large mosaic made in 1927 from ceramic tiles commissioned from a factory in Portugal and called *La Madonna del Fascio*. The mosaic depicts two women offering the Virgin Mary with infant Jesus a *fasces*. Its survival is due to the cunning of the nuns. At the end of the Second World War they painted over this *fasces* with red roses to avoid it being destroyed by partisans.

Today the Palazzo Varano is still the town hall and councillors sit on chairs with red leather backs on which are still visible the embossed *fasces* – despite the attempts to scratch them off at the end of the war.

Visible above all this on the crest of one of the steep hills eighteen hairpin bends above Predappio is a large tower in the Florentine style. The tower belongs to the castle of *La Rocca delle Caminate*, Mussolini's summer residence from 1927. The castle was a gift from local people who organised the raising of the funds required to buy and rebuild it. There were 70,000 signatures on the register of donors.

Originally built in the thirteenth century the castle had been devastated by an earthquake in 1870. All that remained were ruins and the tower in a perilous state. The new castle was a replica of the original and on top of the restored tower was installed a lighthouse which, said journalists at the time, sent out a beam of light with the strength of 8000 light bulbs in the colours of the Italian flag deep into the countryside. When the light was switched on it was a sign that Mussolini was in the castle. In the document handing over the castle to him the castle committee described their gift as a 'pledge of love and faith from the Romagna to its Greatest Son'.

In his autobiography, *La mia vita*, written between December 1911 and March 1912 when he was only twenty-eight, but not published until 1947, two years after his death, Mussolini wrote, 'I was born on 29 July 1883 at Varano de' Costa, an old farmhouse on a little hill above the village of Dovia, part of the Comune of Predappio. I was born on a Sunday, at two in the afternoon, the feast day of the patron saint of the Caminate, the old ruined tower which being on the last of the Apennine spurs descending to the undulations of Ravaldino, dominates, loftily and solemnly, the entire plain of the Forlivese. Eight days earlier the sun had entered the constellation of Leo.'[3]

Mussolini was deeply superstitious, like so many Italians. As a child he was fascinated by a thrice-married old woman, Giovanna, who was avoided by everyone else in Dovia and practised witchcraft. She warned him about the malevolence of the moon. She told his future with cards and stories about the unnatural behaviour of hares. Still today in the Romagna there is a fascination with the supernatural. Professional card readings are a regular part of bar life; dreams and activities of the moon taken very seriously. Throughout his life Mussolini was scared of the evil eye. If he encountered someone he thought possessed it, he used the standard defence. He scratched his testicles. He used to say frequently, 'My blood tells me – I must listen to my blood ... I am like a beast; I sense what is about to happen. If I trust my instinct, I never make a mistake.'[4] The castle, as with everything else associated with Mussolini in Predappio except his tomb, has never been open to the public, though in the late 1990s the Council finally opened the *Casa Natale* as an exhibition centre.

For many years after the war Mussolini's widow, Rachele, who died in 1979, ran a restaurant near the castle gatehouse, where she served, among other things, *tagliatelle alla camicia nera* (black shirt). Nowadays with legal entry to the castle difficult and nothing left to take, thieves have begun to steal the black metal studs riveted to the entrance gate. 'I bet you know where Mussolini's treasure is buried,' the caretaker said to me with a wink as we emerged from the castle at the end of my tour. 'I'll go fifty-fifty with you if you tell me where to dig. I've got a metal detector. I've searched everywhere. I've even had a video camera down the well. Nothing. But it's got to be here somewhere.' The missing Mussolini treasure is yet another legend Mussolini bequeathed to the world.

Many people feel aggrieved, particularly those keen to cash in on the tourist potential, that these buildings associated with Mussolini should remain locked up. But perhaps it is better that way so as to be able to contemplate Mussolini and the evil he did, as well as the good, in silence and so more keenly, uninterrupted by the confusions and distortions which are the inevitable results of mass tourism.

2

THE YOUTH OF THE DUCE

In the end Mussolini did speak. According to his sister, Edvige, so worried had his parents become that their son was mute that they called in a doctor from Forlì to see if anything could be done. The doctor, having examined the boy, said, 'There's nothing to worry about. He is late in speaking but he will speak. In fact, to judge from his lively eyes, I have an idea that if anything he will speak too much.' The doctor was right. Mussolini spoke – 'a strange mixture of Italian and Romagnol phrases,' said Edvige.[1] He quickly grew into a disobedient little brute. In an attempt to instil discipline his father, Alessandro, used to beat him with a leather strap. But the boy was stubborn and the strap made him rebel more. It would not be long, however, before the father would come to exercise a powerful influence on the son. Where the strap failed, Socialism would succeed.

There had been Mussolinis living in and around Predappio since the 1600s. In the rush to trace the origins of the dictator after he had come to power in 1922 authors searched high and low in particular for traces of former greatness – in vain. But they discovered that the city records of Bologna frequently mention a Mussolini family who were muslin merchants. In 1878 the city council named a small street after this Mussolini family – Via de' Mussolini.

In a second autobiography[2] (published in 1928 in English only) Mussolini wrote that he was descended from this merchant family and that an eighteenth-century forbear was a composer of some note who lived in London. The book adds, 'and perhaps it is from him that I inherit the love of the violin, which even today in my hands gives comfort to moments of relaxation, and creates for me moments of release from the realities of my days.' Mussolini loved music from a very early age.[3] As a child, he played the trumpet in the school orchestra. As an adult he continued to play the violin competently – often to the irritation of his family. He is said to have had more passion than technique and wielded the bow like a sword. In 1932 he told the German journalist Emil Ludwig, in a remarkable series of revealing interviews between 23 March and 4 April published in book form – that he had given up the violin and not played for two years.

'At first it is refreshing but after a while it induces nervous exhaustion. It's like a poisonous drug, which may be useful in very small doses and is deadly in large ones.'[4]

But as time went on, Mussolini became keener to play up his peasant origins. The plaque put up in 1935 at the farmhouse in Predappio where his father, Alessandro, was born testifies, 'from 1600–1900 – in this farmhouse called Collina – lived and worked – the peasant generations of Mussolinis.' Regardless of this, Bologna's post-war left-wing council took no chances. It renamed Via de' Mussolini Via de' Tessitori. Muslinmaker Street became Weaver Street.

In 1927, overwhelmed with requests for help, usually financial, from a never-ending stream of people claiming to be related to him, Mussolini decided to establish the precise details of his family once and for all. He ordered the *podestà* of Predappio (under Fascism the elected *sindaco* (mayor) was replaced by the unelected *podestà* who had absolute power locally) to draw up an accurate list and distribute 60,000 lira among real relatives. It did little to stop the flow of requests. Two years later the exercise was repeated, again to little effect. In 1942 it was done for a third time. 'I want to know how many of them there are and how much they have pumped me for!' Mussolini shouted.[5] This investigation concluded that 334 'relatives' had received cash help since 1922, of whom 105 were 'related' to Rachele, his wife, and 229 to him. These figures excluded close members of the family.

Was Mussolini of Jewish stock? This was the embarrassing question posed by one author, Giovanni Comisso, to his cost. In his 1941 book, *Agenti veneziani nel 1700* he quoted a letter, dated 4 August 1760, which had been found in the state archives in Venice which said, 'Moisè Mussolin, a Jew, went about all over the place with the news talking with such heat, that he showed himself to have a predominant passion for the Prussians ...' When this was drawn to his attention Mussolini ordered all copies of the book to be seized.

Mussolini's father, Alessandro, was born on 11 November 1854 in the hamlet of Montemaggiore, half an hour's walk from old Predappio. He was the oldest of four children. His mother, Caterina Vasumi, died in 1878 soon after her fortieth birthday. His father, Luigi Mussolini, who owned a small farm and had been born on 28 August 1834, had once been a second lieutenant (*sottotenente*) in the National Guard, the citizens' militia set up in 1847 to keep order in the papal states by Pope Pius IX. But he had got into debt through drink, cards, mistresses and sloth. In the end he had to sell the family farm to his brother and move into a smaller house near-by.

His father's lack of money meant Alessandro was forced to leave school at the age of thirteen, scarcely able to read and write more than a few words. He became an apprentice blacksmith in Predappio and in 1877, aged twenty-three, he moved to Dovia to set up his own forge. That same year his future wife, Rosa Maltoni, the daughter of a vet from San Martino in Strada, one mile from Forlì, was appointed the village schoolteacher in Dovia, on a salary of 50 lira a month. She moved with her parents into Varano de' Costa where the one-room village primary school was housed. Born on 22 April 1858, she was just nineteen.

Alessandro was a reluctant blacksmith. His passion was politics and he was among the first Socialists in the Romagna, initially known as Internationalists. In 1864, Marx and Engels had started the International Association of Working Men – soon known as the International, then the First International. Nation states, they argued, were the creation of Capitalism. The proletariat of the world were part of no nation. Their revolution would sweep away national boundaries. Or so the Internationalists thought. The Italian section of the International was formed at a congress in Rimini in 1872.

Like so many Romagnoli, the blacksmith of Dovia was an atheist and fiercely anti-clerical – a 'mangiapreti' ('priest eater') as they were called. Socialism, not Catholicism, was Alessandro's religion. But Mussolini's mother, Rosa, had an unshakable faith in God and though of modest means her family were members of the petit bourgeoisie. Alessandro's family – peasant landowners – had fallen down at least one social class since his father's destitution.

Already, at the age of twenty-two, Alessandro was described in the police files, which also noted that his eyes were blue (cerulei), as 'a subversive'. Rosa's father had vehemently opposed the marriage but relented when Alessandro the revolutionary atheist priest eater agreed to a formal church wedding. The couple married on 25 January 1882 in the church of San Cassiano, near Dovia. Alessandro moved into the schoolhouse with his new wife and transferred his forge from premises elsewhere in Dovia to the ground floor.

When Mussolini was born Rosa insisted on having him baptised. As for Alessandro, he insisted on christening the boy – Benito, Amilcare, Andrea – not after famous saints but famous rebels: Benito Juarez, Amilcare Cipriani and Andrea Costa – the first a Mexican, the other two Italians. Juarez had become Mexican president after leading the successful liberal revolution in the 1860s against conservative Catholics and a French army sent by Napoleon III to install Archduke Maximilian of Austria on the throne of Mexico. On seizing power Juarez had Maximilian tried for treason and shot, to the horror of the royal families of Europe – but to the delight of Alessandro Mussolini.

Amilcare Cipriani had fought alongside Garibaldi in the attempted seizure of Rome from the pope in 1862 (Rome was finally captured in 1870, leaving the pope a virtual prisoner inside the Vatican. Not until the 1929 Lateran Accords would the Catholic Church recognise the sovereignty of Italy). Cipriani had then gone to France where he fought as a colonel with the revolutionary Communards in their failed attempt in 1871 at revolution in Paris. He was captured by French troops and dispatched to the French penal colony of New Caledonia in the Pacific. In 1880 he was granted an amnesty by the French government and returned to Italy where he was hailed as a martyr by Italian Internationalists.

Andrea Costa was, like Alessandro Mussolini, a Romagnolo. By the mid-1870s he had become one of the most prominent Internationalists in Italy. Alessandro knew him as an acquaintance. Initially, Costa advocated armed revolution as the means to create a Socialist state. But then he changed his mind about revolution, arguing instead that the way to achieve Socialism was by getting elected to parliament and instituting reform. This caused a bitter row with Cipriani and others who continued to advocate armed revolution and echoed the split within the Internationalist movement as a whole on the issue.

Alessandro had taught himself to read and write, and had articles published in local Socialist newspapers. This was no mean feat in a country of 28 million people of whom 70 per cent were illiterate. He even read Marx's impenetrable *Das Kapital*, or at least bits of it, and would recite extracts to his children. At some point between 1878 and 1879 he was imprisoned for six months for his Socialist agitation in Forlì and on several occasions between 1874 and 1882 the police declared him to be 'a danger to society and to public security' and placed him under *'ammonizione'* – a formal caution commonly used against political agitators because of the difficulty in getting juries to convict them. These *ammonizioni*, which lasted various lengths of time, imposed a curfew on Alessandro requiring him among other things to report to the local police station every Sunday, to keep out of cafés, and banned him from standing for public office. The last of these *ammonizioni* was revoked on 4 October 1882, nine months after his marriage. In October 1889 Alessandro was elected a 'social-liberal' councillor in Predappio which, according to the 1901 census, had a population of 4231. He lost his seat in 1894, regained it in 1899 and remained a councillor until 1907.

His most noted contribution to local politics was his organisation of the first co-operative of farm labourers to local life and the purchase in 1891 of the first local steam-threshing machine. In an 1891 article entitled 'What is Socialism?' published in *Rivendicazione*, a Forlì Socialist newspaper on 10 February, he wrote: 'Socialism ... is open rebellion, violent and moral, against the inhumanity of things as they are.'

When he died on 19 November 1910 his son, Benito, by then a journalist and revolutionary Socialist agitator, wrote an obituary of him in the small Socialist weekly newspaper, *La Lotta di classe*, which he had edited in Forlì. He said, 'I do not know at what time and under what influences he became a follower of the International. But it is certain that when he arrived at

Dovia he was already carrying on a great propaganda, and had formed the first organisation of the Internationale. He was thrown into prison. When he returned he remained under police supervision for forty-two weeks. His house always offered shelter and friendship to those pursued by the authorities. Later, when the Socialists had come to take part in municipal politics, my father became mayor (*sindaco*) of Predappio. In 1892 he formed in Predappio the first labour union ... In 1902 he was again arrested ... The clergy, the police and the moderates persecuted him ceaselessly ... He left me no material heritage, but he left me a moral one – his treasure: the Ideal. ... And after this sorrowful burial, I pursue my way, following in his footsteps.'[6]

Alessandro was never mayor of Predappio – though he was at one point deputy mayor (*pro-sindaco*). The 1902 arrest – the second – referred to by Mussolini led to Alessandro being held in the Forlì jail for 167 days after being accused with others of smashing the ballot box in Predappio on polling day – 6 July – in the local elections. At his trial he was acquitted but aged forty-eight, the lengthy spell in custody had taken its toll on his health.

Alessandro's passion for politics meant that he worked in his forge only sporadically. Consequently, the Mussolini family was forced often to rely on Rosa's meagre primary-school teacher's salary of 50 lira a month – and the occasional inheritance from a dead relative. Later, in a book to commemorate the death of his brother Arnaldo in 1931 Mussolini would recall that the family ate meat, half a kilo of mutton, only on Sundays, which formed the basis of a stew. This stew carried on as soup, becoming thinner as the week progressed.[7]

This then was the atmosphere in which the young Mussolini grew up – in the seething Romagna in a world where the new religion, Socialism, was sweeping through Europe – a world on the brink of the twentieth century. He looked like his mother. In particular, he had inherited her big black eyes – the eyes which would later captivate so many men and women. But like his father and unlike his mother he was a rebel from the word go. His mother was his first teacher at the school in Palazzo Varano, which he attended from the age of six until he was eight, and he spent his third year as a pupil at the school up the hill in Predappio. Each day, except when it was too cold or wet, he used to walk there, one mile each way, barefoot, carrying his shoes, laces tied together and slung round his neck, to keep them clean and not wear them out. It was a habit he would continue into adulthood.

The future dictator's childhood interests, however, lay not in the classroom but in the countryside. He stole birds' eggs and fruit, kept birds he had caught as pets, especially little owls with which he was particularly fascinated. 'His best friends as a child were owls,' wrote Margherita Sarfatti, an early biographer, and for many years his mistress. 'Each year, he quivered with impatience to go with a long rod, under the arches of the bridge where they had their nests, to trap the young ones with lime.' He especially loved cats. There is a photograph of him taken in 1923 hugging a female lion cub, which had been given to him as a gift. He kept the lioness, which he called Italia, in a room next to his study in his Rome home, until it was a young adult when it was moved to the Rome zoo.[8]

He swam in the Rabbi, pinched girls and brawled with boys. He was tough and a bully. He was also quick-witted. He shared a bed with his shy, fat brother, Arnaldo, fifteen months younger than him, and was fiercely protective of him. He admitted later that he was violent and a thief as a child. 'I was a restless urchin free with my fists,' wrote Mussolini in his first autobiography *La mia vita*. 'I was the head of a small band of urchins who roamed, the riverbeds and the fields. ... I was a bold rural thief,' he added.

Like his father, who as an adult had gone to church once only to marry, he too hated church. He rarely remained for an entire service, to the despair of his mother, and would sit instead in the branches of an oak tree outside waiting for her to come out. In *La mia vita* he said that the 'red light of the lit candles, the penetrating smell of the incense, the endless singing of the faithful and the sound of the organ, disturbed me profoundly. Once I fell to the floor unconscious.'[9] While his mother did her best to instil religious faith in her eldest son, his father did the opposite. His wild tirades in local Socialist newspapers against the church would include such lines as this, in *Rivendicazione* on 25 May 1889: 'Oh priests, the day is not far off when you will stop being useless and false apostles of a religion based on lies, and in which, leaving behind the lying and obscurantism, you will embrace truth and reason, and throw the cassock into the purifying flames of progress and put on the honoured doublet of the worker.'

Despite Mussolini's loathing of church his parents sent him aged nine to a boarding school, L'Istituto Salesiano, run by monks of the Salesian Order, in Faenza twenty miles from Predappio. It was the idea of the richest woman in Predappio, Palmira Zoli, 'an idiotic bigot', wrote Mussolini in *La mia vita*.[10] His father gave his consent because he thought the monks might be able to do what he had been unable to do – discipline the boy. The Salesian college was fee-paying – 60 lira a month for the sons of 'nobles', 40 for the sons of the 'middle class' and 20 for the sons of the 'common' such as Mussolini – nearly half Rosa's teacher's salary. But the 'common' Mussolinis must have had some money to spare. In fact, they possessed at least one small farm called Vallona. Furthermore, both Mussolini and his brother Arnaldo, who were educated at different schools, remained in full-time education until they were eighteen which was unusual.

Alessandro and his eldest son Benito travelled the twenty miles to the Salesian college for the start of his first term there in mid-October 1892 by means of his donkey-drawn cart. The journey took six hours. Mussolini recalled the event in *La mia vita*, 'I don't remember feeling much pain at leaving my brother and sister: Edvige was three, Arnaldo seven. I was distressed instead, profoundly, at leaving a *lucherino* (siskin) that I kept in a cage under my window.'[11]

Mussolini hated the college: the monastic way of life ruled by the sound of the bell; the hours of enforced silence; the daily mass; the frequent corporal punishment; and the segregation of the 200 or so pupils at mealtimes at three different tables according to the wealth of their families. The pupils were not allowed to speak during meals. The food was 'repugnant' and the coffee an 'indecent soup', he wrote in *La mia vita*.[12] The headmaster was a 'terrifyingly thin man ... a walking skeleton'. The pupils had to get up at 6 a.m. in winter, 5 a.m. in summer, and immediately attend mass. Each evening before going to bed there was a ceremony in the assembly hall at 7.30 p.m. in which they had to line up to kiss the rector's hand. They were only allowed to go outside the walled precincts once a week on Sunday for a two-hour walk around Faenza escorted by monks. Imprisoned in the college, he pined for the countryside around his home. During his first few weeks he was 'devoured by melancholy', he wrote.[13] In July the summer holidays began and Mussolini could at last escape. But when he arrived home he found to his dismay that his beloved *lucherino* had disappeared. His family had forgotten to feed it and it had died.

He failed to convince his parents, in particular his mother, to take him away from the college and so in October 1893 back he went. The punishments continued – as did the indoctrination. The secular world consisted of sinners and the corrupt, said the teachers, and only monks were pure. 'I feared the world,' he wrote, adding, 'I imagined it as full of turbid people out to grab me and turn me into one of the fallen.' Then, in April 1894 aged ten, came the day when he was due to celebrate communion for the first time. This caused in him 'a very serious internal crisis'. In the weeks beforehand he and his fellow communicants did not attend classes. They spent each day, supervised by a monk, learning psalms in Latin by heart, praying and reading the Bible. The monk told the group that if they had not confessed every single sin before their confirmation they would go the way of a boy in Turin who had been 'struck down by a serious illness' which killed him. 'This episode terrified us. I thought it was true.' Duly, all confessed like mad, even to things they had not done or thought, just to be on the safe side. But after the confirmation service and their first communion none of them died. 'All my companions were pure because none of them was struck down,' wrote Mussolini wryly, adding that he could discern no 'visible changes within myself'.[14] Despite his dislike of church, monks and priests, however, it is clear that he believed in God, even if as some kind of devil.

But his days at the Salesian college were numbered. On the evening of 24 June 1894 he stabbed another pupil, a friend, in the hand, during a fight, the cause of which he did not record. His immediate punishment was to be locked in the college courtyard with the college guard dogs. To escape the dogs, in desperation he ran over to the locked gate leading back into the school. But as he climbed, they snapped at his heels. They missed his flesh but tore his trousers. The rector wanted to expel Mussolini on the spot. But Mussolini's mother and father came to the school to plead on their son's behalf. The rector agreed that Mussolini could remain until the end of the academic year – a month later. Much has been made of this stabbing incident as an early sign of a violent psychopath – particularly by post-war authors, but Mussolini freely admitted to it in *La mia vita*.[15]

The Faenza college archives contain a lengthy report on Mussolini's expulsion in the summer of 1894. It described him as possessing a 'lively intelligence, an impressive memory, but of a totally disorganised kind'. However, the report went on to say that he was 'passionate and unruly' and that he was unable to adapt to the college where he felt he had been sent by his parents as punishment. 'He opposes every order and discipline of the college. Nothing fulfils him: in a group of people he feels sad and lonely. He wants to be alone.' The report referred only obliquely to the stabbing.

In October 1894 Mussolini, now aged eleven, was sent by his parents to another school: the Collegio Giosuè Carducci in Forlimpopoli ten miles from Predappio. The school was a new lay institution named after the famous Italian poet, and the headmaster was the poet's brother, Valfredo Carducci. Mussolini was still a boarder but this time he could come home at weekends. The Salesian friars meanwhile sued Mussolini's parents for recovery of 250 lira in unpaid school fees and forced them to take out a mortgage on one of their smallholdings to pay off the debt. It took his parents 'ten to twelve years' to pay this debt off, recalled Mussolini, yet somehow the Mussolinis found the money to pay the fees at the new school. But they were going through a very difficult time financially. For example, Mussolini's mother wrote a letter the following year – in September 1895, just before Mussolini's second year – to her employer, the prefect of Forlì, begging him to subsidise her son's education. Addressing him as 'Your Excellency' she referred to the local economic hardship which had reached 'the absolute limit' and that year's 'total absence of grapes, the only product in these parts'. She said that her family was in dire financial straits. The prefect, however, did not help. But yet again she and her husband managed to find the money.

Mussolini was much happier at the Collegio Giosuè Carducci. In *La mia vita* he wrote, 'No priests, nor the footprints of priestiness.' Mass was voluntary. He did not go. 'I had passed from hell to heaven.' Discipline was 'more human'. 'I was truly happy.'[16]

But one day he stabbed again. He was doing homework when another boy came up and scribbled all over his work. A quarrel started. The other boy, he said, slapped him. So he stabbed him in one of his buttocks with his knife. If we are to believe his version of events, however, he did not start the fight. This time Mussolini was not expelled but was only allowed to stay on at the school as a day boy. He rented a room in a house in Forlimpopoli belonging to a vet whose wife was a cripple. He would return to Predappio each Sunday.

Authors searching for early signs of a deeply disturbed mind use the two stabbing incidents, the throwing of stones, the brawling, the rebelliousness, the bullying and so on as evidence. Mussolini certainly thought his adult character had been formed by his background. He told the German journalist Emil Ludwig, 'My father was sent to prison as a Socialist agitator. When he died, thousands of his comrades followed his body to the grave side. All this provided a definite trend to my aspirations. Had I had a different sort of father, I should have become a different sort of man. The fact that I was born among the common people put the trump cards in my hand.'[17] It is doubtful if thousands of people turned up at Alessandro Mussolini's funeral. And, though true that Mussolini was born 'among' the common people his family, though poor, was better off than most. The influence of his father's politics got stronger the more he went out into the world on his own. In the train that took him from Milan to Rome in October 1922 to become prime minister he was asked what he was thinking about and replied, 'I am thinking about my dad.'

The idea that the child bully became the adult dictator is less easy to sustain. Stone-throwing, bullying, rebelliousness and brawling were part of life, then, in the Romagna as everywhere else. They still are – to a certain extent.

The year 1900, the start of the new century, saw the king of Italy, Umberto I, assassinated at Monza by an Italian anarchist, Gaetano Bresci, who had emigrated to America and just returned. The assassination occurred on 29 July 1900 – Mussolini's seventeenth birthday. That year also saw Mussolini have sex for the first time – with a prostitute. He felt absolutely no shame or embarrassment whatsoever in writing about his blossoming sex life – at any rate in the unpublished *La mia vita*. This first sexual encounter occurred in a Forlì brothel one Sunday in 1900. He had gone there with a friend. 'When I went in I felt the blood surge to my face. I did not know what to say or do. But one of the prostitutes took me on to her knees and began to excite me with kisses and caresses. She was an elderly woman who spilled out lard from all parts of her body. I gave her the sacrifice of my sexual virginity. It only cost me 50 centessimi. I left that house head down and tottering like a drunk. I felt as if I had committed a crime.' But he added, 'Naked women entered my life, my dreams, my desires. I undressed, with my eyes, the girls that I met, I lusted after them violently with my thoughts. I frequented, at carnival time, public dances and I danced. The music, the rhythm of the movements, the contact with the girls and their perfumed hair and glistening skin with its pungent smell of sweat, awoke in me the appetites of the flesh and I found relief on Sundays in the brothels of Forlì.'[18]

It was at about this time that Mussolini began to write poetry – nearly all of which he burned several years later. One poem which survived began, '*Ridon tremuli i rii, tra la fiorita / erbetta nel languor del di novello / mentre la Primavera esce verita / nell'oro verde del suo broccatello.*' His family's financial situation improved as well when his mother inherited a large sum of money, 10,000 lire when an aunt died.

The academic year 1900–01 was Mussolini's final year at school. He was allowed back into the school as a boarder. In an essay in 1900 on how a teacher should grade children he wrote, 'The teacher should take into account the individual psycho-physical conditions of the pupil; the atmosphere in which the child spends most of his day; and never forget above all that, because of social inequality, the intellectual product of the poor pupil is not as impressive as the product of the rich pupil, not because of any deep difference in their mental powers, but simply because the poor one finds in his domestic environment not peace, but discord, not bread, but the leftovers discarded by the charity of the bourgeois; while the rich one does not experience worry and starvation, and enjoys instead all life's expensive comforts. The teacher must take these things into account when he grades, if he wants to provide at the very least a grade based on a semblance of justice.' He was awarded nine out of ten by his teacher.

On 27 January 1901 Giuseppe Verdi died aged eighty-seven. Italy mourned. By now Mussolini had become interested in public speaking and was already good at it. The headmaster chose him to give the memorial speech on Verdi to the school and public in the theatre at Forlimpopoli on 10 February. This was a great honour and evidence of his gift as a public speaker. Verdi, though appointed a senator by the king, had always remained aloof from politicians and refused to take his seat in the Senate. Mussolini used this point to launch an attack on the ruling class. Finally, the headmaster got up to stop the speech, but too late because Mussolini was about to finish. Rino Alessi recalled the event, 'The applause cut short the scene. The assembly was electrified.' The speech received a small mention in the Socialist Party's newspaper *Avanti!* which described it as 'an applauded speech'.[19] Another fellow pupil, Sante Bedeschi, who would remain a friend into adulthood, described Mussolini at this time as 'chock-a-block with books, magazines, prohibited newspapers'.[20]

By now Mussolini was reading avidly. Among his favourite authors was

Dante. In 1932, asked by the German journalist Ludwig if he still read Dante, Mussolini replied, 'Again and again; always, in fact. He was the first writer to give me a vision of greatness; and at the same time he showed me the heights to which poetry can attain.'[21] By the time of his final year at school, according to Alessi, Mussolini had read among others Bakunin and Zola. He had also read Hugo's *Les Misérables* and been so impressed by Gustave Le Bon's (1842–1931) *La Psychologie des Foules* (*The Psychology of the Crowd*), published in Paris in 1895, that he mentioned it in *La mia vita* and on other occasions throughout his life as a major influence. He would read it and reread it. He would write in 1926, 'I have read all the works of Gustave Le Bon and I don't know how many times I have reread his *Psychology of the Crowd*. It is a masterful work, to which even today I still go back.'[22]

Le Bon was not a Socialist. But he believed in the importance of harnessing the crowd. The crowd was volatile, dangerous and had to be controlled. It would do things no one individual would dare do on his own. But what motivated it to action was emotion, not reason. To appeal to emotion the orator, wrote Le Bon, must achieve simplicity of language and syntax. He must make a simple assertion and he must repeat that assertion. Later Mussolini would say that his were not speeches in the traditional sense of the word but 'allocutions, making contact between my soul and yours, between my heart and yours'.[23] He also quoted Le Bon's hostility to democracy approvingly in 1937, 'He [Le Bon] said, "Democracy is that political system in which from time to time the people are given the illusion that it is sovereign." A useless illusion and a ridiculous sovereignty. The authentic people does not know what to do with it.'[24]

Le Bon wrote of the crowd, 'Alone, he [man] was perhaps educated, careful, timid; in the crowd he becomes driven by instinct, a barbarian.' The crowd, Le Bon went on, was also conservative with a horror of the new and though capable of explosions of violence incapable of revolution. He added, 'The crowd ... instinctively seeks a leader ... It is better for the leader to be authoritarian and a little tyrannical. Crowds respect strength and are rarely influenced by goodwill, which they often consider weakness. The leader must be a man of willpower and action, not of thought ... Individuals united in a crowd lose their willpower and their own thoughts, and transfer everything to the leader ... The so-called ideas of the crowd are not ideas but feelings. They are ideas of force, energy and myth. The crucial substance of the crowd is not made of rationality, but of religiousness: religiousness towards the so-called spiritual values: fatherland; nation; courage; heroism; sacrifice; order; family; state; justice; liberty.'

In 1901 Mussolini passed his final school examinations with distinction (*licenza d'onore*) receiving 132 out of a possible 150 marks. His best subjects were history, Italian, literature and choral singing. On 29 July he celebrated his eighteenth birthday. That summer he went on holiday to Cattolica on the Adriatic coast not far from where the River Rubicon flows into the sea, and stayed with a school friend. He did not return to Dovia until October where he found his former friends all destined to become farm labourers and peasants. Several times a week he would travel the ten miles to Forlì, often on foot, newspaper or book under his arm, for violin lessons and to read in the city's library. Already, he called himself a Socialist of the anarchist kind.

Mussolini had started smoking cigarettes and drinking red wine. He had also acquired a nickname in Predappio: '*E Mat*', '*il Matto*' – the Mad One. As Vittorio Emiliani, former editor of *Il Messaggero* and himself from Predappio, noted, 'To be called '*strambo*' (odd) in a land full of odd people such as the peasant Romagna, then you needed to try very hard.'[25] His eyes and eccentricities fascinated and scared people.

The eighteen-year-old Mussolini, Il Matto, was tough but thin, short though not by Romagnol standards – five feet five and a half inches tall (1m 69cm according to his military service file, which noted he had a mole on his neck, and even shorter according to his Forlì police file – 1m 67cm – five feet four and a half inches) – rarely shaved and wore crumpled, usually black, clothes. He also wore a black cravat – the symbol of the anarchists – Socialists wore red cravats. He also adored playing the violin and dancing. He composed a song, which for a time was popular in Predappio. '*Bimba non mi guardare / forse tu m'ami di un affetto serio / ma questo cor che tu sognando brami / è pieno di veleno.*'[26]

Mussolini now began to confront his destiny. His *licenza d'onore* qualified him to be let loose on children as a primary-school teacher. He sometimes stood in for his mother at the Dovia primary school – and it was while doing so that he met his future wife, Rachele Guidi, for the first time, who was a pupil at the school. It was also at this time that he raped a young woman – by modern definition at least – and by his own admission, though such behaviour was common in turn-of-the-century Romagna. She was a neighbour in Dovia whom he referred to as Virginia B. 'One fine day,' he wrote, while most of the village was in church listening to a 'portentous missionary friar' he pounced. 'I grabbed her on the stairs, threw her into a corner behind a door and made her mine. She got up weeping and humiliated and through her tears she insulted me. She said that I had robbed her of her honour. It is not impossible. But, I ask you, of what honour was she speaking?' Clearly, Mussolini did not see the incident as rape. He was proud of it. As for the girl, she had not consented but once Mussolini had 'made her' his, as he put it, she wanted more – if we are to believe him. 'She wasn't in a sulk with me for long. And for at least three months we loved each other not much with the mind but much with the flesh.'

Mussolini dwelled at length in *La mia vita* (which was not published in his lifetime) on his sexual conquests. Once in power, however, any mention in print of his sex life ceased – except in the context of his wife, Rachele. This is not because once married, he was faithful to Rachele. Far from it. Mussolini slept with hundreds of women. His sexual technique, according to those who spoke out, was always the same – the same as his own description of it that 'fine day' on the Dovia staircase. But once in power he did not have to pursue women. They pursued him; queuing up to leap into bed with him. Few, however, made it to the bed. He preferred the wall or the floor to the bed. The bed meant time and intimacy. He wasted no time on preliminaries. The sex was furious; over quickly. One woman who lived near his Rome residence, the Villa Torlonia, said that one day she waved at him from her kitchen window when she saw him ride past on his horse. He promptly sent her a pass to the Palazzo Venezia – the headquarters of the regime. No sooner had she been shown into his enormous marble-floored office than he thrust her up against a wall and began to squeeze her breasts as if they were rubber automobile horns.[27] Claretta Petacci, who superseded Sarfatti as his principal mistress, is said to have sighed to trusted friends, 'He doesn't even take his breeches off.'

In 1932, speaking to the German journalist, Emil Ludwig, Mussolini complained that his raw material, the Italian people, unlike the raw material of an artist was subject to the influence 'of the dead and even the influence of women.'[28] By then he had read and agreed with Otto Weininger (1880–1903), the Viennese psychologist, who believed that women were a negative and evil influence, the cause of all that was bad, including madness. Women did not feel the need and as a result certainly did not have the ability to achieve political emancipation. Mussolini wanted big-breasted women with powerful hips and rosy cheeks to breed sons. 'Woman must obey ... Has she in history ever done architecture? Ask her to build a cabin, not even a temple. She can't. Architecture, which is the synthesis of all the arts, is alien to her. ... My view on the role of woman in the State is opposed to any kind of feminism. Naturally she must not become a slave; but if I gave her the vote, she would laugh at me. In our State she must not count.'

Asked by Ludwig if a dictator could ever be loved, Mussolini replied, 'Yes, provided that the masses fear him at the same time. The crowd loves strong men. The crowd is like a woman.' For Mussolini women, like the crowd, needed, wanted, to be taken by force.

3

THE DUCE AS TRAMP AND TEACHER

Mussolini's attempts in the late summer of 1901 to find a teaching post failed. Already suffering from the typical depression of young people embarking on adult life, he became gloomier still. 'I have absolutely no prospects in sight and I'm condemned to vegetate. Painfully! I wait. What for? Bread. Will it come soon? I don't think so ...' he wrote in December to Sante Bedeschi, his schoolfriend (the bulk of his letters to Bedeschi were not published until 1939). But in another letter to Bedeschi he wrote, 'All sorts of things happen to me! The other day in Fiumana, I came within a hair's breadth of stabbing a peasant who had insulted me; a month ago a hail storm destroyed ... the entire grape crop. But you see philosophy has made me the perfect stoic. I observe and I smile. What is our miserable existence compared to the "*macrocosmo*" ... So I laugh. Laugh, laugh always!'[1] But it was a bitter laugh. Languishing thus in Dovia, he found some relief in reading and sex with local girls including another neighbour – Venezia Proli. She at least thought the relationship was destined for marriage.

Then, in late December 1901, the council in Gualtieri, some hundred miles north-west of Dovia on the south bank of the River Po, near Reggio Emilia, wrote saying that his application as a primary-school teacher had been successful. The council was the first in Italy to be run by Socialists. The councillors would have known of Mussolini's father. This no doubt explained why he got the job. He was preferred to older better qualified candidates and he took up his post in February 1902. His pay was 56 lira a month and he lodged with a family who charged him 40 lira a month rent. The school was three-quarters of a mile outside the town and he walked there and back each day barefoot – carrying his boots as of old[2] tied together round his neck. Each day he wore the same clothes: black suit, broad-brimmed black hat, black cravat, black cloak. He carried a knife and a knuckle-duster concealed about his person. Later he would carry a revolver as well. Local people found him odd – and scary.[3] They called him 'The man in black'. Often at night he used to stagger about town drunk. Sometimes he slept in the street outside his favourite bar. The class contained around forty children who were, he said, of reasonably mild temperament. He was always in debt and frequently wrote to his friend, Sante Bedeschi, asking for loans. He also asked many people in Gualtieri for loans.

It took Mussolini only a month to find a new woman. The highlight of the week was the Sunday evening dance where the favourites were the polka and the mazurka, and where fights in which he was involved frequently broke out. There, one evening, he met Giulia Fontanesi, the twenty-year-old wife of a soldier stationed elsewhere, and mother by the soldier of a small boy. He danced with her all night and refused to let anyone else do so. Subsequently he wrote to her seeking a meeting. She wrote back. But she lived with her husband's parents. They therefore arranged to meet in a room elsewhere 'on the evening of 20 March at house number nine in the Vicolo Massa, on the second floor ... Giulia F. was waiting for me at the door. She had a pink blouse on which stood out in the chiaroscuro light. We climbed the stairs and for two hours she was mine. I went home intoxicated with love and desire.'[4] The husband's parents found out about the affair and La Fontanesi was forced to move into the room she used to conduct her affair with Mussolini. He wrote, 'Now we had more freedom. .... I went to her every evening ... Those were enchanting months. Our love was violent and jealous ... Little by little I made her get used to my exclusive and tyrannical love. She obeyed me blindly. I did with her what I wanted.' The affair between the eccentric primary-school teacher and the soldier's wife caused a 'scandal' in the town. But the lovers did not care. They even attended public feast day parties together.

Mussolini was an extremely possessive lover. In Giulia's case he would erupt in fury if she danced with other men and he even ordered her not to leave her home unless with him. One day he spotted her in the street on her own and in the row that followed, he said in *La mia vita*, he stabbed her in the arm with his knife. But a friend of La Fontanesi's, Teresa Landini, interviewed aged 101 in 1983 by the journalist Fabrizio Castellini, said that Mussolini's story about stabbing her in the arm was nonsense. She was adamant: Mussolini had bitten Giulia *à la* Mike Tyson![5]

Mussolini left the school when the academic year ended in late June 1902. In *La mia vita* he said that the reason for his departure was that he had decided to emigrate to Switzerland to 'seek my fortune'. He intended later to 'send for' Giulia, he added.[6] But this desire to emigrate was not the whole story. The school had decided not to renew his contract. The reason, even if not recorded, is clear: his highly public affair with an absent soldier's wife. But he was restless anyway, and did not like teaching. He wanted to travel. The council decision merely forced his hand. In May he wrote to his parents to apply for a passport for him from the council in Predappio. He was under twenty-one and needed their permission.[7]

Before his departure for Switzerland he wrote to his mother asking her for the money for the train journey to Switzerland. He told her untruthfully that a job awaited him. She duly obliged and sent him 45 lira – nearly her entire monthly wage. He spent his remaining days in Italy with Giulia before leaving on 9 July. Her friend, Signora Landini, remembered, 'Mussolini left for Switzerland, promising his woman, thrown out of her home by her husband because of him, with a little child to feed, that he would get in touch and rejoin her as soon as he had sorted himself out. But it was a sailor's promise.' Mussolini recalled, 'I remember every detail of my last night. Giulia cried and kissed me. I too was moved. At five in the morning I kissed her for the last time. The train left at six. I made a sign to her with my hand at the bend in the lane; then I continued on my way, towards my new destiny. Ten years have gone by. I have not seen her since.'[8] They did, however, correspond for several years, he said, even though the husband had returned home to resume the marriage. But the husband, Signora Landini said, 'could not cope with the embarrassment and fled to America'.

When he left Gualtieri Mussolini even owed the cobbler money and his landlady rent. She, however, followed him to the station demanding the money. Reluctantly Mussolini handed over the one thing he had of value on the platform – his precious black cloak. Mussolini would spend the next two and a half years of his life between the ages of nineteen and twenty-one in Switzerland with one short two-month break back in Italy. These were to be crucial years in completing the development of his personality and his politics. Poverty, anger and envy were to play a powerful part in the process.

His train reached the frontier with Switzerland at Chiasso on the evening of 9 July 'at 10.40' and while waiting to switch to a Swiss train he picked up a newspaper and read a small item which said that his father had been arrested after being accused with others of smashing the ballot box in Predappio on the day of the local elections – 6 July. 'This news placed me in a dilemma. Turn back or go on? I imagined it was nothing serious and decided to continue my journey.'[9] But it was serious. His father was to spend the next 167 days in prison, held in custody, awaiting his trial at which he was acquitted just before Christmas 1902. Thirty years later Mussolini told Ludwig, 'I left my job as teacher, left my father in prison – not that I could free him – and penniless, went to Switzerland as a labourer.'[10] He had no idea where he was going to go in Switzerland nor what he was going to do, despite what he had told his mother. But at this time Switzerland attracted thousands of people like him from around Europe in desperate search of a better life – many of them economic migrants and many political refugees, often from Russia, such as Lenin, as well as from Italy, such as him. Switzerland was a smaller but easier to reach version of America.

Mussolini decided on the spur of the moment to get off the train at Yverdon, on Lake Neuchatel, on 10 July. He sold the knife he said he had used to stab Giulia for 5 lira. 'I could live for one week,' he wrote but he failed to find work, ran out of money, and on 13 July moved on by foot to nearby Orbe. He worked as a labourer on a site where a chocolate factory was being built but found the twelve-hour day unbearable – '121 trips with a barrow full of bricks up to the second floor,' he wrote in a letter on 3 September 1902 to his friend Sante Bedeschi. He soon quit and on Sunday, 21 July took the train to Lausanne twenty miles away and was forced to sleep rough in a box beneath the arches of the Grand Pont. In *La mia vita* he wrote that he slept in this box 'for several nights'.[11] In a later 1914 letter to a friend he said, 'I was penniless and lodged under the arches of the Grand Pont.'[12]

Probably he spent just one night in the box – not even an entire night, merely a few hours – because on 24 July, his third night in Lausanne, he was arrested for the first of many times in his life, this time for vagrancy. He was jailed eleven times in all before coming to power. Prison taught him, writes Sarfatti in *Dux*,[13] 'physical and moral patience'. But it also gave him a lifelong fear of being enclosed in small spaces. The police report on Mussolini's arrest dated it as 4 a.m. on 24 July and noted that his possessions were: a passport; a licence to teach and 15 centimes. He himself wrote that the only coin he had at this time was a nickle medal depicting the face of Karl Marx.

Two months later he wrote a vivid, powerful and moving letter to Sante Bedeschi dated 3 September. He told his friend that he was about to relate to him 'the sad memories of a desperate youth'. He then described events leading up to his night in the box. At dusk that day sitting beside Lake Leman he had contemplated suicide.

I was assailed by an infinite melancholy and I wondered ... if it was worth the effort to live for another day. But a soft harmony like the singing of a mother over the cot of her child interrupted my thoughts. I turned round. There were forty musicians in an orchestra playing in front of the Grand Hôtel Beau Rivage. I leaned against the gates of the garden, observing through the green canopy of foliage of the fir trees, inclining my ears and I listened. The music consoled both my mind and my stomach. But the intervals were atrocious: cramps attacked my bowels like flaming needles. At length, along the pathways of the park came the throng of pleasure-seekers, I hated the rustle of silk and the murmur of languages I did not understand. A venerable old couple passed me by. They seemed English. I wanted to ask them *'l'argent pour me coucher ce soir'*. But the words died on my lips. The woman, stumpy and bald, glowed with gold and gems. I did not have a single penny, I had no bed, I had no bread. I fled swearing. ... I passed the rest of the night under the Grand Pont ...

In the unpublished *La mia vita* he said that the police released him three days later.[14] There is no evidence that he slept rough again. On the day of his release another Italian, a sculptor and Socialist, allowed him to sleep in his attic free for a while.

It was in Switzerland that Mussolini first tried his hand at journalism, writing for *L'Avvenire del Lavoratore*, a Lausanne Socialist newspaper for Italian immigrants and exiles. His first published article appeared on 2 August 1902 and he had nine pieces published between August and December. He also worked sporadically as a waiter in a bar and as a builder and then, on 30 August, he was appointed secretary of the mainly Italian Lausanne Labourers' and Builders' Trade Union. The secretary's pay was a pittance – 5 lira a month – but at union meetings held above a café food and drink were free. He was now able to afford to rent a room on the top floor of a large house whose view was fantastic. He wrote in *La mia vita*, 'In that room I spent the winter of 1902–1903.' He had begun journalism: the career at which he was to prove brilliant and which would establish him as a figure of national importance in his native Italy within ten years.

But money, as ever, was a problem and this kind of journalism paid virtually nothing. By Christmas 1902 he was penniless again and had to rely on the generosity of friends to survive. His was a miserable existence and he was miserable. He contemplated suicide frequently. In March 1903, however, he met a woman who would transform his life: Angelica Balabanoff, the daughter of a wealthy Ukrainian landowner, an intellectual who spoke many languages, a Jew and a fervent revolutionary Socialist. The introduction took place at a meeting Balabanoff had organised in Lausanne to celebrate the anniversary of the March 1871 Paris Commune. Born in 1869, the youngest of sixteen children, she was fourteen years older than Mussolini. Balabanoff was plump and manly, and a driving force of revolutionary Socialisim in Switzerland, and she knew most of its leading lights including Lenin and Trotsky. Balabanoff was a pioneer champagne Socialist but rarely washed, according to Sarfatti, who wrote, 'The saving grace of humour failed her completely. She lacked a sense of beauty even more. This was fortunate for her! Otherwise she would probably have thrown herself down the nearest well. As things were she had very little acquaintance with water.' Sarfatti referred to Balabanoff as 'the spinster Angelica', 'hunch-backed' but 'extraordinarily intelligent' – 'a strange hysterical creature with a flashing mind', without a sense of humour, who had embraced Socialism 'like a fetishistic and monomaniacal religion'. 'I can well imagine her as an obsessed flagellant in a medieval procession, or perhaps in the grotto at Lourdes ...' Balabanoff's oratory, however, had 'magnetic power'.[15]

Balabanoff was the first and one of the few women apart from his mother to exercise influence on Mussolini. Mussolini would tell his biographer, Yvon de Begnac, in the 1930s that Balabanoff was his 'only political teacher' without whom he would have remained merely 'a small-time activist'. She herself later wrote at length about Mussolini – by which time she had become his bitter enemy. In a 1938 book, she recalled the occasion when she first met him at that March 1903 Lausanne meeting:[16]

> My attention was distracted for the entire meeting by a man whom I had never seen before and what distinguished him from the other workers gathered in the room was his restless demeanour and slovenly clothes. At the end of the meeting I asked one of our activists who he was. The man explained that the stranger was an Italian deserter who had turned up one evening at the club recently. Another of the workers added, 'We all manage to find a job, but he says he cannot, that he's too ill.' I felt very concerned about the young man's situation and went over to where he was sitting all alone. 'Can I do anything to help you?' I asked. 'I hear that you're unemployed.' In a hysterical voice, without even looking up, he said, 'There is nothing that can be done for me. I am ill and incapable of work and effort.'

In another book, this one published in 1927, Balabanoff wrote,

> But what surprised me most in him at that epoch was his great help-lessness; it was that which had inspired my pity for him. Later I had occasion to observe very closely his psychological and political development, while he was assimilating some literary culture, initiating himself into Socialist doctrine, taking part little by little in political action. I was able to follow attentively his anti-militarist and anti-clerical expressions. He had set himself to propagate by word and by writing the doctrines which came from the depths of his moral and material misery. I never lost sight of him until the moment he betrayed us all.

But soon after this first meeting with Balabanoff Mussolini left Lausanne and went to Berne where he did manual work and began to learn German, because he wanted to impress a blonde German woman, he wrote. In June the city's carpenters went on strike and Mussolini gave a speech in which he urged violence. As a result, the next day he was sacked from his job and arrested by the police who accused him of threatening behaviour and held him in custody for twelve days. He was then expelled from the canton of Berne and on 1 July deported to Italy. But at Como he got straight back on a train to Lausanne, where he did various factory jobs until October 1903 when his brother Arnaldo telegraphed to say that their mother was very ill. He returned to Dovia. But the doctor would not let him into his mother's bedroom, because 'the emotion of seeing me again after two years might kill her', he wrote.[17]

He set off on 27 December 1903, this time with his brother Arnaldo who had finished school in August 1902 – the Scuola Agraria at Cesena near Forlì – and, like him, had since drifted about. To help finance the trip they had borrowed 300 lira – a considerable sum – from a friend of his father's who had just returned from Brazil. In Geneva Mussolini worked giving Italian lessons and writing for Socialist newspapers – for *L'Avvenire del Lavoratore*, which had moved its offices to Lugano, the revolutionary syndicalist publication *Avanguardia Socialista* in Milan and even *Il Proletario*, an Italian-language daily published in New York.[18]

He also became more active in politics. On 18 March 1904 he gave a speech at a conference to commemorate the Paris Commune. According to Renzo De Felice, Mussolini's most famous biographer,[19] this is the only time he met Vladimir Ilyich Ulyanov, better known by his pseudonym 'Lenin', who was also at the conference. He could, however, also have met Lenin – and Trotsky – during his short stay in Berne in 1903. Mussolini used to eat at a canteen in Berne, La Mensa Spysi, where both Lenin and Trotsky ate at this time. Mussolini sometimes said in later life that he could not recall meeting Lenin and on other occasions he said that he had. Lenin would later say to Italian Socialists, 'Mussolini was the only one among you with the mind and temperament to make a revolution. Why did you allow him to leave?'

On 19 and 20 March 1904 Mussolini was in Zurich for the Eighth Congress of the Union of Italian Socialists in Switzerland, where he spoke, and on 25 March 1904 he was in Lausanne, where he debated God with Alfredo Taglialatela, an evangelical pastor from Rome, before an audience of 500. It was in this debate that according to Balabanoff[20] – though it does not appear in the printed text of the debate – he asked for a watch and made what was to become a famous though utterly banal call to God to strike him down dead within ten minutes. If God did not strike him down this proved He did not exist, argued Mussolini. Among his recorded views on the subject of religion at this time were that religion was a disease of the psyche and science had proved God did not exist. Furthermore, any God or church which preached resignation and sacrifice, as did Christianity, were for the weak – not the strong.

But it was not so much God that he did not believe in but the Catholic Church and at least until the start of the 1920s the Catholic God. For him, Catholicism and its God represented tyranny and the Catholic Church corruption. In 1911–12, he would write a pamphlet, in praise of Jan Hus (1369–1415), the Czech priest who, like Luther later, passionately opposed the corruption and decadence of the Catholic Church and was as a result burned to death at the stake.[21] Later in the 1920s, Socialists in particular would seize on this work in an attempt to show what they said was the hypocrisy of Mussolini. But the pamphlet on Hus shows that Mussolini was not a hypocrite at all. In fact, 'Giovanni Huss il Veridico', is an attack not on God but on the Church, not on religion, but on the corruption of religion and the tyranny of the Church. Its protagonist, Hus, was as passionate a believer in God as anyone. The pamphlet is also an attack on empire and a defence of nation – brave little Bohemia trying via Hus to shake off the yoke of the Holy Roman Empire. The execution of Hus led to what Mussolini wrote was 'one of the biggest and bloodiest popular insurrections in history'. The main theme of the pamphlet is the theme of Huss himself – that the Catholic Church had simply become a vast, corrupt, tyrannical, money-making machine and that the only solution was independence from both it and its secular champion, the Holy Roman Empire. 'With wealth the entire Christian Church was poisoned and corrupted,' Mussolini wrote. The Hussite movement comprised 'two inseparable elements: the religious and the nationalistic. Both had a social and Socialist appendix,' he added. Critics have also often insisted that Mussolini ditched international Socialism for nationalism merely as a cynical means of getting power. His only interest in life, so the argument goes, was power. But here, as early as 1911–12, is Mussolini, the revolutionary international Socialist, already talking about the importance of nationalism as well as socialism.

The pamphlet shows too how important the idea of a charismatic leader already was to Mussolini. Hus was the man in whom, he wrote, were 'concentrated and directed all the forces of religious and moral liberation ... His doctrine grew more noble with his martyrdom. His followers grew in numbers and strength.' The insurrection which followed Hus's death failed, Mussolini wrote, because it no longer had a charismatic leader and without him his followers split into factions. In the pamphlet's preface Mussolini wrote, 'I hope that this [book] kindles in the soul of readers a hatred for any form of spiritual or profane tyranny: whether theocratic or Jacobin.' Mussolini was against religious tyranny but he had a strong thirst for religion. He needed faith and he found it, first in Socialism, then in Fascism, then in a fusion of Fascism and Catholicism. And he was, as we have noted, obsessively superstitious.

In Switzerland, between the summer of 1902 until the spring of 1904 at least – a very long time indeed by Mussolini's standards – Mussolini does not appear to have had much sex. One explanation is that his morale was still rock bottom – despite his increased involvement in politics and journalism. He was often ill through lack of food and he was shamed and angered by his poverty. He looked like a tramp, rarely washed or shaved. He was not a pretty sight. He also feared he had syphilis. The fear merely added to his depression in Switzerland. In Italy, as a teacher in Gualtieri, at least he had enjoyed status and some money. In Switzerland he had no status and no money. He often thought about suicide.

Many authors say that Mussolini had syphilis. What is the truth? The Geneva University Library records of the sixteen books consulted by Mussolini on his eighteen visits there show that one was about syphilis. In 1905 he had told his cousin Venusta Mussolini that women had ruined him and that he had caught syphilis in the Forlì brothel he had first visited aged seventeen.[22] In 1919 an Italian police report on Mussolini and the Fascists noted, 'Benito Mussolini has a strong physical constitution even though he is infected by syphilis.'[23] Similarly, in her book *Il Traditore Mussolini*, Balabanoff wrote that Mussolini had told her he had syphilis. But it could not have been syphilis, which is fatal if untreated and was incurable then, because Mussolini did not die. According to Dr Luigi Covassi (interviewed by the journalist Fabrizio Castellini in 1984), 'My brother-in-law Dr Umberto Cecchetti treated him at Tolmezzo in 1907. It was not syphilis, as many have claimed, but gonorrhea or clap, a very common infection in those days, which young men usually caught from prostitutes in brothels.'[24] Of course, Mussolini could have caught syphilis after 1907. But again he did not die and his doctor between November 1942 and July 1943, Arnaldo Pozzi,[25] wrote after the war, 'The relevant tests were done and were all negative, no symptoms of any sexually transmitted disease were ever noted. And there was no damage to the heart or nervous system.' Nor did the autopsy on Mussolini on 30 April 1945 by Professor Mario Cattabeni of Milan University, find any sign of sexually transmitted disease.[26]

In early April 1904, Mussolini was imprisoned when he went to the police station to get a *permis de séjour* which he required to attend Geneva University and for which he needed to present his passport. The police noticed that he had changed the date of expiry on the passport from the end of 1903 to 1905. He had done this to avoid returning to Italy to do his military service. The police locked him up for three days then deported him by train. By now, Mussolini had gained a certain notoriety and Swiss Socialists staged an emergency debate in the parliament of the canton of Ticini about his case. Consequently the police allowed him to remain in Switzerland. A Geneva newspaper which had reported the matter called him 'The grand local Duce'. It was the first time that he had been called Duce (the word comes from the Latin *dux* and means literally leader or chief). Originally, Socialists used it to describe their leaders.

Barred from Geneva, Mussolini returned to Lausanne and on 9 May signed on as a student at Lausanne University's Social Sciences faculty, which he attended, he said, each morning. He got a six-month *permis de séjour* on condition that he did not take part in political demonstrations. 'So began another period of life *à la bohème*. . . . I lived in misery.'[27] But he had become much more energetic and driven. He gave lessons in Italian, did translation work, wrote articles, was active in politics and spent many hours in the university.

Among the lectures he attended at the university were those of the famous Italian economist and sociologist Vilfredo Pareto (1848–1923) who taught there. Many biographers have doubted this. But Pareto wrote in a 1923 letter just before his death that Mussolini did indeed attend. Mussolini would draw heavily on Pareto's theory that the world was ruled by elites and democracy was just another form of rule by an elite – an oligarchy. He also said that the majority had no absolute right to rule because it was physically impossible for the majority to rule. A willingness to use force by an elite was the sign of a vigorous elite; reluctance to use force the sign of a weak one. All other political theories were bogus, especially Marxist and democratic theories. Subsequently, Mussolini, like Lenin, did not believe revolution would happen on its own. Men had to act to bring about revolution and he took as his Marxist watchword the famous phrase of Marx from *The Treatise on Feuerbach*: 'The point is no longer to study the world, the point is to transform it.' Mussolini and Lenin, both revolutionary Socialists, came up with the same solution for starting and sustaining the revolution: a revolutionary elite. The masses would not rise up on their own. They had to be stirred to revolution and led to it. The elite would use the masses to seize power and use power to introduce Communism by force on their behalf.

This idea of a revolutionary elite developed from the thought of Pareto in Lausanne and the revolutionary syndicalism of men such as Georges Sorel in France. Sorel was among the first on the left to start talking about the need for a revolutionary elite in his *L'Avenir Socialiste des Syndicats* and later in his 1906 *Les Réflexions sur la Violence*. Sorel's elite would consist of pure, uncontaminated workers – a workers' elite unwilling to make any compromise with the bourgeoisie or its politicians. The bourgeoisie and the politicians would have no role in the new scheme of things. This concept of total non co-operation had sprung from widespread disgust at endemic political corruption especially in France and Italy. To gain power, the workers' elite, once strong enough, would call a general strike which, if sustained, would paralyse the economy and cause the collapse of Capitalism. But to succeed, the strike would require mass support which meant the creation, first, of an ideology that stirred the masses to action. What stirred people to action, however, was not logic but myth. So what mattered about an ideology was not its rightness but whether it had the power to create a myth. Later, in 1914, many revolutionary syndicalists were in favour, unlike Socialists, of intervention in the First World War. In 1918 the 'left-wing' revolutionary syndicalists, led by Filippo Corridoni, would even fuse with 'right-wing' nationalists to form a single group – the *Sindacato Nazionale*. Many of these people would then become Fascists.

Mussolini had also started to read Nietzsche and was very impressed by his ideas about the superman, the whipping of women and the will to power. He took as his personal motto the philosopher's words 'Live dangerously'. In 1924 he would tell the *New York Times* journalist, Oscar Levy, that Nietzsche had 'cured me of my Socialism' – and of politicians who speak hypocritically of 'the consensus of the governed, of parliament and of universal suffrage'.[28]

On 30 April 1904 a military court in Bologna had convicted Mussolini of desertion *in absentia* (for failure to present himself for military service) and sentenced him to one year in prison. But to celebrate the birth on 15 September of Vittorio Emanuele III's first son, Umberto, the king announced an amnesty for military service deserters. Mussolini wrote, 'Two conflicting ideas raced around my brain during the first weeks of autumn. Go back to Italy as my mother wanted or leave for New York?'[29] Mussolini decided to return to Italy in November to do his military service – via Lugano and Milan.

This time he had left Switzerland for good. He was twenty-one. He stayed in Dovia with his family until 14 January 1905, when he set off for Verona to join the Number 3 Company, 2nd Battalion of the 10th Bersaglieri Regiment (*bersagliere* means targeteer). His mother's health, he wrote, was 'first class'.[30] But then, at the end of January 1905, his father wrote to say that she had fallen ill once again. In mid-February he received a telegram saying that her condition was very serious and was given compassionate leave. He arrived at Forlì station on the evening of 18 February and walked the ten miles to Dovia. His mother was still alive but semi-conscious, did not recognise him and could not speak. 'Only her hands moved grasping nervously the sheets ... her forehead was wet with the cold sweat of death.'[31] She died shortly after 2 p.m. the next day – 19 February. She was forty-six. Mussolini does not mention what illness caused his mother's death but it is generally said to have been pneumonia. Arnaldo had not come. He was still in Berne. Later in 1905 Arnaldo returned to Italy to work as a teacher at his old school in Cesena – unlike his brother he did not become involved in politics or journalism until much later. Mussolini wrote that the day his mother died was 'the saddest day in my youth'.[32] As for his father, 'He was no longer a man, just the shadow of a man.'

The loss of his mother and the deep grief he said he felt did not prevent him, however, from indulging in another affair in Dovia – with the young schoolmistress who had replaced his mother at the Dovia school, Paolina Denti. 'We loved each other deeply,' he wrote.

Mussolini completed his military service on 4 September 1906. He had been a good soldier, which was odd given his politics. He was on file with both the Swiss and Italian authorities as a dangerous political agitator and under surveillance, yet he enjoyed his military service.

Mussolini disliked teaching intensely. But Switzerland, despite his involvement in Socialism and journalism and encounters with Socialists from all over Europe, had meant poverty. He would not go back. Instead, he decided to stay in Italy and apply once more for primary-school teaching posts. He was successful. On 23 October 1906 he set off for Tolmezzo, in the mountains of the Carnia, north-west of Venice, to teach in a primary school. His pay was 75 lira a month. 'I remember that it rained all the time.' He also recalled that he could not control his class of around forty children. 'Some of them were incorrigible and dangerous urchins ... I did everything in my power ... but from the word go I was incapable of solving the problem of discipline.' His time at Tolmezzo was a period of 'brutishness and dissipation both physical and spiritual'.[33]

Nor was it long before Mussolini, while professing by letter his love for Paolina Denti, found other women closer to his new home. In March 1907 he began a blazing affair with his landlady at La Locanda della Scala where he lodged, Luigia Paggetta, who was about thirty, married, and 'still beautiful'. 'She loved me madly.'[34] Her husband soon found out, and a fight occurred.[35] 'Naturally the husband, older and weaker than me, came off worse,' wrote Mussolini. Once again, as at Gualtieri, Mussolini's affair with a married woman had caused a scandal. And once again he was not asked to stay on a second year at the school and so had to quit at the end of the summer term.

The report on him by his superiors noted that as a teacher he was 'incoherent in his procedure', 'was not a teacher' and his work bore 'very little fruit'.[36] Despite his hatred of the Church he took Latin lessons from a local priest. He also used to go to the cemetery at night to shout out poetry and sometimes wandered about pretending to be a ghost wearing a white sheet. Meanwhile, his name began to appear in local Socialist and Catholic newspapers in connection with speeches he had made – often spelled wrong, 'Bussolini' or 'Mussolino'.

Mussolini left Tolmezzo at the end of August 1907. 'I had scandalised the zone,' he would recall.[37] He disliked teaching and had effectively been sacked both times that he had tried it. He thought of going abroad again and even applied for another passport, but decided that teaching older children might make the job more tolerable. He enrolled at Bologna University to take the examinations in November 1907 for a diploma as a secondary-school French teacher. He passed the written examinations on 15 November and ten days later turned up for the oral examinations unshaven and with a cigarette stuck to his lower lip to the bemusement of the other candidates and the examiners. He passed.

In March 1908, thanks to his teacher's diploma, Mussolini was appointed by the Socialist-controlled town council in Oneglia, in Liguria, on the Italian Riviera, as French teacher in its Collegio Civico Ulisse Calvi, which was a boarding school. He could now call himself *'professore'* instead of *'maestro'*. But he wrote, 'I was in the same old trap.' His interests lay outside school. Thanks to Giacinto Menotti Serrati, the leading Socialist he had befriended in Switzerland, whose two brothers lived in Oneglia, he started to write for their local Socialist weekly newspaper – *La Lima* – and began to sign articles with the pseudonym *'Vero Eretico'* (true heretic). He was soon appointed editor. This was his first editorship. He ran the newspaper in dictatorial style and wrote violent articles attacking the Church. Priests, for example, were 'black gendarmes in the service of Capitalism'. He wrote, too, of the need for a revolutionary elite. 'The workers have only a vague concept of their mission and of their importance, and above all of their strength.'

But at the end of the academic year Mussolini was sacked yet again. As usual, he had run up debts and as usual there was a woman – this time Giovannina Amoretti. He left Oneglia for good that summer.

4

THE DUCE AS JOURNALIST

Mussolini returned to Dovia in July 1908. It was harvest time. There was serious rioting by casual farm labourers (*braccianti*), who tended to be Socialists, against share-croppers (*mazzadri*) who tended to be either republicans or pro-clericals. The argument was over pay and conditions as a result of the widespread introduction of steam threshing machines between 1904 and 1905. Such machines obviously meant fewer people were needed to do the harvest. There was also the question of who should manage them – the *braccianti* or the *mazzadri*. Mussolini took the side of the *braccianti*.

On 18 July he was arrested and charged with threatening violence against the manager of some steam threshing machines, and subsequently condemned to three months in prison and a 1000 lira fine. He was released on bail after twelve days. In November the court reduced his sentence to the twelve days he had already served.

Meanwhile Mussolini rekindled relationships of old, but by the end of the year he had another female target in mind. In November 1908 Mussolini's father Alessandro decided to move from Dovia to Forlì to become landlord of an inn called the Trattoria del Bersagliere near the station. When his wife had died in February 1905 Alessandro had had to move out of the Palazzo Varano to make way for the new teacher, Paolina Denti – one of his son's girlfriends – and in May 1905 had gone to live at Vallona, the family farm. He had had a mistress for many years: Annina Lombardi Guidi, the widow of a local peasant farmer. She had moved in with him at the farm and then come with him to Forlì. Meanwhile he rented out the farm for 490 lira a year. Annina Guidi had five daughters of whom the youngest was Rachele, born on 11 April 1890. Rachele began work as a waitress at the inn in January 1909. Her father had died in September 1899 when she was nine.

By now, Mussolini had also moved to Forlì, living in lodgings there from November 1908 to January 1909. He was frequently at the inn to help his father as a waiter – and talk politics. According to Rachele, Mussolini was an excellent waiter – most servile. That January of 1909 he saw a lot of Rachele, whom he already knew of old as he had taught her at the Dovia school when he had stood in for his mother when she was ill and whom he had once rapped across the knuckles in class because she would not keep quiet.

Like him, she was a very unruly pupil who threw stones at other children and climbed trees, she recorded, 'like a squirrel'. He wrote, 'Rachele was no longer the little girl whom I had taught so many times when standing in for my mother; she was instead a girl in the full bloom of youth and from the moment I saw her, I liked her and decided to make her mine, which is in fact what happened.'[1] What did Mussolini see in Rachele? She could hardly read and write, she was afraid of snakes and thunderstorms and years later she would sign letters with the word 'bachi' for 'baci' – kisses. One reason why he decided to make her his was no doubt that she was probably a virgin. Where women were concerned his revolutionary Socialism never got the better of old-fashioned values. She was a peasant girl who had tended herds of pigs and flocks of turkeys and who would always retain the sneaky mentality of a Romagnol peasant. But above all she was of his beloved village. She was of his 'terra'.

Rachele, who had blonde hair, herself recalled, 'His eyes always persuaded me to obey him. They were sharp, penetrating, with pupils like bright lamps. I used to say they were phosphorescent.'[2]

In November 1908 Mussolini went back to Bologna University to take examinations for a diploma to enable him to teach German as well as French. But he failed so badly in the written examinations that he was not even asked to attend the oral ones.

At this time he wrote an essay called 'The Philosophy of Force' published in the Republican weekly *Il Pensiero romagnolo* in three instalments in November and December 1908, which illustrates well which way his political thought was heading, despite his revolutionary Socialism.[3]

The 'super man' is the great Nietzschean creation ... Nietzsche has rung the bell of an imminent return of the ideal. But it is an ideal fundamentally different from those in which past generations believed. To understand it, there will come 'free spirits' of a new kind fortified by war, by solitude, by great danger, spirits who will have experienced the wind, the ice, the snows of the mountains and will know how to measure with a serene eye the depth of the abysses – spirits equipped with a kind of sublime wickedness – spirits who will liberate us from the love of our neighbour, from the desire for the void (*nulla*) giving back to the earth its purpose and to men their hope – new, free spirits who will triumph over God and over the Void!

The reference to God is a reference to the idea of the Christian God – rather than God.

Sarfatti in *Dux* spoke of Mussolini's 'religious anti-clericalism'.[4] What he especially despised was the Christian doctrine of turning the other cheek, of forgiveness, of loving one's neighbour regardless. 'With Christianity it is the moral of renunciation and resignation which triumphs ... The love of one's neighbour has caused twenty centuries of war and above all – don't forget – modern Europe, this *mostriciatello* (little monster) bloated by its irredeemable mediocrity ...'[5]

Mussolini would never teach again. The Socialists in Trent, capital of the Trentino, which was at that time part of the Austro-Hungarian Empire, offered Mussolini the post of general secretary of the Camera del Lavoro in the city and the editorship of its Socialist weekly newspaper *L'Avvenire del Lavoratore*. He accepted. He had been recommended by his Socialist friends and mentors in Switzerland, Serrati and Balabanoff.

The night before he left Forlì on 6 February 1909 there was a leaving party for him at his father's inn – *Il Bersagliere*. He played his violin and danced with Rachele who wrote, 'Towards the end of the evening he took me to one side and fixing me with his sparkling eyes he surprised me by saying, "Tomorrow I leave, but on my return you will become my wife. You must wait for me." '[6] Mussolini arrived in Trent on the evening of 6 February 1909. It was snowing. The newspaper announced his appointment by describing him as a 'proven fighter ... fervent propagandist, particularly expert on the subject of anti-clericalism ... he speaks German perfectly'. His German was far from perfect – he had failed even to pass the exam to teach it in Italian secondary schools in Bologna the previous November. But his seven months in the Trentino, where both German and Italian were spoken, improved it.

In Trent, he found his vocation and for the first time in his life had a proper outlet for this ambition. Circulation of *L'Avvenire del Lavoratore* increased from '1600 to 2400' he said. He also started working for *Il Popolo* – the local Socialist daily newspaper owned by a wealthy lawyer and Socialist, Cesare Battisti, a firm believer that the Trentino should be part of Italy. He became consumed by journalism and politics. It was in the Trentino – as a result of the constant debate about unification – that Mussolini began to think seriously not just about Socialism and internationalism but about nationalism and the nature of nations.

At this time the Trentino with the Alto Adige formed the Austrian province of South Tyrol. The political issue in the province around which all other issues revolved was: should the South Tyrol remain part of the Austrian Empire or should it become part of Italy. Of the inhabitants of the Trentino, 70 per cent were Italian in the sense that they spoke not German but Italian dialect. However, in the Alto Adige the split was fifty-fifty. The leaders of the Italian Catholic People's Party and most Italian Catholics, by nature conservative, favoured staying with the devil they knew – Catholic Austria. What of the minority Socialists? The German speakers wanted to stay with Austria – the Italian speakers wanted to unify with Italy. What of Mussolini? Like Socialists at large he vacillated. Initially, Socialists opposed nationalism as a tool of the bourgeoisie. But in the end reality forced the party to water this down. So the party line changed: nationalist movements against a foreign colonial oppressor were fine as long as they were led by Socialists and did not become tools of the bourgeoisie. This was also Lenin's view – on, say, Ireland.

Soon after leaving the Trentino Mussolini wrote an essay, 'Il Trentino Veduto da un Socialista', serialised in part in May 1910 in *La Voce*, a Florence-based weekly newspaper owned by Giuseppe Prezzolini, a nationalist heavily influenced by Nietzsche. (The Italian Nationalist Association was founded in 1910.) In the essay Mussolini gave only lukewarm endorsement of unification with Italy and said that anyway in the immediate future there was little chance of it happening. But his experience in Trent forced him for the first time in print to confront the issue of nationalism head on. In the pamphlet, he noted that Italian-speaking workers in the Trentino refused to renounce their *Italianità* or the Italian language. He said that as the majority of workers spoke Italian and the majority of the bourgeoisie spoke German the language of the workers should prevail. His opposition to unification with Italy was essentially pragmatic: Austria was too strong. When, later, Mussolini became a passionate nationalist, Socialists would say that in Trent he had been anti-nationalist and that here, once again, was an example of his hypocrisy and opportunism. But the truth is that in Trent Mussolini was already veering to nationalism.

His employer at *Il Popolo*, Battisti, like most local Socialists, was a reformist Socialist (i.e. he believed in revolution via the ballot box). But he was fiercely in favour of Trentino unification with Italy. Mussolini was a revolutionary Socialist and in two minds about unification. This did not stop Battisti appointing Mussolini editor of the daily *Il Popolo* on his twenty-sixth birthday, 29 July 1909. Mussolini said he produced the newspaper almost entirely on his own. It was the first daily paper that he had edited. He used it and the weekly *L'Avvenire del Lavoratore* to assault with fury, wit and humour much more easily identifiable enemy targets than Trentino national status. These targets were the Church and democracy.

The Catholic Church was 'a great big corpse' (the next year he would use the same expression to describe his own party), he wrote, and the Vatican a 'den of intolerance and a gang of robbers'. The Italian-speaking Catholics responded through their newspaper *Il Trentino*, edited by Alcide De Gasperi. De Gasperi was Catholic, bourgeois, conservative and pro-Austria. He represented the majority view among Trentino Italian speakers – Socialism the minority view. Like many of Mussolini's opponents De Gasperi, who forty years later would become prime minister of Italy, would criticise Mussolini for changing his political spots to get power. But De Gasperi, like Mussolini's other critics, was no different and when the time came he would switch sides over unification with Italy. Where once he had been comfortable calling himself Austrian he would soon be just as comfortable calling himself Italian.

Mussolini's printed assaults were frequently libellous in the extreme. He dismissed De Gasperi as a man 'without ideas and without courage'. He described him and his Catholic colleagues variously in print as 'donkey', 'liar', 'barbary ape ... somehow escaped from Gibraltar' and 'rabid priest'. Jesus, 'the sweet vagabond of Palestine', was a Socialist, not the son of God, who could not resist the passionate onslaught of Mary Magdelene. De Gasperi in turn wrote, 'The only thing Mussolini and his friends are is violent, they consider public life as a tournament of insults and beatings ... the socialist bosses are criminals.' But De Gasperi – like so many others after him – missed the point. Mussolini was not at all how De Gasperi portrayed him.

What was compelling in Mussolini was not actual violence, nor even the violent content of his words. It was the form of his words. The language of Mussolini was his special gift both spoken and written. It was not actual violence people found attractive in him – there was never very much of that – it was his violent use of words. And he was funny. He used ridicule and sarcasm. And what was also compelling was his refusal to swallow dogma, whether the dogma of the Church or that of Socialism. This enabled him to change his mind.

Mussolini quickly became a brilliant popular journalist. He developed a style – unlike the traditional style, which was dominated by the concept of elegance which usually meant convoluted sentences expressed in lofty language. His sentences were short, concise, emotional and written in simple language. 'Oh, if it were possible to strangle it ... verbose, prolix, inconclusive, eloquence ...' he said.[7] His aim in his writing – and his speaking – was to strip away 'all that is decoration, frippery, superficiality, annulling all the flotsam of fifteenth centuryisms, all vain chit-chat'.[8] Insult, sarcasm and ridicule were frequent weapons in his verbal armoury: nauseating, imbecile, cretin, paranoid, mental deficient, revolting reptile – the kind of words used. Of De Gasperi and the priests in Trent he said they were a 'zoological species of black anthropoid'.

As well as the Church, Democracy came under heavy fire from Mussolini in Trent. At a meeting on 22 April 1909 he said, 'Who says democracy, says rabble of money-grubbers from the political sewer, says lawyers in search of clienteles, teachers in search of teaching jobs, journalists beating at the counter for secret funds, speculators buying the silence of judges, worried consciences which pretend to be anti-clerical but who are in bed with freemasonry which has become today a universal association of mafiosi.' The only solution was 'physical, material and muscular' violence because 'so long as ideas remain in libraries, they are completely innocuous'. Reformist Socialists who wanted to use democracy as the means to revolution he dismissed as 'Tagliatelle Socialists'. This hostility to dem-

ocracy was not something Mussolini had come to gradually. It was something he had had from the start. He was never a democrat. But much of
him was always and remained a Socialist. Both Mussolini and Lenin came
to the same conclusion. Revolution was impossible via parliament and
democracy. Inevitably, these dissipated the power of the revolutionary
idea. For Mussolini there was no contradiction between Socialism and
what would become Fascism. It was the Socialists who had, for him,
betrayed Socialism, not he. In fact, he continued to think of himself as a
Socialist to the end of his life.

Not surprisingly, Mussolini was frequently arrested, jailed and fined
during his seven months in Trent for his offensive articles. His office was
searched by police and publication, in particular of *L'Avvenire del Lavoratore*,
often stopped.

In September 1909 the Austro-Hungarian authorities ordered Mussolini's
arrest as a dangerous political agitator, which prompted the Trentino
Socialists to call a general strike, and Mussolini to go on hunger strike.
The next day the police escorted him by horse-drawn carriage, then train
south, to the Italian frontier at Ala. Only the Socialist journalists heeded
the call for a general strike. But the expulsion made front-page news in
Italian and Austrian newspapers nevertheless and was debated briefly in
the Italian parliament. While in Trent he had not written a single letter to
Rachele and only one postcard to his father in which he included a
sentence telling him to remind her of his desire to marry her.

Mussolini returned to Forlì on 5 October 1909. He was already, aged
twenty-six, going bald from the front backwards. Once more he was
without a job. Once more he thought of going abroad, once more the idea
of America cropped up. He decided to stay in Forlì. Battisti wrote to ask
him to write a historical novel – *Claudia Particella l'Amante del Cardinale* –
for serialisation in his daily newspaper, *Il Popolo*, to boost sales. The novel
was published in fifty-six instalments amid much fanfare between 20
January and 11 May 1910. It was Mussolini's one and only novel and was
about a seventeenth-century cardinal king and his lover. He had written
it, he told the German journalist Ludwig in 1932, 'for political reasons' to
embarrass the Catholics. 'It's a horrible little book,' he told him. 'In those
days the clergy was truly polluted with corruption,' he added. By 1932, of
course, he had only recently signed the Lateran Accords with Pope Pius
XI. This might explain why in Italy the novel was never published in
book form. But in 1929 it was published in English – without Mussolini's
permission. His other motive in writing the novel was financial: he was
desperate for money.[9] His situation, he wrote to Battisti, was 'very acute'.

The novel was based on the story of Carlo Emanuele Madruzzo, the last
bishop-prince of Trent in the first half of the seventeenth century and his
twenty-year love affair with Claudia Particella, the much younger daughter
of his prime minister (*primo consigliere*). In reality, Madruzzo died of old

age after failing to get permission from the Pope to leave the church and marry Claudia. In Mussolini's novel Claudia, described as having 'the black eyes of the devil', is murdered with poison just as she has fallen in love with a young Hungarian knight and is about to betray the old cardinal for the first time. All the characters in the book are bad – except a servant called Rachele.

Meanwhile, in real life Mussolini continued his assault on Rachele. 'In the weeks that followed [his return to Forlì from Trent] I declared my love to Rachele, who responded in kind. While waiting to unite myself with her I sent her, between 1909 and 1910, to San Martino, to stay with one of her sisters. I wanted to detach her from the atmosphere of that inn, and anyway there was no longer an absolute need for her to work there.'[10] San Martino was a hamlet just outside Forlì. Mussolini, as usual, was jealous, but this time with reason. While he had been away, a surveyor with lots of land from Ravenna had proposed to her. Even Mussolini's father, Alessandro, thought the marriage a good idea. She recalled, 'I could not make up my mind ... But already destiny had me in its grasp.'[11] Mussolini then wrote to his rival and ordered him to leave Rachele alone. As for her, she wrote, 'I loved him, but I was hesitant. He was very, very jealous. At a certain moment he banned me from leaving the house to go and work in the *trattoria*. Then he banned me from his meetings because he insisted, "When you're there I am speechless." '[12]

Both his father and his father's mistress, Rachele's mother, were strongly opposed to him marrying Rachele. Mussolini merely said that they each had their own reasons – without specifying what these were. But their opposition might be explained by their knowledge that if Mussolini married Rachele he would be committing incest. Since for many years before the death of his wife Annina Guidi had been Alessandro Mussolini's mistress there has always been much speculation – but no evidence – that Alessandro was Rachele's father and that as a result Mussolini was about to marry his half-sister. Both Rachele and Alessandro had blue eyes which was – still is – rare in the Romagna. For every hundred pairs of brown eyes only one pair is blue. She was often referred to as Benito's half-sister. To get the permission of Rachele's mother and his father Mussolini employed dramatic tactics. One night in early January 1910 he said to Rachele, she recalled, ' "I want to make a life and a family. You must be my woman and the mother of my children." The next day he called my mother and his father; he took out a revolver and some bullets and said gravely, in my presence, "Here there are six bullets: one for her" and he pointed at me, "the others for me." '[13]

On 17 January 1910 Mussolini married Rachele, as he put it, 'without official ties, neither civil, nor religious'.[14] He was twenty-six. She was seventeen. This so-called marriage could not have amounted to more than a decision to live together. There was nothing in writing. There was no honeymoon. Mussolini simply went to Rachele's sister's house just outside Forlì where she lived and told Rachele to pack. The couple then walked through heavy rain the mile or two to Forlì to spend their first night together in a hotel. Rachele must already have been pregnant as the couple's first child, Edda, was born seven and a half months later, on 1 September. Rachele would always feel unable to address her man with the informal '*tu*' and would use the formal '*lei*' throughout their life together.

Many are convinced that Edda was not Mussolini's first child. That honour, they say, belongs to an illegitimate boy, born in far-off Innsbruck, Austria, on 19 May 1910. The mother was a woman from Trent called Fernanda Oss who christened her baby boy Benito Ribelle Oss – '*Ribelle*' was Mussolini's nickname in Trent. The boy would die aged two and his mother of consumption in Trent on 22 February 1922 aged thirty-eight. The existence of this alleged first Mussolini child did not become public until after the Second World War. But the child cannot have been Mussolini's – unless conception occurred in the first week or so of September 1909 and the birth was late. This is because Benito Ribelle was not born until 19 May 1910. A normal pregnancy of nine months would mean that the child was conceived in the third week of September 1909. But Mussolini was arrested in the second week of September 1909, on the 10th, and held in custody until his expulsion from Trento and Austria on 26 September. So the idea seems very far fetched and means that the boy was born after at least a ten-month pregnancy.

Mussolini and Rachele moved into a small two-room flat in Forlì, which they rented for 15 lira a month. On 27 January his father had a stroke, which paralysed his right side. He recovered enough to walk about with a stick. Mussolini used to play his violin over Edda's cot and then, when she fell asleep, lift her eyelids with his fingers to contemplate her eyes. This terrified the child. Edda, said Rachele, suffered always from insomnia as a result. Mussolini claimed in *La mia vita* that as a result of Edda's birth he now promised Rachele that he would give up alcohol for good and did. Her story was different: he did not come home one night until 5 a.m. and was so drunk that two friends had had to carry him. He began to smash every object he could lay his hands on. 'If you come home again drunk I will kill you,' she told him the next day. But Mussolini did not give up drink.

On 19 November 1910 Alessandro Mussolini died aged fifty-six. He was buried in the cemetery at Forlì. (But in 1932, after Mussolini had been in power for nine years, his remains were transferred to the new Mussolini family crypt at the San Cassiano cemetery in Predappio.) His three children sold the farm, Vallona, and received 3000 lira each. His mistress decided to give up the inn and when in December Mussolini and Rachele moved into a larger apartment in Forlì she joined them. Mussolini used to lock Rachele in the flat when he went out, she claimed, and to stop her going down the stairs to the communal standpipe he did the washing-up.[15] And as he always used to cut himself when shaving, she shaved him each morning. Later a barber would shave him. The week before his 'marriage' to Rachele, Mussolini had started as founding editor of a new Socialist newspaper in Forlì, *La Lotta di classe*, a small four-page weekly, which he wrote himself. He had also been appointed general secretary of the Federation of Forlì Socialists.

On 9 January 1910 *La Lotta di classe* published its first edition. Mussolini's pay was 120 lira a month, a lot more than he had earned as a teacher. The newspaper was funded by the 1400 members of the Forlì Socialist party. Initially the circulation was 1200 but soon reached 3000, said Mussolini in *La mia vita*, as the newspaper became in his words the 'organ of Socialists in the entire province'. The main thrust of his editorials was to urge Socialists not just to talk, but to act – and to attract anyone, not just Socialists, who supported revolution. By action he meant violent action. A bomb could be more effective than a thousand speeches. Rachele recalled that the success of the newspaper led to an offer from Italian Socialists in America to edit *Il Proletario* – to which he was a regular contributor.

Mussolini now set his sights on the destruction of the reformists who controlled the Socialist party. At the party's annual conference in October 1910 in Milan he took part in an unsuccessful attempt to get the revolutionary wing of the party to split and form a new party. He saw another opportunity in March 1911 when Leonida Bissolati, a senior figure on the party's National Executive, founding editor of *Avanti!* from 1896 to 1903 and Socialist MP, took part in discussions in the *Quirinale* with the King, Vittore Emanuele III, over the formation of a new government following the collapse of the previous one. Discussions with the monarch were sacrilege to revolutionary Socialists such as Mussolini. In *La Lotta di classe* he demanded the party expel Bissolati 'otherwise we go', but only the Forlì Socialists supported him. So he and they announced that they would leave the party after its twelfth annual congress in Modena in September.

On 29 September 1911 Italy declared war on Turkey over Libya, ostensibly to protect Italian citizens living in and around Tripoli. But the real aim of Giovanni Giolitti, the Liberal Italian prime minister, was to take Libya from Turkey and make it an Italian colony. Italy, a new nation, was determined to join the scramble for Africa even at this late stage. Libya was one of the few places left to grab.

Mussolini fiercely opposed the Libyan war, which put on hold the thorny question for him and his Forlì comrades of whether to stay out or try to rejoin the Socialist party. The moderate Socialist party leadership did not call a general strike in protest at the war – to the fury of revolutionaries such as Mussolini. But the workers' trade union, the *Confederazione generale del Lavoro*, and some regional Socialist parties did. In only a handful of places, however, did a general strike take place. Nationalism had a stronger hold over the mind of the Italian proletariat than Socialism. This was something Mussolini noted and would later exploit. The Romagna, including Forlì, was one place where the strike enjoyed for a brief period a measure of success. It was not so much a strike as a riot. In Forlì both Socialists led by Mussolini and Republicans led by Pietro Nenni – often enemies but united on this issue – went on strike on 26 and 27 September. Thousands took to the streets – 4000 according to the police, 10–12,000 according to Mussolini. There was much damage done, particularly at the station where a troop train was unable to depart. On 14 October Mussolini and Nenni were arrested, jailed, and accused of resistance to the forces of law and order, violation of the liberty of shopkeepers, and criminal damage to railway, telephone and telegraph lines. At their trial on 18 November 1911 Mussolini admitted among other things that he was in favour of sabotage. He also said that to oppose the war was the truly patriotic thing to do. Mussolini and Nenni were found guilty, and sentenced to one year and one year and fifteen days in prison respectively. On appeal, the sentences were reduced in the case of Mussolini to five and half months and Nenni to seven and a half months.

Mussolini would later arrest Nenni and send him into exile, but save him from the Nazis. Later still, Nenni would be leader of the Socialist party which fought – unsuccessfully – the 1948 general election in a united front with the Communist party. On 10 December 1911 Mussolini wrote an article,[16] smuggled out of prison, for La Lotta di classe: 'Monarchy! Army! War! These are the three spiritual and ideological beacons around which are gathered the moths ... of Italian nationalism ... We have ... looked with sympathy on nationalism within the nation, a democratic-cultural movement of progress ... of the renovation of the Italian people ... They [the nationalists] should reflect that before conquering Trento or Trieste or Tripolitania they should conquer Italy first; they should bring water to Puglia ... justice to the South, literacy everywhere!'

While Mussolini was in prison, Rachele was left without any money and had to rely on the generosity of his Socialist friends. One day she visited him in prison and complained that she had eczema on her head. 'Shave it,' he told her. She did. 'Benito thought he had found a solution to stop other men chasing me and deep down I felt flattered by his jealousy.' But her mother brought Rachele a wig. Years later, one day in Rome in 1923, Mussolini lured Rachele into the barber's where he used to get shaved. 'He was sitting in front of the mirror and I had to bend down to hear what he wanted. Then, before I could stop him, he whipped out a big pair of scissors and chopped off my plaits.'[17]

Mussolini was released from prison on 12 March 1912. He and his Forlì Socialist colleagues had already drawn up their plan to rejoin the party. In June 1912 they did so.

The success of the general strike in Forlì, Mussolini's arrest as a result, and the temporary secession of the Forlì Socialists from the party had made him known to the party leadership if not the party at large. Bissolati and his reformist colleagues were the dominant force and controlled its National Executive. But the Libyan war in particular had made Bissolati and them vulnerable. Mussolini set his sights once again on their destruction. The battleground was the Italian Socialist party's thirteenth annual congress between 7 and 10 July 1912 in Reggio Emilia – near Bologna. This time his tactics were different. The previous year he had tried to take like-minded Socialists with him out of the party. This time he would do the opposite: try to expel the reformists from the party and put the revolutionaries on its commanding heights. He decided to move a motion demanding the expulsion of Bissolati and the other reformists on the National Executive on the grounds that they were class collaborators and had renounced revolution. It was Mussolini's first important political speech.

For revolutionary Socialists like Mussolini universal suffrage – most men had got the vote in 1912 in Italy increasing the electorate from 3 to $8\frac{1}{2}$ million – could not deliver the Socialist revolution. 'The experience in other nations shows us that universal suffrage does not solve the social question,' he wrote[18] in 1912 around the time of the Reggio Emilia congress, adding, 'For us universal suffrage has a value insofar as it is a consultation of the nation, insofar as its use demonstrates to the proletariat that if it wants to redeem itself it cannot, and must not give up on revolution.' Or, 'The usefulness of universal suffrage is, then – from a Socialist point of view – negative: on the one hand it slows down the democratic evolution of the bourgeois political regimes, on the other it demonstrates to the proletariat the necessity of not giving up other more effective methods of struggle.' Or, 'Universal suffrage is the oxygen bag which prolongs the life of the dying.'

For Mussolini democracy and parliament were a dead end. In Italy, in particular, once they became MPs Socialists got bogged down in the mire of the Italian parliament, where nothing of substance ever happened, and corruption and party machine politics were the norm. Outside parliament, trade unions even, thought Mussolini, were all very well but they merely turned the worker into 'a passive petit bougeois' whose only concern in life was pay. The party and revolution were the only answer. The party must saturate the workers in 'an heroic-religious atmosphere'. No other organisation, not trade unions, not co-operatives, not MPs, could do it. The party was the elite which would prepare the proletariat for revolution and lead it to revolution and beyond. The party was 'an aristocracy of intelligence and will power'. The party was Pareto's necessary elite. The reformists, on the other hand, argued that the revolutionaries, not they, were out of date and had failed to move with the times. Revolution on the streets was the old idea. Only via a majority in parliament could there be a revolution. There had only been extra-parliamentary revolution in France and all that had really done was substitute an emperor for a king. Since Marx there had not been one single revolution worthy of the name.

But when Mussolini walked up to the platform in a suit, once black but so threadbare it had turned green, to speak at the congress in Reggio Emilia that afternoon on 8 July, delegates in the hall had barely heard of him. Certainly, he was not in any sense leader even of the revolutionary wing of the party. He did, however, have four powerful supporters within the party, Giacinto Menotti Serrati, Angelica Balabanoff, Costantino Lazzari and Francesco Ciccotti. He began with a full-frontal attack on Bissolati, whom he had never met, and targeted his visit to the king after the failed assassination attempt. 'Tell me, Bissolati, how many times have you paid homage to a builder who has fallen from scaffolding? How many times to a muleteer fallen from his cart? How many times to a miner struck by a boulder? Well? What is an attempt on the life of a king, if not a hazard of the job?'[19]

At Reggio Emilia in July 1912 it was not Mussolini's oratory, however impressive, that really won the day. It was his Machiavellian skill for intrigue. He and his allies had been active and cunning behind the scenes in the inevitable deal-making preceding a Socialist party congress debate on who would vote for what and what they required in return. As Gaudens Megaro, an early American biographer, put it, 'No man, in the socialist movement, had ever risen, so lightning like, from a more or less second division position to a position of primary importance.'

Mussolini's motion demanding the expulsion from the party of Bissolati, Ivanoe Bonomi (a later prime minister), Angiolo Cabrini and Guido Pod-recca (later a Fascist) for 'very serious offence to the spirit of the Socialist doctrine and tradition' was carried by 12,566 votes to 5633 with 2027 abstentions. The congress then elected a new National Executive whose thirteen members included Mussolini and Angelica Balabanoff. The decision to expel the reformists – who then formed their own reformist Socialist party – was noted with approval by among others Lenin, now in Vienna, in his newspaper *Pravda*. 'The theory of Professor Mussolini', noted *Il Nuovo Giornale*, 'was somewhat mad', but added nevertheless that he was 'a truly original thinker' whose oratory was 'crude' but which 'the crude Romagnoli love'. The *Resto del Carlino* spoke of his 'abundance of gestures and mimics' which made him look 'like a Chinaman'. *La Giustizia* described his personality as 'hysterical and neurotic'. The journalist of *Il Nuovo Giornale* of Florence noted that on his way to the podium Mussolini had embraced a hunchback whom he had kept close to him throughout the congress for good luck (in Italy hunchbacks bring luck).

Mussolini himself wrote on 18 July in *Avanti!*,[20] 'The religious soul of the party wrestled once again with the realist pragmatism of the rep-resentatives of the economic organisations [unions] . . . the eternal conflict between idealism and utilitarianism, between faith and necessity ... We want to believe, we must believe, that humanity needs a faith. It is faith which moves mountains because it gives the illusion that mountains move. Illusion is, perhaps, the only reality in life.' Faith was what counted. He had seen this as a child, at school, in his mother, and in himself when he prepared for his confirmation. He had seen it all around him in Catholic Italy. Later that month, on 29 July, Mussolini celebrated his twenty-ninth birthday. But even now he could not have been that sure of his position within the party, nor in politics, because that same day he applied for another schoolteaching post in Crespellano.

In the last paragraph of *La mia vita* Mussolini summed up his life so far (his life up to the age of twenty-eight, written before the Reggio Emilia congress, while languishing in Forlì prison like his father before him, and completed 'on 11 March 1912, on the eve of my release, at 3 p.m. in the afternoon'),[21]

> I have had a pretty adventurous and tempestuous youth. I have known the good and bad in life. I have given myself culture and sound science. The time abroad helped me to learn modern languages. The past 10 years I have wandered about from one horizon to another: from Tolmezzo to Oneglia, from Oneglia to Trent, from Trent to Forlì. I have been in Forlì now for three years [actually two and a half years] and already I feel in my blood the ferment of nomadism compelling me to go elsewhere. I am a restless man, with a wild temperament, averse to popularity. I have loved many women, but now on these distant loves oblivion spreads its grey veil. I love my Rachele and she too loves me profoundly. What does the future have reserved for me?

In the introduction to *La mia vita* he had written, 'I am 28. I have reached, I believe, that point which Dante called "the middle of the walk of our life". Will I live the same again? I doubt it.' He was only wrong by five years.

5

AVANTI!

Mussolini went back to Forlì and his little local weekly newspaper *La Lotta di classe*. But not for long. Another consequence of his triumph at the Reggio Emilia congress was that the leading reformist Claudio Treves, editor of the party's national daily newspaper *Avanti!*, was sacked by the new party executive, which controlled the appointment. Treves, like all left-wing reformists, had no intention of resigning from the party in protest at the expulsion of the right-wing reformist Bissolati and his three colleagues. He and they remained in the party determined to wrestle back control from the revolutionaries now in charge. Of those senior party figures who had supported Mussolini at Reggio Emilia it is interesting to note how quickly their dizzy support for the party's bright young thing would change to fervent hatred. Within two years they would all – Lazzari, Ciccotti, and his two old friends and mentors from Switzerland, Balabanoff and Serrati – become his sworn enemies.

On 10 November 1912 the National Executive, now controlled by the revolutionary wing of the party and of which Mussolini was now also a member appointed him editor of *Avanti!* 'You will tell me that Mussolini is young, lacking in experience; but I repeat, that we must encourage the young. In fact, because he is young we will be able to guide and control him more easily . . .' Constantino Lazzari, party secretary, told the meeting, according to executive member Balabanoff.[1] How wrong he would be. Neither he nor anyone else would be able to guide and control Mussolini.

Mussolini left Forlì for Milan. He would never again live full time in his native Romagna. He took up the editorship of *Avanti!* on 1 December. Treves had been paid 700 lira a month. Mussolini had to take less – 500. His salary was a pittance compared with the salary of mainstream national newspaper editors, which were in the region of 20,000–25,000 lira a year.

Like Treves most of the staff of *Avanti!* were reformists. Mussolini had agreed to take over the editorship on condition that Balabanoff be appointed deputy editor. Immediately he stamped his authority on the newspaper. The defeated moderates remained convinced, however, that Mussolini was nothing but a flash in the pan. But the circulation of *Avanti!*, which was 28,000 when Mussolini took over, soared. By the time he left two years later it had risen to an average 60,000 – sometimes reaching 100,000. He replaced the heavy ramblings of his predecessors with shorter articles. The headlines were bigger, vicious, hard-hitting and funny; the content simpler, powerful and punchy. To begin with Rachele had remained in Forlì with her mother and the infant Edda. But one day in early 1913 she turned up in Milan at the *Avanti!* offices with Edda. Mussolini told her to go straight back to Forlì until he had found a suitable home. The peasant girl from Predappio would never take to life in the city, whereas he loved it. But she was not prepared to let him out of her sight for long. She refused to leave Milan and found an apartment which the Mussolinis had to share with her mother and a woman from Forlì who had murdered her husband.

Mussolini did not have to wait long for an event which he hoped he could use to stir up revolution. In January 1913 serious unrest broke out in various parts of Italy. In the worst violence troops killed seven demonstrators and wounded dozens of others at Roccagorge, near Rome. By 1914 the Socialist party had nearly 60,000 members – compared with 30,000 at the end of 1912. The expulsion of Bissolati and his faction had not damaged the party as Bissolati had warned – quite the contrary.

The main hope of those in the party who wanted to get rid of the young loose cannon was that he would be sacked from the editorship of *Avanti!* In March 1913 – just four months after his appointment – the party executive debated the matter. Narrowly, they supported him. He still had the backing in particular of Lazzari, the party secretary, and Balabanoff. According to the latter – writing many years later and by then irreconcilably embittered – Mussolini was a weak editor. All the big ideas were hers, she claimed, not his. 'In the period of my collaboration at *Avanti!* he did not write a single important article without consulting me or modifying it, if I believed it necessary. I have never met anyone so weak, so dependent on the help of others and in particular of me ...'[2] This could not have been true. In Trent and Forlì, for example, Mussolini had already proved how strong an editor he was. When Balabanoff wrote about Mussolini she was writing as his bitter enemy. Hell hath no fury like a Socialist scorned. Mussolini said of her, 'She knows and understands many things and she knows the Marxist texts; but while juices circulate in her body ... in her mind ideas wither.'[3] Were they lovers? It is impossible to say. Mussolini denied it to Rachele who confronted him over the matter because of gossip that Balabanoff was Edda's mother, not Rachele. 'If I was in a desert and she was the only woman, I would prefer to seduce a monkey,' he told her. Balabanoff herself, by the time of her collaboration with him at *Avanti!*, unmarried and in her mid-forties, did not say. She wrote, 'He spoke about himself, only himself, when we were alone; with no reserve whatsoever, he revealed his weaknesses, his fears, he envied my strength of will, my self-discipline and everything which made me a normal human being. So much weakness and strangeness in him I attributed to his black depression, promiscuity, and his illness [a reference to the false rumour that Mussolini had syphilis], about which he spoke very often, almost boasting about it.'[4]

Apart from Rachele and Balabanoff there were at least three other women in Mussolini's life in Milan at this time: Leda Rafanelli, an anarchist, author and Muslim convert bewitched by the Middle East where she had been born, Ida Irene Dalser, a masseuse from Austrian Trent, and Sarfatti, *Avanti!*'s rich Jewish art critic, who was married to a Socialist lawyer, Cesare Sarfatti. Mussolini was especially entranced by Rafanelli, who used to dress in the clothes of the harem and believed that she had lived once before in Egypt at the time of the pharaohs. Rafanelli first came across Mussolini at a meeting in Milan in March 1913 at which he was a speaker. In an article about his speech for the anarchist weekly *La Libertà* she wrote, 'He is the Socialist of heroic times. He revealed himself to me as an artist of word and thought – an artist who is crude and colossal.' He sent her a thank-you note for the article and she wrote back asking to meet him. 'I feel that between the two of us something has begun,' he replied. Mussolini became a regular visitor to her Milan apartment where the furniture consisted of low divans and exotic cushions scattered over the floor, and the air was thick with the smell of incense. 'When I want to have a break in my tumultuous busy but lonely life I will come to you. You will make me live oriental hours. We will read Nietzsche and the Koran.' He asked her to teach him Arabic. He lied to her, saying that romantically he was unattached – 'free as the air'. Two women were, however, madly in love with him, according to Rafanelli,[5] who wrote that he had told her, 'One is very ugly, though she has a noble and generous soul. The other is beautiful but has a deceitful, greedy and stingy nature. Naturally, she's a Jew.' The ugly woman with the noble soul was Balabanoff. The beautiful woman with the ugly nature was Sarfatti, he told her. Even though Balabanoff too was a Jew, Mussolini did not mention this. The beautiful Jew would follow Mussolini from Socialism to Fascism. The ugly Jew would not. But both, in the end, would become his bitter enemies. Of Sarfatti Mussolini said – according to Rafanelli – that she 'persecutes me with her love, but I can never love her. Her stinginess disgusts me. She is rich and lives in a grand palazzo in Corso Venezia. When one of her articles is published, she sends her servant to *Avanti!* to get three copies gratis, to save a few cents. And she has a newsagent right next door.' But Rafanelli knew about Rachele anyway and, if we are to believe her version, written years later after she too had become an enemy of Mussolini's, she did not find him in the least sexually attractive. So when one evening he pounced, she rebuffed him.

Mussolini had more success with Ida Dalser but the consequence was acute embarrassment for him – and acute pain, then tragedy, for her. She became pregnant by him and had the child, whom she christened Benito Albino. Mussolini was eventually forced to recognise the boy legally as his and pay Dalser monthly maintenance. Dalser came from Austrian Trent, where Mussolini first met her when he was there in 1908–9, and they met again in Milan by chance. She had opened a massage parlour, Mademoiselle Ida's Oriental Hygiene and Beauty Salon, and one day she turned up at the offices of *Avanti!* to place an advertisement for it in the newspaper, according to her niece, Alda Cimadon.[6] She was thirty-three – three years older than Mussolini – and very beautiful. She also had a wild temper. The handful of surviving letters from Mussolini to her – in Signora Cimadon's possession – written between autumn 1914 and early 1915 are signed 'your Benito', 'your BM', even 'your wild friend and lover Benito'. In one he says, 'I love you too.' Benito Albino was born on 11 November 1915. By then, Mussolini had founded his own newspaper, *Il Popolo d'Italia*. Dalser would sometimes turn up at the newspaper's offices which overlooked a courtyard, carrying the baby boy in her arms. On one occasion she screamed up from the courtyard, 'Coward, pig, assassin, traitor. You hide eh! Come down if you're brave enough.' On another she interrupted a party meeting at which Mussolini was present to hold up the child and shout, 'Comrades, this is Mussolini's son, who, after seducing me, abandoned me and him.' Dalser would hound Mussolini for years to come.

Rachele did not seem to blame her husband for his serial infidelities. She blamed instead his mistresses. In her opinion his infidelity was their fault. For example, she said, 'Only three women made me suffer. Against each one of them I fought with all my strength. They were Ida Dalser, Margherita Sarfatti and Clara Petacci.' It was the mistresses, not the husband, who had made her suffer. 'Anyway, after the Ida Dalser experience, I pricked up my ears because I realised that with Benito the danger did not come from him, in these relationships, but from the women who clung to him and did not want to let him go.'

Dalser was a serious threat – especially with Benito Albino in tow. But first Sarfatti, then Claretta Petacci, his most famous mistress, would prove much more so. Sarfatti, born on 8 April 1880 in Venice, was the daughter of a rich Jewish landowner and businessman who despite his own religion had close links with Italy's Catholic establishment and knew the Pope, Pius X. When Mussolini took over at *Avanti!* Sarfatti had been the newspaper's art critic since 1908, signing her articles *'El Sereno'*. It was there, probably, that they first met in 1912–13, though she worked from home.

Unlike Mussolini, she and her husband were reformist Socialists – followers of the party's leading lights, Anna Kuliscioff and Filippo Turati. The Sarfattis were regulars at the salons they held in their shared apartment in Milan overlooking the cathedral in the Piazza Duomo. By 1912 she was already well established as a leading art patron and art critic. She boasted that she was the first person in Italy to recognise the genius of Toulouse-Lautrec. Cesare Sarfatti, her husband, became a Socialist city councillor in Milan – but failed to become an MP. Initially Sarfatti was in awe and envious of the older Kuliscioff. But her star would soon burn much bigger and brighter. Sarfatti had a buxom figure, grey-green eyes, reddish blonde hair and was, like Dalser, three years older than Mussolini. She did not possess beauty. But she was sensuous. And she had a big sex drive. Possibly, this was because her husband, whom she had married in 1898 when she was eighteen, was thirteen years older than her. 'She found bourgeois sexual morality stifling and psychologically destructive. (There was some evidence that she had affairs with women as well as men.)'[7] Sarfatti had already had a number of affairs, with men that is, before Mussolini stormed into her life. Probably as a result of this, a nickname she had acquired as a teenager – 'The Red Virgin' – had stuck. Unlike many middle-class Socialist women who deliberately dressed down, Sarfatti dressed up. She always wore the most expensive clothes. Her interest in Socialism had started as a teenager when she had fallen in love with a very much older man – a Socialist professor. By early 1913 she and Mussolini had become lovers. Their affair would continue for twenty years.

Politics, not women, however, were Mussolini's principal passion. In the pages of *Avanti!* he towed the party line. But he had meanwhile founded his own monthly publication, *Utopia*, in which much more flexible ideas were expressed. In the first issue he dismissed the Marxist theory of history as class war between capital and labour won at the moment the proletariat became conscious of its condition. He wrote, 'The great masses called upon to found the new realm do not need so much to "know" as to "believe".'

The massacre in January 1913 at Roccagorge had not led to revolution, and though Mussolini despised parliament and democracy, this did not stop him standing for election for the first time as an MP in Forlì in the October 1913 general election. In his campaign speeches he attacked militarism and imperialism. Though hostile to democracy he saw the elections as an important test of support for Socialism and as a means of raising the revolutionary temperature. The Socialists had their best ever general election result and got nearly 1 million votes – 11.3 per cent of the total – and won 53 of the 508 seats. With the expulsion of Bissolati from the party in 1912 and his formation of the *Partito socialista-riformista italiano* the number of Socialist MPs in parliament had dropped from 40 to 25. So this was a major success. But Mussolini himself failed to get elected. He blamed the 'bourgeois spirit' of the electorate.

For Socialism to triumph revolution was needed. How was this to happen? On 8 February 1914 Mussolini spoke at a conference in Florence of the need for a revolutionary minority – an elite – and the need for a swift revolution. Unless quick it was doomed. He said, 'Civil society today is extraordinarily complex. Either you succeed in establishing the "*novus ordo*" rapidly, with the institutions which you have worked out before-hand, or if not you run the risk of plunging society into chaos from which will spring the hydra of counter-revolution.' Then, in June 1914, came 'Red Week'. Hopes of revolution were high – but only for a few days. The trade unions called a twenty-four general strike for 7 June – officially to protest at the confinement in a lunatic asylum of an anarchist, Augusto Massetti, who had shot dead an army officer in the unrest at Roccagorge in January of the previous year. The case became a cause célèbre and all anti-government groups demanded Massetti's release. In all about 1 million people took part in the general strike. But there was little co-ordination. There was little violence, except at Ancona on the Adriatic coast. There, the army was called out to separate the demonstrating strikers from conservative counter-demonstrators. The strikers attacked the troops who opened fire, killing three and wounding at least ten others. That night trade unions in Milan proclaimed an indefinite general strike. But apart from in Ancona, only in Mussolini's native Romagna did the general strike have real bite. Across the region strikers seized town halls and raised the red flag. They even proclaimed the Romagna a republic. The government was forced to send 10,000 troops there to crush what had become open insurrection.

The violence in Red Week had caused the deaths of at least seventeen people and left more than a thousand injured. So much for revolution. In *My Autobiography* – the one written mostly by his brother Arnaldo and published in 1928 – Mussolini said that Red Week was 'not revolution' but 'chaos'.

The preoccupation of Socialist minds with the failure of Red Week was short-lived. War now came for the second time to the political rescue of Mussolini – though for a while it looked as if it would cause his political death. On 28 June 1914 Archduke Franz Ferdinand of Austria, heir to the Habsburg throne, and his wife, Sofia, were assassinated by a Serb nationalist in Sarajevo, the capital of Bosnia-Herzegovina which Austria had annexed from Turkey in 1908. Under the Triple Alliance, signed as long ago as 1882, Italy was allied to Germany and Austria. Italy had signed the treaty in a fit of pique at the French seizure in 1881 of Tunisia, which it had always regarded as its own in all but name. France and Britain, meanwhile, were allied with Russia.

At midnight on 28 July Austria declared war on Serbia. That night Sarfatti was in Venice for a masked ball on the Lido at which the rich and titled women of the nations of Europe paraded with parrots on their arms, naked except for strings of enormous pearls, or wearing fabulous jewels and costumes. The men would soon become deadly enemies. At midnight – the deadline for the Austrian ultimatum – the band struck up a tango. In *Dux*[8] Sarfatti wrote, 'The diabolic cadenza of "Irresistible", the latest tango, *ritmava* the shipwreck of the beauty, the joy, the peaceful civility of an epoque, despatched into the abyss.' Mussolini meanwhile was in Milan in the offices of *Avanti!*.

A few days later, on 1 August, Germany declared war on Russia, which had mobilised in support of Serbia. On 3 August Germany invaded Belgium with the intention of moving swiftly into France. On 4 August Britain declared war on Germany. The official reason was that Britain was bound by an 1839 treaty to protect Belgian neutrality. In fact, Britain was not bound to intervene because, as the British Foreign Office had noted in 1905, the 1839 treaty was not 'a positive pledge to use material force'. Britain went to war, as Prime Minister Asquith noted privately, for reasons of 'policy' rather than out of 'legal obligation'. While Britain and the other nations got down to the grisly business of trench warfare the Italian government remained neutral. Yet despite the Triple Alliance Italians, many of whom had been ruled by Austria until half a century beforehand and some of whom such as those in the Trentino still were, had never been friends of Austria. The alliance had been purely tactical. Furthermore, since reunification the new nation Italy had increasingly become its stronger and older neighbour's rival for territorial expansion, especially in the Balkans.

Neutrality was not only the policy of the Italian government but also of the Italian Socialist party – and of Mussolini himself. In general, Italian Socialist opposition to the war was based on the traditional Socialist idea that any war between nations was a bourgeois war in which the blood of the proletariat was spilled to further bourgeois interests. The only exception – for certain Socialists at any rate – was a nationalist war of liberation against a colonial or imperial oppressor. The initial cause of the First World War – Austria's ultimatum to Serbia – could have been regarded in this light as Austria, the imperial power, threatened to invade Serbia and deprive it of its independence. So too could the chance it provided, however slim, of liberation of the Trentino from Austria. But the war quickly escalated into something entirely different.

Initially Mussolini supported absolute Italian neutrality. Yet within little more than three months he had changed his mind. This change of mind was to have extraordinary consequences not just for Italy but Europe as well. First, in October 1914, he would switch from strident support of absolute neutrality to what he called 'active neutrality'. To his Socialist colleagues the article proclaiming this was a bolt from the blue. It caused his immediate resignation from *Avanti!* and within a month expulsion from the Socialist party and the foundation of his own daily newspaper, *Il Popolo d'Italia*. Then, in the first issue of *Il Popolo*, Mussolini supported war outright against Austria and Germany.

Even though Mussolini's article abandoning absolute neutrality had come as a shock the signs had been there from the start of the crisis. On

26 July 1914, two days before Austria declared war on Serbia, Mussolini wrote an article in *Avanti!* headlined DOWN WITH WAR![9] Whoever got involved – Russia, France, Britain, Germany – Italy, he insisted, should remain neutral. The war was not 'a cause' which involved Italy. And if the war – at this stage only Austria was threatening war on Serbia – escalated into 'a European conflagration' Italy should still stay out 'unless she wants to precipitate her total ruin'. This was the reasoning not of a revolutionary Socialist, but of a realist. The 'cause' was not Italy's and involvement would mean Italy's 'total ruin'. His argument – by its prominent reliance on the word Italy – was also curiously nationalistic in tone for a revolutionary Socialist. (In Trento, as we have noted, he had already conceded that nations should exist based on language. His opposition then to Trentino liberation had been pragmatic – Italy could not defeat Austria.) In the 26 July 1914 article Mussolini then reverted to type. He warned the Italian government to stick with its policy of neutrality 'or else the proletariat will know how to impose it on it with all its means'. This was more like a revolutionary Socialist. But again what the proletariat would be doing would be to impose neutrality in the interests of the Italian nation. He ended the article with the slogan, 'Not one man! Not one coin!'

Now came an event which challenged to the core Mussolini's thinking on Italian neutrality – the collapse of the second Socialist International. On 4 August the German Socialist party, which was the leading Socialist party in Europe, decided to support the German government's invasion of neutral Belgium which had taken place the day before. The nationalism of the German Socialists had triumphed over their internationalism. Other Socialist parties in other countries, including Britain and France, also supported their governments' decisions to go to war. The International was dead.

It was not long before Mussolini questioned Italian neutrality in print. On 23 August he wrote,[10] 'Whether or not Italy can remain neutral until the end of the conflict we do not know; either way ... intervention will depend on circumstances which cannot be predicted.' He then went on to leave aside the 'Socialist principles' for opposing the war to discuss war 'on the terrain of reality, of actual national reality, if you wish'. He asked, 'With what purpose? With what objectives? Simply, moral and political objectives or also territorial objectives?' He said that he opposed Italian intervention even on these real – as opposed to theoretical Socialist – terms. Perhaps the objective of Italy was to annex Trent and the Trentino from Austria, he asked. But how could she? He replied, '700,000 of the 4 million men mobilised by Austria, would be sufficient to hold, if not repel, the Italian offensive.' His attitude to Italian intervention, it is clear, was not just based on blinkered adherence to the standard Socialist line that the war was a bourgeois war – his opposition to war was also based on common sense.

54

The war escalated. Increasingly, Mussolini became consumed with conflicting ideas. Reality was challenging theory in a much more powerful way than ever before. Like everyone else, Mussolini faced a brutally hard choice. According to the classic revolutionary Socialist model the proletariat in the countries at war with each other would react against war with an indefinite general strike and refuse to fight. This would cause two things to happen: the governments of these countries would be unable to fight the war and they would collapse. The revolution would begin. The more countries declaring war on each other, the more general strikes, the bigger the revolution. The beauty of it was that it required no war actually to take place – the general strikes would stop war starting. There would be relatively little blood shed. But the decision of the Socialists in Germany and elsewhere in Europe to support their governments going to war meant that there was now no hope according to this theoretical model of an international revolution. The dream was dead.

Mussolini's confusion did not go unnoticed. The newspaper *Azione Socialista* ran an article headlined THE TWO MUSSOLINIS[11] on 19 September. 'Which of the two will win?' it asked. September 1914 saw the first pro-war demonstrations in Milan organised by the Futurists Filippo Tommaso Marinetti and Umberto Boccioni. Marinetti had published his Futurist Manifesto in Paris in February 1909 exulting instinct, violence, dynamism, speed, machines, danger and war, and denigrating common sense, culture, the good life, pacifism and neutralism. Futurism was a political as well as an artistic movement. The things the Futurists exalted so too did Mussolini. In September he spoke at a Socialist party meeting in Milan where he was expected to argue in favour of absolute neutrality. Sarfatti wrote of her 'stupor' in *Dux*[12] when he spoke instead of his doubts. 'It was a shock when he told us of his torment in all its nakedness.' Mussolini's confusion was shared not just within the Italian Socialist movement but within Italy as a whole.

But there was another Socialist way of looking at war and its relationship with revolution, which was different from the standard line that if the proletariat opposed war, revolution would result. This other way involved the opposite – supporting war. It involved much sacrifice and the shedding of much blood. Far from destroying the dream of revolution, the bloodbath of war between nations could in fact turn the dream into reality. War would mean the deaths of many members of the proletariat, the economic exhaustion of the fighting nations and thus terminal political instability within the nations. The proletariat, furious and stirred at last from sloth, its revolutionary consciousness finally in place, would turn its weapons away from the national enemy abroad and on to the class enemy at home – the ruling class which had sent it into battle. Revolution would result. The bloodbath of war would give birth to revolution. Marx himself – as usual contradicting what he wrote elsewhere – said that social revolution usually followed war. It had not happened in his lifetime. But it would happen in Russia in 1917 and almost happen in France when large sections of the French army mutinied. It would happen in Italy – in 1922. But, of course, no Socialist could easily argue this line. 'Comrades, off you go to die and thanks to your deaths we'll have a revolution after you've gone.' This is what the revolutionary syndicalists, led by Alceste De Ambris and Filippo Corridoni, were arguing and Mussolini had always been very keen on revolutionary syndicalism. Many in the mainstream political establishment on the other hand argued that war would unite the nation and stop – not start – revolution.

Mussolini became increasingly convinced of the revolutionary possibilities of war offered by this second bloodbath model: that revolution would result from going to war – not from opposing war. He was also increasingly convinced that people were more attached to the idea of nation than class. He would soon fuse this second theory of revolution with nationalism. The German Socialists had decided to support war for nationalistic not revolutionary reasons. Their nationalism was stronger than their Socialism. This had persuaded Mussolini of the motivating power of nationalism. The Libyan war of 1911–12 which he had opposed and gone to prison over, had been a clear-cut imperialist war. But the First World War was different. It was not a war between nations over distant colonies. It was a war between nations involving invasion of those nations. The threat such a war posed to those nations, particularly Italy and the people of Italy, made him revise his views on nationalism. He had always been furious at Metternich's dismissal of Italy as a mere 'geographical expression'.

Mussolini began to question something else. Why was it all right for Socialists to kill people in their own country, their class enemies, but not abroad? He had addressed the matter in a 13 August 1914 article in *Avanti!*[13] in which he wheeled out the traditional party line. Violence at home was violence against the ruling class, he wrote, while violence abroad was violence by the ruling class using the proletariat as passive instrument of that violence. War was 'supreme madness'. But he then spelled out what he called 'the tragic dilemma' in which, with the First World War, the bourgeoisie had placed the proletariat: 'either insurrection easily repressed in blood, or participation – solid – in the slaughter'. Either revolution doomed to bloody failure or war and bloody slaughter. Absolute neutrality meant revolution doomed. War it must be. But not just yet.

Whatever Mussolini still said publicly either in print or in speeches, privately he had long expressed his doubts about neutrality. Sarfatti recalled,[14] 'His state of mind was in truth a complex one. It was not the Socialist in him that was for neutrality and the Italian in him for war. Rather it was the contrary.'

Mussolini delivered the thunderbolt which would prove to be one of the single most significant political events in twentieth-century Italian history on 18 October 1914 – a Sunday. The rest of the Socialist party executive picked up their copies of the party newspaper en route for a three-day meeting of the executive in Bologna to discuss the war. The front-page splash astonished them. It was headlined FROM ABSOLUTE NEU-TRALITY TO ACTIVE WORKING NEUTRALITY.[15] Essentially, Mussolini had real-ised the absurdity of absolute neutrality – it meant impotence. 'A party which wants to live in history and to make – insofar as that is conceded – history, cannot submit – that's suicide – to a rule on which is conferred the value of an unquestionable dogma or eternal law subject to the iron necessities of time and space.' Anyway, Mussolini wrote, Socialists had conflicting opinions on the subject of war – three in particular: first, all war, even war to defend one's country, is wrong because it is bourgeois; second, only defensive war against a foreign conqueror is right; and third, war on behalf of a small foreign nation threatened by a larger imperial nation is right. The party's insistence on absolute neutrality had been based on the first opinion. But, said Mussolini, the party had not been absolutely neutral. Its neutrality had only ever been 'partial'. It had, for example, criticised Austria for attacking Serbia and Germany for invading Belgium. It had threatened that if the Italian government entered the war on the side of Austria and Germany it would call for a general strike and insurrection. It had in effect been pro-Serbia, pro-Belgium, and by implication pro-France and Britain. 'We have condemned the war ... but this has not impeded us from distinguishing – logically, historically, and socialistically – between one war and another ... To evaluate all wars in the same way would be absurd and – one is permitted to say it – cretinous.' The party had even given tacit approval, he added, to the call-up of conscripts to guarantee neutrality and accepted mobilisation of the army as a precautionary measure against invasion. 'We have made then the first important concession to the historical national reality.' He said, 'Absolute neutrality threatened to bottle up the party and deprive it of any possibility or liberty of movement in the future.' Socialists could not ignore 'national problems'. 'If the concept of "nation" is "obsolete", if "national" defence is an absurdity for the proletariat who have nothing to defend, we must have the courage to disavow the Socialists of Belgium and France who in the face of the German invasion have confused – temporarily mind you – nation with class and deduce in consequence that there is only one genuine, authentic, pure Socialism in the world: Italian Socialism ... But that is an act of arrogance which for lots of reasons is not worth it for us!' Mussolini then cited a number of internationally known Socialists who supported Italian intervention against Austria and Germany including the old revolutionary hero of his father, Amilcare Cipriani, who would not die until 1918. 'Do we want to be – as men and Socialists – inert spectators of this great drama? Or do we want to be – in some way or another – the protagonists?' he concluded.

The 18 October 1914 article, then, was not an attempt to argue in favour of Italian intervention in the war at all. It was an attempt to convince the Socialist party to be free to react to events – that it must make history, not be the victim of history. Making history, however, may or may not mean entering the war. Within less than a month Mussolini would decide to support war itself.

Many observers then and since – of whatever political persuasion – have seen in Mussolini's decision to defy his party or as it is often put – to betray his party – and his support first of flexible as opposed to absolute neutrality, then of war itself, as the decision of a cynical opportunist. But what opportunistic reason could there possibly have been? It is absolutely impossible to believe that Mussolini at this stage regarded himself as even remotely close to getting political power. His decision to support war and thus lose at a stroke his prominence in the Socialist Party was much more likely to result in his consignment to the political wilderness. Indeed, this is precisely what most Socialists were convinced would happen to him. Other observers, especially those weaned on the Allied wartime propaganda image of Mussolini as nothing other than a grotesque, unprincipled buffoon, insist that Mussolini simply changed his mind on the war because Britain and France were doing well on the Marne in late 1914 – repelling the German advance on Paris – and looked like winning quickly.

On Monday, 19 October Mussolini went to Bologna to confront his colleagues on the party executive. He had the support of only one of its members and so the next day, 20 October, he resigned his editorship. Within a month he would launch his own newspaper – *Il Popolo d'Italia*.

Mussolini's resignation from the editorship of *Avanti!* thrust the issue of whether Italy should remain neutral or not into the forefront of public debate. Many others on the Italian Left had abandoned the sacred principle of absolute neutrality. They included the Republicans, the reformist Socialists such as Bissolati, whom Mussolini had forced out of the Socialist Party at the Reggio Emilia party congress in 1912 and who had subsequently founded the first reformist Socialist Party – the *Partito socialista-riformista italiano* – the revolutionary syndicalists such as De Ambris and Corridoni, and the Futurists such as Marinetti, who had called war 'the only hygiene in the world' in the Futurist Manifesto of 1909.

Even Antonio Gramsci, a revolutionary Socialist like Mussolini, later founder of the Italian Communist Party and the Italian Left's greatest political theorist, was critical of blind support for absolute neutrality. In *Il Grido del Popolo*, on 31 October, he wrote, 'Revolutionaries who regard history as a creation of their own spirit ... and who prepare to the hilt the conditions favourable for the definitive breach (the revolution) must not content themselves with the provisional formula "absolute neutrality", but must transform it into "active working neutrality".'[16]

But Mussolini's opponents, especially his former Socialist Party comrades, claimed that he had changed his mind over the war not as a matter of conscience but only because he had been offered a bribe to do so which he had accepted. *'Chi paga?'* they bellowed. Indeed, this was the headline in *Avanti!* day after day.[17]

Mussolini – who had no money of his own – received funds to finance his new newspaper from – among others – Filippo Naldi, the editor of the Bologna newspaper, *Il Resto del Carlino* and, via Naldi's contacts, from Italian industry sources such as Fiat and the arms manufacturer, Ansaldo, and – although well after the launch of the newspaper – from the French government and the French Socialist Party no less.

Later in the war – in 1917 – with Italy staring defeat in the face after the rout at Caporetto, he also accepted money from the British government as part of efforts to keep Italy in the war. This was the idea of Samuel Hoare who was a lieutenant-colonel with Military Intelligence in Italy in charge of British propaganda.

Allegations of British Mussolini money never surfaced at the time. But Hoare, who would become Foreign Secretary in 1935 and lose his job when his secret attempts to appease Mussolini over Ethiopia were revealed, disclosed these earlier secret dealings with Mussolini in his 1954 auto-biography.[18] He had told the story, however, on at least one occasion previously – a dinner party in January 1939 at which Sir Henry 'Chips' Channon was present.

In his diaries, Channon wrote: 'He [Hoare] was told that there was a powerful Socialist – a fellow called Mussolini – in Milan who owned a newspaper there. He might be able to keep Italy in the war, at least he would be able to guarantee Milan and the north – if sufficiently bribed. Sam Hoare "for a very considerable sum indeed" bought the newspaper ... So English government funds did much to create the Fascist revolution. This is very secret...'[19]

That the French and British governments should have financed Mussolini should come as no surprise. All warring governments were involved in trying to buy up newspapers in Europe and America to support their cause. Lord Northcliffe, the British press baron, for example, was believed to have under his supervision 1400 British agents active in the propaganda field[20] and the German government financed Lenin in 1917. Nor should it come as a surprise that the French Socialist Party should finance Mussolini – the man whom Italian Socialists accused of betraying Socialism; after all, they supported the war.

Naldi was an establishment liberal. His motive in helping Mussolini, whom he had met in the summer of 1914, was to split the Socialists and promote the cause of Italian intervention. There are no reliable figures but the money, though it enabled Mussolini to launch *Il Popolo d'Italia*, was short-lived and by April 1915 the newspaper was in 'terrible financial trouble'.[21]

So Mussolini turned to the French. Precise figures are unavailable but it seems that the French Socialist Party gave Mussolini a 100,000 lira lump sum in March 1915 and 10,000 lira a month thereafter. The size of the French government subsidies, which began to arrive in May 1915, is not known.[22]

In March 1915 Mario Montet, the French Socialist MP, handed one instalment of Socialist Party money over to De Ambris, Mussolini's revolutionary syndicalist ally, in the office of French War Propaganda Minister, Jules Guesde, a Socialist, who was present. Montet told De Ambris, 'Take this envelope to Comrade Mussolini. It contains the monthly contribution that the French comrades are giving his newspaper for the interventionist campaign.'[23]

Marcel Cachet, the French Socialist MP, later leader of the French Communist Party and editor of *Humanité*, was among those who acted as the conduit for the French money.[24] Cachin first came to Italy in December 1914 – a month after the launch of *Il Popolo d'Italia* – to meet selected Socialist leaders such as Mussolini.[25]

In the 1920s, when Cachet's involvement became known it caused him severe embarrassment. By then, Mussolini had become the *bête noire*, not just of Italian Socialists, but Socialists everywhere – not to mention Communists. The most convincing exposé of Cachin's role was by Paul Faure, another French MP, whose source, he said, was Guesde, the War Propaganda Minister, himself. In a 1928 article in the French newspaper, *Populaire*, about Mussolini's French money, Faure wrote, 'I do not know more precisely who was the material carrier of the money, but Cachin, if it pleases him, could inform his readers in *Humanité*. He was in Italy at the time to seek out Mussolini on behalf of the French government.' Cachin felt compelled to retain a highly conspicuous silence.[26]

Without money from the French government and the French Socialist Party there would perhaps have been no *Popolo d'Italia* and no Fascist Party. But receipt of the money does not prove bribery despite 'Chips' Channon's flowery interpretation. To begin with, when Mussolini wrote the article in *Avanti!* on 18 October 1914 that led him to resign from the newspaper two days later all that was certain was a pledge by Naldi that money for a new newspaper would be forthcoming. It was not until 13 November, two days before publication of the first issue of *Il Popolo d'Italia*, that he and Naldi went to the Hotel d'Angleterre in Geneva to meet the French for the first time[27] and no French money arrived until well into 1915.

But more important, Mussolini had changed his mind on the war in any case regardless of the money. His new position was perfectly defensible for a Socialist; it was the position, after all, of Socialists more or less everywhere, except in Italy. The money the French and others gave him was to sustain and promote a man who already supported their cause. For

Mussolini had realised, unlike most leading Socialists in Italy, that absolute neutrality was an absolute dead end. It meant standing on the sidelines. It meant impotence. Mussolini made his dramatic change of tack because he was determined to give Marx a shot of Nietzsche in order to escape the straitjacket of Marxist determinism. Men were not condemned, he believed, to lie back and think of history. Men could make history. Men could and must act. The proletariat must make the war of the bourgeoisie their war. But war also made Mussolini realise something else: that nation had a stronger grip on men than class.

As the 1919 police report on Mussolini and Fascism concluded, Mussolini's volte-face was not the result of 'calculated interest or money' but of his being 'a sincere and passionate apostle first of vigilant armed neutrality, then of war'.[28] The report is surely correct. Even an inquiry by the Socialist majority group on Milan Council into the origins of the funding of *Il Popolo d'Italia* concluded in February 1915 that Mussolini had conceived and financed the newspaper after his resignation from *Avanti!* and that he was not guilty of moral or professional misconduct.[29] It was conviction, not bribery, which created Fascism.

In November 1914, Mussolini's former comrades in the Italian Socialist Party thought that he was destined for oblivion. But it was they, not he, who were thus destined. The Italian Socialist Party, which formalised its pacifist stance in May 1915 with a thumb-twiddling policy neither to support nor sabotage the Italian war effort, would remain impotent, more or less, until the end not just of the First World War but the second as well. The rot set in almost immediately. In 1914, party membership stood at 58,326, in 1915, 41,974, and by 1917, 27,918.[30] If it had supported the Italian war effort, as its comrades did elsewhere in Europe, the party would probably have swept to power after the war with Mussolini as its leader. Instead, Mussolini's brand of Socialism – Fascism – would sweep it aside.

Fearing violence from his enemies and for show, Mussolini kept a revolver and three hand grenades on his desk at the *Popolo d'Italia*'s grotty little office. The first issue – 30,000 copies – came out in Italy's major cities on Sunday, 15 November 1914 and sold out by 10 a.m. Underneath the masthead in the centre were the words 'Socialist Daily' and on the ears, the slogans 'The revolution is an idea that has found bayonets' from Napoleon and 'He who has iron has bread' from the nineteenth-century French revolutionary, Louis-Auguste Blanqui. Rachele said that she had to ask her husband what this last slogan meant.

The two slogans would remain until March 1918. The newspaper was subtitled 'Socialist Daily Newspaper'. The newspaper offices in Via Paolo da Cannobio, not far from the Duomo, were according to Sarfatti[31] 'two tiny rooms furnished with only four tumbledown chairs and a rickety table' in a squalid street. The front-page splash in the first issue on 15 November 1914 carried the headline AUDACIA![32] It called for Italian intervention in the war on the side of France, Britain, Russia and Serbia. Mussolini's argument in this and subsequent articles in favour of war was not the bourgeois one of national interest but of the national and international interest of the proletariat.

Mussolini wrote, 'The destiny of European Socialism is linked very closely with the various possible outcomes of this war; to ignore it means to detach oneself from history and from life, to work for reactionism – not for the Social Revolution.' Neutrality, he wrote, was 'anti-revolutionary' and the 'propaganda of cowardice'. Quite apart from the Socialist party, those who supported neutrality included monarchists, priests, the bourgeoisie – and the government. Their motive, said Mussolini, was to preserve the international status quo. By supporting the same policy as them Socialists were being anti-Socialist.

We are men and living men who want to make our contribution, however modest, to the creation of history. Inconsistency? Apostacy? Desertion? Never again. It remains to be seen on which side are the inconsistent, the apostates, the deserters. History will reveal it tomorrow ... If tomorrow there is a little more liberty in Europe, an atmosphere ... politically more adapted to the development of Socialism, and to the creation of the capabilities of the classes of the proletariat, those who at the moment when it was necessary to act, slothfully placed themselves to one side will be the deserters and apostates: if tomorrow – on the other hand – Prussian reactionism triumphs in Europe and – after the destruction of Belgium – with the projected annihilation of France – the standard of human civilisation falls, all those who did nothing to stop the catastrophe will be the deserters and apostates.

I do not have aggressive intentions towards the Socialist party, or against the organs of the party in which I intend to remain, but I am ready to fight anyone who attempts to impede me from the free criticism of a position which I maintain for various reasons is detrimental to the national and international interests of the Proletariat.

He ended this first article for *Il Popolo d'Italia* with what he called his 'inaugural shout ... The shout is a word that I would never utter in normal times ... a fascinating and frightening word: War!'

Foreign observers were quick to notice the new newspaper and its distinctive early tabloid style. These included the travel writer Freya Stark who later wrote, 'I admired the *articoli di fondo* so much that from that moment on I never abandoned the *Popolo*.'[33] She wrote that she had been 'struck in particular' by Mussolini's writing style.

Mussolini had given up on international Socialism. But he had not given up on Socialism. Socialism in the shape of the Italian Socialist party, however, now gave up on Mussolini. The Milan section of the party in which Mussolini was inscribed held a special meeting on the evening of

24 November 1914 – nine days after the launch of *Il Popolo d'Italia* – at which was proposed his expulsion from the party on the grounds of 'moral worthlessness' (*indegnità morale*). Mussolini attended the packed meeting – determined to defend himself. He still wanted to remain within the party. As he walked to the podium there was chaos. There were shouts of '*Venduto! Traditore! Sicario!*' Paolo Valera, who was there, said the atmosphere in the hall was that of a 'lynching'. Dalser was also present. She slapped a man who hurled insults at Mussolini. Mussolini wore a shabby black suit whose trousers were too short and was as usual unshaven. The audience drowned out much of what he said in his speech. It bombarded him with coins – the symbol of Judas – balls of paper, even the odd chair. It brandished the core evidence against him – copies of the first issue of *Il Popolo d'Italia*. Mussolini was in severe physical danger. But he stood firm and bellowed,[34] 'I tell you you are wasting your breath ... You will be forced into the war. ... You cannot get rid of me, because I am, and will always be, a Socialist ... You hate me ... You hate me because you still love me! What divides me from you now is not a small question, it is a big question which divides all Socialism.' The Milan party voted in favour of his expulsion. Sarfatti and her husband Cesare were conspicuously absent from the meeting. Sarfatti, in particular, was a follower of the tide. It was unclear which way the tide was turning. Paolo Monelli,[35] a post-war biographer, remarked that Mussolini had used the language of a lover's tiff in his speech to the party which he said was typical of Italian politics – the language of a woman, not a man, lover.

Still, the Italian government, presided over by the liberal Giovanni Giolitti, remained in favour of neutrality. At this time Giolitti was replaced by a new prime minister, the conservative Antonio Salandra, who like him favoured neutrality – initially. The line of both men, in common with a majority of Deputies (MPs), was that Italy could use neutrality to bargain for territorial concessions from Austria. It was in this climate, Mussolini claimed later, that he formed in December 1914 the first *Fascio di azione rivoluzionaria* (the word *fascio* means literally bundle and had been used for a long time as an alternative to union), a pro-intervention pressure group of left-wing revolutionaries. This, he said, was the start of Fascism. But in fact the first *fascio* – called initially the *Fascio rivoluzionaria di azione internazionalista* – had been formed in October 1914 by others, in particular by the revolutionary syndicalists led by Corridoni and Massimo Rocca. They had issued their manifesto on 5 October. Two months later Mussolini had simply given his support to this group after his departure from the Socialist party, helped write it a new manifesto urging Italian expansion to its 'natural frontiers' and then more or less taken over spokesmanship via *Il Popolo d'Italia*. He was instrumental in the dropping of the word '*internazionalista*' from the title. The key themes at this stage were populism, idealism, adventurism, Futurism, action, revolution. By the end of

February 1915 there were 105 *fasci* with a total membership of about 9000. That month Mussolini was already writing 'We Fascists . . .' During the second half of 1914, Mussolini had felt like Hamlet: unable to act. But now his procrastination was over. His instinct had triumphed. He also had his own newspaper – in those pre-television and radio days a tool of enormous influence. As the months went by, he became increasingly nationalistic – nationalistic on behalf of small nations against the expansionism of the Austrian and German empires. He and the former *Avanti!* editor Treves exchanged a furious polemic with each other, which culminated in them fighting a duel on 29 March 1915 in which both were injured but Treves came off worse. Mussolini had accused Treves, among other things, of being '*Claudio il coniglio* [rabbit]', '*Claudio tremens*', 'nauseating', 'vulgar' and 'wife'. According to Rachele, this was the hardest of the duels Mussolini fought. He lost a small piece of ear and his shirt was soaked with blood. Rachele kept the shirt – nicknamed the Shirt of Treves – as a memento. She also kept several dozen splinters of bone, which he lost over the years for one reason or another, in a bottle.[36]

On 1 April, Mussolini wrote an article, 'Down With Peace!', in which he said that to remain neutral was anti-revolutionary because it would mean the triumph of Austro-German imperialism.[37] In January, he had written, 'Today it is war, tomorrow it will be revolution. Our intervention has a double scope: national and international . . . It means we contribute to the ruin of the Austro-Hungarian empire; it means perhaps revolution in Germany, and as an inevitable consequence, revolution in Russia; it means, in summary, a step forward, for the cause of liberty and revolution.'[38]

Italy finally declared war on its ally Austria, but not its other ally Germany, on 24 May 1915. (Italy would not declare war on Germany until 28 August 1916.) Mussolini continued to press for war on Germany as well. He regarded the Germans, though further away, as the real enemy. The Germans were a nation of 'robbers and murderers' whose 'bestial pride' had caused the war, he wrote, and Krupp, the Essen arms manufacturer 'a pederast'.[39]

The King, in cahoots with the Prime Minister, Salandra, had taken Italy into the war without consulting Parliament. Parliament, where the majority had been in favour of neutrality, accepted the fait accompli. Yet under the Triple Alliance, Italy was allied to Austria and Germany. Salandra had first tried to use Italian neutrality to extract territorial concessions from Italy's allies. When that failed, he used the same tactic with the countries of the Triple Entente – Britain, France and Russia. This bore fruit in the shape of the secret Treaty of London signed on 26 April 1915. The treaty promised Italy – if she entered the war on the side of the Triple Entente and in the event of victory – the Trentino, Trieste and Istria, Jubaland in British East Africa (later Kenya) and much else besides in the Mediterranean.

The Salandra government, unlike Mussolini, had accepted a bribe. It had declared war on its ally Austria, thinking the war would be short, as a result of a promise of territory. It would be the Soviet Communists who revealed the existence of the secret Treaty of London in 1917. The failure of Britain and France to ensure that its terms were honoured and the failure of successive Italian governments to insist that the terms be honoured would blacken still more the mood of anger and bitterness in postwar Italy – a mood which would enable Fascism to flourish.

In 1924, Mussolini would tell George Seldes, the American journalist, 'The turning point in my life was the war. The war showed the world plainly, I think, the utter bankruptcy of internationalism. We had been fighting for a hollow fraud. I had fought for internationalism all my life, preached it, gone to prison for that same cause, and suddenly the war came and I realised first that internationalism was dead because it had never really lived, and that I had a real duty in my life, and that was my country.'[40]

6

TRENCH WAR IN THE ALPS

When Italy declared war on Austria on 24 May 1915, Mussolini called it a 'revolutionary war'. Later, speaking to Ludwig in 1932, he would say, 'When we celebrate our entry into the war, on 24 May 1915, we do not do so as a triumph over the vanquished. This fact will give you the key to my whole political attitude. For us the date is a revolutionary landmark, seeing that then the people came to a decision in defiance of the wishes of the parliamentarians. It was really the beginning of the Fascist revolution.' War declared, Mussolini's opponents immediately heaped scorn on him in print for not volunteering; they accused the warmonger of being a coward. As a result of one such article Mussolini fought another duel with its author, the anarchist Libero Merlino. Both men were injured. In Italy the traditional method of settling differences for journalists was the duel – though illegal – rather than the libel writ. Each newspaper office had a room where journalists learned how to fence. At first blood, the unwritten rule was that both sides should attempt a reconciliation. But often reconciliation was impossible and the duel would continue until one side could carry on no more. As duels were illegal they took place in secret such as a field on the edge of town in summer, or a gym in winter. General Carboni, Mussolini's fencing teacher, noted, 'In action on the board he never fenced cleanly, but invariably searched for the successful or spectacular strike with dangerous and incorrect movements ... ever ready to argue about the hits he sustained.' Mussolini fought at least five duels in his life[1] – the last in 1922.

Many have written that Mussolini only became a soldier when forced to by conscription. They are wrong. He was thirty-two on 29 July 1915 – a little long in the tooth to be at the front. He had volunteered immediately but was turned down partly for political reasons and partly because the call-up for those born in his year was imminent anyway. In fact, Mussolini was very keen to get to the front and even wrote to an influential friend, the republican MP Salvatore Barzilai, urging him to pull strings. Already, the fifty-two-year-old poet warrior Gabriele d'Annunzio had enlisted and would become a war hero. The revolutionary syndicalist leader Corridoni had also volunteered and would die – as had many of the Futurists including Marinetti, noisily, Umberto Boccioni and Mario Sironi. The Futurists formed the Lombard Volunteer Cyclist Battalion. Cesare Battisti – Mussolini's old newspaper boss in Austrian Trent, had come to Italy and volunteered. In 1916 the Austrians executed him as a traitor after he was captured. Even Bissolati, the reformist Socialist enemy turned ally, had volunteered at the age of fifty-eight. Marinetti soon returned from his bicycle duties at the front suffering from a hernia.

Mussolini's year was called up on 31 August 1915 and on 3 September he joined the Bersaglieri with whom he had done his national service, arriving at the front two weeks later more than 6000 feet up on Monte Nero. In November he applied for officer training but the request was turned down after being considered by Prime Minister Salandra. This was a sign of the fame Mussolini already enjoyed and the fear he instilled. Mussolini's commanding officer offered him the chance to remain safe behind the lines at regimental headquarters to write a diary of the regiment. His death would have been a serious propaganda blow and behind the lines he would be less able to foment trouble among the troops. He refused the offer and spent the rest of 1915 – when not in hospital with typhoid – at the front in the mountains, near Austrian Trieste, 5000 feet up above the River Isonzo with the 33rd Battalion of the 11th Bersaglieri Regiment. That winter temperatures, he recorded in his diary, fell as low as minus 20°C. The Italian war aim was a swift strike to seize the irredentist territories it had long had its eye on such as the Trentino and Trieste from Austria. But the Italian army was badly equipped and badly led. Disease was rife. Cholera and typhus swept the ranks. By the time Mussolini reached the front to experience mountain trench warfare for himself in September 1915 the Italians had already suffered 130,000 casualties (defined as: dead and wounded) on the Austrian front since the outbreak of hostilities in June 1915 and progressed a matter of yards. They would suffer another 116,000 casualties by Christmas. This mountain warfare was as deadly in its way as that on the plains of France and Belgium.[2]

Sarfatti had kept in constant touch with Mussolini since his departure from *Avanti!* but she agonised about what she should do. Whereas Mussolini had left the fashionable Socialist party for the unfashionable wilderness, it was too risky for her – from a fashion point of view – to join him there – yet. But her fashionable friends the Futurists had volunteered. On 29 December 1915 she gave a speech[3] in Milan commemorating the death earlier that month of the British nurse Edith Cavell, executed by the Germans after being captured in Belgium and accused of harbouring enemy soldiers. 'In this war which we did not want, but which we must now fight to the last man, she is the purest and most radiant example of a martyr,' she said. The Socialist party made up her mind for her – though she must have been aware of the effect the speech would have. The party expelled her.

Mussolini did not formally marry Rachele until December 1915 in a civil ceremony – five years after the unofficial marriage to her in Forlì. The main factor behind the decision was Dalser. Everywhere she went she said she was Mussolini's wife. On one occasion she set fire to a Milan *pensione* and Rachele was briefly held in the police cells because police confused the identities of the two women.

By the time Rachele and Mussolini married he was a soldier and in hospital behind the front lines at Treviglio, near Bergamo, suffering from typhoid. He had contracted typhoid on 15 November 1915. The wedding ceremony took place one month later – on 16 December – in the hospital ward and so ill was the groom that he was unable to get out of his sick bed. 'He had yellow eyes and was wearing a big woollen balaclava which came down over his forehead and neck,' she recalled.[4] She had to be asked three times if she consented to marry him by the registrar before she confirmed that she did 'in a low voice'. Mussolini, duly recovered from typhoid, returned to the front where he spent Christmas Day 1915 according to Rachele. He ate just five chestnuts that day, he wrote to her.

But Mussolini was soon back in Milan on leave during which he secretly recognised Dalser's son, Benito, as his. In July, he eventually agreed to pay her maintenance of 200 lire per month. Sarfatti had arranged the lawyer to draw up the documentation. Despite ownership of *Il Popolo d'Italia* Mussolini was still very poor. 'The money Mussolini offered must have been pledged by the Sarfattis.' On 22 May 1917 the Italian authorities interned Dalser as an enemy alien – she was Austrian – and a serious danger to public order because of her threats of violence to Mussolini and his family. They despatched her south from Milan, first to Florence, then to a camp at Caserta near Naples.

Mussolini was soon back at the front and in March 1916 promoted to lance corporal (*caporale*). That month his regiment received orders to move from the mountains above the Isonzo in the east, west to the other end of the front, to the mountains of the Carso. On the way he had to pass through Tolmezzo – twenty miles behind the lines – where he had taught in 1906-7. In the street he saw Luigia Paggetta, the married woman with whom he had had a scandalous affair. They spoke to each other. But that was all. Three days later he arrived at the front, 5000 feet up in the mountains of the Carso. The worst of the winter was over and though the snow was deep the sun shone.

In 1916, Mussolini was regularly under fire. On one occasion in July he volunteered to lead his platoon back and forth across enemy lines for thirty-six hours on reconnaissance patrol under constant artillery, mortar and machine-gun fire. Italian casualties for 1916 on the Austrian front totalled 403,000.

Mussolini's second child by his wife was born on 27 September 1916 while he was at the front. He saw the boy, Vittorio, for the first time only in January 1917 when he returned to Milan on leave. His wife said he looked 'ragged and emaciated . . . his uniform was in shreds'. The year 1916, spent almost entirely at the front, demoralised Mussolini: the corpses; the rats; the lice; the disease; the foul, freezing, damp, wet, snowy weather; the absence of action – the absence of victory. War was not the beautiful poem the Futurists described. He despised the practice of promotion based on length of service not merit. The only words in his war diary for 27–28 January 1917 were: 'Snow, cold, infinite boredom. Order. Counter-order, disorder.'[6]

The entries in the war diary are sparse, bleak and very perceptive. 'A little further on the body of an Austrian, abandoned. The dead man still grips in his teeth a bit of collar from his tunic which strangely is still intact. But underneath, through the putrefying flesh, you can see bone. His shoes are missing. It is obvious why! The shoes of the Austrians are much better than ours' (20.9.15). 'Bombs, bombs, bombs all night, until dawn. No one dead, several injured. A morning of sun and cannonade' (24.9.15).

He was still drinking despite his promise to his wife to give it up. 'Tonight guard duty. Snow. Snow. I am drunk on white . . . But at dawn tiredness gripped me. To defeat it I swallowed half a bottle of rum' (2.3.16). The weather and the stars featured prominently. 'Night already. In the sky a timid sprinkling of stars. I look at them with the awestruck adoration of someone in love.' He spent Christmas 1916 in his Alpine trench. 'Like yesterday, like always, for a month around here, it rains. Today is Christmas . . . The date does nothing for me . . . Modern civilisation has "mechanised" us. The war has brought to the point of exasperation the process of the "mechanisation" of European society' (25.12.16). Only men understood war. 'The psychology of woman skims over war and is absolutely incapable of penetrating its intimate tragic substance. For woman, the man who returns from war presents the same attraction of "exoticism" as the man who returns from California and nothing else' (29.12.16). Men made war. War bound men together. From this would come a powerful idea: that of *la trincerocrazia* (the aristocracy of the trenches) – the elite who would be the vanguard of his revolution.

But his days as a soldier were numbered. On 23 February 1917 he sustained serious shrapnel injuries when a mortar he and others were using for firing practice exploded. Five died. He was lucky. He was taken to a field hospital where one day he met the King, Vittorio Emanuele III, who spent much of his time at the front and was nicknamed 'the Little King'. 'How's it going, Mussolini?' the King asked. 'Not very well, Majesty,'

Mussolini replied. Five weeks later he was well enough to be transferred, first to a hospital in Udine, then one in Milan.

In the Milan hospital the women in his life were able to see him once again. 'Forty-two wounds ... like the arrows of St Sebastian,' wrote Sarfatti.[7] 'His leg was never the same again,' said Rachele.

In February 1917 Dalser turned up at the hospital. Rachele – who when referring to Dalser usually called her either 'the Austrian' or 'the mad one' – was also there. She said, 'One morning, on a visit to see him, I met a brunette with an unpleasant appearance. I didn't recognise her as Ida Dalser ... It was she who recognised me. In the room where my husband was she flung herself at me, insulting me and shouting, "I am the wife of Mussolini! Only I have the right to be near him ..." The soldiers present found it all madly funny. Then, wild with anger I threw myself at her and battered her with kicks and punches. I ended up even putting my hands round her throat and squeezing. From his bed, like a mummy whose bandages stopped him moving, Benito tried to intervene. He raised himself out of the bed to stop us. Luckily, some doctors and nurses intervened before I could strangle her. Ida Dalser fled and I burst out crying.'

Once in power, Mussolini would have Dalser locked up in a lunatic asylum in Venice where she would remain for the rest of her life. Signora Cimadon recalled the night the Fascists came to the house in Trent to take away her aunt who had by then returned there from Milan:[5] 'It was three in the morning. The Fascist militia surrounded our house ... They searched every inch of the house. They looked for letters that Mussolini had written her ... But she wasn't mad.' The reason behind her detention, however, was her behaviour during a 1927 visit to Trent (which, after the First World War, became part of Italy) by Pietro Fedele, then the Fascist Education Minister. Dalser turned up at the Hotel Bristol where Fedele was guest of honour and flew into a rage. She would die in the asylum in December 1937 at the age of fifty-seven – officially from a stroke. Benito Albino – who was adopted by Giulio Bernardi in Trent in 1938 – would die aged twenty in July 1942 in circumstances that remain unclear.

Many have tried to dismiss Mussolini's shrapnel injuries as slight but they were not. He did not leave hospital until the summer and he was granted one year's sick leave. The worst injury was to his left leg. It meant that the riding boots he became famous for had to be a zip-fastened version to stop the scar inflaming and chafing. He finally left hospital on 1 August 1917 on crutches and would never see action again.

Mussolini had been a good soldier. In August 1916 he had been promoted to full corporal (*caporale maggiore*) and in February 1917 – after his injury – sergeant (*sergente di squadra*). On his own admission he had killed enemy soldiers – though only from the safety of his trench by firing mortar shells or throwing grenades at them. He had never been involved in the fiercest of fighting. He had, it seems, never had to go over the top and charge an enemy position. But he had been under heavy fire for long periods. His service record states that he had 'been of good conduct' and served 'with faith and honour'.[8]

While Mussolini had been at the front the financial situation of *Il Popolo* had become dire. In July 1916, for example, it had been forced to reduce the number of issues per week to three and the number of pages to two. But in April 1917 a Milan police report noted that the newspaper 'had up to a point overcome the grave crisis experienced'. The report explained the upturn in fortune as the result of money from new subscriptions, subsidies and advertising. The subsidies, it noted, came from rich Milanese industrialists,[9] which it did not name. According to a February 1917 personal note by a member of staff in the office of Orlando, then Italian interior minister, after Mussolini was called up for military service at the front all the newspaper's previous sources of funds including French government money had dried up. One of Mussolini's first acts on his return to the helm was to launch a massive subscription appeal through the pages of the newspaper, which raised the impressive sum of 100,000 lira in two months.

On 1 August 1917 Pope Benedict XV had urged the warring nations to stop what he called 'the useless slaughter'. Few listened. The autumn brought monumental developments across Europe. The Russian Revolution, which had begun in March, triumphed in November with the seizure of power by Lenin's Bolsheviks who immediately sought peace. Large numbers of French troops mutinied, America entered the war and Italy's darkest hour arrived – the catastrophe at Caporetto.

In August, the Italian Commander-in-Chief, Luigi Cadorna, had launched his eleventh offensive since the start of the war. At a cost of 182,000 Italian casualties it got nowhere, like nearly all of the previous ten. The front line had remained more or less static since the start. That was all about to change. On 24 October, boosted by seven German divisions no longer needed on the Russian front, the Austrians launched an offensive on the eastern end of the line. With the help of poison gas and flame throwers the Austro-Germans broke through at Caporetto – a little town on the Italian side of the River Isonzo. The Italian troops abandoned their positions and fled in total disarray. The next day, 25 October, the Italian government resigned. Within days the Italian troops had retreated as far as the River Piave – twenty-five miles inside Italy. Already, Italian losses in those few days alone were 40,000 dead or wounded and 280,000 taken prisoner. Equally bad, 350,000 Italian troops had deserted and there was serious rioting in Turin. A senator committed suicide. The whole of Italy, it seemed, lay at the mercy of the Austrian and German forces. Cadorna refused to accept the blame himself. He blamed the Pope, who he called a defeatist for his August 1917 public plea for peace and Giolitti who had done the same – and the Italian Socialist party. Cadorna also blamed his troops who 'cravenly withdrew', he said. Mussolini did not blame the troops. He blamed Cadorna and the general staff, Socialists, war profiteers and the government.

Caporetto had a seminal impact on Italy and on Mussolini. The defeat caused the triumph in Mussolini of his nationalism over his Socialism, of nation over class. Most Italians, like the Italian government and parliament, had been reluctant entrants into the war. Caporetto forged for the first time in Italy a real sense of nationhood. Until then, the war had been fought at the frontier. But now Italy had been invaded and was fighting to exist.

The new government – led by Vittorio Emanuele Orlando – removed General Cadorna and replaced him with General Armando Diaz. The Italian army regrouped behind the Piave and somehow managed to hold the enemy on the north bank with the crucial help of six French and British divisions – a total of 216,000 troops – reluctantly dispatched from the Western Front. The enemy would advance no further. Among the Italian dead was Roberto Sarfatti, Sarfatti's eldest son. Desperate to go to war he had tried to enlist at the age of fifteen. Two months after his seventeenth birthday in July 1917 he had finally been able to join up. He was killed in action in January 1918. A recklessly brave soldier he was awarded a posthumous *medaglia d'oro* – Italy's Victoria Cross. Mussolini wrote a glowing obituary of him in *Il Popolo d'Italia*. He said that the young Sarfatti had 'immolated himself serenely and heroically for the well-being of our beloved Italy ... His offering to the *patria* was complete, his devotion total ...' Sarfatti was devastated by the loss of her son. Though previously her sister had committed suicide she had not known deep suffering such as this before. But the death of Roberto became a potent symbol to Italians of the defiance of Italy.

Post-Caporetto Mussolini received financial support once again from Ansaldo, the arms manufacturer – though not nearly as much as had been given to start the newspaper in 1914. In the last three weeks of 1917, for example, Ansaldo took out four half-page advertisements in *Il Popolo d'Italia*. Mussolini also received Samuel Hoare's British money.

Mussolini, meanwhile, developed the concept of the '*trincerocrazia*', a group of men who were both an elite and a mass. What bound the group was not class consciousness but war consciousness. The war had created a new class. Those who had fought in it – the war class. He first used the word '*trincerocrazia*' in an article published in *Il Popolo d'Italia* on 15 December 1917. Italy would be divided, he wrote, after the war 'between those who were there and those who were not there; those who fought and those who did not fight; those who produced and the parasites'. These men – *trinceristi* – had the moral right and the necessary strength he said to create the new post-war Italy. Marinetti and the Futurists were saying much the same thing. In September 1918 they would publish a political manifesto in the weekly *Roma Futurista* which exalted the *arditi*: 'The *ardito* (commando) in war must be the Futurist in peace.' The *arditi* were formed after Caporetto and wore a black shirt under their jackets and they would form the majority of the first Fascists.

Mussolini's third child by Rachele, Bruno, was born on 22 April 1918. She told her biographer, Anita Pensotti, that Mussolini was very considerate towards her after Bruno's birth – he had been at the front when Vittorio was born. He even insisted on doing some cooking, she said, but was hopeless at it. 'I gave him suggestions (the bedroom was next to the kitchen) but very soon I realised I was wasting my time. Benito, in fact, had burned all the pans and wasn't able even to fry an egg. In addition he had spent in two days the amount that was enough for me to get through to the end of the month. So, twenty-four hours after the birth of Bruno, I was forced to get out of bed to avoid worse disasters.'[10] Mussolini prided himself on his physical fitness and physical prowess. But according to Rachele he was very prone to catching colds. When he had a cold he used to 'blow his nose every five minutes' with handkerchiefs the size of napkins.

Mussolini's relationship with Sarfatti, his other woman, deepened. He described himself in one letter[11] to her as 'your most devoted savage', adding, 'Give me a little of the blood from your lips.' In another he wrote, 'I kiss you with a violent tenderness.' In a poem, Sarfatti wrote: 'Other women you take, leave, and retake. / I smile and suffer: I know. / The day will come: you will find that I am inside you, / In your spirit and flesh, always.'

Sarfatti was entranced by the atmosphere at the pokey offices of *Il Popolo d'Italia* in a wretched building in a run-down part of central Milan – by the 'comradeship of brotherly bohemianism, which enlarged the heart … what happiness, how much fervour, how much fun …'[12] A bookcase was full of grenades, as was the stove. Mussolini drank milk all the time – hot milk in winter, cold milk in summer. He used to dip biscuits in the milk. Occasionally, he smoked cigarettes. He disliked beards – even though he had spent many years if not bearded, severely unshaven. 'He had a superstitious hatred of old-fashioned enormous beards, which provided a camouflage of false external gravity, behind which was fatuous nonsense. Such (bearded) men are unsporty, undynamic types, anti-life types …'[13] Those who produced *Il Popolo d'Italia* worked and lived in what Sarfatti called 'heroic poverty'.

Cesare Sarfatti must have known about his wife's affair with the man who had been his close political associate in the Socialist party. But he retained a stiff upper lip. As for Rachele, wrote Edvige, Mussolini's sister, 'Rachele realised, in her simple way, that in Margherita S. lay a special danger and perhaps hated her alone among all the women who "created" problems for her.'[14]

It would not be until exactly one year after Caporetto – October 1918 – that Italy would exact revenge for her humiliation and restore her pride. The Italian army had ensured that the Austro-German advance ground to a permanent halt on the Piave front when it repulsed a massive assault on it in June 1918. That saved Italy. But Italy wanted more than salvation. She wanted revenge for Caporetto. On 25 October the Italian forces, assisted by the British and French, attacked the Austrian line and fought their way across the river, taking back the key strategic town of Vittorio Veneto on 29 October. It was a famous victory – a victory etched in the collective memory of Italy as Waterloo is in Britain. The Italian army then drove the Austrians back across the border and occupied the Trentino. Everywhere in Europe by now the German and Austrian war effort was collapsing. The end, when at last it came, was swift. Austria asked for an armistice with Italy on 3 November, which became active the next day, and a week later Germany followed suit. On 9 November revolution broke out in Germany and the Kaiser fled to Holland. The guns which had left so many millions of young men dead in Europe fell silent on 11 November.

7

THE BIRTH OF FASCISM

The 4 June 1919 police report on Mussolini and Fascism (by the chief of the Pubblica Sicurezza's special investigations office, Inspector General Gasti, to the interior minister[1]), summed up Mussolini's character and daily routine well:

> He sleeps until late morning, leaves home at midday, but does not return until three in the morning, and those fifteen hours, except for a brief pause for meals, are devoted to journalistic and political activity. He is a sensualist and this is demonstrated by his various relationships conducted with women of which the most notable are those with Guidi [Rachele] and Dalser.
>
> He is an emotional and impulsive person and these characteristics make his speeches impressive and persuasive but, though a good speaker, one cannot say he is an orator. He is a deeply romantic person, who attracts much sympathy and many friendships. He is uninterested in and lavish with the money he has and this has given him a reputation for altruism and philanthropy.
>
> He is very intelligent, shrewd, cautious, thoughtful, with a good understanding of men and of their qualities and their weaknesses. He is quick in his likes and dislikes, capable of sacrifice for friends, and resolute in his hostilities and hatreds. He is courageous and bold; he has organising ability.

Victory in war plunged Italy into crisis. There was rampant inflation. By the end of 1920 the lira was worth just one-quarter of its value in 1914. In 1913 a gramme of gold had cost 3.49 lire in Italy. By 1920 it cost 14.05 lire. In July 1919 the new government of Francesco Nitti, who had become prime minister in June, imposed a compulsory price reduction of 15 per cent in the face of widespread rioting and strikes, but it had little effect on the situation. By 1921 the cost of living was 400 per cent higher than in 1915. Yet average real wages increased by only 1.8 per cent in the period 1913–22. By the end of 1919, the number of unemployed Italians was 2 million, and there was acute social unrest. In 1914 there had been 781 strikes by a total 170,000 workers. In 1919 there were 1860 strikes by $1\frac{1}{2}$

million workers and in 1920 more than 2000 strikes by nearly 2 million workers.[2] The British ambassador in Rome, Sir George Buchanan, who had witnessed the 1917 Russian Revolution, recorded that in his opinion Italy was not on the verge of revolution but the atmosphere was so explosive, especially in the north, that he thought the government might lose control of large areas of the country.

Returning soldiers, with tiny war discharge payments, unable to find employment, were also angry. Of the 5,758,277 Italians mobilised during the war, 670,000 had been killed and 950,000 injured, of whom 220,000 were disabled.[3] In the summer of 1919 there were still 1,575,000 soldiers serving in the army and 117,000 officers – half deployed in the former war zone on the Austrian and Yugoslav frontiers. But of the rest, half were deployed within Italy to guarantee public order. That so many men should be deployed in such a role shows how strong was the fear of revolution: so deployed they might stop revolution but if demobilised their numbers would swell the ranks of the unemployed and thus increase its likelihood.

Something else angered Italians, especially returning soldiers – what soon became known as the '*vittoria mutilata*' (the phrase was coined by the poet-soldier Gabriele d'Annunzio when he proclaimed: 'Oh victory, thou shall not be mutilated') – the mutilated victory. But under the Treaty of Versailles, signed on 28 June 1919, Italy got only Trieste and the Trentino. American President, Woodrow Wilson, had refused to recognise the terms of the Treaty of London. Wilson, who did not much like Italians, believed that the entire eastern Adriatic coast apart from Trieste should be part of the new Yugoslavia. Italy had won the war, felt Italians, but lost the peace. Yet as Mussolini had written at the start of the war, the war had been Italy's baptism as a nation. It had shown that men were more loyal to their nation – even a young nation such as Italy where most people still spoke dialect not Italian as their first language – than their class. Men had gone off to fight the national enemy in a way that for fifty years Socialists had hoped in vain that they would fight the class enemy. By now Mussolini had abandoned completely the idea of the proletariat being the only group of people that mattered and began to speak publicly of quality as well as quantity – of the importance of merit not just of the masses. He agreed that all men should have equal opportunity. But he was well aware that not all men were born equal as Socialists insisted. Some men were born with more talent than others.

On May Day 1918 he had written an important article in *Il Popolo d'Italia*[4] which illustrates his thinking:

> You [the proletariat] represent work but not all work, and your work is only one element in the economic game ... You have the numbers, but numbers are not enough to make you worthy to govern nations and the

world. Numbers are 'quantity'. We must transform them into a 'qualitative' factor. You will arrive if you deserve it. It is possible that out of your mass – by means of a refining process – will emerge organisms capable – not just for you, but for all – of governing the state politically and economically ... Liberate yourselves above all from the notion of a simplistic socialism *alla russa*, which is too expropriatory and 'egalitarian'. It is not a question of 'taking over ownership' of goods; it is a question of 'producing' more of them, without interruption. It is not a question of making men equal in the sense of *aplatir* [flattening – he uses the French word] but of establishing with fortitude hierarchies and discipline. So long as men are born differently 'gifted', there will always be a hierarchy of ability ... It is a question of organising the state to ensure the greatest individual and social well-being.

In March 1918, he had dropped the two quotes from Napoleon and Blanqui on the ears of *Il Popolo d'Italia* and on 1 August changed the front page sub-title from 'Socialist Daily' to 'Daily Newspaper of Combatants and Producers'. The 'combatants' were the *'trincerocrazia'*; the producers, the productive element in society regardless of class – the productive workers as well as the productive bosses. The class war Mussolini had in mind would pit producers against parasites.

Early in 1919, Mussolini and his family moved from the suburbs of Milan to a much smarter flat in Foro Bonaparte in the centre. His wife, like millions of others, caught Spanish flu which killed more people than the war – 400,000 in Italy alone. Mussolini would be thirty-six in July 1919. What now? Looking back, according to Hitler in 1942, 'The Duce himself told me that at the moment in which he began the struggle against Bolshevism he did not know exactly where he was going.'[5] The 1919 police report on Mussolini and Fascism noted that despite the mutual hatred between Mussolini and his former colleagues in the Socialist Party 'he will always want to appear, and deludes himself perhaps that he will always be a Socialist'.[6] Since 1915, Mussolini had been using the expression 'we Fascists' – pronouncing the word in his Romagnol accent *'Fassisti'* – to describe his brand of Socialism. It was now that Fascism was born.

The Crisis of the Italian Liberal State

The war and its aftermath plunged Italy into economic, moral and ideological crisis. The political system – a constitutional monarchy based on the British model – was not strong enough to survive the crisis. The worse the crisis became the less able were the men at the centre of the system to do anything about it. Between 1914 and 1922 there were, for example, eight different prime ministers – one a year – compared with just one more or less continuously, Giovanni Giolitti, in the previous decade.

The reasons for the political crisis were partly historical; partly to do with the war and its immediate aftermath. In reunified Italy the democratic element had been democratic only in name, at least until the introduction of near universal suffrage for literate men aged twenty-one and over, and illiterate men aged thirty and over by Giolitti in 1912. For much of the period after Italian reunification the chief characteristic of Italian politics had been the absence of a small number of clearly defined political parties. Government was by coalitions of different factions of MPs – not by single parties. The Italian political system at the turn of the twentieth century was like that of eighteenth-century England: ruled by patronage. This style of government by faction was known as *'trasformismo'*, a phrase coined in 1882 to describe the alliance of the two main opposing factions of the day. The word had soon become a term of abuse to describe the worm at the heart of the Italian political system. In fact, *trasformismo* would never go away in Italy.

Italy had finally experienced industrial revolution in the last decade of the nineteenth and first decade of the twentieth centuries. But this had happened really only in the northern triangle formed by the cities of Genoa, Turin and Milan. In 1914, for example, double the number of Italians were still employed in agriculture as in industry. Illiteracy rates in the north were relatively low, varying between 10 and 15 per cent, but in the south they were extremely high, varying between 50 and 70 per cent (this compares with an average national illiteracy rate in 1861 at the time of Italian reunification of 74 per cent – 85–90 per cent in the south). Then, the war over, came economic depression, rampant inflation and mass unemployment.

As a victor in the First World War Italy expected, as promised by the Treaty of London, handsome territorial gain. Instead it got just the Trentino and Trieste. The *'vittoria mutilata'* became a symbol of Italian failure – another rallying cry for nationalist forces.

Mussolini admired and was friends with nationalist leaders such as Alfredo Rocco and Enrico Corradini who would both later become Fascists. The nationalists had founded the Italian Nationalist Association in 1910. It was never a party, for the nationalists despised parties. Like Mussolini, they had been among those who had shouted loudest for Italian entry into the First World War – initially on the side of Austria and Germany, subsequently against. Though what would be described today as right-wing extremists, the Italian nationalists, again like Mussolini, had much common ground with the left-wing extremist revolutionary syndicalists, whose main inspiration was Georges Sorel. Sorel aimed for the syndicalisation of the state via a revolution, after a general strike – the last strike – had brought down the government. Both nationalists and syndicalists despised parliamentary democracy and the middle classes; both exalted the use of violence. They agreed that what counted was not whether a policy was right or wrong but whether it created a myth which moved men to action.

There was a further weakness – running like a fault line through Italy. The Vatican had never recognised the Italian state as legitimate because much of reunified Italy included chunks of territory seized from the Vatican – the former papal states such as Mussolini's native Romagna, not to mention Rome. Furthermore, popes traditionally had been hostile not just to the idea of Italy but to the idea of democracy. Therefore many Catholic Italians, taking their lead from the Pope, were also hostile. But under the Gentiloni Pact of 1913 the Vatican had given Catholics permission to vote but only for pro-Catholic candidates – though not to be politicians. This Vatican reticence undermined the major new political force with mass support to emerge after the war: the Catholic *Partito Popolare Italiano* (*Popolari*), founded by a Sicilian priest, Don Luigi Sturzo, on 18 January 1919 who was then forty-seven.[7] Don Sturzo had entered politics by marching at the head of peasants carrying aloft a large crucifix to occupy the fields of wealthy landowners – many of whom were absentee. He was mayor of Caltagirone from 1905 to 1920. 'He was truly the shepherd of his flock and his flock was all the poor and oppressed of the country.'[8] '*Vogliamo le fabbriche, vogliamo la terra, ma senza guerra, ma senza guerra,*' sang the flock.

Like the Vatican, the Socialist party did not recognise the legitimacy of the Italian state either – seeing it as something to be destroyed. The extremists managed to take the Socialist party with them, and official party policy switched between 1917 and 1918, from the reformist wing's strategy of a democratic revolution via parliament (the position stated in the May 1917 party programme) to that of outright revolution along Russian lines (the policy adopted in December 1918 by the party executive). At the party's annual congress in October 1919 it expelled all moderates from the executive – as had happened in 1912 as a result of Mussolini's Reggio Emilia Congress speech – and announced firm support for a Russian-style revolution in Italy.

The new strategy ruled out any rapprochement or alliance with other parties in parliament. This meant that the chance of forming Italy's first left-wing government via the ballot box was lost. The Socialist party was further weakened because while the party had adopted the revolutionary line the parliamentary group remained reformist. Mussolini noted on 6 April 1919, 'The crisis [between the two] must, one day or other, explode.' Yet in 1919 Socialist revolution looked very likely in Italy. The Socialist party, its policy now revolutionary, attracted huge support. Party membership, which had plummeted in the war, surged to all-time highs. Italy, it seemed, was indeed on the verge of revolution.

The instinct of the dominant Italian politician of the twentieth century until the war, the liberal Giovanni Giolitti, was the classic instinct of a *trasformista*: embrace the enemy, if possible so as to reduce his ability to stab you in the back. But after the war Giolitti's style of politics could not contain the powerful forces the war had thrown up.

The Fascist Movement Is Founded

Just as Don Sturzo founded the *Popolari* in early 1919, so too did Mussolini found the Fascist movement. He had not been a member of a political party since he quit the Socialist party in 1914. He insisted, however, that Fascism be a movement not a party. A movement had broader appeal than a party. It was more spontaneous – more like a crowd – and more flexible. Nor would a movement become corrupt, it was felt, and ineffectual like Italy's existing political parties.

So it was that on the morning of 23 March, a Sunday, Mussolini and other like-minded people organised a meeting in a hall in Milan's Piazza San Sepolcro. Barely noted by the press at the time, the San Sepolcro meeting would later achieve legendary status. The aim was to unite all the pro-war revolutionary groups into a single organisation. Many of these groups already called themselves *fasci*. The name given to the new movement was the *Fascio di Combattimento*. Among the 120-odd people to attend the inaugural meeting of Fascism were Futurists including Marinetti, revolutionary syndicalists, ex-soldiers and a number of nationalists and Republicans – the party led by Pietro Nenni, Mussolini's old friend from Forlì with whom he had once been in prison. They came from all classes, even the nobility. The 'professional' politicians were mainly revolutionary syndicalists or, like Mussolini, former Socialists. It is impossible to say for sure precisely how many people attended the meeting. Once the Fascists had seized power those claiming to have been there numbered several hundred. Mussolini himself said in his 1928 autobiography that there were 54 people present, Sarfatti 145 in *Dux*. Sarfatti was also there, she would claim.

Many of the ex-soldiers were *arditi*, many officers. These people – spat at by Socialists in the street and unable to readjust to civilian life – would prove to be the most important element of early Fascism. Many wore black shirts at the meeting and carried *manganelli* (clubs), knuckle-dusters, riding crops and black flags. In the centre of these black flags – the flag of the *Arditi* – was a white skull whose teeth gripped a dagger. Black was the colour of death – of war. Red was the colour of the enemy – Socialism. The group was united by the war and the *vittoria mutilata*; by nationalism; by the new; anti-clericalism (not God necessarily); and by a hatred of both Socialism (not the working class necessarily) and privilege (not Capitalists necessarily). As Ferruccio Vecchi, the ex-*arditi* captain and Futurist, wrote, 'With the end of the war, we are precisely those who have no direction any more, those surrounded by the abyss, those without bread. ... The war has by now become our second nature ... Where shall I go? What shall I do? I don't know ...'[9] They would become Mussolini's civilian trenchocracy.

In his speech to the meeting, Mussolini rejected both Italian Socialism and Russian Bolshevism, and proposed a system that would put the interests of the nation above those of class. To promote class unity not class hatred he called for the introduction of corporations to represent the various economic groupings in the nation. This idea – which would eventually become the Fascist idea of the Corporate State – derived, via revolutionary syndicalism, from the medieval corporations, those bodies whose members were bound together according to profession that performed both an economic and a political role in the days before the establishment of parliaments. Government by corporation was therefore a potential alternative to government by parliament. Its attraction was that it would abolish class hatred because the corporation would represent the interests of the group not those of the individual.

Yet immediately, the Italian Left branded Fascism a reactionary force in the service of the bourgeoisie. It would keep on saying so. History, by and large, has accepted this definition of Fascism. But Fascism was anything but a right-wing movement.

The first Fascist programme, which was not officially adopted until June 1919 and published in *Il Popolo d'Italia* on 6 June, reflected the predominance of the Futurists and was very left-wing. By now there were in Milan 'about 3000' Fascist members, according to Inspector Gasti's report.[10]

The programme's demands numbered: universal suffrage from the age of eighteen for everyone including women (in Britain women aged thirty and over had been given the vote in 1918); an electoral system based on proportional representation; a lowering of the minimum age of deputies (MPs) from thirty-one to twenty-five; abolition of the monarchy and the upper house, the Senate and hereditary titles; Chamber of Deputies to form a National Assembly which would decide what form of government should emerge from the Fascist revolution; a maximum eight-hour working day; workers' representation in the management of industry; confiscation of 85 per cent of war profits; confiscation of ecclesiastical property and land from the rich; a progressive tax on capital; and the ceding to Italy of Fiume and Dalmatia.

The first branch of the *Fascio di Combattimento* was formed in Milan and the second in Genoa. By August 1919 there were branches in nearly all major Italian cities.

Socialists, meanwhile, had started to beat up and sometimes kill workers who refused to join their unions and take part in the waves of strikes which characterised 1919. Even modestly dressed women, wrote Sarfatti,[11] were sworn at: *'Porca borghesia'*.

Soldiers and former soldiers, wearing medals or uniforms in the streets, were spat at and abused. Train and tram drivers sometimes refused to move if officers were on board. In retaliation, strike breakers and ex-servicemen formed armed squads. Squad members called themselves *'arditi'* or *'squadristi'*. Mussolini, meanwhile, hired ex-*arditi* to guard the offices of *Il Popolo d'Italia*. It was on 15 April 1919 that the Fascists used violence for the first time in response to a call by the Milan Socialists for a general strike in protest at the killing of a party official by the police at a recent demonstration. That day a gang of 200–300 Fascists, nationalists and *arditi*, marching in a column like soldiers, many armed with pistols and carrying burning torches, attacked Socialists demonstrating in the city's Piazza del Duomo, in front of the Cathedral. They then marched on to the Milan offices of *Avanti!*, the Socialist party newspaper, in Via San Damiano, which they sacked and burned. Four died – a soldier and three Socialists – and thirty-nine were injured. The shot which killed the soldier came from the first floor window of the *Avanti!* offices. It is not clear who fired it. The leadership of the *Fasci di Combattimento* had not officially ordered the assault but leading members such as Marinetti and Vecchi had marched at the head of the Fascist column.

Mussolini, who had not taken part, was jubilant. He told the newspaper, *Il Giornale d'Italia* that the violence had been the spontaneous reaction of the 'crowd, of combatants, of people fed up with Leninist blackmail because Milan wants to work'. 'We Fascists did not organise the attack on the Socialist newspaper, but we accept all the moral responsibility.' In *Il Popolo d'Italia* on 18 April,[12] he wrote, '... they were not reactionaries, they were not bourgeois, they were not Capitalists those who moved in a column ... They were people, genuine, authentic people! ... We combat openly and proudly, together with the majority of Socialists throughout the world, that obscure phenomenon of regression, of counter-revolution and importance which is called Bolshevism.' The next day he wrote that if the attack had been a reactionary act, 'the reaction was of the people'. *Avanti!*, he said, was reactionary: 'the newspaper of Caporetto'. It and the Socialists wanted a Russian-style revolution, which had 'killed' Russia. On 1 May in *Il Popolo d'Italia*[13] he described the Socialist party as a class of '20,000 or 30,000 men' who aimed to replace the bourgeoisie as the dominant class, 'who have never worked and will never work because they have found their career in Socialism'; who wanted to introduce a dictatorship, the dictatorship of the proletariat with themselves as dictators. 'The party is an extraneous fact to the workers' movement.' He defined the Fascist movement as 'an anti-party without statutes and without rules'.

Several months later he wrote, 'Fascism is pragmatic. It does not have a priorisms. It does not promise the usual utopian paradises. It leaves those charlataneries to the party card tribe. It does not pretend to live for ever. It will live only until it has achieved the task it has set itself.' So too was Sarfatti jubilant at the attack. In *Dux* she wrote, ' "God, I thank you," I prayed in my heart.'

Significantly, the authorities took no action to prosecute any of the Fascists who had taken part in the assault on the Socialists and the *Avanti!* offices. But in Florence the Socialists retaliated by killing a Fascist. The message was not lost on Mussolini that the police and army – and the government that gave them their orders – were prepared to tolerate violence committed against Socialists because of their fear of Socialist revolution. It was at this time that Mussolini started to keep a revolver and several hand grenades on his editor's desk at the *Popolo d'Italia* offices – next to his habitual large glass of milk. He also hung the black flag of the Arditi, depicting a skull with a dagger in its teeth, on the wall behind his chair. That summer Mussolini personally encouraged the formation of armed Fascist squads from his newspaper offices Via Paolo da Connobio. As he could not stand the cold, not least because he was terrified of catching colds, he always insisted on keeping the heating on very high. When in power it was never lower than 24°C[14] in his office at Palazzo Venezia. At *Il Popolo d'Italia*'s offices the combination of the stove on full blast, whatever the weather, near the grenades he kept on his table terrified staff. On one occasion, Sarfatti discovered him hard at work next to a lighted cigarette that he had absent-mindedly placed on top of one of the grenades.

Mussolini and Sarfatti meanwhile continued to work side by side where her main role was to oversee *Ardita* – the newspaper's monthly literature and arts review, which had been launched in March 1919. If nothing else, Mussolini was producing his best journalism. He would write articles very quickly in about twenty minutes with the aim that they should be 'electric' and 'explosive.'[15] Mussolini was obsessive about order and kept his editor's desk very neat and tidy. He always used the same type of square-nibbed fountain pen and the same Faber pencils – either red or blue.

Just as it had failed to intervene to stop or punish the Fascist violence against the *Avanti!* offices in April the Italian government also failed to intervene to stop the wave of Socialist strikes and frequent riots over the high price of bread which swept Italy that summer of 1919 – especially in the industrial north. The motive for this government inertia was the same in both cases: fear of Socialist revolution. So it stood by doing nothing when Socialists went on strike just as it stood by when Fascists used violence against the strikers. It feared that to intervene with troops against the strikes might provide the spark of violence which would ignite revolution. The Socialist party did not shrink from violence, using intimidation and arson to force employers to grant wage increases. Large parts of Italy, both cities and the countryside, were under the de facto control of the Socialist party. Yet by July 1919 Mussolini was already writing in *Il Popolo d'Italia* of the triumphal development of Fascism – a gross exaggeration.

It was in July 1919 that Mussolini started to take flying lessons, probably paid for by Sarfatti, and so began a lifelong obsession with aviation – though in the next ten months he only managed fourteen lessons and six and a half hours' flying. Just as the Futurists were fascinated by machines – especially planes – so was Mussolini. It suited the image he wanted to project of being the new man. He also loved fast cars, which he drove at reckless speed. In a 19 August 1919 article in *Il Popolo d'Italia* he echoed the mood of most of Italy when he described the state of the nation as one of 'civil war'. The country had been split in two by those who had supported Italian intervention in 1915 and those who had not – the neutralists. The same division continued after the war. The battle, he said, was not a battle between labour and capital but a battle between 'anti-national forces' and 'national forces'. Such forces were to be found in each and every class. Chief among the anti-nationalist forces was the internationalist, neutralist Socialist party, which he said had 'tried to assassinate the Italian nation' and was still trying.[16]

If d'Annunzio's March on Fiume Was Comic Opera
Mussolini's March on Rome Was *Opera Lirica*

Two months before the November 1919 elections an event of seminal importance occurred for the destiny of both Mussolini and Italy. On 11 September the poet Gabriele d'Annunzio, despite suffering from a high fever, rose from his sickbed in his house in Venice – the Red House – to lead a force of 2000 Italian soldiers who had deserted from the Italian army to seize the important Adriatic city port of Fiume on 12 September – nowadays Rijeka, in Croatia. Fiume had been part of the Austro-Hungarian empire which had collapsed at the end of the First World War and was now situated in the new nation of Yugoslavia. Its status was supposed to have been decided at the Versailles peace talks but was not by the time the Versailles Treaty was signed in June 1919. Just outside Fiume, General Vittorio Emanuele Pittaluga, in charge of local Italian forces, confronted d'Annunzio and told him to turn back. D'Annunzio, mimicking Napoleon, drew back his coat to expose his war medals, which included the *medaglia d'oro* and said, 'All you have to do is order the troops to shoot me, General.' General Pittaluga did not, could not, have the poet shot. Instead, he embraced him and wept. Together they entered Fiume. The city was taken without a single shot being fired.

That same month Nitti had outraged officers by announcing an amnesty for wartime deserters and issuing orders to officers not to wear uniform in public so as to avoid inflaming the volatile situation on the streets. This amnesty did not apply to post-war deserters and the punishment for them remained execution. That so many soldiers were prepared to desert to join d'Annunzio's cause and that even General Pittaluga was unable to bring himself to stop d'Annunzio gives an idea of how high passions were running in Italy and its army over Fiume and the *vittoria mutilata*.

The seizure of Fiume electrified public opinion in Italy and threatened to bring down not just Prime Minister Nitti but the Italian state as well. This is exactly what d'Annunzio hoped would happen. The flame lit at Fiume would engulf Italy. The March of Ronchi, as it became known, reminded Italians in particular of their tradition of marching at key moments in their history to achieve great success – such as Julius Caesar's crossing of the Rubicon to march on Rome and the march of Garibaldi's Thousand which secured Italian reunification. D'Annunzio, with a single bold action, had got Fiume. The Italian government, with endless diplomacy, had not.

Nitti was as afraid of a coup by the army as he was of Socialist revolution – indeed, he appealed to the workers and peasants to stand with him against d'Annunzio. He felt unable to order the army into Fiume against d'Annunzio for fear of a civil war – a war which would pit nationalists against Socialists and both against the government. His only alternative was a waiting game. So despite his promise to the Allies to expel d'Annunzio swiftly by force if necessary, he did no such thing. He felt able to order the army and navy merely to blockade the city. Nitti then announced the first general election since the war to be held in November.

D'Annunzio managed to hold Fiume in defiance not just of the Italian government but of Italy's allies, America, Britain and France, and the new Yugoslavia in whose territory Fiume was. Until d'Annunzio decided to make Fiume the symbol of the *vittoria mutilata*, few Italians had heard of it. But what happened at Fiume is crucial to understanding the success of Fascism. D'Annunzio at Fiume set the tone for all that followed. He had already achieved considerable fame as a poet, playwright and war hero. He had volunteered in 1915 for military service as soon as Italy had entered the war. He was fifty-two at the time and his only military experience had been the odd duel. Yet during the war he had taken part in a number of daring military escapades, which captured the imagination of Italians. Initially he had joined a cavalry division as a commissioned officer but was soon given free rein to do more or less whatever he chose. His most famous exploits were to command a squadron of planes over Austria to drop propaganda leaflets in the colour of the Italian flag on Vienna and despite being a sufferer of severe seasickness to command a torpedo boat attack on the Austrian fleet at anchor. He also charged an enemy trench in a flowing cape armed with a pistol. He ended the war, minus one eye, lost in a flying accident, and with Italy's highest military honour – the *medaglia d'oro*.

D'Annunzio had also gained notoriety for his scandalous private life. This bald, near-hunch-backed, tiny, one-eyed poet-warrior, with rotting teeth, who rumour had it had had a rib removed so that he could perform oral sex on himself, had the reputation of being one of the great lovers of his day. He had affairs with a long line of beautiful women. His mistress between 1897 and 1904, for example, was Eleanor Duse, the ravishing and internationally acclaimed Italian actress. Of baldness he said that in future all 'beautiful people' would be bald. Indeed, if not baldness, the shaven head certainly, did become one of the hallmarks of the Fascists. D'Annunzio was deeply superstitious – even more so than Mussolini. When faced with a decision, he would often let the flip of a coin decide the matter. He was particularly superstitious about dates and numbers. He settled on the date for the start of the move on Fiume – 11 September – because the number eleven felt lucky.

Despite his physical repulsiveness and lack of physical strength, d'Annunzio had become the symbol of Italian military, sexual and cultural prowess, and a national hero of such importance that the Italian government feared his every move. So too did Mussolini, who admired and envied d'Annunzio. Both men despised the Italian parliament and Italian political parties. Both despised the Socialist party – rather than Socialism – and bourgeois society. Both admired heroic violence and heroic action. Both exalted machinery but rebelled against the mechanisation of men caused by industrialisation. But Mussolini realised all too painfully that it was d'Annunzio not he who was in a much stronger position in 1919 to lead the kind of political movement he had in mind. Publicly, in his speeches and writings, he gave d'Annunzio his whole-hearted support at Fiume. But in fact – in terms of material support – he did little to help the poet's cause and *dietro le quinte* ('behind the choir stalls', as the Italians say) quite a lot to sabotage him – certainly his dream of using Fiume as a base for a march on Rome. If the poet's Fiume venture failed, Mussolini did not want to be associated too directly with that failure. But if it succeeded and spread to Italy it would mean d'Annunzio, not Mussolini, would be its undisputed leader. But most importantly Mussolini quickly decided, rightly or wrongly, that a move on Rome would benefit neither him nor d'Annunzio, but the Socialists who would use it to start their own revolution. He gave the poet full support for the seizure of Fiume in his newspaper and raised money for him. In his letters to him he spoke in favour of extending the action to Italy.

Politically, d'Annunzio – the John the Baptist of Fascism – was an extremist but he cannot be classified as either extreme left- or extreme right-wing. Like Mussolini he was very right-wing when it came to the idea of Italian greatness but veered left when it came to social policy. Certainly he hated parliamentary democracy *'all' Italiana'* – a corrupt, inept parliament. It was he who had coined the phrase *vittoria mutilata*, it was he who coined the phrase *'mare nostrum'* to describe the Mediterranean and provide a slogan for Italian colonial aspirations. And he it was who first called Prime Minister Nitti *'Cagoia'* (untranslatable but suggestive of excrement). Mussolini had taken such phrases up as his own. In *Il Popolo d'Italia* of the 24 October 1919[17] he noted the impossibility of talking about 'left' and 'right' in the Italy of his day: '... We use this terminology ... but we add immediately that in the majority of cases the only value that right and left have today is purely retrospective.'

D'Annunzio was not and would never become a Fascist – though in October 1920 he did become a member of the Fascist Movement.[18] Yet much of the inspiration for Fascism came from d'Annunzio – particularly what Fascism looked and sounded like, and why it was able to seduce so many Italians with its emphasis on politics as theatre: the idea of the dialogue between the leader and the crowd in which the crowd shouted *'aia, aia, alala'*, *'si'* or *'no'*, in response to the leader, the Roman salute, the cult of the leader, the appeal to the young and the new, the singing of the *arditis'* song, *'Giovinezza'*, which would become the anthem of Fascism, the public use of sacred and ancient Roman images ... All these helped transform the piazza into a political theatre. All these gained fame with d'Annunzio at Fiume. Art for d'Annunzio was politics and vice versa; the sacred secular and vice versa. What mattered were action, glory, virility, creativity, the Latin people, youth, nobility, excitement, the sacred, the spiritual, the defence of the Adriatic, the redemption of Italy, *mare nostrum*, the *vittoria mutilata*, the idea of Greater Italy. Above all, d'Annunzio despised inaction and impotence.

D'Annunzio like Mussolini wanted to transform Italians into heroes and Italy into a reincarnation of the heroic Roman empire. Both aimed to transcend the conflict and chaos which characterised post-war Italy with a political movement whose principal strength was an appeal to the subconscious desire of mankind for faith in a cause. D'Annunzio and Mussolini could only have succeeded on such a grand scale in Italy – that country whose people are so deeply superstitious, religious, noisy and theatrical. The appeal of both was the appeal of the cult – an appeal driven more by emotion than by reason. They succeeded because they were able to create a myth which moved men to action.

Sigmund Freud once said that everywhere he went in his studies of the human psyche the poet had been there first. Mussolini might have said the same about d'Annunzio. He would tell Ludwig,[19] '... the poet is almost always a prophet ... "the mirror of the gigantic shadows which futurity casts upon the present". Dante is a signal instance of this. He foreshadowed the liberation of the mind which was then about to begin. ...' But Mussolini added, '. . . a poet is not the herald of a specific revolution. The course to be taken by a revolution cannot be accurately predicted; its outlines are continually reshaping themselves. Thinkers and poets are like stormy petrels; they feel that a storm is brewing, but do not know from what quarter the wind will blow or what changes it will induce.'

As Michael Ledeen notes in *The First Duce – d'Annunzio at Fiume*[20] the poet's seizure of Fiume made him 'one of the pivotal figures of the twentieth century'. The style of politics seen at Fiume for the first time – the direct dialogue between leader and crowd – set the tone for a style of politics which would become the hallmark of the twentieth century. Ledeen adds, 'Everyone from Mussolini to Francesco Saverio Nitti realised that d'Annunzio could have led a successful march on Rome during his reign at Fiume and an analysis of the diplomatic correspondence of the period shows that this concern was exceedingly widespread throughout the Western world . . . and it was only the poet's lack of political acumen that prevented him from eventually seizing power in Italy.'

Mussolini had first met d'Annunzio on 23 June 1919 at the Grand Hotel in Rome where he had gone from Milan to drum up support for the new Fascist movement. The two had corresponded before that since the end of 1918. The meeting was the start of a long love–hate relationship between them. According to Nino Daniele, a d'Annunzio supporter present, Mussolini urged caution, telling the poet that 'you can't do a revolution without the army'.[21]

On the eve of his departure from Venice for Fiume d'Annunzio informed very few people not directly involved that the invasion of the city was imminent, but Mussolini was one of them. D'Annunzio asked him to publish an article about the march in *Il Popolo d'Italia*, which he did. The day after the seizure of Fiume Mussolini splashed in *Il Popolo d'Italia* with an article headlined VIVA FIUME!. Conspicuously, the article did not, however, urge the re-enactment of Fiume in Italy. In a subsequent article he heaped scorn on Nitti with a barrage of insults – 'jesuitic', 'bourbonic', 'odious', 'useless', 'acrid' and 'bestial'. 'The real men, today, are at Fiume, not in Rome. The capital of Italy is on the Carnaro, not the Tiber,' he wrote.

That d'Annunzio should inform Mussolini must mean that he regarded him as a crucial ally both in retaining Fiume and in the planned move on Rome. But he quickly became furious with Mussolini. He did not just want words of support from him but material help. On 16 September he fired off an angry letter[22] to Mussolini demanding to know why he had not sent men and funds. 'My dear Mussolini, I am stupefied by you . . . I have risked all, given all, and had all. . . . And you tremble with fear . . . I haven't slept for six nights; and I am devoured by fever. But I am on my feet,' he fumed.

Mussolini replied[23] on the 18th from Venice where he had gone so as to go to Fiume if necessary. He advised d'Annunzio that it was too early to make any move on Italy and that it was necessary to see which way the wind was blowing first. Such a move might spark off Socialist revolution. The next day Mussolini launched a Fiume appeal in *Il Popolo d'Italia*, which would raise an enormous amount – 3 million lire in little more than a month. His wild enthusiastic support for d'Annunzio at Fiume had the added advantage of boosting the newspaper's circulation.

Finally on 7 October Mussolini went to Fiume – by plane. This time he had something concrete to give the poet – the money so far raised by the *Il Popolo d'Italia* appeal. He stayed until noon the next day. During his two-hour meeting with d'Annunzio he once more said they should do nothing until after the elections. The elections would give a far clearer picture of how weak the Nitti government's position was and whether to move on Rome or not. They would also give a clear idea of how strong support for the other enemies was – the Socialist party and the *Popolari*.

The 1919 General Election: Fascism Fails

The Fascists fought their first general election on 16 November 1919. Mussolini was one of seventeen Fascist candidates in Milan as were Marinetti and the conductor, Arturo Toscanini, who were close friends. Toscanini had donated 30,000 lire to the campaign. The election was fought for the first time under a system of proportional representation which divided Italy into fifty-four districts, each to elect between five and twenty MPs. The new system gave smaller parties a better chance of representation in the Chamber of Deputies.

Giolitti's 1912 electoral reform had given the vote to literate men aged twenty-one and over, and illiterate men aged thirty and over, thus increasing the electorate from 3 to 8.6 million. A more recent reform had abolished the literacy qualification increasing the electorate to 11 million. The 1919 election, then, was the first election in which the Italian people – Italian men at least – really did count.

But this first Fascist attempt at getting power by trying to reconcile the two seemingly opposite ideas of nationalism and Socialism was a devastating failure. The only Fascist success was in Liguria where the crypto-Fascist, Valentino Coda, was elected[23] and in Milan – the Fascist stronghold – the Fascists received just 4657 votes out of a total 270,000 votes cast there. In Mussolini's home village of Predappio in the Romagna the Fascists did not get a single vote. To rub salt into his wounds his leading Socialist opponent in Milan, Turati, one of his arch enemies, obtained 180,000 votes.

The Socialist party, on the other hand, enjoyed its best ever election result. It got 1.76 million votes and won 156 seats – up from 52 – to become the largest single party. The new Catholic party – Don Sturzo's

Popolari, forerunner of the dominant post-World War Two political force in Italy, the Christian Democrat party until its virtual wipe-out by the corruption scandals of the early 1990s – also did very well. It won 100 seats. The *Popolari* did not aim to be the Pope's party – simply a party representing Italian Catholics. But until 1913, the Vatican had not permitted Catholics to vote nor, until this 1919 election, to take part in politics. Now it had given Don Sturzo its informal blessing, though it did not formally cancel the papal *non expedit* of February 1868, which said that Catholics could not take part in elections in Italy, until just after the 1919 election. This papal change of heart was a highly significant moment for the relationship between the Vatican and Italy, and between Italian Catholics and the Italian state. Most of the politicians responsible for the reunification of Italy – much of it achieved at the expense of the Vatican – had been priest-eaters (*mangiapreti*) like Mussolini, however conservative their views in other matters. Unlike the Fascists, the *Popolari* also had the advantage of a ready-made electoral machine in every Italian town and village: the priest. But the anti-Church essence of the *ancien régime* meant that any alliance between any of the factions and the *Popolari* would be very difficult to achieve.

The 1919 election results were a clear indication that the liberal oligarchy, only ever democratic in name, was in mortal danger. The Socialists and the *Popolari* were now the two dominant parties in Italy. Had they been able to combine to form a coalition Italy would have had its first ever left-wing government. But although they had much in common on social matters they were doomed to remain vigorous opponents because of the traditional antagonism between Socialism and Catholicism. The *ancien régime* factions, meanwhile, saw the number of their combined seats slump from 427 to 252. The liberals won 129 seats and had the support of 50 other MPs from traditional factions.[24]

The Socialist party had come back, it seemed, from the dead and now stood on the brink of power. Between 1912 and 1914, when Mussolini had been editor of *Avanti!*, Socialist party membership had nearly doubled to just under 60,000. But during the war the party – thanks to its pacifist stance and the growth of nationalist sentiment – had lost members in droves. Then as a result of the suffering of war, the post-war economic crisis, the collective mood that things must change and the beacon of encouragement provided first by the 1917 Russian Revolution, then in late 1918 by the fall of the Kaiser in Germany, membership began to soar once again. By October 1919 it was 71,000 and by January 1921 220,000.

For now, though, the liberal Nitti, who had become prime minister in June 1919, was able to cling on by creating yet another old-style coalition. But to do so he was forced to include the *Popolari*. The Socialists, who had decided not to participate in such coalitions, were confident that their moment had at last arrived – either with an outright majority in the next general election or via revolution on the streets.

Mussolini, meanwhile, slumped into a profound depression. He would later tell his eldest son Vittorio[25] that the humiliation at the polls in 1919 made him lose faith in himself for the first time in his life. So downcast was he that he once again considered emigrating. Fascism had, it seemed, been destroyed in infancy, squeezed to death between the populist Left – the Socialists – and the populist Right – the *Popolari*. He spoke of abandoning politics and becoming a playwright or wandering minstrel. Failure at the elections caused circulation of *Il Popolo d'Italia* to plummet – just as it caused membership of the Fascist movement to collapse.

The Socialists, cock-a-hoop at their spectacular performance in the polls and the spectacular failure of their despised former comrade, Mussolini, marched through Milan carrying a coffin – the coffin which they said contained the corpse of his political career. They stopped outside Mussolini's home.

They made a lot of noise but did not try to get into the building and went off instead to throw the coffin in one of the *navigli* (canals) which criss-cross the centre of Milan. On the 18th a brief article in *Avanti!*, the paper Mussolini had once edited, gloated, 'There is a corpse in a state of putrefaction which has been fished out of the canal. We are talking about Benito Mussolini.'

On the 18th, Mussolini was one of the thirty-six Fascists arrested for the illegal possession of weapons – but swiftly released. What happened, it emerged later, was that Nitti had been swayed by a telephone call from Luigi Albertini, influential editor and co-owner of the *Corriere della Sera* and senator, who said there was no point making a martyr of Mussolini - a man who was 'a relic.'[26] Mussolini spent just one night in prison and was released the following afternoon. On the 21st he wrote about the elections again to say that regardless of Socialist success at the polls revolutionary Socialism would exhaust itself in the effort to translate 'easy talk of revolution into the impossible revolutionary fact'.[27] But the elections also convinced him that any move by d'Annunzio on Italy from Fiume would be a grave error, providing the spark to start the Socialist revolution the Socialist party was unable itself to supply.

A few days later, on 26 November, he went to Venice by train to join Sarfatti for a two-day holiday and lick his wounds – as usual under the careful surveillance of government spies[28] who trailed him everywhere. Sarfatti and Mussolini occupied separate rooms on the same floor of Venice's luxurious Hotel Danieli. They went for rides in gondolas and strolls through the sinister little streets of the city of her childhood.

Back in Milan Mussolini wrote an article, published in *Il Popolo d'Italia*[29] on 6 December, which spelled out his attitude to the working class and how it was different from that of the Socialist party:

Only a criminal or an imbecile can hate the working class, that is the class which earns its living by working honestly with its hands in the fields and factories ... The workers, the so-called proletariat, are not, as in the stale and old nomenclatura of revolutionary Socialism, something homogeneous, compact, sharply distinct from all the other classes. Even within the proletariat there are distinctions ... There are workers on the fringes of science. There are workers who touch the threshold of the arts. There are, alongside the workers who make books, those who love books ... The truth is we fight the evil spiritual tendencies of one part of the mass of workers; not, note, its yearning for a better political system, a yearning that we believe useful, in the interests of general progress ... we fight Socialist megalomania, the wildly exaggerated and obsequious Socialist adulation of the workers, of those who would have us believe that only manual workers have the right to life and government, even if they are devoid of virtue and talent.

We fight the speculation which the official Socialists – a political party composed only minimally of workers – practise on the so-called proletariat. We fight the absurd idea which attempts to reduce the enormously complex life of Western society to a single 'dato' of manual work.

We fight anything which brutalises or bestialises the workers: from clerical doctrine to red catechism. ... We do not fight the organisation of classes: when possible we assist the process. Our ideas on this are well known: we long for a trade union organisation that is completely autonomous of parties and sects; which develops by itself, according to circumstance, place and experience, the right tactics and the right ideals; that is flexible ... which moves beyond the war of the classes to active and passive collaboration ...

We preserve, for everyone, from top to bottom, our most precious treasure: independence. This is what distinguishes us from the grey sheep-like party card-carrier, and which makes the evil shepherds who exploit it with the deceptions and trickery of demagogy our enemies.

The liberal Prime Minister Nitti's lenient treatment of Mussolini was yet another sign that already in 1919 he and the political old guard thought that the Fascists would prove a weapon they could use on the streets against the Socialists and their strikes and demonstrations. The old guard did not support Fascism – certainly not its initial left-wing incarnation – but thought it could use Fascism to defeat the much greater threat, Socialism, and so preserve the status quo and its own grip on power. The effect of this tolerance of Fascist excess, once that excess really took off in 1921 and 1922, would be the opposite. The policy of turning a blind eye – increasingly relied upon – would prove fatal. It would achieve its aim of the defeat of Socialism in Italy. But within just three years it would also cause the defeat of the old guard and the triumph of Fascism.

For, astonishingly, it was the Socialists who were destined for oblivion. First, even though the Socialist party was the largest party the other parties were able to combine to keep it out of power because it refused to contemplate taking part in coalition government. Second, the party was hamstrung by its traditional weakness – the split between reformists (*riformisti*) and revolutionaries (*massimalisti*). This had caused yet another expulsion of '*riformisti*' at the party congress one month before the elections and at the party congress in January 1921 would cause the fatal departure of the '*massimalisti*' to form the Italian Communist Party.

Membership of the Fascist movement, on the other hand, would soar during the next two years. At the start of 1920, in the wake of the 1919 election débâcle, the party was virtually wiped out. Yet by the end of 1921, there would be 834 *fasci* and 249,036 members.[30] For now, however, the threat of Socialist revolution was what terrified the Italian government as it terrified governments everywhere in Europe.

At the end of November, Mussolini wrote to d'Annunzio to say that although politically the election result was not a disaster, from a moral point of view it was 'mortifying'. He urged d'Annunzio not to launch a move on Italy. 'I believe that any march on the interior at this moment would throw the country into very serious turmoil. It is necessary to wait until we recover ... It is impossible to ignore reality, however sad.' They should wait therefore until the new parliament showed its 'total inability to function' and meanwhile convince the workforce that they were not anti-working class. 'This is necessary to stamp out the imbecilic *pussista*[31] depiction of us as the guard dogs of parasitic Capitalism.'[32]

Life at Fiume

At 6 p.m. on 12 September 1919, the day of his entry into Fiume, d'Annunzio – despite his raging fever – delivered the first of what would become regular speeches from the balcony of the governor's palace which he had made his headquarters. Once over, his audience shouted the oath of allegiance 'against all and everything' and there was much singing. Politics had left parliament and come down into the piazza. The crowd, people, mattered at last, it seemed.

Osbert Sitwell, who was there, recalled in his *Noble Essences*, 'The general animation and noisy vitality seemed to herald a new land, a new system. We gazed and listened in amazement. Every man here seemed to wear a uniform designed by himself: some had beards, and had shaved their heads completely so as to resemble the commander himself ... others had cultivated huge tufts of hair, half a foot long, waving out from their foreheads, and wore, balanced on the very back of the skull, a black fez. Cloaks, feathers and flowing black ties were universal, and every man ... carried the Roman dagger.'

It had to end but not before d'Annunzio and his followers drew up a constitution finally promulgated in September 1920 – *La Carta del Carnaro*. Many of the document's ideas – especially its corporatist ones – derived from revolutionary syndicalism. Fiume would be a parliamentary republic with a regent as head of state – but the post of regent, as with dictators in ancient Rome, would only be filled at times of extreme peril. Furthermore, the aim was to decentralise politics as much as possible – to bring politics out of parliament and into the piazza. Parliament would rarely meet. Nine corporations – each representing a specific area of economic activity – would govern. These corporations, which all citizens had to join, could tax members, with the idea that their existence would ensure an end to the class war between labour and capital. A tenth corporation would exist to promote the spiritual aspect of work. *La Carta del Carnaro* was similar in many respects to the programme published by the Fascists in June 1920.

D'Annunzian Fiume collapsed when the new prime minister – it was Giolitti once again – who had succeeded Nitti in June 1920, signed the Treaty of Rapallo with Yugoslavia on 12 November 1920. Nitti had fallen, not over Fiume but over the price of bread. To check inflation he had been forced to end the bread subsidy. The Treaty of Rapallo defined the boundaries between the two countries. It was not that bad a deal for Italy. She got Istria – the area east of Venice – and Fiume it was agreed should become an independent city state. In addition, Italian-speakers living in Dalmatia could become Italian citizens if they so chose. When d'Annunzio still refused to budge from Fiume Giolitti decided that force had to be used. He did what Nitti had dared not do. But by now the fizz had gone out of Fiume. The flame of the holocaust ignited in Fiume had not ignited Italy, let alone the world.

By late 1920, the danger of Socialist revolution in Italy was much greater than anything d'Annunzio could now come up with. But the Socialists missed their chance – if not to join d'Annunzio's bandwagon then to use the upheaval it had caused as Lenin is reported to have told them to start their own revolution. As Giuseppe Giulietti, Seaman's Union boss, said, if the Socialists had exploited the situation 'offered them by the d'Annunzio rebellion, and had not been afraid of the response of the military, by now we would be a republic and many banking trusts and many sharks would be biting the dust.'

On Christmas Eve, 1920, Giolitti ordered the Italian navy to bombard Fiume. One shell struck d'Annunzio's headquarters in the Governor's Palace and he had a narrow escape. Italian troops then invaded the city. There were fifty-two deaths in the fighting and four days later d'Annunzio's forces surrendered.

On 20 December, speaking in Milan, Mussolini had described Rapallo as 'a bastard, but necessary solution'. As he realised, the reputation of d'Annunzio had been damaged by Fiume after the initial euphoria had died down, but the reputation of the Fiume rank and file – the trench-ocracy – had been enhanced. His own reputation, meanwhile, by not becoming directly involved at Fiume, was left untarnished. He was not associated with the failure. Now, with d'Annunzio out of the way, the revolutionary torch would pass to Mussolini.

The Fascist Phoenix Rises

Fascism could boast a handful of highly talented and charismatic people such as Mussolini, Toscanini and Marinetti but little else at the start of 1920. Most of the Fascists of the first hour – especially those of left-wing origin – had gone. What remained of the rank and file seemed to be made up largely of ex-soldiers and urban misfits keener on regeneration of the nation than the people's revolution.

On New Year's Day 1920, Mussolini – who said he was still a Socialist – wrote in *Il Popolo d'Italia*:[34]

> We don't believe in programmes, schemes, saints, apostles; above all we don't believe in happiness, salvation, the promised land. We don't believe in a single solution – whether of an economic, political or moral kind – a linear solution to the problems of life, because – oh illustrious ballad singers of all the vestries – life is not linear ... Two religions vie today for dominion over spirits and the world: the black and the red. From two Vaticans, today, encyclicals depart: from the one in Rome and the one in Moscow. We are heretics of these two religions. We, alone, are immune from the contagion.

Mussolini could have been forgiven for not believing in the salvation of Fascism either.

The second Fascist national congress took place in Milan on 24 and 25 May. Mussolini told the congress, 'Not against the proletariat, but against the Socialist party, so long as it continues to be anti-Italian ... Only collaboration between the productive proletariat and the productive bourgeoisie can succeed in advancing civilisation. We must not sink the bourgeois ship, but get inside it and expel its parasitic elements. Fight then all parasites: those of the Socialist party, who are all just a bunch of evil shepherds; and those in the bourgeoisie, the bureaucracy and the civil service.'[35]

The significance of the congress is that Fascism, in response to its electoral wipe-out the previous November, moved right. The new programme it agreed abandoned, for example, the call for the abolition of the Senate and decided that only 'unproductive' war profits not 'excessive' war profits should be confiscated. In his congress speech, Mussolini also opened the door to the Vatican. This caused the fiercely anti-clerical

Marinetti to resign as a member of the central committee and leave Fascism – though he would always remain a supporter of Mussolini. 'As for the papacy, it needs to be understood: the Vatican represents 400 million men around the world and an intelligent politics must make use of this colossal force for the sake of its own expansion,' Mussolini had said. 'I am, today, completely outside any religion, but politics is politics. No one in Italy, unless he wants to start a religious war, can launch an attack on this spiritual sovereignty.'

Italy came closest to Socialist revolution in the late summer of 1920, though this would only become clear with hindsight. In June 1920 an army battalion had mutinied in Ancona after refusing to embark for Albania, which Italy had partly occupied since the war, and workers in the city came out in force to support the mutineers. For a few days, until the army snuffed out the rebellion, it looked as if it might spread. But then at the beginning of September workers, especially in the major cities of the industrial north, began to occupy factories and in the countryside peasants took over farms. They locked out their employers and ran the factories and farms themselves. About 1 million workers were involved. Mussolini was in favour of the occupations, he wrote, so long as they did not become a Bolshevik experiment.

For most of September 1920 the red flag flew over the factories and farms. Giolitti did not deploy the army. Whatever the truth, it looked as if Italy was about to become the latest country to go red. Where would it end? The international press descended on Italy to witness the revolution. American tourists asked, 'Where's the revolution? Can I see the revolution?' Charles H. Sherrill, an American general, diplomat and author, wrote, 'At Turin a Red Tribunal, composed partly of women caused men to be thrown alive into the blast furnaces ... Some sailors ... were ambushed by a band of Socialists, men and women, and literally torn to pieces, every last one of them, with all the excesses of the French revolution – the women ripping off ears with teeth ...'[36] The American general's view, though typical of reports at the time, was somewhat over the top but George Seldes, the American journalist, was more sanguine: 'For us of the press it was a terrible disillusion. There was simply no story. We did see the red flag waving from chimneys but there was smoke issuing from them, too, and all the sounds from within were those of ordinary industry and progress. Occasionally someone shouted, "*Viva* Lenin", or, "Long live the revolution", and sometimes a patrol of workingmen would go by. The police let them alone even when they bore arms. There was much joyful singing.' Red September was a story, of course, but not a news story because it was largely peaceful. Seldes was grateful when a bad earthquake occurred near Pisa.[37]

Given the situation in Italy it is easy to understand why Mussolini feared that Socialists would hijack any move by d'Annunzio from Fiume. It was now that secret contacts began between Mussolini and Giolitti in the autumn of 1920. Giolitti, true to form, had decided to try to embrace and absorb the enemy. Both he and Mussolini wanted to stop Socialism and he wanted to distance Mussolini still further from d'Annunzio. As for Mussolini, his Fascists were too insignificant even to attempt to absorb and embrace Giolitti, but an alliance with him might enable Fascists to enter Parliament for the first time. The contacts between the two led first to an informal agreement that Fascist candidates stand on the same ticket as Giolitti's at the November 1920 local elections and then a formal agreement to stand together in what was called the *'blocco nazionale'* in the May 1921 general elections. The Giolitti–Mussolini pact would open the doors of power to Fascism.

Under pressure from Giolitti, the employers were forced to concede pay rises and the principle of worker participation in the management of factories. This diffused the crisis. But then – with the holy grail at last within its grasp – the Socialist party split once again, this time with fatal consequences. At the party congress in Livorno in January 1921, the *'massimalista'* wing, whose leaders included Amedeo Bordiga, Palmiro Togliatti, Nicola Bombacci and Gramsci, quit the party to form the Italian Communist party. They did so because the party executive refused to carry out instructions to Socialist parties everywhere from the Communist International (the Comintern) to abandon the ballot box in favour of revolution. It would have meant the expulsion from the party for the umpteenth time of those considered to be *'riformisti'*. The Comintern had been formed in Moscow in March 1919 with Balabanoff as a founder member. She was soon even more disaffected in Russia than she had been in Italy. Mussolini wrote, 'The party that was supposed to give the present of paradise to the proletariat has split into two enemy factions. That is the sad reality. It is the end of an illusion. Will it be the beginning of wisdom?'[38] In October 1921, the Socialist Party would at last comply with the Comintern instruction and expel the so-called class collaborators who included Treves, Turati and Giacomo Matteotti. Those expelled formed the *Partito socialista unitario* (PSU) thus bringing the number of Socialist parties in Italy to four.

Fascism's hour finally came in the winter of 1920–1 when property owners, both big and small, decided that if the state would not protect them and their property they would have to do it themselves. They encouraged and financed the formation of Fascist squads to act as body-guards and strike-breakers. It was not just the property owners who turned to Fascism for help. Fascism also appealed to workers who did not have the party and union card and were thus excluded from the factory or the farm by the closed shop. Fascism had been a city phenomenon up until now. But the majority of those who had fought in the war were *'contadini'* – peasants (the Italian word *'contadino'* does not have the same negative ring to it as the English 'peasant'). During the winter of 1920–1 Fascism spread like wildfire through the Italian countryside. Mussolini had found his '*trincerocrazia*' at last.

By April 1920 largely Socialist peasant leagues had seized 27,000 hectares of farmland from 191 landowners and handed over the land to 101 workers' co-operatives.[39] The authorities did nothing to stop these seizures partly because of a law which decreed that war veteran peasants should be given leases on uncultivated agricultural land. Over every town and city hall controlled by the Socialists flew not the Italian tricolour but the red flag of revolution. In 1920 strikes and arson caused the loss of one-third of the hay crop, one-fifth of the grain crop and one-quarter of the grape harvest. In the province of Ferrara alone there were 192 arson attacks on farmland in 1920 and the prefect wrote that 'columns of hundreds of leaguists had committed serious crimes against people and property'.

'In 1919–20 the power of the "leaguists" was almost absolute; the proprietors, local authorities, the government were virtually impotent against them.'[40] Landowners lived in a state of terror and any peasant who did not join a league became an outcast. What this meant in practice is summed up well by Angelo Tasca:[41]

> The baker has to refuse him bread; he is treated like a leper, so are his wife and children ... so that either he gives in or he abandons the area ... Certain *Camere del Lavoro*, such as that in Bologna, Reggio Emilia, Ravenna, control virtually all the economic life of their province. They have organised the salaried workers, the small farmers, the peasants; they decide the price of the produce which they distribute in a large number of communes via the network of co-operatives. Landowners, traders, middlemen of all kinds witness, day by day, their 'vital space' reduced by the development of the co-operatives and municipal Socialism ... These institutions ... are absorbing little by little all the political and economic life of the region.

It was to break free of this tyranny that rural Fascism began. Rural Fascism turned Fascism into a force of national importance virtually overnight. Its explosive growth and violence would change Fascism for ever. In January 1921 Mussolini stated his position on the agricultural issue in *Il Popolo d'Italia*. 'Faced with the agrarian problem the position of Fascism is tendentially this: land to him who works it and makes it yield. No "socialisation of the land", a meaningless phrase and – above all – no agricultural state.'[42] In return for *squadrista* support against Socialists, the Fascists persuaded the landowners to hand over large areas of land to the peasants on long leases – especially in Emilia Romagna. Fascist agrarian policy aimed to replace wage labour whenever possible with leases or ownership of small plots. The Fascist agrarian programme published in June 1921 stated that 'land should belong to him who works it'.

Squadrismo

The first major success of organised *squadrismo* had been on 13 July 1920 in Trieste on the frontier with Yugoslavia where there was a particularly well-organised *fascio* in readiness for the endlessly talked-about d'Annunzian March on Rome. The action was not against Socialists but Slovene Slavs. Two Italian naval officers had been killed – by Slovenes it was assumed. The Trieste Fascists used the incident as an excuse to march to the Balkan Hotel, the headquarters of the city's Slav community organisation, and burn it down. Further raids on Slav associations in the countryside followed. Army officers had supplied the Fascists with trucks and weapons for these. A week later, on the 21st, Fascists in Rome burned down the offices of *Avanti!*. Two days later Mussolini wrote in *Il Popolo d'Italia*,[43] 'What difference is there between a crowd which burns down a newspaper and Socialist deputies (MPs) who have practically taken away free speech from deputies of other views?'

The Fascist squads were organised like a military unit and their members wore uniform – beige trousers or riding breeches and black shirts. They had a commanding officer, a *ras* – the name of the semi-independent Abyssinian tribal chiefs. These *ras* were usually ex-officers. The men under their command were called *squadristi*. The chief means of transport was the lorry. The chief weapons were the *manganello* (club) and the revolver. In keeping with their black sense of humour the *squadristi* would often force victims to drink castor oil. More often than not, it is said that the violence was all one way. The truth is that Socialists and Communists gave as good as they got. Between January and April 1921, according to Italian Interior Ministry figures,[44] violence between Fascists and Socialists led to the deaths of 102 people – 25 Fascists and 41 Socialists – and 388 people being injured – 108 Fascists and 123 Socialists. During the month-long 1921 election campaign there were 105 deaths – 3 a day – and 431 people injured – roughly 15 a day.

The success of Fascist violence bred success for the Fascist movement. At last, many thought, someone was fighting back against the Bolshevik menace. It was in Mussolini's native 'red' Emilia Romagna that Fascism enjoyed its most rapid expansion. Bologna – capital of the region and birthplace of Italian Socialism – is a case in point. The grip of the Socialist leagues on agriculture was stronger in Emilia Romagna than anywhere.

On 21 November 1920, armed *squadristi* in Bologna opened fire when the new Socialist mayor – elected in that month's local elections – appeared on the balcony of Palazzo d'Accursio, the city hall, to deliver his inaugural speech. Whether their intention was to kill him remains unclear. Either way, they missed. In retaliation, Socialists on the balcony threw grenades into the crowd below, killing nine and wounding dozens more. The Fascists charged into the city hall and in the ensuing mayhem the Socialists shot dead Giulio Giordano, a Nationalist councillor, Fascist sympathiser and war hero. Two days later 1000 Fascists – mainly war veterans and students – marched through Bologna. They included Dino Grandi, a twenty-five-year-old lawyer and former captain in the Alpini – who until this moment had not been a Fascist. Grandi would rise to the top of the movement with as much speed as the movement itself grew. That day, in *Il Popolo d'Italia*, Mussolini wrote, 'The reality is this: the Socialist party is a Russian army camped out in Italy. Against this foreign army, the Fascists have launched a guerilla war which they will conduct in an exceptionally serious manner.' Giordano was perhaps killed, he added, by 'one of those deserters that the foul Cagoia (Nitti) amnestied three times.'[45]

Hard times also attracted those to Fascism who felt that Socialism could not provide an answer. According to *La Stampa*, Fascism comprised unemployed former officers, poverty-stricken public employees, slump-hit shopkeepers and contractors, students and young graduates, disaffected youths and ex-revolutionaries who had supported the war.[46] According to a November 1921 census in *Il Popolo d'Italia*, 24.3 per cent were agricultural labourers, 15 per cent factory workers, 13 per cent students, 12 per cent owner or tenant farmers, and the rest a mix of shopkeepers, traders, professionals and factory owners. Nearly two-thirds had served in the war, which also meant that they were young. These figures undermine the claim that Fascism was simply a bourgeois counter-revolution.[47]

Agostino Lanzillo, a member of the Fascist central committee and former revolutionary syndicalist, wrote,[48] 'Fascism is composed in the large cities of new men. They formed the crowd which before the war watched political events with indifference and apathy, and which has now entered the contest. Fascism has mobilised its forces from the twilight zone of political life, and from this derives the unruly violence and juvenile exuberance of its conduct.'

The most dramatic Fascist violence in early 1921 took place in Ferrara, in Emilia Romagna, near Bologna, where the dashing twenty-four-year-old Italo Balbo became the local squad leader and *fascio* secretary in January 1921 – though he was still nominally a member of the Republican party until February 1921. As Fascism was a movement, not a party, Balbo's membership of the Republican party was not a problem. Anyone could become a Fascist as long as they were pro nation and anti Bolshevism. Balbo had served with distinction as an Alpino officer in the war and fought at Vittorio Veneto. He had said in a letter home that those who advocated Italian neutrality should be whipped. After the war he studied social sciences at Florence University until November 1920, when he returned to his native Ferrara. Later, he wrote,

When I came back from the war, just like so many, I hated politics and politicians, who in my opinion had betrayed the hopes of the combatants, reducing Italy to a shameful peace and systematic humiliation of any Italians who supported the cult of heroes. Fight, combat, to come back to the country of Giolitti, who offered every ideal as an item for sale? No. Better to deny everything, to destroy everything, so as to rebuild everything from scratch. Many in those days ... turned to Communist nihilism. It was the ready-made revolutionary programme and, apparently, the most radical: in struggle against the bourgeoisie and Socialism ... It is certain, in my opinion, that, without Mussolini, three-quarters of the Italian youth which had returned from the trenches would have become Bolsheviks...[49]

When Mussolini came to Ferrara in April 1921 to speak Balbo had managed to assemble 20,000 Fascists to listen. This was the first of the oceanic rallies for which Fascism would become so famous.

In May 1921, when police arrested Balbo for illegal possession of a revolver, hundreds of Fascists besieged the *Prefettura* demanding his release. The prefect, Samuele Pugliese, a Fascist sympathiser, ordered Balbo's release. In December a group of Socialists killed three Fascists in Ferrara during a Fascist demonstration outside the favourite Fascist meeting place, the Caffe Mozzi, near the Cathedral. Their funeral was attended by 14,000 people. On 21 January 1921 Balbo led the first of many Fascist raids into the Romagnol countryside against the Socialists. In February 1921 the reformist Socialist deputy Giacomo Matteotti had unsuccessfully moved a motion in parliament critical of the government's failure to crack down on Fascist violence. Significantly, only the Socialist and Communist deputies voted in favour. For many Italians it was the height of hypocrisy that Socialists should demand protection from the police and army – who according to the Marxist theory were tools of the bourgeoisie, the class enemy, they were determined to overthrow.

On 2 March 1921, Mussolini nearly died in a plane crash. He was doing take-off and landing practice at an airfield near Milan when the engine of his plane stalled. He was once more back on crutches. On 22 March the first of many attempts on his life took place when an anarchist, Biagio Masi, turned up at his home on the pretence of looking for work. Mussolini told Masi to come to the offices of *Il Popolo d'Italia* and he would see what he could do. But once there, Masi's nerve failed him and he handed Mussolini his pistol. Mussolini let him go but he wrote about the matter in his newspaper and Masi was arrested. In an article to mark Fascism's second anniversary the next day – the 23rd – he wrote that it did not matter that Fascism had no rigid programme or that many of its ideas were similar to those of Socialism. 'Fascism is not a church. It is more like a gymnasium. It is not a party, it is a movement; it does not have a programme ... for the simple reason that Fascism constructs day by day the edifice of its will and passion.'[50] On the night of the 23rd an anarchist bomb exploded at Milan's Teatro Diana killing 21 and wounding 200. But instead of urging the *squadristi* to exact revenge, Mussolini urged restraint. He wrote, 'We must not with ill-considered gestures, help *pussismo* to rebuild its reputation ... Currently, certain acts on individual initiative are not good for Fascism and distance it from strong sympathy because they put it almost automatically on the same moral and material plane as the enemies it so strenuously combats.'[51]

In April 1921 Giolitti was forced to ask the King to dissolve parliament and call a general election for 15 May because the *Popolari* had refused to support a government stock market bill which would have hindered the Vatican's investment opportunities. Mussolini, determined to succeed at the polls this time, agreed to Giolitti's idea of the creation of a *blocco nazionale* to present a united front against both Socialists and *Popolari*. Giolitti would have preferred to form an alliance with reformist Socialists. Tendentially Socialist himself, their presence in government would cool the revolutionary heat in the nation, he thought. But after the Livorno Congress in January 1921, which split the Socialist party left, not right, that became impossible. Meanwhile Fascist squad violence continued. Giolitti issued firm instructions that any violence, whoever was responsible, should be punished.

His instructions all too often fell on deaf ears. Many prefects sympathised with Fascism, but even if they did not many of those under their control did. Furthermore, many prefects were loath to intervene with force for fear of causing the violence to escalate. In March, an Interior Ministry report[52] to Giolitti on the mood in Tuscany noted that the forces of law and order there were fed up with the 'constant verbal and actual violence and the hostile and vitriolic propaganda of the subversives and their press' – in particular with *Avanti!* which urged shopkeepers to refuse to serve them and to treat their wives and daughters as 'whores'.

The violence got worse. On a single day, 8 May, a week before the election, there were 1073 acts of violence[53] committed in Italy by Fascists and Socialists: only 396 Fascists were arrested compared with 1421 Socialists. These figures could mean one of two things only: either the Socialists were the more violent, or the authorities were more prone to ignore Fascist violence. In the five-week period 8 April–14 May 1921, there were 105 people killed and 431 injured compared with 102 people killed and 388 injured in the three months prior to that.

In vain, Mussolini tried to stop the violence by writing in *Il Popolo d'Italia* on 28 April that while initially the violence of the *squadristi* had been necessary to counter Socialist violence and destroy Socialist tyranny, enough was enough. 'We must not turn from being the oppressed into tyrants ... The Fascist victory must not limit its significance in relation to the *Pus* alone, but must be constructive with regard to the nation as well. Having rendered the *Pus* innocuous, we must not put the nation in turmoil, but help to get it back on the difficult path towards internal and external peace. The warning, the commandment of the day is this: If Fascism loses its "sense of limit" it will lose its victory!'[54] Ten days later he denied Socialist accusations that armed Fascist squads were 'terrorising a large part of Italy', describing the charge as a lie. The truth was that Fascist violence had not unfairly affected the result except in 'one or two agricultural regions, the province of Ferrara and Rovigo, or Perugia.'[55] In the elections the *blocco nazionale* won 275 seats, enough just for Giolitti to stay on as prime minister. The Fascists had only put up 75 candidates and had won 35 of these *blocco nazionale* seats, so they had done well. Mussolini now divided his time between Rome and Milan, often making the trip by plane.

On the 'left' the Socialists won 122 seats, but this was 34 less than in 1919. The new Communist party, standing for the first time, got 15 seats. The *Popolari* got 107 – 7 more than in 1919. In the 'centre' the reformist Socialists got 26, the democratic Socialists 41, the democratic liberals 24, Nitti's liberals 36 and Giolitti's liberals 42. These were the so-called centre parties. On the 'right' Salandra's liberals got 21 seats, the nationalists 11, the agrarians 23 and the Fascists 35 (a year later, three of the Fascists had their elections annulled because they were not over twenty-five at the time of the election and ineligible to stand).

The old liberal–conservative groups saw the number of their MPs plummet yet again as in 1919. Mussolini had joined Giolitti's *blocco nazionale* to get into parliament and had justified the alliance on the grounds that it was designed to defeat the Socialists. That task achieved, he promptly withdrew the support of the Fascists for Giolitti. Within little more than a month Giolitti was forced to resign when the *Popolari* withdrew their support as well.

The first decision of the newly elected Fascists, however, after a heated debate which reflected the deep rift within Fascism between Republicans and monarchists, was to vote in favour of a boycott of the royal speech to parliament by King Vittorio Emanuele III on 11 June. In October 1920 Mussolini had written in *Il Popolo d'Italia*[56] that Fascism was 'tendentially Republican' but not necessarily anti-monarchy. If the monarchy served the nation, fine. But the nation was what counted. *Il Popolo d'Italia* of 24 May 1921[57] reported a speech by Mussolini in which he said of the imminent royal opening of parliament, 'They shout, "*Viva il re!*" The Fascists shout, "*Viva l'Italia!*" Our symbol is not the shield of Savoy; it is the *Fascio Littorio*, Roman and even, if you don't mind, Republican. In the fundamental postulates of Fascism every prejudice is rejected (therefore even Republican or monarchist ones) but to this we add that no one can consider the *fasci* as monarchists or dynasticists. Now, faced with the issue of the royal opening, disinterest is really the only Fascist attitude.'

Mussolini did not fraternise with other MPs and rarely went to the

Chamber of Deputies except to make the odd speech. As a provocative gesture, he and his Fascists had decided to sit in the seats on the extreme right of the Chamber to make the point that the right did not exist. On 21 June 1921 he made his maiden speech[58] and began by saying how proud he was to be sitting on the extreme right where in the days of triumphant Socialism no one had dared sit. The speech, which lasted well over an hour, would be 'distinctly anti-democratic and anti-Socialist', he said. The Socialists would find what he – 'the heretic' – had to say – 'the man whom they expelled from their orthodox church' – especially interesting.

Communism – 'Russian Socialism' – had caused nothing but 'misery and desperation', he said, and Lenin was forced to abandon Communist economics almost immediately as useless. He praised the unions, in particular the Socialist union, *Confederazione Generale del Lavoro* (CGL) and he urged the CGL to abandon the tyranny of Marxist dogma and break with the Socialist party (the CGL would finally do this in October 1922). The CGL had much in common with Fascism, he said: 'We do not even oppose experiments in *cooperativismo*. But I tell you immediately that we oppose with all our strength attempts at *socializzazione, statizzazione*, and *collettivizzazione*! We have had enough of State Socialism ... We deny that there are two classes, because there exist many more; we deny that you can explain the whole of human history with economic determinism. We deny your internationalism, because it is a luxury good, which can only work among the upper class, while the people are desperately tied to their terra nativa.'

He then turned to the *Popolari* with whom he said Fascism also had much in common. He agreed with them, for example, that peasants should own the land they worked so long as they were 'productive' not 'anti-productive'. But there remained the problem of the schism between Church and State which had bedevilled Italy since re-unification. To end it, Mussolini said, the Vatican had only to abandon its dream of temporal power (i.e., its claim on the former papal states) and the Italian state offer in return to fund church schools, hospitals and churches.

Fascism could not succeed against the Catholic Church, with '400 million people' worldwide 'who look to Rome', as Mussolini realised only too well. He acknowledged this: 'I affirm here that the Latin and Imperial tradition of Rome is today represented by Catholicism. If, as Mommsen said twenty to thirty years ago, no one can remain in Rome without a universal idea, I think and affirm that the only universal idea which today exists in Rome, is that which irradiates out of the Vatican.'

Mussolini ended his maiden speech by saying that the only way to save the state from 'the civil war' was 'a surgical operation' to reduce the size of the state. 'For us violence is not a way of life, it is not an aesthetic, let alone a sport: it is a brutal necessity to which we have subjected ourselves.

And might I also add that we are prepared to disarm, if you in turn disarm, above all your spirits.' The speech had lasted well over one hour. 'I have finished,' Mussolini said – at last.

1921: *'L'Anno Fascista'*

The situation in the Italian parliament after this, the last general election before the Fascists came to power, was that as usual no single party had a majority. In the past, Giolittian horse-trading would have ensured a workable coalition government. The *ancien regime* had governed by means of alliances between myriad shoals of current and tendency, in a state of endless transformation, pasted together by patronage rather than policy. But the emergence of modern political parties, largely the result of the introduction of universal male suffrage, had mortally wounded the ancien regime.

Before the 1919 election, the patrons of the liberal–conservative old guard such as Giolitti, Salandra, Nitti and Orlando controlled 427 seats out of a total 508, after it only 252. Now they could rely on just 108. The new parties had the vast majority of seats but, because they were parties not factions, were against the idea of coalitions. Yet none on its own had enough MPs to form a government.

Giolitti resigned at the end of June. The reformist Socialist, Ivanoe Bonomi, his War Minister, took over.[59] Bonomi managed to cobble together a flimsy coalition with the lukewarm participation of the *Popolari* whose withdrawal of support had toppled Giolitti.

Red September had fizzled out but failed to cool the revolutionary heat in the country. The violence got worse with the left giving as good as it got wherever it could. In the worst incident, a column of blackshirts launched a raid on Sarzana, near La Spezia, on 21 July but the police opened fire and put the blackshirts to flight. Communist redshirts – the *Arditi del Popolo* – and a hostile crowd then attacked the fleeing blackshirts with pitchforks and billhooks – eighteen blackshirts were killed and thirty seriously injured. The crowd then strung up the dead Fascists.

But two days later it was blackshirt, rather than redshirt violence that Mussolini criticised when he wrote, 'More than once in these columns it has been said that violence must be knightly, aristocratic, surgical and so, in a certain sense human. Here and there in recent times the violence of Fascist individuals and groups has assumed characteristics *assolutamente antagonistiche* to the spirit of Fascism ... To overcome the mortal dangers of this crisis, mortal for the nation and for Fascism ... We must re-establish *prontissimamente* a sense of individual and collective discipline, remembering that ... Fascism began as a movement for the restoration of discipline ... we must not respond to offences of an individual nature with reprisals of a collective nature, since this tactic has damaged us enormously unleashing against us waves of hatred and misunder-standing.'[60]

To stop the violence, Bonomi launched talks for a pact of peace between the warring parties. Mussolini took part because he knew that much of the violence was the wrong sort of violence. It was not, as he put it, surgical, and was therefore counter-productive. Indeed, throughout 1921 Mussolini spoke out against the violence not so much of his opponents but of the Fascists in his speeches and writings.

The Socialists also took part in Bonomi's peace talks but the Communists and the *Popolari* refused. On 2 August Mussolini and the parliamentary Socialist party – not the Socialist party itself – and the CGL, the Socialist trade union, signed what they called the Pact of Pacification.

The pact put Mussolini on a collision course with *squadrismo*. His problem was that the provincial Fascist leaders – the *ras* – were unaccount-able to the leadership in Milan for two reasons: Fascism was a movement not a party; and provincial fascism was funded provincially. But as he had warned: 'The nation came to us when our movement declared itself as the twilight of a tyranny; the nation will reject us when our movement takes on aspects of a new tyranny.[61]

In *Il Popolo d'Italia*[62] of 3 August – the day after the signing of the pact – Mussolini said that it had saved Italy from a 'very serious crisis which might have been and might still be mortal'. 'Right now, the nation needs peace in order to recover, to rebuild ...' Fascism, he added, 'having exer-cised its muscles, must exercise its brains ... If Fascism does not follow me, no one can force me to follow Fascism.'

This was the crux of the matter. Would Fascism follow Mussolini? Fascist provincial leaders such as Grandi and Balbo, for example, were furious at the effect the pact would have on their highly successful efforts to replace Socialist and Communist unions in the workplace with Fascist ones. By June 1922, there were 2126 Fascist unions with 458,284 members.[63]

On 30 July 400 Tuscan *fasci* met in Florence and voted against the pact. On 16 August 600 *fasci* met in Bologna and agreed Balbo's proposal that d'Annunzio should replace Mussolini as the Duce of fascism. Fascism, like Socialism, was in danger of splitting itself to death. In response, Mussolini resigned from the fascist executive two days later (18 August). In reply to the Bologna decision Mussolini wrote in 18 August's *Il Popolo d'Italia*[64] that renunciation of the pact had led Fascism down a 'blind alley'. 'How will you achieve peace now? You think, perhaps, you can achieve it through the extermination of 2 million citizens who voted for the *Pus*? ... With the Pact of Rome, Fascism could have prepared ... to demonstrate not only its pugilistic and bombing (*bombardiera*) superiority, but its moral and cerebral superiority.'

Mussolini's position as the Duce of Fascism was in serious jeopardy. But the executive – whose members, unlike the provincial leaders such as

Grandi and Balbo, supported the pact – refused to accept his resignation. And when Grandi and Balbo visited d'Annunzio at Gardone to offer him leadership of the Fascist movement the poet was suitably poetic. 'The poet – after three days of "meditation" – gave them a highly evasive response: he had wanted to consult the stars, but the sky had been cloudy.'[65] If d'Annunzio had accepted, Fascism would have split in two.

But with sporadic violence still going on in the country at large, largely initiated by Communists who were not a party to the pact, and the intransigence of leading provincial Fascists, the pact was doomed. On 9 September in *Il Popolo*, Mussolini accused the Socialists of breaking the treaty and published the names of fifteen Fascists killed by Communists between 5 August and 4 September. Though those responsible were Communists, who had not signed the treaty, not Socialists, in the eyes of Mussolini who often lumped both together as *'socialcomunisti'* this made no difference.

The next day Balbo's blackshirts responded: 2000 of them from all over Emilia Romagna began to converge on Ravenna – burial place of Dante – near the Rubicon which Julius Caesar had crossed en route to seize Rome. Officially, the blackshirts were there to commemorate the second anniversary of d'Annunzio's seizure of Fiume on 12 September and the 600th anniversary of Dante's death. The idea was to occupy Ravenna for twenty-four hours, then withdraw in perfect order. Though not a technical breach of the pact the 'March on Ravenna' was a deliberate act of provocation. Indeed, once in Ravenna the blackshirts ran amok, sacking and torching Socialist clubs and other targets. The Fascists, said an Interior Ministry report, were 'uniquely responsible' for the violence. The March on Ravenna[66] signalled the end, to all intents and purposes, of the short-lived Pact of Pacification. Grandi and Balbo, it seemed, had triumphed over Mussolini. Two weeks later, on 26 September in Modena, the *Regie guardie* opened fire on a crowd of blackshirts who had attacked them, killing eight Fascists and injuring fifteen. Three *regie guardie* were injured.

Fascism, whose membership had exploded in 1921 and which now had thirty-five MPs, was in disarray. To salvage his own situation as much as that of Fascism, Mussolini agreed with Grandi and Balbo that he would abandon the Pact of Pacification. But in return Mussolini insisted – this was the clever trick up his sleeve – that the Fascist movement become the Fascist Party. A party with a clearly defined chain of command and set of rules, he correctly reasoned, would give him more control over *squadrismo* and the provincial *ras* less.

Mussolini's reputation with the *squadristi* received a timely boost in October when he fought yet another duel, which was widely reported even by *The Times* in London on three consecutive days. In *Il Popolo d'Italia*, he had described Francesco Ciccotti, a Socialist MP who had been among those to back him as editor of *Avanti!* in 1912, as 'the most exquisitely shameless person who walks the streets of Rome'. Mussolini had published his acceptance of Ciccotti's challenge in his newspaper to ensure the widest possible publicity. *The Times* had said that Mussolini had favoured swords over pistols as usual and that the contest would take place near Livorno. The two men and their seconds duly drove out to Livorno but were unable to give their police minders the slip. Just as the duel was about to begin in the garden of a villa the police intervened. Both sides rushed inside the villa and locked the doors. The duel at last took place and lasted one and a half hours but was abandoned after the fourteenth assault because Ciccotti, who had a weak heart, thought he was about to have a heart attack.

The Socialist party, meanwhile, was thrown into further turmoil when the '*massimalisti*' finally carried out the Comintern's instructions to expel as class collaborators all those left who still favoured parliament rather than revolution as the means to the end. The Socialist party thus split for the second time in 1921. There were now four 'Socialist' parties in Italy: the PSI, the PCI, the PSRI, and the PSU.

By contrast, the Fascist movement – the anti-party – which was also threatened by schism, survived thanks to Mussolini's brilliant man-oeuvrings. Instead of splitting, as looked likely after the signing of the Pact of Pacification, it grew ever more united. Yet nevertheless many observers thought that it too was destined for oblivion. *Il Secolo*, a leading anti-Fascist daily, for example, noted on 4 November, 'There isn't a party or political movement in Italy in which there are, as in Fascism, so many currents which flow in opposite directions, each one acting for itself, with no respect either for discipline, or central leadership.'[67]

The Fascists approved the switch from movement to party at the annual congress in Rome on 7–8 November at the Augusteo – the ruins of Emperor Augustus's mausoleum. The new party would be called the *Partito nazionale fascista* (PNF). No one had uttered a word, however, about the subject all wanted to discuss – the pact – until Mussolini mentioned it almost casually in his speech. This caused Grandi, a leading opponent of the pact, to leap on to the podium and embrace Mussolini. The audience greeted the scene with wild applause. The theatrical embrace served two purposes: it stifled debate on the pact and ensured Mussolini's reinstatement as the Duce of Fascism. Crucially, the PNF's first programme, which described the *squadristi* as the essence of the party, would state that they were to be under the command not of the provincial *ras* but the party leadership.

Justifying the switch from movement to party, Mussolini wrote, 'Fascism will not lose any of its characteristics. It will lose, instead, and it is good that it does, much of its dross; it will leave behind and it must leave behind the violent ones, of violence not as a means, but as an end, those ambiguous elements which here and there have tagged on to Fascism to use it for the defence of their own private interests.'[68]

Mussolini had to pay a price, however, for the transformation of the movement into a party – the Pact of Pacification. On 15 November he told Bonomi that the Fascists would no longer adhere to the pact. Bonomi's reaction was to order the prefects to dissolve all armed organisations such as *squadrismo*. But the Fascists had pre-empted him by issuing a directive on the 16th that all Fascist party members would henceforth also be *squadristi*. This meant that if Bonomi had disbanded the squads he would also be dissolving the Fascist party. He was afraid to do so.

The number of Fascists who had gone to Rome for the congress was 40,000 but the Augusteo only had room for 10,000. The Socialists and Communists staged a general strike in protest at the Fascists' presence in Rome, which included railway workers. This meant that the Fascists unable to get into the Augusteo could not go home either. The Bonomi government did nothing to intervene and the Fascists marched about Rome threateningly. In Trastevere, a working-class area, the local people resisted and the resulting violence left 6 dead and nearly 200 injured on both sides.

On 28 December in *Il Popolo d'Italia*,[69] writing about the new Fascist party programme, Mussolini said that 1921 had been *'l'anno fascista'* in which 'Italian politics ... has been dominated and nearly obsessed by Fascism'. The new party programme contained the spirit, not the letter of d'Annunzio's *Carta del Carnaro*, he said, adding 'it is a successful attempt ... to reconcile and balance theory and practice ... the necessary absoluteness of principles with the inevitable "relativity" of life ... Fascism, in this its programme, does not claim originality. There is nothing truly original in the world and especially today it is impossible to be "original" in politics.' The programme was 'not perfect' and would be subject to 'incessant revision'. The *anno fascista* – 1921 – was over. Fascism was now a party. By the end of 1921, there were 834 *fasci* and 249,036 members, and Mussolini was back in charge. Socialist claims that by the winter of 1921–2 there would be 3 million unemployed had not materialised. But there was severe economic crisis in late 1921. Many industrial firms collapsed – even the giant arms manufacturer Ansaldo. There remained, above all, the crisis of the Italian parliament and its inability to govern – a problem which, said Mussolini in *Il Popolo d'Italia* on 29 December, was 'nearly insoluble'.

8

THE MARCH ON ROME

'All things considered, the situation is dreadful, the country is getting nearer and nearer the precipice every day,'[1] wrote a despairing Anna Kulisciof, the grand old dame of Italian Socialism, to Flippo Turati in February 1922. In December 1921 alone, the Italian authorities issued 637,000 permits to possess rifles and 208,000 permits to possess revolvers.[2] That so many Italians should want firearms in a single month gives an idea of how tense was the state of Italy at the start of 1922.

In the second issue of *Gerarchia*, the new monthly review launched by Mussolini in January 1922 and edited by Sarfatti, Mussolini wrote an article, 'Which way is the world going?', in which he attacked the 'principles of 1789' and predicted that the twentieth century would see the demise of democracy and the rise of authoritarianism. The war had killed democracy, he said, and new aristocracies were emerging in its wake. Such thoughts reflected Mussolini's disgust with the peculiar Italian version of parliament and the anti-democratic impulse he had always harboured, especially as a Socialist. Parliament, in the words of Mussolini and other Fascists, '*fa schiffo*', is a '*bordello*' and a '*troiaio*', or as Grandi put it 'a low oligarchy of little and average merchants who seriously think they have rented it'.[3] Most Italians thought the same.

In the *Gerarchia* article Mussolini wrote, 'It may be that in the nineteenth century Capitalism needed democracy; now it can do without it ... Democracy in the factory has lasted only as long as a bad dream. What has happened to the German *Betriebsrate* (factory councils) and the Russian factory councils? Now it is the other democracy, the political one, which is about to end, which *must* end.' The Fascist revolution that would sweep democracy away would be, he wrote, a 'Paretian revolution' by which he meant a revolution of the new aristocracy – the Fascist trenchocracy.

In February 1922, Pope Benedict XV died and was replaced by Pius XI, the former Archbishop of Milan, who had allowed Fascists to hold uniformed memorial services in the Duomo. The former *mangiapreti* Mussolini even went to St Peter's Square for the traditional official announcement. Whatever his views on the Christian church Mussolini realised the power of faith to move men.

'We are working to translate into fact the aspiration of Giuseppe Mazzini: to give the Italians a "religious concept of their nation" ... To establish the foundations for the greatness of Italy in the world, starting with the religious concept of *Italianità*, which must become the essential impulse and directive of our lives,' he had written in *Il Popolo d'Italia* on 7 December 1921. In April 1923 the anti-fascist newspaper *Il Mondo* would say of Fascism, 'For Fascism the possession of power is not enough: it wants possession of the private conscience of all citizens, it wants the "conversion of the Italians".' As Mussolini had said as long ago as 1912 in *Avanti!* on 18 July, 'Humanity needs a credo. It is faith that moves mountains...'

Between 2 and 13 January 1922, Mussolini was in Cannes to report for *Il Popolo* on the meeting of the supreme council of the Allies attended, among others, by Bonomi, David Lloyd-George and Aristide Briand. The heads of state decided to invite a representative of the Soviet government to talks in Genoa in April. This caused bitter controversy. While in Cannes Mussolini interviewed French premier Briand and, fearing that his down-at-heel shoes would create a bad impression, covered them up with white spats before the interview. He would continue to wear spats from now on even when in his black shirt. The spats would sometimes be grey as well as white. In this period Mussolini's usual attire, when not in black shirt, was an ill-fitting pinstripe suit, wing collar and bowler hat.

Nenni, his old friend from Forlì, the Republican who had joined Fascism only to leave it in early 1920 for Socialism, was also in Cannes. One night the two stayed up talking until dawn. Later Nenni[4] recalled that Mussolini had told him that the ideal solution for Italy was the destruction of the liberal regime and in its place a coalition of the mass parties – Socialists, Fascists and *Popolari*. But this had proved impossible and so the only solution now was war. 'Your friends must understand,' Mussolini said as they parted, 'I am just as ready for war as for peace.' 'You have lost the possibility of choosing,' replied Nenni. 'In that case, war it shall be.' George Slocombe of the *Daily Herald* also met Mussolini in Cannes and recalled him going everywhere with blackshirt body guards who also stood guard on his hotel room.[5]

On 7 March Mussolini went to Berlin for his first visit to Germany, where he met a number of government figures and remained about ten days. The German Socialist press called him the 'traitor of the Italian proletariat'. He met the German Chancellor Joseph Wirth, the Foreign Minister Walther Rathenau and Gustav Stresemann, subsequently Foreign Minister, in his capacity as a journalist. Probably he also met representatives of the far right in Germany, though not Hitler. In November 1923 the young Hitler, inspired by Mussolini, would attempt to seize power by means of the beer hall putsch. He would fail and be imprisoned. It would take him another ten years to win power in Germany. Mussolini wrote in *Gerarchia*[6] that Germany was 'neither Republican or pacifist' and felt the Versailles Treaty 'shameful'. He thought Britain's more lenient attitude on war reparations was imperative to keep Germany peaceful, rather than France's ruthless attitude, which would only lead to trouble.

Unsurprisingly, the Bonomi government did not last long and collapsed in February 1922 largely over the domestic crisis. Don Sturzo refused to allow the *Popolari* to support a return of Giolitti because Giolitti's group in parliament had voted down the Bonomi government, which had included *Popolari* ministers and the priest was furious. The Sturzo veto, as it was called, ruled out the one man – Giolitti – who might have been able to save the liberal regime. In typical Italian style, two weeks of intense talks between all and sundry followed in an attempt to create either an anti-Fascist coalition government or else its opposite, a coalition government drawn from the three big mass parties – Socialists, Fascists, *Popolari* – or some other Italianesque government by *imbroglio*. The talks failed and the King in desperation turned to Luigi Facta, a member of Giolitti's clique, who became prime minister on 25 February. Without *Popolari* support, Facta could not have become prime minister. Reluctantly Sturzo agreed to his candidacy.

With the appointment as Prime Minister of the weak but complacent Facta, the *ancien régime* moved inexorably towards extinction. The problem, though, was not Facta; the problem was the regime itself which had lost the capacity to function. For as Mussolini would say in a speech in the autumn of 1922, 'Make thirty crises in the Italian Parliament today, and you will have thirty reincarnations of Signor Facta ... The Liberal State is a mask behind which there is no face.'[7]

In February he wrote, 'Today in the light of new parliamentary experience, the eventuality of dictatorship must be seriously considered.'[8] That month the Fascist executive voted to transform the squads into a paramilitary force – the Fascist Militia – under a unified command. Despite the illegality of what they did the *squadristi* did not regard themselves as criminals. Theirs was *'opera santa'* (sacred work). The pay was good too: 40 lira a day when on the job. In 1928, Gaetano Salvemini, the anti-Fascist historian, journalist, ex-Socialist and founder of *l'Unità*, would admit, 'Given that the police and the courts were incapable of defending the citizens from the arrogant and capricious stranglehold of the union organisation, these same citizens might be forgiven for defending themselves by means of illegal methods. A Fascist, in this early period, had to possess a certain amount of physical and moral courage. He had to face unpopularity, he was exposed to the physical violence of crowds, he risked being injured or killed, a risk which was not as great as Fascist propaganda would lead us to believe, but which was real enough to chill the ardour of most men.'[9]

The Fascist violence of 1922 began in earnest in the spring and was on a much bigger scale than before. In March, 1000 blackshirts occupied Fiume. Facta did nothing. Elsewhere, sometimes thousands of blackshirts would descend on a targeted town. But the Left gave as good as it got whenever it had the chance. Between March and July 1922, for example, 899 Fascists and 959 Socialists were arrested for alleged acts of violence.[10] But the scale of Fascist violence made Italians once again fear rather than welcome Fascism.

In May 1922, Mussolini fought a duel – his last – with Mario Missiroli, editor of the anti-Fascist newspaper, *Il Secolo*, who kept calling him an agrarian slave in his columns. On 10 May Mussolini wrote that Missiroli was 'a treacherous Jesuit and a most solemn coward'.[11] The duel lasted seven rounds. Neither man won but nor was there a reconciliation.

Without Mussolini, Fascism would not have survived the wipe-out at the polls in 1919, the turmoil which threatened to tear it apart in 1921, or achieved power in 1922. Mussolini was evidence that the great – or bad – man theory of history rather than the Marxist determinist one is correct. As Giuseppe Bottai, the thinking man's Fascist and former *Arditi* officer, would write: 'Inflated, overflowing, explosive. An uncontainable vitality, which gave even his most simple and ordinary gestures ... a boundless breadth, the movement of a hand, the picking up of an object from the table, the depiction of an idea in the air.'[12]

The escalation of blackshirt violence damaged Facta, who failed to stop it, more than it damaged Fascism. As a result, Facta resigned on 22 July. Balbo decided to force the pace. Between 28 and 29 July his blackshirts launched what came to be known as the 'Column of Fire' in the provinces of Ravenna and Forlì in Emilia Romagna. In Ravenna he forced the prefect to provide lorries for his men who then drove out into the countryside burning Communist and Socialist Party offices wherever they went. Neither the police nor the army intervened. Between May and September the Fascists had become the de facto government in much of the Po Delta after they had physically thrown out the elected Socialist councillors from town and city halls.

The King failed to find an alternative and so he had no choice but recall Facta on 31 July. The Column of Fire and the return of Facta caused the Left to call a general strike from midnight on the 31st. This was a fatal error. The general strike and the return of Facta alarmed Italians and enabled the Fascists to present themselves as the defenders of the nation once again. They enabled the Fascists to represent the absent state.

Mussolini ordered the mobilisation of the blackshirts and gave the government forty-eight hours to stop the strike or else the blackshirts would do so instead. On 2 August fearing Fascist violence, the strike leaders called off the strike. But the Fascists launched a week-long rampage nevertheless against left-wing targets. On the 3rd, 1000 of them besieged the city hall in Milan in Piazza della Scala, next to the opera house, which was guarded by about 150 soldiers. The soldiers did not open fire and they swarmed past them.

D'Annunzio was in Milan by chance and the blackshirts convinced him to deliver a speech from the balcony of the city hall. The poet told the crowd that *'nulla di vitale* is possible outside the nation, *nulla* against the nation' and ended his speech not with the words *'Viva il Fascismo!'* but *'Viva L'Italia'*. Relations between d'Annunzio and Mussolini were as strained as ever but his speech, regardless of his intention, was taken as a sign of his support for Fascism. The next day – the 4th – the blackshirts sacked and torched the *Avanti!* offices in Milan. Finally, on the 5th, the government ordered prefects in the north to impose martial law. This was enough to cause Mussolini to order the blackshirts to withdraw. On the 11th he told the Naples newspaper, *Il Mattino*, that a march on Rome was 'strategically possible' though not 'inevitable'.

Politicians of all hues, meanwhile, including Mussolini, continued labyrinthine talks to try to cobble together an alternative to the second Facta government. By now, it was unthinkable that such a government could exclude the Fascists but so was it unthinkable that they would be its dominant force.

Mussolini delivered an important speech at Udine on 20 September. He had driven there with Sarfatti with whom he spent much time during this period. She had lent the Fascist executive 1 million lira for the much talked-about March on Rome. 'That march had to be made, it could not be put off any longer. And I did not want to lose my money, which was not a negligible sum,' she told a friend.[13] At Udine, Mussolini spoke of the two forces at play within Italy, within Fascism, within himself: reaction and revolution. 'It is only with the conciliation, and equilibrium, of these two forces that we have been able to achieve the unity of the *patria*.' He emphasised that the monarchy had nothing to fear because perfect political systems existed only in books. 'Why are we republicans? In a certain sense because we see a monarchy not sufficiently monarchical.' He implored Fascists not to indulge in indiscriminate violence – violence that was not 'very moral, sacrosanct and necessary'. But he insisted, 'Violence is not immoral. Sometimes it is moral . . . our violence compared with that of the Bolsheviks in Russia, where 2 million people have been executed, and another 2 million languish in prison, our violence is child's play.'[14]

To march or not to march?

Mussolini had three things to fear: the King, Giolitti and the army. 'If Giolitti returns to power we're fucked . . . Remember that at Fiume he bombarded d'Annunzio,' Mussolini said.[15] And yet Mussolini was talking secretly with Giolitti about forming a coalition government just as he was talking with Salandra. Everyone was talking to everyone else. Even d'Annunzio was in touch with Giolitti – the man who had bombarded him out of Fiume – and had agreed to take part in a rally of national reconciliation in Rome on 4 November. But then, after a row with his mistress, d'Annunzio fell out of a window at his villa at Gardone on Lake Garda and was badly injured which gave conspiracy theorists much to talk about.

Instead of rallying, the Italian Left, livid at the failure of the general strike, disintegrated still further. In early October the CGL, the Socialist union, decided to become independent of the Socialist party and at its annual congress the party itself split yet again as it had done twice in 1921. Those expelled this time included Treves and Turati who now started secret talks about forming coalitions with the class enemies Giolitti and the King. Italian Socialism had tried to ride two horses – Parliament and revolution – and had fallen off both. The other party with mass support, the *Popolari*, also suffered a severe setback when the Vatican withdrew its support. Pius XI, who had become Pope in February 1922, was no Fascist but like so many he saw Fascism as the best chance of a restoration of peace in Italy.

On 11 October Mussolini, who had got to hear about the injured d'Annunzio's secret contacts with Giolitti, went to see the poet at Gardone. No record exists of the result of the meeting. But it was now that Mussolini finally grasped the nettle and decided to organise the March on Rome. On the 16th he called a meeting of the leaders of the Fascist Militia – Balbo, Cesare De Vecchi, and Emilio De Bono, a reserve army general who had only just joined the PNF in July. Serving generals Gustavo Fara and Sante Ceccherini were also there, as was the PNF secretary Michele Bianchi. Those present agreed that four Quadrumvirs – Balbo, De Vecchi, De Bono and Bianchi – be appointed to organise and command the March on Rome. According to Balbo, Mussolini told the meeting that d'Annunzio was 'in favour' of the march.[16] Balbo wanted to march immediately but Mussolini overruled him: the date would be set at the annual PNF congress in Naples on the 24th.

Yet Mussolini still kept on with his secret negotiations to form part of a legally constituted government. En route for Naples he stopped off in Rome briefly where he met Salandra and in vain demanded five ministries as his price for the support of Fascism. Mussolini was keeping his options open to the very end.

Benedetto Croce, the philosopher, who heard him speak in Naples in 1922, found himself applauding. When asked if he did not think Mussolini and his physical gesturing and posturing – chest and jaw thrust out, hands on hips, or else hands dancing up and down like an orchestra conductor, the theatrical swivelling of his eyes – as well as his words, each one delivered in a high-pitched falsetto tone, were farcical rather than charismatic, Croce replied that all politicians 'must be more of less comedians and their success depends on how good they are at it': it seemed to him that Mussolini played his part brilliantly.[17]

For his appearance at the PNF congress in Naples Mussolini certainly dressed the part of a man keen to march. He wore black shirt, black trousers, white sash across his chest, white spats on his shoes and yellow-and-red cravat round his neck – the colours of Rome. In his speech he emphasised that the monarchy was safe with Fascism but he insisted, 'Either they give us the government, or we will take it by going to Rome ... It is now a question of days and perhaps hours.'[18] When the speech was over, De Vecchi urged Mussolini to shout *'Viva il Re!'* but Mussolini refused.[19] It was in Naples at the Hotel Vesuvio that the Fascist leadership set the date for the March on Rome. The blackshirts would move on the provincial cities at midnight on Friday, 27 October and the next day on Rome where they would assemble at three towns outside the capital: Civitavecchia, Monterotondo and Tivoli. Their orders were to avoid armed conflict with the army 'as long as possible'.[20]

Immediately, De Vecchi, the monarchy's Fascist, scuttled off to Rome to meet Salandra and reveal that the march was on and urge him to warn the King. Salandra was unable to do so because the King was at his country residence, San Rossore, near Pisa. So he told Facta instead. Facta did not believe him. The March on Rome was no secret. But would it happen? Then what?

On his way back to Milan from Naples Mussolini stopped off in Rome to change trains and at the station met Raul Palermi, Grand Master of one of the two Italian Masonic lodges, that of Piazza del Gesù. Mussolini told Cesare Rossi, another ex-revolutionary syndicalist, who was with him on the train journey, that Palermi had assured him that army and police officers who were members of his lodge would help the blackshirts in their task. Crucial figures who were members of the Piazza del Gesù lodge included Admiral Paolo Thaon di Revel, commander in chief of the navy, and General Arturo Cittadini, aide-de-camp to the King.[21]

The Quadrumvirate – minus De Vecchi – had set up its headquarters for the march in a hotel in Perugia. If it came to an armed conflict with the army the Fascists had no chance whatsoever of winning. What on earth was going on? On the 27th Bianchi had to wire De Vecchi to urge him to come forthwith to Perugia. De Vecchi ignored him and remained in Rome where he tried to get the idea of a Salandra government with Fascist participation off the ground. His efforts had the unintended effect of convincing Salandra that the march was a bluff. But the man in charge was not De Vecchi in Rome; it was Mussolini, barricaded inside the offices of *Il Popolo d'Italia* in Milan, with his telephone.

The King returned to Rome from San Rossore by train just after 8 p.m. on the 27th and was met at the station by Facta. Later that evening Facta had an audience with the King at the Villa Savoia, the royal residence in Rome, at which he offered to resign. The King would not let him. Instead, they agreed that the King should proclaim a state of emergency the next morning. Facta went to bed.

In Milan, meanwhile, Mussolini emerged from behind his barricades to go to the theatre – the Teatro Manzoni. There is some dispute about whether he was with his wife or his mistress on this the biggest night of his life so far and which play was on. Subsequently, both women would claim the honours and while Sarfatti would omit to say what play it was, Rachele would say that it was *The Merry Widow* yet omit the name of the playwright. Others would say that the play in question was a farce, *The Swan*, by the Hungarian Ferenc Molnár.

No one seems to dispute that on the previous evening Sarfatti and Mussolini had been together at the Teatro Verme where they had seen Wagner's *Lohengrin*. But the 27th was Mussolini's big night, not the 26th, and his wife was adamant.[22] She recalled, 'I have suffered so much for that woman. It is not that I was afraid of her. Benito always used to say that if his wife had been too educated, a teacher, for example, he would not have been able to rise so high as he did with me by his side. But many used to tell me: "Mussolini let himself be influenced by La Sarfatti", and this, I really could not put up with.'[23]

Whichever woman he was with and whichever play it was, he did not stay until the final curtain because a journalist from *Il Popolo d'Italia* arrived midway through the second act with an urgent message delivered to the newspaper's offices by a motorbike messenger nicknamed 'Old Fox'. The Old Fox had driven like a bat out of hell from Cremona to Milan with his message which was from Roberto Farinacci, the *ras* of Cremona. It said that Farinacci had been unable to contain his blackshirts and they had jumped the gun, moving on their targets in the city well before the appointed hour – midnight. Indeed, it was in Cremona that the Fascists would suffer their worst casualties – ten dead (a total of thirty Fascists died in all).[24] The army had fought back, it would transpire, and recaptured the *Prefettura*. The *Il Popolo* journalist was certain that Mussolini was with Sarfatti and that the play was *The Swan*.[25]

While Facta slept, others were busy. The Fascists began their assault on the major provincial cities in the north and midlands. Efrem Ferraris, Facta's chef de cabinet, wrote, 'At the *Viminale* (Interior Ministry building) the telephones connecting the *Prefetture* with the ministry rang ceaselessly and after midnight the news became alarming. In the dead of night, I witnessed in the silence of the great rooms of the *Viminale* the disintegration of the authority and power of the state. On the large sheets of paper I kept in front of me, there grew ever thicker the names of the occupied *Prefetture* that I was noting down, the details of the telegraph offices invaded, of military garrisons which had fraternised with the Fascists, furnishing them with arms, of trains requisitioned by the militia which set off loaded with armed men, towards the capital.'[26]

At 3 a.m. Bianchi telephoned Mussolini in Milan from Perugia to urge him to end all attempts at a negotiated settlement. Mussolini, barricaded once more inside his newspaper office, hedged as usual. Fewer than 30,000 Fascists marched on Rome itself. They gathered at the three pre-arranged assembly points well outside the city and waited. In some cities of the north, the army and police repelled Fascist attempts to seize key buildings. But in cities in the midlands, army and police commanders would later complain that they had been confused by the absence of precise orders from the government. What orders did they need? The Fascists were guilty of all manner of illegality marching about Italy in this way. The south, except Puglia, was uninvolved.

Most of the Fascists who marched on Rome had not marched at all but arrived at the assembly points by train like football supporters for an away game. The government could have stopped the trains but did not. The Fascists were lightly armed with rifles, pistols and *manganelli*. They had no proper means of communication and the weather was atrocious. It was cold, there was heavy rain and there was mud. General Emanuele Pugliese, on the other hand, in charge of the defence of Rome, had 28,400 troops under his command armed with machine guns, artillery and armoured cars.[27] Four thousand nationalist blueshirts – the *Sempre Pronti* – had rallied to the King ready to stand with General Pugliese if required. As dawn came up on the 28th the two sides faced each other – waiting.

'Their weapons and clothes were of an infinite variety. There were black shirts of ordinary cloth, wool, cotton, yarn, and silk . . .. They had in their hands rifles, muskets, sticks, whips, short clubs, double-barrelled shotguns and carbines . . .' said the Spanish journalist Sanchez Mara for the *ABC* newspaper of Madrid. General Pugliese ordered his men to stop the black-shirts, which they did. The two sides fraternised; the soldiers gave the blackshirts food. They had guitars, bicycles, flasks of wine, dogs, hats of every kind . . . One blackshirt wrote to his mother, 'Dear Mum . . . If they tell you that in the south the weather is always beautiful, don't believe them . . . the peasants, even those who don't know who we are, respect us or perhaps it is only fear, but we are fighting for them too . . . The royal *carabinieri* have given us food and blankets, it seems that when the moment comes to advance they will give us arms as well . . . Tell Dad to forgive me, but I could not stay at home while the others went to save Italy.'[28]

Facta had gone to sleep but not for long. He was woken at about 3 a.m. on the 28th and briefed about the degenerating situation. Among those he contacted in the next few hours were Giolitti and Mussolini, inviting both to Rome to talk about a new government. Why do that if he was about to send the army in against the blackshirts? It must have been because Facta, like everyone else, was playing a double game. He then called an emergency meeting of the Cabinet at the *Viminale* for 6 a.m. at which it was agreed to proclaim the state of emergency and order the army to stop the march. Posters to that effect went up in the streets of Rome from 8.30 a.m. Just before 9 a.m. Facta went to the *Quirinale* to ask the King to sign the state of emergency proclamation, which should have been a mere formality. Incredibly, the King refused to sign – a breach of constitutional convention. Later that morning Facta, after a further meeting of the Cabinet during which he hardly spoke and his face was pallid, returned to the *Quirinale* to offer his resignation once again. The King, this time, accepted.

But if the Fascists did march on Rome what would the army do? And what of the commander-in-chief of the army – the King – to whom each soldier had sworn his oath of allegiance? Would the King order the army to open fire on the Fascists? The King and Mussolini were the two people who counted in the end – regardless of all the talking. The decisions both took would decide the fate of Italy.

Vittorio Emanuele III had met Mussolini for the first time in 1917 on a visit to the hospital where Mussolini was recovering from shrapnel injuries. He had met him again in June 1921 when he had consulted Mussolini in his capacity as head of the Fascist party over the formation of a new government in the wake of the failure of the Giolitti government. He had first heard his name mentioned at the time when Mussolini became editor of *Avanti!* in 1912. The King was a strange, shy little man. He had been brought up *all'inglese*, spoke French at home, was five foot three, had never left the front in the war and had been a good but simple soldier who did not like ostentation, and as a Savoy was hostile to the Vatican. Like his subjects, he was exasperated by the incompetence of the Italian parliament. But he viewed Mussolini – by then the most talked-about politician in Italy – with grave suspicion – especially because of the equivocal views of this so-called Duce about whether the monarchy should be abolished. Like Mussolini, he was probably in favour of surgical black-shirt violence against the Bolshevik menace and alarmed by blackshirt excesses. His principal concern was to hold his constitutional monarchy together and stop civil war. Yet, over the last decade, the constitutional part of the monarchy – parliament – had shown itself increasingly incapable of effective government. The Queen Mother, Queen Margherita, on the other hand, openly sympathised with Fascism.

What of the army? Would the army open fire on the marching black-shirts if so ordered to do? According to General Pugliese, speaking after the general strike, the army would always obey 'whatever order from the King and the government'.[29] The message of the general, a Jew, who like many in the army did not hide his sympathy for Fascism, was clear: the army would fight if called on to do so. In his seemingly straightforward statement, however, General Pugliese highlighted the essence of the problem: what if the government ordered one thing and the King another? As for General Pietro Badoglio, Chief of the General Staff between 1919 and 1921, he is reported to have said in mid-October, 'At the first shot, Fascism will collapse entirely.'[30]

The King's change of mind overnight was not only the crucial decision which brought Mussolini to power, it would prove one of the crucial decisions of the twentieth century. Why did the King change his mind? Recalling the event at the end of his life, in 1945, after the fall of Fascism and just before the abolition of the monarchy, he wrote in a book, 'In 1922 I had to call to the government "these people", because all the others, in one way, or another, had abandoned me. For forty-eight hours, I in person had to give orders directly to the *Questure* and the commander of the armed forces, so that the Italians did not butcher themselves.'[31] This is the only time the King made public comment about his fateful decision. It is not a great help in aiding us to understand why he took the decision which let down the drawbridge to Fascism. Certainly, the King knew what the attitude of the army was and whether it would fight the blackshirts or not if forced. The answer was that the army would fight – but reluctantly. 'Majesty, the army will do its duty, but it would be better not to put it to the test,' was what General Armando Diaz, the army Chief of Staff between 1917 and 1919, is said to have told him.

It is said that the King also feared his cousin Emanuele Filiberto, the Duca d'Aosta, who had driven to Bevagna thirty miles from the Fascist headquarters in Perugia. But the duke favoured the nationalists, who were ardent royalists, over the Fascists, who had strong Republican tendencies. It is difficult to believe that the King was influenced overridingly by the plotting of his cousin. Certainly, the King did not refuse to sign the state of emergency proclamation because he sympathised with Fascism. On the 28th he tried every other alternative government first. But, given the uselessness of government after government in post-war Italy, who can really blame the poor King for calling on Mussolini? In so doing he was in tune with what the majority of Italians wanted and felt they needed.

Throughout that Saturday – 28 October – frantic attempts to form a new government took place. Giolitti, meanwhile, remained in his villa at Cavour in Piedmont and Mussolini was still barricaded up in Milan. Among those the King received were Salandra and De Vecchi, who said that Mussolini was ready to join a Salandra government. This might have been true the day before but not any more now that the King had refused to sign the state of emergency. The telephone in Mussolini's newspaper office bolt-hole rang constantly with offers of one sort or another. In the early evening Salandra asked General Cittadini, the King's aide-de-camp, to telephone Mussolini to make him a formal offer of Fascist participation in a Salandra government. Mussolini declined. In his last article in *Il Popolo d'Italia* as editor – written on the 28th – he wrote: 'The victory cannot be mutilated by last-minute combinations. There was no point mobilising just to achieve a Salandra deal.'[32] Lamely, Gramsci's *L'Ordine Nuovo* noted on the 28th 'The proletariat cannot participate: it can today only wait on the turn of events.' For the Left, the March on Rome, it seemed, was an entirely bourgeois affair of no concern to the proletariat.

If the King had declared the state of emergency, De Vecchi and monarchist Fascists would have defected. Mussolini would not forgive De Vecchi and Grandi, who was also involved, for their machinations on behalf of Salandra. He would ensure that neither held important office for a long time. 'On 28 October 1922 he [De Vecchi] was ready to betray and join a ministerial combination of concentration [i.e. a Salandra government],' Mussolini would say.[33] He would tell Grandi just after the March on Rome, 'You did not believe in my lucky star ... You preferred to believe in the non-existent courage of our enemies ... some people call you a saboteur, a traitor even, of the revolution. It is not true. You acted in good faith. Your predictions were obviously erroneous.'[34]

As d'Annunzio had done on the eve of his march on Fiume, Mussolini telegrammed the poet on the 28th, 'We will be sufficiently fair and intelligent not to abuse our victory. I am certain that you will salute it was the best possible consecration of Italian youth reborn.'[35] The next day d'Annunzio replied, in the words of De Felice, with 'a rather sibylline letter devoid of enthusiasm'.[36]

On Sunday morning – the 29th – Salandra finally threw in the towel and to stop his enemy, Giolitti, being called on to form a government urged the King to call for Mussolini. On the 27th Giolitti, who was now eighty, had decided to leave his estate at Cavour, in Piedmont, to go to Rome. By the time he was ready to depart, however, the army had banned train travel.[37] But in any case the King had not called him. The new government had to be 'right' wing. The Salandra option gone, the only choice was Mussolini. A member of the King's staff telephoned Mussolini to inform him. Mussolini insisted on seeing the request in writing. A telegram, signed by General Cittadini, duly arrived at midday.

Mussolini left Milan by train at 8.30 p.m. that evening, arriving in Rome the next day just before 11 a.m. Briefly, he had gone home where his wife had packed his suitcase. From now on she called him 'Presidente' sarcastically. The newsagent at the kiosk below their home asked her if she was going to Rome too. 'No, I'm going shopping,' she replied.[38] She was and would remain a peasant in the Italian sense of the word. Mussolini's mistress, Sarfatti, not his wife, accompanied him to the station.[39] Before his departure, he told the Milan station master, 'I want to leave on time. From now on everything must work perfectly.' This was the origin of the joke that at least under Fascism the trains run on time. The wife of Sir Ronald Graham, British ambassador in Rome, Lady Sybil, was on the same train as Mussolini by chance. When it arrived in Rome it was met by several thousand Fascists. By then, about 50,000 Fascists had arrived in the city. Graham wrote to Lord Curzon, the Foreign Secretary, 'Considering that the Italian race is temperamentally undisciplined, the order and discipline shown by the Fascisti has been remarkable.' Mussolini was 'completely master of the situation', he said.[40]

Mussolini went briefly to the Hotel Savoia where he normally stayed when in Rome and which would be his base for the time being, then to the *Quirinale* to meet the King. He was with him for about an hour. Like d'Annunzio at Fiume, Mussolini had triumphed with hardly a shot being fired. The army had parted like the Red Sea to allow the Fascists to enter Rome. Mussolini's brilliant bluff had paid off. He is said to have told the King, 'I ask forgiveness of Your Majesty for presenting myself still in my black shirt, a veteran of the battle, fortunately bloodless, which we had to undertake. I bring Your Majesty the Italy of Vittorio Veneto, reconsecrated by our victory.' His opponents would soon brand him a coward for remaining in Milan. But as Balbo was forced to concede through clenched teeth, it had been a 'telephone revolution'. Asked by Ludwig in 1932 why he, as a former soldier, had remained in Milan, he replied, 'I was in command in Milan.'

The next day – the 31st – the Fascists marched past the *Quirinale* in a display of loyalty to the King who stood on the balcony with the First World War heroes, General Diaz and Admiral Thaon di Revel, to take their salute. There was a festive atmosphere in Rome. Happy crowds lined the streets. Newspapers reported that the Eternal city was gripped by a fever of delight and that florists had run out of flowers.[42] The Italian people appeared pleased that the liberal–conservative *ancien régime* had collapsed and that the nation was delivered to Fascism. Mussolini was determined to show how disciplined the Fascists were and ordered the Fascists to leave Rome immediately, which they did within three days by specially arranged trains.

The only senior figure to make any sort of a stand against the arrival of the Fascists in power was Count Carlo Sforza, Italy's ambassador to France, who resigned. The only dramatic consequence was that Mussolini, head of a party with just thirty-two MPs (thirty-five had been elected in May 1921 but three banned as too young), was Prime Minister as a result not of an election but a lot of telephone calls and a paramilitary day out. But there were glorious precedents: had not Caesar crossed the Rubicon to march on Rome; had not the House of Savoy itself marched on Rome?

One year later – on the first anniversary of the March of Rome – Mussolini would say, 'They said – one of them was a philosopher of history, a sad masturbator of history – they said that the Fascist government would last no more than six weeks … It will last, *camicie nere*. It will last because we, deniers of the doctrine of materialism, have not expelled free will from the history of mankind.'[43]

Mussolini was Prime Minister at the age of thirty-nine – the youngest Prime Minister since Italian reunification. Balbo was twenty-six, Grandi and Bottai twenty-seven, Farinacci, thirty. The oldest was the quadrumvir, General De Bono, at fifty-six. *The Times* noted, 'The nationalist revolution is a lawful one since it succeeded, without changing the regime and without derangement of public services or private property . . . The impression created by the new Prime Minister is essentially one of strength . . . His eyes are black and very expressive . . . he looks far younger than his forty-eight years . . .'[44] *The Times* had got his age wrong. But it was right about his eyes. Mussolini had created a myth which had delivered him power.

9

POWER: YEAR ONE OF THE FASCIST ERA

Mussolini did not seize power. That was the Fascist version of history. He was given power by the King. Nor was Fascism a bourgeois counter-revolution against the working class. That was the Marxist version of history. The Fascists opposed the bourgeoisie as much as they opposed the Socialists because both exalted one class at the expense of the other. The Fascists exalted the nation, united not divided.

The popular definition of Fascism as right-wing is misleading even though Mussolini in 1922 described it as 'of the right'.[1] The intellectual driving force behind it was left-wing. Most Fascists had either been Socialists or syndicalists. However right-wing the manifestations of Fascism became, its guiding star was always left. Its opposition to Socialism *might* be described as right-wing, its republican tendencies left-wing. Its opposition to the principle of parliamentary democracy might be described as right-wing, its opposition to the undemocratic reality of the Italian parliament left-wing. Its defence of private property *was* right-wing but its support for the big state to bridle Capitalism – its Corporate State – left-wing.

Like the Socialists, the Fascists wanted class war: theirs, however, was not a war between the bourgeoisie and the proletariat but between productive people and parasitic people. They sought the victory not of the working class but of productive people from whichever class they came. This meant, for example, collaboration between productive employers and productive workers, not confrontation.

It was the Fascists who made popular the phrase Third Way between the first and second ways, Capitalism and Socialism, to describe their Corporate State which would ensure class collaboration and end class war. Mussolini would write, 'The force of Fascism consists of this: that it takes from all programmes the vital part and has the force to put them into practice.'[2] It is ironical, therefore, that three-quarters of a century later, after the collapse of Eastern bloc Communism, the Fascist Third Way should become the leitmotif of the millennium Left for whom the word 'Fascist' remains the worst of insults.

Whereas the Socialists wanted to '*socializzare*' the workplace, the Fascists wanted to '*fascistizzare*' life. Both sought a congregation of believers. The Fascist parish was not the Internationale but the nation; the values of the spirit more important than those of the market. 'For a century *la materia* remained the holy grail,' wrote Mussolini, 'today, it is *lo spirito* which takes its place.'[3] The twentieth century would be the century of 'anti-democracy' because people had begun to realise, he said, that 'the democratic justice of universal suffrage is the most resounding of injustices; ... government by all ... leads in reality to government by no one.'[4] Democracy had been mortally wounded in the First World War and died in 1919–20. Bolshevik Russia, where Lenin ruled like a Czar, was the prime example of this. 'As always happens, the nation which swerved most violently to the left, is that which ... strides most quickly to the right ... New aristocracies are rising up ... Where this orientation to the right will go, it is impossible, today, to be sure: certainly a very long way.'[5]

Having defeated Socialism in the piazza, the Fascists now turned their sights on the bourgeoisie in their parliament. What could be more bourgeois, after all, than this Italian parliament groaning with so many lawyers, which like lawyers in general, never seemed to conclude anything? What, as Mussolini was fond of saying of the Italian parliament, could be more 'invincibly nauseous'?

Fascism was not, as the Left insisted, the creature of big business. It had mass appeal: in October 1922 membership of the PNF stood at 300,000 and a year later at 783,000. Nor was it, as the Left also insisted, financed by big business alone. Its money came from many different sources as De Felice has demonstrated beyond doubt.[6] As Adrian Lyttelton has observed,[7] 'Mussolini was borne into power on the shoulders of a mass movement.' But it was not the mass movement which delivered power to Mussolini. He came to power as a result of a *coup d'état* which was unlike all other *coups d'état* for two reasons. First, all normal *coups d'état* involve the army, or a section of the army, taking matters into their own hands. This did not happen. Second, this *coup d'état* was legal: the King invited Mussolini to become prime minister. The King, interpreting the will of the nation, delivered the government to Mussolini – but not the state.

To many Italians (those who formed that difficult to define concept, public opinion, especially in an age which had no opinion polls, television and radio) exhausted by three and a half years of war followed by four years of virtual civil war – two years of 'red' violence, then two years of 'black' violence – Mussolini represented the best chance of a return of order but also the best chance, if not of revolution, of resurrection.

Mussolini had wanted power. But he did not have complete power. Nor was it clear to anyone, least of all himself, what precisely he would do with power. The composition of his first Cabinet, drawn up just hours after his meeting with the King at the *Quirinale* on 30 October at which he wore a black shirt and presented to the King that evening for which he wore formal dress (each ill-fitting bit borrowed from a different member of his entourage, even the cufflinks were borrowed),[8] reflects the limited and non-revolutionary reality of his triumph. For the moment, at least, he had no choice but to work in coalition with the other parties – just like every prime minister before him. But anyway Mussolini insisted that Fascism stood for a government of national pacification above political party open to the best regardless of political party. He wanted 'collaboration with men but not with parties', he said. He even made overtures to Socialists and offered a Cabinet post to at least one, Gino Baldesi, director of the CGL and member of the reformist PSU, whose party secretary was now the MP Giacomo Matteotti. Matteotti would never have countenanced such a thing, had he known. Baldesi accepted. But the offer came to nothing because Mussolini dropped it after protests from the nationalists and extremist Fascists who got to hear about it.

Though Mussolini appointed himself Minister of the Interior and ad interim Minister for Foreign Affairs – something that no previous Italian prime minister had ever done – only three of the remaining thirteen Cabinet positions went to Fascists.[9] Three Fascist sympathisers, from outside parliament though not members of the Fascist party, were also appointed to the Cabinet: the First World War heroes, General Diaz and Admiral Thaon di Revel, became respectively Ministers of War and the Navy; and the philosopher Giovanni Gentile became Minister of Education. Only one member of the Cabinet, who had served in the Facta government, had experience of government. He was the lone representative of the liberal–conservative *ancien régime*.

The composition of Mussolini's first Cabinet angered Fascist extremists. They wanted a Fascist revolution proper, which to them meant primarily that the Fascist party should run the state, not the state the Fascist party, and they would continue to press for it.

On 16 November Mussolini presented the new government to the Chamber of Deputies for the customary vote of confidence and made his first speech to the Chamber as Prime Minister. He told MPs that 'the revolution has its rights' and asked the Chamber to grant him emergency powers to rule by decree for one year to carry out urgent reform. He warned, 'I add, so that everyone may know, that I am here to defend and strengthen to the utmost degree the revolution of the blackshirts … With 300,000 young men *armati di tutto punto*, utterly committed and almost mystically ready for an order from me, I could have punished all those who have defamed and tried to throw mud at Fascism. I could have turned this deaf and grey Chamber into a bivouac for my legions … I could have barred up parliament and formed a government only of Fascists. I could have: but I have not wanted to, at least not for the moment.'

Mussolini then praised the '*masse lavoratrice italiane*' (Italian working class) for their 'passive solidarity' with the '*moto Fascista*' (Fascist rebellion) and the King for his refusal to give in to 'uselessly reactionary attempts' to use the army against the blackshirts, which meant that civil war had been avoided. He concluded 'God help me conduct my arduous task to a victorious conclusion.'[10] This mention of God was taken as a clear message of conciliation to the Vatican.

The Chamber duly approved the vote of confidence in the new government by an enormous majority – 306 votes to 116 with 7 abstentions. Only the Socialists and the Communists voted against. Among those who voted in favour were five ex-prime ministers Bonomi, Giolitti, Orlando, Facta and Salandra. (In October 1922, before the March on Rome, the liberal factions in parliament – Giolitti's group (forty-one MPs), Salandra's group (twenty-one MPs) and De Nava's group (twenty-four MPs) – had formed the liberal party in an attempt to attract mass support.)

Without the support of the *Popolari* Mussolini would not have secured a majority. But the *Popolari*, though broadly hostile to Fascism, could not act against the wishes of the Vatican. And the Vatican had made it clear that it had decided to support Mussolini. The Vatican's overriding concern was for what the pope had called 'the pacification of souls' in a recent letter to the bishops. Following the Vatican's lead, the *Popolari* voted in favour of the new government. Their leader in parliament (Don Sturzo was not an MP) was De Gasperi – Mussolini's enemy of old in Trento and future post-war prime minister.

One hour later, Mussolini spoke to the Senate. His majority was even larger. The liberal philosopher, Croce, who had so enthusiastically heard him speak in Naples just before the March on Rome, voted in favour of the new government; only nineteen senators voted against. Fascism was 'like a working man, impetuous, violent even, but generous and a lover of the *patria*', Croce wrote.[11] Albertini, editor of the *Corriere della Sera* and a senator, said that Fascism had 'saved Italy from the danger of Socialism'.[12]

Among his first official tasks as prime minister, Mussolini attended the Lausanne Conference which began on 20 November involving Britain, France, Russia, Turkey and Greece. The Swiss government had to cancel the deportation orders against him which were still in force from his time as a down-and-out in Switzerland in 1903–4. He stayed at the Beau Rivage, as everyone did.[13] The Beau Rivage was the same hotel outside which he had stood in desperation as a down-and-out all those years ago, watched the rich, and contemplated suicide.

The purpose of the Lausanne Conference was to decide the terms of the armistice with Turkey, which were yet to be settled, and also of the more recent war between Turkey and Greece. This war had ended in October 1922, after bringing Britain and Turkey to the brink of war and forcing the resignation of Lloyd George as British Prime Minister, with the rout of the Greeks and their withdrawal from Asia Minor.

At Lausanne, Mussolini wanted to discuss the twelve Dodecanese Islands which Italy had seized from Turkey in the war of 1911–12. In principle, Italy had agreed under the 1920 Treaty of Sèvres to hand the islands, which included Rhodes and whose population was largely Greek, back to Turkey. But under the 1915 Secret Treaty of London, Britain, France and Russia had promised these islands to Italy in the event of victory. In the end, under pressure from British Foreign Secretary Lord Curzon and French Prime Minister Raymond Poincaré, who pointed out that the most important thing for the Allies was to present a united front against the Turks, Mussolini agreed not to raise the issue of the Dodecanese. Their future, he was assured, could be discussed later.

Mussolini contributed little to the talks and remained for only two days. He had no experience whatever of foreign affairs and much more pressing matters to attend to at home. Harold Nicolson recalled how he 'chafes uneasily against his white stiff cuffs, rolling important eyes. He said little – *"Je suis d'accord"* was the most important thing he said.' But Nicolson added in brackets, '(His *d'accord* was very important, however, because it confirmed the unity of the Allied front).'[14]

Despite what the British delegation thought of him, during those two days Mussolini was the undoubted centre of attention – not they. Foreign journalists queued up to meet the man who had the month before marched on Rome and who seemed to offer a viable and exciting alternative to both Communism and Capitalism. Ernest Hemingway was among the journalists present. He wrote that Mussolini appeared much more interested in creating a headline than contributing to the congress. According to him, at one press conference Mussolini started off proceedings by ostentatiously reading a book and ignoring the assembled journalists. So Hemingway sneaked over to take a look at the book and noticed, he wrote, that it was a French–English dictionary held upside down.[15] Perhaps Hemingway was telling the truth. But he was a notorious embellisher of facts who, for example, famously lied about Scott Fitzgerald's fears that his penis was too small.

Another observer, Clare Sheridan, was far less two-dimensional in her assessment. Her account of this and subsequent meetings shortly afterwards with Mussolini, and the electric effect his presence had on people, not least herself, is unique. Sheridan was young and beautiful but also rich and well-connected (she and Winston Churchill were cousins). She was a Socialist, a successful journalist and sculptress and, though Anglo-Irish, had lived much of her life in Italy. She had already interviewed among others Lenin and Kemal. She recalled, 'The fact was, nobody was interested in anyone but Mussolini. Whenever he appeared in the foyer, surrounded by his bodyguard of young blackshirts, there was a flutter of excitement. He must have appreciated the interest aroused, but he adopted the expression we came to know so well of haughty disdain.'[16]

Through her Italian diplomatic contacts she managed to interview Mussolini in his hotel suite and conversed in French, which he spoke well,

When Mussolini made his entry from the next room, he stood and surveyed me fiercely, his bulgy bull's eyes showing the whites all round them. For long seconds we stood and faced each other. The first thing which struck me about him was that his legs were too short. He was in fact very ill-proportioned...

He talked in staccato sentences: at the end of each he'd close his eyes, snap his jaw, and give an emphatic jerk to his head ... I chose to be provocative to see how he would react, and so I referred to 'the Bolshevik ideal, of awakening the people'.

He exploded, no other word could describe his reaction: '*The People!* And what does that word *People* signify? What are the people? What is this vague herd. That I hear so much about? I only recognise what I can *touch*, what I can measure with my eye, bend.' (The word he used was *plier*, which he repeated several times with an emphatic illustrative gesture.) I visualised him at once as a bully; he seemed to gain the deepest satisfaction from the gesture, as though his pleasure were to force, to bend, if necessary to break, people to his will.

The masses, he went on, always would and always must be governed by a strong minority. 'Inequality and discipline, these are the substitutes for the democratic cry of Equality and Liberty.' ... Suddenly, with his huge bull's eyes fixed on me he suggested I should go with him to Rome: 'Come and see my *fascisti dans toute la gloire de leur jeunesse.*'

That evening, 22 November, Sheridan did indeed take the same train as Mussolini back to Rome. She wrote, 'All night long, half awake, half asleep, I heard the "Giovinezza" march like a persistent refrain. As soon as the frontier was crossed, one heard it at every station. Crowds assembled to greet the Dictator, one could tell the singers were young by their strong, clear voices. Enthusiastic spontaneous cheers pursued the train as it gathered speed, and then faded out into the distance.'

On 25 November the chamber approved Mussolini's request made on 16 November during the bivouac speech, to be granted emergency powers for one year to introduce reforms of the economy, bureaucracy, education system and army without recourse to approval by parliament.[17] Effectively, this gave him *carte blanche* to rule by decree. The support of parliament can only mean one thing: an overwhelming majority of MPs and senators felt that given the turbulence in Italy since the end of the First World War, Fascism was the only answer.

To say, as so many have done and do, that there was no threat of civil war in 1922 Italy, no threat of Bolshevik-style revolution and therefore no need to give Mussolini power, is beside the point. Regardless of how real or not was the threat, the fear of such a revolution in Italy, given events both inside and outside Italy since 1914, was very real. As late as January 1931, according to an eavesdropper in the pay of Fascism, listening in on a conversation Orlando had with a third party, the former prime minister said, 'I am convinced that if Fascism collapsed we would get Bolshevism: and confronted with such a danger, I feel ten times a Fascist.'[18] Quite apart from the threat, or lack of it, of Socialist revolution, parliament had shown itself incapable of governing Italy. Clare Sheridan,[19] summed up this mood well: 'Winston Churchill (who is talked of as the likely leader of a *Fascisti* party in England) says Fascism is the shadow of Bolshevism, and that if we must be ruled by one or the other, he would rather be ruled by *Fascisti* than by Bolshevik violence.' Churchill was far from alone among British Conservatives in sharing such favourable views of Fascism.

Mussolini had raised the eyebrows of serious-minded Romans when in November 1922 he took up residence with his blackshirt bodyguards and Fascist spooks in the lavish Grand Hotel, which was the nerve centre of the richest gossip and intrigue in the Eternal City. (From the March on Rome until then, he and they had stayed at the Savoia.) The Grand was also a favourite with rich American women tourists who were very excited by the presence so close to them of the Duce. During the morning Mussolini would work at the *Viminale* (Interior Ministry) and the afternoon at Palazzo Chigi (the Foreign Ministry) in Piazza Colonna. He gave orders to ban women from entry. 'They obstruct active production of work. They create delays and do not appreciate the urgent nature of work . . .'[20]

Women were for after hours. It was at the Grand that Clare Sheridan, who on her return from Lausanne on Mussolini's train was also staying there, had her next encounter with him. Clearly, he had taken a fancy to her for at 9 p.m. on the very same day of their arrival in Rome he sent a messenger to her room requesting another meeting. But the Roman social season was 'in full swing', she wrote, and she was out 'dancing somewhere'. The next evening Mussolini sent a second messenger but this time earlier, at 7.30 p.m., and she was in. So she went to his suite where he was eating a frugal meal served on a tray. He came and sat beside her on the sofa and they resumed where they had left off in Lausanne.

Sheridan gave two accounts of what happened at the Grand – one in *To the Four Winds* written in 1957, the other in *In Many Places* published soon after the event in 1923. In this first account – written long before Mussolini became the second most despised man in the world after Hitler – Sheridan is much less critical of Mussolini. Her reference to Churchill being the likely leader of a Fascist party in England is not repeated in the 1957 account either.) The second later account shows all the signs of distortion by hindsight. 'The man in the street . . . blindly adored him,' she wrote[21] in *In Many Places*, adding, '. . . he told me that sometimes he feels impelled as by a mystic force that he does not understand ...' She asked him why he had abandoned Socialism and he replied, 'German militarism.' He reminded her that when war broke out the German Socialists had given up on the creed of international working-class brotherhood and decided to fight their brother workers in other countries such as France and Britain. She said goodbye and he kissed her hand.

Soon afterwards (she says 27 November) Sheridan went to hear him speak in the Senate and that evening, Mussolini, who by now had half agreed Sheridan could do a sculpture of him, sent yet another messenger to her room at 10 p.m. Once again she was out dancing. But he did not give up and sent for her again the next evening at 9 p.m. This was their last meeting. She hoped to get him to pose, but wrote,[22] 'He was in a queer mood, charming one moment, aggressive the next. Varying from compliments to threats ...' But in her later account she revealed that he had made a pass at her. It is unclear whether she succumbed or not. Reading between the lines, it would appear she did, and hated herself for doing so, for she wrote:[23]

> I was somewhat disconcerted when he went to the door and locked it. He had no finesse where women were concerned, one attitude only, intimidation. That too was his attitude to the world, to bluff, to bully, to menace. It succeeded, more or less ... In vain I tried to induce him to pose, even for a few minutes. He insisted I sit by him on the sofa: '*Vous êtes une femme pour qui on pourrait avoir une grande passion,*' he said breathlessly ... I was to learn how difficult it can be for a young woman to keep a dictator in his proper place ... He said, '*Vous partirez d'ici à l'aube, blessée et meurtriée.*' ... Exasperated by his failure to impress me, Mussolini lost his temper.

Then the telephone rang. 'If eyes could rivet, his eyes almost pinned me down as he lifted up the receiver ... I felt mesmerised ... That night remains painfully imprinted upon my memory ... I hated Mussolini to his death ...'

On 7 December Mussolini left for the Allied conference in London on German failure to pay war reparations imposed by the Treaty of Versailles. Germany had been unable to raise a foreign loan to pay the crippling debt and the French wanted to occupy the Ruhr as a result and seize German coal. The British proposed granting Germany a four-year moratorium on the reparation debt instead. The British and French argued bitterly and failed to reach agreement. Mussolini blustered and vacillated.

He travelled to London by train arriving at Victoria Station on the evening of 8 December, where he was greeted by Italian Fascists based in London wearing black shirts and singing '*Giovinezza*'. He remained in London for three days, met King George V at Buckingham Palace and stayed at Claridge's, where he complained that the French delegation had been given better rooms and tried to have them ejected.

He would never return to Britain. Indeed, he would hardly ever travel abroad at all for sixteen years until the 1938 Munich conference. The British press was virtually unanimous that Mussolini was a great leader and Fascism, as *The Times* put it, was 'a healthy reaction against the attempt to spread Bolshevism in Italy'.[24]

The London conference, which adjourned to Paris, failed to reach agreement and so the French took matters into their own hands. On 9 January 1923 French and Belgian troops occupied the Ruhr. The German mark, which in July 1923 stood at 160,000 to the dollar, collapsed. By August it was 1 million to the dollar and by November 133,000,000.[25]

Mussolini's policy on German war reparations is well summed up by Sir Ronald Graham (British ambassador Rome 1922–34) who quickly established a good rapport with Mussolini: his only concern was what was best for Italy. Mussolini for his part soon came to regard Graham as a friend and this was of great benefit to Anglo-Italian relations, according to Sir Ivone Kirkpatrick who was head of chancery at the Rome embassy 1930–3 and a post-war biographer of Mussolini. When Graham left Rome, Anglo-Italian relations deteriorated. Kirkpatrick, who was at the British embassy in Berlin from 1933–9, wrote,[26] 'I had known Hitler very well, but there was no doubt that of the two dictators Mussolini was by a long way the most complex and interesting.'

On 15 January, Graham wrote to Curzon,[27] 'In any case his foreign policy will be pure opportunism, and Italian friendship is on offer to highest bidder. My impression is that he would prefer to work with Great Britain, at a price. If we can give nothing he will turn to France. Failing France he may deal with Russia or the Turks. It is a policy of sacred egotism carried to extremes.' In the end Mussolini sided with the British over the French occupation of the Ruhr, which lasted until July 1924 when a much more lenient reparations payment plan was agreed, based on the Keynesian premise that the victors in a war could not flourish while the vanquished starved.

Back from London, Mussolini took his first steps – more like tiptoes – towards dictatorship, each one justified in the name of what all desired; what was called '*normalizzazione*' or else '*pacificazione*'. But in Italy at large Fascist violence had not ceased. On 18 December 1922 Fascist blackshirts killed eleven workers in Turin, and shortly afterwards thirteen at La Spezia. Paradoxical as it may seem, it was the need to curb Fascist violence and try to bring the blackshirts under his control which made Mussolini make these first moves towards dictatorship. First, he and the Fascist leadership established the Fascist Grand Council, which met unofficially for the first time at the Grand Hotel on 15 December 1922. The aim was to exercise greater control over Fascism – not parliament. (The first official Grand Council meeting was on 12 January 1923.)[28]

The Grand Council, whose members were to be appointed by Mussolini who would also decide when it met, would reduce the power of the PNF leadership and other Fascist organisations such as the Fascist trade unions and increase that of the government. But the formation of the Grand Council, as Lyttelton notes, was 'a revolutionary act'[29] because the Grand Council clearly had the potential to become a parallel Council of Ministers (Cabinet). So while it appealed to Mussolini as a means of controlling both the PNF and parliament, it also appealed to Farinacci and the provincial *ras* as a means of exercising control over the government.

At its first meeting it decided to abolish the *Regie guardie* – set up by Nitti in 1919 to maintain public order – and replace it with a national militia comprising the blackshirts to become effective on 1 February. The Cabinet duly issued the necessary decree on 28 December under the emergency powers which parliament had granted Mussolini's government for one year. The formation of the militia – the *Milizia Volontaria per la Sicurezza Nazionale* (MSVN) – was also a revolutionary act; it set up yet another parallel organisation. Its members – there were 300,000 blackshirts – would swear an oath of loyalty not to the King, as was the case with the police and the armed forces, but to Italy.[30] Mussolini, therefore, with the rank of corporal of honour (he had been a corporal in the army) – perhaps inspired by Napoleon's nickname '*Le Petit Caporal*' – would be its Commander-in-Chief. The names of the militia ranks were the same as those of the blackshirt squads – consuls in charge of legions of 1500 centurions at full strength. The uniform was different: an army-style *grigioverde* tunic over a black shirt and cravat, and black fez.

Mussolini appointed the Quadrumvir and Chief of Police, De Bono as *luogotenente generale* of the militia, whose role would be 'to defend the revolution of October 1922'.[31] Whereas before all ranks up to that of consul were either elected from below or appointed by the local PNF, from now on they were to be appointed from above. The ranks of consul and above would be on a permanent salary – the equivalent of an army colonel's. This infuriated the army, which was anyway hostile to the whole idea. All other ranks would be part-time, and paid as and when summoned to work. To get the support of the army, Mussolini pledged among other things that the militia would only do police work. The King agreed because he felt it better to have a militia under the control of the government than continue with blackshirt squads each answering to their respective *ras* out in the provinces; better to have the blackshirts inside the state than out. From Fascism's point of view the militia provided it with its own legally sanctioned national paramilitary police force. From Mussolini's point of view it meant that his control over the blackshirts increased and that of the *ras* decreased. The King, the army and liberal–conservatives accepted the creation of the militia for the sake of '*normalizzazione*'; they hoped that turning the squads into a militia would decrease the chance of blackshirt violence.

Mussolini would describe the Grand Council's role as the 'co-ordination and propulsion' of the revolution; that of the militia its 'defence and armed guarantee'.[32] In 1927 he described the formation of the Grand Council and the militia as 'the bases and tools of this revolution'.[33]

In December, too, De Bono, Chief of Police, gave orders to the prefects to disband d'Annunzio's armed legionaries and next the Communist party was targeted. In the next two months 2236 Communists were arrested, of whom 602 were charged with public order offences. In the month to 10 April large numbers of weapons, including 29,257 rifles, were seized.[34] In early 1923 Mussolini ordered a crackdown on dissident Fascist violence and in June he telegraphed prefects to 'repress inexorably' illegality 'whoever is responsible'.[35]

December also saw the start of talks which led in March 1923 to the fusing of the PNF with Federzoni's jingoistic and fiercely royalist nationalists who had ten MPs. Though they had much in common, nationalist squads and blackshirt squads had frequently clashed in the provinces, especially in the south, and the nationalists' blueshirts – the *Sempre Pronti* – had been ready to stand against the blackshirts in the event of the blackshirts attacking the army during the March on Rome. Mussolini called the fusion of the two parties a 'marriage of convenience.'[36]

Like the Fascists, the nationalists despised the liberal state. If anything, authoritarians in the armed forces favoured them over the Fascists. But the nationalists also scorned the idea of political parties based on mass support. They did not seek mass support nor did they have it. Instead, they aimed to convert key figures in society to their cause such as industrialists, army officers, clergymen, university lecturers, lawyers and civil servants. The fusion of the PNF with the Nationalist Association on 26 February was a serious blow to left-wing Fascists. But the nationalists' good contacts with Italy's elites meant the Fascists were less reliant on right-wing liberal support as a result. It also meant the amalgamation of the *Sempre Pronti* with the militia.

The fusion with the nationalists coincided with the Grand Council decision in February 1923 to ban members of the PNF from being freemasons. The nationalists were pro-Church and anti-freemason. But Fascism teemed with masons including Rossi, Balbo, Acerbo, Grandi, De Vecchi, De Bono, Finzi, Bottai, Giunta, Farinacci, Rocca and Marinelli. Though he had courted their support for the March on Rome, Mussolini had always had – and always would have – an obsessive loathing of freemasonry and as a Socialist had been behind a similar ban on freemasonry in the Socialist party. Given the secretive nature of freemasonry, however, such a ban could hardly be enforced. Till now, the two masonic lodges, Palazzo Giustiniani and Piazza del Jesù, had supported Fascism. Now Palazzo Giustiniani withdrew its support.

Mussolini's antipathy to freemasonry probably stemmed from his deeply superstitious nature and his fear of the occult. He also hated going through tunnels in a train or car because he felt intense claustrophobia. 'For this too, masonry repulses me. I cannot stand anything that is enclosed, subterranean, and which takes place in caves instead of in the light of the sun,' he told Sarfatti.[37]

That Fascism was in control of Italy did nothing to stop King George V and Queen Mary making an official five-day state visit to Rome in early May 1923 – far from it. The king bestowed the Order of the Bath on Mussolini. Indeed, the visit was seen as representing the British seal of approval for Mussolini and Fascism. For as Graham wrote to Curzon, 'The personal impression created by their Majesties has been very great, and the whole visit has done much to strengthen the ties of that Anglo-Italian friendship which may at times be strained or dormant, but is, I sincerely believe, deep rooted in this country ... At the present moment we can count on a satisfactory measure of Italian co-operation and support. But it must be remembered that Italian foreign policy ... is frankly opportunist and egotistic ... He [Mussolini] has proclaimed from the first, and has since emphasised, that his foreign policy will be in the sole interests of Italy and one of "nothing for nothing".'[38]

Mussolini now turned his attention to holding a general election in order to give Fascism the mandate of the people that it lacked. He was trying to walk down both the revolutionary path and the parliamentary path; the path of force and that of consent. Parliament was useful to him to curb Fascist excess. The PNF was useful to him to curb parliament.

But without electoral reform, despite what many believed, an outright Fascist election victory was not certain. Italy had had proportional representation (*proporzionale*) since 1919 by which it was virtually impossible for one party to get an outright majority. This would have to go, he decided, in favour of a return to some form of single-member constituency formula (*uninominale*). The *Popolari*, committed to PR because it had enabled them to get their first big electoral breakthrough in 1919 and with ministers in the government, were the main obstacle to such electoral reform. The Socialists, who had benefited in the same way, were also opposed. But there was little chance of them as a party agreeing anything with Mussolini – despite his overtures to individual Socialists. Giolitti, Salandra, Orlando and the rest of the liberal–conservative old guard, on the other hand, were keen for a return to the *uninominale*, which in the past had helped secure them political dominance. All depended, therefore, on the *Popolari*. If they voted against Mussolini he would never be able to secure a Fascist majority in parliament for electoral reform.

The electoral reform bill brought before parliament as a result was called the Acerbo Bill after Giacomo Acerbo, the Under-Secretary at the Presidenza, who drafted it, and was breathtaking in its boldness: two thirds of the seats would go to whoever got more than 25 per cent of the total votes cast (the rest of the seats would be divided along PR lines). If no one got more than 25 per cent all the seats would be divided up according to the existing PR system. Constituencies would be abolished. There would only be one constituency, Italy, divided into sixteen electoral districts.[39] Each party or coalition would draw up a list of candidates. The electorate would choose between the various lists. Equally breathtaking was that parliament agreed to pass the Acerbo Bill. For a start the Fascists, even after their fusion with the nationalists, only had forty-two deputies.

Fascism, like all political movements, was riddled with divisions as to what Fascism was and how it should develop. If it were too violent and revolutionary it would lose the support of the *'fiancheggiatori'*[40] – all those such as Giolitti who though not Fascist tolerated it, as did the King and the Vatican. If it were not violent and revolutionary enough, it would risk losing the support of at least one of its two extremist wings and so risk tearing itself apart or falling prey to Giolittian *'trasformismo'*. These two extremist wings were known as *Fascismo intransigente* and *Fascismo revisionista*. The *revisionisti* were more revolutionary but less violent than the *intransigenti*. They opposed the use of *squadrismo* as the means to the end. Passion not policy had united Fascists. But as Giuseppe Bottai, the leading *revisionista*, noted, 'calm revives their disagreements'.[41]

Within Fascism Roberto Farinacci, the *ras* of Cremona, was the leading *intransigente* and the biggest threat to Mussolini. Farinacci was of Neapolitan stock and born in 1892. He was the son of a police officer and, like Mussolini, an ex-revolutionary Socialist. He had tried to fight in the First World War but was not allowed to until near the end because he was a railway stationmaster and skilled telegraphist.[42] In 1924 he obtained his degree in law at Modena on a fast-track course for war veterans by copying a fellow student's thesis, a freemason, a bully, a talented networker, fiercely anti-clerical, deeply corrupt and on the proceeds of his corruption owned his own newspaper *Cremona Nuova* – as many of the *ras* did. Elected a Fascist MP in 1921, he had to resign immediately when it emerged that he was too young to be one – though he would return as an MP in the 1924 elections. His favourite word to describe the Chamber of Deputies was *'troiaio'* – (brothel). He despised culture and the cultured, and liked to project an image of himself as an honest down-to-earth man of the provinces. But his power in his province depended – as did that of all the *ras* – on money and force.

Mussolini kept a file on Farinacci – as he did on thousands of people. From this file – which is bigger than anyone else's – it is clear that Mussolini had proof that Farinacci had copied his degree thesis because in it is a letter from Farinacci to Mussolini in which he tries to defend himself: 'Duce, I did not want to copy [it],' he begins.[43] It also contains proof that the closest Farinacci got to the front line in the First World War was six kilometres and he never saw action. Whereas Mussolini feared Balbo because he had true charisma he loathed Farinacci. Nevertheless, until the end, Farinacci would be both an indispensable prop to Mussolini and a thorn in his side. Already, by the end of 1922, Farinacci and the *intransigenti* felt that the March on Rome – i.e. the Fascist revolution – had been betrayed by Mussolini once he became prime minister. They spoke for the Fascism of the 'Provincia Pura' (Pure Province) against the Fascism of 'Roma Troiaio' (Brothel Rome), for the Fascism of the *squadristi*, against that of the *politici*. They wanted – like the Nazis afterwards – to make the state subordinate to the party. They called with increasing urgency for what they termed 'the second wave' to begin.

Against the *intransigenti* stood the *revisionisti* who included Dino Grandi and Giuseppe Bottai, who had founded a magazine, *Critica Fascista*, to promote the views of the *revisionisti*. It was they who spoke most of '*normalizzazione*' and '*riconciliazione*' – for the squads to be disarmed and for violence to be abandoned. But in terms of ends, not means, the *revisionisti* were much more left wing than the *intransigenti*. They believed that an elite should run the state, not the PNF, not parliament. It was they who pushed hardest for a corporate state. But the Fascist revolution, they felt, should proceed legally, not illegally, peacefully, not violently. Unlike the *intransigenti*, they did not enjoy mass support. The division between the *intransigenti* and the *revisionisti* was similar to the division within Socialism between the *massimalisti* and the *riformisti*. Massimo Rocca – an ex-anarchist who used to write scathing articles under the pseudonym Libero Tancredi, turned strident *squadrista* then strident *revisionista* – headed the list of talented contributors to *Critica Fascista*. Balbo, though a Republican and the only senior Fascist to possess similar charisma to Mussolini, was too much of a maverick to be a threat to Mussolini. Between the *intransigenti* and the *revisionisti*, of course, were many other shades of opinion. But the difference between the *intransigenti* and *revisionisti* always turned on the same dilemma at root, as Indro Montanelli, Italy's most famous post-war journalist, noted, 'Should the revolution become the state or should the state become the tool of the revolution?'[44]

Mussolini, somehow, had to keep the conflicting forces inside and outside Fascism from tearing his government apart. But as the reformist Socialist and former prime minister Ivanoe Bonomi, wrote, 'All these discordant elements he has himself ... assimilated and melted in his personality, assuming almost the figure of a referee who, in the chaos of ideas and feelings, chooses the vital elements for his creature.'[45]

What of the *Popolari*? On 14 June the parliamentary group – in line with Don Sturzo's view – decided to oppose the Acerbo Bill. This attracted the wrath not just of the Fascist press but also of the liberal press. Fascist squad violence against Catholic lay targets escalated and then a prominent article in the *Corriere d'Italia* – one of the most authoritative Catholic newspapers – of 25 June 1923, intimated that Pope Pius XI had withdrawn support for Don Sturzo and the *Popolari* as a result of their opposition to the bill and that Don Sturzo should step down. Don Sturzo, as a priest, felt unable to ignore the views of the Pope and resigned on 10 July. Pope Pius XI, the former Archbishop of Milan who had once allowed uniformed Fascists to hold a service in the Duomo and been elected Pope in February 1922, supported Fascism insofar as it contributed to 'the pacification of souls'. Naturally the Pope was disturbed by the strong streak of anti-clericalism which ran through both Fascism and Mussolini himself. But unbeknownst to Don Sturzo, for one, since January 1923 Mussolini had begun secret negotiations with Cardinal Pietro Gasparri, the Vatican Secretary of State.

Cardinal Gasparri, referring to Mussolini's 16 November speech to the Chamber, had confided to the Belgian ambassador to the Holy See, 'Since 1870 (date of the seizure of Rome from the pope) there has never been any invocation of Divine Providence from the mouth of a single Italian sovereign or minister ... And it is a convert revolutionary who gives the example of a return to religious practice. Providence works in strange ways to ensure the happiness of Italy. As far as I am concerned I do not cry for Italian parliamentarism, when I see Mussolini move resolutely towards a conservative government.'[46]

The first meeting between Mussolini and Gasparri took place in January 1923 – either on the 19th or 20th.[47] Mussolini told Gasparri that Fascism could not have got power without Catholicism. Gasparri assured Mussolini that he would attempt to steer Don Sturzo towards the 'right'. But what Gasparri especially wanted was help to bail out the Banco di Roma, which financed all Catholic organisations and their newspaper the *Corriere d'Italia*, which was in desperate trouble. This Mussolini did at the price of the Vatican withdrawing support for Don Sturzo.[48]

Gentile's first reforms of the education system, introduced soon after-wards, pleased the Vatican, because they made religious instruction in schools and universities mandatory and another new law insisted that the crucifix – banned until now – be displayed in classrooms, barracks, public buildings and courts. Contraceptives and swearing in public were also made illegal. The Vatican was pleased, too, with the Grand Council deci-sion to ban PNF members from being freemasons.

The debate on the Acerbo Bill began on 10 July 1923 – the day Don Sturzo had resigned. The Fascists staged menacing demonstrations in Tuscany and Umbria, and Catholic clubs were sacked. Many feared the Fascists would break into the Chamber during the debate to launch the much threatened 'Second Wave'. Mussolini, for example, at the start of the debate wore a black shirt. The militia stood guard at the doors of the Chamber. Many appealed to the King to intervene. But in any case, however much the House of Savoy and the Vatican were at daggers drawn the King, like Pius XI, was broadly in favour of Mussolini. Likewise, out of an expedient desire to avoid conflict the liberal–conservatives, as usual, decided to support the government and vote for the bill. The Socialists and Communists would vote against.

The pressure from the Vatican meant that the *Popolari* parliamentary group now decided by 41 votes to 39 votes to abstain. This meant the bill's passage was certain and on 21 July it was carried by a hefty majority of 223 votes in favour to 123 against.[49] Those who voted in favour included Giolitti, Orlando and Salandra. In the Senate the bill was passed 165 to 41.

Fascist violence did not diminish against Catholic targets as a result of the abstention by most *Popolari* MPs. Just over a month later, on 24 August, two Fascists beat to death a priest, Don Giovanni Minzoni, at Argenta in the Ferrarese – Balbo's fiefdom. Don Minzoni, a First World War veteran decorated with the *medaglia d'argento*, was a fervent anti-Fascist.

There were other Fascist excesses such as the ransacking of Nitti's house on 29 November 1923. A month later (on 26 December), Giovanni Amendola, the leading liberal, was beaten up by Fascist thugs in the street in Rome. On 12 March 1924 Matteotti was treated likewise.

Mussolini, in a furious exchange of telegrams with Farinacci in August 1923, made no bones about his opposition to squad violence. 'I declare that I want to liberate the militia not from Fascism but from the party which is a vast pitiful panorama of imbecilic bigots and interminable object of mirth and daily scorn on the part of all our opponents. Stop. For months and months Fascism has been the only unsettling element in the life of the nation ... government has confronted and solved formidable problems, while provincial Fascism has never exited the bickering of the belltowers ...'

But *The Times* on 31 October 1923, to mark the anniversary of the March on Rome, commented,

It is beyond question that Italy has never been so united ... The Italians are impressed that Fascism is not simply a typical political revolution which has succeeded, but a genuine spiritual revolution. Fascism has abolished the parliamentary chess game; it has simplified the tax system and has greatly reduced the national debt, has improved public services enormously, especially the railways; it has reduced redundant bureaucracy, without causing serious unemployment; it has pursued an energetic and fortuitous colonial policy. All this is a difficult and praiseworthy achievement in its own right, but the greatest gain for Italy is that she has got back internal security and national pride.[50]

Mussolini was not confident enough to call immediate elections. But two foreign policy successes gave him considerable kudos at home, if not abroad, and undoubtedly influenced his decision to call them early in the new year. First, he sent the Italian navy to bombard Corfu on 31 August 1923, killing about a dozen civilians before sending in Italian troops to occupy the island. It was his first serious brush with the great powers – in particular Britain. The bombardment was Mussolini's response to the murder of an Italian delegation, headed by General Enrico Tellini, near the Greco–Albanian border inside Greece, where they were involved in an international effort, under the auspices of the Conference of Ambassadors, to define the border between the two countries. It was unclear who was responsible for the murders but regardless of that Mussolini sent the Greek government a seven-point ultimatum demanding various humiliating types of apology and swingeing compensation of 50 million lire. The Greeks accepted most of the Italian demands but said that 50 million lire was excessive. Mussolini reacted with the bombardment. There is some evidence[51] that he had planned to annex Corfu anyway and the murder of Tellini and his colleagues was a mere pretext. Soon after the invasion by Italian troops, for example, Italian stamps, overstamped Corfu, went on sale.

Naturally, the Greek government was furious at this act of war and so too was the British government. The Greeks took the matter to the League of Nations as a breach of the league's covenant which, among other things, carried the threat of sanctions. Mussolini insisted, however, that the only competent organisation to resolve the matter was the Conference of Ambassadors currently meeting in Paris to discuss the Greco–Albanian border issue. Reluctantly, the British agreed that the League of Nations hand the matter to the Conference – mainly because the French sided with Mussolini, hoping to get Italian support over their deeply controversial occupation of the Ruhr. The British, though very irritated with what Harold Nicolson, then a first secretary, called Mussolini's 'exuberant petulance' and his belief in 'might is right', decided they could not risk the Anglo-French entente.

A month later the conference had drawn up a slightly watered-down version of the Mussolini ultimatum and put pressure on Greece to accept it, which she did. In return, Mussolini agreed to withdraw Italian troops from Corfu. The Italian press saluted Mussolini for what it regarded as a triumph. Here was a prime minister, thought many Italians, who could stand up to the world on behalf of Italy – unlike his predecessors. But when Mussolini met Graham in October he admitted he had misjudged Britain over the Corfu incident and hoped for a return to good relations between Italy and Britain. He would do little to jeopardise those relations for more than a decade. Corfu was a diplomatic smack in the face for Britain and an early defeat for the League of Nations – a version in miniature of Mussolini's aggression in Abyssinia in 1935, which had such fatal consequences for the world.

Mussolini's second foreign success came on 27 January 1924 when he signed a treaty with Yugoslavia by which Italy finally got the city of Fiume. Fiume, after d'Annunzio had seized and lost it, retained enormous psychological importance for Italians. Under the Treaty of Rapallo, soon after Giolotti's gunboats had evicted d'Annunzio, it had become a free city. But in March 1922 a Fascist force had briefly re-seized it. New talks began but reached an impasse. Mussolini solved the impasse by offering Yugoslavia the adjoining delta zone and port, Porto Barros, in return for sovereignty over Fiume and its port. As a result the King awarded Mussolini the highest honour in his gift, the *Collare dell'Annunziata*, which made him a cousin of the sovereign. Mussolini had refused the King's offer of this the previous year.[52] On 16 March, the King took possession of Fiume in person.

January 1924 also saw Fascist Italy become the first nation to recognise the legitimacy of the Bolshevik government in Russia, now called the USSR, and in addition to sign a commercial treaty in particular for the import of Russian raw materials which Italy lacked, along with Britain, whose prime minister since December 1923 had been James Ramsay MacDonald as head of Britain's first Labour government. Given Mussolini's hatred of Bolshevism, this was a very odd thing to do. But Mussolini, who had already decided that the Bolsheviks had abandoned their attempt to run the economy along Marxist lines as hopeless and resorted to Capitalism, felt convinced that Bolshevism was not for export because of the crucial decision of the German people to reject it and his own triumph over it in Italy. Defending the move in the Chamber, he said that the 'spiritual relations' between the two countries were 'excellent'. He added that the Russian press alone had stood up for Italy against Britain, Greece and the rest, over Corfu. He justified it thus: 'The problem must be posed in terms of pure and, I would dare to say, brutal national interest: is it useful for Italy, for the Italian economy, for the expansion of Italy, for the well-being of the Italian people, is the *de jure* recognition of the Russian Republic, in as much as this recognition facilitates economic relations and therefore the growth of the Italian people? I answer yes.'[53]

His confidence boosted by these foreign policy successes, Mussolini decided to go to the polls in search of the popular mandate he craved. He dissolved parliament on 25 January 1924 and set the date for the elections as 6 April 1924. The opposition parties – the Communist and various Socialist parties, for example – might have swallowed their differences to form a joint list of candidates to contest the elections against that of the Fascists. But as usual they were unable to unite. As for the liberals and the *Popolari*, many in both parties, like Mussolini, felt that if the Fascist list won the elections, this would make Fascism less likely to resort to violence or dictatorship. This is what Mussolini had kept on saying. In the end the opposition parties presented twenty-three lists,[54] of which seven belonged to factions within the new Liberal party,[55] which had agreed to allow members to make up their own minds whether to join the government 'listone' – as it was called – or form their own parallel lists, though not to form opposition lists. Fascism was able to present itself to the country once again – just as it had in the summer of 1922 – as the only force capable of government.

Mussolini was determined that the election be peaceful and fired off numerous telegrams to prefects ordering them to stamp out violence from whichever quarter, especially Fascists. He told them to use 'all necessary preventative measures' to achieve this, adding, 'You must impede totally vandalistic acts especially against opposition newspapers.'[56] Where dissident Fascists were concerned, he ordered prefects and the provincial Fascist *ras* to stifle their propaganda and to make their lives 'impossible'.[57]

When finally drawn up, the government's *listone* represented a triumph for the *revisionista* position. The *listone* included many non-Fascists such as Orlando and Salandra, and other liberals seduced by Mussolini's siren cry – though not Giolitti who had decided to run his own list (one of the seven parallel liberal lists) while insisting he was not campaigning against Mussolini – as well as important industrialists such as the President and Secretary of the employers' organisation, Confindustria, Antonio Benni and Gino Olivetti. Incredibly Croce, of all people, urged Italians to vote for the government *listone*.

Mussolini could control the PNF at the centre but not out in the provinces and during the election campaign Fascist thugs sacked hundreds of opposition clubs and offices, assaulted hundreds of opponents and murdered the *massimalista* Socialist candidate, Antonio Piccinini, who was dragged out of his house in Reggio Emilia on 28 February 1924 and shot dead.

About 7.6 million Italians voted which was a turn-out of 63.8 per cent and up 5.4 per cent on the 1921 elections.[58] The government *listone* polled 4,305,936 votes and a parallel government list 347,552 votes – 66.3 per cent of the vote. This gave the government 374 deputies, of whom 275 were Fascists, out of a total 535 in the new parliament.[59]

The *Popolari* polled 637,649 votes, the numerous liberal-conservative lists 199,024 and the Republicans 112,906. As for the parties of the left, the two main Socialist parties, the *massimalista* PSI and the *riformista* PSU, polled 341,528 and 415,148 votes respectively, the PCI polled 268,191, and Bonomi's *riformista* Socialists, now called the Social Democrats, 100,174. Between them the two main Socialist parties – down from a combined total of 123 seats at the 1921 elections to 22 (PSI) and 24 (PSU) now – and the *Popolari* – down from 108 to 39 seats – had lost well over half their seats. The Communists, on the other hand, had increased their vote by a third and the number of their seats from 15 to 19.

Mussolini had only needed 25 per cent of the vote. He had 66.3 per cent. Fascist violence had not delivered him consent. Italy had. The King, at the opening of the new parliament, praised the new intake of MPs as the 'youth of the war and of victory who broke the circle which had encircled and withered the existence of the State'. Mussolini told the *Chicago Daily News*,[60] 'Italy is made [*fatta*]. Now we must make [*fare*] the Italians.'

Mussolini had his mandate from the people. But how should the people be governed, by force or consent? In the March 1923 edition of *Gerarchia* he had written an essay entitled 'Force and Consent' in which he said,

> I beg the liberal *signori* to let me know if ever in history there has been a government based exclusively on popular consent. There has never been such a government, there will never be one. Consent is as mutable as the sands on the seashore ... mankind is perhaps tired of liberty. It has had an orgy of it. Liberty today is no longer the severe chaste virgin for whom the generations of the first half of the last century fought and died. For the intrepid, restless, tough youths who face the twilight dawn of the new history other words exercise a much bigger fascination, and they are: order, hierarchy, discipline ... Let it be known, then, once and for all, that Fascism recognises no idols, worships no fetishes. It has already trampled, and if need be will step quietly once again, over the more or less putrid body of the Goddess Liberty.[61]

He returned to the theme in an introduction to Machiavelli's *The Prince*, (originally intended as a thesis in return for the proposed award of an honorary degree from the University of Bologna, which never materialised but published instead in the April 1924 issue of his monthly review, *Gerarchia*,[61a] edited by Sarfatti). In it he said that Machiavelli's view of the people was one of 'acute pessimism' which he says is 'sad but true'. He wrote, 'Like all those who have occasion for continuous and extensive intercourse with their own kind, Machiavelli is a despiser of men ... Men, according to Machievelli, are wicked, more fond of their possessions than of their own families, quick to change their opinions and feelings ...' He quoted Machiavelli variously to support this interpretation. For example, 'Men are more grieved by the loss of a farm than by the death of a father or brother, because death is sometimes forgotten but property, never.' Or else, rulers 'must assume that all men are wicked and will demonstrate their evil dispositions whenever given the chance ... Men never do anything good unless forced to, but where liberty abounds and where there is freedom everything immediately falls into confusion and disarray.'

Mussolini used his interpretation of Machiavelli's view of human nature as the basis for a critique of parliamentary democracy and the phoneyness of the idea of popular sovereignty. Referring to the English and French revolutions of the seventeenth and eighteenth centuries he said that in an attempt to end the discord caused by wicked men, rulers had introduced systems of government which attempted to allow 'power to rise up as an emanation of the free will of the people'. But he said,

> This is a lie and a delusion. First of all there is no definition of the people. Considered politically, it is a purely abstract entity. It is not known where it starts or where it ends. To apply the adjective sovereign to the people is a tragic farce. The people can at most delegate, but can never exercise any sovereignty ... Their cardboard crowns of sovereignty – acceptable when times are normal – are torn away at such moments, and the order comes to acquiesce in a revolution or to make peace or to march towards the unknown destiny of war ... You see, the sovereignty graciously extended to the people is snatched back from them at times when its need is realised. It is left in their hands only when it is innocuous or is felt to be so, namely in times of normal administration ...
>
> Can you imagine a war being declared by referendum? ... Regimes based completely on consent have never existed, do not exist, and probably never will exist ... Therefore one should rightly arrange matters so that when they (the people) no longer believe, they can be made to believe by force.

He ends by quoting *The Prince*: 'That is why all armed prophets have conquered and unarmed prophets have come to grief.' To understand Mussolini's political credo, one need look no further than this April 1924 essay of his on Machiavelli. To him, parliamentary democracy was 'a tragic farce' and the idea of the sovereignty of the people a 'cardboard crown'. But what was his alternative to be?

In addition to being a shrewd political thinker, Mussolini was a master political tactician. He had absorbed or destroyed à la Giolitti the parliamentary 'right' and 'centre' and he now looked to do the same to what remained of the parliamentary 'left'. Matteotti, first elected an MP in 1919 and since 1922 PSU party secretary, a fanatical personality, was determined to stop any such manoeuvre. The liberals had collaborated lying down. The *Popolari* had collaborated standing up. Mussolini, the ex-Socialist who always would regard himself as a man of the left, now tried collaboration with the Socialists. He had tried this before, most notably with the short-lived 1921 Pact of Pacification. Matteotti, Secretary of the PSU, for one, however, was bent on confrontation.

Carlo Silvestri, a Socialist and *Corriere della Sera* journalist, who knew Mussolini both in this early period and much later at Salò after his fall from power in 1943, said subsequently that he saw documents that Mussolini had with him which showed the extent of Mussolini's attempts in 1924 to strike a deal with the left – not just with the CGL but also the PSU.

During the fourth Matteotti trial, after the fall of Fascism in 1947, Francesco Giunta, in 1924 one of the most influential *ras*, member of the Grand Council and MP, who replaced Bianchi as PNF Secretary in October 1924,[62] said on oath, 'Mussolini did not have the courage to bring the Socialists into the government in 1922, but he would have brought them in at the end of June 1924.' King Vittorio Emanuele III's son, Crown Prince Umberto, would recall that his father had told him the same.[63] So would De Bono and so too Cesare Rossi, then Mussolini's press office director. The idea of a return to Socialism was deeply rooted in Mussolini at this time, Rossi said.[64]

On 30 May 1924, Matteotti spoke to the new parliament. His speech should have lasted an hour but constant heckling, whistling, and banging of fists on table-tops by the massed ranks of Fascist MPs meant it lasted four hours. When he said that the election had not been free because of violence and intimidation and had been rigged to boot, there was pandemonium. Matteotti knew exactly what he was up to with his pro-vocative speech. So inflammatory was his language that the speaker, the liberal Enrico De Nicola, ordered him to speak 'not prudently nor imprudently but parliamentarily'. Matteotti knew his speech would destroy all possibility of a deal between the Socialists and the Fascists.

Mussolini, who had sat watching the speech impassively throughout, marched out of the Chamber when it was over back to his office in Palazzo Chigi. In the reception area outside he ran into Giovanni Marinelli, treasurer of the PNF, and Rossi, director of his press office, and is said to have shouted, 'What's the Ceka doing? What's Dumini doing? If you weren't cowards, no one would ever have dared to give such a speech!'[65] The Ceka to which Mussolini is said by Rossi to have referred was the secret squad – more a gang than a squad – set up at some point in early 1924 to conduct punitive strikes on political opponents deemed in need of a lesson – often Fascist dissidents. Marinelli, PNF party treasurer, ran it. Subsequently, Mussolini denied the existence of a 'Ceka' in the Chamber. In a sense, he was telling the truth. For it did not have a name until the opposition gave it one, taken from that of the Bolshevik secret police – the Tcheka. And it was – certainly at this stage – no more than an informal organisation and tiny by comparison: a dozen or so thugs to be called on to target an individual politician when necessary.

Amerigo Dumini, born in St Louis, Missouri, in 1896, Fascist of the first hour, war veteran and holder of the *medaglia d'argento*, was the Ceka's chief hit man. Dumini was in the habit of introducing himself as 'Eleven Murders' Dumini. Rossi used him as a fixer and bodyguard. Despite his pedigree as a thug, he had intellectual pretensions and used to frequent Sarfatti's salon.

The 'Ceka' had not, so far as is known, murdered anyone to date. It had merely beaten people up. But Dumini had been at Sarzana in July 1921 when eighteen blackshirts had died and shot dead a *carabiniere*, for which he had been amnestied. He had also participated in the more recent ransacking of Nitti's house and the assaults on Amendola and Matteotti.

On 7 June Mussolini delivered his first speech to the new parliament at the end of the debate on the King's speech and everyone had expected him to reply in kind to Matteotti. But instead he appeared to hand the Socialists an olive branch. He said that the Socialist (PSU) MP Giuseppe Modigliani, with his characteristic *'acutezza'* had tried hard to 'unbottle' and 'refloat' the part of Socialism which was 'still possible' from that which was 'a prioristic, and thus negative' referring to the Socialism of, among others, Modigliani's fellow PSU MP Matteotti.

Two days later, on 9 June, Britain and Italy signed the treaty which ceded Jubaland to Italy – another foreign policy success for Mussolini. But the next day – 10 June – Matteotti disappeared and with him any hopes Mussolini might have had for a deal with the Socialists. Matteotti lived in Rome, in the area where the Ministry of the Navy is today near Piazza del Popolo. He left his house at about 4 p.m. on foot and walked along Lungotevere Arnaldo Di Brescia – along the Tiber – in the direction of the Chamber of Deputies at Montecitorio. It was extremely hot. He did not notice that a blue Lancia was parked in the shade of the plane trees opposite his house. But the concierge of another house, suspicious at the length of time the Lancia had remained parked there, did notice and took down its number plate. There were five people inside the Lancia: Dumini, Albino Volpi, Giuseppe Viola, Amieto Poveromo and Augusto Malacria who was the driver. The Lancia moved off and pulled up alongside Matteotti. Four of the five men got out and pounced on him. After a violent struggle they managed to bundle him inside the car, which then sped off towards Ponte Milvio. Matteotti continued to struggle and managed somehow to throw his MP's identity card out of the window – later found by a passer-by. He also managed to break the glass dividing the driver's compartment from the passenger's. But he was stabbed in the throat and died. His five abductors drove out of Rome fifteen miles along the Via Flaminia to a wood – the Boschetto della Quartarella – where a hundred metres from the road they buried the corpse in a grave less than half a metre deep. They had no shovels in the car and had to use the car jack.

It is probable – though there is no proof – that Matteotti's attackers had not intended to kill him. If they were going to kill him, the last place to do so would be in a car driving through central Rome. Secondly, they would also have worked out a proper plan to dispose of the body. If they were going to bury it they would surely have come equipped with shovels. As to whether or not Mussolini gave them their orders and what precisely those orders were – once again there is no proof either way. Even so, it is equally probable that Mussolini did not give orders to anyone to murder Matteotti. He was far too shrewd a politician to order such a thing, whatever he might have shouted in a fit of anger. Quite apart from scuppering his hopes for a rapprochement with the Socialists, to murder Matteotti would plunge the regime into a crisis which would threaten its survival. As Mussolini told Camillo Barrère, the French ambassador, who had gone to see him immediately he had heard the news, 'The idiots! They've killed him!'[66] Barrère was convinced that Mussolini had known nothing about the crime before it happened.

The news of Matteotti's disappearance appeared in the papers on Monday, 12 June. It caused a wave of revulsion in Italy. That afternoon Mussolini spoke to the Chamber and said that he did not know where Matteotti was but that he had issued orders to the police to launch an urgent inquiry. Opposition MPs greeted his words with wild heckling and a Republican MP, Eugenio Chiesa, shouted, '*Allora e complice!*' The words had the effect of pricking the bubble of awe around Mussolini and pointing the finger at him.

The concierge who had noted the number plate of the suspicious Lancia he had seen parked underneath the plane trees opposite Matteotti's house now went to the police, who swiftly traced the owner of the vehicle. It was none other than Filippo Filippelli, the Fascist editor of the *Corriere Italiano*, who had, it transpired, lent it to Dumini and was a close associate of Rossi. Filippelli claimed he did not know why Dumini wanted to borrow the car. The locating of the Lancia meant that a full-blooded investigation was inevitable – a cover-up now would have been far too risky. That evening the Fascist Grand Council met and it became clear that to survive, Fascism would have to sacrifice at least Finzi, Under-Secretary at Interior, Rossi and Marinelli. Mussolini agreed also to resign as Interior Minister.

That same evening, Amendola, leader of the non-'*listone*' liberals, and Turati, the PSU leader, decided that their MPs would boycott the Chamber in protest. This was the prelude to the so-called Aventine Secession, named after the withdrawal of the plebeians from Rome to the Aventine Hill in *c.*494 BC in protest at patrician rule. As a result the plebeians were given a voice in government. The secession proper took place on 27 June and involved all opposition parties – though not the '*listone*' liberals who had stood on the same ticket as the Fascists at the elections and not the Communists. But the Aventine MPs would fail to emulate the success of their ancient predecessors because what began as a walkout ended up as a lockout. For as Lyttelton notes, 'The maintenance of the "secession", once the initial effect of the crime and the protest had worn off, led the Opposition into a blind alley ... by remaining outside parliament, they gave the King the pretext to wash his hands of the situation.'[67] After all, the behaviour of the Aventine was unconstitutional. Furthermore, as Umberto II, the King's son, said, '... even admitting that the Crown was disposed to facilitate the counter-attack of the opposition, I do not understand why it should have done it from the moment when it was clear that the majority of the opposition was preparing a real and proper insurrection directed not only against Mussolini, but also against all institutions, including the monarchy.'[68]

The next day, 13 June, Mussolini spoke again to the Chamber. He admitted that Matteotti was the victim of a crime, that those behind it had already been identified and two of them, including Dumini, had been arrested. Dumini had been arrested at Rome station the previous day, the 12th, it would later emerge; sitting in a first-class compartment of the night sleeper to Milan awaiting its departure. Mussolini told the Chamber,[69] 'If there is anyone in this Chamber who has more right than anyone to be saddened by and, might I add, exasperated, it is me. Only an enemy of mine, who for long nights had been thinking of something diabolical, could have perpetrated this crime, which today fills us with horror and wrenches from us a cry of indignation.' The speech over, the President of the Chamber, Alfredo Rocco, on instructions from Mussolini, adjourned the Chamber *sine die*. Meanwhile Mussolini gave orders for the mobilisation of the militia in Rome, Florence, Bologna, Ferrara and Milan.[70] Rumours spread that Mussolini was planning a coup. Early that evening Matteotti's wife came to see him at Montecitorio. 'I know nothing, *Signora*,' Mussolini lied.[71]

Parliament was adjourned *sine die* but there was still the press, and the opposition moved swiftly to try to turn the Matteotti affair into the trial of Fascism. D'Annunzio broke his long silence and in a newspaper interview described the Fascist government as a *'fetida ruina'*. The view that at the very least Mussolini would have to go gathered momentum.

The waiting room outside Mussolini's office at Palazzo Chigi, normally chock-a-block with people keen to see him, was suddenly deserted, his *usciere* (usher), Quinto Navarra,[72] later recalled. One day during this period, Navarra, hearing only silence from Mussolini's office for an inordinate length of time, peeped around the door to see if he was all right and saw him kneeling on an armchair, banging his head against the wall. Senior Fascists who saw him in July found him with a three-day stubble. He was like 'a businessman about to declare himself bankrupt', recalled one.[73] The crisis affected his health badly as well and he had an attack of the excruciating stomach pains which would plague him for the rest of his life. Several of the doctors who treated him said that these were caused by a stomach ulcer. But the autopsy done on him in 1945 would find no evidence of an ulcer.[74] The illness was not caused by either alcohol or cigarettes, which he had more or less given up by now, or diet as he rarely ate meat. Nor was it caused by a wild social life. Mussolini hated social occasions – 'the distractions of what is termed "society" ' – and tried hard to avoid them at all costs. Likewise, he disliked Sundays because even if he was at work no one else was – and Christmas. 'The day in which he worked most relentlessly was the first of January; he never spent it with his family,' recalled Navarra.[75] His stomach trouble would haunt him for the rest of his life at times of stress.

Despite being extremely generous with money, Mussolini had never had genuine friends with whom he could unburden himself because he did not want them – he was afraid of friendship. Men inevitably sought 'profit and advancement' from friendship, be believed.[76] 'I cannot have friends. I have no friends. First of all, because of my temperament; secondly, because of my view of human beings. That is why I avoid intimacy and discussion ... Only from a distance do I follow the careers of my former comrades.'[77] 'Fundamentally I have always been alone. Besides, today, though not in prison, I am all the more a prisoner ... Contact with ordinary human affairs, an impromptu life amid the crowd – to me, in my position, these things are forbidden.'[78] He ensured, he said, that the droves of people with whom he had contact daily did not 'come into contact with' his 'inmost being'. 'I preserve my loneliness untouched.' In August 1943, held prisoner on the island of Ponza after his overthrow, he would write in the diary he kept there, 'In my life I have never had a single "friend" and I have often wondered if this were an advantage or a disadvantage. Today I think it has been a benefit. In this way many people are exempted from "feeling sorry for me", that is "suffering with me".'[79] He would tell Ludwig, 'I classify them [human beings] primarily into those whom I like and those whom I dislike.[80] Only his brother Arnaldo was a genuine friend – as opposed to someone he liked. But Arnaldo was in Milan. So too was Rachele, where she still lived with the children, and he had hardly seen her since becoming prime minister. Besides, she was a woman. He saw Sarfatti more than his wife because she came to Rome from Milan once a week to see him. But their relationship would never be the same. He did not have time to see her any more at her whim – only his. Furthermore, his sexual attraction for her – she was anything but a head-turner anyway – had waned. Snobbish, egotistical, arrogant, spoiled, this made her hit the roof.[81] But she found power irresistible. Once he got power she became even more obsessed with him. She wept. She whined. She waited, sometimes hours, to see him in vain. She accused him of insane jealousy. The truth was the other way round. 'My absurd lover, tyrannical and adored!' she wrote in March 1923.[82] Sarfatti had spent her adult life accumulating important people either as trophies or for what they could do for her. Mussolini, now her most important trophy, became ever less hers. The Rome-based American journalist Thomas B. Morgan acidly wrote of her, 'She ... basked in his reflected glory, satisfied to *meditate* that she had been a stimulation to the superman and *inwardly thinking* that he was partly her creation' (my italics).[83] The idea that Mussolini was in any way the creation of Sarfatti was, of course, nonsense. Without his occasional patronage her ambition to create a purely Italian school of art which she called Novecento – and defined as 'modern classicism' – would have foundered. Mussolini was interested only in the sexual conquest of women. Women bored him as people. At best, by now, Sarfatti had become an occasional shoulder to cry on. But Sarfatti was obsessed with her 'creation'. In an attempt to control him, she had found him a flat in the Palazzo Tittoni, in Via Rasella, near Piazza Barberini, where he had moved from the Grand Hotel in March 1923. The flat, which was on the top floor, 'was always filled with a strong smell of cheap eau-de-cologne, which he used instead of washing for which he didn't have the time or the inclination', wrote Monelli.[84] The bedroom was painted red and black with a big red carpet on the floor on which Mussolini was fond of despatching his lovers. In one corner was a small table on which were placed medals, crosses and religious trinkets. Through superstition, rather than faith in the Christian God, Mussolini never threw away objects of this kind given to him. In the drawing room was a piano and on a table 'two or three violins'.[85] There was no kitchen. The owner of the flat, Baron Fassini Camossi, who lived on the floor below, used to send him up cooked meals in the evening.

Sarfatti also found Mussolini a housekeeper, Cesira Carocci, a peasant aged about forty whose nickname was *La Ruffiana* (roughly translatable as 'The Arse-licker') and who called everyone '*mio cocco*' ('my coconut'). Sarfatti thought that this way she could exercise more control over Mussolini with a spy in his midst. The opposite happened. La Carocci, who was unmarried, worshipped Mussolini. She helped him tie his ties, she ironed his clothes and she listened to him play his violin. Mussolini preferred Beethoven to Wagner – he could not stand *Parsifal* though he loved Wagner's 'earlier, more melodious works' such as *Tannhäuser*. 'The language of music is international but its essential nature is purely nationalistic. Music seems to me the profoundest means of expression for any race of man ... If we Italians play Verdi better than do Frenchmen or Germans it is because we have Verdi in our blood.'[86]

In addition to *La Ruffiana*, the flat was also home for a while to Italia, Mussolini's lion cub, whose smell combined with that of the eau-de-cologne. Naturally the deeply bourgeois Sarfatti found the animal's stench deeply unpleasant. After several months Mussolini reluctantly gave Italia, which he took for walks on a lead, to Rome's zoo after she pounced on him one day and scratched him.[87] Mussolini loved animals, in particular cats. 'If I could do whatever I liked, I should always be at sea. When that is impossible, I content myself with animals. Their mental life approximates that of man and yet they don't want to get anything out of him: horses, dogs and my favourite, the cat.'[88] In 1943 he wrote that 'animals are superior to men because they have instinct and not reason'.[89]

It was during the summer of 1924, at the height of the Matteotti crisis, that Sarfatti began to write her biography of Mussolini – *Dux* – at her country house Il Soldo, near Lake Como, completing it that winter. It appeared first in English as *The Life of Benito Mussolini* in September 1925, and in June 1926 as *Dux* in Italian. Sarfatti must have worried that he would be a busted flush before it was published. Rachele was aware of Mussolini's relationship with Sarfatti, as she was aware of his philandering in general. She recalled, 'He didn't like them thin: whether they were blonde or brunette, tall or short, didn't matter to him much, but they shouldn't smell too much of perfume ... Today I can say that his *carnet* was abundant, but not all that much more so than the normal Italian who finds women pleasing and whom women too find very pleasing. I'm not trying, of course, to minimise the importance of my rivals, but ... I want to get one thing straight: my husband always slept *a casa*, in his own bed, except when he was travelling.'[90] Mussolini told his wife that Napoleon did not like perfume either[91] and Ludwig[92] that he would fall from power for the same reasons as Napoleon 'because of the contradictions in his own character ... that is what always leads to a man's downfall'. He admired Caesar more than Napoleon because he 'combined the will of the warrior with the genius of the sage' but Jesus Christ most of all. 'Just think to start a movement that has lasted 2000 years, which has 400 million adherents ... That is unparalleled.' Mussolini detested slippers because they were bourgeois and forbade his children to wear them.[93] As for shoes, once he had found a pair to his liking he would never throw them away.

Italy, unlike Britain, say, is a country where the conspiracy theorist is often right. So even where there is no conspiracy Italians invariably see one. This is what happened with the Matteotti affair. The truth here, as nearly always in life, is as banal as it is simple. Matteotti died by mistake as the result of a cock-up by a gang of Fascist thugs. That is not to say that Mussolini was not morally guilty of the crime nor actually guilty of the initial attempt to cover up the crime. He was in serious trouble. Public opinion had swung against him overnight.

On 14 June four ministers, Giovanni Gentile, Luigi Federzoni, Aldo Oviglio and Alberto De Stefani, threatened to resign unless Mussolini got rid of the leaders of his entourage at Palazzo Chigi – Rossi and Marinelli – as well as Aldo Finzi, Under-Secretary at Interior. He agreed. Finzi went, so did Rossi, and so too did De Bono, the Chief of Police and commander of the militia.[94] Rossi, who prided himself on being Mussolini's right-hand man, immediately went into hiding and wrote to him threatening to expose all he knew about the Matteotti murder if he did not help him avoid arrest. Mussolini did not reply and a week later Rossi gave himself up to the police and was held in custody. Given his anger with Mussolini for jettisoning him, Rossi's testimony must be treated with caution. He told the investigating magistrates that Mussolini had given him, Marinelli and De Bono orders to set up the Ceka to intimidate members of the opposition and kill them if necessary. The Ceka had been responsible for previous assaults on, for example, Amendola and for sacking Nitti's house. Mussolini had given the orders, he said, in those instances. But crucially he did not know whether this was also true in the case of Matteotti.[95]

Mussolini appeared doomed nevertheless. But who would cast the first stone? The opposition had retreated to the Aventine. What about the King? He had been away on a state visit to Spain and Britain but returned to Rome by train on 16 June. The next day Mussolini, who as prime minister usually met the King twice a week on official business, went to see him at the *Quirinale*. He handed the King the decree appointing the fiercely royalist ex-nationalist Federzoni in his place as Interior Minister, which the King signed. Later, his son, Umberto II, would say that his father had already decided that Mussolini was not involved in Matteotti's murder. The King did nothing.[96]

On 24 June Mussolini spoke to the Senate on a vote of confidence. Here, there had been no Aventine secession. The Senate was untouched by the Acerbo Law, and its members largely the same as when he came to power. During the debate the *Osservatore Romano*, the Vatican mouthpiece, went on sale to espouse the views of the Vatican for the first time. Mussolini should stay for the sake of stability, otherwise chaos would result, it commented. The Senate, like the King and the Vatican, sided with Mussolini. It voted 225 to 21 in his favour with 6 abstentions. Croce, as usual, voted for. He did so, he told a newspaper, because he believed that by supporting Mussolini this would force him to reject intransigent Fascism and lead him to a liberal–conservative government. To placate the King and the army Mussolini agreed that from 28 October the militia would swear an oath of loyalty to the King, not Italy. *The Times* on 5 July commented, 'For ourselves, we hope that Signor Mussolini, who is unquestionably a great administrator and a great political foreman of the works, will not lose his hold on the people.' The *Daily Mail*, an even greater admirer of Mussolini than *The Times*, said, 'We in England have confidence in Signor Mussolini; so have the Italians.'

However, on 9 July intransigent Fascism reared its head once more, when thousands of Fascists, led by Farinacci, marched through Florence to protest at Mussolini's attempt at a constitutional solution to the Matteotti crisis. Curzio Suckert (later he changed his name to Malaparte), chief intellectual of intransigent Fascism, fiercely criticised Mussolini in his publication, *La Conquista dello Stato*, and called on the forces of provincial Fascism to save the Fascist revolution with violence – the often talked about 'Second Wave'.

Throughout the torrid summer of 1924 an uneasy equilibrium prevailed. But then, on 16 August, a gamekeeper out with his dog found Matteotti's body after the dog began to dig furiously. Press coverage of the Matteotti affair became intense once more. Senator Albertini's *Corriere della Sera* – the voice of industry – turned against Mussolini, urging the disbanding of the militia and the restoration of statutory liberties. The Matteotti affair, however, did not stop Luigi Pirandello, the playwright, now becoming a member of the PNF – joining, among others, Guglielmo Marconi and Toscanini. (Pirandello would win the Nobel Prize for Literature in 1934.) By early November investigating magistrates had charged Rossi, Marinelli, Dumini and six others with offences relating to the abduction and murder of Matteotti. But their trial was postponed when the Catholic newspaper, *Il Popolo*, accused De Bono, the sacked head of the police and the militia, still a senator, of complicity in the murder and demanded his impeachment in the Senate.

There were to be four Matteotti trials in all. The first was the impeachment trial in the Senate in 1925 of De Bono, at which he was acquitted in 1925, and the second in November 1925 when Rossi and Marinelli went on trial and were found guilty but only of organising an act of violence against Matteotti – not murder. Not long afterwards, however, Marinelli was appointed the PNF's inspector general. Rossi fled to France but in August 1928, while staying in Lugano, Switzerland, was lured to the nearby Italian conclave of Campione by Fascist agents posing as tourists and arrested by Italian police. He was convicted of high treason and sentenced to thirty years in prison, though after ten years Mussolini commuted this to confinement on the island of Ponza.

The third trial, that of Dumini and the other four in the car, took place in March 1926. They were defended by Farinacci who heaped venom on the character of Matteotti to show that Matteotti had deserved to die. The court found three defendants – Dumini, Volpi and Poveromo – guilty of killing Matteotti but decided that the crime was not premeditated and the result of his provocation of the defendants. They were each sentenced to five years, eleven months in prison. The other two, Viola and Malacria, were acquitted.

The fourth trial took place in January 1947. The only interesting new evidence to emerge here was that of Carlo Silvestri, the Socialist journalist, who had known Mussolini well since the end of the First World War. Initially he believed Mussolini had ordered the murder of Matteotti and this led to his imprisonment for a time. Despite this he was very close to Mussolini at Salò, after the fall of Fascism in 1943 when Mussolini set up a rump Fascist State in the north of Italy. Gradually, he said, he had changed his mind about Mussolini's guilt. He told the court that on several occasions he had acted as an intermediary between Mussolini and the

Socialists, beginning in August 1922 – just prior to the March on Rome – and that in his opinion intransigent Fascists determined to place an insurmountable obstacle between Mussolini and the Socialists, and also the *Popolari*, were behind Matteotti's murder. 'I intend to reach the agreement because collaboration with the Socialists and the *Popolari* is the only possible solution for the salvation of Italy,' Mussolini had told Silvestri, he said. Mussolini could not have ordered the murder of Matteotti, he said, because he came from the PSU whose MPs included Baldesi and Buozzi, the same people he wanted to join his government. Dumini, Volpi and Poveromo were convicted of kidnap and premeditated murder, and sentenced to life. The court passed no judgment on whether or not – via Marinelli – Mussolini had given them their orders.

Mussolini and Fascism were becoming increasingly isolated. But the Aventine MPs continued their boycott of the Chamber. As Giolitti noted, 'Mussolini has all the luck. With me the opposition had never let up. With him it left the field wide open.' In early November Balbo sued *La Voce Repubblicana* for libel over a 1923 article, based on letters of his leaked to the newspaper by his enemies within Fascism, accusing him of being behind the murder of the priest Don Minzoni. He lost the case. This forced Mussolini to sack him as militia commander on 1 December, little more than a month after his appointment. He was replaced by a regular army officer, General Asclepia Gandolfo, which pleased the King and the army but displeased the *ras*.

Provincial Fascist *intransigenti* in several cities remobilised blackshirt squads and extremist Fascist newspapers attacked not the opposition but moderate Fascist ministers, especially Federzoni. Farinacci's *Cremona Nuova* fulminated against the '*politica rinunciatoria*' of the past two years.

It was now that thirty-three militia consuls – close to Balbo and probably acting with his knowledge – decided to try to end the impasse. In early December a group of senior Fascists including Balbo had met and decided to nominate a committee of five to take control in the event of an emergency. On 31 December the thirty-three consuls arrived at Palazzo Chigi with the excuse of wanting to wish Mussolini a Happy New Year. They gave him an ultimatum instead in the shape of a letter from the Florentine *ras* Tullio Tamburini: 'I am in Florence ... either you, guided by God, pursue a grandiose programme, as we hope, or we before becoming an object of ridicule will engage battle.' In particular, the consuls told him, either we all go to prison or none of us does. They left, unconvinced at his attempts to placate them and at a meeting immediately afterwards they talked of assassinating him. Farinacci, Tamburini and other *intransigenti* leaders then ordered 10,000 armed *squadristi* to converge on Florence, where they indulged in a wave of violence – including setting fire to opposition party offices and newspaper offices such as *Il Nuovo Giornale*.

But Mussolini dared not risk ordering the forces of law and order to clamp down on this resurgence of *squadrismo*.

He had, however, one democratic option left:[97]: he could get parliament to agree his proposal for electoral reform, dissolve parliament and hold new elections well before the conclusion of the Matteotti trial, which was anticipated in the spring. But he needed the consent of the King. If the King consented it meant, among other things, that the army still wanted him as prime minister. But the King might refuse. In which case Mussolini would have to resign.

On 2 January Mussolini went to the *Quirinale* to see the King but did not speak about the matter and left. Instead, at 6 p.m. that day, he instructed the Under-Secretary at the Presidenza, Giacomo Suardo (he had replaced Acerbo on 3 July 1924), to take the decree of dissolution with the date left open (*decreto in biancho*) to the King to sign. The King, recalled Suardo later, was perplexed and perturbed. He paced up and down. He agreed to sign out on one condition: that Mussolini came in person to retrieve the decree.[98] Mussolini duly returned to the *Quirinale* late that evening. There is no record of what occurred at this meeting. But the King would not sign the decree. He did, however, intimate to Mussolini that he would sign if the Chamber passed a new vote of confidence in Mussolini and approved Mussolini's proposal for electoral reform first.

Overnight, however, Mussolini decided on another, far bolder course of action. His request to the King to sign the decree dissolving parliament was in some ways similar to Facta's request to the King to sign the state of emergency decree at the time of the March on Rome. The King reacted similarly on both occasions. He changed his mind. First yes, then no. But Mussolini, unlike Facta, decided to ignore the King. We do not know exactly why. But it is probable that because the King had not given a point-blank no to Mussolini's request but a conditional yes, a maybe or, as the Italians say, a '*ni*', Mussolini felt that he had given his consent without formally giving it.

But after his meeting with the King Mussolini abandoned the idea of electoral reform and played instead what he had called in December 1921 in the Chamber the 'big card, which one plays once only, which imposes terrible risks and, once played, can never be played again'. Mussolini was an impulsive man who said that he always acted on instinct. Later he would tell Ludwig that he often had 'premonitions' and 'ominous fore-shadowings' and that he sensed 'spiritual atmosphere'. These things 'led' and 'troubled' him.[99] 'I have superstitions,' he added. 'I fear a *jettatore* (evil-eyed man) more than an anti-Fascist!' he told Navarra.[100] Mussolini judged people according to whether he felt they were lucky or unlucky – whether they were born under a good or bad star. He was keen on astrology and the reading of palms. He would often sideline highly competent people if he deemed them unlucky.[101] He trusted his instinct or, as he often put it, his blood. The big card, which Mussolini's instinct now told him to play, was dictatorship. This time, unlike in the case of Facta, the King did not stand in the way. *The Times* of 2 January reported that Mussolini was 'finished' and the next day predicted that he was about to announce his resignation.

That afternoon he went to the Chamber for the first session of parliament after the Christmas recess and spoke.[102] He began, 'Article 47 of the Statute says: "The Chamber of Deputies has the right to accuse ministers of the king and to send them to the High Court of Justice." I ask formally if in this Chamber, or outside this Chamber, there is anyone who wishes to invoke Article 47.' For several minutes there was noisy conferring. No one took up the challenge. Mussolini then issued a denial. 'It's said that I've founded a Ceka. Where? When? How? No one can say ... Truly there has been a Ceka in Russia, which has convicted, without trial, between 150,000 and 160,000 people, according to official statistics ... But in Italy the Ceka has never existed.' He then made a confession. 'All right, then, I declare here ... that I assume, I alone, the political, moral and historical responsibility for all that has happened.' But he warned, 'You are full of illusions! You have believed that Fascism was finished because I had repressed it, that it was dead because I had chastened it ..... But if I put the hundredth part of the energy that I have put into repressing it, into unleashing it, then you would see ... Italy, *o signori*, wants peace, she wants tranquillity, she wants *la calma laboriosa*. This tranquillity, this *calma laboriosa*, we will deliver it to her with love, if it is possible, and with force, if it is necessary. You can be certain that within the forty-eight hours succeeding my speech, the situation will be clarified across the board.' Mussolini moved that the Chamber be adjourned.[103] The Chamber, still minus the Aventine, agreed.

Back at Palazzo Chigi Mussolini now set in motion the moves which would, as he had said, clarify the situation. He ordered Federzoni, the Interior Minister, to telegram orders to the prefects to close down all 'suspect' organisations which might contain under whatever pretext '*elementi turbolenti*' or which 'tend to subvert the powers of the state'. Under existing Italian law this was legal because of the wide powers of discretion enjoyed by the prefects. The telegram also ordered prefects to confiscate all illegally held weapons. The telegrammed orders led to the closure of about 400 such organisations, even wine shops suspected of being gathering points for subversives, and more than 100 arrests within days. Another telegram sent at the same time explicitly ordered provincial fascist leaders to ban 'meetings ... processions, public demonstrations' by Fascists.[104] The next day Mussolini himself sent a telegram to the prefects ordering them to inform provincial Fascist leaders that any form of 'illegal disorder' by Fascists would seriously damage the government. This was the start of a process – rubber-stamped by parliament where the Fascists already had an enormous majority even without the absence of the Aventine – which abolished the rights of assembly and association, and by the end of 1926 would lead to the abolition of all political parties except the PNF.

But the King, the Senate, the Church, the army and industry, still remained potential reservoirs of opposition. Mussolini's dictatorship would never be absolute. Without the murder of Matteotti, however, it might not have happened. Yet Mussolini did not order the murder of Matteotti. He did not want Matteotti murdered. He was furious when he found out. Mussolini's speech of 3 January 1925 doomed liberal democracy in Italy. But it also doomed Fascist *intransigentisimo*.

From now on the *intransigenti* would be doing battle not with a prime minister but a dictator. As for the King, as usual, he had done nothing. And, by doing nothing, though he had no way of knowing, he had waved in dictatorship. But the *revisionisti* were also unhappy. Bottai's *Critica Fascista* described the crackdown as a 'liberal counter-revolution' designed to restore 'bourgeois normality'. It added, 'Perhaps without realising it ... we are reinforcing all those public institutions which we ought to have destroyed.'[105]

Mussolini, unlike the King and the opposition, had acted. In 1932 he would tell Ludwig, 'It has become ever more plain to me that action is of primary importance. This even when it is a blunder. Negativism, quietism, motionlessness, is a curse. I advocate movement. I am a wanderer.'[106]

Abroad, as at home, the Matteotti crisis caused if not outrage, certainly the wringing of hands. But Mussolini had at least one important foreign supporter – an Irishman and a Socialist to boot – the grand old man of letters, George Bernard Shaw. In 1927 Shaw, who used to holiday in Italy at Stresa on Lago Maggiore, wrote an article headlined A DEFENCE in the *Daily News*, in which he skilfully criticised the newspaper for writing a series of contemptuous articles on Mussolini 'as if the whole situation could be disposed of by representing the country as writhing in the grip of a brutal dictatorship', as he put it subsequently in a letter to Dr Frederick Adler, a fellow Socialist who was furious with his article.[107]

In another 1927 letter about the *Daily News* article to an unnamed recipient Shaw said that the Italian nation had accepted Mussolini *'faute de mieux*, several of them with enthusiasm', adding, 'Some of the things Mussolini has done, and some that he is threatening to do go further in the direction of Socialism than the English Labour party could yet venture if they were in power. They will bring him presently into serious conflict with Capitalism; and it is certainly not my business nor that of any Socialist to weaken him in view of such a conflict.' Italian anti-Fascist refugees in London and Paris, concluded Shaw, 'have it all their own way when they represent Italy as groaning under an unbearable tyranny. All the tyranny I saw was of the kind which our Capitalist press denounces as characteristic of Socialism ...'

In his reply to Adler about the *Daily News* article, Shaw had said,

It [the article] was a demand for common sense and common civility in dealing with a foreign statesman who had achieved a dictatorship in a great modern state without a single advantage, social, official, or academic, to assist him, after marching to Rome with a force of Black shirts which a single disciplined regiment backed by a competent government could have routed at any moment. To tell us that this extraordinary success was achieved by murdering one hostile deputy and administering castor oil to his supporters is childish. The obvious retort to it is 'If dictatorships can be established in Italy as easily, why did not the Communists establish the dictatorship of the proletariat by the same simple means? They have as much castor oil at their disposal as the *Fascisti*; and they have not hesitated to shoot and throw bombs.'

He went on,

In your letter you speak of the restoration of democracy in Russia and Italy. But do you seriously attach any value to the *status quo ante* in Russia and Italy? ... After the war the government in Italy was so feeble that silly syndicalists were seizing factories, and fanatical devotees of that curious attempt at a new Catholic church called the Third International were preaching a *coup d'état* and a Crusade in all directions, and imagining that this sort of thing was Socialism and Communism. Mussolini, without any of Napoleon's prestige, has done for Italy what Napoleon did for France, except for the Duc d'Enghien you must read Matteotti ...

As it is, the murder of Matteotti is no more an argument against Fascism than the murder of St Thomas à Becket is an argument against Feudalism ... Mussolini may have to hang some of the cruder Fascists for *trop de zèle* before order is completely restored in Italy. Meanwhile nothing is to be gained by pretending that any indictment can be brought against him by us or anyone else that he cannot meet by a crushing *tu quoque*. The blots on his rule are neither specifically Fascist nor specifically Italian: they are blots on human nature.

Still furious, Adler sent Shaw's letter to the *Manchester Guardian* who published it, provoking an equally furious response from readers, especially the exiled grand old men of Italian Socialism such as the historian and journalist Gaetano Salvemini. Salvemini trotted out the standard Socialist line that Mussolini was simply a creature of the bourgeoisie and that Shaw was a victim of Fascist propaganda fed him by Fascist diehards on his visit to Italy. The Fascists had 'bludgeoned, maltreated, wounded, arrested, deported, or forced to flee fifty deputies; murdered no less than a thousand followers of those deputies' and so on. Such violence was, of course, very small beer indeed compared with Bolshevik excess and Shaw felt forced to leap to his own defence. He wrote to the *Guardian* to say that Salvemini had revealed himself to be 'politically hopeless', adding, 'His letter exactly confirms my estimate of anti-Mussolinian Liberalism and explains how he has provoked the Fascist leader to describe Liberty as a putrefying corpse.' He had not spoken to any 'Fascist diehards' during his stay in Italy but had been 'stuffed with polemics against Mussolini'. He added, 'As far as I could work out, the ordinary middle-aged or elderly citizen gave Mussolini a Pragmatic Sanction ... The young people seemed to me to have what I can best describe as the Boy Scout mentality, and to associate their *esprit de corps* with Fascism.' Salvemini had accused Shaw of failing to recognise that Mussolini had got power only thanks to funds from the bourgeoisie and the support of army officers. Shaw's reply hit the nail on the head: 'The question is, why did Mussolini get that support instead of Signors Salvemini, Giolitti, Turati, Matteotti, and their friends, in spite of the fact that he was farther to the Left in his opinion than any of them?' Shaw was a Socialist who despised, not Socialism, but Socialists. So too was Mussolini.

On 19 December 1925 Rachele and Mussolini finally became man and wife in the eyes of the Catholic Church at a special ceremony presided over by a priest in the Milan apartment (they had had the three children baptised in the summer of 1923). He arrived with the priest and his witness, Raffaele Paolucci, while Rachele was cooking *tagliatelle* in the kitchen. A servant went in to tell her they were there. She would not come out. Finally he came into the kitchen and said, 'Come on, Rachele, don't make me beg.' Still she ignored him, so he untied her apron and propelled her into the drawing room.

Rachele did not visit Mussolini's Rome apartment until December 1926 – but as Mussolini dreaded Christmas, left before it. Her husband, she noted, had stopped smoking completely, got up each day at 6 a.m.[108] and went riding in the grounds of the Villa Borghese for an hour. He then had a shower, she noted with approval, followed by breakfast of fruit, bread and milk. He came home for lunch – pasta always, meat rarely, lots of raw and cooked vegetables. He returned from work at about 9 p.m. and ate a light supper followed by camomile tea, and went to bed at 10.30 p.m. He slept very soundly. The only material luxuries power had given him that he was passionate about were a red Alfa Romeo Torpedo, clean sheets, expensive ties, the flying and the riding – and women. Rachele stayed for less than a month – enough time to 'realise that the life of important people ... is a real bore'[109] and to become pregnant with their fourth child, Romano. Furthermore, she was furious. 'I found Benito in the care of *una domestica* called Cesira and it seemed that she was *la padrona*,' she recalled. But there was worse. 'In those days my husband had lived alone in the capital for four years. When he visited us he behaved like *un signore serio*, a good *padre di famiglia*. But in Rome I discovered that he was *un vero playboy*: very elegant, sports car, lion on a leash to impress beautiful women ... I burst into tears ... That row was useful, though, and even led to his good brother Arnaldo intervening to advise him to conduct a more ordered life, a life more in keeping with that of a married man with obligations to a wife and family ...'[110] Mr and Mrs Mussolini had, after all, been man and wife in the eyes of the Catholic church for a year by now.

10

DUX

Within two years of Mussolini's speech on 3 January 1925 to the rump Chamber of Deputies he had become a dictator. He achieved dictatorship by means of the force of law not the force of violence. There was violence, though few deaths, between 1925 and 1927. But he did not order it. For he knew that violence placed Fascism in great jeopardy. Without Mussolini, Fascism would have quickly torn itself apart. For as the famous Italian journalist, Paolo Monelli, no Fascist, wrote in 1950, 'They were both agreed, those first few years, Mussolini to want to become the *padrone assoluto* of Italy and the Italian people to encourage him in this ... and they shouted at him, and it was true: "*Sei tutti noi!*" (You are all of us!) ... These were also the years when Lady Chamberlain [Ivy, wife of Sir Austen] came to Italy wearing her Fascist brooch.'[1] It was difficult 'to resist the seduction of his eloquence', conceded Monelli who was a witness.[2]

Mussolini was proud of his dictatorship. In his famous May 1927 Ascension Day speech to the Chamber, for example, he would describe it as 'the regime of champions' and dismiss the criticism that under a dictatorship there is no opposition thus: 'Here arises the problem: but how can you live without an opposition? ... We reject in the most perfect and scornful manner this way of reasoning. The opposition is not necessary to the functioning of a healthy political regime. The opposition is silly, super-fluous in a totalitarian regime like the Fascist regime ... we have the opposition inside ourselves, dear *signori*. We are not old nags who need to be goaded on. We control ourselves severely. Above all, we find the opposition in things, in the objective difficulties of life, which give us a mountain of oppositions, which could exhaust spirits even superior to mine.'[3] Anyway, he added, '... the people has the perfect right to judge the regime of champions ... and if these champions are not up to the situation, the people has the right to manifest its severe judgement.' But the people had judged. Fascism had a broader consensus, he was con-vinced, than parliamentary democracy had had. 'This regime ... is a regime which rests on a party of a million individuals, plus another million young people, plus millions and millions of Italians ... No other government, anywhere in the world, has a more vast and profound base than the Italian government.' He went on, 'What is this universal suffrage anyway? We have seen it in action. More than 11 million citizens had the right to vote, and there were 6 million who every now and again couldn't give a damn. And the rest of them, what value could they have had, when the vote is given to the citizen simply because he is over twenty-one years of age ...?'

The dictatorship arose, however, not from megalomania but necessity – it was the only way to govern the Italy of the day. The road to dictatorship was 'the legal insertion of the Fascist Revolution in the State'.[4] The core of the creed was 'everything in the state, nothing outside the state, nothing against the state'.[5] The state – the totalitarian state as the Fascists called it – had to become the nation; the nation, the state. It was in Italy in 1925, that the word 'totalitarian' first gained widespread usage in a political context.[6]

Hegel, who struggled heroically to allow mankind free will, wrote, 'The great man in an era is he who knows how to translate into words the will of an era, to explain what this will is and to make it reality.' Mussolini, it seemed to many, was that man. On 29 July 1940, Bottai[7] wrote – somewhat ironically – in his diary that Mussolini was 'all instinct, "*da bestia*" [that of the beast], as he likes to repeat, very sensitive to historical connections, to the secret meaning of events, gifted with an admirable, miraculous power of intuition, a kind of *rabdomanzia* [divining] of history, a genuine genius of history, of which once conscious he immediately translates into action'.

British Ambassador Graham would write in 1935, 'My constant impression is that of a man who is the victim, not the master, of his destiny.'[8] Yet if destiny exists then by definition no man can be its master – only its victim. Destiny, possession, instinct, the stars, blood, Mussolini spoke of all these as things which did not just influence but governed his actions. And yet he spoke too of will, force, action and the lion's claw. But he was determined that man could challenge, defeat, use, manipulate destiny.

In July 1925, speaking about freedom, he spoke of destiny as well when he told peasants that 'true' liberty was the liberty 'to work, to own, to move, to honour publicly God, to exalt the victory and the sacrifices that he has imposed, *to be conscious of oneself and of one's own destiny ...*' (my italics).[9] In December 1925 he told the Chamber, 'To live for me means struggle, risk, stubbornness ... never to submit to destiny ...'[10] In October 1926 he told farmers in Rome, 'Those who reduce the entire complexity of the phenomena of life to certain formulas will have to admit ... that between the forces of life and of history there is also the force which is called human will.'[11] In March 1926 he said, 'The wheel of destiny passes. He who is wise is he who ... seizes it in the minute in which it passes by in front of him.' Destiny if good could be seized; if bad wrestled. And yet, in March 1945, a month before his death, it was as if his destiny, not free will, had been in charge all along. He told a journalist, 'I will go where destiny wants, because I have done what destiny told me.'[12]

By the end of 1927 Fascism had stamped its mark on the era. As if to confirm this, from December 1926 the *fasces* – the axe encased inside a bundle of rods – became incorporated in the state insignia. In October 1927, the Fascist calendar was introduced and it became obligatory to put the Fascist date, in Roman numerals, next to the traditional date on official communications: '*Anno I*' of the *Era Fascista* beginning on 29 October 1922 – the date when the King appointed Mussolini Prime Minister.[13]

The biggest threat to Fascism came from within Fascism. Farinacci and many of the most powerful provincial leaders wanted the party which was their power base to control the state. This had happened in Soviet Russia and would happen in Nazi Germany. But it would mean getting rid of the monarchy which Mussolini dared not do because that would have led to a civil war, which the Fascists would probably have lost. Whether his motive was to keep power or to preserve peace, he was determined not to alienate the King and the army.[14]

The most obvious schism within Fascism was between Farinacci and Bottai; between *intransigentismo* and *revisionismo*. Mussolini said that they were merely 'two keys on the same piano' but Bottai's *Critica Fascista* said that while he was Fascism's 'Holy Water' Farinacci was its 'Devil'.[15] Bottai did not believe that the party should control the state but that it should connect the state with the nation via its officials who should be elected by members and enjoy complete freedom of speech.

There were many other currents of opinion within Fascism – the unions, the ex-nationalists, the *fiancheggatori* – notably described in an article in *Critica Fascista* in 1925 as 'The Five Souls of Fascism' – each one more or less at odds with the other.[16]

The 3 January speech and the closure of organisations deemed subversive, and the related mass arrests in the forty-eight hours which followed it, took the King, as everyone, by surprise. The three remaining non-Fascist ministers resigned and the grand old statesmen, Giolitti, Orlando and Salandra, finally passed over to the opposition – though unlike the Aventine secession they remained in parliament. The King, as usual, who said, 'I wasn't expecting it and I wasn't even warned,'[17] could have put a stop to Mussolini and, it seemed, he was not pleased with the speech. His aides even told Amendola, the Liberal MP and driving force behind the Aventine secession, to continue to wait on events as the King had finally decided to get rid of Mussolini. Probably, the King had decided to do no such thing. The aides had tried to push him to do it and he had given them one of his typical ambivalent responses which they had interpreted as agreement. Even the Socialists – who had not so long ago staged a walkout of the Chamber during the royal address – having lost faith in their own ability to affect events either via the Aventine secession or working-class protest, now regarded Vittorio Emanuele as the only hope of ousting Mussolini.

So, placing its faith in the King, the Aventine still refused to return to parliament, where it would have had some effect. The only positive response it made to the 3 January speech was a moral protest in the shape of a pedantic manifesto. But the King, despite his unhappiness with the turn of events, as usual did nothing. It was not so much that he actively wanted Mussolini to remain. It was that by now he had lost all faith in the opposition as a viable alternative. He was especially irritated by the continued refusal of the Aventine to return to parliament. Yet as late as June 1925 the Aventine still expected the King to move against Mussolini. Meanwhile it continued to remain off stage, waiting. The longer it refused to attend parliament, the more convincingly the Fascists could say that it had forfeited its right to be in parliament. The King, undoubtedly, agreed. Anyway, if he had forced Mussolini to resign the likelihood of civil war – or at the very least the return of widespread squad violence – was very strong. Gino Sarrocchi, a supporter of Salandra and one of three ministers who resigned as a result of the 3 January speech but who remained in parliament, later said that the reason why he and other liberal-conservatives did not oppose Fascism even now was fear of Socialist or Communist revolution – that 'in that historical moment, whether right or wrong, the liberals of the right did not believe it possible to consider that the end of the revolutionary danger was near ...'[18] Despite this others noted that the Fascist and Bolshevik regimes had many similarities – a fact not lost on the Soviet government, which had been recognised by Mussolini in 1924 and which actively sought an alliance with him in 1925–6.[19] When, in June 1925, the Senate acquitted De Bono in relation to Matteotti's murder and the beatings of Misuri and Amendola, the King's mind was made up. In July 1925 Amendola's political career ended when Fascist thugs beat him up again, this time so severely that he decided to leave Italy for France. Eight months later he died of a brain tumour in Cannes. Despite the removal of its driving force, the Aventine continued its boycott of parliament.

Il Duce, as he was increasingly called, had survived the Matteotti crisis and would soon come to enjoy semi-divine status. But on the evening of 15 February 1925 he fell gravely ill. Still only 41, he collapsed after vomiting blood and was forced to take to his bed. He did not re-appear in public again until 23 March when he made a brief speech from the balcony of his office at Palazzo Chigi. News of the illness could not be kept quiet. Rachele was not allowed to come to Rome from Milan as part of an attempt to stifle rumours that the Duce was dead. If Mussolini died now, so too would Fascism – so crucial was he to its survival. No other Fascist had his charisma and cunning. Fascism without him was quite unthinkable.

Neither Mussolini nor anyone else ever made an official comment as to the nature of the illness – unofficially, it was said to be flu. The situation was so serious that a famous Italian specialist, Professor Sir Aldo Castellani, was called from London to treat Mussolini. Castellani diagnosed a duodenal ulcer, he later wrote, and he also discovered a notable enlargement of the liver. He put Mussolini on a strict diet and treated him with doses of alkeli.[20] Mussolini had suffered excruciating stomach pains before, notably in 1924, at the height of the Matteotti crisis,[21] but not as bad as this. No doubt because of Professor Castellani's diagnosis, he was convinced that he had an ulcer. But, as his autopsy would reveal in 1945, he did not have an ulcer. The probable explanation is that he suffered from 'hypochondriacal nervous symptoms . . . which got worse or better depending on external circumstances'.[22]

After several days Castellani felt confident enough to return to London. He had also taken a blood sample to check among other things for syphilis, which Mussolini had once tested negative for, and which he might have contracted subsequently, given his continued libertinism. In addition his absence in public had naturally caused rumours to spread like wildfire about the state of his health – these included resurrection of the old one about the syphilis which the gossips insisted he did have and which now they said had finally got the better of him. Impatiently, Mussolini telegrammed Castellani in London for the results of the blood test. Castellani telegrammed back to say that the test was negative.

By 1922 Mussolini had given up cigarettes and banned others from smoking in his office[23] and the only alcohol he drank was red wine in moderation. He had become obsessive about his diet. He hardly touched coffee at all but drank as much as three litres of milk a day (these days, anyone suffering from stomach ulcers is under strict orders not to touch milk). As for food, he ate lots of pasta, fresh fruit and vegetables, but little meat. He said that he spent no more than ten minutes eating a meal and aimed for three. In 1937 he would tell an American journalist that he had not been ill since 1925 and if he felt any slight discomfort he fasted for twenty-four hours.[24] When Castellani conducted a check-up on Mussolini a year after his collapse he found him in good health.

Mussolini had destroyed the parliamentary opposition *de facto* and it would not be long before he delivered it the coup de grace *de jure*. With the King quiet the greatest threat to Fascism came from within – specifically from the PNF. Before the March on Rome the party had been Mussolini's only power base. Thanks to the party he had got the government. Now he wanted to get the state as well. Though the aim was the *fascistizzazione* of the Italian people, this had to be a 'spiritual, not a mechanical or quantitative process',[25] not via the violence of *squadrismo*. That would have the opposite effect.

Farinacci and the *intransigenti* on the other hand saw the party as the guardian of what he said was the movement's 'apostolic spirit'; its task to interpret 'the will and thought of the Fascist masses'.[26] The squads were the priest soldiers of the revolution. 'Heroic violence attracts youth, calmness repels them', commented Balbo's *Corriere Padano* in September 1926.

Initially, in the summer of 1925, the main target of *squadrismo* was the Catholic lay organisation *Azione Cattolica*, accused by the Fascists of being a political organisation. In June the Pope himself had protested in person about one incident – an attack on a religious procession in Rome to which Farinacci retorted '... Fascism, just as it has defended religion, so will it combat furiously ... those who use religion as a political instrument.'[27] According to Interior Ministry figures, 35 Fascists were killed and 355 injured in 1925, compared with 27 non-Fascists killed and 388 injured.

Much of Farinacci's support came from the agrarian *piccola* and *media borghesia* – the very people, many of them small owner or tenant farmers, who had been so crucial to the success of Fascism in its early days. They were an extremely significant group in a country of 40 million people whose economy was still largely agricultural. In 1921, for example, there were 4,177,800 privately owned farms in Italy, compared with 2,257,266 in 1911.[28] This phenomenal growth in small owner farmers in the first quarter of the twentieth century – a new class – was due to the breaking up and selling off of the enormous feudal estates by the aristocracy. Understandably, this new rural-based class wanted no truck with trade unions and so were virulent opponents of Fascist syndicalism. They were also hostile to big business. Later they would avidly support Mussolini's imperialist ventures and anti-Semitic laws. Many were Republicans.

But Mussolini's hands, for the moment, were tied. He felt he had no choice but to make a significant concession to the Fascist *intransigenti*. Consequently, on 12 February 1925 – three days before his collapse with stomach trouble – Mussolini, via the Fascist Grand Council which agreed the proposal unanimously, had appointed Farinacci General Secretary of the PNF. Federzoni, the ex-nationalist, was still Minister of the Interior. While Farinacci stood for illegal violence, Federzoni stood for legal violence. Mussolini knew that apart from Balbo, Farinacci was the only person who had sufficient grass roots support to win the confidence of the party. By promoting him to the second most powerful position within Fascism, Mussolini hoped that both he and the *intransigenti* would feel they had won a victory. He hoped that it would diminish their desire to resort to *squadrismo* and the use of the *santo manganello* as the solution for everything.

But in the summer of 1925 Farinacci started to encourage the reforming of the squads and the use of violence. The previous summer at the height of the Matteotti crisis, the squads had begun to spring up again, especially in the big cities with a large working-class opposition to Fascism, often thinly disguised as sporting clubs with suitable sporting names. The squads were highly informal organisations bound by personal ties, 'coming together when specific needs or opportunities presented themselves; little communities gravitating round a particular café or brothel. It followed that the problem of *squadrismo* could not be solved by organisational measures alone; so long as the "spirit of opposition" to official directives survived, and so long as individuals within the Fascist movement preserved their old ties, the squads could reappear in times of crisis as if by magic.'[29] Once again, as before the March on Rome, these squads soon became rivals to the regular police; a form of political police force – or mafia – who kept opponents of Fascism in a state of permanent intimidation. Increasingly, they became involved in enforcing protection rackets and other corrupt activities of the provincial *ras*. Farinacci, himself steeped in corruption, encouraged the process.

As a counter to Farinacci, Mussolini knew he could rely on his Interior Minister, Federzoni, the ex-nationalist, who was a rigid opponent of illegal squad violence. But the trouble was that Federzoni in turn had to rely on the provincial prefects to enforce the rule of law. And to date the prefects had proved far from reliable when it came to showdowns with the Fascist squads – both before and after the Fascist takeover. This was because the prefects, appointed by central government, needed the support of the PNF, and hence the local PNF bosses, to retain their posts and also because to quash civil disorder they had to rely on the militia which had replaced the *Regie guardie* in 1923. But given that the militia was formed from the disbanded squads which had marched on Rome, its sympathies were likely to be with the squads. In his memoirs, Federzoni wrote, 'One of the most perfidious bright ideas of the extremists, with the aim of maintaining the country in that state of continuous turmoil which it hoped would subject it to the uncontrollable domination of the party, was the reconstitution of the *squadre d'azione* ... Farinacci was responsible for their resurrection and multiplication ... In the years 1925 and 1926 the revival of the *squadre d'azione* became a truly pernicious cause of disorder.'[30] But as Federzoni wrote to Mussolini in April 1926, 'If a disgraceful act of whatever kind took you away even only temporarily from the direction of the state, there would be chaos. This constitutes the tragic greatness and, at the same time, the only weakness of our situation.'[31] Mussolini's great strength was that outside Fascist circles he, not the likes of Farinacci, enjoyed extraordinary prestige. The Italians never gave their consent to Fascism; they gave it to Mussolini.

A much bigger threat to Mussolini's life, and hence to Fascism, than his stomach was assassination. There were four attempts on his life between November 1925 and November 1926. Two came within a whisker of killing him. There would be more in the future but all those were foiled at the early stages of plotting. 'In Italy today it is said, generally, that Mussolini has escaped sixteen attempts,' the American journalist George Seldes would write in 1935.[32] But these early ones, when Fascism was still there despite the Matteotti crisis but still vulnerable, were the most dramatic. The longer the Aventine secession failed to achieve results, the more the murder of Mussolini came to seem the only answer.

In such a climate it suited Mussolini that attempts on his life receive as much press coverage as possible. For each one presented him with an excuse – in the interests of stability – to introduce legislation which increased his grip on power. Later, with the dictatorship established, news of such attempts would have had a negative propaganda effect. It would call into question the claim that Mussolini ruled by consent. Indeed, in these early years in power, attempts on his life suited him in another way, as long, of course, as they failed. For his survival of them contributed to the growing idolatry of him and the feeling that, if not invincible, at the very least destiny was on his side. But his lust for the crowd always left him vulnerable to assassination.

The first assassination attempt took place on 4 November 1925, the seventh anniversary of Italian victory over Austria in 1918, and ended without a shot being fired. Tito Zaniboni, a member of the Palazzo Giustiniani masonic lodge and PSU MP (Matteotti's Socialist party), was arrested in possession of a sniper's rifle with telescopic lens in room 90 on the fifth floor of the Albergo Dragoni fifty metres across Piazza Colonna from Palazzo Chigi where Mussolini was due to appear on the balcony that morning at 11 a.m. to make a speech to mark the occasion. Zaniboni had donned militia uniform so as to be able to enter the area without attracting suspicion. That Zaniboni was both a Socialist and a freemason was a red rag to the Fascist bull. Throughout 1925 the Fascists had stepped up their campaign against Freemasonry.

The month before Zaniboni decided to act, Florence was the scene of an appalling outburst of squad violence, largely directed against the freemasons though also against Socialists which had been whipped up by the Fascist press. Precise figures for the number of dead in the *Fatti di Firenze* do not exist, but there were at least eight and they included the ex-Socialist MP Gaetano Pilati, shot in his bed in front of his wife by three Fascists who had broken in at dead of night.

It was in this febrile atmosphere that the Socialist freemason Zaniboni seized his moment. Originally, he had been among those Socialists who had been most keen to negotiate some sort of working relationship with Fascism and had been among the promoters of the 1921 Pact of Pacification. But since Matteotti's murder he had spent many months in secret talks with many different people trying in vain to garner support among anti-Fascists for various plans to overthrow Mussolini including a *coup d'état*. He had even gone twice to see the King to urge him to get rid of Mussolini – to no avail. He had been given 5000 lire by the Palazzo

Giustiniani masonic lodge to organise an anti-Mussolini demonstration but that was as far as the lodge was prepared to go. The masons had supported the March on Rome but turned against Fascism when in 1923 the party – even though many senior Fascists such as Farinacci and Balbo had been masons and may, many suspected, still have been – banned members from being masons. In the end Zaniboni, having failed to attract anything other than lukewarm support for his other ideas to oust Fascism, decided to assassinate Mussolini. His action was a sign of how impotent was the position of the Aventine. Unfortunately for him, an acquaintance he talked to about the plan tipped off the authorities. The police waited until he was inside the hotel room complete with rifle before arresting him at 9 a.m. Mussolini had been informed by the police of the plot to kill him and appeared on the balcony only ten minutes late.

General Luigi Capello, who held a senior position within the Palazzo Giustiniani lodge, was simultaneously arrested in Turin. The general was accused of being a party to the plot, which he denied. He admitted that he had conspired with Zaniboni in the recent past to plot a *coup d'état* among other things, but insisted he had not been in contact with him for several months before the assassination attempt except once in October when he refused to take part. But he, like Zaniboni, was sentenced in 1927 to thirty years in prison. Despite the insistence of the Fascist press that the Zaniboni attempt was a plot by freemasonry rather than the action of one man acting more or less alone – given that both Zaniboni and Capello were masons – all attempts to implicate other senior Palazzo Giustiniani masons failed. But just as with the Jews, so with the freemasons. Certainly, it was true that freemasons occupied positions of influence in Italy, as elsewhere, and it is true that by now they opposed Fascism. And it is true also that Zaniboni was a mason.

Following the Zaniboni attempt, Mussolini staged a press conference for foreign journalists at which he was asked, 'Could your excellency explain the reason for the Fascist war on masonry?' Mussolini could. He replied, 'I am very glad you asked that question because there is a lot of misunderstanding in Anglo-Saxon countries over this question. We must once and for all make clear the great difference between English and American masonry and the political masonry of Italy ... Italian masons have nothing in common with English masons except the name ... The work of masonry on behalf of our independence has been much exaggerated.' (This is a reference to the fact that Garibaldi was a mason who called masonry his bulwark of liberty.) 'The sect must be absolutely abolished because its influence is deleterious to discipline in the army, to the impartiality of the courts, and a subversion of order that should obtain in all public offices ... Fortunately, Fascism has struck Italian masonry such a blow that it will be difficult for it to regain its legs again for some time ...'[33] Elsewhere Mussolini described masonry as 'this shady institution with its secret nature has always had in Italy a character typical of the briber and the blackmailer ... Its secret character throughout the twentieth century, its mysterious meetings, abhorrent to our beautiful communities with their sunlight and their love of truth, gave to the sect the character of corruption, a crooked concept of life ... This is a war without quarter, a war of which I am a veteran ... Italians won this battle for me. They found the cure for this leprosy ...'[34]

Raoul Palermi, grand master of the Palazzo Jesù lodge, left Rome on the advice of police, for Palermo. Charges against Domizio Torrigiani, grand master of the Palazzo Giustiniani lodge, in connection with the Zaniboni attempt were dropped for lack of evidence – the same Torrigiani that Mussolini had been so keen to get the backing of just before the March on Rome. Nevertheless he was sent to *confino* (enforced exile) on the remote island of Ponza.[35] There is no doubt that Italy's freemasons had been plotting to overthrow Mussolini. There is no doubt too that, egged on by Capello, Zaniboni had acted alone.

The Zaniboni assassination attempt promoted a wave of support for Fascism. 'You can't find an anti-Fascist if you paid him in gold,' wrote Balbo.[36] The reaction of the Fascist government was to ban the party Zaniboni belonged to – the PSU – and subject the masonic lodge to which Zaniboni belonged – that of Palazzo Giustiniani – to a campaign of harassment. Fascist squads, acting on their own initiative, sacked opposition newspaper offices and the homes of masons.

The *Fatti di Firenze* had infuriated Mussolini. He objected to such wanton squad violence on both a tactical and moral level. But Farinacci saw violent *squadrismo* as the only way, however risky, to establish the Fascist Revolution – the total destruction of the *ancien régime* not just the dressing of it up in a black shirt, the so-called Second Wave.

For Mussolini violence, to be practical and moral, had to be ordered from the centre and in a good cause or not at all. 'The French Terror merely hastened the Restoration,' he wrote to Farinacci in August 1926.[37] His view on violence had always been the same. In 1927, he would tell the Chamber in the famous Ascension Day speech, that whereas once *squadrismo* had been '*grande*' and '*eroico*', it was now '*assurdo*' and '*idiota*'.[38]

Mussolini would use the *Fatti di Firenze* of October 1925 to strike a deadly blow at Farinacci, who defended the violence as 'legitimate exasperation', and *squadrismo*. On 5 October Mussolini vented his rage at a Grand Council meeting. His speech notes illustrate his fury: 'It is not Fascist, not Italian – not timely, chivalrous or surgical violence ... And all this under the noses of 10,000 English *and* Americans.'[39] He despised tourists because they were idlers who treated Italy as a museum and in particular the animal-loving English ones who had even complained when he placed a live wolf – symbol of ancient Rome – in a cage at the *Campidoglio*.[40] But he realised how influential such tourists were in forming opinion. Apart from anything else, his daughter, Edda, was due to start any day now at the exclusive Florentine finishing school – the Collegio di Poggio Imperiale (which she would hate).[41]

The Grand Council agreed a motion instructing the prefects to order all Fascist *federali* – the official title of the provincial party leaders colloquially known as *ras* – to disband any squad still in existence 'of whatever kind with whatever name and with whatever uniform' and enlist them in the militia, and to expel from the party any *federale* who refused to comply. *Squadrismo*, said the Grand Council motion, 'no longer has, three years after the March on Rome, any historical or political justification' and that those responsible for it 'sabotage the legal insertion of the Fascist Revolution in the State, the work to which the Fascist Government dedicates its energies every day'.[42]

Mussolini also dispatched Balbo to Florence – and conspicuously not Farinacci whose task it should have been as PNF General Secretary – to conduct an inquiry into the violence. As a result, the Florence *fascio* was dissolved and fifty Florentine Fascists expelled from the party. In December the *ras* of Florence himself, Tullio Tamburini, was dismissed and dispatched to a politically harmless sinecure in Libya. In addition, the prefect of Florence and chief of the city's police were replaced. Perhaps most significantly, the cosy link between the leaders of the local party and the commanders of the local militia, who were said to be 'completely tied and enslaved' to the local party, had been severed.[43] Balbo had done what the Duce wanted.

The *Fatti di Firenze* led to a purge of the PNF throughout Italy. In a telegram to the prefect of Cremona dated 13 October Mussolini said, 'Please communicate to the honourable Farinacci the following ... "I do not accept *squadre* of any kind ... My orders are precise. All *formazioni squadristiche* ... will be dissolved at whatever cost, repeat whatever cost. It is high time to make the necessary distinction: Fascists with Fascists, criminals with criminals, profiteers with profiteers and above all it's necessary to practise moral intransigence repeat moral." '[44] In an attempt to retain his post, Farinacci complied with the prefects to help demobilise the squads elsewhere in Italy and purge the PNF of its violent and criminal elements.

The *Fatti di Firenze* and the shake-up of the PNF which followed signalled the defeat of the bid by Farinacci and *intransigenza* to dominate Fascism by means of the PNF. Farinacci remained as PNF secretary only until March 1926. The final straw for Mussolini was when Farinacci insisted on acting as defence lawyer for Dumini and the other defendants in the 1926 Matteotti Trial. Mussolini was determined that the trial, which began on 16 March and ended on the 24th – deliberately staged to avoid publicity in distant Chieti like similar lesser political trials – should not be used either by Farinacci or the opposition for propaganda purposes. Farinacci refused to comply. He wanted the trial to be the trial not of Matteotti's murderers but of anti-Fascism. The Grand Council sacked Farinacci on 30 March. He retired, temporarily he thought, to his Cremona fiefdom. Federzoni was said to feel 'trionfante' at the news.

Mussolini continued to be exasperated by Farinacci and was especially furious when Farinacci paraded himself as poor, as a telegram he sent to the prefect of Cremona in September 1928 shows: 'Communicate the following to the honourable Farinacci "... I do not doubt that you were a beggar in 1922, but I deny in the most rigorous manner that you have remained a beggar even in 1928 ... Real beggars do not travel by auto-mobile and frequent luxury hotels ... I find false beggary odious like exhibitionism pescecanesco (dogfish-like)." '[45]

Deprived of a major role in the regime, Farinacci sulked and raged by turn in his Cremona fiefdom. He would never hold a party or government post again. But he would remain a member of the Grand Council to the bitter end.

When speaking to Mussolini, the new general secretary, Augusto Turati who had been the leader of the Fascist unions in Lombardy, used the formal 'lei' and called him 'Presidente', whereas Farinacci always used 'tu' and called him 'Benito'. Mussolini's relationship with Turati was not emotionally charged, as it was with Farinacci. But under Turati the PNF became what Mussolini wanted it to be: 'the conscious tool of the will of the state'.[46] Under Farinacci the party had been a thorn in Mussolini's side and hence to the survival of Fascism – though that is not how Farinacci viewed things. From now on the party became Mussolini's tool. On 18 October 1926 the Grand Council reformed the PNF constitution: Mus-solini became formal head as 'Il Duce del Fascismo' and the Grand Council the 'supreme organ of Fascism'. Together these two would now appoint not just the general secretary but all party officials from top to bottom especially the federali – previously provincial officials had been elected by provincial party members. The chief weapon of the PNF from now on in its mission to instil what Turati called the 'spirit of the revolution' in the Italian people would not be the manganello but propaganda.

During 1926 party membership had grown from 600,000 to just under 1 million by the end of the year, at which level it would remain for several years. By the end of 1927 Turati had expelled 2000 party bosses and 30,000 party members who were die-hard intransigenti, and suppressed around thirty of their newspapers.

Naturally, the intransigenti did not approve of what had become of the PNF; but nor did Bottai and the revisionisti. While the revisionisti welcomed the destruction of squadrismo, they opposed the replacement of elections for senior party posts with nominations from the top, the opening up of party membership and the reinforcement of the powers of the prefects at the expense of the federali. Like the intransigenti their view was that the party should be the vanguard of the revolution; its driving force, based, however, not on brawn, but brain. The party should be the breeding ground for the revolutionary elite, which would rise to the top via elections within the party. Unlike many Fascist gerarchs, and like Mussolini, Turati was not in the least corrupt when it came to money, but several of those close to him in Milan and Lombardy were. In 1930, however, Mussolini sacked Turati who had become the victim of a vicious whispering campaign, orchestrated gleefully by Farinacci, about his penchant for paedophilia and sado-masochism.

As Montanelli wrote, 'In effect Mussolini wanted to see triumph not the illegality, but the legality of the revolution. The watershed between the two concepts is often, in authoritarian states, uncertain. But the essential difference is this: the punishment and repression of opponents had to come, in Mussolini's opinion, from government, not from the initiative of groups or individuals.'

The second attempt on Mussolini's life was made on 7 April 1926 by a mentally unstable Anglo-Irish aristocrat, the Honourable Violet Gibson, daughter of the late Lord Ashbourne, a former Lord Chancellor of Ireland, and sister of the second Lord Ashbourne, an eccentric recluse who lived in Compiègne near Paris. Gibson, aged fifty-four, a Catholic convert spinster, had been a fiercely anti-British pacifist in the war and lived in Paris where, as a member of Professor Rudolf Steiner's Anthroposophical Society, she spent much time radiating German peace propaganda. She suffered from what documents in the Public Record Office[47] relating to her case describe as religious mania with homicidal tendencies but experienced long periods of complete sanity. In October 1923 she had been confined to an asylum in London but released in March 1924. Subsequently, she had come to live in Rome and attempted suicide. Later, she said that she had orders to kill either the Pope or Mussolini. But Popes rarely appeared in public. Indeed until the current one, Pius XI, no Pope had appeared in public since 1870 when Pius IX, the last Pope-King, had declared himself a prisoner inside the Vatican. Mussolini, who loved *bains de foule*, was an easier target. 'A supernatural force entrusted me with a lofty mission,' she explained.

Gibson was in the crowd gathered on the steps of the *Campidoglio* to greet Mussolini after a speech to open an international conference of surgeons. She charged forward and shot him at close range with a revolver. At that very moment he threw back his head to give the Roman salute to a group of students singing *'Giovinezza'*, according to one account. According to another, he had moved his head to look up at a woman who had thrown him a bunch of flowers from a nearby balcony. Either way, the bullet merely struck his nose but did no serious damage. As Gibson was about to fire a second shot, the police disarmed her. This saved her from being lynched by the crowd. In her other hand she clasped a stone with which she explained later she planned to break the windows of Mussolini's car if necessary so as to shoot at him.

Surgeons at the conference treated Mussolini and soon afterwards he reappeared before the crowd sporting a large plaster on his nose. He gave a short speech in which he coined one of his most famous sayings: 'If I advance, follow me; if I retreat, kill me; if I die, revenge me!' The next day he set sail for Libya where he delivered a speech on horseback and was greeted by shouts of '*Ave! Caesar!*'

On the instructions of Sir Austen Chamberlain, the Foreign Secretary, the British authorities gave every assistance to the Italian police in their inquiry. Among other things, they found out that Gibson had once tried to kill a woman friend with a knife in order to repeat the sacrifice of Abraham and Isaac.

Gibson was charged with attempted murder and extremist newspapers insisted that she be punished for her crime regardless of her mental state because, as *Il Resto del Carlino* put it, 'mad dogs are killed, although no blame can be attached to them for their ferocious madness'. The newspaper, *Impero*, convinced of her guilt, reported that 'our country ran the gravest risk of being afflicted, through the murderous hand of a foreigner, with a terrible disaster, which Providence, for the good fortune of Italy, brought to nought ... The projectile fortunately only passed through the nostrils and divisional membrane of the nose thus slightly wounding the Prime Minister who, after undergoing rapid first aid treatment, without losing either his calm or his time, returned shortly afterwards, to the exaltation of the nation, reassured at his escape from danger, to carry on his marvellous and incessant activity.'

But privately, Mussolini promised British ambassador Graham that he would ensure that no political bias affected her trial. Initially, she was held in prison but in July moved to a private nursing home. Finally, in early 1927, the charges against her were dropped on the grounds that her insanity meant that she was not responsible for her actions and in May she was deported after the British government had assured Mussolini that it would use its discretionary powers to confiscate Gibson's passport and refuse to reissue a new one.

But the government had been unable to assure her family that she would automatically be detained in a mental hospital. This was because it had no powers to give such an assurance. So Graham, the British ambassador in Rome, with the blessing of Sir Austen Chamberlain, in cahoots with Foreign and Home Office officials and one of Gibson's sisters, the Honourable Miss Constance Gibson, concocted an elaborate, more or less illegal plan to kidnap her. Constance Gibson went to Rome 'assisted' by three psychiatric nurses and a Cook's courier, and accompanied her sister back to London by train without telling her, of course, what lay in store for her. At Dover a psychiatrist was on hand to certify her insane on the train up to London and at Victoria a car to take her straight to a private mental hospital in Northampton where she was detained on an urgency order indefinitely. But as Constance Gibson had warned beforehand in a letter to the Foreign Office official handling the case, 'Legally she will not be a lunatic from the time she leaves Italy till she is certified in England. Can you get the French authorities to forbid her staying in France? She is very cunning and may very cleverly sham illness or give trouble going on the boat. We cannot give her a sleeping draught or she could not be certifiable on landing.' There was nothing, after all, to stop Gibson staying in France if she managed to give her sister and minders the slip. But the British official assured Constance Gibson that he had secured private assurances from the French that her sister would not be allowed to remain on French territory 'beyond the bare time required for the journey'.

The Gibson attempt on the Duce's life and his extraordinarily lucky escape inspired a fourteen-year-old schoolgirl to write to Mussolini that same month. 'Duce, my life is for you,' wrote the girl who added that she wanted 'ardently' to 'rest my head on Your broad chest so as to hear still alive the beating of Your great heart'. Her name was Claretta Petacci. The Duce did not reply. By now he received thousands of similar letters. But a decade later Petacci would become his mistress and end up being killed with him in 1945. The letter is interesting, not just because it is from the teenage Petacci, but because it is typical of the adulation so many Italians already felt for Mussolini. 'Duce, my *grandissimo* Duce, our life, our hope, our glory ... Why couldn't I have been there to strangle that woman assassin ...? Why couldn't I have been able to take her away for ever from Italian soil, which has been marked with Your blood, Your great, good, sincere Romagnol blood! ... O, Duce, You who are the man of our future, who are the man loved always with a growing fervour and passion by the Italian people ... I love You profoundly as *una piccola Fascista* of the first hour ... Duce, my life is for You! The Duce is saved! W [abbreviation for *viva*] the Duce!' The following month Petacci sent Mussolini poems she had written, the paper rolled up and tied with a ribbon in the colours of the Italian flag and a note in which she said again that she loved the Duce and in addition that she was ready to cut her veins if he told her that it would suit the cause of Italy. In another letter she begged him to reply, just one word would suffice; in another she begged to be able to look at his 'beautiful', 'black', 'profound', 'warm', 'vibrant' eyes. Petacci signed each letter with her name, age and address. Curious, Mussolini told his secretary, Chiavolini, to write a thank-you note, which he did: '*Gentile signorina*, the expression of your youthful and fervid devotion, rich with ingenuous intimacy, has reached *S.E. il Capo del Governo*. He, sympathetic to the *piccola Fascista*, has asked me to pass on his genuine thanks.'[48]

Three days before the failure of Gibson's lofty mission Clementine Churchill, the wife of Winston Churchill, at this time Chancellor of the Exchequer, had left Rome. She arrived back at Folkestone by ferry on the evening of 7 April – the day of the assassination attempt. She and a woman friend had spent two weeks staying with British ambassador Graham and his wife Lady Sybil, who were friends, at the British embassy. She had met Mussolini, who subsequently sent her, care of the embassy, a signed photograph of himself. On 20 March Clementine wrote to Churchill from the embassy,

> I have seen Mussolini – He came very privately to tea with Sybil the day after we arrived – He is most impressive – quite simple and natural [underlined], very dignified, has a charming smile & the most beautiful golden brown piercing eyes which you see but can't look at – When he came in everyone (women too) got up as if he were the King – You couldn't help doing it ... He fills you with a sort of pleasurable awe ... He loves music and plays the violin. Sybil had arranged a lovely little concert for him – I had a few minutes talk with him – He sent you friendly messages & said he would like to meet you. I am sure he is a very great person – I do hope nothing happens to him. He looked pale & thin but not I thought ill – It is certain that he inspires fanatical devotion in his followers ... He seems to like the Grahams very much.

On 25 March, Churchill replied, saying, 'The description of Mussolini is vy vivid. No doubt he is one of the most wonderful men of our time.'[49]

Churchill himself met Mussolini for the only time[50] in January 1927 in Rome after a Mediterranean cruise with his son Randolph and brother Jack, in the course of which he played his last game of polo in Malta. Churchill arrived in Italy at Genoa and wrote to his wife to say, 'This country gives the impression of discipline, order, goodwill, smiling faces.' The Fascists 'have been saluting in their impressive manner all over the place'. In Rome he met Mussolini twice – once at Palazzo Chigi and then at a British embassy reception.[51] Before leaving Rome on 20 January, Churchill read a statement to journalists: 'I could not help being charmed, like so many other people have been, by his gentle and simple bearing and by his calm, detached poise in spite of so many burdens and dangers. Secondly, anyone could see that he thought of nothing but the lasting good, as he understood it, of the Italian people, and that no lesser interest was of the slightest consequence to him.' Churchill then made some comments on Fascist Italy which he said, like any political issue, could not be judged 'apart from its atmosphere and environment'. But his view was nevertheless forthright. He said it was 'quite absurd to suggest that the Italian government does not stand upon a popular basis or that it is not upheld by the active and practical assent of the great masses'. He added, 'If I had been an Italian, I am sure I should have been wholeheartedly with you from start to finish in your triumphant struggle against the bestial appetites and passions of Leninism. But in England we have not yet had to face this danger in the same deadly form. We have our own way of doing things. But that we shall succeed in grappling with Communism and choking the life out of it – of that I am absolutely sure ... the great mass of the people love their country and are proud of its flag and history. They do not regard these as incompatible with a progressive advance towards social justice and economic betterment.' These remarks caused a furore in Labour and Liberal circles. 'We always suspected that Mr Winston Churchill was a Fascist at heart,' wrote the *New Leader* on 28 January. 'Now he has openly avowed it.'[52]

The third attempt on Mussolini's life happened less than six months after Gibson's and also in Rome. Just after 10 a.m. on 11 September 1926 a twenty-six-year-old anarchist, Gino Lucetti, a marble mason who had lived in France for some time and mixed with anti-Fascist exiles, threw a grenade at the Lancia ferrying Mussolini from the Villa Torlonia to Palazzo Chigi. Mussolini still lived in the small flat in Via Rasella but in the summer frequently stayed at this neo-classical early-nineteenth-century villa set in a park on the Via Nomentana, owned by Prince Torlonia who was an admirer of the Duce's. In 1929 Mussolini moved to Villa Torlonia permanently and virtually for free – the prince charged him rent of just 1 lira a year. Rachele and the children joined him there from that date. Mussolini had not lived with his family since leaving Milan after the March on Rome seven years beforehand. Rachele and the children had remained in Milan, living either there, or at Villa Carpena, the family's house in the Romagnol countryside near Predappio. Rachele had taken no part whatsoever in Mussolini's political life and hardly been a part of his private life either for seven years.

Quinto Navarra,[53] Mussolini's usher at Palazzo Chigi, was in the car and recalled hearing something strike it as it slowed down in a piazza, Porta Pia. He turned round and saw a man on the street with his arm raised. He thought the man was giving the car a Roman salute. But Mussolini had realised that it was a grenade and ordered the chauffeur to drive off at speed. Seconds later the grenade exploded in the road, injuring eight pedestrians. Lucetti was arrested at the scene and like Zaniboni and Capello sentenced to thirty years in prison, latterly on the island of Ponza (liberated in 1943 by the Allies he died soon afterwards in an Allied bombardment). Mussolini had remained calm throughout the incident, said Navarra. The Pope was among those to send him a message expressing his 'immense joy' at his survival and describing the attempt as 'a wicked crime'.

Though they sparked off unwanted *squadrismo*, these assassination attempts by incompetent individuals acting more or less alone rather than as part of some concerted campaign against Mussolini worked in his favour, not against. They created a mood of alarm in the Italian psyche –

and that of the King in particular – which made it easier to introduce the laws that transformed the regime into a dictatorship and in the Fascist psyche a mood of fury which made it necessary to do so. Without them, Mussolini would doubtless have proceeded towards dictatorship but he would have had to do so much more cautiously.

Despite mounting pressure from within Fascism, Mussolini resisted introducing the death penalty for attempts on the life either of members of the royal family or himself. It was now, in January 1926, that the *Popolari* attempted to return to parliament, but Mussolini refused to let them. What remained of the Aventine – the PSU by now was banned – continued its boycott. After the failed attempt of the *Popolari* to return, it was clear that the Aventine MPs could not return now anyway. But they had given up hope that the King would remove Mussolini and so prayed that if an assassin did not kill him, illness might. At the end of 1925 rumours began to circulate that Mussolini's ulcer had turned into a malignant tumour.[54] The rumours were unfounded.

Between November 1925 and January 1926, capitalising on the 'rush to Fascism' prompted by the Zaniboni attempt, Mussolini pushed past the Chamber, the Senate and the King a mass of draconian legislation. In November 1925 all secret organisations such as freemasonry were banned and all organisations, secret or not, including political parties had to submit names of members to the police for scrutiny or face imprisonment. In December 1925 a law gave the government the power to sack any public employee whose conduct in or outside work was deemed hostile to the government. The first victims of this law were a number of university professors. Another law that month set up a register of authorised journalists, which was used to exclude non-Fascist journalists from being able to work. And in January 1926 another gave the government the power to withdraw citizenship from any Italian abroad guilty of activity damaging to the peace and security of Italy or Italy's national interests or prestige. Punishment included the power to confiscate the Italian property of the offender. This was aimed at the increasing number of anti-Fascists who had gone into exile, especially to France (in all 10,000, according to best estimates). Among early victims was the historian and journalist Gaetano Salvemini. Salvemini, a former Socialist who had quit the party in 1911, had remained on the left – but after his arrest in 1925 for anti-Fascist activities had decided to leave Italy, going first to France, then, via Britain, to America, where he remained until 1947.

Two more new laws, rubber-stamped by a servile parliament, directly altered the constitution and increased the power of the prime minister at the expense of parliament. The first, which came into effect in December 1925, changed the title of the prime minister to *Capo del Governo e Duce del Fascismo*. It abolished the right of parliament to pass a vote of no confidence in the prime minister which, in the past, had acted as a break on prime ministers with dictatorial tendencies. The new law meant that from now on only the King, who remained *Capo dello Stato*, had the right to remove the prime minister. The second new law, which came into effect in January 1926, granted the *Capo del Governo* the right to make law by decree. In the past, under the Italian Constitution – the *Statuto* of 1848 – only the King had the right to do this or delegate that right to the prime minster in an emergency.

The fourth assassination attempt took place in Bologna on 31 October 1926 as Mussolini's motorcade drove through the crowd-lined streets en route to the station after the city's fourth anniversary celebrations for the March on Rome. Someone in the crowd fired a shot at the open-top car in which Mussolini was travelling with Leandro Arpinati, the *ras* of Bologna, and Dino Grandi. Balbo was in the car behind. Miraculously, the bullet passed through a sash Mussolini was wearing without injuring him. Balbo leapt from his car to shield Mussolini. The crowd pounced on a sixteen-year-old boy, Anteo Zamboni, and killed him on the spot (his injuries included thirteen stab wounds). Rachele and Edda, now sixteen, had joined Mussolini in Bologna as it was only a short distance from Mussolini's Romagnol home, Villa Carpena near Forlì, but did not witness this latest attempt on his life.[55] Mussolini proceeded to the station where he reviewed a guard of honour before catching a train as planned. His wife and daughter joined him at the station. The crowd meanwhile carried the severed limbs of the dead boy through the streets of Bologna.[56] That evening Mussolini stayed at Villa Carpena where he played the violin as if nothing untoward had happened. He told a United Press reporter, 'I don't know what it is that protects me from assassins. Certainly, it is a mystic something.'[57]

The Zamboni assassination attempt remains the most mysterious of the four. The idea that a sixteen-year-old boy should take a pot-shot at the Duce acting off his own bat seems very far-fetched – as it did at the time to Italians. Furthermore, it is incredible that the bullet should tear the sash Mussolini was wearing but not draw a drop of blood. The explanation for the lack of blood might be that Mussolini was wearing a bullet-proof vest – though this was never admitted. In September 1935, however, the *New York Times* published an interview with a Vienna manufacturer who said he had sold Mussolini a bullet-proof vest.[58] Nor did the police believe that the boy had acted alone. They arrested his father, brother and aunt, who denied that they had been involved in any way and indeed that Zamboni himself had been involved. Nevertheless they were charged in connection with the crime in September 1928. The court acquitted the brother but found the father and aunt guilty, sentencing them to thirty years in prison.

Perhaps Mussolini knew that they were innocent and sacrificed them for reasons of realpolitik – to satisfy the conviction at large that the boy could not have acted alone. Subsequently, for example, he gave the boy's brother money to see him through his university medical degree and then in 1932 surprisingly amnestied the father and aunt. Yet powerful rumours circulated that Fascist *intransigenti* close to Arpinati or Farinacci, not members of his family, had given him his orders. There could be no doubt that the death of Mussolini would cause a wild bout of violent *squadrismo*, which whoever was behind the plot might harness and exploit. The police investigated these rumours. Zamboni's father, a printer, though of vaguely anarchist persuasion, was a friend of Arpinati's. The boy, who had been a member of the *Balilla*, the Fascist youth organisation, had been wearing a black shirt, newspapers reported.[59] But the police found no evidence.

If it was a plot by dissident Fascists then Arpinati, a former anarchist – rather than Farinacci – is most likely to have been the mastermind despite the fact that Mussolini would subsequently appoint him Under-Secretary at Interior in 1929. Arpinati was among those Fascists keenest on a rapprochement between Fascism and Socialism. Perhaps this is why Mussolini amnestied Zamboni's father and aunt, and paid money to his brother. It was hush money to stop them revealing the truth: he did not want news to become public of a plot from within Fascism to destroy him. Though it is true that in 1929 Mussolini appointed Arpinati Under-Secretary at Interior, which would suggest that he did not believe him involved, it is also true that he sacked him in 1934 and subsequently had him sentenced to five years in *confino*, and twenty of his Bolognese associates dismissed from the party. And in 1945 Torquato Nanni, a leading Socialist, would be shot by partisans trying to save Arpinati's life in vain.[60] Yet, after the fall of Fascism, Zamboni's father insisted that the simple truth was that his son was guilty and had acted alone. Police had found a notebook at the boy's home full of scribblings about the attractions of tyrannicide.

The news of Zamboni's assassination attempt caused yet another wave of *squadrismo* to erupt beginning that very night. Those targeted included the philosopher Croce, whose home in Naples was sacked. Mussolini issued orders for the guilty to be arrested and given the maximum sentences.

The fourth assassination attempt also caused yet another round of draconian laws. These put the final nails in the coffins of both the opposition and *squadrismo*. Within a week (5 November) the Cabinet agreed the introduction of capital punishment for attempts on the life of the King, the regent, the Queen, the heir to the throne and the *Capo del Governo* – Mussolini. Federzoni, who had already come under intense criticism from his rival Farinacci and the *intransigenti* as a result of the previous assassination attempts, resigned as Interior Minister. At the same meeting the

Cabinet agreed to ban all publications and political parties guilty of 'actions against the regime'. Effectively, this meant that from now on there was just one political party in Italy – the PNF – and one press: that approved of by Fascism. To try political crimes the Cabinet agreed to set up a new type of court, the Special Tribunal for the Defence of the State, chaired by a general to be appointed either from the armed forces or the militia. Defendants were to have no right of appeal. (It was the Special Tribunal that tried the Zamboni family.) In its sixteen years and five months of existence, the Special Tribunal sentenced the 4596 political offenders who came before it to a total of 27,735 years in prison and handed out forty-two death sentences of which thirty-one were carried out – just under two executions a year.[61] This, of course, was nothing by the standards of the Nazis in Germany or the Communists in the Soviet Union. Nor by those of the French Revolution.

On 9 November the Chamber voted through these latest Cabinet proposals with only twelve deputies voting against (in the Senate on 20 November, only forty-nine voted against). The same day the Chamber put the Aventine MPs out of their misery once and for all by voting to exclude them permanently on the grounds that their continued absence meant that their parliamentary mandate had lapsed. The Chamber also banned the Communist party – whose MPs had remained in the Chamber throughout. Earlier that month, after the Zamboni assassination attempt, Mussolini had ordered the arrest of all the leading Communists including Gramsci, who was an MP and arrested in the Chamber. In May 1928 Gramsci and seven comrades were tried by the Special Tribunal for conspiracy to incite civil war and class hatred. Gramsci was sentenced to twenty years in prison from where he wrote the works which made his name as one of the leading Marxist theorists of the twentieth century. His main contribution to the debate was that it was not enough to take over the means of production; Communism also had to capture the culture. This is exactly what Mussolini believed as well. Gramsci had always suffered from poor health and died in 1937 in a clinic where Mussolini had latterly allowed him to serve his sentence. Among other ousted MPs were De Gasperi, the leader of the *Popolari*, and the grand old men of Socialism, Turati and Treves. The King did not protest. There was much talk at this time of a plot by Fascist *intransigenti* to overthrow the monarchy. Perhaps this helps explain the King's silent acquiescence in the legal transformation of his kingdom into a dictatorship. The Aventine, which had begun as a strike, had ended as a lockout. The violence orchestrated by the provincial *ras* after the Zamboni attempt, and the laws imposed by Mussolini as a result had persuaded many Aventine MPs to leave Italy anyway. They included Turati, now aged seventy. The Chief of Police had ordered Turati to leave his Rome house on the night of the Zamboni attempt as, recalled Turati, he was 'unable to guarantee my immunity from aggression and invasion by the Fascists' – more evidence that the violence was not authorised from the centre.[62]

To survive, Mussolini had to put a stop to *squadrismo* once and for all. His solution was to use the prefects who were the enforcers of the authority of the state in the provinces. In January 1927 he sent them a circular which ordered them to control any excess by the PNF. This circular spelled out, for the first time under Fascism, that the state, via the prefect, was a higher authority in the provinces than the party, via the provincial leader – the *federale*. Before Fascism the prefects had represented the authority of the state in the provinces but *squadrismo* and the powerful position of the party within the regime had created a de facto rival. The prefects had been loath, either through fear or ambition, to confront the *federali* and their *squadristi*.

Mussolini was determined to reverse this situation, to ensure that the state, not the party, was in charge. He described the January circular a few months later as a 'fundamental document; because it has stabilised the position of the party in the regime, in a way which will not tolerate any more equivocation.'[63] In addition to their traditional role as enforcers of public order – i.e. the suppression of illegal activity – Mussolini now also gave them a new role as enforcers of moral order – the suppression of immoral activity. In the past, although the prefects had very wide-ranging powers, they had not usually arrested citizens until they broke the law. In addition, in February 1927 elective local government was abolished. A *podestà* and an advisory group, appointed by the prefect, replaced the *sindaco* (mayor) and councillors.[64]

The most famous prefect during the Fascist era was Cesare Mori, the prefect of Palermo. His fame stemmed from his suppression not of Socialists or *squadrismo* but of the Mafia. Mussolini had decided to take on the Mafia after a visit to Sicily in the spring of 1924 in which he realised that the Mafia – using its usual tactic – had infiltrated the local PNF to such an extent that it controlled it. The Mafia had sprung up in the mid nineteenth-century and by now controlled much of Sicily's main economic activity: agriculture. On the advice of Federzoni and De Bono, Mussolini appointed fifty-two-year-old Mori, an orphan, the prefect of Trapani, then as now the nerve centre of the Mafia, in May 1924, then of Palermo in October 1925. It was Mori, it will be recalled, who as prefect of Bologna had confronted the blackshirts of Balbo and Arpinati and, unlike so many other prefects, had stood firm. Mussolini had described him at the time in *Il Popolo d'Italia* as not worth 'one drop of blood from the last Fascist left in the province'. To appease the Fascists, Facta had transferred Mori to the backwater of Bari and, a month after the March of Rome, Mussolini had sacked him. Perhaps it was his bold stand against the blackshirts in Bologna which made Mussolini recall him. Furthermore, Mori had worked in Sicily as a young police officer and so had knowledge of the problem.

By the end of 1925 Mori had begun to use with a vengeance the absolute power and 800 men that Mussolini had given him to tackle the Mafia, rounding up its members and, unable to prove them guilty of specific crimes, had them convicted of the general Mafia offence of criminal association. (Ironically, it would be the reintroduction of this law in the 1990s that would deal the Mafia the only significant blow of the post-war period.) He issued threats that if those who had gone into hiding in the mountains did not surrender he would imprison their wives and children.

Many *mafiosi* including significant numbers of the *capi* fled to America, to return with the Allied forces in 1943 as soldiers and be used by the Americans to weaken Fascist authority. 'If the Sicilians are afraid of the *mafiosi* I will show them that I am the strongest *mafioso* of all,' said Mori.[65] Mori's war on the Mafia meant taking on the PNF in Sicily as well, which he did, forcing Mussolini to dissolve the Palermo *fascio* in 1927 and put its *federale*, Alfredo Cucco, who was also an MP, on trial. Mussolini was still very pleased with Mori's work nevertheless and telegrammed him in January 1928, 'I am satisfied *vivamente* with round-up operation province Agrigento ...'[66] Then in June 1929 Mussolini sacked Mori out of the blue.

It was said at the time that Mussolini had got rid of Mori because by hitting the bosses as well as the foot soldiers of the Mafia he had upset too many Sicilian Fascists with strong links to the Mafia. But it was also said that Mori had become a fanatical wearer of the black shirt and punch-drunk with power, and that this did not fit the image of Fascism Mussolini wanted to put across, nor was it his idea of what Fascism was either. Mori was appointed a senator but died, largely forgotten, of old age in 1942. Many said at the time and have continued to say that Mussolini, via Mori, was the only Italian head of state ever to solve the problem of the Mafia. The *New York Times Magazine*, for example, wrote that the Mafia was dead and a new Sicily was born. And it is true that until the end of the Second World War the Mafia was largely inactive. British Ambassador Graham, however, wrote to Austen Chamberlain on 1 August 1928 that Mori had only prosecuted the 'lesser villains' and 'a number of innocent people by very doubtful means, including fabricated police evidence'.[67]

Like Graham, Mussolini was much too realistic to believe he had destroyed the Mafia. In the May 1927 Ascension Day speech he reeled off statistics on Mori's successes. But he was also quick to emphasise how entrenched a problem the Mafia was in Sicily and that no one should be fooled by those who insisted that to say the Mafia existed was a lie told to slur the '*tradizioni nobilissime*' of the island or by those whose image of the Mafia was one of 'poetry'. He said, 'Some ask me: when will the fight against the Mafia finish? It will finish, not only when there are no longer any *mafiosi*, but when the memory of the Mafia has disappeared definitively from the memory of the Sicilians.'

*

Crucial too to Mussolini's dictatorial ambition were the police. To enforce the authority of the state, prefects required an effective police force. Unlike in other totalitarian states such as Soviet Russia and Nazi Germany, the police had not played a significant role in the imposition of Fascism on Italy. *Squadrismo* had performed that role. But just as Mussolini was adamant that the party – via *squadrismo* – would not control the state, neither at the centre nor in the provinces, so was he adamant that it would not control the police either.

The *intransigenti* for their part, had lost the battle to have the PNF dominate the state; they now tried to have the party dominate the police. When Federzoni resigned as Interior Minister in November 1926 the *intransigenti* regarded this as a victory for them. In the same way they regarded the barrage of dictatorial laws passed as a result of the assassination attempts as a victory. Mussolini, however, was now Interior Minister as well as Capo del Governo and he soon dashed their hopes. The police, under Fascism, were never controlled by the party. They remained controlled by the state.

After the third assassination attempt, Lucetti's, in September 1926, Mussolini had sacked Crispo Moncada, the Chief of Police, and appointed the prefect of Genoa, Arturo Bocchini, instead. This was to prove an inspired move from Mussolini's point of view. The portly Bocchini, a forty-seven-year-old Neapolitan, was more interested in lobster and beautiful women than politics and never had more than a superficial commitment to Fascism. But he was a brilliant policeman and remained in his post until his death in 1940. His first important success was to destroy the sophisticated clandestine network of the Communist party, which his predecessor had failed to do. That Mussolini insisted the police remain firmly under the control of the state not the party meant there were far fewer arbitrary arrests and persecution than otherwise is certain to have been the case. But the police had a battery of powers at their disposal to use if they so chose. Many of these pre-dated Fascism such as *confino* (banishment to a remote place) – often one of the many small islands off the Italian mainland which are today exclusive tourist resorts – of those suspected of intending to engage in subversive political activity. The numbers employed in the various police forces escalated. Then, at the end of 1927, Mussolini set up a secret political police force, known only by its initials – OVRA – (the Fascists never revealed officially what these initials stood for but it is thought *opera di vigilanza e di repressione dell'anti-fascismo*) and headed by Bocchini. The OVRA was not an organ of repression by force, such as beating or torture, but by prevention via knowledge. It employed 700 full-time agents who were served by thousands of informants recruited from all walks of life including waiters, concierges, even writers. It tapped telephones, steamed open correspondence and even drew up reports on the graffiti in public urinals.[68] Its archives groaned with files so as to be able at a moment's notice to reveal 'the total number of subversives resident in the kingdom, abroad and in the colonies; the number of subversives divided by political tinge and by province; the number of political confinees ... the priests existent in the kingdom'.[69]

It was the OVRA which provided the Special Tribunal for the Defence of the State with most of its work. Between 1927 and 1929, 5046 people came before the tribunal of whom one-fifth were convicted. It sentenced one to death, six to twenty-five–thirty years in prison, forty-two to fifteen–twenty-five years, 370 to five–fifteen years. But this was all very small beer indeed compared with the appalling atrocities inflicted on their citizenry by other dictatorships whether of the right or the left. Mussolini also gave orders that the OVRA spy on the senior Fascists. Balbo and Farinacci both found out and wrote to Mussolini to complain. But their complaints fell on deaf ears. As Montanelli wrote, 'Fascism passed in this way definitively from the disorganised indiscriminate and barbaric violence of the *squadre d'azione* to a rational and systematic system of surveillance and repression.'[70]

The Battle for the Economy and the Corporate State

Fascism's big idea was the corporate state – the so-called Third Way between Capitalism and Communism – which would abolish the class war. Both Capitalism and Communism meant class war. In the class war, Capitalism, via the free market, gave the bosses the upper hand, and Communism, via the state, the masses. Fascism, via the corporate state, would incorporate both bosses and masses inside the state and so abolish class war.

Until 1925 Fascism's main concern was survival. Consequently, it left the economy largely alone. The economy did well until 1924 when industrial production passed the previous peak reached in the First World War but this was accompanied by rapid inflation. If in 1913 the cost of living index was 100 it had reached 480 by 1923 and 657 by 1926. Wages did not keep up with prices. Compared with a base rate of 100 in 1913, by 1925 the cost of living had risen to 623, wages only to 513. The lira, meanwhile, plummeted in value. In July 1925 the sterling exchange rate was 132 lira, by July 1926 it had fallen to 154 (in 1922 the exchange rate had been 90).[71] Inflation was rising, the lira falling. The stock market crashed.

Fascist economic policy at this stage was in favour of a reduction of state intervention which was what laissez-faire liberals of course had always wanted. During the period 1922–5 Mussolini benefited from a general economic upturn in Europe. But wages fell: from a base of 100 in 1913: they were 101.8 in 1922 but 97.6 in 1923 and 92.3 in 1924.[72] The number of strikes, however, plummeted: from 680 between 1 November 1921 and 31 October 1922 involving 7,336,393 working days lost, to 156 in the same period of 1922–3 involving 246,975 working days lost.[73] Unemployment also plummeted. The number of people officially out of work (the true figure was much higher) more than halved from 381,968 in December 1922 to 150,449 in December 1924.[74]

By mid 1925 the economy was in serious trouble. It was now that Mussolini launched a series of economic 'battles' – the battle for grain and the battle for the lira being the most famous. The impulse behind these two battles was the same: protection from the hostile forces of the market. Mussolini fought the battle for the lira because he was convinced – he had a point – that a country without a strong currency could not play a major role in the world. When he had been in France in January 1922 with his brother, Arnaldo, to cover the Cannes conference for his newspaper, he had been deeply depressed by the feebleness of the Italian lira against the French franc. In Cannes, Arnaldo had gone into a bank to change 10,000 lire and been given 5200 francs in return. 'This little experience made a profound impression on me,' Mussolini wrote in *My Autobiography* (the second, published in 1928). He was determined to protect the lira from the market.

His first move was to sack Alberto De Stefani as Finance Minister in July 1925. De Stefani was a supporter of traditional laissez-faire policies; he was against state intervention and for free trade and privatisation. Mussolini appointed Count Guiseppe Volpi di Misurata, an avid protectionist, as De Stefani's successor. Count Volpi, an absolutely typical *fiancheggiatore*, was the son of a Venetian builder and nicknamed the Doge of Venice. He had not finished his university law degree but had made money in the murky world of import–export and then a fortune selling electricity – an industry that had traditionally enjoyed heavy government subsidy. Volpi was close to Giolitti of all people, who had appointed him governor of Tripolitania (Libya) in 1921, the post he held when Mussolini appointed him Finance Minister (he would last three years until 1928). The King, on Giolitti's advice, had appointed Volpi first senator then count for services to Italy. Though no Fascist, Count Volpi quickly aped *lo stile mussoliniano* – hands on hips, chin thrust forward.

Count Volpi's policy – and it became long-term Fascist policy – was to persuade Italy's creditors to spread out repayment of debts over much longer periods – to transform them from short-to long-term debts. He did this with the dangerously high domestic national debt, so reducing it – as a figure in the annual budget at least – from 28 billion lire to 6. He did the same thing with Italy's massive war debts with America and Britain – striking deals between November 1925 and January 1926 – the British deal on especially favourable terms with Churchill who was Chancellor – by which Italy was given sixty-two years to pay them off. These moves helped restore confidence in the lira and enabled Count Volpi to borrow substantial sums from big foreign banks, notably $100 million from the American bankers J. P. Morgan.

But though this helped, it did not help enough. Italy had to come up with something else to tackle the economic crisis – in particular the severe inflation. Volpi decided that the government would protect the lira by using government money to buy the lira. This policy enjoyed some success initially, but by July 1926 the lira had slumped to 153 against sterling. Volpi, like the banks, agreed that revaluation was necessary but, like them, did not want to fix the lira any lower than 125. Rightly, he feared deflation if the rate was lower. Mussolini, who had no expertise in economics apart from peasant common sense, had other ideas (interestingly, so too at the same time did the Tories in Britain who pursued a similar sterling revaluation policy with similar consequences). Mussolini was adamant that the sterling exchange rate should be fixed at 'Quota 90' – 90 lira to the pound – the level at which it had stood in 1922 when he came to power. He rightly believed that the fate of the lira and that of Fascism were inextricably linked. The battle for the lira was a battle for the survival of the regime as his enemies such as Nitti, from exile in France, kept on reminding everyone in print. Yes, Mussolini revalued partly for reasons of propaganda. But the propaganda served a concrete purpose. If you talk up the value of something long and cleverly enough, its value does tend to rise.

On 18 August 1926 Mussolini made public his intention in a speech at Pesaro. He said, 'I want to say to you that we will conduct most strenuously the economic battle in defence of the lira, and in this place, I say that I will defend the lira until my dying breath, until the last blood.'[75]

A few days later he wrote to d'Annunzio, 'I think only of one thing, I suffer only from one pain: the lira.'

During the course of the next year Count Volpi revalued the lira in stages until in July 1927 it stood at 92.46 lire to the pound.[76] Mussolini was satisfied. In December 1927, the lira–sterling gold standard exchange rate was fixed permanently at this rate.[77] In the spring of 1927 it had strengthened still more to 85 lire against the pound at one point – a clear sign that the markets backed Mussolini.[78]

But the social cost of the 'Quota 90' was high. Employers went bankrupt or laid off workers to stay afloat; those retained were put on short time and reduced wages. In Florence the PNF conducted a campaign against the foreign straw hat.

Mussolini had said at Pesaro in August 1926 that the Italian people would be prepared to make the necessary sacrifice. It had made the sacrifice, prepared or not. Unemployment, which in 1924 was 150,000 according to official figures[79] increased to 225,346 by January 1927 and 439,000 by January 1928.[80] Yet the situation among the masses, though delicate, reported the Interior Ministry, was not of 'serious concern', given the 'total absence of demonstrations'.[81]

With the full backing of Mussolini, Volpi had also pursued a vigorous protectionist policy to defend the economy from foreign competition. Half the 8 billion lire deficit on the import–export account was due to cereal imports, he liked to point out.[82] The tariff on imported wheat, for example, was reintroduced in 1925 at 27.5 lire per *quintale* (50 kilos), was more than 40 lira per *quintale* in 1927 and 75 per *quintale* in 1931 – and the same year, that on sugar doubled. The revaluation of the lira, despite the austerity it caused, and the policy of protection – as such a policy usually does in the short term – yielded positive results. By 1928 the economy was in recovery. But then in 1929 came the Wall Street Crash and depression worldwide.

Perhaps Italy's major economic handicap was that it did not possess raw materials such as iron and coal, and it had to import huge amounts of wheat. Mussolini was determined that at least so far as staple food production went, Italy should become self-sufficient. So in June 1925, amidst an immense propaganda fanfare, began the first of several battles for grain. Tariffs on imported cereals, especially wheat, and a major propaganda campaign to instil enthusiasm in the peasantry were the main weapons in the battle. Mussolini himself would frequently thresh wheat bare-chested for hours on end at harvest time and inevitably ensure that the picture be published. Pictures of Mussolini in rural or sporting situations are much more common than pictures of him in factories. The battle was a success. Wheat production increased from 50 million *quintali* in 1925 to 80 million *quintali* at the start of the 1930s,[83] and between 1925 and 1935 grain imports decreased by 75 per cent.[84] But fertiliser had still to be imported which, when the Second World War broke out, created severe problems.

The battle for grain suited two other battles which Mussolini held most dear – the battle for *ruralità* and the battle for births. The rapid industrialisation in the north of Italy had caused cities like Milan and Turin to mushroom in size and such cities, where the working class was enormous and confined closely together especially at work, were breeding grounds not just of dissent but also of disease and material suffering. Mussolini decided to try to stop the growth of the big cities and to do this he launched the battle for *ruralità* – rurality.

The Fascist flirtation with Futurism, which glorified the city, violence, speed, industry and the machine, and its bear hug with the (essentially urban) bourgeoisie which it despised, was not as strong as its deeper romance with the countryside. The countryside was where Mussolini – and the majority of Italians – came from; it was his *terra natale*. The support of farmers and peasants had been why Fascism achieved such swift success before the March on Rome. Though not a peasants' revolt, Fascism was certainly a provincial revolt. Oswald Spengler's *Decline of the West*, which Mussolini knew well (he had written an introduction to a book on demography by the German, Richard Korherr, which had a preface by Spengler. The introduction was published in *Gerarchia* in September 1928 under the title '*Il Numero come Forza*'), provided his view with philosophical weight. Spengler's main idea was that to be powerful a nation had to have a large and growing population. He spoke of the sterility of the city and the fecundity of the countryside. Mussolini spoke of the city as a place where the cots were empty and the cemeteries growing ever bigger.[85]

The battle for wheat and the battle for rurality fitted well with the Fascist frame of mind. The other big battle, the one for births, stemmed from Spengler's idea that numbers equal power; that a low birth rate was a symptom of decline. Mussolini was determined to increase the population of Italy. At first sight such a view would seem to be at odds with his determination to stop the growth of the cities, especially those in the northern industrial triangle. But the battleground once again was to be the countryside not the city. Peasants led healthier lives than the urban working class and would, he believed, breed more and better children. The battle for births, spearheaded by its own government department – *L'Opera nazionale per la protezione della maternita e dell'infanzia* – led among other things to handsome cash prizes for the most prolific mothers, handed out on the Day of the Mother and Child, and the much derided bachelor tax introduced in 1926[86] on unmarried men aged twenty-five to sixty-five which affected roughly 3 million men (unmarried women were not taxed as it was assumed that, unlike bachelors, they had not chosen to remain single). Mussolini introduced the tax, he said, to give the nation a 'demographic whipping'.[87] Militia officers gave the Roman salute to pregnant women in the street. Newspapers published details of birth rates comparing city with city. In 1928 a law gave prefects powers to stop people leaving rural areas for the cities. The battle for births also pleased the Vatican. Mussolini led by example, producing two more children ten years after the birth of the last one, Bruno: first Romano, on 26 September 1927, the year the battle for births was launched, then on 3 September 1929 Anna-Maria. He continued as well his extramarital activities. The Fascist slogan 'Many enemies, much honour' became 'Many women, much honour'. Here at least, the regime had the unequivocal consent of Italian men.

Mussolini would have liked to have been editor of every newspaper at the same time but that was physically impossible. Nevertheless, detailed instructions went out daily to newspaper editors on what they should emphasise and what they should play down or ignore in their coverage. The battle for births figured frequently in these instructions. In July 1932, for example, one such missive said, 'One calls attention to the newspapers of the necessity of applying in the strongest possible fashion, the dispositions already given to avoid publication in papers and periodicals of pictures of thin women. The phenomenon of the slim woman has no other significance than the reduction of the birth rate.'[93] He spelled out his view on the importance of a growing population in his 1927 Ascension Day speech to the Chamber. This speech came as the economic crisis, aggravated by the battle for the lira, began really to bite – in both the city and the countryside. He said '*Signori!* If Italy wants to count for something, she must present herself on the threshold of the second half of the twentieth century, with a population not less than 60 million inhabitants ... What are 40 million Italians [Italy's population] in the face of 90 million Germans and 200 million Slavs? And in the face of the 40 million French plus the 90 million inhabitants in their colonies, or in the face of the 40 million English, plus the 450 million who people their colonies?'[88] He concluded that 'a certain type of urbanisation' was 'destructive' and 'leads populations to sterility', namely, 'industrial urbanisation'; as was the 'infinite cowardice of the so-called superior classes in society' – i.e. the bourgeoisie. The 'small rural farm' was the answer. The Fascist disgust with the bourgeoisie – more specifically with the bourgeois spirit – was something it had always had and always would have. But Fascism was never able to free itself of the bourgeoisie – though it would have been interesting to see what it came up with alone. This explained why he was determined to build up the countryside, he said. Between 1930 and 1940 an average 70,000 people a year left the countryside, compared with 250,000 a year in the previous decade.[89]

The four battles – lira, grain, rurality, babies – achieved more in propaganda terms than they did in reality. But regardless of the propaganda, they were 'a decisive aspect of the consensus that Fascism managed to achieve around Mussolini between the end of the twenties and the middle of the thirties.'[90] And they went hand in hand with what was undoubtedly a significant achievement of Fascism: a vast public works programme launched in 1928[91] whose crowning glory was the draining of the malaria-infested, largely uninhabited Pontine Marshes to the south of Rome which emperors, popes, kings and the odd prime minister had all tried and failed to make habitable. The programme also involved the creation of new medium-sized and small model towns such as Pontinia and Littoria, new Predappio where the Duce had been born, even one, in Sicily, called Mussolinia. The draining of the Pontine Marshes was part of a massive programme, which made millions of hectares of unusable land farmable.

The new Fascist towns and Fascist additions in the old towns were fine, the structure sound, the style – neo-classical *alla Fascista* – grand, not gross, nowhere near as cold and repellent as the knee-jerk descriptions of the critics would have the world believe; the results are still there throughout Italy today. But when Mussolini sent the bulldozers into the heart of

Rome to demolish medieval and Renaissance buildings – the years of decadence – the critics had a point. The buildings had to go, said Mussolini, to make way for a wide road to link the Colosseum with Piazza Venezia – the piazza in which stood the Vittorio Emanuele II monument and Palazza Venezia from whose balcony he delivered his speeches to the crowd. The road, called the Via Imperiale, was part of a five-year programme begun in 1925 to make Rome 'vast, ordered, great'. Sarfatti, the arbiter of taste, was closely involved in all this. WOMAN REBUILDS OLD ROME ran the headline, for example, on an American article about it.[92] The project included a large sports complex – away from the centre of the city – with football stadium, competition swimming pool and athletics track, the Foro Mussolini, complete with marble statues of naked athletes – forerunner of the athletics stadium built by Hitler for the 1936 Olympics.

In addition, the Fascists introduced electrification on 2100 kilometres of Italy's railway network by the end of 1929, adding a further 1600 kilometres by the end of 1933. Mussolini not only made the trains run on time but he made them run faster – halving the journey time, for example, between Rome and Siracusa. Milan station remains today the giant marble symbol of the Fascist achievement in the field. And the programme included as well the construction of thousands of kilometres of roads and Europe's first motorway, of 400 bridges including the one connecting Venice to the mainland and of aqueducts for regions where water was scarce such as Apulia. The Fascists would later boast that in ten years they had spent more on public works than the liberal regime in sixty years.

Such projects were tangible, photographable signs of Fascist achievement but what Mussolini wanted to be Fascism's major contribution to economic history was much less tangible: the corporate state. The corporate state was established in principle in late 1925–early 1926 when parliament passed the *Legge Sindacale*; and in practice in June 1926 when the Grand Council established the rules on the application of the law. Often called the Rocco Law after the Justice Minister, Alfredo Rocco, who drafted the final text (Rocco, an ex-nationalist, also drafted the laws which transformed the regime into a dictatorship), the Fascist press described the *Legge Sindacale* in triumphant headlines: HISTORIC, THE END OF THE LIBERAL STATE!, THE MOST DARING LAW IN THE WORLD'.[94] Either the Fascist State is corporative or it is not Fascist,' said Mussolini in 1930. The guiding principle was that both workers and employers would be represented in the same unions – called corporations after the medieval corporations. This would mean that the employers were unionised for the first time. The task of the corporations would be to 'co-ordinate and better organise production'.[95] The idea of such corporations pleased the Catholic Church as it infused much of its social teaching. In 1892 Pope Leo XIII's encyclical, *De Rerum Novarum*, was a rebuttal of class war in favour of class collaboration. The current Pope, Pius XI, set out the position of the Catholic Church when he said that Capitalism and Communism were united in their 'satanic optimism'.

But while the corporations of old were set up to protect the medieval merchant from the state, the Fascist corporations would be part of the state – in the words of the Grand Council, 'organised and controlled by the state', and thus unlike traditional trade unions as well, organs of the state. Bottai hoped that this would make the unions work for the good of the state not against it. The modern roots of the Fascist corporate state were revolutionary syndicalism. D'Annunzio had popularised the idea when he put a version of it into practice during his brief reign at Fiume. In the corporate state the corporations would have a political as well as an economic role. It would be from the corporations that candidates for both houses of parliament would be chosen. The emphasis was *not* on the nationalisation of the means of production – private property in other words – but on the nationalisation of the people – the forces of production. The aim was the abolition of class war – the creation of class collaboration.

There would be a corporation for each of the six main sectors of the economy. Each corporation would comprise two confederations – one for the workers, one for the employers. There would also be a corporation for the professional and intellectual classes comprising one confederation – not two (there was no easy distinction between employer and employee in this field). That each corporation – apart from the last – comprised a workers' and an employers' confederation was a clear admission that class conflict was there to stay.

The armed forces, teaching professions and magistrates would be exempt. Strikes and lockouts would be banned and industrial disputes arbitrated by a labour tribunal. The state would supervise the corporations via a new ministry, the Ministry of Corporations, which among other things would approve the membership of each corporation – this effectively killed off non-Fascist unions for good. Mussolini appointed himself the first Minister of Corporations in July 1926 and Suardo as Under-Secretary, replaced in November by Bottai, the leading *revisionista* (Bottai would become Minister in September 1929). State employees would be organised in separate corporations, controlled by the PNF.

Mussolini wrote in an official press release:

Fascists of all Italy! ... For the first time in the history of the world a constructive revolution as ours is has achieved peacefully, in the field of production and labour, the organisation of all the economic and intellectual forces of the nation, so as to direct them towards a common goal. For the first time a powerful system of thirteen organisations[96] has been created, all placed on the same level of parity, the legitimate and reconcilable interests of all recognised by the sovereign State ... Blackshirts! Raise up your banners! Celebrate, with an act of will and of faith today's date! It is among the most brilliant of our revolution. *A Noi*!

Despite the Fascist fanfare, it was immediately obvious that the workers had got a very raw deal. Mussolini – forced to mediate – had tipped the scales in favour of the employers. This was because he knew that attempts by Fascism to gain support among the urban working class, despite the best efforts of the leader of the Fascist unions, Edmondo Rossoni, had not been a great success. There was no point, he had decided, flogging a dead horse. He had given up on the urban workers – for now. He had decided to place his faith in the urban workers of the future. In the May 1927 Ascension Day speech, for example, he freely admitted this. He said, 'The unions are going well. Especially those which organise the solid, faithful rural masses. But we must not delude ourselves too much over the so-called specifically industrial proletariat: it is for the most part distant, and, if not against as it was once, absent.' He added, 'The generation of the stubborn, of those who have not understood the war and who have not understood Fascism, at a certain moment will eliminate themselves by the laws of nature. The young will arise, workers and peasants will arise to create *l'Italiano nuovo, l'Italiano fascista.*'[97] The corporate state proper, Mussolini had already decided, would have to wait for the future.

The *Legge Sindacale* was a bad blow for Fascist syndicalism and Rossoni, and also for Bottai who, though hostile to Rossoni's syndicalism which he felt increased not decreased class conflict, still wanted the immediate introduction of a proper corporate state. Furthermore, the corporations had been set up but how they would actually operate in practice remained vague. The new law had fudged the issue of whether members of the confederations were to be elected or not. In an attempt to solve these problems the Grand Council approved a workers' charter, the *Carta del Lavoro*, in April 1927 setting out thirty principles which would govern the relationship between workers, employers and the state. The charter was neither a law nor a decree and so not legally binding, merely a manifesto. Bottai conceded that the charter was only 'a formal pledge for further action by the legislative organs of the state'[98] but nevertheless he claimed that it was 'not an antithesis, but an overtaking' of the French Revolution because it proposed genuine equality between employers and workers.[99] And it was a great propaganda coup. In 1932, for example, Albert Thomas, the British trade unionist, and President of the International Workers' Congress held annually in Geneva, said that the corporate state meant that in Italy 'you couldn't say there was social regression'.

The charter stated, among other things, that the 'Italian Nation' had needs 'superior' to those of the 'individuals' of the nation and that the nation was 'a moral, political and economic unit which is fulfilled completely within the Fascist state'; that work was defined as 'a social duty' which was 'protected by the state'; that the workers' confederation – their union – within each corporation was 'free' but only if 'legally recognised' and 'controlled' by the state; that the 'intervention of the state' in the economy would happen only when private enterprise was 'lacking or else inadequate' or when 'the interests of the state' were at stake. With regard to workers' pay and conditions, the charter guaranteed among other things holiday pay, higher pay for unsociable hours, redundancy pay and social security pay.

But by 1927 the Italian economy was suffering from the effects of Mussolini's battle for the lira. The reality of wage cuts, short time and the dole was in stark contrast to the lofty words of the *Legge Sindacale* and *Carta del Lavoro*. A Ministry of Corporations report in 1932 said that between June 1927 and December 1928 industrial workers' wages had been cut by 'about 20 per cent' and by a further 10 per cent in 1929 and that in 1930 – this after the 1929 Wall Street Crash – there had been a reduction of wages in all sectors of '18–25 per cent'.[100] In June 1929 Mussolini admitted to the Chamber that in parts of Sardinia and southern Italy 'the inhabitants have to live on wild plants'.[101]

In 1930 Bottai did manage to introduce new rules which obliged the labour tribunal to treat the grievances of the workers more favourably. But the corporate state never got off the ground except in name. When Bottai tried hard to implement it in the early 1930s Mussolini blocked him and in 1933 sacked him as Minister of Corporations, taking over the post himself once again. In 1944–5 Bottai would admit that the corporate state 'was never born, strangled by the umbilical cord that attached it to the dominant class'.[102] We shall never know if the corporate state failed because it was never tried (though Mussolini did try at Salò, by when it was too late, to introduce 'a right-wing State with an economic and social structure of the left').[103] As set out in the *Legge Sindacale*, the Fascist corporate state failed to tackle the core issue of the ownership of the means of production and hence the control and management of production. The closest it got was the phrase that the role of the corporations was 'to co-ordinate and better organise production' or the clause in the *Carta del Lavoro* that the state should intervene if it absolutely had to but privatisation was best. The Fascist corporate state hardly even managed to deal with pay and conditions and when it did it nearly always favoured the employers – let alone production. An abyss separated aspiration and achievement. Mussolini did, however, become increasingly interventionist in his economic thinking and action – especially after the 1929 Wall Street Crash. But it was not via the corporations that the Fascist state intervened in the economy.

Just as Mussolini had to neutralise Fascist *squadrismo*, so too did he have to neutralise Fascist *sindacalismo*. Before the March on Rome the PNF and the Fascist unions had been united in a common aim. But after it they grew apart and became rivals in the struggle for control of Fascism. Farinacci, for example, when PNF General Secretary, had tried unsuccessfully to bring the Fascist unions under the control of the party – as he had tried to bring everything under the control of the party. Employers, especially the big industrialists, were hostile to the Fascist unions just as they were to all unions. Rossoni, President of the umbrella organisation of the Fascist unions, wanted the employers to recognise only Fascist unions in the workplace. To weaken the unions the employers preferred to have different unions in competition with each other. But Rossoni wanted much more: in particular, he wanted his unions to have a say in management. In May 1924, in what was seen as a move to the left, Mussolini said in a speech to the Fascist unions that he supported the right to strike, adding that the 'conditions of the mass of industrial workers should not deteriorate'.[104] A year later the Grand Council recognised the need to strike.[105]

Between 1924 and 1925 the Fascist unions had begun to flex their muscles and there was a notable increase in strikes in which they were involved – the biggest of which began in February 1925 by 6000 metalworkers in Brescia belonging to Fascist unions and led by Augusto Turati, who would replace Farinacci as PNF General Secretary a year later. This rapidly spread, involving 100,000 workers – belonging to Socialist, Communist and *Popolari* unions – in the north of Italy.[106] The strike ended with a pay increase after the government, embarrassed by the hijacking of the strike by the non-Fascist unions, had put pressure on the employers to negotiate. The Brescia metalworkers strike convinced Mussolini that the government and the party, not the unions, should be the ones to call the shots in the workplace from now on. In April 1925 the Grand Council announced that strike action, though legal, was an 'act of war' for use only as a last resort and that in future all strikes would require the permission of the PNF and Fascist union's central leadership.

Naturally, such strikes jeopardised the support for Fascism of the *fiancheggiatori*. But they also incensed Farinacci and the *intransigenti* who wanted the unions to be under the strict control of the PNF. And they irritated Mussolini because they threatened, as did *squadrismo*, the implementation of his vision of Fascism. He wanted the unions to be within the state and not a threat to the state. On 2 October 1925 *Confindustria*, the employers' organisation, and Rossoni's Fascist union organisation, signed an agreement at the headquarters of the PNF, Palazzo Vidoni. Under the Palazzo Vidoni Pact, as it was called, the industrialists agreed that only the Fascist unions had the right to represent the workers, a victory of sorts for the Fascist unions (in December 1923, the two sides had agreed the same thing, but it had not been adhered to). A Communist union missive urged the workers to stage a mass protest in the factories immediately. None did.[107] But by 1927 both Bottai and Turati wanted to destroy Rossoni's ambitions for the Fascist unions and so too did Mussolini. So in November 1928 Mussolini announced what was called the *sbloccamento* (unblocking) of the unions. This deprived Rossoni's umbrella organisation – the *Confederazione nazionale dei sindacati fascisti* – of control over the seven national federations that formed the worker element of the new corporate state. These federations would from now on be autonomous. At a stroke Rossoni lost control of the Fascist unions. From now on, Mussolini via the PNF would control them.

Mussolini had emasculated the Chamber of Deputies and the only opposition left within it after the Aventine had been locked out for good was a handful of liberal MPs grouped mainly around Giolitti.[108] Now he made the Chamber an integral part of the corporate state by transforming it into the political forum not of the people of the nation, but of the nation's producers – productive employers and productive workers.

On 16 March 1928 Mussolini presented a new electoral reform bill to the Chamber. The Chamber would comprise only 400 MPs. These would be chosen by the Grand Council from a list of 1000 names submitted mainly by the new Fascist employer–worker corporations, though 200 would be submitted by other approved organisations such as the National Combatants Association. Those entitled to vote were men aged twenty-one and over who paid a union due or minimum 100 lire per annum tax or owned property or were employees or pensioners of the state – or priests.[109] The electorate would have the choice of either accepting the entire list or rejecting it. A simple majority of 50 per cent plus one of the votes in favour of the list would send all 400 candidates to the Chamber. Though there had been talk of abolishing the Senate or reforming it as well, in the end Mussolini left it alone. To have done so would have enraged the King and it had always done Mussolini's bidding anyway.

The Chamber duly passed the bill (216 in favour, 15 against). Giolitti, by now well into his eighties, made his last speech to the Chamber describing the bill as a violation of the constitution which signalled 'the decisive detachment of the Fascist regime from the virtuous regime of the *Statuto* (albertino)'. Two months later the Senate passed the bill, 161 in favour and 46 against, of whom Croce and Albertini. The new Chamber would be 100 per cent Fascist, 100 per cent corporate. The plebiscite – for that is what it was rather than an election – took place on 24 March 1929. It was a great victory and a genuine success for Mussolini with 8,519,559 – 89.63 per cent – voting 'yes' and only 135,761 'no'. There was no violence and no intimidation. Of the 400 on the list, nearly half had been MPs in the previous parliament.[110] Mussolini, who by now held seven ministries, gave up all but Interior.

Several senators had complained that the Grand Council had no constitutional status and therefore no right to choose the list of candidates. The regime gave it that status with a bill in December 1928, which made it the supreme organ of state whose role was to 'co-ordinate all the activities of the regime' – duly passed by both the Chamber and the Senate. The bill further eroded the royal prerogative by giving the Grand Council the right to be consulted over the succession to the throne and to draw up a list of names from which the King would choose the successor to the Capo del Governo. The King was furious, in particular about the idea of the Grand Council having a say in the succession to the throne. By granting the Grand Council constitutional status – by bringing it inside the structure of the state – Mussolini also weakened the influence on it of the party. Equally, because the Grand Council was 'the supreme organ of Fascism' it gave the state formal authority over the party.

Marriage and the Man

It was at the end of 1929, after the birth of their fifth child Anna-Maria, that Rachele came to Rome to live full-time for the first time and the family moved into the Villa Torlonia. From Predappio, she summoned a gang of relatives to Rome to transform the villa into something more to her liking. The main effort was directed at the kitchen, which she moved from the basement to the ground floor.[111] Mussolini and Rachele slept in different rooms and did not lunch together. During the week the family met only for dinner and afterwards sometimes watched a film together, a Western or a comedy, in the conservatory which had been turned into a projection room.[112]

Rachele meanwhile baked her own bread and made her own pasta. She was convinced the Villa Torlonia was haunted. She made the antique furniture shiny by painting it with varnish and replaced the heavy dark curtains with frilly lace. Outside the Villa Torlonia she soon made her mark as well, turning part of the park into a farmyard, no less, with vegetable garden, chicken coops and rabbit hutches, pigsties, turkeys, geese and cats on the loose, and dovecotes, and kennels for her many dogs. Space also had to be found for more exotic creatures given to Mussolini by admirers, such as more lion cubs, a jaguar from Brazil, a monkey, a deer, a pair of Libyan gazelles, a falcon, a royal eagle, parrots, singing birds, and giant tortoises. Prince Torlonia, a former cavalry officer who had lost an eye somewhere along the way and lived elsewhere in the park in a large mock-Gothic horror, the Casina delle Civette, complete with bow windows, like an English semi gone mad, did not approve of Rachele. She used to shoot at the sparrows and play cards with the servants in the laundry. Mussolini, meanwhile, had his horses, including his favourite Fru-Fru, a white stallion, which one day he rode up the entrance steps of the villa and inside the hall. The horse defecated and, afraid of Rachele's fury, he hid.[113] In addition, he played tennis, badly, and continued to fence, well, with his fencing master who had been with him for years, Camillo Ridolfi, a former cavalry officer.[114]

At the beginning of July 1927 he paid an Englishwoman 5000 lire to give Edda English lessons for three months during the summer.[115] The teacher's name was Lillian Gibson but she was no relation to the would-be assassin of 1926. He retained her to improve his own English of which, unlike French which he spoke well and German adequately, he had only a rudimentary grasp. In an article in the *New York Times Magazine* in February 1929 Miss Gibson said that the lessons, which never lasted more than twenty minutes and took place at Palazzo Chigi (Mussolini moved his office from Palazzo Chigi to Palazzo Venezia at the end of 1929), were sporadic. But he had an 'iron memory' and 'enormous concentration' which were a help and by 1929, she said, he could 'now read and get a good sense of any English book or article', translate well from Italian into English and speak it 'slowly and carefully'. He was very keen on idioms such as 'It never rains but it pours', learnt one rainy afternoon, she said.

Rachele preferred to speak in Romagnol dialect rather than Italian let alone anything foreign and her views on life were those of the Romagnol proverbs she used to speak her mind to her husband such as, 'When the fox grows old the chickens shit on his snout'.[116] While Mussolini ran Italy, she went out shopping in Rome on her own unrecognised. The First Lady of Fascism very rarely appeared in public at official occasions. She visited Palazzo Venezia only 'two or three times' in all and came carrying a bag 'containing cold food', which she ate in the reception room.[117]

But at home Rachele was the dictator. She was the exact opposite of the 'placid, patient, submissive, woman of legend', Edda would tell a Swiss psychiatrist who treated her for depression during her exile in Switzerland in 1944–5.[118] 'She was very jealous ... She had constant violent scenes with her husband,' wrote the psychiatrist in his lengthy report on Edda for the Swiss authorities, which includes much information about life in the Mussolini household. Also contrary to the myth, Rachele meddled in politics all the time. 'She had her favourites and her *bêtes noires* for whom she made life hard, she threatened, she stormed ... When angry she spoke only of having people shot, deported, etc ... *En famille* she ridiculed him [Mussolini] constantly, treated him like an imbecile, an idiot, a coward, etc. in front of the children and the servants.' Once, the psychiatrist continued, when Edda went upstairs to visit her father who was ill in bed with flu, Rachele shouted up after her, 'You should take a look, poor little old man, what a handsome man he is in his night shirt ... and that continues to chase women.' Mealtimes were very noisy indeed at the Villa Torlonia where 'everyone shouted louder than everyone else ... The servants joined in ... gave their opinions on everything. Mussolini listened to them quite happily ... Theirs, he used to say, was the true voice of the people.'

The awful Sarfatti was never very far away either. No sooner had the Mussolinis moved into the Villa Torlonia than she moved into an apartment in the Via Nomentana virtually opposite. Rachele apparently did not know. If she had, she would have hit the roof. But Mussolini nevertheless often used to nip over secretly to see Sarfatti. Sarfatti re-created her vaunted Milan salon in her Rome apartment, described by one writer who visited it as 'the apartment of a pretentious blue-stocking'.[119] Sarfatti, who had once criticised Pirandello, described Alberto Moravia's first novel, *Gli Indifferenti*, which was a masterpiece, as 'crudely devoid ... of every intelligent and healthy attitude' in *Il Popolo d'Italia* in September 1929. Sarfatti's own novel, a love story about a teenage girl and how marvellous Fascist and male domination is, that year sank with little trace. G. K. Chesterton, a supporter of Mussolini's, met Sarfatti and found her obsequiousness intolerable at a reception for him at Rome's Foreign Press Club and turned his back on her.[120] Harold Nicolson described her as a 'questing woman' and the 'daughter of a Venetian Jew who married a Jew'.[121] American journalist Kenneth Roberts described her as a 'dumpy, hard-voiced, coarse-skinned, bleached blonde, from North Italy'.[122] But Sarfatti's days as the unofficial First Lady of Fascism were numbered because her days as Mussolini's mistress were numbered. The one thing she did which enjoyed genuine success was her biography of Mussolini. But that too depended entirely on him. It was reprinted five times in 1926 alone, seventeen times in the next twelve years, and translated into twenty languages including Turkish and Japanese. Sarfatti does not even mention Rachele or Mussolini's children once in the entire work.

In 1928 Sarfatti converted conveniently to Catholicism;[123] conveniently, not because of anti-Semitism in Italy, of which there was no more than anywhere else, but because she knew that Mussolini's secret talks on conciliation with the Vatican were close to fruition.

The Conciliation of Church and State, 1929

By 1922 Italy existed in name but not as a nation. The experience of fighting for King and country in the First World War had helped bind Italians together; but the war had also given a big boost to Socialism which was anti-nation. Garibaldi had begun the process of the creation of Italy. Mussolini would complete it. He had said that he would use the state to make the nation, to make Italians, as he put it, Italian: everything within the state, nothing outside; nothing against the state. But since Italian reunification in the second half of the nineteenth century a powerful force within Italy had stood not just outside the state but against it: the Catholic Church. Italian Catholics, therefore, had divided loyalties; their *Italianità* was in doubt. To make them Italian, Mussolini had to solve the '*Questione Romana*'.

Until 1870 the pope had exercised not only spiritual power throughout the world as head of the Catholic Church but temporal power in Italy as absolute ruler of the papal states – Lazio, Umbria, Le Marche and Mussolini's native Romagna – whose capital was Rome and whose population was 3 million. During Italian reunification the forces of Savoy had annexed this papal territory in stages, culminating in the capture of Rome in September 1870. Consequently Pope Pius IX had locked himself inside the Vatican and refused to come out, or negotiate even, let alone recognise the theft of his temporal kingdom. He declared himself a prisoner inside the Vatican and his jailers wicked. It was not just the seizure of the papal states which the Pope regarded as wicked but the politics of those responsible. 'In philosophy liberalism was immediately singled out by the Church as the *summa* of all heresies ... In 1888 the theologist Felix Sarda y Salvany published a work with the significant title *Il liberalismo e peccato*. And even in 1926 Abbot A. Roussel, in his *Liberalisme et Catholicisme*, wrote, "Liberalism is a sin, a grave sin of the spirit, sin itself, because it is essentially a revolt against God and against the order established by him".'[124]

In 1871 the Italian government attempted to solve the impasse with the *Legge delle Guarentigie*, which permitted the defeated Pope to have use of and be ruler of the Vatican, and employ an armed guard to protect himself, and which also offered him an annual sum towards the running costs of the Vatican. But the Pope refused to recognise the law or accept the money; he refused to renounce his claim to temporal sovereignty over his lost territory. Subsequent popes followed suit.

This papal refusal to accept the loss of the papal states left Italy vulnerable – initially at least – to invasion by a stronger foreign power such as France, which had been bound by treaty to defend them but which had not, reeling as it was from crushing defeat in 1870 in the Franco-Prussian War. More important in the long run, it placed Italy's Catholics in serious difficulty. As a result, for example, all popes had refused to permit Italian Catholics to participate in Italian politics. It was not until Benedict XV that this policy was abandoned after the First World War, which helps explain the sudden rise of Don Sturzo's *Popolori* and their spectacular success in the 1919 general elections. But until a pope officially recognised the loss of the papal states the loyalty of Italy's Catholics to the kingdom of Italy – and so to Fascism – would remain in doubt. That Italy's politicians were traditionally anti-clerical, as was the House of Savoy, had made the chances of a solution remote.

Mussolini, the former *mangiapreti* who in 1904 during a public debate in Lausanne had given God five minutes to prove his existence by striking him down with lightning, was determined to solve the *Questione*

Mussolini's parents. Rosa Mussolini (left), the village school teacher, was a devout Catholic who insisted that her son be baptised. Alessandro Mussolini (right), the village blacksmith, was a devout Socialist and *mangiapreti* (priest-eater) who insisted that he be given the names of famous revolutionary figures.

The infant Mussolini in his mother's arms. The boy did not speak for three years.

Corporal Mussolini on crutches after being wounded on the Isonzo Front in February 1917 when his mortar blew up during firing practice. His shrapnel wounds were like 'the arrows of St Sebastian', said his mistress Margherita Sarfatti.

Mussolini practising with his fencing master in the grounds of the Villa Torlonia, his Rome residence. Mussolini fought at least five duels in his life, though none after he had come to power.

Rachele Mussolini, the daughter of a peasant farmer, as a young woman. 'His eyes always persuaded me to obey him,' she would say of her husband.

Mussolini's three most significant mistresses and the Anglo-Irish woman who claimed that God had given her a 'lofty mission' to assassinate him.

TOP LEFT: Margherita Sarfatti, wealthy Venetian Jewess, art critic and Fascist of the first hour, once wrote a poem to Mussolini in which she said, 'The day will come: you will find that I am inside you, in your spirit and flesh, always.' TOP RIGHT: Claretta Petacci, the daughter of a Vatican doctor, was twenty-eight years younger than Mussolini. Their first contact was when she wrote to him as a fourteen-year-old schoolgirl, 'Duce, my *grandissimo Duce* … my life is for You!' BOTTOM LEFT: Angela Curti Cucciati , mother of Elena Curti. 'Everyone knew', it was said, that Mussolini was Elena's father. BOTTOM RIGHT: The Honourable Violet Gibson, daughter of Lord Ashbourne, who came within a whisker of assassinating Mussolini in April 1926.

Fascist election propaganda on the Palazzo Braschi, Rome, in March 1934.

Mussolini (note the spats) and Fascist leaders in the streets of Rome at the conclusion of the March on Rome in October 1922. On his right (white beard and medals), is Emilio De Bono; on his left, Michele Bianchi (bald with medals), the PNF general secretary, and Italo Balbo (black hair and breeches), the *ras* of Ferrara.

Mussolini was as popular with women as he was with men – if not more so.

TOP LEFT: Women agricultural workers, next to a large *fasces* made of wood and wheat, at a parade before Mussolini in Milan in October 1934. TOP RIGHT: A woman in the crowd whispers in Mussolini's ear. BOTTOM: Mussolini strides past gleeful members of the *Piccole italiane*, the Fascist schoolgirl organisation, in the *Stadio dei Marmi* in Rome.

Fascist women auxiliaries, at the time of the *Repubblica Sociale Italiana* (RSI), 1943–45, stand to attention in the snow.

ABOVE: '*Duce!* Give us weapons!' Fascist women auxiliaries, daggers drawn, at the time of the *Repubblica Sociale Italiana* (RSI).

LEFT: Young Fascist women during the 1930s giving the Roman Salute. Mussolini banned the handshake because it was bourgeois.

Mussolini with his pet lioness, Italia, in 1924. Mussolini loved animals because they were motivated by instinct not reason. His favourite animal was the cat.

Mussolini with plastered nose just after the attempt to assassinate him by Violet Gibson in April 1926.

Romana – in order to bring Italian Catholics within the state – to make them Italians. Though talks had occurred before the March on Rome, most notably between Benedict XV and, first Orlando then Nitti, it is unlikely that they would have succeeded had they continued, given the fractiousness and feebleness of the Italian parliament and the anti-clericalism of its political leaders and the King. The liberal-conservatives of the *ancien régime* regarded the *Legge delle Guarantigie* of 1871 as the perfect embodiment of Cavour's formula *'libera Chiesa in libero Stato'* and therefore sacrosanct. They refused to contemplate its repeal and thus doomed their attempts to solve the *Questione Romana*. But as he was not part of the *ancien régime* and despised it, Mussolini felt no such attachment. The new Pope, Pius XI, who had succeeded Benedict XV in February 1922, was keen to unblock the impasse. But the situation called for a political leader who represented a clean break with the past and had the will and the power to achieve a solution.

Mussolini had made overtures to the Catholic Church from the start. In his first speech to the Chamber as an MP in 1919, for example, he had said that the 'only universal force which still exists today in Rome is that which shines out from the Vatican'. Once in power, his first Education Minister Gentile's education reforms in 1923 made compulsory the crucifix in classrooms and the teaching of religion in primary schools for the first time since 1877.[125] He had made swearing in public a crime, closed fifty-three brothels in Rome and 25,000 bars, made contraception a criminal offence, described modern negro-inspired dance rhythms as 'evil germs that will breed immorality in the minds of my people'[126] – in 1930, the regime would ban jazz[127] – and banned PNF members from being freemasons. In his determination to stifle the *Popolari* he had already held successful secret talks in 1923 with Cardinal Gasparri, the Vatican Secretary of State, during which he had agreed that the Italian government would bail out the struggling Banco di Roma – the bank of the Vatican – and Gasparri had agreed that the Vatican would distance itself from the *Popolari*. He had also baptised what he called his 'first series' of children in church in 1923, got married in a private religious ceremony in his Milan flat in 1925 and baptised Romano (1927) and Anna-Maria (1929) immediately.

Much has been written on whether or not Mussolini believed in God – most of it concludes that he did not. As a young man he was a strident atheist. But this atheism, as we have seen, was the result both of the immortal confidence of youth and of a hatred of the Catholic Church, which like so many he regarded as tyrannical and corrupt; the result, therefore, not of a lack of belief in God but of a lack of belief in a Catholic God. Mussolini believed in the supernatural and was deeply superstitious. A careful examination of his several utterances on the subject of God shows that he did believe in God but that Christianity did not have a monopoly on God. God, for Mussolini, was only partly Christian. At the Lausanne conference in 1922, just after he came to power, he told foreign journalists, 'My spirit is profoundly religious.'

Ludwig asked Mussolini if he believed in God for his book, *Talks with Mussolini*, first published in 1932, and received perhaps the most frank and full statement ever made by Mussolini on the subject.[128] But this answer was cut from the second edition of the book which appeared immediately after the first, so huge was demand. Mussolini had made only small changes, corrections mainly, to the original manuscript, written in German, before publication of the first edition. But he and the censors then made many changes, mostly small ones, to the original manuscript for the second edition of which the passage containing Mussolini's views on God was by far the largest. In the original, uncensored version of the manuscript, Mussolini replied, 'In my youth I did not believe at all. I had uselessly appealed to God to save my mother; and she died just the same ... But I do not exclude completely ... that at some point, in the course of millions of years, there took place a supernatural apparition, and that nature therefore is divine. But I did not witness it ... In recent years the belief has gathered strength in me that there could be a divine force in the universe.' 'Christian?' asked Ludwig. 'Divine,' he repeated ... 'Men are able to pray to God in many ways. We must leave each completely free to his own way.' Ludwig then asked Mussolini how he squared his famous fatalism with his equally famous will – predestination with free will. Mussolini replied, 'One must react against fatalism with the will. This is an interesting struggle. The will must prepare the terrain on which destiny must develop.'[129] Mussolini told a science congress on 31 October 1926 that 'there is no doubt that science, after studying phenomena, tries strenuously to explain the why in them. My humble opinion is this: I do not believe that science is able to arrive at an explanation of the why in phenomena, and therefore this will always remain a zone of mystery, a brick wall. The human spirit must write on this wall one word only: God. Therefore, in my opinion, a conflict between science and faith cannot exist.'[130]

When his younger brother Arnaldo, who had taken over as editor of *Il Popolo d'Italia* when he became Prime Minister in 1922, died unexpectedly of a heart attack on 21 December 1931 – he had just dropped their sister, Edgive, off at Milan station in his car – Mussolini wrote a short book, an extended obituary, that Christmas in memory of his brother, *Vita di Arnaldo*[131] which was published in 1933. Arnaldo's death had deeply depressed Mussolini. In the book he described Arnaldo as 'for twelve years my most precious collaborator', with whom he had 'the most full and reciprocal confidence' and to whom he spoke each evening on the telephone 'at about 10 p.m.' – had always had faith in God, wrote Mussolini, quoting Arnaldo, ' "not in a generic God which is at times called Infinite, Cosmos,

Existence, to diminish him but in God our Father creator of heaven and earth and in his son..." '.

The book concluded with Mussolini saying that he would never make a will and that he had only one wish: to be buried in the family crypt at the cemetery of San Cassiano in Predappio where 'my spirit, by then liberated from matter, will live after earthly life the immortal and universal life of God'. In 1941, when his second eldest son, Bruno, was killed while test-flying a bomber at Pisa, Mussolini, once more devastated, wrote a similar testimony, *Parlo con Bruno*, in which he wrote, 'How much time must pass before I descend into the crypt of San Cassiano to sleep beside you the sleep without end?' Mussolini believed, it is clear, in 'divine design'. His hostility to Catholicism was not caused by disbelief in God but by the actions of the Catholic Church. Elsewhere, he wrote, 'All of us, who from fifteen to twenty-five years of age saturated ourselves in *letteratura carducciana*, detested a "cruel old Vatican wolf" ...'[132]

Pius XI, who had been elected Pope in February 1922, was keen to continue the process begun by Benedict XV, his predecessor. Obviously, he disapproved of the violence of *squadrismo* but he much preferred Fascism to the anti-clericalism liberals of the *ancien régime* liberal-conservatives, the Socialists and the even more anti-clerical Communists whose violence he had seen when Papal Nuncio in Warsaw and the Bolsheviks were knocking on Poland's door in 1920. It was clear immediately that Pius XI wanted to break with the past from the day of his election by the cardinals as Pope when he appeared before the crowd on the balcony above St Peter's Square – the first pope to appear in public since Pius IX had shut himself away in 1870.[133] He would appear and speak in public fairly often which, given the trappism of previous popes, meant that his public utterances carried great weight.

But though keen, Pius XI was pessimistic. Given the violence of *squadrismo*, the anti-clericalism of the Fascist *intransigenti*, and the spiritual nature of Fascism and its determination to control the spiritual education of the nation, he was deeply suspicious of Fascism. Privately in 1925 he had said that the time was not right to solve 'this difficult problem' and it should be left to his successor.[134] Yet within a year he had changed his mind. We do not have documents or statements to tell us why. By then Fascism, having survived the Matteotti crisis, had become a dictatorship but on the other hand it provided strong, stable government, there was much less violence than before, and as a result of Mussolini's subjugation of the PNF the *intransigenti* now had much less influence. It helped too that Fascism and Catholicism shared many of the same enemies: liberalism, Communism, freemasonry, even democracy. But it was the Pope's appraisal of Mussolini rather than Fascism, we can be certain, which made him change his mind. Publicly, for example, he described the latest attempt on Mussolini's life in Bologna on 31 October 1926 as 'insane' and 'dangerous to the country'.[135]

Like the Pope, Mussolini was unable to proceed as quickly as he would have liked. For despite their reduced influence, he could not ignore the anti-clericalism of the *intransigenti* and their chief spokesmen Farinacci, Balbo and Arpinati. Quite apart from their hostility to Catholicism they believed, contrary to Mussolini, that any alliance Fascism made with non-Fascists weakened and diluted Fascism. Certainly, the bigger the support base of Fascism became, the weaker the influence of the *intransigenti* over it. Nor could Mussolini ignore the views of Fascist intellectuals such as Gentile, chief philosopher of the regime, whose idea of the ethical state meant that the state should govern not just the temporal life of the nation but its spiritual life as well. To separate the temporal and the spiritual in the ethical state, said Gentile, was impossible. The Catholic Church should be free but any deal which gave it a role within the Fascist state was anathema. He wrote, 'The separation of the spiritual and the temporal is ... a Utopia. Undoubtedly. And so the *Questione Romana* will live for ever.'[136]

In addition there was the King, who was notoriously anti-clerical – he had threatened to abdicate in 1919 as a result of Orlando's negotiations on the *Questione Romana*[137] – and who did not want to lose territory, even if the territory in question amounted to only 480,000 square metres.[138] But by the end of 1926 Farinacci was no longer PNF General Secretary and Mussolini had survived four assassination attempts, banned all opposition parties and become a dictator. It is a mark of the power and prestige Mussolini now enjoyed that he felt able to start formal negotiations. It helped, of course, that those negotiations took place in secret.

The talks on the *Questione Romana* – as it was called – began in the second half of 1926 and, like those on the Banco di Roma and the *Popolari* in 1923, were held in the utmost secrecy. An informal sounding-out process produced favourable results and in August 1926 Mussolini, via Domenico Barone, a Councillor of State whose ties with the Vatican were close, informed Pius XI, via Francesco Pacelli, a papal lawyer and brother of Eugenio, the next Pope, Pius XII, that if the Vatican renounced all temporal claims in Italy he was ready to proceed. The Pope, via Pacelli, agreed on condition that the *Legge delle Guarantigie* be regarded as non-existent. Mussolini agreed. On 10 December 1926 Vittorio Emanuele, unenthusiastic, gave his consent. On 31 December, Mussolini wrote to Barone authorising him to start formal negotiations.

The Pope, however, refused. The fourth attempt on Mussolini's life at the end of October 1926 had prompted yet another explosion of violence against opposition targets, including Catholic organisations. The Pope informed Mussolini that unless he publicly deplored the violence, the negotiations could not proceed. Mussolini refused, but he handed Padre Pietro Tacchi Venturi copies of the order to stamp out the violence and punish those responsible that he had sent to the prefects and *federali*. The padre had been involved in the 1923 talks between Mussolini and Cardinal Gasparri and was once more involved. This placated the Pope.

But then in early December, the Pope received news of imminent regulations on the running of the *Balilla* – the new Fascist youth organisation – which included the banning in towns with less than 10,000 inhabitants of all non-Fascist youth groups. The *Balilla* – whose full title was *Opera nazionale balilla per l'assistenza e l'educazione della gioventù* (ONB) – had been founded in April 1926 for the 'spiritual' education (in the Fascist–Gentilean sense of the word) of the nation's youth – in other words their *'fascistizzazione'*. 'Balilla' had been the nickname of a teenager who, according to legend, had thrown the first rock at Austrian troops in a rebellion at Genoa in 1746.[139] Boys were *Balilla* from the age of eight to fourteen, *Avanguardisti* from fourteen to eighteen, then *Giovanni fascisti* until they joined the PNF and/or the militia at the age of twenty-one.[140] Girls enrolled in separate organisations such as the *Piccole Italiane*. Only boys wore black shirts, but girls wore black skirts.[141] By July 1927 the total membership of the *Balilla* was 1,236,000.[142] In 1939, 7,891,547 young Italians were members of the *Gioventù italiana del littorio* (GIL) which had replaced the ONB in 1937.[143] It was only in 1939, however, that membership became compulsory. By 1941, the total figure had risen to 8,830,000.[144] The GIL took as its motto the Fascist slogan 'Believe Obey Fight'. Its role was the 'spiritual, sporting and premilitary preparation' of the nation's youth.[145]

The proposed ban on non-Fascist youth groups would mean the end of the Catholic youth groups belonging to the Church's lay organisation, *Azione cattolica*, founded at the turn of the century. These included the *Giovanni esploratori* and the *Gioventù cattolica* – launched by Pope Benedict XV in 1916, which by now had a combined total of roughly 200,000 members.[146] The Pope demanded that Mussolini stop the ban going ahead. Mussolini refused, which prompted the Pope to speak out in public – in the same speech in which he described the Bologna assassination attempt as 'insane' – against this threat to the Church in the field of the spiritual education of Italians.[147] And in January 1927 he told Pacelli to inform Mussolini that as a result formal negotiations could not begin. But after Mussolini had given assurances that he had no intention of touching *Azione cattolica* itself and that this could be written into any agreement, the Pope agreed that informal contacts at least could continue. This they did.

The situation improved throughout 1927. There was little Fascist violence and this, noted the *Osservatore romano*, the Vatican's mouthpiece, in September was 'undeniably' thanks to the Fascist government. The talks proper began on 28 January 1928. But then in April, Mussolini extended the ban on non-Fascist youth organisations to towns of more than 20,000 inhabitants. The Pope once more threatened to abandon the negotiations. In response, Mussolini watered down the ban to affect only 'semi-military' organisations, which meant the 28,000 members of the Catholic scout movement, the *Giovanni esploratori*, but not the *Gioventù cattolica* and other groups.

On 4 January 1929, as the talks neared fruition, Barone died and was replaced by Mussolini himself and Rocco, the Justice Minister, who had drafted the laws establishing Mussolini's dictatorship and the corporate state. Mussolini met Pacelli fifteen times in January and February 1929 in his Via Rasella flat after dinner. Often these meetings continued until well after midnight.[148] Pacelli himself had 129 audiences with the Pope in all on the matter.[149]

For months, there had been rumours of an imminent agreement. Nitti responded from exile to the rumours with an article published in several foreign newspapers in which he said that there was absolutely no chance, now or in the future, of such a treaty between the Italian government and the Holy See. Nitti, as so often, was wrong.[150]

There were two separate agreements which collectively became known as the Lateran Accords after the papal palace in which they were signed by Mussolini and Cardinal Gasparri just before midday on Monday, 11 February 1929: a diplomatic treaty establishing the Vatican as an independent state which recognised and was recognised by Italy and which agreed to compensate the Pope for the loss of the papal states; and a concordat establishing the status of the Catholic Church in Italy.

The stumbling block was not the original problem – the *Questione Romana* – at all: the recognition of the Vatican as an independent state by Italy and vice versa, nor the issue of compensation. These were dealt with relatively easily. Indeed, Mussolini had made them a precondition of the talks. Consequently, the Pope formally renounced all claims to temporal power except over the Vatican and several small possessions elsewhere such as Castelgandolfo, the papal summer residence, and he recognised the sovereignty of the House of Savoy over Italy and Rome as the capital. Article 1 – there were twenty-seven articles in the treaty – defined Catholicism as 'the religion of the State'[151] but stated that all other faiths were 'tolerated'. Under the financial agreement, Mussolini agreed to pay the Pope 750 million lire in cash (*contanti*) by way of compensation plus the equivalent of one billion lire in government bonds[152] – an enormous sum which equalled the total deposits in the Catholic Church's 2500 rural banks.[153] A famous song released in 1938, for example, was '*Mille lire al mese*' and went, 'If I could have *mille lire al mese*'. So, looked at another way, this billion lira represented the annual salary of 100,000 well-off

Italians. But the compensation was half what the Vatican had initially pressed for.

The stumbling block, as it was bound to be, was the issue of the Catholic Church's role within Italy; in particular its role in the education of the nation's youth but also in the family life of the nation. Fascism aspired to *fascistizzarre* the Italian people. This required the people to have faith in Fascism. Catholicism aimed to *cattolicizzare* the people. It too required faith. Both needed to capture the spiritual in the people – especially the young. Conflict here was inevitable. On a strictly political level, it had been clear for some time as well that the banned *Popolari* were attempting resurrection by means of *Azione cattolica*. In general, the Church was prepared to concede ground, and did, on the issues of temporal sovereignty and compensation but not on this issue of its spiritual role in Italy.

Mussolini agreed that Catholic marriage would have legal status and that divorce would be illegal unless such a marriage were annulled, or dispensed with on the grounds of non-consummation, by the ecclesiastical court. (It is hard to believe, but from 1870 until 1929, a religious marriage in Italy had had no status in law.) Mussolini also agreed that religious education would be compulsory in all schools – not just primary schools as before – and that both the teachers of the subject and the texts used would be approved by the Catholic Church. In return, Pius XI agreed that *Azione cattolica*, whose continued existence was assured, would not take part in political activity of any kind. Article 43 of the Concordat recognised *Azione cattolica* and its youth groups 'inasmuch as' they conduct 'their activities independently from all political parties'.[154] Article 11 even guaranteed the Catholic Church the right to communicate with Catholics via the Catholic press whose main titles were *L'Avvenire d'Italia* and the *Osservatore romano* and which had remained like Croce's *La Critica* relatively free of censorship, compared with the rest of the press. The *Osservatore romano* had a daily circulation estimated at 250,000 in 1939.[155]

The Lateran Accords were a stunning propaganda coup for Mussolini; proof to the world that he, if not Fascism, was a force for good. Once again he had shown that Fascism was not dominated by dogma, that it was flexible; that the strength of Fascism – Mussolini's Fascism at any rate – was not a programme set in stone but a vision: the creation, by means of the state, of a nation. Francesco Crispi, Prime Minister several times between 1887 and 1896, had said, 'The greatest Italian statesman will be he who resolves the *Questione Romana*.'[156] Mussolini had done it.

The accords also had a concrete political consequence in Italy: they brought over Italy's Catholics not just to Italy, but to Fascism. The accords were a crucial reason why unquestionably from now on Mussolini enjoyed the consent of the majority of Italians. They also weakened still more the influence within Fascism of the *intransigenti* and they undermined the attempts of the banned *Popolari* to re-emerge via *Azione cattolica* as a political force – though to start with the *Popolari* were confident that the opposite would be the case.

On 13 February 1929, two days after the signing ceremony, Pius XI told an audience at the Catholic University in Milan, 'Perhaps it required a man like him whom Providence has made us encounter, a man for whom the preoccupations of the school of liberal thought were foreign.'[157] In the popular imagination this notorious phrase became quickly transformed into 'the man sent by Providence' to untie the Gordian Knot of the *Questione Romana*. Arnaldo Mussolini, writing in *Il Popolo d'Italia*, said that despite his 'unquiet spirit', which in youth made him question everything, his brother had 'known how to bring himself back to the great divine truths that withstand the assault of the centuries'. Mussolini quoted this article in *Vita di Arnaldo*, adding, 'With these words, Arnaldo demonstrated that he knew the intimate and tormented battles and vicissitudes of my spirit.'[158]

On 14 May the new Chamber, elected in the 24 March 1924 plebiscite before which *Azione cattolica* and the Catholic press in the wake of the agreement had urged Catholics to vote 'yes', ratified the accords with 357 MPs in favour and two against after a four-day debate during which Mussolini had spoken for nearly four hours.[159] Mussolini's speech appeased the Fascist *intransigenti* but certain passages irritated the Vatican intensely. He said, for example, that had Christianity not left Palestine and come to Rome, it would 'probably' have remained just one of many sects in the Middle East such as 'the Essenes and the Therapeutae'. Its presence in Rome – the Rome of the Roman Empire – ensured it became a world religion.

On the crucial issue raised most notably by Gentile of the separation of the temporal and the spiritual, Mussolini conceded that a clear-cut separation between Church and state was impossible because 'the citizen is Catholic and the Catholic is citizen'. But he added, 'The Fascist state ... is Catholic, but it is Fascist, in fact above all exclusively, essentially Fascist. It integrates Catholicism, and we declare it openly, but let no one think of changing the cards we have on the table.'[160] The Pope was not amused. The next day, speaking at the Jesuit College of Mondragone, he said, 'The state should interest itself in education but the state does not exist to absorb, swallow, annihilate the individual and the family; it would be absurd, it would be against nature, given that the family exists before society and the state ... In a certain sense one can say that it is called to complete the work of the family and the Church.'[161]

In the Senate on 25 May, Croce and Albertini were among just six senators to vote against approval of the accords after a two-day debate. Croce said that he was not opposed to a resolution of the *Questione Romana* but he objected to the Lateran Accords because they opened the door to the '*confessionalizzazione*' of the state. To the extent that Catholicism was now the religion of the State, religious teaching compulsory, and religious marriage had legal status, this was true. Mussolini delivered a much shorter, more conciliatory speech than in the Chamber. He said that when he had spoken of Christianity owing its success to Rome he had not meant to exclude the role of 'divine design' in that success. Later he told his sister, Edvige, that his statement to the Chamber that but for the Roman Empire Christianity would have remained a sect had been a mistake. It was absurd to suggest that Christianity owed its success to the Roman Empire, which by then had become decadent. He told her that the impulse behind the remark had been envy of the power of the Catholic Church.[162]

Outside parliament, Italian Communist leaders admitted that the accords would widen popular support for the Fascist state temporarily but Fascism had nevertheless capitulated to the forces of reaction. Exiled anti-Fascists said that the accords betrayed the Risorgimento principle, '*tutta la libertà alla Chiesa Romana, ma nessuna sovranità giuridica e temporale del Papa*' (complete freedom to the Roman Church but no judicial and temporal sovereignty to the Pope). The Jews were worried that with Catholicism now the official religion in Italy they would suffer persecution. They were wrong – for now. As Mussolini told the Chamber, 'The Jews have been in Rome since the time of the kings; perhaps they provided clothes after the Rape of the Sabines; there were 50,000 of them at the time of Augustus and they asked to weep on the tomb of Julius Caesar. They will remain undisturbed, as will those who believe in any other religion.'[163] The *intransigenti* and the *Gentiliani* were silent. The King seemed happy.

The formal exchange of the ratifications of the Lateran Accords was due to take place on 7 June. But right up to the evening before the haggling continued. Finally, at 10.30 p.m. on 6 June the two sides arrived at a form of words which both could accept. Pacelli described his trips to and fro that day between Mussolini and the Pope as 'perhaps the most laborious and difficult' of the entire negotiations.[164] Pacelli wrote in his diary, 'I regarded with infinite admiration the man in front of me, and for whom neither day nor night ever brought repose, but only a continuous empassioned work in the service of the nation.'[165]

The next day the exchange of documents took place. Mussolini appointed the Quadrumvir De Vecchi Italy's first ambassador to the Holy See. In December the King and Queen became the first members of the anti-Pope House of Savoy to meet a pope when they went to the Vatican. The scholarly and pious Jesuit priest, Tacchi Venturi, meanwhile became Mussolini's spiritual guide.[166]

The *Questione Romana* was closed. But the battle for the heart and soul of the nation was not. It was quickly clear that the accords had resolved the temporal issue but not the spiritual one. 'As we understand the controversy between Church and state in Italy,' wrote the American commentator

Howard Brubacker, 'the whole question is who gets the custody of the child.'[167] Mussolini was prepared to allow the Catholic Church to be the religion of the state – the Fascist state – and to be in charge of the religious education of the nation. But he was not prepared to allow religious education to verge on political education. The trouble was that the dividing line between the two words 'religious' and 'political' was impossible to define. Mussolini, in his speech to the Senate on the accords, spoke of Fascism's *'politica religiosa'*.[168] For in matters spiritual, where did the Fascist field of influence end and that of Catholicism begin? The problem was all there in Mussolini's phrase, 'The Fascist state is ... Catholic. But it is Fascist, in fact above all exclusively, essentially Fascist.' Gentile was right. To separate the temporal and the spiritual was impossible – at least in the ethical state which Fascism aspired to create.

In 1930 the Fascists founded the School of Mystical Fascism for the teaching of Fascist doctrine in Milan which they dedicated to Sandro Italico, the son of Mussolini's brother Arnaldo, who had died aged twenty in 1930 of leukemia[169] and in which Arnaldo was closely involved. In February 1940 the school would organise a conference entitled 'Why We Are Mystics'.[170] The Fascists of the first hour were by now in middle age. Fascism was determined to create both a ruling class to replace them and a people willing to follow them; the creation, as Bottai put it in 1930, of the *'massima intensità spirituale'* in the nation's youth. 'The problem of the *giovanni* is the central problem of Fascism,' he wrote.[171]

As a result, in 1931 there was a serious crisis between Church and state over the activities of *Azione cattolica* whose youth groups had increased their membership by one quarter to 246,000 since the Lateran Accords. The Fascist press launched a campaign against *Azione cattolica* accusing it of being a political party. It denied this. But to the extent that it had become a refuge for Catholic anti-Fascists and a forum for Catholic social teaching, which on many issues obviously was quite at odds with Fascism, the charge was true. Bottai's *Critica Fascista* accused *Azione cattolica* of 'invading the field of the syndicalist and corporatist system', of trying to create a rival ruling class and to channel Italy's youth towards 'the old programmes and rotting carcass of the Sturzian world'. There was a resurgence of Fascist violence against Catholic targets. The Pope insisted that the Catholic Church had the right to be present in the workplace. He also criticised Fascism for promoting the participation of women in sport, which even pagans had realised was wrong.[172] He added, 'Fascism says that it is and wants to be Catholic: well, to be Catholics not only in name but in fact, to be true and good Catholics ... there is only one way, one only, to obey the Church and its Head...'[173]

On 31 May Mussolini ordered the prefects to close 'youth organisations of whatever kind and for whatever age group which are not under the direct control of the *Partito Nazionale Fascista* or the *Opera Nazionale*

Balilla'. This meant that the *Gioventù cattolica* and *Federazione universitaria cattolica italiana* guaranteed under the Lateran Accords, faced the same fate as the *Giovanni esploratori*.

The Pope responded with several public criticisms culminating on 29 June[174] with his famous encyclical, *Non Abbiamo Bisogno*, in which he accused Fascism of pagan statolatry. Mussolini would not allow its publication in the Catholic press in Italy and the Pope was forced to publish it in France. In the encyclical he acknowledged the benefits of Fascism but deplored Fascist attempts to 'monopolise entirely the young from childhood to adulthood, for the exclusive advantage of a party, a regime, based on an ideology, which is openly transforming itself into a genuine pagan statolatry'.[175] He added, 'We have seen, in fact, a species of religion which rebels against the directions of higher religious authorities, and imposes or encourages the non-observance of these directions ... A conception of the state which makes the young generations belong entirely to it, without any exception from childhood up to adult life, cannot be reconciled by a Catholic with the Catholic doctrine and cannot either be reconciled with the natural right of the family...'[176]

Mussolini would not back down and that month decreed that PNF members could not be members of *Azione cattolica* as well.[177] But after Mussolini had assured the Pope that if its role were to be strictly religious, *Azione cattolica* would be allowed to carry on, the two sides reached a compromise. On 2 September 1931 the Vatican and Mussolini signed an agreement, treated as a codicil to the Lateran Accords, by which the Pope agreed that *Azione cattolica* was 'essentially diocesan' (i.e. would be decentralised, controlled not by the Vatican, but by the bishops), that none of its leaders could be from any of the banned opposition parties and that it would not 'be involved at all in politics' or in 'work of a trade union kind'. Mussolini revoked the ban on simultaneous PNF and *Azione cattolica* membership and permitted the Catholic youth groups to continue on condition that they stopped 'any activity of an athletic or sporting kind'.[178]

In 1929 schoolteachers had been required to swear an oath of loyalty to Fascism and now on 23 August 1931 so too were university teachers.[179] Turati, the then PNF General Secretary, had said in 1930, that teachers had to 'vibrate in unison' with the Fascist conscience.[180] Of 1225 university teachers in Italy only a handful refused to take the oath.[181] That same month Mussolini inaugurated the *Accademia d'Italia* – designed to emulate the *Académie Française* – whose first members included Enrico Fermi, (the nuclear physicist and Nobel prizewinner whose wife was Jewish, who would leave soon after the 1938 race laws for America where he would help make the atom bomb), Marconi, Pirandello, Marinetti, d'Annunzio (after initially refusing) and Gentile. Croce, nominated, declined.[182]

After 1931, there was no more open conflict between the Church and state until the anti-Semitic laws of 1938. Even then, Pius XI and the

Catholic Church, which was much more anti-Semitic than Fascism, objected only to the ban on marriages between Catholics and converted Jews. As De Felice has noted, Pius XI, in so doing, 'endorsed, if not in law certainly in the consciences of many Catholics, the principle of the persecution of the Jews.'[183]

Catholic anti-Semitism, which used as its justification the crucifixation of Christ by the Jews, had led in 1890, for example, to the diffusion by the Catholic Church in every Italian parish of a booklet, *La Questione giudaica in Europa*, which argued that the Jews merited divine castigation because they were 'the sworn enemies of the nations in which they found themselves' and 'do not have the right' to be treated like other citizens. In 1922, *Civiltà cattolica*, the Jesuit publication, claimed that Marxism was 'the perversion of a Semite fantasy' (Marx was Jewish) and the Soviet Union a 'Jewish Communist republic' (many Bolshevik leaders were Jewish).[184] In 1929 Padre Agostino Gemelli, the Franciscan founder of the University of the Sacred Heart, defended the justness of 'that terrible sentence which the *popolo deicida* has brought upon itself and for which it goes roaming around the world, incapable of finding the peace of a homeland, while the consequences of the horrible crime persecute it wherever and whenever'. Blunt as ever, Farinacci, who was an anti-Semite, said in a 1938 speech, 'If, as Catholics, we have become anti-Semites, we owe it to the teachings given to us by the Church for twenty centuries ... We cannot in the space of a few weeks renounce the anti-Semite conscience that the church has formed in us down the millennia.'[185] When Mussolini met Pius XI in February 1932 for the one and only time on the third anniversary of the Lateran Accords the Pope, worried about Communism, told him 'When I was in Warsaw, I saw that in all the Bolshevik regiments, the civil commisar or commisaress was Jewish.'[186] Most Fascists, on the other hand, until very late on, objected to the Jews, if they objected to them at all, only because they saw them as the epitome of the detested bourgeois spirit. For Mussolini the spirit, not race, is what counted.

The Catholic clergy supported much of the Fascist doctrine, especially on issues such as prolific mothers and the corporate state. And though they did not approve of totalitarian government or Gentile's idea of the ethical state, they did support hierarchical government and, for missionary purposes, imperial expansion. Many clergymen had no qualms at all about doing the Roman salute and marching through the streets, and mass became an integral part of Fascist ritual; nor, unlike the Pope, did many especially object to Mussolini's view that Christianity owed its success to the Roman Empire. In 1935 Cardinal Ildefonso Schuster, Archbishop of Milan, during a service to commemorate the March on Rome, emphasised 'the importance of this date, 28 October, which opened a new chapter in the history of the peninsula, in fact, in the history of the Catholic Church in Italy'. Italy had just invaded Abyssinia and Cardinal Schuster praised the invasion, which 'brings in triumph the Cross of Christ, breaks the chains of the slaves, smooths out the roads for the missionaries of the Gospel'. Pius XII, who became Pope in 1939, described the invasion and colonisation of Abyssinia as a 'Crusade'.[187]

But *Azione cattolica* continued as the only serious forum of opposition within Italy to Fascism – though from now on, a clandestine forum. In 1943, for example, it had 2.5 million members. Many of the leaders of the Christian Democratic party, which dominated post-war politics in Italy until the 1990s, were members such as De Gasperi and Giulio Andreotti. Mussolini was right that it was a breeding ground for Catholic anti-Fascists and a political organisation. When Mussolini had met Pius XI in 1932, the Pope bestowed on him the *Speron d'oro* (the Order of the Holy Sepulchre)[188] – the highest civil honour in his gift. It is not known whether, as was customary, Mussolini kneeled before the Pope and kissed his hand during the audience, though this was the subject of intense press speculation at the time.

Ludwig asked him about it for his book, *Talks with Mussolini*, and it would seem that Mussolini did not kiss the Pope's hand. In the second edition of the book – the censored one – Ludwig wrote, 'In general,' answered Mussolini, 'I "do as the Romans do". That is to say, I accept the customs of a country where I am being entertained. At the Vatican, I was left to follow my own bent.'[189] This answer was equivocal. It is the version usually relied on by historians. But in the original version, the reader is left in no doubt. In it Ludwig wrote, 'Mussolini answered, "In general I follow the customs of a country when I am a guest there. Here I had myself dispensed beforehand, expressly, from the duty of kneeling and of the kiss of the hand."'[190]

11

THE FASCIST FAITHFUL
AND THE CULT OF THE DUCE

Fascism was not rational, let alone scientific. But it did make 'rational use of the irrational'.[1] One can talk of a Fascist 'spirit' or 'mentality', therefore, but not a Fascist 'policy'. In 1932 – the tenth year of Fascist rule – Mussolini wrote, 'The elaboration of the principles of the Fascist state has not been rapid, nor easy. Fascism did not have a programme ready and waiting to activate ... This explains why the Fascist revolution is still young and fresh.'[2]

In 1932 the clearest statement on Fascist ideology – the *Dottrina del fascismo*[3] – written by Gentile and Mussolini, proclaimed, 'Fascism is a religious conception of life' which aims to found 'a spiritual society'. In this spiritual society, the bourgeois spirit would be replaced by the Fascist spirit. The state, which was the embodiment of 'a superior law, an objective will', would accomplish this task. The state would transform the individual with whom it was in 'immanent connection' into a 'conscious member' of the spiritual society.[4] Fascism, said the *dottrina*, was 'first and foremost a system of thought'.

The trouble was that in reality the state – 'the conscience and will of the few, even of One' (*Dottrina del fascismo*) – was Mussolini. And Mussolini, though superior, was not objective. Apart from anything else he was human. This he realised. In 1944, after his overthrow, he would write, 'Have you ever seen a prudent calculating dictator? They all become mad, they lose their equilibrium in the clouds, between quivering ambitions and obsessions. And it is actually that mad passion which brought them to the place where they are. A good *borghese* would never make himself so uncomfortable.'[5] But at about the same time he told a journalist, 'All dictators ... have slaughtered their enemies. I am the only passive one ... I believe I have ennobled dictatorship ... Stalin sits on top of a mountain of human bones. Is that good? Is it bad?'[6]

The consent Italians had for the Fascist religion sprang from faith *and* reason. But it was faith which enabled it to endure and which made unnecessary the violent coercion of Italians by Fascism. There was no Leninist or Stalinist terror in Fascist Italy. There was no need. Fascism, said the *Dottrina del fascismo*, had 'created a faith' which had 'conquered souls'[7] and faith, as Mussolini was fond of saying, unlike reason, moves mountains. Until Fascism, only the army and the Church had 'captured the heart and imagination' of the Italian people, Ardengo Soffici, the Fascist polemicist had written.[8] But Fascism did not aim to create its own God as Robespierre had tried to do, nor did it aim to banish God as Communism did. Fascism aimed to coexist with God.

Perhaps the most poignant evidence of the nature of Fascism and depth of faith in it was the reaction of Italians to Mussolini's decision to invade Abyssinia in October 1935. On 18 December, after the imposition of sanctions on Italy by the League of Nations, Mussolini called on Italians to donate their wedding rings – in exchange for steel ones – and other gold to help the invasion effort. Hundreds of thousands of Italians heeded the call and handed over a total of 33.622 metric tons of gold. They included Marconi and Queen Elena, who handed over their wedding rings, Pirandello, who handed over the Nobel Literature prize medal he had won in 1934, and even Croce, opponent of the regime, who gave his senator's medal. Mussolini called 18 December 'La giornata della fede'. The Italian word 'fede' means wedding ring – and faith.[9] Marinetti, the Futurist, meanwhile, went off to fight in Abyssinia as a volunteer. He was sixty.[10] But, of course, the faith Italians had in Fascism varied in its strength and origin just as does that of a congregation gathered in church for midnight mass on Christmas Eve.

Debate rages on the issue of consent: whether or not Italians supported Fascism and if so, whether their support was active or passive, or the result of brainwashing; how long it lasted and for what, Fascism? Mussolini? Both? Even in a modern democracy, bristling with opinion polls and elections, it is difficult to measure consent. Quite apart from anything else, all democratic governments rule with less than 50 per cent of the vote and most with much less. Just as it is impossible to prove beyond reasonable doubt that the Italians did support Fascism, so too is it impossible to prove that they did not. The best that can be done is a judgement based on the balance of the probabilities given the available facts. The late Renzo De Felice caused howls of protest in 1974 when, *Mussolini il duce, vol. I, Gli anni del consenso 1929–36*, book 3, volume 1 of his labyrinthine biography of Mussolini, was published. A bomb was even thrown at his house. All he had claimed was that by the beginning of the 1930s the majority of Italians had accepted Fascism and that this acceptance could not be explained as resulting from fear. He did not claim that Italians had become fanatical supporters of Fascism, nor even that they had become active supporters. But his claim, nevertheless, was a cardinal sin of the most heinous kind – and still is – against the cultural consensus in post-war Italy, which claims that Fascism was imposed by violence and maintained by violence, and that Italians did not accept it, let alone support it. If there was support, it was not genuine, but the result of brainwashing.

The dominant force behind the creation of this cultural consensus in Italy was the Left, which insists that it was the true representative of the Italian people in the *Ventennio* (the Italian epithet for the Fascist period), not Fascism. The Left has had cultural hegemony in Italy throughout the post-war period. But anti-Fascists of all hues have been happy enough to go along with the view. It is easy to see why. For all anti-Fascists, of whatever political persuasion, Fascism was evil. If Italians supported it, Italians too were evil – or if not evil, brainwashed, and so not compus mentis. Or worse still, Fascism was not evil and that is why Italians supported it. Naturally, anti-Fascists could not and cannot possibly accept that.

Precisely the same argument was used by General Charles de Gaulle in France when for the sake of post-war national unity he allowed the lie to exist and grow ever fatter that the French were a nation of *résistants* during the war. The truth, of course, was the opposite. Unlike de Gaulle, the vast majority of Frenchmen – including François Mittérrand – were *collabos*. But the truth is the first casualty not just of war but of history. I believe, however, that where Fascism is concerned, the truth is that a critical mass of people in Italy did actively support Fascism and an even larger proportion, a clear majority, did actively support Mussolini. But I do not believe that Italians were evil. This is not because I believe Italians were brainwashed into supporting Mussolini and Fascism. It is because I do not believe Mussolini or Fascism were evil and that is why Italians supported them. I do believe, however, that Mussolini and Fascism did do evil – in the end. But there was nothing inevitable about their evil deeds. Nor were these evil deeds the responsibility of one man, Mussolini, or a handful of Fascist gerarchs. They were the responsibility of Mussolini and his gerarchs and the Italians. Mussolini gave the orders. But the Italians carried out those orders. To maintain that what the Italians as a nation got up to in the second quarter of the twentieth century was the result of brainwashing is quite simply nonsense. The 1937 novel, *Vino e Pane*, by Ignazio Silone, expelled from the Italian Communist party in 1930, is pertinent. It is about an anti-Fascist exile who comes back to Italy in 1935 to stir up insurrection against Fascism. No one is interested. They do not mind Fascism at all. As Josef Goebbels, the master propagandist, conceded in his diary on 30 June 1941, 'The listeners can see through our manipulation of the news, too clearly. It is all laid on too thickly.' Writing in 1946, the American journalist Herbert I. Matthews said, 'The Duce truly did have in those years an enormous popular consensus.'[11] Luigi Barzini wrote, 'His success seemed incredible. He was more popular in Italy than anybody had ever been and probably will ever be.'[12]

The core ingredient of the consent which Fascism enjoyed was faith – faith demanded by the spiritual essence of Fascism. As Gustave Le Bon had written, 'A religious faith or politics is founded on faith, but without rites and symbols faith will not last.'[13] In 1944 Mussolini wrote, 'I did not create Fascism: I extracted it from the subconscious of the Italians. If it had not been like that, they would not all have followed me for twenty years, all I say ... The gestures, the rites and the uniforms introduced into the life of the nation came to be an accusation against me of a personal mania for *grandezza*. Personally they would have left me indifferent had I not been sure that they appealed to the picturesque nature of the Italians.'

Despite all this a fashion among scholars – especially Anglo-Saxon ones – is to draw up scientific-looking columns and tables containing checklists of very dull words said to define Fascism, if not scientifically, academically. More often than not, these things are deployed with a short defining sentence containing strange words such as 'palingenetic' as in: Fascism was 'a type of ideological politics whose mystical nucleus, in its various permutations, is a palingenetic form of populist ultra-nationalism.'[14] According to another academic, Stanley Payne, the palingenetic definition has 'elegance, concision and exactitude'.[15] Many other academics agree that it is most persuasive. It may well be. It does seem to contain something about the spiritual essence of the beast. But, given the baffling language, who can say for sure? The Marxists, meanwhile, define Fascism as a bourgeois counter-revolution and call it and its variants elsewhere by the false umbrella term '*Nazifascista*' (Fascism was not National Socialism). The liberals, for their part, taking their lead from Freud, define Fascism as a moral sickness. To the man in the street – influenced by both these definitions but not to the best of his knowledge by the 'palingenetic' one – Fascism means what it always has meant since the Second World War and always will mean: 'right-wing', 'dictator', 'world domination', 'holocaust', 'evil', with much sado-masochism thrown in for good measure.

It is possible, however, to say a few things for sure about the nature of Fascism in Italy (hereafter Fascism) – where it began and made its name, as distinct from the hybrids of Fascism elsewhere such as National Socialism in Germany, from which it was very different but from which nevertheless all three of the definitions above derive. Fascism, unlike National Socialism, was optimistic about the future; it exalted the values of Ancient Rome – *Romanità* – which were real, not mythical, and eternal and with which it aimed to create the *uomo nuovo*. 'It is not a restoration but a renovation, a revolution of the idea of Rome,' wrote Bottai.[16] Fascism believed that mankind could progress, though Mussolini had quickly lost faith in the pre-Fascist generations. Italians were 'a race of sheep', he said privately, in need of 'beating, beating, beating'. 'It's the raw material which I lack. Even Michelangelo needed marble to make his statues.'[17] This is why Fascism focused such an enormous amount of energy on the *fascistizzazione* of youth.

The Nazis, on the other hand, did not look forward but back, aspiring to re-create a mythical Aryan. For them the modern was bad. For the

Fascists it was not. The Fascists did not burn books or ban modern art. Fascism did contain a strong current which has been labelled – wrongly – reactionary because it exalted the countryside, the provincial, the Latin and the Mediterranean, and the culture, values and wisdom of the peasantry, and because it detested the bourgeoisie, industrialisation, the city, the foreign and intellectuals. Its chief political supporters were the *intransigenti* – especially the Florentine Fascists – and its intellectual driving force, *Strapaese*, the movement founded by Mino Maccari, Ardengo Soffici, Leo Longanesi and Kurt Suckert – who changed his name to Curzio Malaparte. Naturally, these people were among those Fascists most keen on the Fascist battles for birth and grain, and against urbanisation in favour of *ruralità*. Actually, they were reactionary only if hostility to Capitalism and liberalism, the monarchy and parliament is reactionary. Soffici was a former Futurist. Malaparte wanted a revolution which was both 'anti-proletarian' and 'anti-bourgeois'. In 1923 he had publicly criticised Mussolini's 'frightful ties'.[18]

Fascism, by and large, was modernist. The Futurists, who exalted speed and the machine, had helped create and sustain it. Its core support came not just from the *piccolo borghese* but from the dispossessed and its core ideas came from the avant-garde. Fascism attracted and allowed all sorts of *avanguardisti*. Mario Sironi, scandalously not reckoned so but unquestionably among the great painters and sculptors of the twentieth century, and also the political cartoonist of *Il Popolo d'Italia*, was an ardent Fascist. He wanted to create a modern art which was a synthesis of the classical and the modern – just what Fascism wanted to do with the Italians. He and others had formed the Novecento movement in the mid-1920s to create a Fascist art and literature, and had secured the patronage of the then extremely influential Sarfatti. But the group was not a group; it was a collection of individuals. Sarfatti's attempts to make the art of Novecento the official art of Fascism failed, despite her best propaganda efforts and skilful use of catchy Fascist-friendly phrases such as 'modern classicity' or 'revolutionary restoration' to describe it. Fascism was not especially interested in having an official art – unlike the Nazis in Germany or the Bolsheviks in Soviet Russia. In July 1929 Mussolini wrote to her accusing her of making 'shameless' use of his name in connection with her manoeuvrings. He said, 'This attempt to make people think that the artistic position of Fascism is represented by your Novecento is both futile and a lie . . .'[19] But Mussolini was very keen on Sironi on his own.

Some of the most talented Italian modernist architects were Fascists such as Giuseppe Terragni, whose masterpiece was the Casa del Fascio in Como. Alberto Moravia's first novel, *Gli Indifferenti*, published in 1928 – a skilful exposure of the emptiness and hypocrisy of the Italian middle classes – was ridiculed by Sarfatti – she remained bourgeois to the last – and severely criticised by Arnaldo Mussolini who said that Moravia was 'the destroyer of every human value'.[20] Yet *Gli Indifferenti* was not banned and ran into four editions. Its target was the bourgeoisie, which Fascism detested, not Fascism. But, by implication, this meant that the Fascist plan to destroy the bourgeois spirit had failed.

Furthermore, the Fascists were not racist – necessarily. Mussolini believed, for example, that race was not a biological phenomenon but a spiritual one. In 1932 he told Ludwig, who was Jewish and whose real name was Emil Cohn, 'Obviously there is no such thing as a pure race ... But precisely from happy mixtures derives the force and beauty of a nation. Race: it is a feeling, not a reality; 95 per cent is feeling. I don't believe one can prove biologically that a race is more or less pure. Those who proclaim the nobility of the German race are by chance all non-Germans ... Anti-Semitism does not exist in Italy. The Italian Jews have always behaved well as citizens, and as soldiers they have fought courageously ... Lots are generals.'[21] A Jew, therefore, could be an Aryan, he told his biographer De Begnac.[22] A Jew could certainly be an Italian. Many of the most committed Fascists were Jews, as was Sarfatti, described by De Felice, who interviewed her before her death in 1961, as follows: 'I have never met anyone in all my life so sick with *Romanità*.'[23] Given Italy's rich racial mix, Nazi style racism would have been quite impossible in Italy anyway. The Fascists did not advocate the extermination of Jews. The Nazis did.

Fascism was a mass movement which was against class war and for class collaboration, born in the trenches of the Great War out of feelings of anger, ennui, impotence, isolation and perplexity, the causes of which were the cruelty of laissez-faire Capitalism and the death of certainty, both religious (theory of evolution), scientific (theories of relativity, the subconscious, chaos) and political (failure of democracy and monarchy). Fascism was left-wing in origin but the terms left and right wing are impossible to apply to Fascism in power; it was neither, even though it described itself as right-wing.[24] Furthermore, within Fascism, as within any political movement there were many Fascisms which themselves changed as time went by; the most obvious Fascisms being those of the *intransigenti*, the *revisionisti* and the *fiancheggiatori*. Above all, there was the Fascism of Mussolini himself.

Fascism despised the bourgeois spirit (parasitical) though not the entrepreneurial spirit (productive). On 18 March 1934 Mussolini said in a speech, 'The *fascista imborghesito* is he who believes that by now there is nothing left to do, that the excitement disturbs him, that there are too many parades, that it is time to tidy up, that one child alone is enough ... The Fascist credo is heroism, that of the *borghese* is egoism.'[25]

Fascism opposed class war because it was destructive not constructive. It was against parliamentary democracy because this had failed; it could not have occurred in a country where democracy worked or where the rationalist and materialist ideas of the enlightenment were strong. Italy's two most famous philosophers of the first half of the twentieth century, Gentile and Croce, were both neo-idealists who opposed the Anglo-Saxon concept of individual liberty. Gentile, a former disciple of Croce's, believed that the true state – his ethical state – was a *corpus* – a body politic – hence corporate state – and that the state was more important than the parts – the individuals – who comprised it because if the state was strong and free so too would be the individuals within it; therefore the state had more rights than the individual. Only within the ethical state could individuals realise themselves as proper individuals. The state is 'like a universal ethical will';[26] the state creates the nation and by so doing 'gives the people, conscious of their own moral unity, a will [*volontà*], and thus a concrete existence [*effettiva esistenza*].'[27] Mussolini said, 'The people is the body of the state and the state is the spirit of the people. In the Fascist concept the people is the state and the state is the people ... The tools with which this *idealità* is achieved in the state, are the party and the corporation.'[28]

But unlike the authoritarian right, which aimed to demobilise the masses and restore the past, Fascism aimed to mobilise the masses so as to create the new society of *uomini nuovi*. This ambition, traceable to, among others, the Jacobins of the French Revolution, has been called 'totalitarian democracy'.[29] Sarfatti, speaking in America in April 1934 on NBC's national radio network, said, 'To truly understand Fascism, one must first understand this truth: that it is not a reactionary tyrannical movement or a blind, ferocious hatred of change. On the contrary, it is and intends always to grow into an even more democratic aristocracy, governed not by the people but for the people and for their interests, ruled by a hierarchy which is always open, in which all can join and in which the interests of all have penetrated.'[30] For Gentile, liberalism and Capitalism created a political class which was remote and separate from the people. Fascism would bridge the gulf.

Nevertheless, Fascism claimed that dictatorship was not inevitable; the decision on dictatorship depended on circumstances. If times were difficult, dictatorship was necessary – as it was in democracies, the Fascists pointed out, in times of crisis. 'When dictatorship is necessary, it must be introduced,' Mussolini told foreign journalists at Palazzo Chigi in October 1923.[31] But given the dominant role Fascism gave the state and its hatred of parliamentary democracy, and given that it regarded its revolution as a 'permanent revolution', it is difficult to conceive of circumstances in which Fascism could govern except by dictatorship – apart perhaps from the Fascist Utopia in which the revolution was over and all Italians had become *uomini nuovi*. Mussolini had told Ludwig, 'My aim is, by degrees, by choice of the best specimens, to establish an elite.'[32]

It was nationalistic but, unlike Communism which wanted to impose Communism everywhere, it was no more imperialistic than, say, Britain, and far less so than Nazi Germany. Fascism, said Mussolini, was expansionist. Even Marx had supported British colonialism as a means of bring-ing progress to backward peoples.[33] But Fascism was militaristic. It agreed with Machiavelli that a nation had to be mentally and materially prepared for war not so much for the purposes of invading other countries but to deter other countries from invading Italy. Furthermore war, it believed, is inevitable. *La Dottrina del Fascismo* said, 'First of all Fascism, as far as the future and the development of humanity is concerned in general, and apart from any consideration of current politics, does not believe in the possibility nor the utility of perpetual peace.'[34] One of the dozens of decalogues the Fascists produced, this one for teenage Fascists, the *avan-guardisti*, stated, 'Use force, violence, arms, only in defence of your honour and ideas.'[35] Like Communism, Fascism regarded violence as morally justifiable in certain circumstances other than in self-defence or as capital punishment. Engels had called violence a purifying force and Sorel, the Marxist revisionist and revolutionary syndicalist whose influence on Mus-solini had been profound, had said that correctly used violence was moral and creative. The Futurists, whose ideas permeated Fascism, had exalted 'aggression ... the slap and the fist' in their original manifesto of 1909 and described war as 'the only hygiene in the world'.[36] But once Fascism was in power, a Fascist terror was unnecessary.

By 1930 *squadrismo* had virtually disappeared. Between 1930 and 1934, the OVRA, the secret political police, arrested 6000 political opponents, mostly Communists or members of *Giustizia e Libertà*, the non-party revolutionary movement which aimed to stir up armed insurrection against Fascism founded by Carlo Rosselli in October 1929 – an average of 125 a month.[37] But few of those arrested went to prison. During the 1930s the Special Tribunal imprisoned no more than several dozen political prisoners a year, though the numbers increased in the second half of the decade – 310 in 1938 and 365 in 1939.[38] Three people in all were executed during the 1930s for plotting to assassinate Mussolini.[39] Of the total of 12,310 Italians who had been sentenced by 1940 to '*confino*' in the islands or remote parts of the mainland, only 2504 still remained in *confino* – of whom about one-third were guilty not of political but criminal offences.[40] Conditions were tough but nothing like those in the Soviet gulags or Nazi concentration camps. Few died either in *confino* or prison.

Fascism aimed to bridle but not destroy Capitalism by means of the corporate state – the so-called Third Way between Capitalism and Com-munism. But unlike Communism, Fascism was not materialistic. It was against materialism; it did not believe that the pursuit of money could bring happiness. What was important was not a man's wallet but his spirit. It aimed to nationalise not property – the means of production – but people. Therefore, what remained constant in Fascism throughout was its policy, not on the economy or foreign expansion, which were secondary, but on people.

Most important, Fascism believed, as the Catholic Church still believed and as had actually been the case in the Middle Ages, that the temporal and spiritual could not be separated; therefore it was wrong to attempt to separate temporal and spiritual power. The Fascist cudgel, the *manganello*, was the *santo manganello*, the caster oil unction administered to purify the sinner, the *fasces* the cross, the progress from *Balilla* to the PNF at the age of twenty-one, each stage marked by solemn ceremony, culminating in the equivalent of confirmation – the annual *leva fascista* when young Fascists who had come of age became members of the PNF en masse and swore the Fascist oath together – and the reverence for the dead who had not died but were '*presente*' in the collective conscious of the living. At a Fascist funeral the senior Fascist would shout the name of the deceased comrade and the congregation kneeling would shout in reply, '*Presente!*'

The *Dottrina del fascismo* had said that Fascism was a result of 'the general reaction of the century against the tired and materialistic positivism of the nineteenth century'. It stated,

The world for Fascism is not this material world which it appears to be on the surface, in which man is an individual separate from everyone else ... governed by a natural law that instinctively compels him to live a life of egotistical and momentary pleasure. The Fascist man is an individual insofar as he is nation and *patria*, and that moral law which clasps together individuals and generations in a tradition and a mission which suppresses the instinct for the limited life of a short-term pleasure to establish as a duty a superior life free of limits in time and space; a life in which the individual, by means of the abnegation of self, the sacrifice of his own particular interests, his own death, achieves that wholly spiritual existence in which lies his value as a man ... Life, therefore, as Fascism conceives it, is serious, austere, religious. Fascism is a religious conception, in which man is seen in his inherent relationship with a superior law, with an objective will, which transcends the particular individual and raises him up to be a conscious member of a spiritual society ... Anti-individualistic, the Fascist conception is for the state; and it is for the individual insofar as this coincides with the state, the universal conscience and will of man in his historical existence. Liberalism denied the state in the interests of the particular individual: Fascism reaffirms the state as the true reality of the individual ... Fascism is for liberty. It is for the only liberty which can be serious, the liberty of the state and of the individual within the state ... Fascism, in summary, is not simply a provider of laws and founder of institutions, but educator and promoter of spiritual life. It wants to reconstruct not the form of human life, but the content, the man, the character, the faith.[41]

This spiritualistic, anti-materialistic view of the world both appealed to and worried the Catholic Church. Clearly, faith in Fascism presented a potentially insurmountable conflict with faith in God and it was this which had caused the 1931 crisis over *Azione cattolica* during which Pius XI had accused Fascism of being pagan. The Fascists insisted, however, that as long as the zones of influence in daily life were properly defined, there could be no conflict as Fascism did not possess a theology but an ethic. By and large, the Pope and the Church went along with this. They preferred to regard the spiritual essence of Fascism as complementary not contrary to the Church.

Mussolini said that the Church should be left free in 'all that concerns the salvation of souls' but he warned, 'We shall fight them ... the moment they try to trespass in the political, social and sporting fields.'[42] He told *Le Figaro* in 1934 that 'the Fascist state retains its right to intervene in religious matters ... only in the case where the facts touch on the political and moral order of the State.'[43]

But nevertheless the Fascist concept of the state meant that the relationship between the citizen and the state, with its emphasis on duty, sacrifice and the spiritual, was similar to that between a Christian and the Church. It amounted to the creation of a parallel religion.

Of liberty, Mussolini wrote in March 1924, 'Liberty is not a right: it is a duty. It is not a gift: it is a conquest; it is not equality: it is a privilege. The concept of liberty changes with the passing of time. There is a liberty in peacetime which is no longer liberty in times of war. There is a liberty in times of wealth which cannot be conceded in times of misery.' In September 1929 he wrote, 'The liberty, of which the democracies speak, is merely a verbal illusion, offered intermittently to the naive.'[44] Speaking at the School of Mystical Fascism in 1940, Mussolini said, 'Fascism must have its missionaries, that is men who know how to instil intransigent faith. It is faith which moves – literally – mountains.'[45]

1932: Year Ten of the Fascist Era

To celebrate their tenth year in power the Fascists staged the 'Exhibition of the Fascist Revolution' in Rome, which Mussolini opened on 29 October 1932 – day one of year eleven of the *Era Fascista*.[46] He also amnestied 659 political prisoners out of a total of 1059 and 595 of those held *in confino*.[47]

The 'Decennale', as it was called, was a Fascist masterpiece. It left the millions of people who saw it until 1935 when it closed in no doubt: Fascism was a religious cult and Mussolini its high priest. Sarfatti was not invited to the opening but turned up anyway. She threw a fit, started screaming and was shown the door in no uncertain fashion – a sign of the eclipse of her status even in her field of art. Her last article for *Il Popolo d'Italia* appeared the next day.[48] In early 1932 she had waited for two hours to see Mussolini at Palazzo Venezia – in vain.

The opening of the exhibition coincided with that of the Via dell'Impero which linked the Colosseum to Piazza Venezia.[49] It became nicknamed the 'Via del Consenso'. The road and other Fascist schemes in central Rome had involved the demolition of Renaissance buildings and the displacement of 4000 people to the suburbs. The aim was to liberate Rome's imperial monuments.

The tenth anniversary exhibition took place in the existing nineteenth-century Palazzo dell'Esposizione in Via Nazionale, not far from the *Quirinale*, which had been completely gutted and converted for the occasion. The intention was to create something '*modernamente monumentale*', the exhibition catalogue proclaimed, which conveyed the 'unconfoundable spirit' of Fascism. The spirit of the exhibition was decidedly modern. In particular, a cubist façade, painted black and red, was built on to the old building; the red representing the 'spirit of the ongoing Revolution'. Above the entrance stood four twenty-five-metre-high copper *fasces*, which looked like ships' funnels. Work on the exhibition – 305,524 man-hours in all – began in August 1932 and continued day and night right up until the opening ceremony. It included the laying of 4000 square metres of lino and the installation of a lighting system which was the equivalent of 600,000 candles.[50] Mussolini insisted that senators, academicians and PNF gerarchs, including Pirandello and Marconi, take it in turns to mount the guard of honour in the uniform of the militia.

Once inside, the first thing to confront the visitor was the Fascist oath of loyalty, sculpted like a prayer on a wall in black capital letters by which Italians promised to follow Mussolini's orders without question and to serve the Fascist revolution with all their strength, if necessary their blood.

The exhibition portrayed in photographs, documents and artefacts such as in a reconstruction of Mussolini's office at *Il Popolo d'Italia*, the history of Fascism and its achievements. It included works of art on the theme by, among others, the great painter and sculptor Sironi. The visitor, having progressed through the various rooms on the different key moments in the march of Fascism, arrived finally in the *Sacrario dei Martiri* (Memorial Chapel of the Martyrs). This was a large, dimly lit, circular room whose walls were painted black and the domed ceiling blue. Running round the black walls were six electrically lit white strips, one on top of the other, on which was the word 'PRESENTE!' repeated hundreds of times. Each PRESENTE! represented a Fascist who had sacrificed his life for the Fascist revolution but who was present nevertheless in spirit. In the middle of the room was a plinth from which glowed a red light – the blood of the martyrs. From this rose an enormous black metal cross on which were written in white the words 'PER LA PATRIA IMMORTALE!'. From somewhere within this temple to the fallen came the muffled sounds of the Fascist anthem 'Giovinezza' ... Blood and sacrifice. As Mussolini would write when his son Bruno died test-flying a bomber over Pisa in 1941, 'One single drop of the blood which gushed from your lacerated temples and flowed across your pale face is worth more than all my work, past present and future. Because only the sacrifice of blood is great; all the rest is ephemeral matter. Only the blood and the spirit, only blood counts in the life of individuals and peoples: only blood gives the purple of glory.'[51]

Duce! Duce!

By now, Mussolini – the Duce – enjoyed semi-divine status. In 1934 even Cole Porter wrote about him in his hit 'You're the Tops' which went, 'You're the tops! You're the Great Houdini! You're the tops! You're Mussolini!'. A peak on the Italian side of Mont Blanc had been renamed Monte Mussolini and a rose which was nearly black was named the Mussolini.[52] In March 1934 he staged a second plebiscite. The turn-out was 96.25 per cent and 10,526,503 voted '*sì*' – for the list of parliamentary candidates drawn up by the Grand Council as had been the case in 1929 – and only 15,201 '*no*' – proof of 'an authentic mass adhesion to Fascism'.[53] The Italian Socialist Lelio Basso, writing from Paris in *Politica socialista*, had to admit, 'Fascism is by now a habit, a reality even if irksome, about which one can grumble or laugh in turns, but which no one would seriously think of debating.'[54]

In June 1935 Mussolini, en route from Ostia to Salerno, survived yet another brush with death when the seaplane in which he was flying was struck by lightning at 3000 metres.[55] 'Chips' Channon wrote in his diary on 6 July, 'There is something classical in Mussolini's seaplane flying to Rome being struck by lightning. It would seem as if the Gods themselves were jealous of this dynamic man.' Channon had heard Mussolini speak in 1926, he wrote, and his 'flowing language' had held the audience 'spell-bound', adding, 'It gave me more of a thrill than my interview with the Pope.'[56]

In 1933, Franklin Delano Roosevelt, who had become President in March, invited Mussolini to America. Mussolini, who would never visit America, sent Guido Jung, the Finance Minister, one of many Italian Jewish Fascists, instead. Roosevelt told Jung that he was very worried about Hitler but that Mussolini was 'his only potential ally in his effort to safeguard world peace' and that Italy was 'the only real friend of America in Europe'.[57]

In February 1933, Churchill said in a speech to mark the twenty-fifth anniversary of the British Anti-Socialist and Anti-Communist League at the Queen's Hall, London, 'The Roman genius impersonated in Mussolini, the greatest law-giver among living men, has shown to many nations how they can resist the pressures of Socialism and has indicated the path that a nation can follow when courageously led. With the Fascist regime, Mussolini has established a centre of orientation from which countries which are engaged in a hand-to-hand struggle with Socialism must not hesitate to be guided.'[58]

Richard Washburn Child, American ambassador in Rome between 1921 and 1924, wrote that 'the Duce is now the greatest figure of his sphere and time'.[59] Child had written the foreword to Mussolini's 1928 auto-biography and it reads as if he were writing about a God. 'So he began. He dictated. I advised that method, because when he attempts to write longhand he corrects and corrects ... So he dictated. The copy came back, and he interlined the manuscript in his own hand – a dash of red pencil, and a flowing rivulet of ink – here and there.'[60] Much of the autobiography, Mussolini later revealed, had been written by his brother Arnaldo whom he had supplied with what he called 'the outlines'.[61]

Mussolini's prestige was phenomenal. In 1935 Salvemini, the exiled journalist and historian, and one of Mussolini's most relentless critics, was forced to concede that Italy had become a mecca for political scientists and economists in search of the Third Way between Capitalism and Communism.[62] On 29 November 1932 the *Morning Post* said that whether or not one approved of dictatorship, what Mussolini had achieved in Italy was 'magnificent', adding, 'History, looking back on the rebirth of Italy begun in October 1922, will be able to write the name Mussolini among those of the noblest Romans who ever existed.' In February 1933 even George Lansbury, the new leader of Britain's Labour Party, told the *News Chronicle*, 'If I were a dictator, I would do as Mussolini is doing.'[63] In April 1933 Sigmund Freud sent a copy of his book *Why War?* to Mussolini with a dedication which said, '*Benito Mussolini mit dem ergebenen Gruss eines alten Mannes der im Machthaber den Kultur Heros erkennt.*'[64] For as George Ward Price, the *Daily Mail*'s Rome correspondent, would write in 1937, the 'overwhelming majority' of Italians 'enthusiastically' supported Mussolini 'according to every test which can possibly be applied' – in other words, Ward Price reminded his readers, 'a much greater proportion' of the population than has 'ever voted for the Government of any democratic state.'[65] Only in 1943, after the Allied invasion of Sicily and the fall of Mussolini, did the anti-Fascists manage to mobilise any mass support at all. It is quite impossible to sustain the view that until then the nation did not support Fascism. Even if the support of most people was passive rather than active, there was not hostility.

Mussolini was Fascism. Mussolini was the state. In the Fascist year 1936–7 alone, Mussolini received 220,000 letters. On average he received 30–40,000 letters a month.[66] To cope with the deluge, Mussolini's *segretaria particolare* (private office) employed dozens of staff. Women in particular, hundreds of thousands of them, wrote to Mussolini. One woman from Bologna wrote a total of 642 letters in the course of five years – seeking a date.[67] In 1937 the French journalist, Magda Fontanges, shot the French ambassador, Charles de Chambrun, because she blamed him for the end of her affair with Mussolini. Here are some examples of other letters from women to the Duce (from *Caro Duce*):

Duce, I saw You yesterday during the tumultuous visit you made to our city. My eyes met Yours ... Of course, in my breast beats a heart and not a sponge drowned in lard like in those rows of common women who welcomed you in piazza endangering Your life. They were on the verge of breaking the windows of Your car to touch You: uncouth assassins. How I hate them! Until Your arrival in our city I was the unhappiest woman in the world. Badly matched to a man as cold as a tight hawser in the throat ... I feared I would never again, in life, know love. Now I know that I love You ... Now here, in the earth of Sienna, there is a flower which waits to be picked. Don't let it wither because, if You draw near, You will discover a passionate, devoted and discreet garden (Michela, December 1925).

Duce, you must ... believe no human figure is superior to You in our hearts. To demonstrate this to you the child I am about to bring into the world will have Your name or if it is a girl the name of Your most devoted wife. (Cesarina, June 1931).

Caro Duce, Tomorrow I return home from the summer holiday camp ... These fifteen days have been unforgettable ... I have to confess to You, Duce, that never having seen the sea I had never learned to swim. Despite the lessons from the signorine *and the instructions of the* bagnino *in the first few days I felt so much fear of drowning in the water and the salt which burned my eyes and my nose really irritated me. Then I remembered Your speech that we must always be brave and never give up until the goal is reached. So I put everything into it and I put up with the salt and I did not lift my head even if I was afraid: in the end, Duce, I learned how to do the first strokes and now I can nearly swim. Duce, I owe my joy to You ... (Silvia, August 1935).*

Eccellenza Mussolini Capo del Governo, Watching the departure of the gallant troops ... for the war against the infidel enemy I cried with emotion and rage because I am a woman and they won't let me fight for our Great Italy ... Other girls, who like me witnessed the departure, have confessed to the same feelings ... Give us weapons, Duce (Annalisa, June 1940).

Italian women adored Mussolini. He was the satisfier of what D. H. Lawrence had identified as the dominant urge in Italians. In *Twilight in Italy*[68] Lawrence wrote, 'I was startled. This, then, is the secret of Italy's attraction for us, this phallic worship. To the Italian the phallus is the symbol of individual creative immortality, to each man his own Godhead. The child is but the evidence of the Godhead.' He added, 'The substratum of Italy has always been pagan, sensuous, the most potent symbol the sexual symbol. The worship of the Cross never really held good in Italy.'[69]

Mussolini's sexual hold over Italian women infuriated the novelist Carlo Emilio Gadda, who had initially been a lukewarm supporter of Fascism. In his bitter post-war diatribe against Fascism, *Eros e Priapo* (first published as a whole in 1967), Gadda reserved much of his vitriol for Italian women and what he identified as the priapic bond between them and Mussolini. He wrote,

He made these delirious women believe that he was the only *genitale-eretto* available in the piazza ... He was the bringer of the sublime, the 'form' achieved by the sublime in the historical evolution of the country and its peoples ... He was the herald of the silver trumpet ... He was after all the dominant procreative organ, the paternal master phallus in chief ... These dear little women drank deeply [*colsero cosi*] the healthy breath of their husband or confidant, thinking of the *kuce* ... holder of the only and the central barrel of sperm ... The maddest women, those most seized by the image, had no need of a husband, lover or fucker ... The Idea was enough, the Idea alone of the *patria*, and of the *kuce*. It was enough just to imagine the *kuce* in the act of saving the *patria* for them to feel saved. One of these mad women succeeded in producing a child: with the portrait of the *kuce* ...[70]

The view of Italian women that the Duce was 'phallus in chief' meant that they queued up – literally – to make love with him. A primary-school teacher in Piedmont even wrote to invite him begging him to exercise the medieval *droit de seigneur* on her wedding night. He declined and sent the police instead.[71] According to Quinto Navarra, Mussolini's usher at Palazzo Venezia, he had sex with a different woman nearly every single day from September 1929, when he moved his office there, until the collapse of the regime on 25 July 1943. No doubt Navarra exaggerated. But the same office – the *segreteria personale* – which read and responded to all letters to Mussolini, also dealt with the constant stream of love letters from women. These letters would be filed initially under the headings 'known' or 'new'. The police made enquiries about promising 'new' women and if deemed suitable Mussolini would be shown their letters to decide whether or not he wished to meet them. The encounters took place at Palazzo Venezia in the late afternoon.[72] Navarra wrote, 'Women of all types and all classes, if not of all ages. He seemed to prefer mature women ... Besides, in this area, he was not fussy, and for me who saw day after day a new woman cross the inviolable threshold of the dictator, it became ever more obvious that beauty was not indispensable in his lovers, confirmation of the ephemeral and bureaucratic character with which he treated these fleeting adventures between official audiences with the regularity of a timetable established in advance.'[73]

Mussolini's office at the fifteenth-century Palazzo di Venezia, which resembles a fortress, was in the Sala del Mappamondo, so named because it was here that the world's first globe was kept. The hall is on the first floor and enormous – sixty feet long, forty feet wide and forty feet high. Apart from the large table at which Mussolini worked at the far end, and a few chairs and two other tables nearby, there was no other furniture. Mussolini kept his work desk in meticulous order. He always used the same square-nibbed fountain pen, and the same type of red and blue Faber pencil to make comments or corrections to the enormous amount of written material that crossed his desk. This included the huge number of newspapers he read every day, as well as the OVRA reports on friend and foe alike. He filed everything that crossed his desk, even invitations.[74] There were three telephones on the desk and inside one of the drawers a revolver. He could not stand umbrellas, sofas or slippers – bourgeois – hearses or funerals, and flies. If he heard a fly, he would ring for Navarra to come with the swat. He could not stand any noise at all either. The use of klaxons was banned in Rome and a café in Piazza Venezia forced to close.

It was in the vast silence of this office that Mussolini received the women. The love-making took place on a stone window seat, against a wall, or on a carpet, and was rapid. Once over, Mussolini would dismiss the women immediately without even offering them 'coffee, liqueur, or even a piece of cake'.[75] And it was here that Mussolini and Claretta Petacci, the daughter of a Rome doctor, became lovers in 1936. Normally Mussolini preferred mature women, perhaps because there was less chance of emotional drama. But Petacci – who had written him letters and poems as a teenager like so many others – was nearly thirty years younger than him. In 1936 he was fifty-three and she was twenty-four. Normally he never sought anything except sexual release. This time it was different.

Chance, or destiny as he would say, not her teenage letters, brought them together. Four years earlier, on 24 April 1932, a cloudy, rainy Sunday, Mussolini was driving to Ostia on the coast from Rome in his red Alpha Romeo sports car – followed by his bodyguards in another car – and overtook a Lancia in which Petacci was travelling in the same direction with her mother, Giuseppina, nine-year-old sister Myriam, and fiancé Riccardo Federici, an air force lieutenant. The Petaccis recognised Mussolini and an exhilarated Claretta urged their driver to chase him. They caught up with him at Ostia and she leaped out and went over to him, followed by her fiancé. Mussolini spoke to both of them briefly and she mentioned her letters to him. Several days later Mussolini telephoned the Petaccis' home and asked to speak to Claretta. He had found her poems to him, he said, and invited her to come and see him that evening at 7 p.m. at Palazzo Venezia. 'I have not slept thinking about you,' Mussolini told her during their brief encounter, she recalled.[76] He was smitten immediately, it seems. 'He was in love because Claretta represented for him the reincarnation of the ideals of his youth,' recalled Myriam.[77] Mussolini invited Claretta to see him fairly frequently after that. It seems that their relationship remained platonic. 'For her it was sufficient to be received by her *uomo-mito*, talk with him, to listen to him,' said Myriam.[78] Quite apart from anything else, Claretta was engaged and duly married in June 1934 to Federici. The marriage was an instant failure and the couple agreed to separate. In 1936 Federici was posted to Tokyo as air force attaché at the embassy, where he remained. Mussolini may well have been behind the posting. It is unclear precisely when Mussolini and Petacci became lovers but it was probably at some point in 1936 after her separation. She started to visit him at Palazzo Venezia again and in October that year – the month of the invasion of Abyssinia – he summoned her mother to Palazzo Venezia and asked her: 'Signora, do you permit me to love Claretta?'[79] That same month Mussolini gave Petacci use of the flat at Palazzo Venezia. Here she would come every day, entering Palazzo Venezia by a side entrance, from just after lunch until about 9 p.m. when Mussolini went home, for the next seven years. She would rarely see him for more than half an hour. While waiting for him in the flat, she would smoke – with the windows open because he hated smoke – listen to music (Chopin's Nocturnes were a favourite) or read, in particular, the poems of Elizabeth Barrett Browning. She was insanely jealous of his other women and would interrogate Navarra, who gave nothing away. Mussolini admitted he was unfaithful in general – though never in particular – but urged her 'not to be jealous of this animal part of my being...'[80]

Once back home at night, she would wait for his brief telephone call. But like most womanisers he too was jealous of her. 'I love you, so much so much ... Jealousy makes me insane,' he told her in one of many telephone conversations between them tapped by the SSR (Servizio speciale riservato). In another she complains that he is tormenting her. He says he too is tormented. She complains that he has been seeing a woman called Romilda. 'But you're mad,' he replies. 'It's useless lying ... she sits where I have sat ... on the same sofa, My God!'[81] But unlike him, she had no life apart from him. She wrote in her diary, 'I feel as if I am sent by God to help him and defend him ... I am necessary to him because he is alone.'[82] She told a friend, 'A woman must, day by day, hour by hour, construct around the man of her heart a building in which he, without realising it, finds himself a prisoner ... What I mean is ... that many women would not cry "afterwards" if "before" they had worked, made an effort so that the circle around their loved man rose up solid and insurmountable.'[83] All Rome quickly knew about La Petacci. But Rachele, who knew about Sarfatti, apparently never knew about Petacci until 1943.

The Glory Years: *I Ragazzi degli Anni Trenta*

In the Thirties Italy had extraordinary success in the sporting and technological fields; success which gave Mussolini and Fascism even more prestige. In 1933, the Italian liner, *Rex*, set a new record for crossing the Atlantic – four days, twenty-three hours and twenty-eight minutes.[84] In both 1934 and 1938 the Italian football team won the World Cup – apart from Italy only Brazil has won the world cup back to back – and the gold medal at the Berlin Olympics in 1936. In 1930 Tazio Nuvolari, driving an Alfa Romeo, had won the *Mille Miglia*, beating a Mercedes to usher in a golden age for Italian motor racing and Balbo, Air Minister since 1929, led fourteen Italian Savoia Marchetti flying boats across the Atlantic to Rio de Janeiro and back. In 1933 Balbo, still only thirty-seven, repeated the feat – this time with twenty-four Savoia Marchettis – touching down in Chicago where he and his fellow flyers received a tumultuous reception and he the honour of having Chicago's 7th Street renamed General Balbo Street and being made a Sioux chief. The planes then flew to New York where they received an even bigger welcome, and he met President Roosevelt. Lindbergh, the first man to fly across the Atlantic in 1924, described the transatlantic flight as the greatest aeronautical achievement ever.[85] As a result Mussolini made Balbo Air Marshal but then in mid-October sacked him as Air Minister, taking over the post himself and banishing Balbo from Italy to be Governor of Libya. Mussolini had already taken over the War Ministry in July and now, in addition to Balbo's job at Air, took over the Navy Ministry as well. Mussolini was always envious of anyone else who threatened to attract more adulation than him. But this is not why he sacked Balbo. Balbo, like Farinacci and many other senior Fascists, but unlike Mussolini, was deeply corrupt. Mussolini knew this from the secret services which steamed open letters, intercepted telegrams, had paid informers everywhere and tapped telephones. Phone tapping was the responsibility of the Interior Ministry's SSR, set up by Giolitti, which by now employed hundreds of stenographers in Italy's major cities. The SSR spied on Fascists as well as the enemies of Fascism. Galeazzo Ciano – married to Edda Mussolini and by now the coming man – thought that one of Balbo's chief characteristics was his 'total untrustworthiness'.[86] But more important than this or Balbo's corruption, Mussolini hated to delegate and wanted to control Italy's foreign and military affairs himself. Already Interior Minister and Foreign Minister (he had sacked Grandi in July 1932), he now held five ministries. Malaparte (Suckert), who had been a firm friend and collaborator of Balbo's, had written in October 1932 to Nello Quilici, the editor of Balbo's newspaper the *Corriere Padano*, that Balbo had lost his revolutionary zeal and grown 'fat'. In December he wrote to Quilici, 'I don't believe in his revolutionaryism. I don't believe in the future of the fat men ... Italo has within him the stuff of the provincial tyrant, that is of the *cabotin* who loves gold and power.'

In 1933 Italy also won the Schneider Cup for air speed and Primo Carnera, from Udine, became the first and only Italian to win the world heavyweight boxing title. In 1932 Fiat had launched the first 'people's car' – the 24-horse power *Balilla* at a cost of 10,000 lire – the equivalent of a skilled worker's pay for two years. In 1936 Fiat launched the famous

Topolino (Mickey Mouse) or *Cinquecento*. But by 1938 only 340,000 Italians had cars and half that number telephones.

The new Italian, *l'uomo nuovo*, Fascism aimed to create was a modern Platonic man – healthy in body and mind, and so healthy in spirit. Consequently Fascism placed an enormous emphasis on sport. The Foro Mussolini in Rome – the enormous sports complex built in the Fascist–Classical style – was the most obvious symbol of this. Under Fascism sport became part of life not just for the few as previously but for everyone. Physical education became compulsory at school for the first time. More important, sport had a central role in the curriculum of the *Balilla* which was responsible, said the 1926 law setting it up, for the 'welfare and physical and moral education of youth'.[87] Indeed, in 1927 the *Balilla* took over physical education in secondary schools and in 1929 in primary schools.[88] In 1929 there were only 502 gyms in Italy, by 1936 there were 5198.[89] In 1941 the GIL (which had replaced the *Balilla* in 1937) organised 83,201 sports competitions involving more than 2 million young Italians.[90] There was a similar explosion in adult involvement in sport organised by The *Opera nazionale dopolavoro*, the Fascist Social Club. In 1922, for example, there were 352 athletics clubs with 832 members; by 1936 there were 3872 with 53,207 members.[91] The *Dopolavoro* ran 11,159 sports clubs at its height.[92]

The Wall Street Crash and the Corporate State

The 1929 Wall Street Crash and the Great Depression which followed hit Italy just as the 1920s Fascist policy of cutting state expenditure and the cold shower of Quota 90 were beginning to pay dividends at last. The index of industrial production, which had fallen from 100 in 1927 to 93 in 1929, had risen to 120 by 1930 and in 1929 unemployment stood at a respectable 300,000.[93] The Socialists and Communists claimed the crash was the final crisis of Capitalism. So too did the Fascists. The crisis did not hit Italy as badly as more developed countries because its economy was less tied to world markets and was still preponderantly agricultural: until 1937 the agricultural sector was worth more than the industrial sector.[94] In addition, Mussolini's battles for grain and the lira – which had involved protecting them from foreign competition with high import tariffs and tough exchange controls – now offered the Italian economy some protection from foreign recession.

But the crisis still hit Italy hard. During the years of the depression, which in Italy lasted until 1936, unemployment rose sharply, hitting a peak of 1.3 million in February 1933[95] as businesses went bust in droves or reduced output and put staff on short time. This was not as bad as the peak levels in America of 11.5 million, Britain of 2.7 million, or Germany of over 5 million.[96] But between 1929 and 1932 production in Italy fell by a third, as did, by 1936, exports and imports. For those still in work there were wage cuts – in 1930 an 8 per cent cut for industrial workers who earned more than 12 lire a day and worked more than three days a week, and in 1934 a further 7 per cent cut. (The average wage of a factory worker was 300–400 lire a month and a kilo of flour cost 3 lire.)[97] State employees had their wages cut by 12 per cent.[98] Farm labourers suffered even more, with wage cuts of 20–25 per cent during the same period.[99]

Mussolini's response to the crisis was not, however, to implement the corporate state as Bottai, sacked as Minister of Corporations in July 1932, for one, wanted. Addressing the crowd from the balcony of Palazzo Venezia on 16 October 1932 – shortly before the opening of the tenth anniversary exhibition – Mussolini said, 'Either this is a cyclical crisis in the system, and it will solve itself, or else it is a crisis of the system, and then we will witness the passage of one epoch of civilisation to another.[100] In 1933 Mussolini wrote several articles on this theme for American newspapers owned by Randolf Hearst as a result of a lucrative Sarfatti-orchestrated deal. In one, he wrote, 'It is no longer an ailment. It is a constitutional disease ... There is no doubt that, given the general crisis of Capitalism, corporative solutions can be applied anywhere.'[101]

The Fascist method of 'bridling' – as Mussolini put it – Capitalism was the corporate state, which it called the Third Way between Capitalism and Communism. In 1932 he told Ludwig, 'The Fascist state directs and controls the entrepreneurs, whether it be in our fisheries or in our heavy industries in the Val d'Aosta. There the state actually owns the mines ... All the same, this is not Socialism, for we do not want to establish a monopoly in which the state does everything. We term it state intervention ... If anything fails to work properly, the state intervenes.'[102] In November 1934 he admitted that the corporate state was still only in its 'experimental stage'.[103]

In practice, in many ways what Fascism actually did on the economic front owed more to Socialist ideas than Fascist corporatist ones and the corporate state, apart from the creation of an enormous bureaucracy, remained largely untried. Mussolini, for example, supported the Keynesian 'pump priming' solution to the depression of increased government expenditure on public works. Between 1929 and 1934, expenditure on public works tripled to overtake defence for the first time as the largest item in total government expenditure.[104] Much of this money was spent on rural projects such as the draining of the Pontine Marshes. Mussolini, who saw the 1929 crash and subsequent depression as yet more evidence of the need for *ruralità*, also encouraged the purchase of land by the peasantry – between 1921 and 1938 the number of farm workers who did not own land fell from 44 per cent to 28 per cent. The battle for *ruralità* and the related battle for births would make Italy self-sufficient and less dependent on the world markets. But Mussolini could not and did not ignore industry. He set up a number of para-state institutions to intervene in the economy more in line with Socialist ideas of state intervention than Fascist ones on the corporate state such as the *Istituto Mobiliare Italiano* (IMI) in November 1931 to lend money secured on property to businesses and to manage them.

The fear among entrepreneurs was that such a move signalled the start of nationalisation but Mussolini insisted that this was not the case. It was merely 'a means to set going energetically the Italian economy towards the corporate phase', in other words a system which 'respects fundamentally private property and private initiative, but wants them as well within the state'.[105] State intervention in the economy continued nevertheless. In January 1933 Mussolini, who had taken back control of the Ministry of Corporations from Bottai in July 1932, set up the *Istituto per la ricostruzione industriale* (IRI) – which survived until 2000 – to save the major banks from collapse by buying the shares they held in ailing or collapsed businesses. This meant that IRI came to own large sectors of the economy – by 1937 44 per cent of the total share capital of all the companies quoted on the Milan Stock Exchange. In 1936 the Banca d'Italia was nationalised. These years also saw the foundation of state holding companies such as Finsider for the steel industry. This policy of state intervention in the economy was driven more by pragmatic than ideological considerations – the necessity of crisis. But as a result, by 1939 the state owned 21.5 per cent of all quoted companies in Italy – a greater percentage of state ownership than anywhere else in Europe outside Soviet Russia.

Fascist economic policy was reasonably successful. By 1938, total Italian production had increased by 153.8 per cent since 1913 compared with 149.9 per cent in Germany and 109.4 per cent in France. And by 1939 industrial productivity had grown by 145.2 per cent since 1913, compared with 143.6 per cent in Britain, 136.5 per cent in France, 136 per cent in America and 122.4 per cent in Germany. By 1935 industrial production had increased to the pre-depression level and by 1939 had increased by a further 20 per cent.[106] The workforce, however, suffered. Between 1922 and 1939 industrial wages had decreased by 14 per cent and the average wage was half that of France and a third that of Britain. But to offset this there were sporadic rounds of enforced price cuts and the beginnings of a welfare state – including pensions, sick pay and paid holidays – introduced between 1928 and 1930. Married couples received lump sum payments for each child they had. In November 1933, 2620 couples got married simultaneously in Rome and were received by the Pope that evening.[107] In December 1933 the ninety-three most prolific mothers were summoned to Rome to meet the Pope and Mussolini, and receive cash prizes. The number of offspring each had produced varied between fourteen and nineteen. Unemployment benefit was introduced in 1933 and by the end of the 1930s 13 million Italians belonged to the state health insurance scheme.[108]

By 1939 social security expenditure was 21 per cent of state expenditure.[109] This helped families with children in particular. In addition, the cheap leisure activities offered by the *Dopolavoro* also offset the financial hardship of the Italian people. In 1935 it controlled 771 cinemas, 1227 theatres, 2066 theatre companies, 2130 orchestras, 6427 libraries as well as all the thousands of sports clubs.[110] The same year the forty-hour week was introduced. In return the workforce was expected to spend Saturday afternoons in sporting, political and paramilitary activities – the so-called *Sabato Fascista*. From 1932, under the *treni popolari* scheme, Italians could travel by train on Sundays for a 70 per cent discount. The average real wage index shows that matters, though not good, were not that bad: 100 in 1913, 127 in 1921, 123 in 1922, 121 in 1928, and 125 in 1934.[111] In November 1919 – it is often forgotten – unemployment had stood at 2 million on the eve of the *Biennio Rosso* (Two Red Years).[112] Mussolini, despite the Wall Street crash, had never been so popular.

Getting Across the Fascist Message

It was not by means of television, which hardly existed, or even radio that Fascism transmitted its message to the people – especially in the backward south and the countryside. The mass media simply did not exist in Italy until late on in the Fascist period. It was only in 1935[113] that Mussolini transformed his personal press office into a ministerial department, the Ministry of Press and Propaganda, which in May 1937 became the Ministry of Popular Culture (known as MinCulpop) and began to exercise direct control over all cultural activity not just the press. The inventor of radio, Marconi, may well have been an Italian and committed Fascist, but few Italians had a radio. In 1924 a million Britons and a half million Germans owned a radio, but only 27,000 Italians did. In 1931 there were 242,000 radios in Italy and in 1939 1,170,000 – out of a population of 43 million – compared with 12.5 million radios in Germany.[114] Newspapers, censored from early on, were important but no newspaper had a mass circulation and much of the population was still functionally illiterate anyway. Increasingly important as well was the cinema newsreel. Mussolini had said that 'the cinema is the strongest weapon' but according to his eldest son, Vittorio, he preferred books and the theatre to watching cinema films. 'My father, if he watched a quarter of an hour of a film, that was already a lot, then he'd go to bed ... I don't think he ever watched a film through to the end.'[115] Between 1923 and 1939 only one cinema feature film was banned and in the entire Fascist period only a couple of dozen propaganda feature films made.[116]

Fascism had to make do with cheaper, simpler ways to get its message across such as the poster or handbill and, from 1930 onwards, the stencilled slogan on walls and buildings everywhere such as 'Mussolini is always right', or 'Believe Obey Fight'. Some of these slogans – there were millions of them – faded now, can still be found, as can the *fasces* which the Fascists even put on manhole covers. 'The advent of the masses in public life creates the same advertising and publicity necessities and procedures as in industrial and commercial life ... We must ... repeat, repeat, repeat. Exactly as in commercial publicity,' wrote Bottai in 1936.[117]

But much more important than the media in getting Fascism across was its physical presence in the daily lives of Italians. The Fascists did not regard the education system as the main indoctrinator of the young – that was the task of the *Balilla*. But there was indoctrination nonetheless. A 1927 primary school textbook, for example, concluded by saying, 'The Duce is semi-divine [*ha del divino*] ... His will is without limits, His courage annuls fear, His Heart is the synthesis of 40 million hearts ... He is Universal.'[118] Standard textbooks for the main subjects in line with the 'requirements' of Fascism were issued in 1928–9 for primary schools and the new primary school curriculum introduced in 1934 required teachers to teach the theories of Galileo so as 'to make evident ... the excellence of Italian genius'.[119] From November that year teachers were required to wear the black shirt in class.[120] In 1939, the Grand Council, at the instigation of Bottai, appointed Education Minister in 1936, approved the *Carta della Scuola* – the Fascist manifesto for schools. This said, 'In the moral political and economic unity of the Italian nation, which is achieved integrally in the Fascist state, school, first foundation of solidarity for all social forces, from the family to the corporations, and the party, forms the human and political conscience of the new generation.'[121] Between 1923 and 1936 the total number of primary school pupils rose from just under 3,981,000 to 5,187,000, secondary school pupils from 326,604 to 674,546 and university students from 43,235 to 71,512.[122] Bottai tried hard to encourage freedom of speech and criticism among young Fascists on the correct grounds that without them the Fascist ambition to create a new ruling class would fail. For a while during the 1930s the young did enjoy remarkable freedom of expression; much more so than adult Italians. Young Fascists openly said that the corporate state, for example, should not just manage but own the means of production. But Mussolini decided that for the young, as for everyone, faith, not freedom of speech, was what mattered most.

Outside school it was the PNF which provided the physical presence of Fascism in both the adult and children's world. Mussolini had stifled the PNF's ambition to be the elite force in control of the permanent revolution; instead, it became the tool of the revolution responsible for the *fascistizzazione* of Italians. One way this happened was by increasing the membership of the PNF. Consequently, between 1932 and 1939 adult male membership rose dramatically from just under 1 million to 2,633,000.[123] Party officials, therefore, became the Fascist clergy.

In addition the PNF controlled, directly or indirectly, numerous organisations – twenty-nine by 1942[124] – which included the Fascist youth organisation, the *Balilla* and the *Dopolavoro*. In 1937 all Fascist youth groups were integrated in a new organisation, the *Gioventù italiana del littorio* (GIL), under the direct control of the PNF.[125] The *Dopolavoro*, the Fascist social club founded in April 1925, had just under 4 million members by 1939. It was never compulsory for Italians to be members of the *Dopolavoro*. Nor did they have to be members of the PNF to join. Indeed, until 1942, non-PNF members of the *Depolavoro* outnumbered the PNF ones.[126] The PNF and its dependent organisations were far more important in securing consent for the regime than the media. In addition, they offered jobs and status to thousands of people as officials.

The PNF established its presence even in the traditional zone of influence of the Socialists and Communists – the factories in the northern Italian cities. In 1932 the Communist Mario Montagna, Togliatti's brother-in-law, wrote in *Stato Operaio*, 'There are thousands and thousands of Fascist cadres (and not only the rank and file) who are not scoundrels, who are not corrupt; who believe, disinterestedly, in Fascism, and whom the people do not scorn, hate, but often feel tied to, in fact, by a thousand threads, which range from the defence of the most trivial daily affairs to personal esteem and faith.'[127]

Fascist architecture, meanwhile, of which there was an extraordinary amount, provided a concrete presence. The *Casa del Fascio*, the PNF building in every town and village, was built to be like a church – and like the 1932 Mostra della Rivoluzione had a *sacrario* – and from 1932 onwards had to possess a bell tower. The aim was to create a new mentality and a new way of life: 'To live courageously, dangerously; to feel repugnance for the comfortable and soft life; to be always ready to dare both in individual and collective life; to love pure sincerity and abhor that which is shifty; to feel at every moment pride in being Italian; to work with discipline; to respect authority.'[128]

Starace and *Lo Stile Fascista*

Though the process was well under way when Turati was PNF General Secretary (1926–30), it was with the appointment of Achille Starace, General Secretary from 1931 to 1939 and holder of the post far longer than anyone else, that the most intense period of *fascistizzazione* took place. This process involved form (ritual) as well as content (mind and body). Naturally, there was overlap between the two areas. But the form part – the visible part – became known as *lo stile fascista*. Mussolini had told Starace he wanted him to 'put Italy into riding boots'.[129] Starace soon became Fascism's first grotesque buffoon. As a result, support for Fascism dwindled, though not support for Mussolini. So as the 1930s progressed the fate of Fascism came to depend even more on Mussolini.

The Roman salute had become the obligatory means of address for public employees in November 1925[130] and in October 1927 the Fascist calendar had been formally introduced – 29 October 1927 being day one of year VI of the *Era fascista*.[131] *'Giovinezza'* had become the unofficial national anthem. In May 1931, prior to conducting a concert at the opera house in Bologna, Toscanini had repeatedly told local Fascists that he would refuse to play it, as was by now customary on such occasions. 'I play only serious music,' he had fumed. Consequently, when he arrived at the opera house a group of Fascists, who included the journalist Leo Longanesi, accosted him and would not let him in. He refused again to agree to play *'Giovinezza'* and so they kicked and punched him. Longanesi slapped his face. The police intervened but the concert was cancelled. Soon afterwards Toscanini, who had stood as a Fascist parliamentary candidate in 1919 but had become disillusioned with Fascism, left Italy for America – though he came back several times until he decided to stay away for good until after the war in 1938. This was a severe propaganda blow to Mussolini who in 1932 had described Toscanini as 'the greatest conductor in the world'.[132]

Starace, aged forty-two when he became PNF General Secretary in December 1931, was in charge of the implementation of *lo stile fascista* in every aspect of Italian life. The aim, in particular, was to abolish the manners and dress code of the bourgeoisie – the old ruling class – deemed guilty of possessing the spirit of the *'pantofolaio'* (pipe and slippers) and *'panciafichista'* (one who stuffs his stomach with figs). It was Starace who abolished the handshake, the top hat and in 1938 *'lei'* (the formal second-person plural)[133] in favour of the much more Roman *'voi'* on the grounds that they were bourgeois, who banned foreign words such as 'film', which became *'filmo'*, and who insisted that the word Duce always be written in capitals in official communiques and newspapers: DUCE.[134] He also introduced the rule that officials should run to and from Mussolini's desk.[135]

Starace, born in San Nicola di Gallipoli, Puglia, in 1889, was a much decorated war hero, ex-*squadrista* in Trento and keep-fit fanatic. He had blind faith in Mussolini. Like Farinacci, he was an *intransigente* but unlike him he was not a scheming trouble-maker. His only ambition was to follow the orders of his idol. Though married with children, Starace's family remained in Puglia throughout his career and the gossips soon decided falsely that he was a homosexual, a paedophile, a sniffer of cocaine, and a participator in orgies. Many of the accusations reached the ears of Mussolini.[136] In fact, he was an insatiable womaniser whose penchant was for singers and ballerinas. He loved riding and dogs, which were guarded by three militiamen round the clock – doing an eight-hour shift each. 'But you realise that Starace is a *cretino*?' Arpinati had said to

Mussolini of Starace's appointment. 'I know. But he is an obedient *cretino*,' replied Mussolini.[137]

Increasingly, as the 1930s progressed, Mussolini and the Fascists wore military uniform in public and increasingly Starace made sure Italians did so as well. Starace adored uniforms and spent much time designing them for the numerous Fascist organisations. He was particularly proud of a coarse woollen cloth, called *orbace*, from the sheep of Sardinia, which he insisted be used for PNF uniforms. He was a stickler for the detail of Fascist ritual such as how many trumpet blasts should precede the salute to the King as opposed to the salute to the Duce, or how many centimetres should separate one militiaman from another at a parade. Continuously he fired off his orders and thoughts in the PNF's official two-page bulletin, the *Foglio di Disposizioni*, on all aspects of *lo stile fascista*. In 1932 he wrote, 'To salute Romanly, remaining seated is ... not very Roman!' In 1937, angry that the handshake was still in use, he wrote, ' "Addicted to the hand shake". This is the right note to mark on the personal file of those who persist in this behaviour, nearly always symptomatic of a scarcely Fascist spirit.'[138] Christmas was all right, though the Christmas tree, bourgeois and Anglo-Saxon, was frowned upon. 'Often, in place of the prescribed long black trousers and short black trousers, with black boots, striped trousers are worn, a residue of *il tight*!!! (morning dress). Comment is superfluous.'[139] 'It is absolutely forbidden to wear the collar of the black shirt starched.'[140] Often these missives would end with a single word to emphasise the point such as 'Style!' or 'Succinctness!' or 'Careful!'.

While the PNF did not present a political threat to Mussolini any more, it failed to create the much talked-about new elite which would take over the running of the revolution after Mussolini and the other gerarchs were dead. At the same time, to get employment in any state institution it became obligatory in 1933 to be a member of the PNF.[141] In 1930 total PNF membership had been about 1 million and Mussolini ordered the last of the major purges. The then General Secretary, Giovanni Giuriati (1930–1) expelled 120,000. But in 1933 PNF membership was opened up again in line with its new role to *fascistizzare* the nation. During the 1930s membership soared, as did the party's activities. By 1942 its twenty-nine organisations had a total membership of 27,376,571 out of a population of 46 million. These included nearly 6 million in the men and women's sections of the PNF itself, 8,754,589 in the youth organisations, and 4,612,294 in the *Dopolavoro*.[142]

Instilling faith in Fascism involved the creation of numerous prayers and catechisms – dos and don'ts called *decaloghi* – memorised by millions, which would be utterly absurd unless seen in the context of the religious nature of Fascism and the faith of Italians in their Duce. A 1935 'Prayer to the Duce' for secondary schoolchildren went as follows: 'For You, oh Duce, who are the life, the hope, the assuredness of the new Italy; for You, oh

Duce, who makes problems light, and even the humblest task noble; for You, oh Duce, who sees everything and feels everything with Your genius as leader and Your heart as father; to You whom I love more than any other thing in the world; to You who has given me a strong, feared and great *patria*; to You, for the joy of an instant, for a smile seen from afar, for the sureness that You give me (*m'odi*), I offer in humility my life, oh Duce!'[143] There were *decaloghi* on all sorts of subjects even the raising of rabbits, pregnancy, hygiene and the crossing of roads.

But, as is the danger with any religion, *lo stile fascista* – the form – became more important than the content. Starace even insisted on summoning Fascist officials – not usually the fittest of men – to take part in an athletics competition in Rome at the Foro Mussolini in which, among other things, they had to jump over hurdles made of rifles with bayonets fixed and dive through circles of fire.

Not surprisingly, Starace became the subject of countless jokes. His obsession with *lo stile fascista* caused many Italians and foreigners to switch from admiring Mussolini and Fascism to regarding them as ridiculous. Starace was the subject of most of the ridicule and jokes. But Mussolini had appointed him and Mussolini did nothing to stop him. Increasingly isolated, increasingly in the grip of the image the world had of him which he and the Fascists had created, Mussolini became ever stranger. Balbo had confided to the journalist Monelli[144] in 1934, 'He thinks from now on he is God. He has lost contact with the country and no one can make him listen to reason any more.'

Foreign Policy 1925–35: An Italian Place in the Sun

When Italians looked at the map of the world they were irritated, as all who were not British were, that a small island – Britain – should own most of it – while their country owned next to nothing. What was so British about Gibraltar? Malta? Cyprus? India? Africa? they asked. Mussolini, naturally, shared this irritation. In his dealings with Britain, and to a lesser extent France, the other major colonial power, this was always in the forefront of his mind.

It is true that Mussolini exalted the Roman Empire. But it was its values he wanted to revive. Even if he had wanted to, he was far too realistic to entertain any serious ambition to revive the Roman Empire itself. Italy, as he well knew, did not have the military clout. In the 1920s Mussolini had said that Fascism was not for export. In the 1930s he changed his tune. He did so not because he had decided that he personally wanted to rule the world but because of the 1929 Wall Street crash. This convinced him – as it had the Communists – that the final crisis of parliamentary democracy and Capitalism had arrived. He believed, therefore, that Fascism and the corporate state would replace them not as a result of external but internal forces. By 1934 there were Fascist parties in thirty-nine countries.[145] On 27 October 1930 he said in a speech from the balcony of Palazzo Venezia, 'The phrase that Fascism is not an article for exportation is not mine. It is too banal. It was adopted for the readers of newspapers ... In any case it must be amended ... Today I confirm that the idea, doctrine and spirit of Fascism are universal. It is Italian in its particular institutions, but it is universal in spirit; nor could it be otherwise, for the spirit is universal by its very nature. It is therefore possible to foresee a Fascist Europe which will model its institutions on Fascist doctrine and practice...'[146] On 25 October 1932, in a speech in Milan to mark the tenth anniversary of Fascism, Mussolini said that 'within ten years, Europe will be *fascista* or *fascistizzata!*'.

Mussolini frequently made bellicose speeches and used bellicose imagery, but these must be treated with caution. In his 1932 *Talks with Mussolini*, Ludwig had said, 'Still, in Italy you train your children for war!' Mussolini replied, 'I train them for the struggle for life ... also I prepare them for the struggle of the nation.'[147] On imperialism Mussolini said, 'There are half a dozen different types of imperialism ... the tendency towards imperialism is one of the elementary trends of human nature, an expression of the will to power. Nowadays we see the imperialism of the dollar, there is also a religious imperialism, and an artistic imperialism as well.'[148] In 1919 he had said imperialism was not 'necessarily aristocratic or military' but could be 'democratic, pacifist, economic, spiritual'.[149] Ludwig had gone into his long series of talks with Mussolini in 1932 extremely sceptical but came away convinced that Mussolini would keep the peace in Europe. By 1946, when Ludwig wrote the introduction to a new edition of his book, he felt able to explain Mussolini's change of mind only in terms of a change in character because he was sure that even in 1938 after the alliance with Germany there was nothing inevitable about Italy going to war in 1940.[150]

Mussolini had not written an Italian *Mein Kampf*. He had no master plan. Nor did he believe in a master race, or detest the Jews. Some of his best friends – as they say – were Jews: Sarfatti, for example. In August and September 1934 he wrote a series of articles in *Il Popolo d'Italia* under a pseudonym – as was his habit by now – which were hostile to the Nazis. In one, poking fun at Hitler's obsessive belief in the superiority of the Nordic races, he said that if this were so then the Lapps were the most superior race of all.[151] In April 1933 he received the Chief Rabbi of Rome to assure him that he had no intention of discriminating against Italy's Jews and in February 1934 he met Chaim Weizmann, the leader of the Zionist movement, who requested and received a signed photograph of Mussolini and who told him, 'Look after yourself well. We still have need of you.'[152] 'Undoubtedly, no contemporary Englishman or Russian had had so much sympathetic understanding of the Jews, as Mussolini with me in 1932,' wrote Emil Ludwig in his 1946 introduction.[153] By 1946, with the war over and the horror of the Holocaust revealed, the German-Jewish historian and jour-nalist was writing with hindsight. Yet still he admired Mussolini.

Mussolini's policy towards Germany was driven by fear of Germany, not a feeling that Fascism and National Socialism should march together to take over the world. Nevertheless, Mussolini was adamant that Italy had to be a nation armed and prepared for war – not for the purposes of attack, of invasion, but for the purposes of defence and bargaining. In a 1934 speech he said, 'It is necessary to be militarily strong. Not to attack, but to be able to face any situation.'[154] Mussolini had no territorial ambitions in western Europe at all and only minor ones in the Mediterranean, such as Albania, a few mainly Greek islands and slivers of Yugoslavia. Unlike Hitler, Mussolini did not want to invade his neighbours. Nevertheless, like all Italians, he was interested in Italian prestige and like them the wound of the *vittoria mutilata* pained him still: the feeling that at Versailles, Italy – a victor nation – had been treated like a nation vanquished.

As Sir Ronald Graham, British ambassador in Rome had warned back in July 1923, 'It would be rash to assume that Italy is inevitably yoked to the cart of the Western Powers. Signor Mussolini is determined that Italy's signature shall be essential to European contracts. My conclusion is that Italy must inevitably gravitate towards the Power or group of Powers ready to assist her in the expansion towards which she must eventually be driven by irresistible force.'[155]

Between 1925 and 1935 Anglo–Italian relations were exceptionally good. This had a lot to do in the early stages with the very good rapport Mussolini enjoyed with both Graham and Sir Austen Chamberlain, the British Foreign Secretary until 1929. On 27 November 1926, for example, Italy and Albania signed the Treaty of Tirana which in effect made Albania an Italian protectorate. Britain gave formal recognition to the treaty, which angered the French, who viewed the Balkans as their sphere of influence, and the new nation of Yugoslavia.

During the important Locarno Pact talks in October 1925 to guarantee frontiers between France, Belgium and Germany, Mussolini sided with Britain. The Locarno Pact, named after the Swiss town where the talks were held, guaranteed Germany's western borders in return for a promise by Germany to keep the Rhineland demilitarised. In addition, if France and Germany went to war, Britain and Italy agreed to defend materially and morally the innocent party. Germany in turn agreed to join the League of Nations, which it did in September 1926. With hindsight it is easy to dismiss such treaties as Locarno, of which there were many during the 1920s and 1930s, as mere bits of paper that bound none of the parties to anything much. But Sir Austen, for one, believed that the Locarno Pact had created a genuine chance of lasting peace in Europe and that Mus-solini's role had been crucial. Mussolini[156] did not like going abroad, partly because of superstition, and very rarely did. He would not set off on a trip anywhere, for example, on Mondays and Thursdays. He felt very uncomfortable abroad. This partly explains why he gave up the Foreign Ministership in September 1929 and appointed Dino Grandi, who had been Under-Secretary, in his place. Grandi, who had learned very good English, was an Anglophile. He survived in the post until 1932, when he was appointed ambassador to London instead and Mussolini resumed the job once more.

During the 1920s there was virtually no contact between the Fascists and the Nazis. Mussolini did not rate Hitler at all and described *Mein Kampf* as 'unreadable'.[157] Hitler, however, had been an ardent admirer of Mussolini since 1922. He had tried his own 'March on Rome' – the beer hall putsch in 1923 – which had failed dismally and led to his imprisonment. Nevertheless he was determined to establish a government based on the Fascist model in Germany. He ate in Italian restaurants and wanted to know everything about Mussolini. 'He seemed like someone in love asking news about the person they loved,' recalled SS Colonel Eugen Dollmann.[158] The Nazi brown shirt was a copy of the Italian black shirt. The Nazis also copied the Roman salute, which they called the Fascist salute, and the SA named a brand of cigarettes the *Balilla*. The title *Führer* was the German translation of *duce*. Hitler kept a bust of Mussolini on his office desk and in 1927 he asked, via the German ambassador in Rome, for a signed photograph of Mussolini. Mussolini – only too happy to give Clementine Churchill and Chaim Weizmann such a photograph – turned down the request with a short note from the Foreign Ministry. In the end, when Hitler seemed close to power, he gave Hermann Göring a signed photograph to give to Hitler when Göring met him in Rome in April 1931.[159] But he continued to ignore Hitler's repeated requests via third parties for a meeting. Mussolini had not bargained on Hitler coming to power. But on 30 January 1933 it happened, when President Field Marshal Paul Ludwig von Hindenburg appointed him Chancellor. Major Giuseppe Renzetti, who had been acting as Mussolini's unofficial ambassador in Berlin, had got to know Hitler well. On 30 January he reported Hitler's words to him that day, 'I have arrived here certainly thanks to Fascism. If it is true that the two movements are different, it is also true that Mussolini has achieved the *Weltanschauung* which unites the two movements: without that achievement perhaps I would not have arrived in this place.'[160]

Sir Austen Chamberlain met Mussolini twice in Italy: over Christmas in 1925 at Rapallo and in September the following year at Livorno where Mussolini ordered a destroyer to give him a nineteen-gun salute. It was during this second visit that Lady Chamberlain had worn a Fascist badge. Subsequently, in October 1926, speaking in London, Chamberlain described Mussolini as 'a very remarkable man' and said that Italy prior to him was a place of 'political corruption, social anarchy, industrial strife, and national degeneracy'. He added, 'Mussolini is a man of shrewd sense and I am confident that he does not mean to embark on a policy of aggression . . .[161] Winston Churchill, as we have seen, shared Chamberlain's admiration for the dictator. In January 1926 Churchill, who was Chancellor of the Exchequer, insisted against stiff opposition from the Treasury on agreeing to Italy's request for a rescheduling of her £576 million war debt to Britain on very generous terms for Italy. Defending his decision, Churchill referred to the secret 1915 Treaty of London by which Britain, France and Russia had persuaded Italy to enter the war in 1915 in return for promises of territory and the eventual cancellation of war debts accrued. Failure to keep these promises had infuriated Italians. Churchill said in a statement, 'We have felt bound to consider this [the treaty] as a factor,' adding, 'Italy is a country which is prepared to face the realities of post-war reconstruction. It possesses a government under the commanding leadership of Signor Mussolini . . .'[162]

It was not only British Conservatives such as Chamberlain and Churchill who looked favourably on Mussolini. So, too, did some Labour politicians including Ramsay MacDonald who became Prime Minister in May 1929 at the head of his and Labour's second minority government – once again reliant on the support of the Liberals. He had already formed a favourable opinion of Mussolini during his first premiership when he had handed Italy Jubaland in 1924. These Labour politicians also included Sir Oswald Mosley. Mosley, who started out as a Conservative before joining Labour, was a minister in the second MacDonald government. He had quickly become the great hope of the Labour left but, unable to shift the party leftwards, he resigned and founded the New Party which, in October 1932, became the British Union of Fascists. Secret British Foreign Office documents show that the BUF was heavily subsidised by Mussolini until 1935. The British government only became aware of this in 1945 when it found papers relating to it among captured Mussolini documents. It decided, however, not to make public what it knew. One of the documents – translated into English in 1945 – was a letter from Grandi, Italian ambassador in London, to Mussolini on 30 January 1934 in which he wrote, 'MOSLEY has asked me to express his gratitude to you for sending him the considerable sum which I arranged to hand over to him today . . . He also spoke with gratitude of the simple generosity with which you accepted as a future commitment his requests for material aid.[163]

Lord Rothermere, owner of the *Daily Mail*, became a convert to Mosley's BUF at this time and his newspapers came out in support of the BUF at the end of 1933. Grandi – who described Rothermere as 'a political figure of the second order (in spite of his claims to be the deus ex machina of English politics)' – explained how

MOSLEY also told me in a tone of especial gratitude that he owes the final conversion of Lord ROTHERMERE entirely to you. For many months negotiations have been in progress between Lord ROTHERMERE, his son (a very serious young man who in fact is now the director of his father's whole vast newspaper business) and MOSLEY ... Once MOSLEY was persuaded there still remained to be persuaded Lord ROTHERMERE, with whom negotiations entered into immediately before Christmas had broken down. It needed but a single word from you to carry ROTHERMERE, quite unexpectedly, to MOSLEY's side ... ROTHERMERE exclaimed ... 'If Mussolini believes in MOSLEY, then full speed ahead with the whole group of papers.' Thus MOSLEY has returned from Rome owing everything to you.[164]

Grandi added,

In political circles in LONDON the sudden conversion of ROTHERMERE to Fascism has for some days been the subject of sour comment in many quarters; yet the effect of the conversion has been at once. Without the support of the *Daily Mail*, the *Evening News* and the few dozen provincial dailies which the ROTHERMERE group controls, the BIRMINGHAM meeting would have passed more or less unnoticed. The fact that the most widely read group in England of papers which give straight news devoted a whole page to the meeting 'compelled' all the English papers, from the comfortable *Times* to the anti-Fascist *Daily Herald* to give a full and faithful account of the BIRMINGHAM meeting.

In his memoirs Mosley said he had donated £100,000 to the BUF of his own money and that Lord Nuffield, the car manufacturer, whom he described as 'the main backer', had donated £50,000. Rothermere also donated money to the BUF, wrote Mosley, 'though not as much as Lord Nuffield' and in addition planned to raise money for the party by selling cigarettes via its 400 party offices. Rothermere abandoned this plan after complaints from Jewish advertisers in his newspapers, said Mosley. When accused of accepting money from Mussolini, Mosley never issued a flat denial but instead challenged his accusers to produce evidence. In his memoirs he wrote that 'my long and secure financial independence rendered me particularly invulnerable to such attacks'. It is only now, thanks to the captured documents, that we know Mosley was lying.[165]

In March 1935 Grandi urged Mussolini to stop funding Mosley. He wrote,

At the moment you are spending a great deal of money in England. At any rate until a few days ago, you were giving MOSLEY about three and a half million a year in monthly instalments of about 300,000 lire. All this money, believe me, DUCE, even on the best supposition simply goes down the drain. At the present time we should concentrate our efforts in a different direction. With a tenth of what you give MOSLEY, that is with a monthly allowance to the Embassy of 35,000 lire, I feel that I could produce results ten times better ... In this country of ... Puritans, almost everybody is corruptible. One only has to be careful to offer the money between two pages of the Old Testament.[166]

Between 1932 and 1936, Mosley met Mussolini 'half a dozen times or so' at Palazzo Venezia. Both spoke French with each other but when Mussolini tried to speak in English Mosley said that he found it difficult to understand him. The meetings ceased after Mosley's highly publicised marriage to Diana Mitford in Berlin in October 1936 at which the guests included Hitler and Goebbels. As a result, Mussolini refused to see Mosley, he said, because he felt antipathy towards Hitler and Germany, and was irritated at Mosley's marriage in Berlin in the presence of Hitler.[167]

At first Mussolini thought he could use Hitler. He aimed to mediate between Britain and France on one side and Germany on the other, in order to gain advantage. In March 1932, Mussolini told the Grand Council, 'It suits us, one way, if Germany should rearm quickly and efficiently to offset France, but on the other hand, so far as we are concerned, we must try to build ourselves up so that we can look Germany in the eyes if and whenever the need arises...'[168]

In Lausanne, meanwhile, the Reparations Conference on the German war debt began on 16 June 1932. MacDonald wanted to wipe the slate clean. Mussolini concurred. But not France. In the end, given the reality of the depression, France agreed the following month that Germany should pay 2.6 milliard marks as final settlement.[169]

But two other equally serious problems remained: rearmament, especially German rearmament, and disputes over national boundaries caused by the creation of so many new nation states under the Versailles Peace Treaty. To solve these problems Mussolini proposed the foundation of a small but powerful new European security arrangement to bypass the large but ineffectual League of Nations with its numerous member nations. The arrangement would involve Britain, Germany, France and Italy forming what he called the Pact of Four. Germany would be allowed controlled rearmament, and Versailles and other related peace treaties would be recognised as revisable. The Pact of Four would guarantee peace in Europe for ten years. Later, he would recall, that Europe, seething under the 'Diktat of Versailles' had a choice: 'revision or war'; a choice which the impotent League of Nations was incapable of making.

He worked out the details of the Pact of Four during a weekend at the beginning of March 1933 at Rocca della Caminate – his castle above Predappio. Given the bitterness and hatred which characterised Franco–German relations – the result of three terrible wars with each other in less than a hundred years – he was convinced that Britain and Italy should together be the mediators in chief. As a result, although Italy was much weaker than Britain she could, he believed, play a key role – the *'peso determinante'* – in Europe.

The Pact of Four was a good idea reminiscent of the Concert of Europe, which had been successful for much of the nineteenth century. But as it gave so much to the Germans and insisted that all treaties be regarded as revisable, it was bound to upset the French and the smaller nations such as those of the Little Entente – Yugoslavia, Czechoslovakia and Romania – who would feel left out on a limb and vulnerable to the loss of territory.

The British, on the other hand, were keen. In Britain a pacifist mood was gathering momentum, which undoubtedly bolstered those advocating a policy of appeasement. Arms races made war inevitable, said the pacifists. On 25 January 1933, five days before Hitler came to power, the Oxford Union passed by a large majority the infamous motion that 'This House will under no consideration fight for its king and country'. Churchill was furious. He believed the opposite to the pacifists. Pacifism would not cause peace but war. On 17 February 1933, speaking to the Anti-Socialist and Anti-Communist Union at the Queen's Hall, London, he described the Oxford debate as a 'disquieting and disgusting symptom', which would arouse contempt in Germany. It was in this speech that he praised Mussolini as 'the Roman genius'.[170]

Given the mood in Britain, Britain's Prime Minister Ramsay Mac-Donald – he had left the Labour party in 1931 and was now head of a cross-party National government – was very keen on Mussolini's plan to guarantee peace. In March 1933, he and the Foreign Secretary, Sir John Simon, who were in Geneva, accepted Mussolini's invitation to come to Rome to discuss it. But subsequently, as soon as France and Germany joined in the discussions, Mussolini's original idea quickly became so watered down as to be meaningless. Hitler agreed, partly because he wanted to be seen as someone with whom it was possible to negotiate and partly to please his mentor Mussolini.

Sir John Simon told the House of Commons nevertheless that Europe 'should be grateful' to Mussolini 'for the work done by him in these difficult weeks'.[171] The Pact of Four was duly signed on 15 July 1933[172] in Rome at Palazzo Venezia by Mussolini and the ambassadors of the other three nations. On 22 June Grandi wrote that Lloyd-George, the former Liberal Prime Minister, had told him of his 'sincere admiration' for the pact, adding, 'Either the world follows Mussolini or the world is doomed. Only your leader has clear vision.'[173] Mussolini's vision was indeed clear, but through no fault of his the Pact of Four bound no one to anything concrete. In any case the French parliament did not ratify it because in October 1933 Germany walked out of the League of Nations Disarmament Conference at Geneva and five days later quit the League itself. This effectively scuppered the pact. Mussolini was furious at the Germans. Ambassador Graham (replaced in October 1933 by Sir Eric Drummond, later the Earl of Perth), who had known Mussolini for eleven years, met Mussolini for the last time on 21 October. He reported that he had never seen Mussolini 'show more annoyance and disgust'. Mussolini said that the Germans had 'broken three windows at once' – the Disarmament Conference, the League of Nations and the Pact of Four.[174]

The Pact of Four was the first time that Mussolini – at the height of his prestige at home and abroad – had tried to establish a framework to guarantee peace in Europe. He would try again, most notably at Munich in 1938.

Austria

The first occasion when it was necessary for Italy to look Germany in the eye came in 1934 over Austria, where the small Christian Democrat Engelbert Dollfuss – he was only four foot eleven – had become Prime Minister in May 1932 at the head of a right-wing coalition government with a tiny majority. Dollfuss was a devout Catholic and had wanted to become a priest but was told he was too small.[175] Most Austrians regarded themselves first and foremost as Germans but at Versailles the French had insisted that Germany should not be allowed to increase in size. Dollfuss was determined to keep Austria independent. In reaction to serious violent unrest caused by Austrian Nazis – who had been part of the German Nazi Party since 1926[176] – Socialists and Communists, Dollfuss suspended parliamentary government and ruled by decree with the consent of the President, Wilhelm Miklas. But Dollfuss was trapped in a fight on two fronts: against Socialists and National Socialists. Meanwhile, the Austrian Nazi Legion – its brownshirts – armed by Hitler, waited at the border for the nod to go in. The *Anschluss*, which Hitler had promised, appeared imminent. The only hope for an independent Austria was the protection of the great powers.

The British and French, however, showed little interest in the fate of Austria. At this stage France was really only worried about what the Germans got up to on its border. As for Britain, already drifting towards appeasement, her main concern was to get Germany back to the League of Nations Disarmament Conference in Geneva which had begun in January 1932 but which had run into the sand even before Hitler had come to power over German insistence on the principle of equality of rights on armaments.

Unlike Britain and France, Mussolini was determined to guarantee Austrian independence and stand up to Hitler. This is hardly surprising, given that unlike Britain and France, Italy shared a border with Austria. Furthermore, in *Mein Kampf* Hitler had said that he wanted not only Austria but also the German-speaking Alto Adige in the Italian Tyrol, which the Italians had got under the Treaty of Versailles from the Austrians. Mussolini and Dollfuss met for the first of several times in Rome in May 1933.[177] They quickly established a strong rapport and became firm allies.

In return for a pledge from Dollfuss to turn Austria, already an authoritarian state, into a Fascist state, Mussolini agreed to give Austria money and small arms and, if required, armed protection against Germany. Dollfuss had already banned the Communist party and in June 1933 he banned the Nazi party. In August 1933 Dollfuss and his wife, Alwine, went to stay with Mussolini in the villa at Riccione on the Adriatic coast which he rented each summer. As a result, in September Dollfuss announced the birth of the 'German Christian-Social Corporatist State of Austria'.

Matters in Austria moved steadily and surely to a head. In early February 1934, after four days of violence in Vienna and Linz between Socialists and the army had left 300 dead, Dollfuss banned the Social-Democratic (Socialist) party and in May decreed that parliament was merely a consultative body. Sir John Simon told a Cabinet Committee on Foreign Affairs on 9 February that the Austrian situation was 'serious'. The British did nothing concrete. Their desire to appease Hitler and get him back to the disarmament talks, and their disapproval of Dollfuss's drift to dictatorship got the better of them. The Germans meanwhile carried on rearming regardless. In May 1935, after more than three years, the League of Nations Disarmament Conference would end, having achieved nothing. On 17 March Italy, Austria and Hungary signed the Rome Protocols on foreign policy and economic co-operation. Grandi told Sir John Simon that Italy had no designs on Austrian and Hungarian sovereignty. On the contrary, the aim of the agreement was to guarantee their sovereignty against German aggression by the creation of 'strong buffer states'.[178] Mussolini had said he wanted to make the Danube 'the European hinterland of Italy'[179] but not Italian. The aim was not just to create a buffer against Germany but also to encircle Yugoslavia so as to force territorial concessions from her. Two days later, 19 March, Mussolini told a meeting of Fascists, 'Austria knows that it can count on us to defend its independence as a sovereign state.'[180]

At the height of the Austrian crisis Mussolini finally agreed to meet Hitler for the first time in Venice on 14 June 1934. Mussolini, who had driven himself to Stra, between Venice and Padua, where he had decided to stay for the Führer's two-day visit in an uninhabited but swiftly refurbished royal mansion, the Villa Pisano, wore his Corporal of Honour Militia uniform. It was Hitler's first foreign trip and he touched down at Venice airport on the advice of his Foreign Minister, Konstantin Friedrich von Neurath, in a suit complete with grey felt hat and mackintosh which observers said was 'yellow'. Hitler felt inferior, and was very irritated with von Neurath. He never forgave him. Observers noted that Hitler had tears in his eyes on meeting his idol.[181] The two dictators held their first talks that morning at the Villa Pisano over breakfast. 'He's mad, he's mad,' said Mussolini during a pause in the first meeting from a window of the villa at those gathered in the courtyard below.[182] The mosquitoes were so bad that Mussolini felt compelled to switch the talks to Venice, where Hitler had been put in the royal suite at the Grand Hotel. During their private conversations, one session of which took place on the beach at the Lido, Mussolini insisted on speaking German – his German was good but not fluent – without an interpreter present. Hitler spoke torrentially. It was like talking to a record player, said Mussolini. Among other things Hitler denied that the *Anschluss* was inevitable for the moment – but wanted nevertheless to see the end of Dollfuss and his replacement with an 'independent' chancellor and the admission of the Austrian Nazis to the government. Hitler also told Mussolini that the Nordic races were superior to the Mediterranean peoples, who were contaminated with negroid blood. Mussolini advised him of the madness of persecution of the Jews and the Church. He took an instant dislike to Hitler. Later, he told Fascists in Forlì, 'Instead of speaking to me about current problems . . . he recited to me from memory his *Mein Kampf*, that enormous brick which I have never been able to read.'[183]

On Hitler's second day in Venice Mussolini delivered a speech to a huge crowd in St Mark's Square, which barely mentioned Hitler. But Hitler, who watched from the balcony of a nearby palazzo, was fascinated by the genuine enthusiasm of the crowd for Mussolini. Later he recalled, 'The people stand in front of him with a humble attitude, as if in front of the Pope, and he assumes the attitudes of a Caesar . . . But all this disappears in informal conversation, when Mussolini becomes simple and charming.'[184] Hitler left Venice on the morning of 16 June. Mussolini told his Foreign Under-Secretary, Fulvio Suvich, as Hitler's plane took off that Hitler was 'a clown'.[185] Hitler, however, had nothing but praise for Mussolini. Major Giuseppe Renzetti subsequently reported back from Berlin that Hitler had told him, referring to Mussolini, 'Men like that are born only once every thousand years, and Germany can be happy that he is Italian and not French.'[186] The two men would not meet again for three years.

Two weeks later – 30 June – Heinrich Himmler's SS murdered Ernst Röhm, the leader of the SA, and a large number of SA brownshirts, on Hitler's orders, in the so-called Night of the Long Knives. Mussolini was with his family, including his sister Edvige, when he heard the news and said, 'Those that he has killed were his closest collaborators, those who had brought him to power. It would be like me killing with my own hands Balbo, Grandi, Bottai . . .'[187]

Dollfuss, meanwhile, had accepted an invitation from Mussolini that he and his family come and stay with them once more in Riccione in a villa near the one Mussolini rented each summer. His wife, Alwine, and the two children arrived on 25 July. Dollfuss was due to arrive later that day. But that morning a convoy of trucks carrying 150 Austrian Nazis disguised as Austrian soldiers drew up at the chancellery. They forced their way inside and opened fire on Dollfuss, mortally wounding him. By evening the army had restored order but a hundred people had died. Mussolini received the news while on a tour of a mental hospital at Cesena[188] – a short drive from Riccione. He was incandescent. Immediately, he drove to Riccione to inform Mrs Dollfuss of what had happened. He then gave orders for four divisions to be sent to the Brenner and returned to Rome. He expected a similar response from Britain and France. It did not happen. There is no doubt that Hitler knew about and supported the planned putsch by the Austrian Nazis. At 9 a.m. on 25 July he told General Adam, commander of Military District VI in Munich, that 'the Austrian government will be thrown out today'. He then told Adam to arm the thousands of Austrian Nazi legionnaires waiting on the border.[189]

But as soon as he heard that Mussolini had sent Italian troops to the Austrian border he backed down. Furious in private, he condemned the murder of Dollfuss in public and disassociated himself from those responsible. Mosley, who saw Mussolini a few days later, believed him to be contemplating a declaration of war on Germany.[190] Mussolini had always been anti-German. In 1917, for example, he had written in the heat of war, '*In fondo*, in spite of the march of the centuries, the soul of the *Boche* has not changed ... The Germans want to strip, sack, destroy Italy.'[191] In 1927 Mussolini had said that European politics would enter into its decisive phase between 1935 and 1940 and in 1932 he said that future conflicts would be caused by a German war for expansion.[192] In 1932 Mussolini asked Ludwig what he thought of Hitler. 'I lowered my right hand to indicate the height of a dwarf and said, "Hitler? Like so." He nodded, evidently satisfied, but he did not say a word, he looked at me with a penetrating gaze and added, "But ... he has six million votes." '[193]

Mussolini had saved Austria from the *Anschluss*. In September Britain, France and Italy signed yet another piece of paper – a joint declaration pledging to preserve Austrian independence. But as Mussolini had told Prince von Starhemberg the Austrian Foreign Minister, 'It cannot always be me alone who marches to the Brenner. Others as well must show some interest in Austria and the Danube basin.'[194] Mussolini's prestige on the world stage had never been so great. The July 1935 issue of *Gerarchia* said that the differences between Fascism and National Socialism were 'profound and unequivocable'.[195] In 1935 the Faculty of Jurisprudence and Political Science at the Elizabethan University in Pecs, Hungary, proposed – in all seriousness – that Mussolini should get the Nobel Peace Prize. Mussolini did not think it a good idea.[196]

12

ETHIOPIA 1935–6:
MAD DOGS AND ENGLISHMEN

Edda Mussolini was the Duce's favourite child. She was rebellious, flighty, hyper and possessed of an elegant thinness. Her family nickname was the *cavallina matta* (mad mare). 'She was an aristocrat born into a family of peasants. Edda had the true nobility that none of us had,' recalled her younger brother, Romano Mussolini, the well-known jazz musician, former husband of Sophia Loren's sister and father of the MP Alessandra Mussolini.[1]

She had also spent a year at the Poggio Imperiale, the famous finishing school in Florence, where she had hoped to escape the family rows and be independent. But there were strict rules there as well and she did not like it. The school did finish her in some ways nevertheless. 'She read books ... She had good table manners, and she spoke English and French while we only spoke Romagnolo,' added Romano. But to the irritation of her father she also smoked, drank, drove, played cards for money and wore risqué bathing costumes. In 1934 she was said to be the first Italian woman who dared to wear a two-piece, which she had ordered from London in secret.[2] She recalled, 'Daddy with all his anti-bourgeois attitudes was in certain things more conformist than a retired colonel. He forbade me, for example, to paint my lips...'[3]

In January 1930 Edda met Galeazzo Ciano, then a very junior member of the Italian delegation at the Vatican, at a party. She was nineteen (born 1.9.10) and Ciano twenty-six (born 18.3.03). Smitten, it seemed, they married swiftly. The wedding reception for more than 500 guests took place on 23 April at the Villa Torlonia. This is said to have been the only party that Mussolini, who loved peasant knees-ups but detested bourgeois phoniness, ever hosted. It was also the first and only time that his wife and he had appeared together at a major public event.[4] Starace was the only guest in uniform. The wedding presents included a gold and malachite rosary from Pius XI, a hand-painted velvet cloak from d'Annunzio and an oriental pearl from Mussolini given to him by a Russian princess. The next day the couple married in a church ceremony, at which Mussolini was present, before departing by car – driven by Edda – for their honeymoon on Capri. They were pursued by her police escort, a servant with the baggage and Mussolini. He had decided to follow them in his red Alfa Romeo with his wife. A few dozen miles down the road Edda told him to get lost.[5]

Ciano was the son of Count Costanzo Ciano, a First World War naval hero from Livorno, Tuscany, who under Fascism had subsequently thrived in business – this being Italy, corruptly. The count – the King had made him one in 1925 – had become a Fascist in 1921 and held various ministerial posts in the 1920s. In 1926 Mussolini had even nominated him as his successor. He remained a member of the Fascist Grand Council until his death in June 1939. His son, Galeazzo, who was also entitled to call himself count, was vain, pompous, frivolous, hedonistic, a snob and devoid of any fixed belief. Though good-looking, he was afflicted by serious ear, nose and throat trouble, and had a high-pitched nasal voice. But he had charm and was intelligent, shining at school and graduating in law from Rome University in 1925. He then joined the Foreign Ministry, after coming twenty-seventh out of 600 applicants for thirty-five places, and was posted to Rio de Janeiro, Buenos Aires and in 1927 to Peking.

Marriage to Mussolini's daughter meant that Ciano was destined for the top. The honeymoon over, Mussolini made Ciano Consul-General in Shanghai. There, Edda became hooked on all-night poker, at which she lost enormous sums of money, and gin, which she drank in a big way. The first of their three children was born in October 1931. From early on, theirs was an open marriage, though something potent bound them inextricably together to the end. Ciano was a serial adulterer and, unlike the Duce whose sexual tastes were more earthy, he had a thing about aristocratic women. Among those the couple knew in Shanghai was Wallis Simpson, the American woman whose subsequent affair with Edward VIII would lead to his abdication in 1937. It is widely believed in Italy that Ciano and Simpson, who was on the verge of divorce from her hard-drinking American husband, Winfield Spencer, a naval officer, had an affair and that, after becoming pregnant by him, she had an abortion which left her sterile.[6]

But Edda, too, was an incorrigible flirt and had many flings. Nevertheless, the Swiss psychiatrist who treated her in 1944–45 would decide that she felt a 'profound disgust' for sex and was 'absolutely frigid'. The psychiatrist felt that the causes of this and all the other problems he had spotted were several: beatings from her mother's broom as a child, bullying at school because of who her father was, constant police protection, parental rows caused by her mother's jealous rages, her father's dominant personality, his extramarital affairs, her 'defective' early education, and her 'exceptional' life. But the psychiatrist was convinced, too, that the problem also had an hereditary aspect: 'It is certain that from a psychiatric point of view the Mussolini family is *héréditairement tarée* [hereditarily tainted].'

There was no doubt that Edda had a serious psychiatric problem. The psychiatrist noted, 'Madame Ciano is disorganised, undisciplined, capricious. She can appear, above all when depressed, perfectly charming, considerate ... full of kindness. Then *brusquement*, she is in a bad mood, tormented, aggressive, in revolt against everyone and everything ...' His diagnosis: 'All these symptoms are *absolument caractéristiques* ... [of] *les psychopathes constitutionnels.*' He found it particularly odd that she found it more comfortable to leave her accommodation at his clinic via the window rather than the door and would sometimes take her shoes off out of doors if they hurt her feet and walk barefoot. He noted too that she dressed in a *'manière ecxentrique et sans discrétion'*.[7] Perhaps Edda's symptoms became chronic only later. Perhaps Ciano saw things differently from psychiatrists, especially Swiss ones.

In June 1933 Mussolini recalled Ciano to Rome and appointed him head of his press office, and the following September he became a junior member of the government when Mussolini elevated the office to an under-secretariat, renaming it the Press and Propaganda Office. Nine months later he made it a ministry. So Ciano was a minister at the age of thirty-two. Ciano, observers noted, had started imitating Mussolini's mannerisms. He, not his father, they now assumed, would be the next Duce. Instead, in the end, he would plot Mussolini's overthrow, and as a result be tried and shot in January 1944. Edda, having tried desperately and heroically to save her husband's life, would refuse to speak to her father again and never did. Ciano had, however, kept a personal diary which, thanks to Edda, survived. The diary provides a rare day-by-day account of what Mussolini and Fascism were like. Unfortunately it does not always have the ring of truth about it and often reads as if it were reworked after events as a means of defending Ciano's reputation.

Galeazzo Ciano: The Son-in-Law the Duce Would have Shot

Mussolini's conquest of Ethiopia, or Abyssinia as the British called it, changed everything. Before it, he was on the side of Britain and France; after it he drew ever closer to Germany. It was also the first major test – and last, it turned out – of the League of Nations in Europe. But the League, set up after the First World War to guarantee peace between nations and once dismissed by Lenin as a 'thieves' kitchen', failed the test dismally. This failure on Ethiopia destroyed the League of Nations. With loud self-righteousness it committed itself to stopping Mussolini's aggression. But it proved to be all mouth and no trousers.

Mussolini believed that the fortunes of men depended on whether they were born under a good or bad star. This made them not good or bad, but lucky or unlucky. He was convinced that his was a good star. Until Ethiopia, events had proved him right. After Ethiopia, his star showed that it had a bad side and that the time had come for the bad side to have its day. But both he and Italians were still either unable or unwilling to recognise this for quite some time to come. The question is: why did Mussolini change sides after Ethiopia and who or what, apart from the stars, was to blame? There is no easy answer to this but Britain played a crucial part in the process. Ethiopia did not really matter very much. Britain, as the more realistic French wanted, should either have got the league to give way to Mussolini or else risk war with draconian sanctions and the closure of the Suez Canal. It did neither. Instead, it huffed and puffed. And so too, as a result, did the league. This did very serious damage to Anglo-Italian relations when with the growing threat from Germany the two countries needed to be closer than ever. It left Italy dangerously isolated in Europe. Mussolini and Hitler, as Professor Norman Stone has written, 'were thrown together by British obstinacy'.[8]

So what did he want? Unlike Hitler, he had no real desire to conquer much in Europe. Certainly, he did not want an alliance with Germany, whom he regarded as an enemy. Quite apart from an *Anschluss*, which he had opposed in 1934, he feared for the Alto Adige (the South Tyrol as the Austro-Germans called it), acquired by Italy under the Treaty of Versailles, where there were 200,000 Germans.[9] Furthermore, in December 1934 Germany was not even invited to an international conference of Fascists at Montreux in Switzerland organised by the Italians. The Fascist press portrayed Hitler as a dangerous megalomaniac and insisted on the differences between Fascism and National Socialism. Undoubtedly, however, Mussolini became determined to conquer Ethiopia at some point in the first half of the 1930s. Why? The cynics insist that he did it because he needed to distract attention from the domestic economic crisis. But sensible examination of the figures shows that by 1935, although things were not good, they were not bad either. There was no particular crisis. (Unemployment was just under 700,000 at the end of 1935 and around 500,000 in 1939.)[10] Others say that the martial logic of Fascism, the uniforms, the violent talk, the holy grail of the Roman Empire reborn, the oft-repeated slogan that only war would make Italians Italian, the unshakeable belief that the Treaty of Versailles had treated victorious Italy as one of the vanquished etc., demanded it. Others say that power had gone to his head or that he was mad. But Mussolini was not especially mad; he was a realist and an opportunist. If a thing was bound to fail, he would not do it, regardless of what Fascist martial logic demanded. If an opportunity presented itself, however, he would seize it. Naturally, in seizing his opportunity in Ethiopia he employed as many arguments as possible, including martial ones, the political one that it was a revolutionary war by a 'proletarian nation' against the imperialism of the rich countries, economic ones such as space for Italians and access to raw materials, and also the moral ones trotted out so often by the British and the French: civilisation of barbarians, conversion to Christianity, abolition of slavery etc. There is no doubt either that he regarded foreign expansion as a means of, if not of completing, then hastening the process of *fascistizzazione* of the Italian people. But Monelli was surely right when he wrote that 'whoever seeks the guiding thread of his actions, a programme or a coherent idea, an immutable principle ... will not find it, except in a hasty, frantic and in a certain sense touching desire to make the country and, as a result, himself great in the brief space of his life.'[11]

Ethiopia was the last piece of Africa, except Liberia, the state of freed slaves, which had not been colonised, mandated, or made a protectorate by the European powers. It was still a slave society, run like a medieval fiefdom by an emperor, known as the *Negus*, presiding uneasily over a number of warring tribes, each ruled by a chief – known as a *ras* – the name taken up by the Fascists for their own provincial leaders. The *Negus*'s Amharic tribe, centred around Addis Ababa, was Christian and had only recently conquered – or united if you prefer – the other tribes. These were of other races and mostly pagan or Muslim. The *Negus* called it an empire, for that is what it was, and he termed himself emperor. Ethiopia was not a nation. And yet it was a member of the League of Nations. In the *Evening Standard* on 13 February 1935 the pro-Mussolini Evelyn Waugh attacked the sentimentalists, liberal humanists and do-gooders who insisted that Ethiopian independence be defended against Italian aggression. He wrote, 'Abyssinia is still a barbarous country ... It was taken bloodily and is held, so far as it is held at all, by force of arms.' The *Negus* had no more right to rule it, he said, than did Italy. Waugh, like so many Catholics, admired Mussolini and Catholic Italy as Europe's best hope of defending Catholic Austria from the pagan bully Hitler. His friends, Diana and Unity Mitford, on the other hand, were fervent admirers of Hitler. Elsewhere he described the Italian conquest of Ethiopia as a 'transition from a lower to a higher form of imperialism'.[12]

In earlier times Italy's claim on Ethiopia would have been regarded in the civilised world as perfectly logical, given her extensive economic penetration of the country. In addition, Italy had three colonies in north and east Africa: Libya (1911), Eritrea (1899) and Italian Somalia (1925), the last two sharing borders with Ethiopia. Attitudes in Britain and France to colonisation, however, had changed. Colonisation might have been the done thing once when they did the colonising. But it was not the done thing any more now that they had their colonies. By the 1930s the term 'sphere of influence' had replaced 'colony' in the jargon of the diplomats as the done thing. The moral justification for continuing with their own colonies – their white man's burden, as they called it – had become the bringing of civilisation and all that entailed.

Italy had long had its eye on Ethiopia. But its earlier attempt at conquest in the last decade of the nineteenth century – encouraged by Britain as a counter to the French – had ended in humiliating failure when the Ethiopian army trounced the Italian army at Adowa (Adua) in 1896. To Italians, Adowa was Italy's colonial Caporetto – on a par with Isandlwana in 1879 for the British. But, unlike Caporetto or Isandlwana, Adowa had not been avenged. The invasion of Ethiopia was not the product of Fascist megalomania; it had far deeper roots in the Italian collective psyche. Initially Mussolini aimed to penetrate it by peaceful means; hence the 1928 Treaty of Friendship between Italy and Ethiopia. But the current *Negus*, Haile Selassie, who became emperor in 1930, had behaved in an increasingly obstructive fashion.

Nor would Britain and France have really minded much in the 1930s if Italy had colonised Ethiopia so long as their national interests were not damaged: in the case of Britain the source of the Blue Nile on Lake Tsana; in the case of France the rail link between Addis Ababa and Djibouti in French Somalia. In 1906 Italy, France and Britain had even signed a treaty which carved up the country precisely along these lines in the event of its disintegration, which at that point seemed likely.[13] The trouble was that Ethiopia had joined the League of Nations in 1923 (against stiff opposition from the British but with Mussolini's encouragement). And according to article 16 of the league's Covenant, an act of war against a member nation was an act of war against the league. Curzon, then Foreign Secretary, had said in 1923 that Ethiopia was 'quite unfit' for entry because of 'rampant slave trading' and 'complete anarchy', and Lady Simon, chairman of the Anti-Slavery Society and wife of Sir John Simon, future Foreign Secretary, called for a crusade to free Ethiopia from slavery.[14] But despite the league's record of failure to keep the peace in its relatively short life to date, Britain and France felt obliged to support it – officially at least. In Britain, especially, public opinion and the Labour opposition had wide-eyed faith in it. Even so, all that was required to avoid a head-on collision over Ethiopia was a behind-the-scenes deal to save the faces of Britain and France at the league. After all, the league had been set up after the First World War not to prevent the conquest of barbarians but to prevent war in the civilised world. As Mussolini told Ward Price,[15] the *Daily Mail*'s man in Rome: 'You ought to be glad I am invading Abyssinia for I am only following an example that your people have so often set in the past.' ... 'Your own imperial history does not entitle you to display so much concern for the independence of the Ethiopians.'

Aware of this, at the end of 1934 Mussolini began diplomatic moves to secure approval from Britain and France for the conquest of Ethiopia. He did not think this would be difficult. Their national interests were not at stake and anyway, he thought, they were decadent peoples whose populations were declining and who would not fight. As he had so often said, a nation whose population was in decline was a weak nation.

Mussolini's diplomatic initiative coincided with an ugly skirmish – the precise cause of which remains unclear – between Italian and Ethiopian forces on 5 December 1934 at the ill-defined border between Ethiopia and Italian Somalia at Wal-Wal, the site of important wells. These wells were garrisoned by Italy, but the *Negus* correctly pointed out that they were his. Some thirty Italian and Somalian soldiers and more than a hundred Ethiopian soldiers were killed in the incident. Wal-Wal provided Mussolini with a pretext to put Ethiopia on the international agenda and to whip up anti-Ethiopian feeling in Italy via the press, radio and cinema newsreels. He demanded that the *Negus* recognise Italian sovereignty over the wells and compensation from the *ras* responsible. The *Negus*, meanwhile, took the matter to the league, which irritated Britain and France who did their best to ensure that this trivial matter did not go formally before the league for a vote but to arbitration.

Mussolini's diplomatic initiative also coincided with secret orders to prepare for an invasion. He told Marshal Badoglio, by now Chief of the General Staff once again, in a 30 December 1934 memo, 'In no other way can we build an empire ... No one in Europe would raise any difficulties provided the prosecution of operations resulted rapidly in an accomplished fact. It would suffice to declare to England and France that their interests would be recognised ...'[16] Given that the league had done little to stop Japan's undeclared war with China over Manchuria in September 1931, except appoint a commission, Mussolini can be forgiven for thinking that the league – dominated by Britain and France – would respond in a similar way on Ethiopia. After all, what he intended in Ethiopia they had recently done in Morocco and Egypt.

But he wanted to be sure. He approached the French first. Here his efforts were hampered by the political and social turmoil in 1930s France which had caused five different governments in just four months between the end of 1933 and the start of 1934. But the new French Foreign Minister, Pierre Laval, like Mussolini an ex-Socialist from a relatively humble background – he was a butcher's son – was a pragmatist disposed to listen. Laval (later executed for his role in the collaborationist Vichy government of Marshal Pétain) was a consummate fixer. He had just replaced Louis Barthou, who had been assassinated in Marseilles with King Alexander of Yugoslavia on 9 October 1934 by Croat 'Ustase' separatists who had then fled to Italy, where they had close links with Italian Fascism. Two of them, including the future leader of the Ustase, Ante Pavelić, were arrested in Turin. Many believed, erroneously, that Mussolini had ordered the assassination. But Mussolini, who had long had his eye on territory and influence in the Balkans, refused to allow them to be extradited to France on the grounds that they were political refugees.[17] (Pavelić would be responsible for the deaths of up to half a million Serbs during the Second World War.) Understandably, this did not please the French. But the overriding concern of Laval and the French

Prime Minister, Pierre-Etienne Flandin, was not the murder of the Yugoslav King or even their own Foreign Minister; it was an increasingly
aggressive Germany. Consequently, both were keen to establish closer
links with Italy in particular to ensure that it continue in its role as guar-
antor of Austrian independence. Their policy was to encircle Germany
and to do this they needed, foremost, alliances with Soviet Russia and
Fascist Italy.

After intense diplomatic preparation Laval arrived in Rome by train on
4 January 1935 for talks with Mussolini. These talks, which produced a
treaty of friendship between the two countries, convinced Mussolini that
he had got the two things he wanted from Laval: French approval, or at
least tacit consent, to conquer Ethiopia and a French commitment to
cover his back in Austria while he was preoccupied in doing so.

On 7 January the two sides signed a wide-ranging series of accords.
Regarding Europe, they agreed that France and Italy would collaborate to
maintain the peace and to protect Austrian independence should it be
threatened, and to use the league to resolve their future differences. All
knew that Mussolini alone could not protect Austria from Hitler; yet in
1934, when he had done so, neither Britain nor France had lifted a finger
to help. Laval's pledge to assist Italy was encouraging and subsequent
military talks produced a secret agreement signed by Generals Badoglio
and Maurice Gamelin of mutual military assistance in the event of German
aggression – described by Laval at Marshal Pétain's trial for collaboration
in 1945 as 'a veritable military alliance'.[18] Regarding colonies, France
agreed to give Italy 114,000 square miles of insignificant desert in the
south of Libya and a 21,000 square mile stretch of coast in French Somalia
adjoining Eritrea. In return, Mussolini agreed to the far bigger concession
of waving Italian rights in the French colony of Tunisia where there were
nearly as many Italians as French.

The two sides had satisfied each other on Austria and Mussolini had
satisfied France on the thorny issue of Tunisia. Yet in return he had been
given only a large patch of useless desert and a small stretch of coast. On
the surface, it looked as if Mussolini had given something for nothing.
But Laval also told Mussolini that as far as France was concerned, Italy
could have a 'free hand' in Ethiopia – though this was not written into
the accords and Laval would later deny it. Even in the text of the accords
themselves, however, it is clear that Laval had given his tacit approval.
This said that the only French interest in Ethiopia was the Djibouti–Addis
Ababa railway and that 'even in the case of modifications to the status
quo in the region in question' the French government 'would not seek
any advantage whatsoever'.[19]

Laval would argue later, unconvincingly, that he had only given Mussolini a free hand for the economic exploitation, not the military conquest,
of Ethiopia. It is probably true that the slippery Laval did not spell it out

in black and white but he was a master of the nod and the wink. Certainly, Mussolini told him of his intention to take Ethiopia. And Laval definitely did not object.[20]

Britain was another matter. Until Laval's visit to Rome, Italy had enjoyed far better relations with Britain than France but the British government could not betray the league because it dared not ignore British public opinion – the majority of which naively believed that the league could guarantee peace in Europe. In addition, the Labour opposition championed the league, demanding that the British government ensure it take a tough stand against the Fascists and the Nazis. Hypocritically, Labour argued fiercely at the same time against British rearmament.

In February 1935, Mussolini began to send troops to Eritrea and Italian Somalia via the Suez Canal – owned by a consortium in which the British government was the majority shareholder – under the noses of the British and the French, which should have made it crystal clear that he was intent on invasion. With this in mind, in March the British government commissioned Sir John Maffey, Permanent Under-Secretary at the Colonial Office, to report on whether British interests were at stake in Ethiopia. In June Sir John's report concluded, 'No vital British interest is concerned in Ethiopia except the head waters in Lake Tsana and the Nile basin.'[21] Mussolini had had an extremely good spy in the British embassy in Rome since the 1920s – one of the servants – and a copy of the Maffey report quickly found its way to him, as had much else of importance in the embassy over the years, thus showing that no matter how good your spies they do not necessarily affect the course of history. The Maffey report merely added to the wealth of evidence Mussolini already had that Britain would not save Ethiopia for reasons of self-interest. There remained, however, the self-interest of the League of Nations to take into account.

In January 1935 the Saar, under French rule for the past fifteen years, held a plebiscite and voted overwhelmingly for its return to Germany. Then, in March 1935, Hitler made it clear that he was determined to rearm on a massive scale in breach of Versailles when he announced the introduction of compulsory conscription. When he came to power in 1933, Germany had seven divisions compared with forty in Poland and ninety in France. By 1935 he had thirty-one divisions and, by 1939, fifty-two.[22] The British, to the irritation of the French, reacted by going to Berlin – Simon and Eden, at this time junior Foreign Minister, went – to talk to Hitler about German participation in a general European peace accord. Mussolini correctly saw this as evidence that Britain preferred to appease rather than confront aggression.[23] It also persuaded him that Britain would do the same over Ethiopia. The French, meanwhile, to the irritation of the British, were on the verge of signing a military alliance with the Soviet Union – the other major potential enemy which, worried by German aggression, had joined the league in September 1934 – against Germany (it was signed on 2 May). This, as the Germans were quick to point out, was a breach of the 1925 Treaty of Locarno.

All Silent at Stresa

It was against this background that, at Mussolini's suggestion, Britain, France and Italy met at Stresa on Lago Maggiore in the north of Italy between 11 and 14 April 1935 to discuss, not Ethiopia, but the growing German menace. Mussolini wanted a concrete commitment on Austria, to leave him free to concentrate on Ethiopia. He had often said that if the Italian army went into Austria to save it from the Germans, the Austrians would open fire. Nevertheless he needed an independent Austria as a satellite and buffer against Germany.

Mussolini got on much better with the French than the British, possibly because his French was very good. With them, he was 'natural and in a good mood', according to a member of the French team, but quite different with the British. 'His physiognomy transformed. He threw, somehow, his chin out.'[24] France, with most to fear from an aggressive Germany, was keen to make a tripartite commitment on Austria, but Britain, in German-appeasing mode as usual, said it would give only moral support. The conference did agree, however, a piece of paper which created the so-called Stresa Front by which 'the three powers, whose political objective is the collective maintenance of peace within the context of the League of Nations, are in complete agreement to oppose, by all possible means, any unilateral repudiation of any treaty which might endanger peace and will act in close and cordial collaboration to this end'.[25]

Ethiopia was not officially on the agenda at Stresa. But by now the ongoing Wal-Wal dispute and the Italian troop build-up via Suez on Ethiopia's frontiers had turned into a complaint to the league by the *Negus* about Italian aggression in general, due to be discussed at the league after the Stresa Conference. Despite this, no one mentioned Ethiopia at Stresa even though the British and Italian diplomatic teams included colonial specialists who had prepared detailed briefs on the subject. Nor did anyone mention Ethiopia when Mussolini insisted on inserting in the agreement the words 'in Europe' after the phrase 'which might endanger peace ...' 'Let's not take on commitments which are too big,' he joked.[26]

Mussolini's request provoked a long silence. Those present – MacDonald, British Prime Minister, and Simon, British Foreign Secretary, and Flandin and Laval, and their aides – knew exactly what Mussolini's game was. He meant to exclude Africa. Despite this they agreed to his change of wording. 'The Duce's proposal was clear to all. MacDonald looked at Simon, and so did Sir Robert Vansittart, the permanent Under-Secretary at the Foreign Office. In the French sector of the table Mussolini's request "provoked a knowing smile on the lips of Sig. Laval". The French Prime Minister, Pierre-Etienne Flandin was silent.'[27]

Mussolini took the silence at Stresa to mean the approval of Britain for his Ethiopian enterprise for which he felt he already had the agreement of France. Grandi, now Italian ambassador in London – whose sayings and writings need to be treated with caution on account of his proven deviousness – claimed that MacDonald had told him at this time apropos of Ethiopia that Britain 'being a lady, appreciates vigorous masculine initiative, provided that things are done with discretion, not in public'.[28] As Lord Hankey, Secretary to the Cabinet, wrote after the Second World War, 'How could MacDonald, Simon and Vansittart have gaily omitted even to mention Abyssinia? ... All the Ethiopian imbroglio sprang from that hideous error. Naturally Mussolini thought he could go safely ahead ...'[29] The silence of the British at Stresa and Laval's nod and wink in Rome convinced Mussolini he could get away with it. He knew that Britain and France did not care what happened to Ethiopia. Unfortunately, they had to care about the League of Nations. At Stresa Mussolini said to Grandi who was also there, 'You told me that the English would reply yes to the Austrian question and no to the African one ... instead, they replied no to Austria and yes to Africa.'[30]

Simon did tell Grandi soon after Stresa that Britain objected to an invasion of Ethiopia because apart from anything else it would undermine the Stresa Front. But then within two months the British – driven by the desire to appease Hitler – made it obvious that there was no such thing as the Stresa Front. To the irritation of the French and the Italians, they signed the Anglo-German Naval Agreement on 18 June without telling them. Under the terms, Britain agreed that Germany could increase the size of its surface fleet to 35 per cent of the British fleet and its submarine fleet to equal that of the Commonwealth. In March, Britain had ignored Hitler's breach of Versailles on troops and now it had agreed he breach it on ships. Mussolini concluded that for all its talk of fair play, Britain was as fickle and untrustworthy as the rest and that if it was not prepared to stand up to German aggression it would not stand up to Italian aggression. The French, meanwhile, had their military alliance with Soviet Russia, to the irritation of the British. British refusal to contemplate a similar move and to commit on Austria at Stresa were grave errors in Laval's opinion. Later, he would write in his prison cell before his execution on 15 October 1945, 'England was not yet ready to envisage this policy of the encirclement of Germany, which alone could stop war, by making it impossible for Hitler to do damage.'[31] As for Hitler, he began to send arms to the *Negus*. He had his reasons: first, he did not want unduly to offend Britain by supporting Italy because at this time he wanted an alliance with Britain; and second, he wanted Italy bogged down in Ethiopia to fracture even further Mussolini's relations with Britain and France, and to make

Mussolini less able or willing to protect Austria. The *Negus* said that Hitler was Ethiopia's only sincere friend in Europe.[32]

Appeasing the Dictators

With the outcry over the Anglo-German Naval Pact in full flow, Eden came to Rome in June 1935 less than a week later to try to appease Mussolini on Ethiopia, as he had appeased Hitler on rearmament. He offered Mussolini far less, however, than he had offered Hitler. Stanley Baldwin, who had become Prime Minister at the head of a new National government on 7 June after MacDonald's resignation, agreed that the policy to date of, as Vansittart put it in a 12 June minute, 'letting things drift on their present disastrous course' had to be reversed. The dangerous implications of the Ethiopian crisis were crystal clear, as another minute from Vansittart on 8 June makes plain: 'Italy will have to be bought off ... or Abyssinia will eventually perish ... That might in itself matter less if it did not mean that the league would also perish (and that Italy would simultaneously perform another volte-face, into the arms of Germany).'[33] There, in a nutshell, it all was: if Italy was not bought off she would invade Ethiopia, which did not actually matter very much, except that the league would disintegrate and Italy switch sides. This is what happened more or less.

Vansittart, like Eden, would become one of the very few to emerge from the 1930s with his anti-appeasement credentials intact. Yet, he was the keenest of all to appease Mussolini. He had toyed with the idea of an Italian mandate in Ethiopia and now proposed instead giving Mussolini the whole of British Somaliland. But the price the Cabinet was prepared to pay when Eden – appointed by Baldwin to the Cabinet for the first time as Lord Privy Seal and minister for the League of Nations – went to Rome was small by comparison. Eden would soon become a hate figure in Italy – the symbol of opposition to Italy's Ethiopian ambitions; the symbol of British hypocrisy and imperial jealousy. And Eden would come not so much to hate but to regard Mussolini as the stereotypical Italian – a spiv – whom it was quite impossible to trust. Eden would prove instrumental in the fatal estrangement of Britain and Italy over the course of the next few crucial years. But his attitude to Hitler was quite different. He had first met him in February 1934 and was impressed, he said, by his sincerity.[34] 'Dare I confess it? I rather liked him,' he told his wife.[35] As A. J. P. Taylor famously wrote, 'Eden did not face the dictators. He pulled faces at them.'[36] In fact, Eden was often ready to appease Hitler and did – but not Mussolini – when what he and the British government should have done was the precise opposite: appease the lesser danger, Mussolini, and stand up to the greater danger: Hitler. And even with Mussolini he was less than tough – going along with the appeasers in the Cabinet, in private at least.

Eden and Mussolini met in Mussolini's office at Palazzo Venezia on 23 June:[37] the tall, thin, suave, pinstripe-suited, upper-class Englishman, the epitome of the British stiff upper lip who played everything by the rules (his British rules naturally); and the short, robust, uniformed, rough-diamond, autodidact, son of a blacksmith Mussolini, whose rules were those of the mob and the piazza, of what his blood and his instinct told him. The day before, Laval, via the French ambassador in Rome, had made it plain to Fulvio Suvich, Italian Foreign Under-Secretary, that regardless of Britain he would ensure that 'the Ethiopian question will be sorted out at Geneva without causing any turbulence ... He will do all in his power to help us obtain all that we want.'[38]

Eden made Mussolini – to Italian eyes – a silly offer. He told him that Britain was prepared to give land-locked Ethiopia the Bay of Zeila in British Somaliland and so access to the sea in return for convincing Ethiopia to give Italy the province of Ogaden, which bordered Italian Somaliland, plus a number of economic concessions. He must have known that such an offer was doomed. Mussolini refused it point blank.

At a reception for Eden in the Albergo Excelsior Eden was, as usual, in his pinstripes but Mussolini wore a white summer suit with open-necked shirt. The two men studiously ignored each other. When one of Mussolini's aides at the behest of British ambassador, Sir Eric Drummond, came over towards the end of the proceedings to urge him to speak to Eden, Mussolini replied, 'The distance between us is exactly equal. If he wants to speak to me, he can come over here.'[39] On the 24th, Eden Met Mussolini again.[40] Mussolini spelled out in detail the parts of Ethiopia he wanted and said that what he had in mind was not a colony but a situation similar to the British mandate in Egypt. But Eden told Mussolini that his proposal was unacceptable. Conspicuously, Mussolini did not attend a lunch afterwards for Eden at a seaside villa, hosted by Suvich. Instead, he stood on the prow of a launch which moved slowly back and forth in front of the villa staring straight ahead. The gossip soon had it that the two men had rowed and despised each other. But in January 1936 Mussolini would say that he had nothing personal against Eden. 'The disagreement is purely political and remains so.'[41] Eden likewise denied that there was any personal animosity. 'Pure balderdash,' he wrote in a minute in response to the rumours.[42] The previous year when he had met Mussolini for the first time he said Mussolini was 'genuinely anxious' to help and had a 'very realistic attitude'.[43] But as one of Eden's biographers has noted there was nevertheless 'a complete failure of personal chemistry' between the two men.[44] Eden himself confessed that in his dealings with Mussolini he had to be 'particularly careful' not to let his personal prejudice colour his attitude 'too much' and that he was 'inevitably influenced by dislike of Italy and her methods'.[45]

Attempts to diffuse the Ethiopian crisis continued throughout the

Mussolini in his vast office at the Palazzo Venezia in 1931 where he insisted on silence. If he heard the sound of a fly he would ring for his usher and the fly swat.

Mussolini in December 1938 at the opening of the new model workers' village in Forlì near his birthplace, Predappio, and named after his father, Alessandro.

ABOVE: Mussolini salutes the crowd in Piazza della Vittoria, Genova, March 1938. His popularity in Italy during the 1930s was extraordinary.

RIGHT: Mussolini in dialogue with the crowd at the Colosseum in Rome in 1929.

BELOW: Agricultural workers in the Pontine Marshes near Rome salute the Duce with their spades in 1932.

Early 1945: Mussolini receives a bouquet of flowers from a little girl as defeat and death come ever closer.

Mrs Mussolini, brandishing a shotgun and flanked by friends, strolls down the high street in Predappio, Mussolini's birthplace, during the 1930s.

Mussolini and clergy-men, including a bishop, Monsignor Bartolomasi, doing the Roman Salute at the blessing of Nuova Guidonia, a Fascist new town, near Rome in November 1937.

Mussolini personally battles for wheat.

Mussolini and Vittorio Emanuele III, nicknamed 'the Little King', on military manoeuvres in the Abruzzi in 1938. The King, who remained head of state throughout the Fascist era, backed Mussolini until the Allied invasion of Sicily in July 1943.

Mussolini listens to Neville Chamberlain, British Prime Minister, at Munich in September 1938. The two leaders had used a secret channel to orchestrate this last serious attempt at peace before the outbreak of the Second World War and were both hailed as heroes as a result.

Hitler, wearing a yellow mackintosh, meets Mussolini for the
first time in Venice in June 1934.
'He's mad, he's mad,' said
Mussolini.

Mussolini meets Hitler and
Göring at German advance
headquarters in the Ukraine in
August 1941 not long after the
German invasion of Russia and
before the first Russian winter. A
German victory in the East still
seemed certain.

Mussolini with Francisco Franco, the Spanish dictator, and Serrano Suner, Spain's Foreign Minister, at Bordeghera on the Italian Riviera in February 1941. Hitler and Mussolini would try repeatedly to persuade *El Caudillo* to join the war on their side but in vain.

A propaganda reconstruction of the last successful cavalry charge in history by the Italian 'Savoia' cavalry near the River Don on 23 August 1942. It was long thought that the reconstruction portrayed the actual charge.

TOP: Mussolini, his wife (veiled) and daughters, Anna Maria (veiled) and Edda (unveiled), at the funeral of Mussolini's second child, Bruno, who was killed when the bomber he was test-flying over Pisa crashed in August 1941.

MIDDLE: Taken in late April 1945, in the court-yard of the Milan *Prefettura*, this is believed to be the last picture of Mussolini before his death.

BOTTOM: Milan, 28 April 1945: Mussolini, his mistress, Claretta Petacci, and Fascist leaders, including Achille Starace and Nicola Bombacci, the former Communist leader, hanging by their feet from the girders of the petrol station in Piazzale Loreto.

summer of 1935 to no avail. Vansittart's view remained that to alienate Italy over 'so relatively petty a matter ... would be lunacy'; what mattered was to stop the collapse of the Stresa Front against Hitler.[46] Eden disagreed but the majority of the Cabinet, not to mention the French government, did not. Their view might have prevailed had it not been for the publication on 27 June of the results of the Peace Ballot organised by the League of Nations to test British public opinion on the league: 11.5 million Britons had voted of whom 10 million agreed that if a member state were attacked, the other states should 'compel' the aggressor 'to stop'. As to how this might be done, 87 per cent said with economic sanctions and 59 per cent military measures.[47] A general election was imminent and so a reluctant Cabinet abandoned the sensible view that Italy should be bought off in favour of the naive view of Eden and the British public that the league should somehow stop the Italian conquest of a country where barbarity, slavery and the parading of decapitated heads on spears were the way of life. The *Echo de Paris* commented, 'What are 100,000 Italians threatening Ethiopia next to 10 million soldiers who are being drilled between the Rhine and the Niemen, and to what end? To defend themselves?'[48] The *Manchester Guardian*, on the other hand, was pleased.

On 11 September, at the sixteenth meeting of the Assembly of the League in Geneva, Sir Samuel Hoare, who had replaced Simon as Foreign Secretary when Baldwin became Prime Minister in June, delivered a speech which gave the unintended impression that Britain was determined to stop Mussolini in Ethiopia by force if necessary. Delegates gave the speech a jubilant reception. Tension increased soon afterwards when the British sent part of the Home Fleet to reinforce the Mediterranean Fleet. In return, Mussolini despatched two divisions to Libya to threaten Egypt. There was much talk of war between Britain and Italy. Eden did not agree but Hoare, in common with most of the Cabinet and the French government, felt that if the league imposed oil sanctions Mussolini would respond with what they called 'a mad-dog act' and declare war on Britain.[49] Mussolini was not a mad dog but we shall never know what he would have done in the event of an oil embargo because there was to be no oil embargo. Certainly, he did not want war with Britain. And whatever he said in public, Hoare was conciliatory in private – as was Laval.

Hoare had written to Mussolini reminding the dictator how after Caporetto, as a lieutenant-colonel in charge of British propaganda in Italy, he had secured British government funds for Mussolini's newspaper *Il Popolo d'Italia*.[50] More directly, at the end of September he wrote to Mussolini assuring him again that he was 'an old friend of Italy' and Britain wanted to see 'a strong and prosperous' Italy, that if it came to it, Britain would urge the league to introduce only limited economic sanctions against Italy, and that the reinforcement of the Mediterranean Fleet was purely defensive. The day before Hoare's speech to the league, for example, Laval,

Hoare and – yes – Eden had talks at which, as Laval would tell the French Chamber of Deputies on 28 December, 'We agreed immediately to exclude military sanctions, an eventual naval blockade, the closure of the Suez Canal ... in a word on the exclusion of everything that might lead to war.'[51]

On 28 September the *Negus* presided over the Mascal (End-of-the-Rains) Feast in Addis Ababa. It was still bucketing down. Evelyn Waugh, who had somehow convinced the *Daily Mail* to send him out as its war correspondent, wrote a funny account of this for the newspaper in which he said, 'At 1.30 p.m. the Emperor, in military uniform, drove to the spot, escorted by soaking lancers. He took his place on the throne, and sat waiting alone and immobile while the rain turned to hail. It swept over the grandstand, burst through holes in the roof, and torrents of water ran down the streets. Priests arrayed in ceremonial vestments huddled together under cover while they waited for the Abuna (archbishop) to begin the celebration at a kind of maypole which had been erected.' Due to 'natural reluctance', however, the 'aged and infirm' Abuna would not leave his shelter. But eventually, two hours later, the rain slackened a little. 'The old man ventured out, walked three times round the "maypole", threw a wand bearing a bunch of yellow daisies to the foot of the pole, and hurried back to shelter.'[52] The 'End-of-the-Rains' that year, of course, had more sombre significance: the Start-of-the-War.

On 1 October Mussolini told Pompeo Aloisi, the head of the Italian delegation at the league, that if he got 'the large vassal regions of Abyssinia' the affair could be resolved without recourse to arms. But the *Negus* – understandably – was in no mood to negotiate away his fiefdom. The next morning, Mussolini saw the King – the commander-in-chief of the armed forces – who told him, 'Duce go ahead. I'm right behind you. Forward I say to you.'[53] By the early evening, Mussolini announced the invasion of Ethiopia from the balcony of Palazzo Venezia to an enormous crowd in Piazza Venezia. The speech was relayed by radio to loudspeakers rigged up in piazzas throughout Italy and announced by the ringing of church bells.

Ward Price, the *Daily Mail*'s man in Rome was in Mussolini's office at the time. He recalled,

From a latticed window in one of the thick walls of the old palace, I looked down on the Piazza Venezia. It was a vast mosaic of pink faces under the soft evening light, gazing eagerly upward at the closed window of Mussolini's room. The square itself can hold 200,000 people, but for as far as one could see down the broad Via del Impero, stretching away to the Coliseum, and in every other street leading to the Piazza, at least as many more were wedged in solid masses. Surging waves of movement swept through the excited multitude ... Every window and roof was crowded to capacity. Slowly, while the nation waited in suspense, a honey-coloured moon rose in the green evening sky. It hung over the broken outline of the huge Coliseum, which in two thousand years has looked down upon so many mighty spectacles. Then at 7.30, a sudden roar like a volcano eruption broke from the crowd. Mussolini, in the grey uniform and round black cap of the Fascist militia, had stepped on to his flood-lit balcony.[54]

He began, 'Listen! A solemn hour in the history of *la patria* is about to strike. Twenty million people are reunited in this moment in the piazzas of Italy. Never in the history of the human race has there been such a gigantic spectacle.' He came to the point: why Italy was invading Ethiopia. It involved – as so often it did in the case of Mussolini – destiny. 'For some months, the wheel of destiny, under the impulsion of our serene determination, has been moving towards its destination ... We have been patient with Ethiopia for forty years. Now *basta!*' Italy was the victim of the league, he insisted, which was trying to deny Italy 'our rights' to a place in the sun with the threat of sanctions. Italy would combat economic sanctions with discipline, sobriety and sacrifice, he said, military sanctions with military force, and war with war. Sarfatti listened from the open window of an apartment on the other side of Piazza Venezia. 'It's the beginning of the end,' she said to the man with her. Asked why, she replied, 'We'll win ... and he'll lose his head.'[55] The next day – 3 October – Italy invaded Ethiopia at dawn. In Addis Ababa, to the wild throbbing of war drums, the *Negus* issued a proclamation which said, 'Arise, each of you, take up arms, and rush to the defence of your country. Rally to your chiefs, obey them with a single purpose, and repel the invader.'[56]

A Proletarian Colonial War

The Italian invasion force – in the end more than 500,000 strong[57] – was the largest colonial army ever put into the field and the consequent financial burden on relatively poor Italy very heavy. Also despatched were a huge number of workers – 100,000 at their peak of whom a significant proportion were criminal, corrupt and incompetent – to enlarge the Red Sea port of Massawa in Eritrea, the main disembarkation point, and to create an efficient infrastructure once inside Ethiopia. The situation was so congested at Massawa that ships sometimes could not unload their cargoes for months. Italy attacked from Eritrea to the north and from Italian Somalia to the south-east. But on 6 October the Italians took Adowa in the north – scene of the massacre of their forebears in 1896 – with hardly a shot being fired and at a cost of the death of just one Italian soldier. Later Alessandro Lessona, the Colonial Minister, recalled how Mussolini's face was 'radiant with joy' when told the news. 'Today is a great date for Fascism,' he said.[58]

On 11 October the league – as expected – voted by an overwhelming majority in favour of economic sanctions against Italy. Only four countries out of more than fifty voted against: Austria – a clear sign of its reliance on Italy for protection from Hitler – Hungary, Albania and Paraguay.[59] The sanctions included arms but crucially not oil. Consequently Italian ships were able to refuel, even at Suez throughout the crisis. Later, at the Munich conference in 1938, Mussolini would tell Hitler that if Eden had had his way and there had been an oil embargo it would have stopped him 'within eight days'.

Such limited sanctions had little effect. Indeed, they had a negative effect. The French government, though it went along with them, was unhappy and only very reluctantly gave a guarantee – even then an ambiguous one – of military help if Italy attacked Britain in the Mediterranean as a result. But also sanctions had united Italy 'as it has never been before' and made Italians 'prepared to fight to the last man'.[60] On 18 December – the so-called *Giornata della Fede* – millions of Italians responded to the call to give their wedding rings and other gold for the *patria* – in Rome alone 250,000 women gave up their rings.[61] Mussolini donated 2262 kilos of precious metal from among the vast collection of presents he had received over the years from admirers.[62] Sarfatti, however, did not donate any gold, let alone her wedding ring.[63]

Though the Pope was largely silent in public, the Catholic Church was right behind the war as well, regarding it as a missionary crusade against barbarity. On 28 October Cardinal Ildefonso Schuster, the Archbishop of Milan, in particular, celebrated a mass in the Duomo in which he asked God to protect the troops as 'at the cost of their blood they open the door of Ethiopia to the Catholic faith and Roman civilisation' and begin 'a new chapter in the history of the peninsula'.[64] Many Italian bishops were seized with a sense of martial ardour. The Bishop of Brindisi described the *Negus* as 'a half-savage king'.[65]

Similarly, all things British became mud and the subject of vicious satire. The Fascist press focused on, among other things, the 30,000 Boer women and children who had died in the British concentration camps during the Boer War. In addition the regime introduced a ban on foreign, especially British, products in the name of self-sufficiency – called *Autarchia*. The ban included coffee and tea but not, for some reason, Shakespeare. The Hotel Eden in Rome – though named after paradise – was obliged to change its name. D'Annunzio, who despised the British and the Germans but adored the French, would write to Mussolini in March 1936 of the 'dictatorship of the English trousers' and of Eden as a 'novice minister fashioned by the hairdresser, tailor and hatmaker'[66] and '*Il signor* Eden dressed as Hypocrisy'.[67] D'Annunzio, who had been such an inspiration and threat to Mussolini, would die on 1 March 1938. Mussolini attended his funeral on 3 March at Gardone – eleven days before the *Anschluss*. The last time they met was at the end of September 1937 at Verona station as Mussolini's train passed through on his return from his meeting with

Hitler. D'Annunzio was virulently against the idea of an alliance with Germany. In his will, d'Annunzio bequeathed Mussolini one of his ears, which he stated should be severed personally by Mussolini with a sword. Mussolini declined.[68]

Mussolini was in a hurry to finish the job in Ethiopia quickly. He needed to capture as much territory as possible before sanctions were strengthened to include oil or, worse, the Suez Canal was closed. Equally, he needed the strongest possible hand for the negotiated settlement he still wanted and to get his troops back to Italy as a deterrent against the growing threat of the *Anschluss*. But the commander of the Italian forces, General De Bono, one of the four blackshirt leaders – the Quadrumvirs – who had led the March on Rome, did not move fast enough for Mussolini. De Bono had retired from the army after the First World War and had been appointed only because of his blackshirt credentials. So in mid-November Mussolini replaced him with Marshal Badoglio, the Chief of the General Staff since 1925 and Governor of Libya until Balbo's appointment in 1933. General Rodolfo Graziani remained in command of the Italian forces in the southeast. Badoglio was due to depart from Naples for the front by boat on the 17th but Mussolini ordered him to postpone his departure until the 18th because the 17th, he insisted, was 'an unlucky date'.[69]

The Hoare–Laval Pact

Despite his warmongering, Mussolini attempted to get talks started the day after the invasion began – 4 October. He instructed Grandi in London to inform Hoare that he was prepared to negotiate. But with a British general election due in November (it was called on 20 October for 14 November) and public opinion firmly against the appeasement of Mussolini, the British government could not reply positively to the overture, as that would have meant abandoning the peace ballot policy on which it had decided to fight the election. MacDonald, now deputy Prime Minister and Lord President, was nevertheless in regular secret contact with Grandi – in contravention of a decision by the Cabinet to maintain total discretion. MacDonald was very worried that the 'unrealistic' peace ballot policy meant that war was imminent between Britain and Italy. He was especially angry with the 'fanatical anti-Fascism' of Eden and the 'liberal tub-thumping' of Baldwin. 'If Mussolini and I had been listened to and followed, Europe would not be in this state,' MacDonald told Grandi, adding, 'I ... who, before I knew him, was a bitter enemy of Mussolini and Italian Fascism, know very well that Fascism is a popular, social and revolutionary movement ...'[70]

The election safely in the bag, however, the situation swiftly changed. The British government was rightly scared of two things: that the estrangement of Italy over Ethiopia would drive Mussolini into Hitler's arms and so cause much bigger trouble for Europe; that the longer the Ethiopian crisis continued the more it would divert energy away from the biggest problem of Germany. It wasted no time in resuming talks. For as the British ambassador in Berlin, Sir Eric Phipps, put it at the time, Ethiopia was 'mere child's play compared with the German problem'.[71] Initially, Hoare said Britain was prepared to allow Mussolini only Adowa and other territory in the north, and an economic monopoly in the rest of Ethiopia. Ethiopia in return would get a sea port. But this was too similar to the offer Eden himself had made back in June. Mussolini refused it.

In early December, however, Hoare, suffering from exhaustion it was said, left Britain for a holiday in Switzerland. But en route he stopped in Paris to meet Laval, who had become Prime Minister in June 1935 as well as Foreign Minister,[72] in secret to try to put together a more enticing package which would give Mussolini enough for him to feel able to withdraw from Ethiopia. Baldwin and the Cabinet – including Eden – had given Hoare a free hand. According to Laval, Eden had an even more direct responsibility for these talks. In Geneva Eden had told Laval that Edward, Prince of Wales, wanted to meet him to talk about politics. Laval, who had already devised the plan with Mussolini but needed British agreement, duly met the prince in Paris. The prince wanted to help find a solution to the Ethiopian crisis. Laval urged him to convince George V, his father, to try to put pressure on Baldwin. Laval believed that this happened and that this is what convinced Baldwin to send Hoare to Paris.[73]

That he should do such a thing reveals precisely the frame of mind of British Conservatives. But theirs was the correct policy – not that of the British Labour party, the British public, or of Eden, the man the public wrongly thought of as its champion. If the league had imposed oil sanctions, Mussolini would have conquered Ethiopia in the end despite what he later told Hitler. Italy could and did buy a lot of oil from America – which was not a member of the league and not involved in sanctions – during the Ethiopian war. Even without oil sanctions, oil imports from America rose from 6 per cent of the total in October 1935 to 17 per cent by February 1936 as Italy bought as much oil as it could to stockpile.[74]

So what, after an oil embargo, would the British have done? Close Suez? Naval blockade? This may or may not have led to war. The French were convinced that a ban on oil would cause war and were determined to avoid it. Whether or not Eden, for all his tough talk, was really prepared for Britain to go to war with Italy for the sake of the league's reputation and the fate of a slave society, few others were. That the British fleet – which would have shouldered the main burden of any military action – had little ammunition could not be ignored either. Mussolini knew this from more documents copied by his spies at the British embassy in Rome.[75] Eden's proposed course of action would have led to a dangerous showdown in which Britain would not have been able to open fire if required. But unlike Eden, the British public and the Labour party, most of the British Cabinet were realists who rightly felt that the league should not stake its reputation on Ethiopia. The realists – the appeasers – not Eden, public opinion, or Labour, were right on Italy – though they quickly managed to cock things up.

In Paris Vansittart, the permanent Under-Secretary at the Foreign Office, was also present at the Hoare–Laval talks. Together those present formulated a new plan – shortly to become known as the Hoare–Laval Pact and achieve pride of place in the demonology of appeasement. The plan would have given Italy sovereignty over much more of Ethiopia than previously conceded, including Eastern Tigre and a vast area in the south which Italy could have for the purposes of 'economic expansion and colonisation'. In exchange, as before, Ethiopia would get a sea port.[76] Laval had been in regular contact with Mussolini and the plan was based on their discussions. Vansittart was in touch with Baldwin by telephone 'every hour and every half-hour', according to Laval.[77]

Hoare left for his holiday in Switzerland where, on 9 December, he broke his nose ice-skating and was confined to his bed. He was unable to return to London until the 16th,[78] where he went straight back to bed at his home in Cadogan Gardens.

The Hoare–Laval Pact was put to the Cabinet minus Hoare on 9 December and agreed. Eden did not protest – despite the astonishment he later said that he had professed – except over one or two details. Mussolini agreed it could form the basis for discussion and called a meeting of the Grand Council to discuss it. That he had agreed to Britain's request as a precondition of the talks to withdraw one of his divisions from Libya and had actually done so is compelling evidence of his sincere desire to reach a negotiated settlement. But then in France, on 13 December[79] details of the plan found their way into the press. The news that the British and French governments had secretly decided to hand a large chunk of another country to the Fascist dictator caused an outcry, especially in Britain.

On 18 December the *Negus* turned down the plan but the same day the Grand Council met and approved it as a basis for negotiation. Then, at midnight, news arrived from London that as a result of the furore Hoare had resigned. Despite their complicity in the Hoare–Laval Pact Baldwin, Eden and the rest of the Cabinet had decided to sacrifice Hoare to save themselves. Hoare, still in bed, was absent but agreed to resign for the sake of the government's survival and he decided for the same reason not to reveal the complicity of his Cabinet colleagues in the pact, which the documents make crystal clear.

The Hoare–Laval Pact was the only serious effort at a diplomatic solution to the Ethiopian crisis. Eden, by now the number one hate figure in Italy, replaced Hoare as Foreign Secretary at the age of thirty-eight. Despite his failure to oppose the pact when it had been secret, he had quickly disassociated himself from it once it was in the public domain. The *Daily Herald* – like everyone outside Cabinet unaware of Eden's true role – commented that Eden was the only person to emerge from the 'miserable affair ... without discredit'.[80] In the popular imagination Eden stood for high principle and strength; the rest of the government for cynicism and weakness. In truth, there had been little divergence between his views and those of the rest of the Cabinet. Eden now became the prisoner of the popular perception of him as the only member of the government prepared to stand up to the dictators. But if details of the Hoare–Laval Pact had not been leaked and if it had been presented cleverly, it would probably have been agreed by parliament, given the alternatives: oil sanctions – which the French would not accept – leading in any case to war; or the continued Italian military presence in Ethiopia. Baldwin had a huge majority. He could have ridden out the storm. He chose not to. Eden, now Foreign Secretary and so in a much more influential position, pressed on with his oil sanctions campaign and by 1936 had convinced a reluctant Cabinet to agree. The idea came to nothing because of the French. Those who shouted loudest for an oil embargo in Britain were the Labour opposition while still as ever opposing with equal noise the rearmament required to back up such sanctions.

Subsequently Eden would write in his memoirs that he was 'astonished' when he first saw details of the Hoare–Laval Pact.[81] Like other members of the Cabinet, he made out that Hoare had done it all off his own bat. When Eden wrote his memoirs the relevant documents in the Public Record Office had not been released, so it was impossible to challenge his version of events. These documents show beyond doubt that either Eden's memory was at fault or he was lying. The Oxford historian R. A. C. Parker's comprehensive study of the documents concludes, 'In fact the Cabinet gave him (Hoare) a free hand, and afterwards approved of what he had done.'[82] In France the Laval government survived a vote of confidence, only to fall in January 1936 over the economy. But the new government, headed by Albert Sarraut of the Radical party, with Pierre Flandin as Foreign Minister, opposed oil sanctions with equal vigour. The last thing the French wanted was to drive Italy into the arms of Germany, which is what they were convinced Eden's policy would do. Their aim remained a deal on Ethiopia to get Italy back on side so as to present a common front against Germany. But it was not to be.

Victory in Ethiopia

With the new year the Italian advance into Ethiopia, which had made little headway during the winter, began to gather relentless momentum – from the north and the south. It was now that Hitler chose his moment to capitalise on the collapse of the Stresa Front and the weakness of the league over Ethiopia. On 7 March he sent troops (only two divisions) into the Rhineland, along the border with France, which had been made a demilitarised buffer zone under the Treaty of Versailles. This was his most serious breach of Versailles to date. It was also forbidden under the 1925 Treaty of Locarno, which Germany had willingly signed. It was a big gamble and Hitler's generals were terrified. If the French had gone in, they would have defeated him in no time. But they would not do so unless the British and Italians did as well. Not surprisingly, given sanctions, Mussolini declined – though Italy did adhere to the condemnation of Germany by the league. But so too did the British decline. Instead, Eden proposed 'to enter betimes into negotiations' with Germany as he put it in a minute.[83] At this Flandin, it was reported, burst into tears. More than twenty years later Eden admitted his error, conceding that military intervention 'would have been the right thing to do and many millions of lives would have been saved'.[84]

But despite his fear of Germany, Mussolini was not altogether unhappy. Hitler's move distracted attention from Ethiopia, while it also increased pressure on Britain and France to restore good relations with Italy. When Flandin proposed sanctions on Germany, Britain refused these as well. Furious, he said France would withdraw its support for sanctions against Italy, which it more or less did. Nor did French policy on sanctions against Italy change when the Socialist Leon Blum was elected Prime Minister in May 1936 at the head of a Popular Front government which saw the Communists enter government for the second time in western Europe (a Popular Front government, supported by the Communists, had been elected in Spain in February 1936). Blum's pacifism was as zealous as his anti-Fascism. Popular Fronts such as his had had the support of the Communists since August 1935 when the Comintern in Moscow permitted them for the first time to make tactical alliances with other left-wing parties in order to get power. The then General Secretary of the Comintern, Dimitrov, described this as the 'Trojan Horse' tactic.[85]

The Popular Front's arrival in power soon spurred British Conservatives such as Chamberlain and Churchill, history's anti-appeaser in chief, to seek a swift end to sanctions. Initially Churchill had thought that, given its antipathy to the Nazis, the Popular Front might strengthen French resolve against Hitler. Instead, there was even more internal social unrest in France and this, combined with the Popular Front's instinctive pacifism, paralysed French policy. So Churchill soon decided it was even more imperative that Italy be brought back on side.[86]

Undeterred, on 10 April Eden urged the Cabinet to close Suez in addition to the oil embargo – in vain. On 19 April Grandi met King Edward VIII, who had just succeeded George V and was well known for his Fascist sympathies. Grandi's aim was to try to persuade the King to put pressure on the government to lift sanctions. The King felt 'a genuinely sincere joy' at the Italian military triumph, according to Grandi. 'I have to tell you that rarely have I found someone in England who understands Fascist Italy and our revolution better than King Edward,' Grandi wrote to Mussolini.

'I am always ... in line with Stresa ... I can assure you there is nothing between Germany and me ... But any worsening of sanctions will necessarily throw Italy into an isolation from which its government will have the overriding duty to free it. It is up to France and Britain not to reject us,' Mussolini told the French ambassador, Count Charles de Chambrun.[87] The French, with Germany right next door, were much more willing to bring back Italy into the Stresa Front than Eden. As late as April 1936 Mussolini still hoped for a negotiated settlement. He made new proposals to the British and French by which most of Ethiopia apart from Addis Ababa and an area around it would become an Italian protectorate or mandate rather than a colony. The French were keen but the plan failed, largely because it was unacceptable to Eden who told the Cabinet that in any case the rain might defeat Mussolini. As Vansittart remarked, 'It's got to rain *very* hard – and *very* quick – and *very* long!'[88]

Ethiopia: Italian Atrocities and Vanity

Among the many senior Fascists who queued up to serve short, glory-seeking spells in Ethiopia were Bottai, Farinacci and Starace in the army, and Ciano, who had a military pilot's licence, in the air force. Farinacci accidentally blew off one of his hands when a grenade he was using to catch fish on Lake Ascianghi exploded prematurely. He claimed that he had sustained the injury in combat and as a result received a *medaglia d'argento* for gallantry. Starace made sure of his moment of glory by insisting on being the first into the captured town of Gondar.

Also present were Mussolini's two eldest sons, Vittorio and Bruno, as bomber pilots. Bruno was not yet eighteen, the legal minimum age to be a military pilot, but Mussolini insisted the rule be waived in his case. They and Ciano all took part in the first bombing raid of the war on Adowa. Vittorio wrote a book about his war experience in which he described it as 'sport' and 'fun'. He added, 'War certainly educates and toughens, and I advise it to everyone ... I believe that it is one's duty as a man to do at least one.'[89] Mussolini wrote to Vittorio on 6 January 1936, 'Your *mamma* complains that you never write. I believe she is right. I embrace you. Papa.'[90] The Fascist press, meanwhile, eulogised Mussolini's sons as heroes and both received *medaglie d'argento*.[91]

But while Italy had about 500 planes in Ethiopia, the Ethiopians had no air force though some anti-aircraft guns. Nevertheless, Ciano was hit four times in all by enemy fire. In December he returned to Rome for surgery to ear, nose and throat problems which periodically caused him temporary deafness and pain – made much worse by flying. But in February he was back once more and at the end of April, with victory imminent, he decided to land at Addis Ababa airport still in enemy hands as an act of bravado. His plane did touch the runway but was hit by enemy fire. He had to give up his plan, pull up, and with leaking fuel tanks, return to base. For this exploit he was awarded a *medaglia d'argento*. Mussolini sent him a telegraph which said, 'I am very proud of your flight over Addis Ababa.'

They denied it at the time but the Italians did use poison gas in Ethiopia – though Mussolini did admit to Ward Price, the *Daily Mail*'s man in Rome, the use of 'tear gas and a mild kind of mustard gas'.[91] But so keen were they for this not to come out that on one occasion they intercepted photographs of victims due to be dispatched to British newspapers and swapped them with photographs of leprosy victims. When these photographs were published, Grandi in London was able to issue a convincing denial. But the Italian use of gas was on a very limited scale by First World War standards. Then, Germany had deployed 52,000 metric tons of poison gas, the French 26,000 and the British 14,000. The 1925 Geneva Convention, which Italy had signed in 1928, banned its use for first-strike purposes – though not its possession as a deterrent or its use if an enemy used it first (the British had large stocks with them, for example, when they invaded Italy in the Second World War). The Italians had also used it in small quantities against unrest in Libya between 1923 and 1931 – but then so had the British in Iraq during the 1920s. Badoglio requested its use and Mussolini authorised it on several occasions, sometimes for purposes of terror but mainly for defensive purposes and retaliation against the Ethiopian use of dum-dum bullets, also banned by international treaty, and other atrocities, such as the ritual mutilation of Italian soldiers including decapitation and the parading of severed heads. It was first used on 22 December 1935. In all, according to the most reliable figures, the air force used it twenty-two times, dropping a total of 972 – 212 kilo, C.500T – mustard gas bombs. It was also used on the ground, most notably at the Battle of Amba Aradam in February 1936 where 1367 poison gas shells were fired and 60 metric tons dropped from the air.[92]

The use of gas had little effect on the outcome of the war. The Italians won for two reasons: their enormous superiority in weapons and equipment, and the decision by the *Negus* to commit his troops to battle – instead of conducting a guerilla war. The Italian advance continued. By May it had reached Addis Ababa. On the 2nd the *Negus* and his entourage of dignitaries and slaves abandoned the capital and fled the country by train on the French railway line to Djibouti. Mussolini turned down a request from General Graziani, commander of the Italian forces in the south, to bomb the train. Addis Ababa became the scene of widespread arson and looting by Ethiopian soldiers, targeted at Europeans and the general population. Three days later, on the 5th, Badoglio arrived in Addis

Ababa on horseback where he was welcomed as a liberator – by the Europeans at least. It was raining very heavily. But the rain had failed to do Eden's bidding.

The human cost of the Ethiopian war to Italy had been small: the Italian forces lost 2500 dead and their native Eritrean and Somalian troops 1600 dead. The Ethiopian losses were many times that – though figures are unreliable. The financial cost to Italy had been enormous and would continue to be so: 57 billion lire in 1935–40 – 20 per cent of total state expenditure.[93] The war also made Mussolini dangerously self-confident about Italian military prowess.

That evening in Rome – the 5th – Mussolini spoke to a crowd of 200,000 from the balcony of Palazzo Venezia at 10.30 p.m. announcing victory. When he had finished the ecstatic crowd brought him back to the balcony for ten encores, so wild was their applause. On the 9th he gave another balcony speech in which he named the King Emperor of Ethiopia and proclaimed the resurrection of the Roman Empire. 'Are you worthy?' he asked the crowd. 'Yes!' it replied. 'Yes!' Each word in the speech was 'like a step forward', commented Ugo Ojetti.[94] This time he was called back to the balcony, it was said, forty-two times. Rachele had driven to a nearby side street in her Fiat *Topolino* with Romano and Anna-Maria to be there.[95] 'He's like a God,' said one of the gerarchs listening from inside Mussolini's office. 'He is a God,' said Starace.[96] The speech over, the gerarchs, with Ciano at their head, marched to Parliament singing 'Giovinezza'. There was wild celebration throughout Italy late into the night.

But in June Mussolini's youngest child, six-year-old Anna-Maria, was struck by polio; her arms and legs paralysed. Mussolini became deeply depressed and remained at home with her for ten days until it became clear that she would not die. Later he confessed to Petacci – she would become his mistress in the autumn of 1936 – that he had prayed to God to save his daughter.[97] His wife said that he kissed his mother's rosary which he kept on his bedside table.[98] In 1968 Anna-Maria would die of cancer. On 9 June Mussolini appointed Ciano Foreign Minister. He was thirty-three.

Badoglio, who had not wanted the war to begin but then not wanted it to end once put in charge, was showered with prizes. He requested from the King, and was granted, the title of Duke of Addis Ababa and was also given a luxurious villa paid for out of government funds – plus a viceroy's salary for life. Later he would be among the leaders of the plot which overthrew Mussolini in 1943. De Bono was promoted to marshal. He too would be a party to the plot and as a result be shot in January 1944. Graziani was appointed Viceroy of Ethiopia and was soon – on the orders of Mussolini – responsible for terrible atrocities against the Ethiopians in the pacification of the interior. Myth would have it, even after the fall of Mussolini, that Italian colonial rule was much more civilised than the

British and French versions. This was true in Libya under Balbo's rule, though not before. Under his predecessor, De Bono, the Italians were responsible for atrocious brutality in Libya as well. Between 1930 and 1931, for example, 40,000 shepherds died in forced deportation marches to distant internment camps where conditions were barbarous.[99] And it was certainly not true in Ethiopia. Italian control in the five short years of conquest over much of the country was always precarious. The efforts to stamp out resistance prompted the brutality. Villages were torched and suspects shot without trial. On 19 February 1937 a bomb attack on an official ceremony in Addis Ababa killed several Italian officials and severely injured Graziani and dozens of others.[100] As soon as he was able, Graziani ordered a bout of dreadful violence by local Fascists. He admitted that 1000 Ethiopians had been killed as a result but the figure could have been as high as 3000.[101] In addition, a system of apartheid was introduced involving segregation in public places and an April 1937 law made sexual relations between whites and blacks a crime punishable by up to five years in prison. A popular Fascist song was 'Faccetta nera' (little black face) about a slave girl freed by Italian soldiers so she can go to Rome and wear a black shirt. Eventually, Mussolini banned the song and ordered Badoglio to punish Italian soldiers guilty of sexual relations with native girls. In November 1937 Mussolini recalled Graziani, replacing him with Amedeo of Savoy, Duke of Aosta. As for Mussolini, the King wanted to make him a prince. But he refused. 'Majesty, I have been and want to remain only Mussolini,' he said. But he did accept the title Founder of the Empire.

There remained the question of sanctions. On 1 May Grandi in London showed Churchill, at this point on the backbenches, a telegram from Mussolini in which he said that an Anglo-Italian rift would have only one result: 'the supremacy of Berlin in Europe'.[102] Churchill, who had been among the most fervent supporters of sanctions at the beginning, had now decided that they were pointless, given Italy's triumph. The most important thing, he felt, was to get Italy back into the Stresa Front. He told Grandi that he would make a speech to that effect in the House of Commons, which he did. The speech severely weakened support for sanctions. He also wrote an article in the Evening Standard in which he said that British policy on Ethiopia had been a humiliating failure because the British people had demanded that the government uphold the authority of the league but also that Britain should not go to war with Italy.

Mussolini told the Daily Telegraph in an interview on the 28th that good Anglo-Italian relations were 'desirable' and 'necessary'.[103] Despite Eden's intransigence, this was the view of the majority of the Cabinet and it was now only a matter of waiting for the right moment to end sanctions. On 11 June Neville Chamberlain annoyed Eden when he decided to take the bull by the horns and become the first member of the Cabinet to call for sanctions to be lifted.[104] Chamberlain, the favourite to succeed Baldwin, told the Conservative 1900 Club that to continue sanctions would be 'the very midsummer of madness' because of the risk of war with Italy. The tide had turned and Eden had to relent. On 18 June he told the Commons that the British government would urge the league to abandon sanctions because there was 'no longer any utility' in them.[105] On 30 June, at the league, the *Negus*, swathed in a black cloak of mourning, urged it to act. It would not. A few days later Britain withdrew its Home Fleet ships from the Mediterranean and on 15 July the league lifted sanctions.

Mussolini spoke once more from the balcony of Palazzo Venezia. 'Today, 15 July, in the Year XIIII, the sanctionist world raised the white flag on its battlements,' he told an ecstatic crowd. The deputy editor of *The Times*, Barrington Ward, wrote that the British government 'have no foreign policy at all'. Reviewing foreign policy in July 1936 the Cabinet decided that the league should not use sanctions again and that a series of regional treaties were a surer way of guaranteeing the peace, though with the ominous proviso 'on the basis that we could not help eastern Europe'.[106] As A. J. P. Taylor wrote, 'No concrete "interest" was at stake in Abyssinia ... But Italy still stood condemned as an aggressor, and the two western powers could not bring themselves to recognise the King of Italy as Emperor of Abyssinia. The Stresa Front was gone beyond recall, Mussolini forced on to the German side. This outcome was unwelcome to him. In attacking Abyssinia, Mussolini had intended to exploit the international tension on the Rhine, not to opt for Germany. Instead he had lost his freedom of choice.'[107] As Laval put it: 'Anti-Fascism ... not only in France, but elsewhere, had been stronger than the love of peace.'[108]

In June 1937 Evelyn Waugh would write a review of De Bono's account of the Ethiopian campaign, entitled *Anno XIIII*, in which he said,

Never, since the American War of Independence, has our prestige in the world fallen so low ... The results of English diplomacy are already apparent. Italy and Germany who in 1934 seemed irreconcilable opponents are now in close and formidable alliance and England is left to seek her friends among nations distracted to the point of impotence by internal dissension, dissensions which have been largely aggravated by the events themselves. We all see the result and are appalled; few trouble to probe farther and enquire into the false ideas which have exposed us to shame. We prefer to harbour a grievance and vent our rage in moral lessons to our neighbours, eagerly accepting any extravagant report which will confirm our belief that foreigners as usual have behaved like cads. It is small wonder that, since our diplomacy is so little understood at home, it should not at all be understood abroad. Marshal Emilio de [sic] Bono, in his book *Anno XIIII*, is only expressing the conviction, not only of every Italian, but of practically every European and Asiatic, when he assumes that our opposition to Italian aggrandizement in East Africa was directed solely from motives of imperial jealousy. Japan had been allowed to flout the League of Nations and still retained unchallenged territories held by her under a League mandate. From that moment the League was dead everywhere except in the minds of the peace-balloters. The sudden revival of League machinery and League principles seemed to the world as malignant and capricious as a prosecution under the Lord's Day Observance Act.[109]

Mussolini told the French Socialist, Jean-Louis Malvy, in June 1936,

The present situation obliges me to seek elsewhere the security that I have lost on the French side and on the English side, with the aim of re-establishing the shattered equilibrium to my advantage. Who should I turn to, if not to Hitler? I have to tell you that I have already had *ouvertures* from him ... I know perfectly well what will happen if I reach an agreement with Hitler. First of all there will be the *Anschluss* within a short time. Then, with the *Anschluss*, it will be Czechoslovakia, Poland, the German colonies etc. To sum up, it is war inevitably. That is why I have hesitated and still hesitate to take that path ... But if the attitude of the French government towards me and the Fascist regime and Italy does not change soon and it does not give me the assurances which I need, then I will accept Hitler's offers.[110]

In Italy, Mussolini's popularity had reached the highest point of its curve. For it was also the moment in which many Italians, especially young Italians, began to turn, not so much against, but away from, if not Mussolini – the Duce – from Fascism. The great Italian journalist Indro Montanelli, who had set off enthusiastically as an infantry officer for Ethiopia, was one who lost his faith at this time. He wrote 'We young people ... had not adhered to Fascism. We were born inside it, and this had exempted us from choice ... For us Liberal Democracy was impotence, disorder, factious division and, lastly, desertion and surrender.' What made Montanelli snap was that even though few Italian soldiers were called upon actually to fight the enemy at close quarters, that did not stop a grotesque 'fairground display of vanities, contests of rhetoric and the race for prizes, decorations and promotion ... It was not a different Italy which was born in Abyssinia, but the same Italy, with its gerarchs, its tedious rituals, its jungle of contradictory regulations, its clienteles, its factions. Our dream of a new world swiftly dissolved.' Back in Italy, Montanelli and others were determined not to overthrow, but to change Fascism. Fascism, however, would not allow them the means. It smothered debate. Fascism would not budge. Montanelli tried instead to turn against Fascism and made contact with the anti-Fascists in France but found them even less impressive than the Fascists. So he bided his time undermining Fascism from within in a hundred tiny little ways.[111] The regime was mummifying and, as Bottai noted, it seemed that Mussolini was no longer a man but a statue – a statue of himself – a 'hard, stony statue, from which a cold voice emanated'.[112] His wife, she later claimed, urged him to retire: 'If I were you, I'd retire to raise chickens at the Rocca. You've done more than enough [Rocca delle Caminate, his castle above Predappio, his birthplace].'[113]

13

THE SPANISH CIVIL WAR (1936–9):
THE BLURRING OF GOOD AND EVIL
AND THE TAKING OF SIDES

His Ethiopian war over, Mussolini quickly joined in someone else's. This time his motive was not to get turf but to stop others getting turf. Spain had become a republic in 1931 with the abdication of King Alfonso XIII after a revolution of sorts and been in turmoil ever since. In February 1936 the Popular Front, a left-wing coalition supported by the Communists, had won the general election by the narrowest of margins. The new government was divided and impotent. Naturally, the turmoil got worse. Priests, among others, were murdered by government supporters; churches desecrated. Spain, it seemed, was ripe for Communist revolution. To stop this General Francisco Franco – *El Caudillo* – started a military uprising in Spanish Morocco against the government on 18 July 1936. In Spain itself, simultaneously, other generals arose. The Spanish Civil War began.

Immediately, Franco sought military help from wherever he could get it. He was – if anything – a nationalist, not a Fascist, though he had the support of the Falange – a party which in some ways resembled the PNF. But he shared similar enemies: Communism and democracy. Democracy in Spain – as everywhere if introduced overnight – meant chaos; chaos meant Communism. If Franco failed, Communism would triumph. So Mussolini agreed to help. He envisaged a swift Franco victory and therefore minimal help. 'Bolshevism in Spain means Bolshevism in France, which means Bolshevism next door,' he told his wife.[1] Independently, Hitler decided to help Franco as well. Blum in France and Stalin in Soviet Russia agreed instead to help the Republicans. Blum and his Popular Front identified with the Republicans and their Popular Front. Both his and their front existed with the support of the Communists who aimed to use these fronts as the Trojan Horse with which they would launch their revolution. A Republican triumph would also inevitably bring Spain and France into alliance against Italy, which Mussolini did not want either. It might cause strife-torn France to fall to Communism as well. Mussolini made no attempt now or later to persuade Franco to try Fascism in Spain though in March 1937 *The Times* repeated a rumour that he had suggested the Duke of Aosta become Spanish king.[2] The 'national' was too significant a part of Fascism for it to become 'international'. But to stop Communism Mussolini was determined that Franco should triumph.

All four intervening countries – Italy, Germany, Russia and France – denied their intervening. In Britain, Baldwin aimed to keep the country neutral but referee the contest nevertheless. Many in his party, such as Churchill, wanted Franco to win, not the elected government, because with Soviet Russia involved the Communists quickly gained the initiative. Like Mussolini and Hitler, they feared that a Republican victory would mean the fall of Spain to Communism. Moscow did all it could to fulfil Lenin's prophecy that Spain would be the next country to go Communist. Pope Pius XI, on the other hand, was especially worried about the murdered priests. In September, in reaction to their ongoing slaughter by the Left, he spoke publicly of the 'truly satanic hatred of God' of the Republicans.[3] During the war, more than 4000 priests and about 300 nuns were killed. An exhibition of the exhumed bodies of nineteen nuns in Barcelona attracted very large crowds.[4]

But the chattering classes of the day saw it differently from Mussolini, Hitler, Churchill and the Pope. For them the Spanish Civil War was a noble cause – regardless of the murdered priests. Poets flocked to the Republican flag. They had gone, they decided, to fight against 'Fascism'; for 'Democracy' and 'Freedom'. Instead, they found themselves fighting not for those things, but for chaos and Communism. For the Communists swiftly hijacked the situation. Some, like Ernest Hemingway, came away disillusioned by 'the carnival of treachery and rottenness on both sides,'[5] but not before their chatterings had entered the conscience of the age. Untruthfully, Communist-inspired propaganda lumped together as one National Socialism and Fascism, and even Franco's nationalism. They called them 'Fascism' or 'Nazi-Fascism'. Equally untruthfully, they also lumped together democracy and Communism and called them 'anti-Fascism'. They said that democrats and Communists were fighting for the same things, which they were not. Actually, Communism had much more in common with Fascism, National Socialism even, than democracy. Regarded as one and the same, the Duce – the revolutionary despiser of the bourgeoisie – and the Führer – the right-wing despiser of the avant-garde – moved closer still. But just as the Spanish Civil War created a Rome–Berlin 'Fascist' axis, it also created an 'anti-Fascist' Madrid–Paris–Moscow axis. The Spanish Civil War saw the launching of the great Communist lie that the Communists were fighting for democracy. They would repeat the lie even more loudly in the Second World War (especially in Italy with regard to their role in the Italian Resistance between 1943 and 1945). The Communists, of course, in Italy as everywhere, were not fighting for democracy at all. They were fighting against democracy. And for Communism.

Recently unearthed Russian archive documents – reports to and from

Comintern agents in the field – reveal the true nature of Stalin's game in Spain.[6] His aim, despite his propaganda which paid so much lip service to an alleged determination to defend democracy, was that Spain should become the first Soviet republic in the West. That is why he was so determined to stamp out – and did, ruthlessly – home-bred Spanish Marxism, using as his justification that it was a tool of Franco and the forces of reaction – of so-called Trotsky-Fascists. If the home-bred variety of Communism had triumphed, his Russia-dominated variety would have failed. Yet even today in Western liberal circles the view that Stalin entered the fray in Spain to defend democracy remains pretty much the unchallengeable vulgate.

Mussolini and Hitler had not even conferred on giving help to Franco. But as Hugh Thomas has written, 'The Spanish war would make Hitler and Mussolini allies.'[7] In 1949 Bottai, the leading representative of the Fascist revolutionary Left which had not died and would survive until the end, would write that the war in Spain had bound Fascism to its 'reactionary imitations, to personalistic dictatorships, to anti-Marxism, blindly disowning the essential truths of Socialism . . .'[8]

Both Mussolini and Hitler opposed Communism, but that was not the whole story: for Mussolini increased power and influence in the Mediterranean and the desire to stop an alliance between Spain and France; for Hitler another chance, as Ethiopia had been, to further weaken ties between Italy and Britain and France and to distract attention from his territorial ambitions in central Europe. Mussolini did not want to weaken those ties if he could help it. Once again, as in Ethiopia, he wanted a swift conclusion in Spain; more so, as he had already expended such a vast amount of money and effort in Ethiopia and this time was fighting principally for a cause not for territory. But Hitler, as in Ethiopia, wanted the opposite. As Joachim C. Fest has written, Hitler's opportunity 'consisted, now as before, uniquely in crisis.'[9] The more distracted Mussolini became in Spain, the less likely he would be to defend Austria against an *Anschluss*. In addition, the Mediterranean was of direct interest to Mussolini but not to Hitler. For these reasons Mussolini's military commitment in Spain was far greater than Hitler's. For example, German manpower never exceeded 10,000 whereas Italian manpower totalled about 80,000 at its height.[10] Franco, on the other hand, was in no hurry either. For he had to win both a military and a political war.

Ulrich von Hassell, German ambassador in Rome, reported, 'Regarding the relations between Italy and France and England, the Spanish conflict could have the same effect as the war in Ethiopia ... the struggle for political predominance in Spain exposes the natural conflict between Italy and France, while the position of Italy as a Mediterranean power puts it in conflict with England. In such a situation, the opportunity to confront the western powers shoulder to shoulder with Germany will become increasingly evident to Italy.'[11]

Initially Franco asked Mussolini and Hitler for bombers to protect and transport his troop convoys between Morocco and Spain from the Republican government's fleet. The first twelve Italian bombers, Savoia-Marchetti 81s, left Sardinia for Spanish Morocco on 30 July. Two crashed and one had to make a forced landing in French Morocco, thus alerting the world to Italian involvement. Hitler sent twenty Junkers Ju 52s at the same time. The French sent some seventy planes to the Republicans. In October the first planes – fighters – and tanks – T-26s – arrived from Soviet Russia, about a hundred of each. This Russian weaponry was far superior to anything the Italians and Germans had sent to date and wherever deployed gave the Republican forces command of the air and on the ground. In October, too, the first contingents of the International Brigades – organised by the Comintern – arrived.

In November Hitler replied by sending the Condor Legion: some hundred planes, mainly bombers and fighters, but supported by tank companies – initially a total of 3800 men rising to 5000. Soon the Condor Legion included the extremely good Messerschmitt 109 fighter and Heinkel 111 bomber. Mussolini also sent tanks, artillery and eighty more planes. None of this matériel from Italy and Germany was given free to Franco. He had to pay for it. Manpower, however, was a different story. Italian wages were paid by Franco and Mussolini. At the end of December the first Italian troops arrived in Cadiz – 10,000 of them of whom two-thirds were blackshirts (i.e. not regular soldiers). Called by Churchill 'armed tourists', the blackshirts were said to be volunteers. No doubt this was true in part as their wages were good – 175 lire a week compared with a Rome bricklayer's 150 lire a week. And they were hardly trained. By February there were just under 50,000 Italian 'volunteers' in Spain – 30,000 of whom were blackshirts, the rest from the regular army.[12] The Italian air force was also present at bases in Majorca. Among the Italian pilots was Bruno Mussolini, who had arrived in the summer of 1937 and remained there on and off until the summer of 1938.[13] He flew a total of twenty-seven missions.[14]

Some 20,000 foreign volunteers had by now arrived to fight on the Republican side as well. In total, about 40,000 foreigners came to Spain to fight 'Fascism' – nearly all in the International Brigades. Most, 60 per cent, were Communists and a further 20 per cent became Communists in Spain.[15] They included more than 3000 Italians such as Luigi Longo, the former Italian Communist party youth leader (later he would lead the partisans in north Italy and after the war be PCI General Secretary from 1964 to 1969) appointed by the Comintern as one of the three commanders of the International Brigades' base at Albacete between Madrid and Valencia. Pietro Nenni, the Socialist leader and friend of Mussolini from Forlì, was also there as was the former Socialist Carlo Rosselli, an Italian Jew married to the Englishwoman Marion Cave and leader of *Giustizia e Libertà* – a left-wing Italian movement in exile aimed at uniting the disunited Italian Left – and it was said 102 Italians aged sixty or more. Rosselli's battle-cry was '*Oggi in Spagna, domani in Italia*'. The Italians called themselves the Garibaldi Brigade, which infuriated Garibaldi's grandson, Ezio. Garibaldi, who opposed Marxism, would have been a Fascist, he insisted, not a Communist.

In addition, Togliatti, the ruthless and obsessively secretive leader of the Italian Communist party in exile and the member of the seven-man Comintern executive in charge of its Latin section, soon arrived to direct Communism in Spain. (Togliatti spent the Second World War in Russia where he would wash his hands – it was only revealed many years after the event – of the fate of Italy's soldiers captured on the Russian Front, tens of thousands of whom were either exterminated or died in concentration camps of malnutrition, disease, or brutality. The Second World War over, Togliatti returned to Italy and became the PCI's General Secretary until his death in 1964.) Many were adamant that Togliatti arrived in Spain in the autumn of 1936 but later he would deny this and say that he did not arrive until June 1937.[16] After the Second World War Togliatti would also claim – untruthfully – that he was not even in charge of the Comintern's Latin section.[17]

He had a good reason to insist that he was not in Spain until June 1937: by then, the Communists on the orders of the Comintern had carried out a Stalinist-style purge of the *Partido Obrero de Unificacion Marxista* (POUM), the anti-Stalinist Spanish Marxist party which opposed control of Spanish Communism by the Comintern. The Communists accused it untruthfully of being pro-Franco and Trotskyite. In May 1937 POUM and Communist forces fought a bitter battle in Barcelona, after the seizure of the telephone exchange from the POUM in which 600 combatants died. Soon afterwards the Communists were responsible for the 'disappearance' of the POUM leader, Andres Nin, falsely accused of espionage, the execution of a number of its members, and the incarceration of forty members of POUM's central committee, and hundreds of rank and file members. The non-Communist majority in the Republican government, desperate not to lose Russian military aid, washed their hands of the affair. George Orwell, who had joined the POUM forces as a volunteer in December 1936, escaped being a victim of the purge by a whisker and came to despise the Communists. He would write that the war produced a 'richer crop of lies than any event since the Great War of 1914–1918.'[18] But there were atrocities by all in the Spanish Civil War. The Germans, using Heinkel 111s, bombed the small town of Guernica, near Bilbao, in April 1937. Estimates for the number of dead at Guernica vary between 100 and 1600.[19] In March 1938 the Italians bombed Barcelona. In the biggest raid, involving mainly Italian Savoias,

1300 people were killed.[20] Mussolini was pleased that Italians should be 'horrifying the world with their aggressiveness for a change, instead of charming it with the guitar'.[21] Farinacci, not the nicest of men, urged Franco to limit the number of summary executions.[22] In Majorca the Italian militia leader, Arconovaldo Bonaccorsi – the so-called Conte Rossi – was responsible for the round-up and execution of an estimated 3000 Republicans.[23] And in February 1939 Mussolini memoed Ciano to say, 'It is understood that if the Spanish prisoners have to be respected by us, it is agreed that the international mercenaries should be shot. And of course, above all, the renegade Italians.'[24]

In total, the Germans sent about 600 planes, 200 tanks and 1000 pieces of artillery to Spain; the Italians 660 planes, some 150 tanks, and 1000 artillery pieces. The Germans lost about 300 dead in Spain, the Italians more than 4000. Russia sent 1000 planes, about 900 tanks, 1550 artillery pieces and 1000 pilots, no troops, but many political indoctrinators responsible for among other things the destruction of the POUM. France sent about 300 planes.[25]

Like Churchill, most members of the British Cabinet and Conservative party preferred Franco to the elected government. Certainly, they did not want to see Spain go Communist and fall within the orbit of Soviet Russia. But at the same time they feared that Mussolini wanted to exploit the civil war for territorial gain – in particular the Balearic Islands. They also feared that the Spanish Civil War could escalate into a general European war. So too did Mussolini, Hitler, Blum and Stalin. But all were determined that the conflict remain local; hence the limited nature of the military aid sent; hence, too, the formation in London in September 1936 of the Non-Intervention Committee whose twenty-six member nations included the intervening nations, Italy, Germany, France and Russia. Of these, only France paid some heed to it. Blum later said that the reason he did not give more aid to the Republicans is that it would have brought about civil war in France where in the 1930s there was serious unrest and weak government – though his policy also had to do with his pacifism and pressure from Britain.[26] Mussolini had signed up to the committee because Franco seemed on the verge of taking Madrid and he thought he could end his intervention anyway. It was not to be. The war would drag on until 1939. Despite their denials, it was crystal clear that each of the four was intervening. But deliberately the committee was unwilling to find sufficient evidence to prove it. Joachim von Ribbentrop, German ambassador in London from 1937 until February 1938 when he became German Foreign Minister,[27] later described it as the 'Intervention Committee'.[28] But membership of the committee did at least show a will on the part of the interveners that the conflict be contained within Spain.

Fatally, however, Italian and German military support for Franco quickly produced for the first time a diplomatic rapprochement between the two countries. Hitler made all the running. He offered German recognition of the Italian conquest of Ethiopia. This was very dear to the Duce's heart; something denied him by the British and the French. So in October 1936 Mussolini dispatched his son-in-law, Ciano, now Foreign Minister, to Berlin for talks with Hitler. The only concrete result of these talks was the German recognition. But Ciano showed Hitler copies of thirty-two secret British government papers, which Grandi had got hold of in London. Mussolini hoped these would diminish Hitler's appetite for a rapprochement with Britain. The papers revealed the strength of British fears about German aggression and the need for swift British rearmament to combat it. Hitler was angry with the British, said Ciano. Germany would be ready for war in three years, said Hitler. Apparently, Austria was not discussed. But at the Berghof – the 'Eagle's Nest' – his mountain retreat at Berchtesgaden, Hitler made a point of ushering Ciano to the large windows which had a view stretching to Salzburg in Austria. Servants appeared with telescopes and Hitler bade Ciano use one to study the view. 'This is how I am constrained to look at my native city, Salzburg,' he said.[29] Ciano told Italian journalists in private that he found it 'incredible' that Hitler who was 'a real madman' was so popular in Germany, that Göring was a 'fat, vulgar ox' though 'capable' and that he did not like Ribbentrop because he did not have the 'stupid frankness' of his colleagues but was nevertheless 'a fool'. Smugly, he concluded, 'Germany is in the hands of very inferior men whom we must exploit.'[30] Hitler thought Ciano a 'repulsive boy' and 'Viennese café ballerino'.[31] The Germans were also well aware that Ciano had the loosest of tongues.

Nothing especially ominous was signed or agreed – apart from recognition of Ethiopia as Italian and a general agreement of friendship. But soon after Ciano's return Mussolini coined the infamous word 'axis' to describe the new relationship between Italy and Germany during a speech in the Piazza del Duomo, Milan, on 1 November in which he said, 'This Rome–Berlin vertical line is not a diaphragm but rather an axis, around which may revolve all those European states with a will to collaboration and peace.' He also said that whereas for Britain, the Mediterranean was 'one of many roads, or rather a short-cut', for Italy 'it is life'. But his tone towards Britain was conciliatory; what was required was a rapid 'recognition of reciprocal interests'. A week later he told Ward-Price of the *Daily Mail* that the 'interests of Britain and Italy in the Mediterranean were not antagonistic, but complementary'.[32] Despite Ethiopia and Spain, an alliance between Italy and Germany was no more than one of several possibilities at the end of 1936.

On 23 January 1937 Göring came to Rome where Mussolini, worried as ever about an *Anschluss*, asked him about German intentions. Göring told him that no move on Austria would be made without prior agreement with Italy. He and Göring did agree, however, that Franco was now amply supplied and they would end military aid. They also agreed that they would do nothing to cause the civil war to escalate into war outside Spain. Göring returned to Rome in April and according to Paul Schmidt, the German interpreter on such occasions, by then Mussolini seemed resigned to the *Anschluss*.[33]

Britain's mistake was this: Hitler wanted an alliance with Mussolini; Britain did not. Britain wanted merely to stop an alliance between Hitler and Mussolini. This was fine as an aim, but to achieve it, Britain would have had to offer Italy an alliance. This it was not prepared to do. Britain should also have struck up an alliance with Russia. As with Italy, it toyed with the idea of a Russian alliance and made belated moves to get one but failed to secure it. Britain behaved towards Italy in the same way as it behaved towards Russia. If it had achieved alliances with both, as Laval wanted, there would have been no world war. But on grounds of distaste it could not bring itself to go for an alliance with Italy and, until too late, with Russia. Incredibly, instead Hitler managed to achieve alliances with both because both felt that Britain would not ally with them. In fact, Italy – not Britain as Grandi had claimed – was the lady. Britain showed only limp interest. Hitler, however, was full of seductive urgency.

Joint military involvement in Spain, the Ciano–Hitler meeting and Mussolini's axis speech did hasten Anglo-Italian talks nevertheless. These resulted in the so-called Gentlemen's Agreement signed on 2 January 1937, which agreed nothing much except that free passage through the Mediterranean was a 'common vital interest' and that neither side would seek to change the territorial status quo in the Mediterranean. Mussolini had failed to get what he most wanted: British recognition of his conquest of Ethiopia. Others in the British Cabinet were keen; Eden put a stop to it. Nevertheless, despite his announcement of a Rome–Berlin axis, the Gentlemen's Agreement makes it clear that Mussolini was still interested in his traditional policy – and that of Italy – of playing one side off against the other.

In Spain, Italy's blackshirt 'volunteers' meanwhile had suffered humiliation of sorts in March 1937 at Guadalajara thirty miles from Madrid after they attacked and were repulsed by a smaller Republican force, which included a large number of Italian volunteers. The Italians fought a civil war in miniature. But it was superior Russian planes and tanks which proved decisive. It did not help that General Mario Roatta, the Italian commander, had only a Michelin road map to guide him. The Italian forces – three blackshirt divisions including the *'Dio lo vuole!'* (God wants it!) and one regular army division – supported by tanks and mobile artillery – totalled 35,000. They lost about 3000 dead; the Republicans about 2000.[34] Hemingway, who was there as a reporter, wrote absurdly, 'I can state flatly that [it] … will take its place in military history with the other decisive battles of the world.'[35] The Battle of Guadalajara was a hiccup, no more, but an excellent propaganda opportunity for the Republicans nevertheless. It was proof that regular Italian army troops were in Spain and it showed that they were anything but invincible. Guadalajara enraged Mussolini. He would not now leave Spain without a military victory which would not come until August 1937 at the much bigger battle of Santander. There, of the total 90,000 troops on the Nationalist side, 25,000 were Italian. They faced an army of 80,000 Republicans. Once again, air power proved decisive. But this time the nationalists had the superior planes.[36] Mussolini was ecstatic. His telegram of congratulations to his commanders in the field was published in the Italian press along with their names. This was the first public admission that Italy's armed forces – as opposed to blackshirt 'volunteers' – were involved in Spain.

At the time of Guadalajara Mussolini was in Libya for the first time since 1926 to open the road from Tobruk to the Egyptian border. In Tripoli he rode about on horseback and native horsemen presented him with a ceremonial sword, which he brandished aloft for the photographers – soon entitled by the Fascist press the 'Sword of Islam'. The horsemen proclaimed him the protector of Islam. Radio Bari began anti-British broadcasts to the Middle East. The British completely misread these propaganda stunts, whose aim was merely to put pressure on Britain, and thought that they were the prelude to aggression by Mussolini in Egypt, the Sudan and the Middle East.

Mussolini said nothing in public about the humiliation of Guadalajara. But on 17 June he wrote an unsigned article in *Il Popolo d'Italia* about the battle in which he claimed, 'Rather than a failure one must speak of an Italian victory, which events did not permit to be exploited in full.'[37] If not a defeat, Guadalajara was definitely a retreat. Mussolini was wrong. But then so too was Hemingway.

Carlo Rosselli, the founder of *Giustizia e Libertà* and Republican volunteer, would have been at Guadalajara but was in Bagnoles-de-l'Orne[38] in Normandy, recovering from phlebitis. On 9 June he and his younger brother, Nello, drove his wife to the station at Bagnoles and on the way back found the quiet country road blocked by a car. They stopped and the occupants of the other car leapt out and stabbed them to death. The murders caused outrage in Europe akin to that of the Matteotti killing in 1924. About 200,000 people attended their funeral in Paris. The culprits, it emerged, were members of the Cagoule, the extreme right-wing political group supported by Francois Mitterand who would later be Socialist French President in the 1980s. The Italian Secret Services were unquestionably involved in some way in the death of the Rosselli brothers, though precisely how remains unclear to this day. At the time the Left insisted that the Cagoule had murdered the Rossellis at the request of Mussolini. In 1945 an Italian Secret Service lieutenant-colonel went on trial for the crime. He testified that he had been given orders by Ciano. Sentenced to life, he was acquitted after a retrial ordered by the Italian Supreme Court. Though Ciano was probably involved, it is unlikely that Mussolini was.[39] Antonio Gramsci had died on 27 April from a stroke in a clinic in Rome after being released from prison, where he had been held for a decade. Despite their post-war adulation of him, Italy's Communists had boycotted him since 1930 on orders from Stalin who had decided that Gramsci was an enemy of Communism. Gramsci had let it be known from his prison cell that he opposed Stalin's decision that the moment had come for Italy's Communists to man the barricades. In a short unsigned note in *Il Popolo d'Italia* in December 1937 Mussolini wrote that Gramsci had 'died of illness, not lead, as happens in general to Communist leaders in Russia'.

Chamberlain's Secret Contacts with Mussolini

Mussolini was still very angry about Britain's treatment of Italy over Ethiopia – first sanctions, then refusal to recognise Italian conquest. And, as Sir Eric Phipps, British ambassador in Berlin, wrote to the Foreign Office, 'the only way to keep the balance of power in Europe is to separate Mussolini from Hitler.'[40] The way to do this was to recognise Italy's conquest of Ethiopia, otherwise as Drummond in Rome warned, Mussolini would make a formal alliance with Hitler. Others such as Vansittart agreed. Eden, however, resisted all such moves on the grounds that Mussolini was totally untrustworthy and therefore any agreement with him was pointless.

But on 17 May 1937 Neville Chamberlain succeeded Baldwin as Prime Minister and the atmosphere changed. Keener than Baldwin on foreign policy, Chamberlain was determined to appease Mussolini regardless of Eden. Chamberlain's view was perfectly defensible. But from a British point of view, in addition to Ethiopia there was now the new stumbling block of the Italian military presence in Spain, especially in the Balearics.

Grandi swiftly set out to bring Britain and Italy closer by cunning and lies. First he sent Mussolini a despatch reporting untruthfully that Chamberlain had told him he admired Mussolini. Next, again untruthfully, he told Chamberlain that he had a letter from Mussolini for the Prime Minister seeking talks. On 27 July Chamberlain came to see Grandi about this letter. The letter did not exist but Grandi read him an extract from a piece of paper which he said was the translation. Immediately, Chamberlain wrote to Mussolini in reply to 'the message you were good enough to send me', quoting the words of his late half-brother Sir Austen (who had died in March) that Mussolini was 'a good man to do business with', stating that good relations could be restored 'if we can only clear away some of the misunderstandings and unfounded suspicions which cloud our trust in one another' and suggesting talks 'with a view to clarifying the whole situation'. On 31 July Mussolini replied, 'The interests of Italy and Great Britain are not opposed either in the Mediterranean or elsewhere ... I am glad to agree with Your Excellency's suggestion that conversation be entered upon.[41]

The Goose is a Roman Animal

Then, at the end of September 1937, Mussolini accepted Hitler's open invitation to go to Germany, arriving on the 23rd. Sooner or later, after a last attempt at an alliance with Britain, Germany would ally with Italy, Mussolini told Filippo Anfuso, the Foreign Ministry's *segretario di gabinetto* (similar to a permanent secretary) and subsequently ambassador in Berlin, prior to departure.[42] Ciano at this point was the 'most pro-German' of them all.[43] Mussolini's meeting with Hitler made Chamberlain more determined to appease Mussolini; Eden less so. With Mussolini were Ciano, Starace, and dozens of Fascist officials and journalists. Hitler laid on the biggest welcome he would ever lay on for anyone. So keenly did he seek to impress Mussolini that he even ensured that a picture of Predappio – Mussolini's birthplace – be hung in Mussolini's room. Unlike the British, Hitler pulled out all the stops in his efforts to seduce the Fascist lady. Mussolini saw the giant Krupps armaments factory in Essen where Hitler caressed the latest weapons as if they were his offspring, and in Berlin German military might and discipline on parade. Göring entertained Mussolini at his home by showing him his model electric train set.[44] It rained heavily during much of the visit and the Italian contingent worried about catching colds.

The climax was an open-air rally on 28 September at the Maifeld in Berlin, part of the sports complex built for the 1936 Olympics. Nearly 1 million people were present inside and outside to witness Hitler and Mussolini speak. No Italian had ever addressed so many Germans. There was the usual marching up and down. The rain got worse. Thunder added portentous embellishment to the proceedings. In his speech, Hitler described Mussolini as 'a genius, one of those rare geniuses not created by history but themselves creators of history'.[45] It was dark when Mussolini took the podium to deliver a speech in German from written notes; the terrifying oceanic scene bathed in neon light. He said his visit was an expression of solidarity between two revolutions whose course had been 'different' but which shared a common purpose, 'the unity and the greatness of the people' and a common enemy, 'the Third International'. No matter how hard anyone tried it would be impossible to separate Italy and Germany. Italy would march with Germany to the very end. To those wondering what would be the consequence of his visit to Berlin he said 'peace'. The vast crowd cheered. There followed a spine-chilling torchlit procession of brownshirts to the sound of slow drum beats. The scene was like a 'kind of Valhalla', said Anfuso who was there. Mussolini was deeply impressed by the enormous size and discipline of the crowd, he added.[46] He left Germany on the 29th 'certain of German invincibility'.[47] But in his report to the King he said that the trip had been purely of a *carattere dimostrativo* (merely for show). He had spoken to Göring about Austria, he added, who had assured him that 'no move would be made in that direction without prior notice to Italy. My impression is that the Reich has not given up on the *Anschluss*; it waits only for events to mature.'[48]

Nothing formal was agreed, let alone an alliance. But ominously a German Foreign Office circular to embassies did state that Hitler had agreed not to obstruct Italian interests in the Mediterranean and Mussolini had agreed that Italy would not obstruct German interests in Austria, but emphasising that 'up till now nothing has been discussed or agreed which Austria could consider damaging or threatening to its independence'.[49] The *Anschluss* was now less than six months away.

Mussolini had decided, furthermore, that a 'little bit of Prussia' would do the Italian people good.[50] No sooner had he returned to Italy than he ordered the goose-step be used by the Italian armed forces which he called the *Passo Romano*. This may have been all right for tall Germans but looked silly when done by small Italians. The King objected – in vain as usual – not because he was even smaller than his subjects but because he did not like Germans. Mussolini commented, 'It's not my fault if the King is a pipsqueak ... They say that the goose-step is Prussian. Nonsense. The goose is a Roman animal ... It saved the *Campidoglio*.'[51] In private, Mussolini gave displays of how the *Passo Romano* should be done. He banned newsreel footage of him doing it at the head of a military parade, though, because it made even him look ridiculous.

Mussolini's fatal drift towards Germany had begun. But, wrote Anfuso, 'It's not true that Mussolini wanted to throw the Italian people into the arms of the Germans through a love of parades or adventures; even less so as to abandon himself to an easy blackmailing of England and France: if he committed an error by encouraging the first steps towards the alliance, it was that of believing that the Italians could march at the same speed as the Germans ... Though obscurely fearing the Germans, he was convinced he could be their equal, because he had under his nose the results of his political successes which had given him the title of founder of a doctrine then used as inspiration by Hitler.[52]

Yet, Churchill, anti-appeaser-in-chief, still felt able to write in October 1937 of 'the amazing qualities of courage, comprehension, self-control and perseverance' possessed by Mussolini.[53] But on 6 November Italy joined the Anti-Comintern Pact against International Communism to which Germany and Japan were already signatories. Many saw this not just as an alliance against Russia – but also against Britain and France. This was the first formal paper agreement between Mussolini and Hitler since the short-lived 1933 Pact of Four. Ciano noted, 'I have rarely seen him so happy. The situation of 1935 is no more. Italy has broken its isolation; it is at the centre of the most formidable politico-military combination that has ever existed.'[54]

By now, Hitler had made loud and clear his intention not just of 'liberating' Austria but also the Germans in the Sudeten areas of Czechoslovakia – one of many nations artificially created at Versailles out of the ashes of the Habsburg Empire. Eden, however, told the French, who were bound by treaty to defend Czechoslovakia, that Britain was 'lukewarm' about giving military assistance to protect the Sudetenland in the event of an attack by Hitler – yet another example of Eden's reluctance to stand up to Hitler.[55] On 11 December Mussolini announced Italian withdrawal from the League of Nations, creating further distance between Italy and Britain and France. His aim, however, was to stop an Anglo-German rapprochement so as to gain more leverage on both Britain and Germany.

But Grandi wanted desperately to improve Anglo-Italian relations before it was too late. So in December he approached Chamberlain once again on his own initiative, using the same tactic as in July: that he had a message for Chamberlain from Mussolini. As a result of Eden's irritation at Chamberlain's July letter, Grandi felt unable to contact Chamberlain direct, so he used intermediaries instead. They reported back to him that Chamberlain would telephone him at the Italian embassy, which he duly did. As before, Grandi had no message from Mussolini for Chamberlain so he invented one. Grandi's deviousness had a positive result once again. Consequently Chamberlain authorised a friend, Sir Joseph Ball, a former MI5 officer and now head of the research unit at Conservative Central Office, to keep in touch with Grandi, which he did almost daily. Later, Grandi wrote that he was sure that this secret channel of communication had persuaded Chamberlain to start new Anglo-Italian talks regardless of Eden.[56]

By now, Chamberlain and Eden were at serious odds over policy not on Hitler but Mussolini. While Chamberlain wanted to appease both Hitler and Mussolini, Eden wanted to appease Hitler alone and though not actually confront, simply ignore Mussolini. With Hitler, what Chamberlain and he had in mind at this point was handing back colonies to Germany. Eden felt that at least with Hitler 'an agreement ... might have a chance of reasonable life whereas Mussolini is, I fear, a complete gangster'.[57] Given that to date Hitler had broken far more serious treaty obligations than Mussolini, Eden's position was not especially logical. While Chamberlain wanted to prise Mussolini away from Hitler to weaken the axis, Eden's view is summed up in utterances such as 'nothing would be more foolish than openly to attempt to woo Mussolini away from Hitler'.[58] Eden agreed with the appeasement of Hitler because he thought it would work; he disagreed with the appeasement of Mussolini because he thought it would not work. No moral principle guided the actions of the man history came to see as the great principled anti-appeaser; the man who is alleged to have faced the dictators. What guided Eden was realpolitik and a deep cynicism about the trustworthiness of Italians, especially Mussolini, whom he described on one occasion in December 1937 as 'anti-Christ'.[59] The closer Mussolini got to Hitler, the more Chamberlain wanted to prise him away. For Eden the reverse was the case. 'Reduced to its essentials, Eden's dispute with Italy was not, "Shall fascism or democracy prevail?" Rather it was "Who shall rule the Mediterranean?" '[60]

Lady Ivy Chamberlain, widow of Sir Austen, was frequently in Rome and that December met Mussolini who – she wrote to Eden on 15 December – insisted he did not want the Balearic Islands, emphasised that 'for the safety of Europe England and Italy must remain friends' and left her with the impression that 'he really wants an understanding'.[61] In February 1938, Lady Chamberlain met Ciano and showed him a letter to her from Neville Chamberlain, her step-brother-in-law, which referred to his hopes of getting talks started by the end of February. Eden was angry about these meetings and urged Chamberlain to ban Lady Chamberlain from seeing Mussolini.

Chamberlain had told Grandi, via Ball, that he agreed talks could now start. Everyone knew the *Anschluss* was imminent; they knew as well that after that, Hitler would turn his attention to Czechoslovakia. On 12 February Kurt von Schuschnigg, the Austrian Chancellor, was forced to meet Hitler at the 'Eagle's Nest' in Berchtesgaden and blackmailed into appointing the Austrian Nazi, Arthur Seyss-Inquart, Interior Minister.

On 16 February, Ciano telegraphed Grandi telling him to impress on Chamberlain how urgent the Anglo-Italian talks had now become because 'tomorrow' post-*Anschluss*, Germany would be on Italy's frontier and there would no longer be any alternative but a rapprochement with Germany. Ciano said that neither he nor Mussolini knew when the *Anschluss* would happen but 'Today we are in the interval between the fourth and the fifth act ... This interval, *and only this interval*, can be utilised for the negotiations between us and London.'[62]

That same day Chamberlain summoned Eden and Grandi to 10 Downing Street. Grandi told them that Mussolini had not agreed with Hitler that he could invade Austria. Chamberlain felt that this was the last chance to hold talks with Italy before Mussolini was sucked irretrievably into Hitler's vortex and was determined to go ahead. Eden disagreed. They decided the matter had to go to the Cabinet where Eden spoke of 'fundamental differences of principle'.[63] It is difficult to see what these differences of principle were. Differences over strategy yes but not of principle. The Cabinet sided with Chamberlain and the following day Eden resigned, giving his reason in the House of Commons disagreement on 'whether official conversations should be opened in Rome now'.

Anschluss

Chamberlain was free to start his talks with Mussolini. And still Mussolini wanted to keep his options open.

But on Sunday, 12 March Hitler's troops invaded Austria to a tumultuous welcome from Austrians. Hitler had not, as Göring had promised he would, consulted Mussolini. But the day before he had sent him a written message which, though it did not state that he would invade the next day, made it pretty clear. Hitler could count on the British and French doing nothing. But could he count on Mussolini? Despite the convergence of Italy and Germany during the past two years, he was far from sure. In a letter to Mussolini, he wrote, 'I have established a clear demarcation line between Germany and France, and now I establish another one, just as clear, between Italy and us. It is the Brenner. This decision will never be changed or called into question.'[64] Mussolini, via the Prince of Hesse – married to one of King Vittorio Emanuele's daughters, Princess Mafalda – told Hitler that he accepted the invasion in a 'friendly manner'. Hitler was overcome with emotion. He told the prince, 'Tell Mussolini that I shall never forget him ... Never, never, never, whatever happens.'[65]

Chamberlain told his sister, Ida, that the *Anschluss* could have been prevented 'if I had had Halifax at the Foreign Office when I wrote my letter to Mussolini, rather than Eden ...'[66] For the man who had said no to Hitler over Austria in 1934 had said nothing now. But the fact is Mussolini, his armed forces exhausted by Ethiopia, partially committed in Spain and no match for their German counterparts in 1938, was powerless to stop the *Anschluss* on his own. This was precisely why Eden himself had opposed any public commitment by the British government to oppose an *Anschluss* because he 'did not want to put himself in a position of suggesting a resistance which we could not, in fact, furnish'.[67] The Germans of the Alto Adige chose this moment to call for an *Anschluss* of their own. Would Hitler now march into Italy as well?

On 16 March Mussolini told the Chamber of Deputies that the crux of the matter was that 'when an event is inevitable, it's better that it's done with us, rather than in spite of us, or, worse, against us.'[68]

Anglo-Italian Talks, 1938

With Eden gone but the *Anschluss* fact, Chamberlain pressed on with his plan to try to prise Mussolini away from Hitler. The much-postponed Anglo-Italian talks had begun on 10 March in Rome – two days before the *Anschluss*. According to Drummond, Mussolini was furious at the *Anschluss* and ready to desert Hitler.

The talks produced the Easter Agreement, which was signed in Rome on 16 April. By now, more than a dozen members of the league had recognised the Italian conquest of Ethiopia. Finally, Britain also agreed to do so but only once Italy had withdrawn its troops from Spain. In return, Italy stated that it had no territorial claim in Spain, agreed to reduce its forces in Libya and stop Radio Bari's virulent anti-British broadcasts to the Middle East. Ciano wrote in his diary, 'I believe it really will be able to serve as the foundation for the new friendship between Italy and Great Britain.'[69] But British insistence on withdrawal from Spain was silly, given the urgent need to isolate Hitler, the British view on balance in favour of victory by Franco and Mussolini's genuine fear of Hitler now that his troops were at the Brenner.

The British should have dropped the condition and tried to form a proper alliance with Mussolini by offering in return, as some such as Vansittart suggested, the enticement of territory. They could have put pressure on the French who really did have territory Mussolini wanted, such as Tunisia. Halifax summed up the wishful-thinking British position: 'Although we do not expect to detach Italy from the Axis, we believe the agreement will increase Mussolini's power of manoeuvre and so make him less dependent on Hitler and, therefore, freer to resume the classic Italian role of balancing between Germany and the western Powers.'[70]

The Clash of the Latin and the Teutonic

On 3 May 1938, little over two weeks after the Easter Agreement, Hitler arrived in Rome for a week-long state visit, bringing with him Goebbels, Ribbentrop, Himmler and Rudolf Hess. Hitler's only previous visit to Italy had been just weeks before the first attempt at the *Anschluss* in 1934. His second visit now came a few weeks after its accomplishment. The visit, which saw a clash of the Latin and the Teutonic in all their diversity, exemplified the strangeness of an alliance between the two men who had been corporals on opposing sides in the First World War. For while the sombre menace of the *'Deutschland über alles'* sent a shiver down the spine, the jaunty allegro of *'Giovinezza'* evoked a desire to smile.

The first sign that Mussolini did not have as much power as Hitler, even personally, was that the King, not Mussolini, was Head of State. Consequently Hitler had to ride in the open royal carriage with the King from the station to the *Quirinale* where, as the King's guest, he was to stay. The King had also been sole head of the armed forces until 30 March when Mussolini instigated a move in the Chamber of Deputies which created the new post of *Primo Maresciallo dell'Impero* to be held jointly by him and the King Vittorio Emanuele. From now on Mussolini was in charge of the armed forces in wartime but *'agli ordini del re'*.[71] The King, as ever, mumbled about this assault on his prerogative but did nothing except huff and puff about abdication as usual. Now he had a petty revenge of sorts, albeit marred by his dislike of Germans and disapproval on sight of Hitler, who he told aides was a degenerate. Nor did Hitler and his entourage care for the King and what Hitler later described as the arrogant aristocratic parasites who surrounded him. Himmler said the *Quirinale* smelled of catacombs and Hitler was annoyed when on his first night no woman could be found to turn back his bed linen while he watched – a bizarre nightly habit of his.

The Italian people was lukewarm, if that, to Hitler and as for the Pope, conspicuously, he had decamped for the papal summer residence at Castel Gandolfo and closed the Vatican's museums in his wake. Nor did Hitler and Mussolini care for each other. Ranuccio Bianchi Bandinelli, the guide and interpreter, recalled that 'Hitler was full of deference, at times almost servile, never familiar. Mussolini, however, treated him with self-confidence, speaking a fluent German quite rich in vocabulary, though with a thick Romagnol accent. But he became wary when Hitler paraded cultural notions.'[72]

The Italians impressed the Germans most in Naples with a display of their naval power, especially in submarines. These did a synchronised submerging, watched by the two sides from a battleship. The sunset in the Bay of Naples that day was wonderful. Vesuvius glowed. Anfuso, who was present, recalled, 'Prince Umberto joked with Ribbentrop; Himmler confided his Mediterranean impressions to Ciano; the King guaranteed Hitler's happiness to Mussolini; Hess tried to explain to Starace that the sky in Naples was beautiful.'[73]

On 9 May in Florence, Hitler was in a marvellous mood. The King for once was absent and the artist turned dictator was able to show off his passion for art at the Uffizi and Pitti galleries. At last, he had seen for himself the city of his dreams, he said. In Rome the crowds had been kept back a long way as the dictators drove about. In Florence they were much closer. Bandinelli described the experience as like an 'electric massage'. 'I had the feeling that, for those two people, this electrifying contact must have become an irrepressible need, which unless satisfied from time to time they would have been unable to live, and which gave them a kind of mute exaltation. It was perhaps, for them, the real reason for their adventure.' Looking out over Florence from the Piazzale Michelangelo, Hitler's throat made strange gurgling sounds and then he said, 'At last; at last I understand Böcklin and Feuerbach.' Bandinelli commented, 'It was as if ... someone had said ... in Paris, "At last I understand Meissonier and Boldini." ' Hitler added, 'And to think that, if Bolshevism had come, all this would have been destroyed ...' Mussolini was becoming increasingly bored, noted Bandinelli. In the Uffizi he made an ushering motion to Bandinelli with one of his hands to speed things up and muttered, 'We'll be here a week.' Hitler, staring in awe at the Michelangelo *Doni con la Sacra Famiglia* tondo, murmured, 'Michelangelo, Michelangelo.' He turned to Mussolini and said, 'If Bolshevism had come ...' Mussolini, 'with a certain surliness and a shrug', replied through gritted teeth in German, 'Everything destroyed.'[74]

Anfuso's overriding memory of the Nazi visit to Italy was from Florence as well, where in the Palazzo della Signoria part of Hitler's entourage found themselves separated from the Führer by a locked and ancient door. They unsheathed their 'ceremonial' daggers and forced it open. 'Hitler ... departed leaving me the memory of those daggers which chiselled away at a venerable door.'[75] When Hitler was about to depart for Germany from the station in Florence, Mussolini told him, 'Now no force can separate us any more.' Hitler's eyes filled with tears.[76]

As in Germany, there had been little official political talk. Ribbentrop had pressed Ciano hard on the issue of a military alliance and handed him a draft document. Ciano had produced a written response but to Ribbentrop's bemusement it was more like a peace treaty with an enemy than an alliance with a friend.[77] Schmidt, Hitler's interpreter, recalled, 'Mussolini and Ciano were obviously trying to evade any serious political discussion – though Hitler, and more specifically Ribbentrop, were constantly seeking it. The programme had been deliberately planned so that there was no time for serious talk ... I inferred at the time ... that the Italians had by no means got over their shock at the Austrian *Anschluss* and especially at Hitler's methods in carrying it out, and that their eyes were still turned westwards.'[78]

The Munich Conference

Hitler now turned his sights on aggression in Czechoslovakia. This time, Britain and France could not stand back and do nothing as they had over Austria. France, for one, was bound by treaty to protect Czechoslovakia. Russia, meanwhile, had a military alliance with France. Mussolini was caught in the traditional Italian dilemma. Just as in the First World War Italy had had to choose between Germany and Austria-Hungary on one side and Britain and France on the other, so had she now. Then, she was allied to the Austro-Germans and, after a year of neutrality, had switched sides. What would she do this time round?

Chamberlain's foreign policy was still dominated by a desire to appease Mussolini. In July he wrote to the French Prime Minister, Edouard Daladier, a right wing radical, complaining that increased tension between France and Italy had jeopardised the British goal of peace in Europe because it made Italy more than ever dependent on 'favours from Germany'; a situation which was not 'agreeable' to Mussolini. He said, 'I consider Italo-British solidarity the keystone of our foreign policy ... We consider the Anglo-Italian accord [Easter Agreement] a valid step forward towards our final goal which is a general European *appeasement*.'[79]

In June 1938 Ribbentrop renewed German overtures for a military alliance with Italy and promised that the alliance, should it be signed, would be void if Germany invaded Czechoslovakia. Ciano wrote, 'Relations with Great Britain have not developed as we might have hoped. The offer assumes a new value. Mussolini is in favour.' In August Ciano wrote that if the British allowed the Easter Agreement to 'lapse' – as he put it – 'our path is clear for a military alliance with Germany'. The situation was nevertheless 'an unpleasant impasse'.[80] Hitler would not, however, give black and white answers to Italian requests about his intentions in Czechoslovakia. But what Mussolini did know, via his spy in the British embassy in Rome who had passed on copies of secret British documents, was that Britain would not defend Czechoslovakia by force.[81] Soon, anyway, Hitler left no one in any doubt in a speech on the 12th in Nuremberg at the Nazi Party annual congress.

On 15 September, when Chamberlain flew to Germany to plead with Hitler on Czechoslovakia, Mussolini told Anfuso, 'As soon as Hitler sees this old man he will know that he has won ... Not only will Hitler not stop, but he wants to tear up Versailles piece by piece, nation by nation ... Better with us than against us.'[82] Hitler told Chamberlain that he would only negotiate if the British and French accepted the principle of Sudeten self-determination and a plebiscite. Chamberlain did not have authority to agree, so left empty-handed.

But a week later, on 22 September, he was back. This time, after securing French agreement, he agreed that Germany could have all the Sudeten areas where more than 50 per cent of the population was German. Hitler reacted by giving him an ultimatum: Czech troops must abandon the Sudeten areas by the 28th or else he would invade. On the 24th the Czechs mobilised. France called up its reserves. Britain mobilised its fleet. But Italy did nothing. Either Mussolini did not think a European war was imminent; or he was determined not to take part.

As in 1937, Grandi in London entered the fray yet again. On 26 September he had breakfast with the former British ambassador in Rome, Sir Ronald Graham, where both agreed that Chamberlain should be persuaded to make a direct appeal to Mussolini to mediate. Graham contacted Halifax who told Chamberlain. On the 28th Chamberlain sent two telegrams: one to Hitler in which he promised Hitler 'all essentials'; the other to Mussolini which, among other things, said, 'I trust Your Excellency will inform German Chancellor that you are willing to be represented and urge him to agree to my proposal which will keep all our peoples out of war.' Whether or not the Grandi–Graham initiative had been the decisive factor in persuading Chamberlain to approach Mussolini we do not know, though naturally Grandi was convinced.

Drummond in Rome took Chamberlain's message to Ciano at Palazzo Chigi, who took it to Mussolini at Palazzo Venezia. On receipt, Mussolini telephoned the Italian ambassador in Berlin, Bernardo Attolico. 'Tell the Chancellor that ... I favour the suggestion, and beg him to refrain from mobilisation.' Attolico interrupted Hitler while he was with the French ambassador to pass on the message. Hitler agreed. 'Tell the Duce that I accept his proposal,' Hitler told Attolico. From the time Chamberlain had sent his telegram to Drummond in Rome, to Hitler's acceptance in Berlin, one and a half hours had passed. Mussolini then contacted Hitler to propose a conference involving Germany, Britain, France and Italy. Hitler agreed. Chamberlain was speaking to the House of Commons that afternoon when just after 4 p.m. he was handed a note informing him of this. There was euphoric applause. Churchill shook Chamberlain's hand but Eden did not. Roosevelt sent a telegram to Chamberlain which simply said, 'Good man.'[83] The Pope and Stalin were the only people in the world, it seemed, who were upset – apart from the Czechs. The Czechs, the subject of Munich, were not invited to take part in the Munich conference.

The next morning Grandi was at Heston Airport, Croydon, for Chamberlain's departure to Munich. Chamberlain shook his hand and thanked him. Back at the embassy Sir Joseph Ball turned up to tell Grandi, 'The Prime Minister has asked me to tell you that you were right, and he is glad he followed your advice to approach Mussolini directly. We owe world peace to Mussolini.'[84] Chamberlain arrived at about midday. Daladier flew from Paris.

Mussolini and Ciano had left Rome on the overnight train the previous day. Mussolini told Ciano, 'When in a country they adore animals to the point of providing them with cemeteries, hospitals and houses ... it is a sign that decadence is at work ... As for the rest ... Four million surplus women. Four million sexually frustrated people who create a load of problems either to excite or placate their desires.' He was referring to the British.[85] Hitler had made a point of going by train to Kufstein in Austria to meet Mussolini early the next morning.[86] They travelled on to Munich together in Hitler's train, arriving at around 11 a.m. But during the journey, to the astonishment of Mussolini, Hitler was keener to speak about his plans to invade France rather than Czechoslovakia. Finally, Mussolini asked, 'What are your demands on Czechoslovakia?' Ribbentrop handed Mussolini a piece of paper.

The Munich conference began at half past twelve at the Führerbau or Brown House – the Nazi Party headquarters in Munich. The Czechs turned up in the afternoon anyway and waited outside the conference room while the fate of their country was decided. The situation was heavy with symbolism. Mussolini and Hitler wore uniform, Chamberlain and Daladier were in pin-striped suits. Only Mussolini was able to speak a foreign language. Thanks to his good French, reasonable German and passable English, he was the only one able to speak without an interpreter. Mussolini produced 'his' proposal from a pocket in his uniform. It was merely the translated version of what Ribbentrop had handed over on the train. But Hitler, the French diplomat André François-Poncet observed, treated Mussolini with deference throughout – as if 'fascinated' or 'hypnotised'.

'If the Duce laughed, he laughed, if the Duce frowned, he too frowned; it was a scene of genuine mimickry.'[87]

The proposal Mussolini put to the conference was no different from that given to him by Ribbentrop on the train to Munich. Yet, soon after midnight, an agreement was ready for signature in four languages. It gave Hitler what he wanted – evacuation of Czech troops from the Sudeten areas to begin on 1 October and be finished with by the 10th. The British and French agreed to guarantee the new smaller Czechoslovakia's borders against aggression.[88] Polish and Hungarian claims to other parts of Czechoslovakia would be settled separately. The British and French told the waiting Czech representatives that unless they accepted the deal, they were on their own. Ciano took SS Colonel Eugen Dollmann to one side and asked him to show him the nightlife of Munich.[89]

Though Hitler was the real victor, Munich *appeared* a triumph for Chamberlain and his policy of appeasement which had included his secret contacts with Mussolini begun via Grandi in July 1937 and his step-sister-in-law at about the same time. Rarely had a man who had decided on such a disastrous course of action enjoyed such enthusiastic praise for having done so. Rarely was a piece of paper such as the one he waved at the cameras on his return to Britain so worthless. Daladier's reaction to the euphoric reception he received in France on his return was more realistic. 'Madmen,' he muttered. Equally, Munich *appeared* a triumph for Mussolini. He was the man who had stepped in at the eleventh hour to prevent world war. It is true that but for him, Munich would not have happened. But it is equally true that if Munich had not happened, Hitler would have invaded Czechoslovakia anyway and neither Britain nor France would have gone to war to stop him. Had they done so, however, as Germany's generals admitted at the Nuremberg Trials, they would have defeated Hitler. In the late summer of 1938 Germany did not have enough war-ready divisions, they said. A year later, however, when Britain and France declared war on Germany, Russia had switched sides and the German army was much stronger.[90]

Mussolini and Ciano left Munich the following morning by train. At Italian stations en route to Rome, crowds waited to cheer the train as it passed. Many sank to their knees in gratitude. This was a clear sign that whatever Mussolini wanted, Italians wanted peace – not war. At Florence the King himself, who was at his country residence in San Rossore, near Pisa, was on the platform to congratulate Mussolini. In Rome, at Palazzo Venezia, Ciano told the anti-German Balbo, 'See, then, the policy of the Axis does have its uses.'[91] Mussolini gave a speech from the balcony in which he said, 'At Munich we have worked for peace and justice. Is this the wish of the Italian people?' 'Yes, Yes,' it replied!

Munich gave Mussolini a fabulous opportunity to capitalise. It brought him to the apex of his power and prestige. Munich might have brought

Britain and Italy closer. On 3 October Ciano told Drummond that Mussolini had decided to withdraw 12,000 troops from Spain as Communism there was more or less defeated and that the British should now allow the Easter Agreement to come into force. But the Fascist carrot, as ever, came with a stick. If Britain did not now recognise Italian sovereignty in Ethiopia, the Italians would have to take 'certain action which up to now they had definitely refused'. It was clear what this meant: an alliance with Hitler.[92] On the 15th, 10,000 Italian troops left Spain and received a hero's welcome in Naples. On 26 October the British Cabinet at long last agreed to implement the Easter Agreement. On 16 November it came into force. Even now, Mussolini had not made up his mind to abandon his – and Italy's – traditional policy of playing one side off against the other; or looked at another way, playing a pivotal role – the *peso determinante* – between Britain and France on one side and Germany on the other – or, as at Munich, the role of mediator. For even now there was no formal alliance with Hitler. And still Mussolini wanted to keep his options open.

The British asked for more talks in Rome if that suited. Mussolini agreed. But he now enraged the French. During the Ethiopian crisis France, unlike the British, had withdrawn its ambassador from Rome in protest. But now, post-Munich, it recognised the Italian conquest of Ethiopia and restored full diplomatic relations. On 30 November, the new ambassador, François-Poncet, was invited by Ciano to attend a sitting of the Chamber of Deputies to hear him speak.[93] In a vicious, obviously premeditated performance, the deputies subjected the ambassador to wild heckling and shouts of 'Tunisia! Corsica! Nice! Savoy!'. Mussolini was present. At the same time the Italian press carried violently anti-French articles and the Fascists staged anti-French demonstrations. These outbursts reflected Mussolini's preoccupation at this time: Italian claims against France. Prior to the January trip, British Foreign Office officials had toyed with the idea of giving Mussolini territory in Africa such as British Somaliland and trying to get the French to make similar concessions. But in the end, given French fury with Italy which nearly caused cancellation of the trip, it was decided to avoid talking about territory altogether and have instead, as Chamberlain so quaintly put it, a heart to heart. But territory, by now, was all Mussolini was really interested in.[94] Chamberlain and Halifax arrived in Rome on 11 January 1939.

Chamberlain had with him his umbrella; symbol of the *vita comoda*. Though Mussolini wore uniform, there were no rallies or displays of military might as there had been for Hitler. Instead, there was dinner and a trip to the opera for which Mussolini wore a pinstriped suit. The Italian people cheered Chamberlain and Chamberlain wondered if Britain might mediate between Italy and France. Mussolini declined. Chamberlain said he was worried that Hitler was on the verge of yet another aggressive move. Mussolini replied that Hitler 'desired a long period of peace' and that further aggression was 'absolutely out of the question'. This, after all, is what the Germans had been telling the Italians. Chamberlain even proposed a toast to 'His Majesty the King of Italy Emperor of Ethiopia', it was said.[95] Before his departure Chamberlain gave a speech at the station. He said without irony, 'We leave more than ever convinced of the good faith and goodwill of the Italian government.' Back in London, he went so far as to say in a report to the Cabinet on his visit that the Duce was 'a charming host and a man of peace'.[96] But Mussolini was annoyed with the British because he realised why they wanted to prise Italy from Germany: not because they wanted Italy as an ally but merely to weaken Germany.[97] The mere sight of Chamberlain – the man with the umbrella – confirmed him in his view that democracy was doomed.

The aim of the British and French, as ever, was the maintenance of the status quo and opposition to revision of the Treaty of Versailles. Mussolini commented, 'These men are no longer made of the stuff of Francis Drake and the other magnificent adventurers who created the empire. They are by now the tired sons of a long series of rich generations. And they will lose the empire.'[98] It was now that Mussolini finally made up his mind to commit himself to Germany.

The Fascist Class War Against the Jewish Spirit

Mussolini had said that Italy needed 'a little bit of Prussia' and in September 1938, the same month that the world hailed him as the angel of peace as a result of Munich, he introduced anti-Semitic laws. His motive was not, as might be assumed, that he disliked Jews. He was no more anti-Semitic or racist than the majority of his contemporaries. Sarfatti, his principal mistress until Petacci, for example, was Jewish, as were many top Fascists. More than 10,000 Jews, about one-third of adult Italian Jews, were members of the PNF in 1938.[99] In 1920, Churchill, then War Secretary, had written an article about the Jews being the driving force behind Communism in which he said that there were three kinds of Jew: the 'National Jew' who was patriotic; the 'Zionist Jew' who aimed for a Jewish state in Palestine; and the 'International Jew', a category which included Marx, Trotsky and most of the Bolshevik leadership, who was 'absolutely disruptive'. These international Jews were 'leaders of a worldwide conspiracy for the overthrow of civilisation', wrote Churchill.[100] Ironically, the Nazis would claim that Churchill was part of the international Jewish conspiracy.

Sarfatti herself, like so many, was racist. In 1934 she had written an article on the dangers of the falling birth rate in countries such as Britain and France and urged the white race to unite against the perils of the black and yellow races.[101] It was now, at the end of 1938, that Sarfatti, die-hard Fascist that she was, decided to leave Italy for good. Initially she went to

France, then South America, and did not return to Italy until after the war. Seeking journalistic work, she wrote to an American friend asking him to pull strings for her. She suggested an essay urging America to save, as she put it, 'what I call "The White Civilisation".'[102]

Nor was Mussolini's motive pressure from the Nazis, of which there was little. The decision was his alone. But the timing of the laws, as Fascist Italy and Nazi Germany converged, was hardly coincidental. This convergence, however, was not the reason for the introduction of the laws – though it was the catalyst. The real motive had deeper roots within the Fascist psyche, which had nothing to do with hatred of the Jews as a race. The Jews had come to epitomise Mussolini's three enemies: Communism, the bourgeoisie and anti-Fascism. Jews were prominent in all three.

Although not anti-Semitic, Mussolini became increasingly anti-Jewish. But his hostility to Jews had an identical cause to his hostility to the bourgeoisie. It was the Jewish psyche or spirit – the epitome of the bourgeois spirit which he scorned as *la vita comoda* – that he wanted to stamp out, not the Jews. It was part of a bigger battle between decadence and renaissance, between the Judeo-Christian and the Greco-Roman traditions: Mussolini persuaded himself that the Jews, like the freemasons, had secret loyalties which conflicted with Fascism. Judaism in general was international; it stood against the nation. Italian Zionists, in particular, who wanted to establish a Jewish homeland in Palestine, also stood against the nation. In Spain, many of those who fought Franco, especially among the Italians, were Jews, as was the anti-Fascist and Socialist French Prime Minister Blum. Soviet Communism, its leadership now purged of the Jews by Stalin, had nevertheless become, felt Mussolini, nothing but state super-Capitalism.

The campaign against the Jews gave Fascism the opportunity to discriminate against 'all those grey zones in which – under the imprint of the meanest "bourgeois spirit" – move those who come from the old ruling classes.'[103] It should therefore be understood as the product of the drive towards the *fascistizzazione* of Italy; the Fascist mission to create a new society in which the community counted more than the individual but as a result the individual lived a more not less fulfilled life – a society in which individuals believed that moral well-being has more value than material well-being. As De Felice has written, Mussolini's campaign against the Jews 'was more against the Italians than against the Jews'.[104]

For *fascistizzazione* to succeed required not the destruction of the bourgeoisie or even of bourgeois wealth but the destruction of the bourgeois 'spirit' which placed the self above all else and aspired only to money. The Jews, therefore, like the bourgeoisie – of which they were seen as the epitome – had an option: they could convert. Mussolini said that for most Jews perhaps a generation would suffice for them to become proper Italians.[105]

The campaign against the Jews formed part of a renewed assault on the bourgeoisie in 1938–9, as did the abolition of *'lei'* and the introduction of the goose-step; and as did the alliance with Germany against the decadent bourgeois nations, Britain and France, nowhere better encapsulated than in the very person of Chamberlain himself – the man with the umbrella. In 1934 Mussolini had said in a speech, 'The credo of Fascism is heroism, that of the bourgeoisie egoism.'[106] On 25 October 1938 he told the PNF *Consiglio Nazionale,* 'I have picked out an enemy of our regime. This enemy has the name "bourgeoisie".' He was determined to give the bourgeoisie, which hated heroes, myths, sport and producing children, but loved the *vita comoda,* 'hefty punches in the stomach', he said.[107] Two major reforms were part of the same process. In February 1939 the Grand Council approved the Schools Charter drawn up by Bottai, now Education Minister. Its aim was to bring the Fascist revolution into the classroom and 'form the human and political conscience of the new generations' and so create a truly genuine Fascist society. Among its proposals was the introduction of manual work experience for school pupils.[108] In January 1939 the last remnants of democracy in the Chamber of Deputies disappeared with its abolition and replacement by the *Camera dei Fasci e Corporazioni* (Chamber of Fasces and Corporations). From now on deputies would not be elected but chosen from the membership of the various Fascist organisations. Starace issued instructions for the slogan *'Abasso la vita comoda'* to go up throughout Italy. A very popular book published in 1939 was *Processo alla borghesia* (*The Bourgeoisie on Trial*) which consisted largely of articles taken from *Gerarchia* and *Popolo d'Italia.* Mussolini had founded a religion and a regime; but there remained the Catholic Church and the monarchy – and the bourgeoisie.

Mussolini's anti-Semitism was not therefore biological racism but spiritual racism and part of his mission for the spiritual regeneration of the nation. For, unlike Hitler, he believed that races existed only in a spiritual not a biological sense. In August 1938 he approved an article in Bottai's *Critica Fascista* which said, 'The foundations, in fact, of Italian racism are and must be eminently spiritual, even if they start, opportunely, from purely biological "data".'[109] The idea of races of the spirit, of course, enabled Mussolini to establish a direct link between modern Italians and ancient Romans, and so reinforce the concept of *Romanità.* The spirit had survived, if not the blood. In 1941 he told De Begnac, 'Does a *razza Italica* exist? I do not believe so, despite the demonstrations of so many scientists … Missiroli gets it right when he speaks of the spiritual values of Judaism in sharp contrast to those sustained by the Roman *civiltà* and the Christian *civiltà.*'[110] Mussolini's mission, as he saw it, was to transform the Italians into Italians. The Jews became victims of this bigger process.

In 1932 Mussolini had told Ludwig, 'Naturally there is no such thing as a pure race, not even a Jewish one ... Race: it is a sentiment, not a reality; it is 95% sentiment. I don't believe that it is possible to prove biologically that a race is more or less pure ... Anti-semitism does not exist in Italy. The Jews have always behaved well as citizens, and as soldiers, they have fought courageously.'[111] In the *Dottrina del Fascismo*, co-authored with Gentile and first published in 1932, Mussolini defined the nation as 'not a race' but 'a multitude unified by an idea'.[112] The section in the 1932 *Enciclopedia Italiana* entitled 'Jews' spoke of 'the inexistence' of a Jewish race. In 1935, when the encyclopaedia reached 'R', under 'Race' it stated that 'a race does not exist, but only a people and an Italian nation. There does not exist a Jewish race or nation, but a Jewish people; there does not exist, the gravest error of all, an Aryan race ...'[113] Until 1938 Mussolini opposed anti-Semitism for tactical reasons anyway. In March 1933 he wrote to Vittorio Cerruti, then Italian ambassador in Berlin, telling him to urge Hitler to abandon anti-Semitism. 'The issue of anti-Semitism could stir up Hitler's enemies, even the Christians of Germany,' he said.[114] In December 1937 Ciano wrote in similar vein: 'Nor do I believe that it is convenient for us to unleash an anti-Semitic campaign in Italy. One must never persecute the Jews as *such* (i.e. as Jews). That would provoke the solidarity of all the Jews in the world.'[115]

Nor were Italians anti-Semitic. The Italians, after all, were the bastard offspring of countless invasions. To talk of an Italian race was nonsense. Anyway, there were only about 50,000 Jews in Italy.[116] So there was not 'a Jewish problem' as there was in countries where there were large numbers of Jews such as Germany, Russia, Poland or Austria (Vienna had 176,000 Jews in 1935) – though between 1933 and 1940 about 20,000 refugees came to Italy, a large proportion of whom were Jews.[117]

Anti-Semitic articles had begun to appear in the Italian press in earnest from early 1937. Yet in Libya, in March 1937, Mussolini had made a point of visiting the Jewish quarter in Tripoli[118] – though at the same time he had wielded the Sword of Islam and proclaimed himself to be the protector of Arabs. But that reflected his decision to curry favour with the Arab world as a means of countering the British and French in the Middle East and North Africa. In September 1937, however, Mussolini had told Ciano that America was a 'country of niggers and Jews' and that by the year 2000 the only 'races' that would count were 'the Italians, the Germans, the Russians and the Japanese. The other peoples will be destroyed by the acid of Judaic corruption.'[119] But then in February 1938, he had the press publish a government denial that he was about to launch an anti-Semitic campaign. The statement did refer, however, to a 'universal Jewish problem' which could be 'resolved only in one way: by creating in some part of the world, not in Palestine, the Jewish State'.

But then came the *Anschluss* in March 1938 and Hitler's visit to Italy in May. On 4 June 1938 Mussolini ordered Farinacci to sack his Jewish secretary, Jole Foa, who had worked for him for twenty years. Farinacci, who was anti-Semitic only for political reasons, protested, 'My secretary is alone in the world, she is fifty and she has worked with me for twenty years.'[120] But Mussolini insisted on the grounds that if the Germans found out they would see her continued employment as 'evidence of the lack of seriousness' on the part of Italians. He gave Farinacci the considerable sum of 50,000 lire to give to her as redundancy money.[121]

The first serious sign of an imminent campaign against the Jews was not long in coming. On 14 July 1938 the *Giornale d'Italia* published a 'scientific' document which soon became known as the '*Manifesto della razza*'.[122] The article claimed that races did exist, that these were purely biological, that the Italians were of Aryan origin and that the Jews did not belong to the Italian race. This was anti-semitism based on the biological argument. It was the first and last time that the Fascists used the biological argument so prominently. But the manifesto then qualified this when it stated, 'All the work the regime in Italy has done up to now has its roots in racism ... This does not mean the introduction in Italy of German theories of racism ... but ... the elevation of the Italian to the ideal of superior conscience of himself and greater responsibility.'[123]

In response, the leading Jewish Fascist and First World War hero Ettore Ovazza wrote to Mussolini on the 15th: 'We remain silent today before the public with our pain ... Is this the end of a reality: that of our feeling one with the Italian people? ... I can't believe it. I cannot consider changing religion, because this would be a betrayal – and we are Fascists.'[124] In October 1943 Ovazza and his family would be assassinated by the Nazis as they tried to cross the border into Switzerland.

On 27 July the *Giornale d'Italia* published an article, signed by Starace but drafted by Mussolini, which used a different argument, attacking the Jews for regarding themselves as a separate and superior race: 'As for the Jews, for millennia everywhere and also in Italy they have considered themselves a "race" different from and superior to the others and it is notable that despite the tolerant policy of the regime, the Jews have constituted in every nation – with their men and their means – the high command of anti-Fascism.'

The first anti-semitic laws soon followed. In September the Council of Ministers approved a decree which stated that all foreign Jews, defined as those who had come to Italy since 1919, had to leave Italy within six months. These included 8000 Jews from Germany and Austria who had found refuge in Italy from the Nazis. The decree defined foreign Jews as those whose parents were both 'of the Jewish race' even if they were not Jews by religion. That same month it approved a second decree which stated that 'no person of Jewish race' could be a teacher or student. But the Fascist definition of Jews, native ones at least, relied – unlike that of the Nazis – on religion not 'race' as the test.

The Grand Council met to discuss the Jewish Question on 6 October and approved the two decrees. Few in the Fascist hierarchy objected except, notably, Balbo and Federzoni. The rest, including the otherwise enlightened Bottai, approved. The Grand Council drew up a document called the *Carta della razza* (Race Charter). The charter targeted foreigners as well as Jews – for example, it banned marriage between Italians and 'non-Aryan' races as well as Jews, and between government employees and 'foreign women of whatever race'. But the Jews were the main target. The justification for the laws, said the charter, was that Fascism since the start had tried to increase the quality and quantity of the Italian race and that since the conquest of the Empire the task of creating 'a racial consciousness' had become 'urgent'. The charter stated, 'World Jewry – especially after the abolition of masonry – has been the animator of anti-Fascism in all fields ... The immigration of foreign elements – considerably on the increase since 1933 – has made the state of mind of Italian Jews worse, in regard to the regime ... All the anti-Fascist forces are headed by Jewish elements; world Jewry is, in Spain, on the side of the Bolsheviks of Barcelona.' The charter defined a Jew as anyone who had two Jewish parents; or a Jewish father and a foreign mother; or who belonged to the Jewish faith. It exempted those born of a mixed marriage who did not belong to the Jewish faith prior to 1 October 1938. In Germany, the definition of a Jew was much stricter: anyone with one Jewish grandparent.[125]

But in addition to teachers and students, the charter extended the banning of Jews from crucial activities. They could no longer be government employees, do government contract work, be members of the PNF, the armed forces, owners of businesses employing more than a hundred people or owners of fifty hectares of land or more. But, in a clear signal that the anti-Semitism of Italian Fascism was only half-hearted and that it was founded on a non-biological definition of 'race' – it included a list of 'loyal' Jews who would be exempted from the bans on account of their patriotism: those over sixty-five, or married to an Italian before 1 October 1938, or who had fought in the First World War, Libya, Ethiopia or Spain, or had joined the PNF between 1919 and 1922, or during the Matteotti crisis. These exemptions were a clear reflection of why the Fascists objected to the Jews. What counted was spirit, not race. Fascist anti-Semitism was, therefore, akin to the hatred of the infidel – of non-believers. But a Jew could embrace the Fascist faith, convert to Fascism, if he so chose. For as Mussolini had said: Jews could become Aryans. For Hitler, however, once a Jew always a Jew. For Mussolini, Jews were not racially inferior; but they were the spiritual enemy of the Fascist faith. Just days before publication of the manifesto in July, for example, Mussolini had confirmed the promotion of a Jew to be commander of an army division. Starace, on the other hand, wanted to expel all Jews from the PNF. Mussolini overruled him.[126]

The hostility of the Catholic Church to the Jews was similar in origin to that of Fascism. Undoubtedly, this helped create a climate in which Mussolini felt able to introduce laws against the Jews. Historically, the Catholic Church had been anti-Jewish because the Jews had crucified Christ. But its hostility was religious, not biological. It ceased from the moment that a Jew converted to Catholicism. A Jew could become a Catholic just as for Mussolini a Jew could become a Fascist.

In March 1937 Pius XI issued a powerful encyclical, *Mit brennender Sorge*, attacking Nazi anti-Semitism which he criticised as being founded on 'the myth of blood and race'.[127] But a powerful force within the Catholic Church, the Jesuits and their organ in Italy, *La Civiltà cattolica*, were stridently anti-Jewish. The arguments the Jesuits used against the Jews were very similar to those used by the Fascists. Communism was a Jewish plot, they said. That there was a world of difference between the Jew as epitome of the bourgeoisie and the Jew as champion of the proletariat did not trouble them. Thus, articles in *Civiltà cattolica*, could say the following, 'The prototype of the Jews is the banker. What property they really have boils down to a drawer and a wallet. The supreme Judaic ideal is to transform the world into a single limited company ... The most rapid means of achieving this is brutal and dictatorial Communism. If not all, a lot of Hebrews [*giudei*] constitute a serious and permanent danger to society.'[128] Or this, 'It is an obvious fact that the Jews are a perturbing element because of their spirit of domination and revolutionary tendencies. The workers are for Marx the tool which the Hebrews [*giudei*] will exploit to become the bosses of the world ... The Socialist or Communist revolution is the quickest and surest road to the concentration of all capital in the hands of the Jews, constituting a kind of state supercapitalism ...'[129] Such views were quite distinct from Nazi anti-Semitism, which was 'intrinsically and explicitly materialistic and anti-Christian', they insisted.[130]

Pius XI, however, criticised the *Manifesto della razza* on 28 July 1938. The human race was one race, he told an audience of students, and he wondered how Italy had come 'disgracefully' to imitate the Nazis.[131] The bulk of the speech, however, dealt not with the Jews but with the renewed Fascist crackdown on the activities of *Azione cattolica*. 'Who attacks Azione cattolica attacks the Pope,' he said.[132] Two weeks later Starace and the head of *Azione cattolica* signed an agreement which ended the friction. The Pope was right about the Manifesto: its racism, like that of the Nazis, was biological. But its argument was not the one used by Mussolini to introduce the laws against the Jews – and it was not the one that he believed in.

In Trieste, on 18 September, Mussolini gave a speech in which he denied that Italian hostility to the Jews was an imitation of that of the Nazis. He said that 'the Jewish problem' was but 'an aspect' of a bigger problem: the need for Italians to gain a racial consciousness in order to gain the prestige necessary to maintain an empire. He added,

> The racial problem has not erupted out of the blue ... It relates to the conquest of the Empire; since history teaches us that empires are conquered with arms, but maintained with prestige. And prestige requires a clear and severe racial conscience that establishes most clearly not just differences but superiorities. The Jewish problem is therefore but an aspect of this phenomenon. World Jewry has been, for 16 years, despite our policies, an irreconcilable enemy of Fascism ... Nevertheless Jews of Italian citizenship, those who have unquestionable military or civil merits ... will find understanding and justice; as for the others, we will pursue a policy of segregation.[133]

But Pius XI – who would die in February 1939 – failed to criticise publicly the laws against the Jews. In letters in November 1938 to Mussolini and the King, he protested only against the ban on marriage between Catholics and converted Jews, and only because such a ban was a violation of the 1929 Concordat which had made marriage subject to Canon Law.[134]

Initially Mussolini claimed that he had no intention of persecuting Jews. What he had in mind was discrimination, not persecution. A government statement in August 1938 said, 'The Jews in Italy ... are 44,000 according to Jewish statistics ... The proportion is thus one Jew per 1000 Italians. It is clear that, from now on, the participation of the Jews in the global life of the state must be and will be adapted to such circumstances.' The Jews themselves, said the statement, had 'always been, always and everywhere, apostles of the most total, intransigent, ferocious and, depending on one's point of view, admirable racism; they have always maintained that they belong to another blood, another race, they have proclaimed themselves an 'elect people' and they have always furnished proof of their racial solidarity over and above all frontiers. And here, we do not want to speak of the equation historically established these past twenty years in Europe between Jewry, Bolshevism and Masonry.'[135]

But the discrimination introduced by Mussolini – though it did not involve violence at all – was indeed persecution. Mussolini had no intention of putting Jews in concentration camps or exterminating them but life for Jews in Italy became very harsh after the bulk of the laws against them came into force in December 1938. Jews, as now defined, were: those whose parents were 'of Jewish race' even if they now belonged to another religious faith; those with one parent 'of Jewish race' and the other 'of foreign nationality'; those whose mother was 'of Jewish race' if the father was unknown; those with one parent 'of Jewish race' who belonged to the Jewish religion. An exception was made for those who had one parent 'of Jewish race' but belonged to a different religion before 1 October 1938.[136]

In June 1939 a new decree banned Jews from being lawyers or journalists and subjected them to severe restrictions in the other professions. In July 1939 a decree set up a Race Tribunal with complete discretion to decide who was and was not a Jew. This swiftly provided a new opportunity for Italians to practise something for which they have always possessed a special flair: bribery and corruption. Thus could Jews at a price become Aryans. As a result of the race laws about 7000 Jews were expelled from the armed forces; expelled too were 181 school and university teachers, 400 state employees and 5600 school and university pupils.[137] Things Jews no longer had the right to do included the employment of non-Jewish servants and the announcement of their deaths in the newspapers. The Jews in Italy did not, however, have to wear a yellow star. The Queen had complained to the King about the race laws. She was worried about the fate of her Jewish doctor. The King had complained about the laws to Mussolini – but only limply. He was worried about his Jewish soldiers.

Some took more drastic action. The scientist Enrico Fermi, whose wife was Jewish and who had won the Nobel Prize for physics in 1938 and would be among those who would develop the atomic bomb, emigrated to America. On the morning of 29 November 1938 Angelo Fortunato Formiggini, the famous Jewish publisher, jumped to his death from the Ghirlandina Tower in Modena. Formiggini was a Fascist. Prior to his death he had written to Mussolini, 'Dear Duce ... You have become mad ... deep down you pain me, because you have fallen into a trap placed for you by destiny.'[138] Formiggini's suicide prompted Starace to comment, 'He died like a Jew: he threw himself off a tower so as to save on a bullet.' The following month in Spain a Jewish Lieutenant-Colonel of infantry, Giorgio Morpurgo, told by his commanding officer that he would have to leave the army as a result of the race laws, walked off alone towards enemy lines. The enemy shot him to death, not knowing why Morpurgo had walked towards them or who he was. As a result he was awarded the *medaglia d'oro*, Italy's highest military honour, for gallantry. The citation stated that he had died singing 'Giovinezza'. It did not mention that he was a Jew.[139]

The Pact of Steel

Mussolini set out his foreign policy aims at a meeting of the Grand Council on 30 November 1938 – the same day that the French ambassador, François-Poncet, was heckled in the Chamber of Deputies. These included Tunisia, Corsica, Albania and the Italian-speaking Swiss canton of Ticino. In the Mediterranean Italy's situation was 'dire', he said. 'We must improve it. Tunisia is necessary; and Corsica.' Albania was also 'necessary', he said, because it would enable Italy to 'counter-act the German line of penetration, along the Danube'.[140] But what did 'necessary' mean? Did it mean invasion? Or what? On 4 February 1939 he told the Grand Council that he now had a bigger foreign policy ambition which he called the *'Marcia all'Oceano'*. 'Italy is closed in the Mediterranean "prison". The bars of this prison are: Cyprus, Malta, Tunisia, Corsica; the gates: Suez and Gibraltar ... The peoples which do not touch the Ocean are only half independent. We are one of them. We must stretch out to the Ocean. March to the Ocean.' Many have seen this speech as evidence of a determination to conquer all these places. But was it? Mussolini did not say that Italy should conquer them. He did not even mention Britain and while he saw France as the major obstacle, he said that war with France was not inevitable. The only country he earmarked for conquest by force in the near future was Albania. Apart from that, only on Tunisia and Corsica was he specific that they should become Italian but only in a distant future.[141]

Hitler persisted with his pressure on Mussolini for a military alliance. He wanted such an alliance because he believed that Italy could bog down Britain and France in the Mediterranean and make it easier for him to pursue his aggressive ambitions in central Europe. He also wanted to ensure that Italy did not declare war on Germany – as Italy had done in 1916. On 27 October 1938 Ribbentrop came to Rome once more to press Mussolini. Ribbentrop, Ciano noted, 'wants war within three or four years'.[142] This time Mussolini gave his approval in principle to a military alliance which would be both aggressive and defensive. On 1 January 1939 he sent word to Ribbentrop that he was now ready to sign up. Talks began. Europe was on the verge of war, but the reason Mussolini wanted an alliance with Hitler is not because he wanted war. It is because he did not want war. Initially he had ridiculed Hitler. Now he feared him. There was a certain affinity, it is true, between Fascism and National Socialism – the uniforms and so on. But this had more to do with what they were against than what they were for. For Latin Italy and Teutonic Germany were like chalk and cheese. Ethiopia had estranged Italy from Britain and France. Spain had thrown Italy and Germany together. But even then Britain and France could have prised Italy from Germany with a concrete offer of turf; instead, they thought that a heart to heart would suffice.

That Christmas and New Year Mussolini spent at Rocca delle Caminate, his castle above Predappio, his birthplace, in the foothills of the Apennines. It was there, in the dense fog of the Romagnol winter, that he made up his mind to ally with Hitler. With war in Europe seemingly inevitable, he decided that Italy could not remain isolated any longer and so the choice was simple: either an alliance with Britain and France, or with Germany. The British had offered only tiny morsels by way of concessions, let alone an alliance – the French even less.[143] Mussolini chose Germany for two simple reasons: fear and greed. If he allied with Hitler and war came, there was less chance of Hitler waging it on Italy. If on the other hand Hitler went to war with Britain and France, he could remain on the sidelines if need be, safe in the knowledge that Britain and France would not attack Italy. As for greed, Mussolini's greed was small beer compared with Hitler's. It had nothing to do, either, with fantasies of world domination. He had got no territorial concessions whatsoever from Britain and France in the Mediterranean. Their concern was to maintain the status quo. Hitler had become a better bet. Also, he wanted a guarantee that Germany would not try to do in the Balkans what it had done in Austria and Czechoslovakia. And there was another reason, a psychological one: Mussolini's belief in destiny. Mussolini told his wife, 'I still feel the pain of having to have detached myself from my former allies, Rachele. But there is a new factor, the formidable military power of the Germans; and then there is History which proceeds in spite of mankind . . .'[144] Mussolini allied with Hitler to control him. He did it not to hasten war, but to avoid it.

Pius XI died on 10 February 1939 aged eighty-two and on 12 March the Cardinals in conclave elected Cardinal Eugenio Pacelli as the new Pope, who chose the title Pius XII. Three days later Hitler 'invaded' the 'Czechia' parts of Czechoslovakia – Bohemia and Moravia. Slovakia was already a Nazi protectorate.[145] This gave Mussolini deep misgivings once again about an alliance with Hitler. 'The very stones would rebel against it,' he told Ciano.[146] The policy of Munich was in shreds. As over Austria, Hitler did not tell Mussolini, let alone consult him. Mussolini was 'depressed', noted Ciano, adding, 'It's the first time I've seen him like this. Even in the period of the *Anschluss* . . .' Mussolini lamented that 'every time Hitler takes a country he sends me a message'.[147] Already, Mussolini feared March because it was when Julius Caesar had been assassinated. Hitler made him fear it even more. 'What need is there to have a go at the Slavs? And, beginning like this, where will he roll next March?' Mussolini said.[148]

Fearing a move by Hitler on Croatia, Mussolini sent troops to the Veneto on 19 March and told the German ambassador in Rome that Italy would not stand by if Germany invaded Croatia. Hitler gave an assurance that he had no intention of doing so. Two days later, however, Mussolini told the Grand Council that Italy had no choice but to stand firm with the Axis. Only Balbo objected. Mussolini made a statement which sums up the driving forces behind his foreign policy decisions. He said, 'I want to make a cynical declaration: in international relations there is only one moral: success. We were immoral when we assailed the *Negus*. We won and we have become moral, *moralissimi*.' But he went on, 'The problem for us is another one. It is the relationship between forces inside the "Axis". The demographic situation has moved in favour of the Germans . . . Militarily, the situation is this: Germany has double our divisions; our navy is double the Germans'; our air force compared to the German one is 1 to 5; industry 1 to 12. So, the annexation of Czechoslovakia has altered the relationship within the "Axis" in favour of Germany. But we have a political advantage: we are the referees of the situation in Europe. If we do not wish it, Germany will not be encircled. This is our security ... Therefore, we must increase our stature, in regard to our comrade in the Axis. When? Where? We shall see.' Bottai noted wryly, 'So, if a success were obtainable by abandoning the policy of the Axis, would it be "moral" to abandon the Axis?'[149]

The British and French, now both bound by treaty to defend Czecho-slovakia, were cross, as usual, with Hitler but did no more than wring their hands. On 20 March Chamberlain wrote another letter to Mussolini to try to get him to put pressure on Hitler. Though angry with Hitler, Mussolini did not reply to Chamberlain until 1 April when he said he would do nothing until Italy's rights had been recognised. He was referring, in particular, to the Italians in Tunisia.[150]

On 28 March Franco took Madrid and two days later Valencia. Togliatti had fled Spain by plane on the 25th. The Spanish Civil War was over. There was widespread celebration in Italy as the Italian armed forces had played a very significant role in Franco's triumph. The Civil War had not begun as a struggle between nationalists and Communists; but that is what it quickly became. If Franco had failed, Spain would have become the first country in Western Europe to go Communist. The war over, Mussolini withdrew his forces from the Balearic Islands. Those such as Eden who had feared that he would seize the Balearics were proved wrong. On 26 March Mussolini gave a speech to the Fascist rank and file in Rome to mark the twentieth anniversary of the first *Fasci di Combattimento*. He said that the Nazi seizure of Czechoslovakia had been 'destined' (*fatale*), the Axis powers stood 'in clear antithesis to all other conceptions of contemporary civilisation' and what counted in international relations was not 'brotherhood' but 'force'. He singled out Italian grievances against the French, 'problems of a colonial character: their names are Tunisia, Djibouti, the Suez Canal'. *The Times* agreed, sort of, commenting that Mussolini's claims on France had 'created a new point of departure' so long as 'able diplomacy' predominated.[151]

To deter Hitler in the Balkans and to emulate him, he decided to invade Albania which had been a de facto Italian protectorate since seized from the Turks during the First World War. As Ciano had put it to Bottai, the aim was the 'creation of a wall of defence against Germany in its march towards the Balkan east. There are many geopolitical elements, which make Germany a "Balkan" nation. The annexation of Austria ... above all: the Danube, which brings German life into the Balkan lands ... The annexation of Albania will give us the prerequisites to confront it [Germany].'[152] Triumph in Spain boosted Mussolini's morale greatly. His doubts about an invasion of Albania evaporated. The same day that Madrid fell, Mussolini finally ordered Ciano, who had been pestering him for some time on the matter, to prepare the invasion of Albania. It took place on 7 April – Good Friday. It was very badly prepared and executed but King Ahmed Zog – a member of a powerful bandit family before he had become Albania's first king and remained there thanks to Italian money – had no army at all with which to respond and fled Tirana in the direction of Greece. Mussolini did not warn Hitler. But Hitler did not seem to mind.[153] The French were indifferent. The British were irritated at this breach of the Easter Agreement which had guaranteed the Mediterranean status quo. Albania, like Ethiopia, was also a member of the League of Nations. But the British did no more than give Mussolini a ticking off. Small European nations, it seemed, did not matter as much as big African ones. Mussolini was in constant contact with the Italian embassy in London with orders to assure the British that there were no plans to move on Yugoslavia or Greece. Chamberlain told the House of Commons that he was 'still not convinced that Italy has made up her mind, particularly the Italian nation, to be involved in national conflict with Great Britain and France in the Mediterranean.'[154] On 16 April a group of Albanian dignitaries came to Rome to present the crown of Albania to Vittorio Emanuele III who accepted it.

Drummond, British ambassador in Rome, had been urging his government to pressure the French into making concessions to Italy since the end of the Spanish Civil War. The war had caused a severe rift between France and Italy. Now it was over. Italy's claims were far from draconian: guarantees for Italians in Tunisia, representation on the Suez Canal Board and Djibouti to be a free port. Drummond had the support of Halifax, the Foreign Secretary. But the French would not listen. In April he was replaced as British ambassador in Rome by Sir Percy Loraine.

The talks on a military alliance between Italy and Germany continued. But no sooner had Mussolini made up his mind to ally with Germany than he started to throw obstacles in the way. Italy, after Ethiopia and Spain, he told the Germans, required several years of peace and would not be ready for a war until 1943. Even that date, he assured Badoglio, the Chief of the General Staff, understandably worried, was only a rough guideline and not a commitment set in stone.

On 6 May Ciano met Ribbentrop in Milan to discuss the alliance in detail. A note from Mussolini to Ciano stipulated that an alliance could only be formed on the basis that 'Fascist Italy does not desire to take part in a war of a European character, though convinced that it is inevitable', which it could only contemplate 'from 1943 on'.[155] Ciano asked about Hitler's intentions towards Poland, which by now had become the obvious next target, and Ribbentrop lied that Hitler had decided to employ conciliation to resolve the matter. On 3 April, unbeknown to Mussolini and Ciano, Hitler had given his generals orders to prepare the invasion of Poland for September. Ribbentrop also told Ciano that an alliance with Soviet Russia – the other totalitarian power – would not be a bad idea; a hint that Germany was attempting to form an alliance with the Communist arch enemy.

In December 1943, while in prison awaiting trial and death, Ciano wrote an introduction to his famous diaries in which he blamed the alliance between Italy and Germany entirely on Mussolini in a pathetic attempt to disassociate himself from it completely. He wrote that from Milan he had telephoned Mussolini to give him an update on the Ribbentrop talks and was astonished, he claimed, to be told to announce the alliance at once. He wrote, 'The decision to secure the alliance was taken by Mussolini, out of the blue, while I was in Milan with Ribbentrop ... By telephone, I received the order ... In this way was born the Pact of Steel. And a decision that had so many sinister effects on the life and future of the entire Italian people was due, exclusively, to the disrespectful reaction of a dictator.'[156] Ciano was as obsequious as he was devious. Quite simply, he was the Duce's yes man, however much whinging he did in private. The truth is, he went along now with what his boss and father-in-law the Duce said, as he always had done. His influence on him – and so on events – was slight and derived from the Duce's belief that he brought him '*fortuna*'.[157] Mussolini agreed to the Pact of Steel because, as he put it, 'Germany alone can take decisions which do not coincide with our interests. The alliance constrains it to consult us and not to decide alone.'[158]

Ribbentrop left Milan to draw up the document. When Ciano saw it for the first time a week later, he wrote in his diary that it was 'truly dynamite' as if, regardless of those endless talks of his with the Nazis, both now and before, he was even more astonished.[159] This comment, like so many in Ciano's diaries dealing with such crucial moments, reads as if it were written after the event either by him or someone else in an attempt to clear his name – just as the introduction to his diaries that he wrote in 1943 was an attempt to clear his name. What was to stop him and Mussolini, after all, refusing to sign or insisting on changes, if they did not like the dynamite? Nothing. And if Mussolini still insisted against the wishes of Ciano, what was to stop Ciano refusing? At the very least, he might have resigned, mightn't he? Edda said that she had urged him to do so repeatedly.[160] Ciano told Bastianini, Foreign Under-Secretary, 'I am ready to do so [resign] if the others do so with me.'[161] Anfuso, who knew Ciano well, was convinced that Ciano's diaries were extensively rewritten, added to and cut, after the event, and that 'the Mussolini portrayed by Ciano is someone who acts *a vuoto* and Mussolini was not like that ... When Mussolini was not being the pragmatist, Ciano was unable to perceive in him anything more ... He [Mussolini] was fascinated by systems, inasmuch as they seemed to him to develop logically only by virtue of an historical reason: his Marxism was in this respect permanent and he amazed no one in claiming that he remained more Socialist than his opponents of the Left.'[162] Sir Percy Loraine, the new British ambassador in Rome, told the Foreign Office on 9 May that the Italians still liked the British: 'To judge by the very cordial welcome extended to myself, by obvious popularity of British show-jumping team at Rome Horse Show that ended yesterday (and equally obvious unpopularity of German team) and other indications ... confirm the impression that the Prime Minister and yourself derived here, there is great friendliness and respect here for the UK.' Two weeks later, after the signing of the pact, Loraine wrote that the pact had placed Mussolini in 'a stronger position to restrain Hitler from moves which would involve Italy in an unwelcome and unpopular war ... On the whole I think that I incline to believe that the alliance is preferable to the Axis. The situation is more positive.' The American ambassador, William Phillips, agreed. But Loraine admitted that he was worried about 'the conviction of the Duce' that 'only' the pact could 'procure gains for Italy', he said.[163]

Ribbentrop's document stipulated that should either country go to war, the other would join it automatically 'with all its military forces' even if that country was the aggressor.[164] There was also a clause on the Alto Adige which gave the Germans there the option of German citizenship. Mussolini agreed to the pact without even getting Foreign Ministry experts to examine it. The only alteration he made was an addition which stated that the border between Austria (now Germany) and Italy remain unalterable. There had been so many pieces of paper signed since the First World War. Here was another.

On 20 May, despite the astonishment he recorded in his diary, Ciano duly left for Berlin by train to sign the alliance which Mussolini, the brilliant phrase maker, soon called 'The Pact of Steel'. Ciano and Ribbentrop signed it on the 22nd. Hitler was present, but conspicuously, Mussolini remained in Rome. Ribbentrop assured Ciano that Germany wanted at least three years of peace, which was somewhat less than the four or five he had previously told him. The King had decided to bestow on Ribbentrop the highest award in his gift – the *Collare dell'Annunziata*. Ciano presented it. Ribbentrop was now a cousin of the Italian King. In addition, Vittorio Emanuele sent a telegram – his first ever to a minister – congratulating Ciano on the pact.[165]

Mussolini had signed the Pact of Steel because he hoped that it would guarantee peace – not war. He claimed it was a defensive, not an offensive alliance.[166] Ciano, as ever the yes man, had simply gone along with the wishes of Mussolini in the same vein. Yet after the Second World War a whole industry sprouted up on the basis of the famous Ciano diaries, which would have us believe – among other things – that Ciano tried to stop the Pact of Steel. Even today in Italy, this view which emanates from the diaries is widespread. Within a week of the signing Mussolini wrote to Hitler on the 30 May to insist that though war against the 'plutocratic nations' was 'inevitable' there must be at least three years of peace first.[167]

Apart from anything else, the celebrations for the twentieth anniversary of the March on Rome, due in October 1942, were a top priority, he said. Hitler now tried to have talks with Mussolini to clarify matters. But the Duce made repeated excuses. No talks occurred.[168] There was much talk of talks between generals as well, and the swapping of military secrets, but nothing much happened. Both sides, it was clear, wanted to keep their options open. Just as in September 1937, Mussolini had told the King that his visit to Berlin had been only for show. So too with the Pact of Steel. For what was the Pact of Steel, after all, but yet another piece of paper? Force and destiny were all that counted in the game of international politics, as Mussolini had said time and again, not the law of contract.

1939: Mussolini, Man of Peace

The day after the signing of the Pact of Steel Hitler told his generals he would attack Poland at the earliest possible opportunity. This was a sign of how much he valued his alliance with Italy. His justification on Poland – he always had one and this time it was morally stronger than ever – was the return of Danzig (later Gdansk), which was very German indeed. Until Versailles, Danzig had been part of West Prussia. Now it was a free city connected to Germany by a thin corridor of land inside Poland. 'The attack must be kept hidden even from Italy and Japan,' he said.[169] On 22 June the German army mobilised in secret. Meanwhile German attempts to secure an alliance with Soviet Russia continued, also in secret. 'They [the British and French] have isolated us: they will pay the consequences! But, if it is possible, we will remain out of the conflict,' Mussolini told De Begnac in July.[170] In February, Mussolini had told Grandi that he would be replacing him as ambassador in London and in July recalled him to Rome where he became Justice Minister. He had done so because of Grandi's pro-Britishness. In October 1939 Churchill would write to Grandi saying that he felt 'genuine grief' that subsequent events had 'saddened' his 'memorable mission' in Britain.[171]

On 11 August Ciano met Ribbentrop at his schloss outside Salzburg and the next day Hitler at the 'Eagle's Nest' in Berchtesgaden in an attempt to persuade them to seek a peaceful solution to the Danzig problem. War now would be 'madness', Mussolini had told Ciano on the 9th, 'because it would be impossible to localise it and a general war would be disastrous for all'.[172] Ciano failed to convince Hitler and Ribbentrop of this. It was only now, said Ciano in the introduction to his diary, that Ribbentrop told him the Germans wanted not just Danzig but all of Poland. 'My arguments slid off their will like water off marble,' he wrote.[173] But for months the Italian ambassador in Berlin, Bernardo Attolico, had been sending frequent messages to Rome which warned of Hitler's determination to seize Poland. Ciano had chosen to ignore or not to believe these. Subsequently, the messages would grow more urgent. Ciano had written in July, 'I am sceptical, very sceptical, now about Attolico, who has lost his head.'[174] But anyway Hitler had insisted that Britain and France would not declare war over Poland and even if they did it would be merely as a gesture not actual war.[175] 'I've never been mistaken,' he said.[176] And then during Ciano's meeting with Hitler a telegram arrived inviting Germany to send a representative to Moscow for talks. Ciano did not believe a Nazi–Soviet Pact possible either.[177] For this belief, perhaps, he can be forgiven.

Ciano wrote in his diary, 'I return to Rome disgusted with Germany, its leaders, their way of behaving ... The Duce's reactions are varied. At first he agrees with me. Then he says honour compels him to march with Germany. Finally, he states that he wants his part of the booty in Croatia and Dalmatia.'[178] Mussolini, angry as well, was racked by doubt and indecision. Ciano, Grandi – now back in Rome – and Bottai urged him to abandon the Pact of Steel. But Mussolini would not do so, because, as Anfuso explained, he was 'most oppressed' by the thought of Italy being accused of betrayal as in 1914–15. He was also very afraid that if he did not march with Hitler, Hitler would march against him.[179]

On 21 August Ciano tried to arrange yet another meeting with Ribbentrop, this time at the Brenner, to urge him once more against invasion of Poland. Eventually, Ribbentrop took Ciano's call but said that a meeting was impossible because he 'awaited an important message from Moscow'.[180] Ciano told Bottai that his train was ready to leave but then, 'At 8 p.m. Ribbentrop called me by telephone: "You know, I am leaving tomorrow. I have to communicate a personal secret to the Duce and you. I will be signing the agreement with Russia" ... "What? Agreement? What kind?"'[181]

On 23 August, in Moscow, Ribbentrop and Vyacheslav Molotov, Soviet Foreign Minister, signed the Nazi–Soviet Pact of non-aggression.[182] In a secret clause they had also decided to carve up Poland between them. Hitler informed Mussolini a couple of hours before he told the press. Simultaneously, the British and French had been attempting to achieve an alliance with Russia. But Hitler had beaten them with Russia, as he had with Italy. One effect of the Nazi–Soviet Pact was to reduce drastically Germany's need of military help from Italy. It also destroyed a core justification for the Pact of Steel; one of the few things Fascism and National Socialism had in common: hostility to Communism. The other core justification, hostility to the imperialist 'democracies', remained. The pact was 'an act of betrayal on the ideological, moral and spiritual front', noted Bottai.[183] But Bottai also noted that there were many similarities, especially on social policy, between Fascism and Communism, such as the championing of 'the people' against 'the bosses', which in the 'Messianic period' of the Fascist corporate state had led to the 1933 treaty between Italy and Russia. From 1935, though, he said, Fascist expansionism had taken over from Fascist social policy as the dominant force in the Fascist foreign policy. But now, perhaps, with the Nazi–Soviet Pact, he suggested, the class struggle might be brought on to the international stage in the shape of war between poor and rich nations: 'War between nations like a war between classes.'[184] The main attraction of the Nazi–Soviet Pact to Hitler, of course, had nothing to do with ideology. It was purely, cynically, practical: he hoped it would deter Britain and France from declaring war on Germany over Poland; and if it did not, enable him to defeat them because of the removal of the threat of a war against Germany on two fronts. Both Ciano and Mussolini, though shocked, thought that the pact was a master blow.

Britain was not, however, deterred and on the 25th signed a defensive military alliance with Poland. But nor was Hitler. The same day he sent a message to Mussolini explaining why he had signed the Nazi–Soviet Pact and why secrecy had been important, and to tell him that the invasion of Poland was imminent. But the boost to Hitler's chances of victory given him by the Nazi–Soviet Pact made Mussolini less belligerent, not more. He was adamant: Italy would not fight. In this he had the support, quite apart from the Italian people, of the King, the Vatican, the big industrialists, the service chiefs and nearly all the Fascists gerarchs, most notably Ciano (only through fear of losing), though not Farinacci, or Starace, who described war as 'like eating a plate of macaroni'.[185] Yet in 1940, once Hitler had conquered the Low Countries and was on the verge of victory in France, many of these – Ciano, the King, the service chiefs, even the Italians – would change their tune.

Mussolini replied to Hitler that if Germany attacked Poland and the conflict remained local, Italy would give economic help. But he said that if, as a result, Britain and France declared war on Germany, Italy would not provide military assistance 'given the current conditions of our military preparation, regularly and *tempestivamente* signalled to the Führer and Ribbentrop' – unless Germany supplied Italy with military aid and raw materials 'to resist the attack which the British and French would predominantly direct against us'.[186] The letter disturbed Hitler and caused him to postpone the invasion of Poland – albeit only briefly.[187] Hitler asked Mussolini what he lacked. On the 26th Mussolini supplied details. So absurdly huge were the quantities of *matériel* involved that it would have required 17,000 trains to supply them. Mussolini, it was clear to Hitler, did not want war.

The Second World War was a week away. But war was the last thing Mussolini wanted. Such a war, he knew, would signal the passing of his moment. He would never now be the chief protagonist of his age whether he went to war or whether he stayed out. Either way he and Italy would lose. If he stayed out, he would be regarded as a coward, hypocrite and traitor. If he joined in, he would subject Italy to disaster because he knew that the Italian armed forces were in a pitiful state. Italian arms production was still proceeding on the basis of a very short war after 1942. Italy's arms manufacturers were still selling more arms to Britain and France than Germany in September 1939. In August 1939 Mussolini ordered work to fortify the Alps to be stepped up. The aim was to create a Maginot Line to defend Italy not so much from the French but from the Germans.[188] He had boasted in October 1936 that he had '8 million bayonets' ready to do battle. Fascist propaganda hammered home an incessant belligerent message. It was all bluff. When the war started the army was seriously deficient in all aspects of firepower and there were no anti-aircraft guns at all. Italian pilots were often excellent and had captured nearly all the major aeronautical prizes. But of the thousands of planes the air force had probably only 1000 were of any use in combat. The fleet was large but did not possess an aircraft carrier and though it had more submarines than anyone else these were already out of date. Nor did the Italian armed forces have radar. The Fascists claimed that they invented radar but did not develop it because the cost was prohibitive.[189]

On the 26th Mussolini wrote to Hitler a second time, telling him that 'forces greater than my will' – certainly not 'considerations of a pacifist nature alien to my spirit' – meant that he could not go to war at Hitler's side and he urged Hitler to seek a 'political situation'. Hitler replied on the 27th that he understood the reasons behind Mussolini's decision not to go to war but asked him to keep it quiet 'at least until the outbreak of the struggle'. Hitler added, 'I should also urge you, Duce, if it is possible, to force France and England at least by a show of military activity to keep committed a part of their forces, or in any case leave them uncertain.'[190]

Mussolini now tried to stop the Second World War. The British and Germans were still talking, just. On the 23rd he had told Ciano to see the British ambassador, Loraine, to offer to mediate at a peace conference à la Munich. Loraine, emotional, collapsed in Ciano's arms, wrote Ciano.[191]

Next, on the 29th, Mussolini appealed directly to Hitler. He sent him a message: 'As a true friend of yours and of the German people I wish to say to you that the English proposals contain in my opinion the basis of a solution favourable to Germany of all the problems in which it is interested.' Neither initiative led anywhere. Then, on the morning of the 31st, Mussolini told Ciano to telephone Halifax and say that he was prepared to put pressure on Hitler once again if he could offer something tangible; and to tell Loraine that Italy would not fight Britain and France. He proposed a conference involving the five powers for 5 September in San Remo. But that afternoon Halifax telephoned Ciano to say that there was nothing more that could be offered.

That evening, Ciano met Bottai alone at his office in Palazzo Chigi. The previous day Mussolini had ordered precautionary blackouts to begin, so in darkness they sat together on a window seat in Ciano's office. Ciano told him, 'We, you understand, must not, we cannot, intervene. We must not . . . The Germans have violated our pact. We have no duty to intervene. And, I add, no interest.' Ciano also told Bottai that Italy and its empire were 'extremely vulnerable' and its armed forces had 'frightening deficiencies'. 'The truth is we are not ready . . . The Italian people does not want *this* war. It does not feel it. It does not believe in it.' As for Mussolini, Ciano added, 'Everything about the Duce, his past, character, temperament, everything brings him to rebel against neutrality; and his high sense of honour brings him to rebel against the abandoning of an ally, a treachery like that of Italy in '14. How can Mussolini do a Giolitti? But then he sees, he knows, he feels that the people cannot be brought to make *this* war in *these* conditions . . . *Ecco, il dramma.*'[192] Ciano and Bottai then went to see Mussolini at Palazzo Venezia. Finding Starace and another gerarch outside Mussolini's office, Ciano flew into a rage. They stood up to give him the Roman salute to which he retorted, ' "And you idiots, fools, imbeciles with no more sense than a cow in those dunce heads of yours – you egg him on, you make him do all this." '[193] After seeing Mussolini, Ciano returned to the Palazzo Chigi where he did the most rebellious thing he had ever done: he switched on the lights.

Germany's invasion of Poland led Ciano 'decisively' to turn against the Axis, said Bottai.[194] Yes, Ciano had turned against Germany, and yes, once war started he tried to convince Mussolini to keep Italy out of it. But as soon as Germany started winning easily in the west in the spring of 1940 he was all in favour of Germany once again. Ciano, the spoiled child of the regime, had never been popular in Italy and it was him rather than Mussolini whom Italians blamed for the Pact of Steel. 'We were better off when Mussolini was in charge,' was by now a popular saying, noted Bottai.[195] Grandi described Ciano as 'the man most hated by the nation'.[196] But of course, it was Mussolini, not Ciano, who was the Duce. It was Mussolini who made all the decisions.

Hitler's troops invaded Poland at dawn on 1 September. The British gave him an ultimatum: unless he evacuated Poland by 11 a.m. on the 3rd they would declare war. Attempts continued to get him to agree to negotiate. At 10 a.m. on the 2nd, Mussolini sent him yet another plea. But he ignored it because of British insistence that his troops withdraw from Poland first.[197] At 11 a.m. on the 3rd, Britain declared war on Germany. At 5 p.m. France followed suit. That afternoon, Italy announced that it would remain neutral. Mussolini called it non-belligerent because he could not bear the idea of Italy being neutral and being accused of treachery. He told the Council of Ministers, 'Our position is clear; and was plainly spelled out to the Führer: Italy would not be ready until the end of '42.' He added, 'It has to be said as well that the Führer has challenged destiny.'[198] Grandi said that Italy should denounce the German invasion. Germany, not Italy, he said, was the traitor; it had contravened both the Anti-Comintern Pact and the Pact of Steel. Though many agreed with him, only he spoke out. That day Hitler sent Mussolini an ominous message which said that 'even if now we march on different paths nevertheless our destiny will bind us one to the other'. The German press talked of Italian betrayal. But the German army quickly overran western Poland and on the 17th Russia invaded Poland as well. Together, as agreed in the secret clause in the Nazi–Soviet Pact, Germany and Russia partitioned Poland a week later. Hitler invited Mussolini to meet him in Berlin. Mussolini declined and sent Ciano instead on 30 September. Hitler urged Ciano to bring Italy into the war. This would enable him to attack France immediately as it would ensure a swift victory, he said. 'Either he is bewitched, or he really is a genius ...' wrote Ciano.[199]

Ciano and the *'Vita Comoda'* at the Nineteenth Hole

Mussolini heaped scorn on golf because it was bourgeois and British. He thought that golf courses would be better off as fields for peasants to cultivate. He suspected that golf courses – he had never visited one – were places where 'afascists' and 'Anglophiles' staged open-air baccanales.[200] Ciano, however, loved golf. This irritated Mussolini. He told him, 'I get continuous reports of this golf club ... Beautiful women and experienced ladies ...' He handed him back a book he had borrowed from him and added, 'I must conclude that when one seeks only beautiful women and one likes terrible books, decadence for a man is certain.'[201] But as a result of Ciano's interest, 'the whole of Roman society took up golf,' wrote Susanna Agnelli, adding, 'The women behaved with a lack of dignity that was embarrassing ... To hold on to Galeazzo's arm in public and to be pawed by him was the sign of success ... Whatever he said, they all doubled up in laughter.'[202] The all-knowing Loraine informed the Foreign Office that Edda had become 'a nymphomaniac and in an alcoholic haze leads a life of rather sordid sexual promiscuity'.[203] The *enfant terrible* of Fascism, Curzio Malaparte, albeit with the benefit of hindsight, would write, 'All the black blood of the Mussolinis is not in the veins of the father, it is in the veins of Edda ... Edda is implacable, obsesses his nights. There will be blood spilled, one day, between that father and that daughter.'[204] Edda told a friend, 'It is true that I have lovers, but I make children only with Galeazzo.'[205] Mussolini's wife took up divining for oil near the family villa at Carpena. So strong was her conviction that she had found it that in 1939 she convinced Mussolini to order the state oil company AGIP to conduct tests. The tests found nothing.[206] As for Mussolini, he became increasingly remote and solitary. François-Poncet, the French ambassador, had noted just after Munich, 'He no longer receives anyone and no one today can say, apart, perhaps, from Count Ciano, what he prepares and towards what objectives he heads.'[207]

In early November Ciano met Bottai and others at his golf club, *Il Golf dell' Acqua Santa* near the Via Appia – the only one in Rome – founded by British residents at the turn of the century and still dominated by them. He told them, 'Between German hegemony and English hegemony, better the latter: it's the hegemony of golf, wisky [*sic*] and comfort.' Bottai noted, 'In sum, the hegemony of the *vita comoda*.'[208]

On 7 December Mussolini told the Grand Council, 'Here, there are two empires at war; two lions. We have no interests at stake, if neither beats hollow the other. If England wins, it would only leave us the sea to go swimming in. If Germany wins, we would feel the weight. One might hope that the two lions tear each others to pieces and each leaves its tail on the ground. And, if so, let's go and pick them up.'[209] Balbo argued in vain at the meeting that Italy switch sides and ally with Britain and France. On the 18th Ciano delivered a strong anti-German speech, with Mussolini's approval, to the Chamber (now called the *Camera dei fasci*) which he described in private as the 'funeral of the Axis'. On 5 January Mussolini wrote to Hitler urging him to abandon the Nazi–Soviet Pact and negotiate with Britain and France. Any move which brought Germany and Russia closer would have 'catastrophic repercussions' in Italy. He said, 'I'm profoundly convinced that Great Britain and France will never succeed in forcing your Germany helped by Italy to capitulate, but it is not certain that we will succeed in bringing the Anglo-French to their knees or even to divide them. To believe it, means to delude oneself.' He added, 'The solution to your *Lebensraum* is in Russia and nowhere else ... Germany's task is this: to defend Europe from Asia ... Until four months ago Russia was the number one enemy in the world: it cannot become and it is not the number one ally. This has perturbed profoundly Fascists in Italy and perhaps also many National Socialists in Germany.'[210] Hitler did not reply until March.

Given the proximity of Germany, France was by now much keener than Britain to make concessions to Italy to keep her at the very least out of the war. The British had decided that it was pointless to try to buy continued Italian neutrality or a mediatory role with Hitler. They believed that Mussolini would not accept, as his Italian predecessors had done in 1915 with the secret Treaty of London, the promise of concessions because apart from anything else the 1915 promise had not been met. He would insist on concessions first. Instead, Britain pressured a reluctant France into agreeing to the introduction of a joint naval blockade of Italy in November 1939. In particular, Italy had little coal of its own, and Chamberlain and the British War Cabinet mistakenly thought that a blockade would deter Mussolini from entering the war. They held this view until April 1940. At the start of March the British tightened the blockade still further.[211]

This was Mussolini's non-belligerent dilemma during the winter of 1939–40 – Italy's traditional dilemma. As Grandi noted, Mussolini was 'fighting the biggest interior battle of his life'.[212] During the months that followed he was 'in the state of mind of someone who had given up the game', said Anfuso, 'but whose intention was to rejoin it when he had recovered his strength'. He hardly appeared at all in public.[213] He could not make up his mind. One minute, 'the idea of intervention with the Germans attracts him', the next 'he openly hopes for their defeat'.[214]

He was 'like a virile recluse smothered in chains'; angry at accusations that Italy, as in 1914–15, was a traitor this time round as well or that the Italians would be more a hindrance than a help to the Germans anyway; and he was envious of Hitler's success.[215] 'For Mussolini, the idea of Hitler's waging war and, worse still, winning it, is altogether unbearable,' wrote Ciano.[216] According to Grandi, Mussolini's desire to do down Hitler had become an obsession. He said he had 'no intelligence, no dynamism, no political instinct'.[217] Grandi also wrote, 'One of the men he hated most in the world was Hitler. It seems a paradox, but it is the honest truth.'[218] But at the same time he 'hates democracies and cannot forgive or forget sanctions', wrote John Colville, Churchill's private secretary, in his diary.[219] But Mussolini feared Hitler at the Brenner more than he feared the British fleet in the Mediterranean or the French army at Ventimiglia. 'He fears the anger of Hitler ...' Ciano wrote.[220]

To make matters worse, Mussolini suffered a recurrence of his stomach pains. To ease the pain he had morphine injections, it was said, and many noticed that his eyes appeared hallucinated. On one occasion, Bottai found him doubled up on the floor of his office with his fists in his mouth so bad was the pain. Ciano, Grandi, Bottai and Balbo wanted Italy to abandon the Pact of Steel.[221] Balbo thought about trying to depose Mussolini but did nothing, because he feared any such move would result in invasion by Germany and there was no guarantee of help from Britain and France.[222] Ciano, once more at the Holy Water golf club, this time with Anfuso, warned, 'What torments him most is to be regarded as a traitor: *italiano-traditore*. When some German puts it about that the Italians are preparing the old game of the Triple Alliance, it's then that he hits the roof. That is a point that might decide it for him.'[223]

Fascist propaganda had emphasised the *virtù* of war for so long that the propaganda had gathered its own momentum. It encouraged 'a state of apocalyptic expectancy', wrote the anti-Fascist historian and journalist Gaetano Salvemini.[224] The Duce had become a prisoner of his own myth.[225] But, as Bottai noted in April 1940, 'His opponent is this [Italian] people.'[226] And as he said, 'The Italian race is a race of sheep, eighteen years would not be enough to transform it, 180 are needed or perhaps even 180 centuries.'[227] The same month, he told Ciano, 'It is humiliating to stand by twiddling one's thumbs while others are writing history; to make a people great, one must take them into combat, even with kicks in the ass. This is what I shall do.'[228]

Sumner Wells, Roosevelt's special peace envoy, met Mussolini twice in this period in Rome – once on 26 February and then on 16 March. On the first occasion he handed over a letter from Roosevelt urging Mussolini to remain neutral and inviting him to talks. Wells recalled, 'He was ponderous and static rather than vital. He moved with an elephantine motion; every step appeared an effort. He was heavy for his height, and his face in repose fell in rolls of flesh. His close-cropped hair was snow-white.' At their second meeting, however, Wells noticed that Mussolini seemed in better shape as if he had made up his mind to enter the war and a great weight had been lifted from his shoulders. On 10 March Ribbentrop had come to Rome with a reply from Hitler to Mussolini's letter of 5 January and Mussolini told him Italy would enter the war on Germany's side but he gave no date. Two days later Mussolini and Ciano went to the Brenner to meet Hitler. It snowed heavily. Hitler spoke of the imminent invasion of France. Mussolini told Hitler that Italy would enter the war on Germany's side – though once again he gave no date. Later Hitler said that Mussolini was like a school pupil who had done his homework badly. Mussolini had told Ciano that the night before he had had a dream in which he had seen the future.[229]

On 31 March Mussolini wrote a memo which he gave to the King on the 4 April and to Ciano on the 6th. It said that Italy had to enter the war, because it was 'in the middle of the belligerents' and not to do so would be 'absurd and impossible' and reduce Italy to the level of 'a Switzerland times ten'. It added,

> Even if Italy changed attitude and passed over ... to the Franco-English, it would not avoid immediate war with Germany ... Excluding the volte-face which anyway the Franco-English do not contemplate ... there remains the other hypothesis which is a war parallel to that of Germany to achieve our own objectives which are summed up as follows: liberty at sea, window on the ocean ... The problem is not therefore knowing if Italy will enter the war ... It is a question only of knowing when and how; it is a question of delaying our entry into the war as long as possible, compatible with our honour and dignity: (a) to prepare in such a way that our intervention determines the decision, (b) because Italy cannot fight a long war, cannot spend hundreds of billions ...[230]

Finally, in early April, Chamberlain reactivated the secret channel of communication via Sir Joseph Ball and Adrian Dingli, a Maltese at the Italian embassy in London, in an attempt to appease Mussolini. Dingli came to Rome on the 5th with a goodwill message from Chamberlain for Mussolini and the offer of talks. Mussolini replied that talks would only be worthwhile if they produced concrete results on territorial issues. Chamberlain felt unable to pursue the matter further. But Mussolini had still not made his mind up, because on 8 April he wrote to Franco to say that Italy would enter the war on Germany's side but that the date 'cannot be predicted'.[231]

Mildly Mad Mussolini

Unable to pursue effectively to his advantage any more the policy of playing one side off against the other, Mussolini had turned to Germany. The Pact of Steel had nothing to do with a shared ideology and now not even shared interests. Hitler's invasions of Austria, Czechoslovakia and Poland were not in Mussolini's interests. Mussolini could have walked away from his alliance with Hitler. But at what price to his prestige, his regime, to Italy? If Fascism were to survive in Italy, it had to ensure it could do so after Mussolini. A successful war would have achieved that.

Nor had the declaration of war on Germany by Britain and France anything much to do with ideology. This was not a war between Fascism and anti-Fascism – not yet, not until Hitler turned on Russia. Anti-Fascism's leading light, the Left, could hardly talk about ideology with Hitler allied to Stalin. At most it was a war between democracy and dictatorship. But the dictatorship the democracies opposed from an ideological point of view was that of Stalin, not Hitler. It was not ideology which caused them to declare war on Hitler.

Mussolini had thought he could control Hitler, the disciple who had hero-worshipped him, but instead helped unleash him. There was no doubt now who controlled the Axis. Later Grandi wrote that Mussolini 'felt isolated ... Germany was slipping through his hands. He believed he could bind Germany to him and he did not realise that he bound himself *a corpo perduto* to Germany. It is certain that if Mussolini had known war was imminent he would not have asked of Hitler, after reflecting on it, the commitment to peace for at least three or four years. He intended the pact of alliance, rather, as a guarantee, even if temporary, of European peace ... What he did later, on 1 September, confirms what I am saying.'[232] The British and French, on the other hand – as Hitler had predicted – having declared war on Hitler to save Poland, did not actually make war on him. Poland, meanwhile, had ceased to exist. Hitler now turned his rapacious gaze west.

De Felice has written, 'I'm convinced that, if Mussolini had kept Italy out of the Second World War, he would have regained a large part of the consent lost, and perhaps he would have increased it.'[233] But equally, it must be said, had Mussolini entered the war and won he would have been even more popular. Winning, however, as he knew, could not depend on him. It depended on Hitler. Mussolini had not intended to abandon Italy's traditional foreign policy objective of playing one set of nations off against another. He had hoped to use the Italian convergence with Germany as a bargaining counter to swing back the other way. But Hitler's continued aggressions swept him along in their wake. Thus did his chance to shape history, rather than be shaped by it, evaporate. The shaping of history now depended on other people. But at least in Hitler, Mussolini thought, he had backed the winner. Britain and France, he believed, were decadent nations and lacked the strength of will to win. But what swung it was an idea: his belief that only such a war could complete the Fascist revolution. The bourgeoisie in Italy wanted peace – *la vita comoda*. Mussolini opted for war. But then so too had the bourgeoisie in Britain and France.

In 1947 a Neapolitan psychiatrist, Dr Tommaso Senise, wrote a pamphlet in which he diagnosed the by now dead Mussolini as mad – but only mildly mad. He had not examined the patient, of course, but he had lived through his dictatorship. He was convinced that Mussolini suffered from 'morbid excitability', more commonly known as 'mania', which he said was a 'manic depressive psychosis'. Symptoms included: 'the vivacity, mobility and incoherence of his ideas, the loquaciousness, the changes in mood (though prevalently irritation and anger), the exaltation of the instincts, of the affections, of the sentiments ... and ... the diminution or loss of the moderating and inhibitory faculties, the lack of judgement, reflection, criticism, self-control ... the disordered conduct ... the proneness to impulsiveness and aggression, the *vagabondaggio*, the dissoluteness of the sexual and family life, the inconsistency and contradictoriness in the political attitudes ...' Such symptoms are common in politicians as a whole but Dr Senise was adamant that in the case of this particular politician they meant only one thing: 'Mussolini therefore was essentially a maniac, a fanatic, a chronic and constitutional *eccitato* ... And seeing as this maniacal state, though habitual in him and generally unmotivated or hardly motivated, was not ordinarily extremely intense, that is to say it did not reach the level of *"furore"* except episodically ... one can with great precision assert that Mussolini was afflicted by *ipomania* ... which means mild, light mania.' But 'unlike Hitler', Mussolini was not 'a megalomaniac', said Dr Senise. Megalomania was an offshoot of paranoia, which was something much more dangerous because sufferers had highly organised delusions of grandeur. The final chapter of Dr Senise's pamphlet was entitled 'How Can We Save Ourselves from the Mad Politicians?'. Among other things, he suggested the regular vetting by a panel of psychiatrists of the sayings and writings of politicians as well as of the politicians themselves![234]

Perhaps Mussolini was mildly mad. But the renowned psychiatrist, Carl Jung, wrote in September 1939 that he was 'rational' (*ragionevole*) and guided by the interests of Italy.[235] In April 1941 John Whitaker 'revealed' in the *Daily Telegraph* that in the spring of 1939 Mussolini had suffered a 'partial paralysis of his sight' which 'in my opinion' caused him to sign the Pact of Steel and enter the war from which 'his peasant guile' would otherwise have saved him.[236] Others blamed syphilis which Mussolini had long been rumoured to have but did not. In the year of his death Mussolini would say that the only mistakes he had made were the result of following his reason rather than his instinct, his blood or the stars. 'Each man has his star. Mine is a good star, but I cannot share it with others without neutralising it ... I have never bluffed. I have often raised my voice, but I have never played blindman's buff with the wheel of fortune. Whenever I did not have force, I had political certainty.[237] He told Ottavio Dinale, an old friend, at the end of 1939, 'I have responsibilities ordained by fate ... they were not chosen by my caprice, they were loaded up on to my shoulders by destiny or Providence ... Responsibilities are the raw material of a mission. And I am constrained to continue to the end, to the completion of this mission which transcends me.'[238] In June 1939 a *Spectator* correspondent had written, 'Mussolini is a peasant, the son of a blacksmith, and this the people does not forget. I have spoken to peasants who, after criticising the Duce say, "But he is one of us".'[239]

What, one wonders, would a good man have done in Mussolini's situation in the spring of 1940? Or a clever man? Or, indeed, a peasant? Last-minute efforts on the part of the British, French and Americans to keep Mussolini out of the war now began in earnest.

14

1940–3: DEFEAT

'I don't know who will win the next war, but I know who will lose it: whoever has Italy as an ally.'

German General von Fritsch in a pre-Second World War post-prandial speech to British First World War veterans in London, quoted in 'La Stanza di Montanelli', *Corriere della Sera*, 27.2.01.

Mussolini's Parallel War

Peeling an orange after dinner at the Villa Torlonia on Easter Sunday 1940, Mussolini told those present – who included his son-in-law, Ciano, and his eldest son, Vittorio – that Italy's entry into the war was inevitable. 'You will see that I shall make the Italians march,' he added. 'We do need to kill a few people,' said his wife.[1]

A week later, however, on 27 April, Mussolini told Grandi, 'I have no intention of entering the war.'[2] In 1944 he would write, 'I did not want war. I could not want war.'[3] In 1945 he would say, 'And I entered more to put the breaks on German greed than for national *cupidità* ... At Palazzo Venezia a fortune teller told me, "If you yourself command everything, even the Germans, then the war will be won; in the opposite case you will have an 85 per cent chance of losing it".'[4]

Throughout the spring of 1940 Mussolini chopped and changed. Just as two lovers cannot quite identify the moment when they fell out of love, so is it impossible to identify the moment when Mussolini decided to declare war. But the triumphs and defeats of others were decisive in bringing him to that moment.

At dawn on 10 May 1940 the German army invaded the Low Countries. Hans von Mackensen, German ambassador in Rome, had woken Ciano in the middle of the night to inform him. Together they went to see Mussolini at the Villa Torlonia just after 5 a.m. with a sealed letter from Hitler. Hitler's letter 'invited Mussolini to take whatever decisions he deemed necessary for the future of his people' in the light of the German invasion in the west.

Later that day Churchill became British Prime Minister in place of Chamberlain and Edda Ciano saw her father at Palazzo Venezia. She told him that 'the country wants war and to prolong neutrality would be dishonourable', Ciano noted.[5]

Hitler's generals had told him that the offensive in the west – he had only 52 proper divisions compared to the Allies' 130 – would be suicidal.[6] Two days later he attacked France not, as the Allies expected, from the Low Countries, or along the Maginot Line, but across the Meuse in the Ardennes. By the end of the month the Dutch and the Belgians had surrendered, the French – who had the strongest army in the world on paper – were in disarray and the British were on the run from Dunkirk. There remained the English Channel. 'By the end of the month I shall declare war. I shall attack France and England by air and by sea,' said Mussolini on 13 May. Ciano observed, 'He has decided to act and he will act. He believes in the German success and the rapidity of the success. Only a new turn in military events can induce him to review his decision ...'[7] In readiness, Mussolini secured agreement from a reluctant but ever pliant King to be made sole, not joint as before, First Marshal of the Empire and so supreme commander of the armed forces. Yet the oath of loyalty of every officer remained to the King.

For Britain and France, especially France, it was now even more important to keep Italy out of the war; an attack by Italy in the south would finish France off and Italy could cause serious trouble in the Mediterranean and North Africa. But equally it was now even more likely that Italy would enter the war. For all his talk of an army of 8 million bayonets, Mussolini knew only too well that Italy's armed forces were too weak to fight a long and large-scale war. So did everyone else in the top echelons of the regime, as is clear from a remark by Ciano on the 14th: 'We must remember that Italy is not ready to go to war, or at most a very short war.[8] Reports to Mussolini in late 1939 had warned that Italian industry would not be ready until 1949 to meet armed forces' needs for one year, though this date was revised down to 1943 in February 1940. In 1939 Italy produced only 2.4 million metric tons of steel compared with Britain's 13.4 and Germany's 22.5.[9] In addition, as soon as Italy declared war the British closed Gibraltar and Suez, which made Italy entirely dependent on Germany for raw materials.[10] But the swiftness and enormity of Hitler's military success convinced Mussolini that this was his moment; and yet also that his moment was a fleeting one. For if he did not seize it now, the war would end and the moment would be gone. Having not declared war he would be unable to demand the spoils of war. In August 1943, while in captivity, Mussolini would say, 'I had to intervene, otherwise we should have had to renounce all hope of any claims against France.'[11]

In late April Paul Reynaud, the new centrist Prime Minister who had replaced the right-wing Radical Daladier on 22 March, had swallowed his pride and written to Mussolini to offer talks on Italian claims against France. In May, Roosevelt and Pius XII made personal appeals to Mussolini to stay out of the war. Roosevelt sent messages to Mussolini on the 14, 25 and 30 May, offering initially to mediate but then threatening to increase

American help to the British and French if Italy declared war.[12]

Mussolini had been seriously inconvenienced by the British ban on exports of British coal and the Anglo-French naval blockade of German coal to Italy,[13] which had begun in November 1939. The British War Cabinet agreed to ease the blockade on 4 May, but such a gesture was irrelevant now. For as Ciano told Sir Percy Loraine, the British ambassador, on the 10th, 'Everything depends on the Allies' ability to beat off the German offensive.' This summed up precisely Mussolini's state of mind. If the Germans looked like winning, he would be in at the kill; if they did not, he would not.

Churchill wrote, 'Given the crisis which we now faced with the disastrous Battle of France, it was clearly my duty, as Prime Minister, to do everything possible to keep Italy out of the conflict though not to indulge in vain hopes, so I used all the means and influence in my power.'[14] At the suggestion of Lord Halifax, still British Foreign Secretary in the new government but still an appeaser, on 16 May Churchill wrote to Mussolini urging him to stay out of the war. In his letter he emphasised the traditional friendship between Britain and Italy, and his two friendly meetings with Mussolini in January 1927. He said that war between the two countries would never be declared 'by us'. He added, 'Is it too late to stop a river of blood from flowing between the British and Italian peoples? ... If you so decree, it must be so; but I declare that I have never been the enemy of Italian greatness, nor at heart the foe of the Italian law-giver.'[15]

Mussolini's reply on 18 May was accusatory. He said that in 1935 Britain had insisted on sanctions against Italy whose only ambition was to secure 'a small place in the African sun without causing the slightest injury to your interests and territories or those of others' and this had destroyed the friendship between the two nations. Given that Britain had declared war on Germany over Poland to honour treaty obligations, he went on, Churchill should understand why Italy now had to go to war to honour her treaty obligations with Germany.[16]

The swiftness of the collapse of the French army and the non-occurrence of a much needed miracle led Reynaud to come to London on the 26th in desperation to urge Churchill to agree that Britain and France ask Mussolini to mediate with Hitler for peace – as had happened at Munich – or failing that to bribe him with hefty chunks of their colonies to stay out of the war. They wanted Britain to offer territory as well, perhaps even some kind of arrangement over Gibraltar, Malta or Suez. Halifax, the appeaser, was in favour of the plan but Churchill was against. He felt that appeasement of Hitler was futile, as was trying to buy off Mussolini. He had the support of Chamberlain (still a member of the government despite the humiliation of Munich and now a repentant appeaser) and the majority of the War Cabinet when it discussed the matter on 27 May. As a result, Halifax threatened to resign but, after persuasion by Churchill, did not.

But it was not greed alone which motivated Mussolini. Fear played its part; fear that if he did a deal with the Allies, Hitler would attack Italy; and fear of German power after the war was over. Mussolini was allied to the country he feared most. As Sir Alexander Cadogan, head of the Foreign Office, minuted, 'Mussolini is not going to, and in fact dare not, make any separate agreement with the Allies – even if he wishes to.'[17]

Not surprisingly, when the French offered territory to Mussolini on their own he now rejected it. He told Ciano, 'Are there Italians who really believe it is possible to remain neutral? Let them tell me how ... It seems clear that we cannot draw back. After France, one day, our turn could arrive: and it would be the last straw having signed a pact which is called steel, to be invaded by Germany ...'[18]

Anyway, Mussolini had at last decided the day before that he would declare war on Britain and France on 5 June. It was too late for talks and bribes. 'In truth it is not that he wants to obtain this or that: he wants war.[19] Mussolini informed Hitler of his decision, who asked him to postpone the announcement for a few days because he wanted to put French airfields out of action first. Mussolini agreed. In 1939 Hitler wanted Mussolini's help; now, having won by himself, he did not. On 1 June the King gave his formal consent to war, telling his family that he was carrying out the wishes of the people. Like Mussolini, he thought the war would be short and profitable.[20] That he was as keen on it as so many others is shown by his passing a letter to Mussolini from Prince Filippo Doria, a Roman aristocrat and former mayor of Rome, imploring him not to declare war. This led to the imprisonment of the prince. 'I think the story about King Victor is really dreadful ... Even a Stuart king scarcely did such a dirty trick [except perhaps James II],' Harold Macmillan, when British minister responsible for the Mediterranean would write in 1945.[21]

On 27 May Mussolini had told Marshal Badoglio, Chief of the General Staff whose reaction was that war would be 'suicide', to which Mussolini replied that Badoglio lacked 'the necessary calm for an exact evaluation of the situation. I assure you that by September all will be finished and that I only need a few thousand dead to sit down at the peace table as a belligerent.'[22]

On 10 June Mussolini, in the uniform of Corporal of Honour of the Fascist Militia, announced Italy's declaration of war from the balcony of Palazzo Venezia. The speech was broadcast live by radio and relayed to loudspeakers in the piazzas of Italy, which were packed for the occasion. He said, 'The hour marked out by destiny beats in the sky over our *patria*; the hour of irrevocable decisions. ... We depart on our campaign against the plutocratic and reactionary democracies of the West, who have always placed obstacles in the way of the march, and often threatened the very existence itself of the Italian people ... We take up arms to resolve, after the resolution of the problem of our continental frontiers, the problem of our maritime frontiers. We want to break the territorial and military chains which hold us asphyxiated in our sea for a people of 45 million souls is only truly free if it has at its disposal free access to the Ocean ...' The war, he said, was the war of 'the poor and strong peoples' against those who had 'the monopoly of wealth and all the gold on the earth'. He concluded, 'There is only one categorical watchword, which is essential to all. Already it circulates and enflames our hearts, from the Alps to the Indian Ocean: win! And we shall win, so to give finally a long period of peace and justice to Italy, to Europe, to the world! *Popolo Italiano*! To arms and show your tenacity, your courage and your valliance.'[23] The response of the crowd, though enthusiastic, was not ecstatic. 'Not a single woman applauded,' noted a police report.[24] Roosevelt said, 'Today, the tenth June, the hand that held the dagger has struck it into the shoulders of his neighbour.'[25] Yet as De Felice has written, 'The common feeling of the Italians, at the end of the thirties was total faith in Mussolini, checking the figures properly, one finds that the participation of volunteers in the Second World War was greater than in the First World War.'[26] And as Churchill would say, 'When a nation allows itself to submit to a tyrannical regime, it cannot be absolved of the sins for which that regime is guilty.'[27]

All politicians, it is said, fail in the end. Mussolini's declaration of war meant that he too was now destined to fail. The decision would lead to the deaths of 300,000 Italian soldiers and 150,000 Italian civilians.[28] But at the time the precise opposite – success, not failure – seemed a foregone conclusion. 'Mussolini got his calculation wrong. It is not true that he had not calculated. He calculated, but he calculated wrong,' Bottai would write in 1943.[29] Mussolini calculated that the war would be short so it did not matter how strong or weak Italy's armed forces were, or that Italy possessed no coal, iron ore or oil of her own. Besides, he believed in his good star, his instinct, his blood – destiny.

Indro Montanelli, in the book in his series on the history of Italy dedicated to the years 1940–1943, wrote in the introduction that the writing of it filled him with more bitterness than any of the others – a bitterness caused in him not so much by Mussolini nor even his generals but by the Italian people itself; by 'the defects of our people, first and foremost their total lack of military *virtù*'. This, in his opinion was the result 'not of lack of courage, but lack of ethical backbone. It is right to place the blame on those in the High Command. But it is comfortable to place it only on them ... The Italy which on 10 June took to the field, convinced it would remain only a few days or weeks, was an Italy not only materially unprepared, but also psychologically "exhausted", tired of warlike rhetoric, and intimately *convinced that the victory would be the victory of the Germans, a much more dangerous thing than defeat* ... [my italics]. Italy has never given such a miserable performance. No chapter in its history is more humiliating, embarrassing and, especially for those who took part, more painful to recall.'[30] But with Hitler seemingly unstoppable, the Russians and Americans uninvolved, most people thought the war would be very short. Mussolini declared war not to wage war but to benefit from the spoils of that war. Consequently it hardly mattered whether the Italian people possessed military *virtù* – so long as the war was a short war. It might well have been a very brilliant decision.

Mussolini's Hundred Hours War

The number of Italian troops mobilised at home and in the colonies on the outbreak of war totalled 1.2 million.[31] Of the seventy-three divisions, however, only thirty-four could be considered efficient and only seven were properly mechanised. Of 3000 planes, only 1000 could be considered modern.[32]

The Allies expected Mussolini to make a move on Malta, defended only by three old Gloucester Gladiators, Corsica, or Egypt. Foolishly, he did not. His first military decision of the war was to order Italian troops to put pressure on, but not attack, France. He hoped the threat of a big offensive would secure territory from the French. But he was worried that if he actually attacked France he would be accused of kicking a man when he was down.

Meanwhile the King, as he had done in the First World War when he was nicknamed 'the little king' by the troops, moved to a castle near 'the front' and Ciano took part in an uneventful sortie with his bomber squadron over the Côte d'Azur in search of French targets. By telephone, exhilarated, he told Edda, 'I led my flock in an impeccable manner in the skies over Toulon, where we carried out a slaughter . . .' Edda: 'Is that all?' Ciano: 'No, dear, it isn't all. Listen . . .' Ciano then begins a long description about a British ocean liner which he had no bombs left to bomb then says, 'How's that, you don't say anything?' Edda: 'What about?'[33]

Four days after Italy's declaration of war – 14 June – the Germans took Paris and the French government moved to Bordeaux. Reynaud resigned on the 16th to be replaced by Marshal Philippe Pétain who had just been recalled as Vice-Premier from Spain, where he was French ambassador. The next day the eighty-four-year-old hero of Verdun and symbol of resistance to Germany in the First World War immediately sought what he called an honourable peace. Prior to the war, France had been close to Communist revolution and Pétain blamed the military defeat on left-wing ideology, which had weakened the fibre of the nation. In this sense the defeat was most welcome to him. It would enable the regeneration of the nation; a process which soon became called the National Revolution and whose watchwords were '*Religion, Patrie, Famille*'. Pétain, who despite his mediocrity enjoyed immense prestige and was very vain, appointed himself *Chef de l'Etat Français* – a cross between a dictator and a king – and suspended the constitution of the Third Republic. Anyway, like everyone else, Pétain believed that soon, having defeated the British, the Germans would depart.

The war in France was about to end and Italy had not fired a shot. Mussolini's thirst for the spoils of war overcame his concern to avoid the stab-in-the-back accusation. He was, after all, an Italian and, as Luigi Barzini reminded us in his classic work, the Italians have never set much store by the English saying 'Never kick a man when he is down'. Barzini wrote, 'They do not believe anybody really obeyed it. They know a man should not be kicked when he is old ... But why not "when he is down"? When else, if you please, should one kick a man more advantageously?'[34] Mussolini needed a handful of deaths and a victory, however belated and small, before it was too late. So on the 17th he ordered his forces to attack France, which they did not do until the 20th, which was too late.[35]

The next day Mussolini nevertheless went to Munich to meet Hitler and press for harsh armistice terms. In particular, he wanted France to cede Tunisia, Djibouti and Corsica to Italy, and for Italy to occupy the southeast of France and take over the French fleet. But Hitler did not think it a good idea and in addition insisted Italy sign a separate armistice with France. Hitler's own terms were not harsh. He was anxious not to encourage the French fleet to desert or for them to restart the war from their colonies, keen to keep the size of his occupation force to a minimum and hopeful even of having Pétain as an ally against the British. (This became a distinct possibility when the Royal Navy destroyed much of the French fleet at Mers-el-Kebir, killing 1300 Frenchmen on 3 July.) So Hitler allowed Pétain to govern France from Vichy and keep its colonies; and while his forces occupied the richer north and west and the Atlantic coastline, he left the rest of France unoccupied. That France might become an ally of Germany worried Mussolini. Ciano noted, 'He fears that as a result we might be defrauded of our booty.'[36]

On the 22nd Pétain signed an armistice with Hitler in the same railway carriage at Compiègne where in 1918 the French had presented the cruel peace terms to the Germans. Hitler had ordered the carriage to be brought from the museum where it was kept. Two days later the French signed an armistice with the Italians in Rome by which time all that Mussolini's troops had managed to do at fairly considerable cost – 631 dead – was to capture the outskirts of Menton at the frontier on the Riviera. Mussolini's hundred hours war with France was over. He had not attended the signing ceremony.

Under the terms of the Franco-Italian armistice the only Italian gain was the occupation of the tiny piece of France captured in the hundred hours war. Mussolini had got none of the French territory he wanted. He could have got it only if Hitler had insisted on his behalf or if he had ordered his troops to continue fighting. He would have to wait for the

German defeat of Britain and another round of talks – or act himself. Correctly, in 1944 Mussolini would single out Hitler's failure to insist that the Axis occupy the southern coast of France and French North Africa in June 1940 as the fatal error because it let the British off the hook in the Mediterranean. He would say, 'Spain would have marched in that moment. I proposed it. In Germany also others proposed it: Göring, the navy. Hitler did not want it. He was already thinking of Barbarossa [the invasion of Russia in June 1941]. He did not know what the Mediterranean was. He never understood the importance of this sacred sea, the most important in the world! He did not feel the Mediterranean!'[37]

By now the Italians had also been involved in minor action against the British in North Africa. There were 200,000 Italian troops in Libya and all that the British had in Egypt were 50,000 British and Commonwealth troops, and roughly the same number of Egyptian troops whose loyalty was open to question.[38] British naval chiefs had advised the withdrawal of the eastern Mediterranean fleet to Gibraltar. This would have happened had Churchill not overruled them. In North Africa the Italians could, if they had moved quickly, have enjoyed dramatic success. But they did not move. Balbo, Governor of Libya and world-famous flier who had a street named after him in Chicago, had opposed Italian entry into the war but, once begun, decided to fight it patriotically. On 28 June he took off from Derna in a three-engined S 79 for Sidi Azeis to review Italian troops. As the plane passed over the port of Tobruk Italian anti-aircraft batteries and an Italian cruiser at anchor opened fire on it, thinking it was British. One of the shells struck Balbo's plane which crashed, killing him and his crew. The British had been bombing Tobruk at the time so the reaction of the Italians on the ground was not entirely beyond comprehension.[39]

Immediately, as is inevitable in Italy on such occasions, the conspiracy theorists swung into action. There are still Italians today who believe that Balbo was the victim not, as was the case without doubt, of a friendly-fire accident, but of a friendly-fire plot to kill him. Mussolini was apparently unmoved by the death of the man who had been with him since the start of Fascism and who had given Fascism such a good name abroad, especially in America, but who had been one of the very few to stand up to him. This fuelled the conspiracy theories. The manner of the death of the most dashing Fascist was an ill omen of things to come. The tragi-comical uselessness of the Italian armed forces in the Second World War would be exposed all too soon. Marshal Graziano replaced Balbo as Governor of Libya and commander of the Italian forces there. Mussolini, whose aim was to drive the British out of Egypt and seize the Suez Canal, bombarded Graziani with messages urging him to attack. But Graziani procrastinated endlessly. If Balbo had lived it might have been different.

*

Once Churchill had rejected Hitler's peace offer of July 1940, only the RAF stood in the way of a German invasion of Britain and total victory. Italy had yet to fight and Mussolini spent the summer waiting for Hitler to win the Battle of Britain. For all his talk of war it looked as if he was loath to start one on his own without Hitler holding his hand.

Petacci, meanwhile, nearly died after contracting peritonitis. She was pregnant and fell ill after what was said, privately, to be a miscarriage on 18 August following an ectopic pregnancy.[40] Peritonitis, however, is usually the result, not of miscarriage, but of abortion, which was illegal in Italy. So it may well be that Petacci had had an illegal abortion, not a miscarriage. On 27 August she underwent an operation – for the peritonitis – at her parents' home in Rome, where she lived when not at Palazzo Venezia, at which Mussolini was present dressed in surgical gown, mask and gloves. He visited Petacci each day for a month during her illness[41] – sometimes two or three times a day according to his chauffeur, Ercole Boratto.[42] But apart from this short period the war meant that he saw her less and less. Nevertheless, she still came each day to the first-floor flat in Palazzo Venezia adjacent to the Sala del Mappamondo – ferried to and fro in a motorcycle with sidecar driven by one of the staff and nicknamed the 'motorcycle of love' – to wait for him.[43] During the summer, when Mussolini was at either La Rocca delle Caminate or at Riccione, she would stay with her family in nearby Rimini. Sometimes she was able to be alone with him for brief moments. Once at the beach, according to what she told a confidant, Mussolini shouted at the sea, 'I love her, this *bambina*, I adore her, know it, oh sea, I am not embarrassed to say it, she is my youth, my spring, the most beautiful thing of my life.' What attracted Mussolini to Petacci sexually was, said his usher Navarra, 'above all' her very generous embonpoint.[44]

Mussolini's wife still knew nothing about Petacci though by now many others did. The previous year, for example, Sir Henry 'Chips' Channon had referred in his diaries to news of another Petacci pregnancy – this one not known to Italian historians – the source for which was Chamberlain's sister, who had just returned from Rome and given him 'much Mussolini news'. On 2 May 1939 he wrote, 'The Duce is about to become a father. The mother is the *petite bourgeoise* with whom he has been consorting for two years or more.' The '*petite bourgeoise*' referred to can only be Petacci. This 1939 pregnancy, then, must have been a previous pregnancy which also ended either in miscarriage or abortion – unless she had the child, which is most unlikely given that no one in Italy has ever mentioned it. Sir Henry added, 'At the same time he [Mussolini] is cohabiting with the fair, south-German girl sent to Rome by the Nazis.' It is unclear who this German woman was. Sir Henry concluded, 'Given up to the practices of love he is losing touch with reality and depending more and more on Ciano, who has become impossible and is almost certainly in the pay of the Germans. Ciano is an erotic too and the whole Italian Government has become a sort of brothel, and is losing touch rapidly with the population which by and large is pro-English.'[45]

On 4 October Hitler and Mussolini met at the Brenner – the latest of many summits during the war. That month, on the 23rd, Hitler was due to meet Franco at Hendaye on the Franco-Spanish border and the following day Pétain at Montoire. By now the *Luftwaffe* had lost the Battle of Britain and Hitler had switched to bombing London. First Hitler told Mussolini that he had for the time being postponed Operation Sea Lion – the invasion of Britain. Then he told him that as he needed Pétain to collaborate the treatment of France could not be harsh and that he would urge Franco to abandon neutrality and enter the war on the Axis side. To the fury of Mussolini, Hitler was adamant about continuing to take a soft line on Pétain: the French colonies would remain under French control until the end of the war and the war had to take priority. During the summit at the Brenner, Hitler told Mussolini of his hope 'to have the French forces on our side in a continental coalition against Great Britain'.[46] As usual, Hitler's will prevailed over Mussolini's. Hitler's will, after all, was backed up by a seemingly unstoppable army.

At Montoire Hitler did not manage to persuade Pétain to join the war on Germany's side but did get him to agree, in Pétain's words, to collaborate with Germany. Nor did Hitler's will prevail over Franco. The Caudillo told Hitler that Spain was exhausted by the Spanish Civil War and he could not even contemplate war against Britain unless Germany sent him massive amounts of food and money. Had Spain declared war on Britain or even allowed German troops into Spain to march on the vital British stronghold of Gibraltar, Britain would probably have lost the war in the Mediterranean. Naturally, Hitler and Mussolini were furious with Franco who, apart from anything else, owed his seizure of power to their intervention in the Spanish Civil War. Hitler contemplated an invasion of Spain from France but decided against it. Göring, in prison at the end of the war awaiting trial, said that Hitler's greatest error was his failure to occupy Gibraltar and North Africa with or without Franco's consent.[47] Göring's view was identical to Mussolini's.

1940–1: Greek Tragedy

Mussolini's war strategy sounded, as did so much in his dazzling repertoire, wonderful. His aim was to fight what he called a 'parallel war', not separate from, but parallel to, that of Hitler, a war centred on the Mediterranean and North Africa. The aim of this strategy was to use, not be used by, Hitler's slipstream; to fight wars and win victories which were parallel. The strategy emanated from the very same things which had inspired Mussolini to sign up to the Pact of Steel: fear and greed. The pact would stop German designs on Italy and Italian spheres of influence (fear), especially the Balkans, and achieve Italian designs elsewhere (greed). It would secure gains for Italy but stop Germany making too many gains. So too would the parallel war. The parallel war was an entirely reasonable idea but it required competence on the battlefield.

It also required the war to be short. Mussolini did not want to fight, nor did he ever fight, a total war. Production in many Italian factories remained at peacetime levels, cars circulated, life went on. Full-scale rationing was not introduced until October 1941 (though bread rationing started in 1940.)[48] In May 1942 Italy's public works programme was bigger than that of any other belligerent nation.[49] As for war production, in 1943 the aim was to produce 240 tanks – the number lost on the Russian front in a single day.[50] Mussolini's near total lack of offensive military action until the autumn of 1940 was due to his desire for a negotiated solution to the war – a solution for which he would be chief mediator because of his influence on Hitler. This is why he was so keen not to see a separate peace deal such as the one offered by Hitler in July 1940 between Britain and Germany and why he opposed Hitler's policy of collaboration with Vichy France.

But the parallel war strategy was doomed to failure for a very simple reason: Hitler's armed forces had the clout to enact his aims while the Italian armed forces did not have the clout to enact Mussolini's. This meant that the only possible war in alliance with Germany was one of convergence. But until the brutal exposure of Italy's lack of military clout this was not clear. With the parallel war strategy in mind, at dawn on 28 October 1940 – the anniversary of the March on Rome – Mussolini despatched a small Italian army of 70,000 men, ominously assailed by torrential rain, into neutral Greece from Albania.[51] Ciano had for ages been telling everyone how against the war he was and how much he despised the Germans. But he had become very warlike again over Greece – just as he had been in April 1939 over Albania. For months he had been scheming to start an invasion of Greece to add to 'his' previous conquest of Albania. He had even bribed Greek generals not to fight though discarded a plan to assassinate the Greek king.[52] The invasion of Greece was Mussolini's first big decision as war leader and it was his first big mistake. Ciano called it 'my war' and it duly became known as 'Ciano's War'. But its bigger significance was that it destroyed the support of the Italian people for the war and began to eat away at their faith in Mussolini as well.

It is by no means entirely clear why Mussolini wanted to invade Greece except that, like Everest, it was there. He had never coveted it, as he had French and British possessions in relation to which at least it could be said he had some sort of moral claim. Strategically Malta, dominating the Sicilian Channel, was much more important and much easier to seize. In

June the British had been amazed when he did not seize Malta immediately. Certainly, Mussolini had never said that he wanted Greece to be Italian though he had always had his eye on one or two Greek islands such as Corfu. Nor was Greece the enemy for ideological reasons. It was a semi-Fascist state whose Prime Minister, General Ionnis Metaxas, had introduced the Roman salute, which he called the Greek salute. The Greek king, George II, however, was pro-British and the British were keen to establish naval and air bases in Greece so as to threaten Italy.

But the real reason for the invasion was that Mussolini's parallel strategy required it. He needed an enemy he could defeat on his own so that he could go to the peace table armed with a victory. He had thought first about an invasion of Yugoslavia but Hitler persuaded him against it as he was trying to get Yugoslavia to join the Tripartite Pact. A secondary but vital reason was that on 12 October the Germans had marched into Romania – as ever without telling Mussolini until the last moment – to 'protect' the oil wells there which had been supplying 7 of the 10 million tons Germany needed a year.[53] In June Russia had occupied the Baltic Republics and then the north-east of Romania. Hitler feared that Stalin would move next on the Romanian oil fields. He also feared British sabotage of them. Romanian oil had to go via Yugoslavia or Hungary to Germany and so the Balkans became a vital German lifeline. But Mussolini considered Yugoslavia and the rest of the Balkans his zone of influence. First in France, now in the Balkans, Hitler's only concern, it was clear, were his own interests not those of the Axis. As Marshal Enrico Caviglia put it at the time, Italy 'little by little, is being buggered' by Germany.[54]

Hitler's move into Romania, wrote Ciano in his diary, left Mussolini 'indignant'. He told Ciano, ' "This time I'll pay Hitler back in kind. He'll find out from the newspapers that I've occupied Greece. Thus, will the equilibrium be restored ..." ' And he added for good measure: ' "I'll hand in my resignation as an Italian if anyone makes any difficulties about beating the Greeks".'[55] Incredible as it may seem, Mussolini wanted Greece, therefore, as a buffer against both the formal enemy – Britain – and against the formal ally – Germany. His mind made up, Mussolini manufactured various spurious pretexts for propaganda purposes such as episodes of Greek violence at the border.

Yet Egypt, not Greece, was his true objective. As late as 22 August, in a military directive, Mussolini had said that Italy's priority was North Africa and the seizure of Egypt from the British and that Greece and Yugoslavia should be the subject merely of 'observation and vigilance'.[56] His aim was to dovetail the offensive with Hitler's invasion of Britain, he had told Graziani in a telegraph of 19 August, for 'maximum impact'. The loss of Egypt, he said, would be the *'coup de grâce'* for Britain.[57] But Hitler's move on Romania combined with his defeat in the Battle of Britain convinced

Mussolini to invade Greece and drop the idea of an invasion of Egypt for the moment.

On 15 October, three days after the Germans marched into Romania, Mussolini told Badoglio and the generals at a meeting at Palazzo Venezia that he had decided to invade Greece and that he wanted to do so in less than two weeks' time on the 26th (the invasion was delayed two days). He gave as his reason for the attack: 'When we have achieved these objectives, we shall have improved our position in the Mediterranean with regard to England.'[58] General Sebastiani Visconti Prasca, commander of the Italian forces in Albania, said he had 70,000 troops and was confident that these could establish a bridgehead in the Epirus which bordered Albania. According to his estimates the Greeks only had 30,000 troops. Later, to save his reputation, Badoglio would try to make out that he objected to the invasion on the grounds of lack of preparation. But the only reservation he expressed at the meeting was that a successful occupation of *the whole of Greece* would require double the number of divisions – twenty. But pressed by Mussolini, Visconti Prasca said that for the moment three more would suffice.[59] Visconti Prasca's estimate of Greek troops was out by a factor of ten.[60]

Mussolini's explanation of his Greek invasion to Hitler told only part of the story. In a letter dated 19 October and penned at La Rocca delle Caminate he informed Hitler that he was going to invade Greece in ten days' time as a pre-emptive strike against the British who had just got permission to set up naval and air bases in Greece. 'Greece is one of the cornerstones of British strategy in the Mediterranean,' he explained.[61] In the letter Mussolini also spoke at length about Italian claims on France, which were 'an essential point' and said that it was time for 'clarification of Axis-France relations'.[62] Essential to Italy, but not to Hitler. The Greek invasion was also an attempt to blackmail Hitler over France.

Mussolini knew Hitler would be vehemently opposed so did not write to inform him until four days after telling his generals and deliberately did not transmit the letter to Berlin until the 22nd, by which time Hitler was on his way to see Pétain and Franco. Hitler read it on the 25th and was furious. Determined to persuade Mussolini to drop the idea, he called an urgent summit. Mussolini agreed to meet in Florence on the 28th by which time it was too late. The invasion had begun at dawn that day. 'Why didn't he attack Malta or Crete?' Hitler wondered. 'At least that would have made some sense in the war as a whole against Britain in the Mediterranean.'[63] What angered Hitler in particular was that, having postponed the plan to invade Britain, he had made up his mind to open up his own second front: the Russian one. It was on 18 December that he ordered his generals to start planning Operation Barbarossa. If Mussolini's Greek invasion did not produce a swift victory, it would place 'his' Romanian oil wells in jeopardy and delay his invasion of Russia.

Just before his suicide in May 1945, Hitler said that Mussolini's invasion of Greece had had 'catastrophic' consequences for the Axis. He said, 'The Italians had the courage to launch themselves into the useless campaign against Greece without asking us for advice and without even warning us. The embarrassing defeats suffered by them ensured the mockery and scorn of the Balkan states ... We were forced, against all our plans, to intervene in the Balkans, delaying in a catastrophic way our attack on Russia. If the war had been conducted only by Germany and not by the Axis we would have been able to attack Russia by 15 May 1941.'[64]

But in early May 1941, with the German army still seemingly invincible, Hitler delivered a much more favourable verdict on his Italian allies when a German woman friend of his made a disparaging remark about the Italian army. He retorted, 'Germany must never forget what it owes Italy and Mussolini. We are indebted to them because we were able to militarise the Rhineland, annex Austria, and eliminate Czechoslovakia. Italy pinned down the French divisions on the Alps allowing us to conquer France, and today must bear the brunt of action by the British fleet. I would exhaust my last resources to support and defend Italy and Mussolini.'[65] In Florence, Hitler concealed his anger. More catastrophic than Mussolini's invasion of Greece, however, would be Hitler's invasion of Russia. For Mussolini, the key to victory was the Mediterranean, for Hitler, Russia. Yet a very convincing case can be made to argue that Mussolini, not Hitler, was right.

The Italian invasion of Greece was ineptly organised and, with winter approaching, badly timed. One symbol, among many, of the ensuing fiasco was the sending of a consignment of left-footed boots. Within days the invasion force, which was far too small, was in deep trouble. The proud and determined Greeks soon humiliated the Duce and forced his troops to retreat back inside Albania.

On 11 November, meanwhile, as part of plans to help the Greeks, the British dealt the Italian navy, considered among the finest in the world, a crushing blow. In a daring raid, twenty-one[66] slow and cumbersome Fairy Swordfish – 'stringbags' – from the aircraft carrier *Illustrious*, torpedoed a flotilla of Italy's finest fighting ships at anchor in the Gulf of Taranto, Puglia, wreaking havoc. Three battleships, including the *Littorio*, the pride of the Italian navy, were put out of action as a result.

Mussolini's own planes had finally arrived in France in the second half of October 1940 – 200 of them. On the same day as the Fairy Swordfish had gone into action at Taranto they saw action for the first time over Britain when ten Italian bombers and eight fighters took part in a daylight raid on Harwich – ten were shot down. This was the only significant operation they took part in. The *Luftwaffe* found them more a hindrance than a help and urged their withdrawal, which happened in January 1941. The chilly northern weather caused serious performance problems for both the planes and the crews.[67]

On 20 November Hitler wrote Mussolini a sharp letter in which he warned of the 'grave consequences' of the unfortunate Greek campaign for the Axis. In addition to planes, Mussolini had also sent troops to the channel coast and Hitler urged him to withdraw them as well because, he said, they were not suited to the cold climate. This especially upset Mussolini. On 22 November, in his reply, he had to admit that his troops in Greece had been forced to retreat. He blamed the bad weather, the Albanians who had deserted and the Bulgarians who had refused to join in after saying they might. The weather was indeed a problem. But the real problem was the generals. They had misled him on 15 October at that meeting at which Visconti Prasca had told him he had enough troops. They had told him the Greeks would not fight and once the Italian army had gone in, they were guilty of tactical and logistical ineptitude. Mussolini also blamed the bourgeoisie. Constantly, he lamented that he had failed to eradicate the bourgeois spirit and *la vita comoda* (to appreciate this favourite expression of his one has to imagine him delivering the words in a speech with a capricious sneer). For Mussolini, Fascism remained an anti-bourgeois revolution whose aim was to eradicate the bourgeosie. 'If, when I was a Socialist, I had not had a purely theoretical knowledge of the Italian bourgeoisie dictated by the reading of Karl Marx, but a genuine physical notion such as I have now, I would have launched a revolution so pitiless that, by comparison, that of Comrade Lenin would have been an innocent joke,' he told Ciano.[68] Ironically Ciano, his son-in-law and Foreign Secretary, was the epitome of *la vita comoda* he so despised. Grandi called his hatred of the bourgeoisie his 'white Bolshevism'.[69]

By now, the Italian High Command on the ground in Greece was in a state of psychological collapse. Rightly, Mussolini sacked the reptilian Badoglio as Chief of the General Staff on 4 December. Badoglio's replacement, General Ugo Cavallero, immediately travelled to Albania to try to set things right. With the terrible winter, the Greek counter-offensive slowed and the front stabilised somewhat in a manner of the First World War. The Italian forces settled down to a deeply unpleasant Christmas in the mountains of Albania. It snowed that Christmas in Rome too. In the comfort of his office at Palazzo Venezia Mussolini opined, 'This snow and cold are very good because as a result the pipsqueaks will die and this mediocre Italian race will be improved.'[70] On 23 December 1940 Churchill, hoping to incite the Italian people to overthrow Mussolini in the wake of the Greek débâcle, broadcast a Christmas radio message to them in which he said that 'one man, one man alone' was responsible for Britain and Italy being at war and for Italian military humiliation: Mussolini. In part this was correct; though one man alone was hardly to blame for Italian military failure. 'Italians, this is the point to which one man has brought you; one man alone!' said Churchill.[71] On 22 December Goebbels noted in his diary, 'The Italians have brought the entire military prestige of the Axis crashing down in ruins.'[72]

On 9 February 1941 the Royal Navy and carrier-based planes bombarded and bombed Genoa, killing 144 and wounding 272.[73] A considerable part of the Italian fleet, which was at nearby La Spezia, failed to come out to engage the British. There was no sign of the Italian air force either. But in a speech in Rome on 23 February Mussolini said, 'Soon the spring will be here, and as the season, our season, demands, so will arrive *il bello* ...'[74] Massive Italian reinforcements were sent to Greece – their total reached 550,000 at its peak.[75] They made no difference.

There was bad news too for Mussolini in North Africa where on 13 September Graziani, who had used gas and gained glory in Ethiopia, had finally attacked the British with his force of 200,000 men. At first he enjoyed some success and got as far as Sidi Barrâni well inside Egypt. Mussolini was 'radiant', noted Ciano.[76] Hitler offered Mussolini two armoured divisions to press on towards Suez. But for the sake of his parallel war Mussolini refused. Then, on 9 December, the British counter-attacked, took back Sidi Barrâni, and quickly forced the Italians to retreat well inside Libya, seizing Tobruk, Benghazi and Derna. The British had only 30,000 troops[77] but won because they had superior armour and air power, and displayed a certain *audace*. Graziani was 300 miles behind the front. He now told Mussolini it would be better if he retreated a further 600 miles! By the end of January 1941 the British had taken 130,000 Italians prisoner. If they had carried on they would undoubtedly have taken all of Libya as well. But they did not. On 8 February Graziani handed in his resignation on the grounds that recent events had 'seriously affected his nerves'. Mussolini accepted.[78] Graziani had pursued a strategy of building defensive redoubts in the desert – a similar concept to that which lay behind the Maginot Line in France. But success in the era of the tank, especially in the desert, depended on mobility. True, Italy had few tanks and the few it had were no use. So perhaps Graziani can be forgiven. But whose fault was the lack of useful tanks? To rub salt into the wounds of Mussolini, the British counter-attacked in East Africa as well in January 1941 and swiftly forced the Italians out of Kenya, Sudan and British Somaliland, bits of which they had briefly occupied.

The British then invaded Ethiopia. In September 1940 Amedeo of Savoy, Duke of Aosta and Viceroy of Ethiopia, had noted, 'Today in the entire Empire, which is six times bigger than Italy, there are six anti-aircraft batteries (of which four are obsolete) ... As for fighter planes we have thirty or so perhaps.' Despite this, at around the same time Badoglio, who perhaps should have known better given that he had conquered Ethiopia and had yet to be sacked as Chief of the General Staff, had said, 'I have no worries about the Empire.'[79]

By April 1941 the Italians – who, although badly equipped and led, vastly outnumbered the British – had surrendered in Ethiopia and Haile Selassie was back on his throne after just five years in exile. There had, however, been moments of Italian heroism in Ethiopia. As for the Duke of Aosta, he insisted on carrying on the fight with 7000 men in the north and did not surrender until 17 May. Taken prisoner, the duke would die of tuberculosis on 3 March 1942 in Kenya. Another Italian force held on to Gondar – the town Starace claimed to have captured in 1936 – until 27 November. Soon after its fall, Mussolini told Ciano, 'The dead in Gondar, in November, are 67, the prisoners 10,000. There is no need to reflect too much, to understand what those figures mean.'[80]

Mussolini's war in Africa, as in Greece, had been an unmitigated disaster. The strategy of the parallel war had failed, though Mussolini tried to pretend otherwise. On 17 January 1941 he ordered all Fascist gerarchs to do a stint at the front without exception, to set an example to the Italian people. This meant that while they were away the government consisted of him alone. The next day he set off by train with Ciano – temporarily excused from the front – for yet another summit with Hitler, this time at the Berghof, the 'Eagle's Nest', in Berchtesgaden. Hitler had planned to invade Russia in May but now agreed to try to bail out his mentor in North Africa and Greece. This delayed Barbarossa. Grudgingly, Mussolini accepted the offer of military help from Hitler and agreed to try, where Hitler had failed, to convince Franco to enter the war on the side of the Axis. Hitler was kind and courteous to Mussolini, and seemed genuinely moved, even, about the Italian military failures.[81] Throughout 1941, however, work on the Italian fortifications in the Alps against German invasion would continue apace.[82]

Shortly afterwards, Ciano encountered Mussolini's wife who was worried about the way the war was going, he wrote, because she felt 'that the barometer signals a storm ... She complained that all the starlings – which she loves to hunt – have deserted the pine trees at Villa Torlonia.'[83] Later that year Ciano would write, 'It seems that she goes snooping about dressed as a bricklayer, peasant and God knows what' and 'She is in a state of unjustified and continuous hyper-excitement. Her arguments are of little importance. She could live quietly, but instead embitters her days by futile controversy.'[84]

On 12 February 1941 Mussolini met Franco at Bordighera on the Italian Riviera and, like Hitler, failed to make any headway. But by now the Italians had been stopped dead in Greece and the British had launched a very successful counter-attack against them in North Africa. If Franco had been convinced of a swift Axis victory he might have joined in at the kill – but not now. Ciano, meanwhile, managed to spend his stint at the front from late January to April 1941 with his bomber squadron at Bari in Puglia.

There, he carried on with what mattered most to him: having a good time. On his birthday – 18 March – he and friends sang, danced and let off fireworks in the streets until the small hours in complete disregard of the curfew. Mussolini got to hear about it and, to humiliate Ciano, ordered a general to conduct an inquiry.[85]

In February 1941, a small German tank force under the command of Erwin Rommel had begun to arrive in Libya. For the sake of face, this Afrika Korps was formally under Italian command but Hitler made sure that in reality it was under German command. The issue of who commanded these and other German forces sent to assist Mussolini mirrored the issue of who commanded the war as a whole. The more German troops sent to the Italian theatres of war, the less control Mussolini exercised over them. Hitler's generals had tried to persuade him that such troops should be formally under German command as well. But as a sop to Mussolini, for whom he still felt admiration and warmth, Hitler overrode them. The Afrika Korps comprised 40,000 men compared with the 150,000 the Italians had left in Libya. But it had a small number of good tanks. With this German help, the Italians at last began to make military headway in North Africa. The Afrika Korps, in combination with the Italians, counter-attacked at the end of March against the wishes of General Italo Gariboldi, the Italian Commander-in-Chief. Remarkably, given the recent capitulation of the Italians, by the end of May this Rommel-led Axis force had driven the British back well into Egypt, apart from at Tobruk, which it bypassed. It did not help the British that they had transferred a hefty slice of their already small force in Egypt to Greece. But Rommel's success was proof, not that it was needed, of the feebleness of the Italian High Command and the effectiveness of tanks and of *audace* – an aggressive rather than defensive strategy. He was unable, however, to press on further into Egypt, because *matériel*, which had to come via Italy, was not forthcoming. Lack of *matériel* – the result of Hitler's obsession with Russia – would always be Rommel's problem in North Africa and in the end cause his defeat.

Mussolini desperately desired a victory in Albania against the Greeks before the Germans who had begun to arrive in Bulgaria with King Boris's permission on 1 March took matters into their own hands. So on 2 March, he decided to go in person to the front in an S 79 which he piloted himself escorted by twelve Macchi 200 fighters. He took off from Bari in Puglia because he had been at Bisceglie where in order to supervise the campaign better than in Rome he had latterly installed himself in a farmer's cottage in the midst of olive groves after refusing numerous offers of more luxurious accommodation.

In Albania, his generals noted how nervous he was about the reception his troops would give him. But everywhere he went the troops cheered. The front was in the mountains, which were like the Carso on the Austro-

Italian border where he had served in the First World War. At his insistence, on the 9th his generals launched an offensive of sorts – the long-awaited 'il bello' spring offensive. But the offensive ground to a swift halt. 'The bourgoisie has betrayed me,' he was heard to murmur.[86] On the 15th he left for Valona. He had received news that the hospital ship, Po, at anchor in the port of Vlore, had just been sunk by British planes with his daughter, Edda, who had joined the Italian Red Cross on board. Edda was reading P. G. Wodehouse in her cabin at the time. 'I remember there was a wonderful moon ... the lifeboats were damaged and could not be launched. ... I climbed on the rail and let myself fall into the water,' she said. Edda survived unhurt, shaken but not stirred. 'Someone recognised me. A sailor gave me a bottle of cognac ... I emptied half the bottle in one gulp and almost immediately felt revived.'[87] Edda spent as much of her war as possible, however, in the Ciano villa on Capri where she dressed scantily, drank and gambled. 'The Countess has not even given up dancing,' noted a police report.[88] Edda referred to such things as 'my caprices'.[89] Like Edda, Ciano lived for the night. For as Bottai noted, 'The evenings of Galeazzo are long and empty. This man who does not smoke, drink, or gamble, has as his vice a loquacious nightwandering [nottambulismo ciarliero] amidst easy women and obliging men.'[90]

By now, Hitler was ready to invade Greece but had to redraw the plan rapidly to include the simultaneous invasion of Yugoslavia. Between November 1940 and March 1941 he had persuaded Hungary, Romania and Bulgaria to join the Tripartite Pact, which had been signed jointly by Germany, Italy and Japan in September 1940 – supposedly as a defensive alliance against international Communism. Hitler thought he had Yugoslavia in the bag as well when the regent, Prince Paul, signed the pact on 25 March 1941. But two days later pro-British Yugoslav generals staged a coup and deposed Paul, and installed instead Prince Peter, the eighteen-year-old heir to the throne (son of King Alexander who had been assassinated in Marseilles by Pavelić's Croat terrorists in 1934), as King.

The Germans invaded Greece and Yugoslavia on 6 April – a Sunday (they had invaded Poland, Norway and France on a Sunday). Yugoslavia surrendered to the Germans on the 18th, the Greeks on the 20th. The Greeks refused to surrender to the Italians but the Germans forced them to for the sake of face. Mussolini's propaganda agencies then tried to pretend that the Italians had played a vital part in the victory. True, in the end they had advanced in Albania but only because the desperate Greeks had withdrawn to fight the Germans. As Churchill, in a radio broadcast on 27 April, said, 'Here surely is the world record in the domain of the ridiculous and the contemptible. This whipped jackal Mussolini, who to save his skin has made of Italy a vassal state of Hitler's empire, goes frisking up to the side of the German tiger with yelps not only of appetite – that could be understood – but even of triumph.[91]

The Greek fiasco had cost the Italians 13,755 dead and 50,000 injured, and the Greeks 13,000 dead and 42,000 injured. In the two weeks it took the Germans to do in Greece what the Italians had failed to do in nearly six months they lost just under 2000 dead.[92] In May German paratroopers captured Crete from the British, who outnumbered them ten to one. That month, on the 16th, out of the blue, Mussolini dismissed Starace as Commander of the Fascist Militia. Rachele Mussolini had informed him that a member of the militia had orders to take Starace's four dogs for a daily walk in Rome. Mussolini told Starace of his decision by letter in which he merely said, 'I consider closed your cycle in the function of *Capo di Stato Maggiore* of the Militia.'

The Balkans, which Mussolini had always regarded as his own sphere of influence, were more or less entirely under German control. The invasion of Greece was the first and last military campaign that Mussolini would undertake on his own initiative – the start and finish of his parallel war.

Things were as bad for Mussolini at sea. On 28 March the British and Italian fleets engaged seriously for the first time off Cape Matapan in southern Greece. The Italian navy, despite the losses at Taranto, was still formidable. But crucially it did not have radar or aircraft carriers. The British ships and carrier-based planes sank several Italian destroyers and numerous other vessels in the action, which led to the loss of 3000 Italian lives.

The Axis powers divided up the occupation of Yugoslavia and Greece between them. Croatia remained nominally free *à la* Vichy, with Ante Pavelić, the leader of the Ustase, the Croatian Nazi Party, becoming dictator – but Italy annexed much of the Dalmatian coast and, with the backing of Vittore Emanuele, appointed the King's cousin, Aimone, Duke of Spoleto, as King of Croatia (reluctant to go, Aimone never did). Pavelić and his Ustase had begun to round up and massacre Jews in Croatia. But the Italian army intervened to protect them. It thus saved thousands of Jewish lives in Croatia, as it would save them elsewhere, notably in France.

But during its first year at war Italy had failed to secure a single significant military victory. Yet when he spoke to the *Camera dei fasci* on 10 June to mark the first anniversary, Mussolini was remarkably upbeat. Britain could not win the war, he said, because it had no ally in Europe and was not present there. He was right but everything was about to change because within less than a fortnight Hitler invaded Russia. He added, 'It is *assolutamente* mathematical that in April, even if nothing had happened to alter the situation in the Balkans, the Italian army would have overwhelmed and annihilated the Greek army.' The war, he concluded, was between the forces of blood and gold. Blood, the Axis, the revolutionary force, would win. 'The just God, who lives in the souls of young nations, has decided: we shall win,' said Mussolini.[93]

But in truth Mussolini was angry, in particular he was angry with the

Germans and Hitler, and what had happened in Greece and the Balkans. Before his speech he had told Ciano, 'I ... feel nausea for the Germans ... and personally I've had my fill of Hitler and his way of doing things. I don't like these meetings proceded by a ring of the bell: you use a bell to call waiters. And then what sort of meetings are they? I have to put up with a boring, near useless monologue for five hours... Meanwhile I will continue with the fortifications in the *Vallo Alpino*. One day they'll come in useful.'[94] He also said at about this time, 'We must put thousands of guns along the rivers of the Veneto, because it will be from there that the Germans will launch the invasion of Italy and not across the ravines of the Alto Adige where they would be easily crushed. But we must hope for two things: that the war is long and wearing for Germany and that it finishes in a compromise, that saves our independence.'[95]

Barbarossa

In the small hours of 22 June 1941 2 million German soldiers[96] invaded Russia, taking Stalin by surprise and, of course, Mussolini. As recently as 2 June Hitler and Mussolini had met at the Brenner where Hitler had told him nothing about the plan. Ciano, also there, wrote, 'The general impression is that for the moment Hitler does not have a precise plan of action. Russia, Turkey, Spain are all subsidiary elements ... Even the Duce is convinced that a compromise peace would be welcomed by the Germans with the warmest enthusiasm. "They are already tired of victories. Now they want the Victory that will give peace".'[97] Apart from the usual secrecy each Axis partner displayed towards the other, this comment of Mussolini's illustrates how little he knew or understood Hitler.

At 3 a.m. on the 22nd Prince Otto von Bismark, of the German embassy in Rome, woke Ciano to hand him a letter for Mussolini from Hitler. Mussolini was on holiday at Riccione on the Adriatic, miles from Rome. Ciano telephoned him. The letter said that having 'taken the big step' Hitler felt 'once again spiritually free'. Hitler, by now only too familiar with the problem, made a point of not asking for Italian troops to help him. Instead, he said that 'decisive help, Duce, you might always furnish by reinforcing your troops in North Africa.' Mussolini was taken completely by surprise. 'This is pure madness; it's *cretinismo*, improvisation ...' Mussolini told Nino d'Aroma, director of Luce, the state cinema newsreel organisation.[98] On 6 July he told Ciano, 'Note in your diary that I foresee a crisis between Italy and Germany as inevitable ... I now seriously ask whether a British victory would not be more desirable for our future than a German victory. Meanwhile the English are flying over Germany even by day – and that makes me very happy. Because – since we shall have to fight the Germans – we must create the myth of their invincibility. That notwithstanding, I have little faith in our race; at the first bombardment that might destroy a famous campanile or a Giotto, the Italians would go into a fit of artistic sentimentality and throw up their arms.'[99]

Nevertheless, he wrote immediately to Hitler congratulating him on making war on Communism as well as pluto-democracy. He was confident that unlike previous failed invaders Hitler would win, he said, because he had motorised transport. Furthermore, he insisted on sending Italian troops to Russia because of his habitual obsession with trying to pretend that Italy and Germany were equal partners in the alliance, that wherever Hitler seemed about to secure victory he too had to be present, that in this way he could exercise more control over Hitler. The Germans sent a total of 3,050,000 troops to Russia in all. The Russians had a total of 4,700,000 troops. The Italian contribution was puny by comparison. The first of the 62,000 Italian troops to fight in this initial phase of the Russian campaign under the name, *Corpo di spedizione italiano in Russia* (CSIR), left Italy by train on 26 June. As usual, they were badly equipped and badly armed, though for once their Commander-in-Chief, General Giovanni Messe, was a good soldier.[100] Hitler's invasion of Russia caused his interest in seizing Egypt and Suez to dwindle. Mussolini would have been far better off using the troops he sent to Russia in North Africa. But nevertheless among Italians, war against Russia was more popular than the war against Britain. To the average Catholic, Communist Russia was a much greater evil than Capitalist Britain. As it was to the average Fascist.

Despite his letter of congratulation to Hitler, Mussolini was 'exalted' when the Germans suffered their first setbacks in Russia. On 1 July he told Ciano, 'I hope for only one thing … that in this war in the East the Germans lose many feathers. It's a falsity to talk about an anti-Bolshevik struggle. Hitler knows that Bolshevism has not existed for some time. No code protects private property like the Russian civil code.'[101] In December, when the first setbacks began Ciano noted: 'The Duce is happy at how the war is going in Russia: by now he talks about it openly, and the failure of the German troops delights him.'[102] Only with hindsight was it clear that Barbarossa was a fatal error. Beforehand, both Hitler's generals and British Intelligence thought he would triumph within six weeks, given the general view that Communist Russia was incompetent.[103] To begin with it looked as if this would happen. By mid-August his troops had nearly reached Leningrad in the north and Kiev in the south, and were halfway to Moscow in the centre.

A personal tragedy did nothing to dampen Mussolini's rekindled enthusiasm for war. Indeed, it caused the opposite. On 7 August his son, Bruno, died at the age of twenty-three[104] when the new bomber he was test-flying at Pisa crashed after its undercarriage failed to come down on landing.[105] It was typical of the Italian war effort that Bruno, like Balbo, had died not in combat but in an accident. The conspiracy theorists were as swift off the mark with the death of Bruno as they had been with the death of

Balbo. They included Rachele Mussolini but not Mussolini. Mussolini wrote a tribute to his dead son, entitled *Parlo con Bruno*, published a few weeks later, as he had when his brother Arnaldo died in 1931. In it he listed the minutiae of Bruno's career as a pilot serving Fascism, the war, his war, him. He wrote, 'I ought to convince myself that it was a perfidious trap of destiny, but from time to time a secret voice presents me with the distressing alternative: trap or predeliction of destiny?' Of Bruno's life, he wrote, 'My "Live dangerously" was how you lived your life.'[106]

In the dying days of August Mussolini travelled with his eldest son, Vittorio, by train to meet Hitler at the Wolf's Lair -the Führer's headquarters at Rastenburg in East Prussia. The two dictators spent the next two days cavorting by plane and train from one part of the Russian front to another. At one point Mussolini persuaded Hitler to let him pilot the plane they were flying in – a four-engined Condor. Back down on the ground, Mussolini reviewed Italian troops at the front 400 miles inside Russia. He returned to Rome content. Ciano, off sick from the war between July and September as a result of his chronic throat problem (so he said), returned to the fray in late September. He noted that despite Bruno's death he found 'the Capo well, physically and spiritually' and his dominant theme 'the military progress of the war'.[107]

But as autumn turned to winter the Russians retreated ever further east, sucking the enemy along in their wake and stretching his lines of supply – the tactic that had defeated Napoleon. A German unit reached the outskirts of Moscow in early December. It was the furthest east the Germans would get. The advance petered out in the perishing cold which sometimes reached 50°C below. That winter the Russians counter-attacked and the Germans suffered their first setbacks of the campaign. In early December Mussolini wrote to Hitler, offering to triple the number of Italian troops in Russia. Hitler, whose plan to defeat Stalin by winter had failed, for once accepted.

On 7 December the Japanese bombed Pearl Harbor. 'Mussolini was happy, for a long time he has been in favour of a clear taking of sides between America and the Axis,' wrote Ciano.[108] Immediately, America and Britain declared war on Japan. Hitler and Mussolini, on the other hand, might have declared war on Japan, even though it was their ally, given their views on the dangers of the yellow peril. But Hitler regarded Japan as useful against Britain and Russia. Mussolini duly fell into line. On 11 December Germany and Italy declared war on America. Ciano handed Italy's declaration of war to the American chargé d'affaires in Rome (the ambassador was absent) who could not believe it. 'He thought I had called him to discuss with him the arrest of some journalists,' wrote Ciano.[109] It was obvious now to the Italian people that the war was not going to be a short war at all. It was now a world war as well. Their faith in Mussolini and Fascism was to be put to an even more severe test.

Mussolini had jettisoned Starace in October 1939 as PNF General Secretary and now in his last big decision of 1941 decided to appoint a twenty-six-year-old, Aldo Vidussoni in that position. Vidussoni, a law student who had a mutilated hand and a *medaglia d'oro* after serving in Spain, was a complete unknown. His elevation to the second most powerful job in the regime was a vain attempt to rejuvenate the PNF and hence the war effort. The dilemma which Italian military failure forced many Italians to confront was: *patria* or *fascismo*? If the nation was more important, Fascism would have to be sacrificed. For young Fascists, however, those Italians born into Fascism in whose minds the two were one, this dilemma did not exist. There was no question of deserting Fascism. Fascism, for all its faults, they felt was a superior system to democracy and Communism. Like Mussolini, young Fascists despised above all the bourgeoisie – the phoney Fascists. The war was 'the pretext ... offered by providence' for a 'surgical operation' on Fascism, wrote a young Fascist, Fidia Gambetti, in 1942. Once over, 'the revolution will recommence with full vigour, with young blood, its journey', he added. For young Fascists like Gambetti the war was a revolutionary war, which would signal the triumph of the left-wing essence of Fascism – a revolution within, not against, Fascism.[110] But what counted was victory. So Vidussoni's appointment was utterly without point except as a gesture. He is remembered, if he is remembered at all, for upsetting Ciano with a suggestion that golf clubs should close, given that there was a war on. It was far too late anyway for root and branch reform of the PNF whatever the age of its general secretary.

Only victory could rejuvenate the PNF – Italian victory. Victory alongside Germany, Mussolini had realised too late, would be nothing of the sort for Italy. The more successful Germany was on the battlefield the more he feared Germany. In October 1941 he had told Ciano that before the war Hitler had regarded Italy as a 'faithful ally, mistress of the Mediterranean, as Germany was mistress of the Baltic' but after it was won Italy would become Germany's vassal: 'The defeated states will be genuine colonies. The associate states will be confederated provinces.' Yet he felt powerless to resist the process. He added, 'We must accept this state of affairs because every attempt at reaction would cause us to be demoted from the status of a confederated province to something worse than a colony. Even if they ask for Trieste tomorrow for the German vital space, we would have to bow our heads.'[111] This in a nutshell was Mussolini's brutal dilemma. Meanwhile, he banned the Italian press from commemorating Christmas in 1941 as it was both bourgeois and Anglo-Saxon.[112]

1942: The Turning Point

From the Axis point of view, however, the situation did not look too bad at the start of 1942 all things considered: the Japanese had scored remarkable successes against the Americans and British in the Far East, and for once things were looking up even for the Italians in the Mediterranean. This was largely due to German help – but not entirely. In late 1941 Hitler had agreed to divert prized but scarce U-boats to the Mediterranean.[113] These immediately made their presence felt by sinking the British carrier *Ark Royal* at Gibraltar. Hitler also sent a decent number of planes to Sicily, which caused serious problems for the Royal Navy and would nearly bomb Malta into submission in April 1942. But for once the Italians themselves had something to crow about: the mini-sub nicknamed '*maiale*' (pig). Essentially, the *maiale* was a torpedo with a timer, piloted very slowly to the target by two frogmen, who then swam off as best they could before it exploded. The most spectacular success of the *maiale* came on 18 December 1941 at Alexandria when three *maiali* put two British battleships, the *Valiant* and *Queen Elizabeth*, out of action.

In November 1941 the British had counter-attacked once more in North Africa and regained some lost ground – but given the huge numerical advantage of the British – they had 700 tanks to Rommel's 174 German and 146 (obsolete) Italian tanks – it was a pretty feeble performance.[114] But Hitler sent Rommel more tanks and men and in January 1942 Rommel replied in kind. Like Hitler, Rommel was a believer in the lightning strike and was now impatient to launch the big thrust to victory which he planned to do in June. The Italian High Command, however, correctly believed that the Axis should seize Malta first.

Malta – lying in the narrow channel separating Tunisia from Sicily – was crucial to the British for two reasons: it was a key link in their supply line from Gibraltar to Egypt and a perfect base from which to strike out at the Axis supply line from Italy to Libya. Mussolini should have seized it from the British in 1940 when it was defenceless but did not. It was of far more importance strategically than Greece, though far less obvious a prize. Now, in 1942 its seizure became a cause célèbre for General Cavallero, Chief of the General Staff. Correctly, he believed that unless it was taken, the Axis supply line to North Africa would be fatally endangered. The Desert Fox, however, had other ideas. He agreed that Malta should be taken first, but if not, his June offensive had to take place regardless. Later, in his memoirs, he would claim untruthfully that he had always insisted Malta be taken first.[115] Between June 1942 and January 1943, 43 per cent of the petrol supplies and 16.7 per cent of the war *matériel* destined for Libya were sunk by the British.[116]

Nevertheless, the Axis High Command drew up a plan, Hercules, for a joint invasion of Malta. During April from its bases in Sicily the *Luftwaffe* pummelled Malta hoping to bomb it into submission without the need for an invasion. They nearly succeeded, but the British clung on. On 29 and 30 April Mussolini, Hitler and the generals met at Schloss Klessheim, Salzburg. Mussolini was keen to talk about Malta. But Hitler, as usual on such occasions, droned on and on, mostly about Russia. Mussolini looked at his watch, General Wilhelm von Keitel nearly dozed off and General Alfred Jodl after an epic struggle, actually did. Eventually, Mussolini was able to get in a word about Malta. Hitler prevaricated and subsequently sided with Rommel. Hercules was postponed.

Rommel was wrong about Malta, as he would find out. He launched his North African offensive early, as was his wont, on 26 May.[117] He made slower than usual progress because of fierce resistance by the British but by 15 June he had reached Tobruk. Meanwhile, the Italian navy delivered a major blow to the British when between 14 and 15 June it attacked two vital convoys bound for Malta – 'Harpoon' from Gibraltar, and 'Vigorous' from Alexandria. Only two out of the six convoy ships in 'Harpoon' and two out of the seventeen in 'Vigorous' reached Malta. In addition, in the engagement of 'Vigorous', German U-boats and the *Luftwaffe* sank five of its Royal Navy escort ships.[118] As a result, the British suspended all convoys to Malta. On the 20th Rommel attacked and overwhelmed Tobruk, taking 32,000 British and Commonwealth soldiers prisoner, and Hitler promoted him to field marshal. The Italian rank and file had acquitted itself well and earned Rommel's admiration. But he held Italian generals, whom he considered snobbish and incompetent, in contempt.

Now, if ever, was the ideal time to take Malta. On the 21st, the day of the surrender of Tobruk, Mussolini wrote to Hitler, 'The action on Malta becomes more than ever necessary . . .'[119] But Rommel had the bit between his teeth and was determined to press on in North Africa to total victory. An invasion of Malta would have required the diversion of resources from there, and delay. The seizure of Tobruk persuaded Hitler that Rommel could take Egypt within days and he sided with him. Replying to Mussolini he said, 'The English 8th Army is practically destroyed . . . If now our forces do not continue to the utmost limit of what is possible into the heart of Egypt itself . . . the situation will alter for us unfavourably . . . This time Egypt can be, under certain conditions, wrenched from England. The consequences of such a strike will be of world importance! . . . If, Duce, in this historic hour, which will never be repeated, I can give you some advice straight from my eager heart, it is this: order the continuation of the operation until the complete annihilation of the British forces. The Goddess of Fortune passes only once to warriors in battle. Anyone who does not grasp her at that moment can very often never touch her again.'[120] Hitler's talk of glory and the Goddess of Fortune had won Mussolini over. To soothe Cavallero's nerves over Malta, Mussolini promoted him to marshal. The plan to seize the island was postponed yet again – fatally never to be resurrected. In 1944 Mussolini would blame the loss of North Africa on the Axis failure to seize Malta and control the Sicilian Channel, 'which might well be called the graveyard of the Italian mercantile marine'.[121]

Convinced by Hitler that nothing could stop Rommel, especially when Cavallero telegraphed him to say the same, now Mussolini flew to Libya on 29 June, complete with his Sword of Islam, ready to preside over the victory. Rommel had reached El Alamein – sixty miles from Alexandria. The British prepared to evacuate Cairo. Mussolini could not ignore that the imminent victory would be Rommel's. Even so, the majority of Rommel's troops were Italian and at least Mussolini could win a propaganda victory with a triumphant march into Cairo. But even Rommel felt unable to go on. He needed reinforcements and supplies, and the Italian soldiers, many of whom were on foot, were exhausted.[122] The British, meanwhile, unlike the Axis, were able to bring in reinforcements and tanks quickly. Back in Libya, Mussolini was forced to wait, as he had had to do in Albania the previous year. His trip had begun badly with an ill omen when his barber, who went everywhere with him, died en route in a plane crash. Rommel avoided meeting him, saying he was too busy. Three weeks later, on 20 July, Mussolini flew back to Rome, via Athens, deeply frustrated.

In captivity, in August 1943, he would say, 'The wheel of fortune ... turned on 28 June 1942, when we halted before El Alamein ... The Germans have never grasped the importance of the Mediterranean, never ... they maintained and still maintain that Russia is a deadly peril to Western and European civilisation. I tried in vain to convince Hitler this was a meaningless phrase ... Stalin has killed Bolshevism ... In contrast to Trotsky he has completely renounced world revolution.'[123] Mussolini was right.

On the 22nd he seemed as concerned that Hitler do something about the starvation he had seen in Athens as North Africa because such starvation was bad press for the New European Order the Axis talked so much about. The brutality and economic exploitation so typical of German occupation everywhere merely caused hatred of the Axis among the populations of those countries occupied. Mussolini was angry with the Germans on this as on so much else. He realised only too well that the jackboot alone was not enough to ensure the foundation of the New European Order. The political war had to be won as well. In October 1942 Ciano would write, 'Mussolini is very worried about the behaviour of the Germans in the occupied countries and especially in Greece. ... He said, "... if we lose the war, it will have been the result of the political bestiality of the Germans who have not wanted to use common sense and restraint and who have made all Europe ardent and treacherous like a volcano".'[124] Hitler replied to Mussolini's letter blaming the starvation on the Greeks and going on about the Russian priority.[125]

Mussolini's terminal political decline dates from the failure of Rommel to advance in July 1942. It coincided with a serious decline in his health. On his return to Rome from Libya he fell ill with terrible stomach pains, which were diagnosed initially as amoebic dysentery. Between August and October Mussolini spent most of his time at Riccione on the Adriatic or at La Rocca delle Caminate, apart from three brief visits to Rome. After he continued to lose weight and show no signs of improvement his family became increasingly worried. For years he had stuck to a strict diet since his first serious stomach trouble during the Matteotti crisis of 1925. Lunch typically consisted of potato pureé, a tiny amount of grilled meat, a little spaghetti sprinkled with parmesan cheese, a glass of watered-down red wine and fruit – according to Pietro Carradori, one of his police bodyguards from 1937 and his personal bodyguard from 1942. Each day at 5 p.m., he drank a cup of unmilked tea with a slice of lemon and two spoonfuls of sugar.[126] On 10 September Professor Sir Aldo Castellani, who had treated Mussolini since 1925, saw him and he too said the problem was an amoebic infection.[127] By 26 September Edda was sufficiently worried – after a night out on the town – to write to Ciano from Capri, 'Dear Gallo [Italian for cockerel but also short for Galeazzo],' she began. '... My father is not well – burning in the stomach, irritability, depressions etc. ... in my opinion we're back on the track of the ulcer ... Radiographs of every type have been done – all negative ...'[128] Two days later, Professor Cesare Frugoni, Mussolini's clinical consultant, was called in. He decided that the illness was a resurgence of the stomach problem of old, complicated by the amoebic infection. He appointed Professor Arnaldo Pozzi to visit Mussolini every day to oversee the treatment and accompany him on trips out of Rome.[129] (This stomach problem of old is diagnosed as an ulcerous duodenal disease [*affezione ulcerosa gastroduodenale*] by a doctor consulted by De Felice which would not have been diagnosable on a live patient because the endoscope did not exist.)[130] But the doctors who did the autopsy on Mussolini in 1945 found only minor atrophic gastritis. Pozzi prescribed sedatives and benzoate of soda.[131]

But Mussolini continued to be ill and to lose weight. By now he had lost about a quarter of his body weight.[132] Professor Frugoni began to fear that Mussolini might have cancer. Dr Petacci, Petacci's father, meanwhile, though not involved in the diagnosis, remained certain that the cause of the pain was psychosomatic. As for Mussolini's wife, she was convinced that the doctors were useless and forced yet another doctor on him on 17 January 1943 at La Rocca delle Caminate. Miraculously, Mussolini got better – though he would suffer a relapse, which caused his doctors to order him to rest for most of June 1943. Bottai had written on 7 October after seeing him, 'But the man does not seem so much ill as dejected and saddened, no longer fighting triumphantly against age ... He has in himself killed the man that he was ... The man who had *sempre ragione* has, by now, for most people, *sempre torto*.'[133]

Celebrations for the twentieth anniversary of the March on Rome on 28 October 1942 – before the war Mussolini had told Hitler that he could not go to war until after they had finished! – were muted, given the circumstances. On 21 October, Hitler wrote,

> I am quite clear that your historic March, twenty years ago, introduced a turning point in world history. The fact that our democratic opponents do not grasp this is not exclusively due to their ill will, nor is it based on the selfish interests which they represent. For just as the deaf can hardly understand the greatness of a musical genius or the blind the beauty of a picture and thereby appreciate the significance of its creator, even less can the average and spiritually hidebound leaders of the ordinary middle-class parliamentary system, even with the best will in the worlds, judge the greatness of an historical turning point ... I am perfectly convinced, Duce, that you were the first man to succeed in combating Marxism not by police methods but by overcoming it through a force able to create a new state and community. You removed the mass of its followers and bound them to a new idea ... I have often studied in retrospect the phases of your Fascist revolution, and I am always convinced anew that fate must have willed that two men and two revolutions in Europe should determine the features of the New Age...

This was Hitler's build-up to an apology for not being present because he felt unable to leave his advance headquarters in the Ukraine where he was living 'in solitude' and 'unhappily tied more and more to the telephone and the tape-machine'. Mussolini's reply on 1 November was short: 'Unfortunately our enemies took pleasure in disturbing the solemn occasion – on purpose – by massive bombardments on Milan, Genoa and Savona.'[134] One of the justifications for the carpet bombing of Italian cities by the Allies was that it would stir up anti-Fascism in the Italian people. It did not have this effect when it hit non-military targets, as it so often did, such as Renaissance city centres and major works of art such as the Mantegna frescos in Padova.[135] The Italians were resigned to the war, as they had been resigned for centuries to foreign invasion. They were not thinking of taking up arms against Mussolini, however much they wanted the war to end.

El Alamein was as far as Rommel would get. While waiting for reinforcements and supplies, he went on holiday. On 24 September he met Mussolini at La Rocca delle Caminate where Mussolini had retreated in an attempt to recover from his stomach illness. Bottai, who saw Mussolini at this time, noted his 'grey face, deadly pale, drawn cheeks, tired eyes, mouth twisted in bitterness ... The man appears, more than tired, mortified, wilted ...'[136] The *Luftwaffe* planes which had nearly bombed Malta into submission in April 1942 had now gone to the Russian front. Malta had become once more a haven for British supply convoys and a mortal threat to Axis supply convoys. Rommel told Mussolini that he needed at least two more divisions and thirty days' petrol in reserve.

On 23 October, Lieutenant-General Bernard Montgomery counter-attacked at El Alamein. He had a huge superiority in men and weaponry, and could hardly fail to win. He had 230,000 men; Rommel 80,000 – mostly Italian. He had a huge advantage in tanks – 1440 to 540 (260 German) and planes – 1500 to 350. Rommel, still on holiday, hurried back to the front, arriving on the 25th. Nevertheless Montgomery made heavy weather of it. In three days he lost 600 tanks, Rommel 150. But after twelve days, Rommel had to retreat.[137]

During the night of 7–8 November,[138] an Anglo-American force invaded French Morocco and Algeria without telling de Gaulle for fear that the news would get back to the collaborationist Marshal Pétain or that he would try to interfere. Soundings had convinced them that the French would not oppose them. By chance, however, Admiral Jean François Darlan, Pétain's head of government from December 1940 until August 1942 and still Commander-in-Chief of what remained of the French armed forces, was in Algeria at the time.[139] But Darlan, no doubt influenced by the size of the invasion force, decided to order non-resistance. Some French units did resist but were soon dealt with. Six weeks later Darlan was assassinated in mysterious circumstances.

Since 1940, Mussolini had been trying to convince Hitler that the Axis must occupy the whole of France and French North Africa because of the importance of the Mediterranean to the outcome of the war and the completely untrustworthy nature of the French. Hitler, however, having meted out military humiliation on France in 1940, had appeased France ever since, thinking this would at the very least stop her causing trouble for the Axis and at best turn her into its ally. Then he had turned his mind to Russia. Events had now proved Mussolini right. On 3 January 1943 he told the PNF directorate, 'Only by wanting deliberately to delude our-selves, could we have thought that a policy *di favore* towards France would have achieved results. France has hated us, hates us and will hate us until the end of time.' In the same speech he said, 'He who does not feel the need to do a little war, for me is not a complete man. War is the most important thing in the life of a man, like maternity in that of a woman ... Only war reveals the nature of a people, the flaws which it carried inside, which went unnoticed by mediocre and superficial observers ... History offers no other possibility for a comparative examination between peoples ... This year will decide if the Italian people has a future or not, if the Italian people must resign itself to being a people of tourists, a large Switzerland ... or a people which is conscious of what it has been, but above all what it must be.'[140] In 1944 he would write that 'the prime origin of the disaster was French and goes back to one date – 8 November 1942'.[141]

The Allies now had sizeable armies in North Africa either side of the Desert Fox and for the first time the Americans were in action in the

European theatre. If only the Führer had granted Mussolini's earlier request to occupy adjacent Tunisia, he lamented, the invasion of Algeria could not have happened. If only the Axis had seized Malta. King Vittorio Emanuele, who had gone along with Mussolini since the March on Rome, now tried to distance himself from what Professor Sir William Deakin has famously defined as 'the brutal friendship' between Mussolini and Hitler. Hitler, his attention momentarily distracted from Russia, finally did what Mussolini had wanted him to do from the start: he ordered the immediate occupation of the whole of France on 11 November without consulting Pétain. The same day a German force moved swiftly into French Tunisia – all that lay between the Anglo-American invasion force in Algeria and Tripoli – the last Axis redoubt in North Africa. The Italians arrived in Tunisia the next day. The Italians, it was agreed, would occupy the southeast of France and Corsica, which they did by fishing boat. What remained of the French fleet was at anchor in Toulon but on the night of the 26–27 November – just before the Germans arrived to seize it – the French blew it up. In November the British also carried out heavy bombing raids on cities in the north of Italy. In Russia, as the Germans faced a second winter there, the catastrophe began to unfold.

Stalingrad

Hitler had 70 per cent of his armed forces tied down in Russia.[142] In the summer of 1942, to bolster his own modest contribution, Mussolini had sent a second much larger army to Russia – known as the *Armata italiana in Russia* (*Armir*) or Italian 8th Army – totalling 150,000 men – under the command of General Gariboldi who had performed ingloriously in North Africa and tried to stop Rommel's offensives. Gariboldi was given command as well of the Italian army already there – the Csir – which meant that he was able to give orders to the competent General Messe who had commanded thus far and had experience of the situation. There were now 230,000 Italian troops on the Russian front.[143] In theory, Gariboldi was in charge not just of Messe but of the Italian forces; in practice, however, as in North Africa, the Germans were.

These troops would now be sacrificed for the sake of Hitler's obsession and Mussolini's failure to break free from Hitler – as if Hitler held him in a trance. Hitler had soon had to abandon the original plan of capturing Moscow and in March 1942 drew up another plan – 'Case Blue' – for a great offensive in the south towards the Volga, on which stood Stalingrad, and the Caspian Sea. The aim was to capture the oil wells of the Caucasus, which supplied 30 million tons of oil a year.[144] Hitler set up a new headquarters at Vinnitsa in the Ukraine to be nearby. First the German army had to repulse several major Russian offensives, which they did. 'Blue' began on 28 June, but it did not go according to plan. By July Hitler was referring to his generals as 'sausages' and by September refusing to dine with them.[145] But the worst was still to come.

In the Ukraine the Italian forces included the Savoy Cavalry Regiment. To them goes the honour of the last successful cavalry charge in history. This took place on 24 August 1942 through fields of sunflowers on the banks of the River Don near Isbusenskij. It was copy-book stuff, beginning at a trot, moving on to a gallop and finally the charge itself to the cry of 'Savoia!'. There were 650 of them and they put the enemy, 2000 Siberians equipped with heavy machine-guns, to flight. They lost 32 dead; the Siberians 150. In addition they took 500 Siberians prisoner. The Germans, for once, were impressed with the Italians. But the last charge of the Savoia made no difference to the outcome of the war in Russia.

A week later, on 1 September, the German 6th Army, commanded by General Friedrich Paulus, attacked Stalingrad, which by now had become the key to everything. He failed to take it and laid siege to it. But it held out. Then, on 19 November, the Russians who had amassed an enormous force for the task, broke through the Axis line to the north-west of Stalingrad, in the part held by the Romanians. Swiftly they swept south and east, so encircling and trapping Paulus's 6th Army, which numbered some 250,000 men. Attempts to save the 6th Army failed. By the end of January 1943 the Russians had defeated it and on 2 February the last of its remnants surrendered. One hundred and fifty thousand Germans had perished and the rest were taken prisoner of whom only a few thousand came back.

On 2 December Mussolini made his last speech to the *Camera dei fasci e delle corporazioni*.[146] He said, 'I have the vague impression that a good part of the Italian people would like to hear my voice again.' His main target was Churchill 'from whose mouth, fetid with alcohol and tobacco, come out such wretched vilenesses' and the British people which, when you took away 'tea at five', was still 'the primitive barbarian Briton with his skin painted in various colours'. Quoting Carlyle on the British, he added, ' "No human race, from Adam on, is covered with such dirty rags of lies as ours. But we wear them proudly and haughtily like a sacerdotal vestment or a royal mantle".' He said that the war was 'sacrosanct' because at stake were 'eternal values … the to be or not to be'. He also disclosed (highly conservative) figures for Italian military and civilian casualties to date – 40,000 dead, 37,000 missing and 232,000 taken prisoner, and that in the British bombings of the industrial cities in the north 1986 had died and 3332 been injured.[147]

In mid-December it was the turn of the Italians to suffer catastrophe on the Russian front when the Russians attacked the Italian 8th Army – the Armir – positioned along the River Don, adjacent to the defeated Romanian army and to the north-west of the German 6th Army at Stalingrad. Within days the Russians had routed the Italians.

By now, Mussolini had begun to believe that the only way out was to make peace with Russia so that the Axis could concentrate on what he was convinced should be its main task: the defeat of the Americans and British in the Mediterranean and North Africa. Already, on 7 November 1942, Mussolini had told the German military attaché in Rome that 'we must make a separate peace with Russia as soon as possible'.[148] Mussolini was right. But that was not the point. Increasingly he confronted Hitler on the matter. But Hitler would not listen. Bottai saw him on 15 December and found him 'unshaven, his face livid and shrunken'.[149]

At this time – 18–20 December – Ciano and Laval had talks with Hitler at the Wolf's Lair, his forest headquarters in Rastenburg, East Prussia, where it got dark very early. Mussolini had felt too unwell to make the journey. He had at least told Ciano to impress upon Hitler the importance of peace with Russia. Hitler would not listen. He said, 'We are at war for world civilisation.' In private, Alfieri told Ciano it was necessary at all costs to break with Germany. 'Ciano looks at him with tired eyes ... then lets fall these textual words: "Nothing, nothing! It remains only to wait for the collapse".'[150]   Of the 230,000 Italians who served on the Russian Front, 95,000 were missing by the end of the campaign. Only now, after the collapse of Communism, has it been possible for Italian historians to establish precisely what happened to them. About 25,000 had died in combat. The other 70,000 were taken prisoner. Of these, about 20,000 died on the forced marches or train journeys to the Russian concentration camps and about 40,000 died in the camps themselves. In some camps the death rate was 500 a day. Cannibalism was common because of lack of food. About 10,000 Italian prisoners survived the horror to return to Italy.[151]

The Italian Communist party had sent a representative, Vincenzo Bianco, to indoctrinate the captured Italian soldiers. He wrote to Togliatti, who was the leader of the Italian Communist party even though still in exile in Russia, to say, 'How can I convince the Italian prisoners to sign up with the PCI (Italian Communist party), if their Russian jailers do not even give them anything to eat, they make them die of deprivation?' In February 1943 Togliatti, who because of his membership of the Comintern was perhaps in a position to do something for the Italians, replied from Moscow, 'In practice, however, if a large number of prisoners die as a result of the reality of the hard conditions, I have absolutely nothing to say. So much the better. And I'll explain to you why. There is no doubt that the Italian people has been poisoned by the imperialist and villainous ideology of Fascism ... The poison has penetrated into the peasants, the workers, not to mention the *piccola borghesia* and the intellectuals, in short, it has penetrated into the people. The fact that for thousands and thousands of families Mussolini's war, and above all the expedition in Russia, is ending in tragedy, with personal bereavement, is the best, the most effective of antidotes ...' The two letters only saw the light of day in 1992 when published by the Italian press.[152] Initially Italy's post-Communists angrily tried to dismiss the Togliatti letter as a forgery, but in the end they had to accept that it was genuine.

That Christmas, once again, Mussolini was badly ill with stomach pains and spent Christmas Day in bed at Villa Torlonia. To begin with his doctors once again feared that he had cancer but in the end resorted to the usual diagnosis of a chronic gastric ulcer aggravated by nervous tension.[153] On 11 January, Mussolini was due to have one of his usual twice-weekly audiences with the King but cancelled and left Rome for La Rocca delle Caminate. There, two specialists saw him and diagnosed acute gastritis caused by nervous tension.[154]

Mussolini and the Jews

What marks Hitler out as evil, rather than just another aggressive leader keen to seize territory, was not a thirst for military conquest. It is the Holocaust. Yet Mussolini was not anti-Semitic, nor was Fascism, unlike National Socialism, an anti-Semitic ideology. Indeed, Mussolini did much to save Jews from Hitler. The idea of Mussolini building gas chambers to exterminate Jews is inconceivable. He did not even dislike Jews. Equally, Britain and France did not declare war on Germany to save Jews, but to save Poland. Nor did Mussolini declare war on Britain and France to kill Jews. The Holocaust, as it must, clouds the issue.

The turning point in the war, 1942, was also the year that saw the start of the systematic extermination of the Jews by the Germans. Professor Norman Stone writes, 'In 1942, Hitler set himself to extinguish the Jews of Europe ... Even so, we do not really know what Hitler's part was in this work.' What set the Holocaust apart from standard ethnic cleansing was its industrial nature and in particular the use of gas. At the so-called Wannsee conference in January 1942, it was decided, in Stone's words, that those Jews 'who could work, would work; those who could not would receive "the logical treatment", that is, they would be gassed'. The deportations of Jews from the Axis and Axis-occupied countries to the death camps, which were all in the occupied East (as distinct from concentration camps such as Dachau in Germany), began soon after the Wannsee conference. Systematic exterminations in these camps continued until November 1944 when Himmler, the head of the SS, gave orders for them to stop. Those who died afterwards died of malnutrition and disease.[155]

But Italy was the only Axis-controlled country in Europe, apart from Denmark, that did not deport Jews. Furthermore, in the Italian occupied territories – parts of Yugoslavia, the south-east of France and the south of Greece – the Italians did not round up Jews for deportation and in many cases stopped those who tried. In France the French had been only too willing to round up the Jews, even in unoccupied Vichy. In 1939 there were 330,000 Jews in France. But already by November 1942 when the Axis powers occupied the whole of France, the French had collaborated in the deportation of 42,000 of the total 75,721 Jews deported.[156] That was pretty good going since the deportations from France had only begun in July 1942. But the Italians prevented the French from carrying on with their *rafles* in the sector of France they controlled – the south-east. They also cancelled the Vichy law which required Jews to wear the yellow Star of David in public.[157] An Italian Foreign Office memo to the Italian Consul-General in Nice said, 'It is not possible to permit the forcible transfer of Jews. The measures to protect the Jews, both foreign and Italian, must be taken exclusively by our organs.' Similar instructions were sent to all *departements* in the Italian zone. To ensure that Jews were not arrested, the Italians insisted that only they could arrest Jews, not the French police or Milice.[158] In Nice, for example, the commander of the Italian *carabinieri* ordered his men to use force against the French police who had turned up at the synagogue in Boulevard Dubouchage to arrest any foreign Jews.[159] Such actions caused Jews to flood into the Italian zone. In May 1943 alone, 4500 foreign Jews sought refuge in the Isère *département*.

In June, the Italian authorities began actively to save foreign Jews who had sought refuge in the zone under their occupation south and east of the Rhone. In March 1943, for example, they told the Vichy authorities in Valence, Chambéry and Annecy that they would not arrest any foreign Jews. In June 1943, they blocked the arrest by the Vichy police of 7000 foreign Jews in Mégève. Of the total 75,721 Jews deported from France to the death camps only 24,000 were French Jews – the rest foreign.[160] But the Italians also did their best to save French Jews. On 14 March 1943, General Maurizio Lazzaro De Castiglioni, Italian commander in Isère, gave written orders to the *département*'s Vichy Prefect to stop the arrests of all Jews. 'The arrest of Jews of whatever nationality, even French, is the task of the Italian military authorities,' the general wrote. In Athens, the Italians did not require the Jews to wear the yellow Star of David in public either and General Carlo Geloso, commander of the 2nd Army, placed guards at the synagogue to protect Jews from Nazi-supporting Greek students.

Hitler did not inform Mussolini at any point of the 'final solution'.[161] But it is certain that Mussolini knew that the Germans had begun the systematic extermination of Jews by the summer of 1942. On 17 August, von Mackensen, the German ambassador in Rome, sought approval from Mussolini to order the round-up and deportation of the 3000 Jews who had taken refuge in the Italian sector in Yugoslavia.[162] That same day Prince Otto von Bismarck, a senior diplomat at the German embassy, had secretly revealed to the Italian Foreign Office that Jews deported to the camps in Poland were being systematically killed. Ciano informed Mussolini of this in a memo on which Mussolini wrote *'nulla osta* ... M' (no objection).[163] On the 24th the Italian Foreign Office informed von Mackensen of Mussolini's *'nulla osta'*. But in Italian government circles, at least, *nulla osta* by itself was not an order; it was a delegation of responsibility to those on the ground – the army.[164] Italian generals and officials in Yugoslavia refused to deport Jews. Subsequently they used the full armoury of Italian bureaucratic trickery to ensure that none were deported. Professor Jonathan Steinberg writes, 'A long process which began with the spontaneous reaction of young officers in the spring of 1941 who could not stand by and watch Croatian butchers hack down Serbian and Jewish men, women and children ended in July 1943 with a kind of national conspiracy to frustrate the much greater and more systematic brutality of the Nazi state. It rested on certain assumptions about what being Italian meant.'[165]

In July 1942 a senior Italian Foreign Ministry official noted in his diary the 'monstrous' measures taken against Jews in Holland and France which offended 'in the most brutal way human dignity'.[166] In October 1942 Vidussoni, the twenty-six-year-old PNF Secretary, who had returned from a visit to the Ukraine in September, wrote a memo to Mussolini in which he said that Italians there had told him that the executing of Jews was 'the order of the day' and that 'whole towns and villages' had seen their populations decimated 'principally by the elimination of the Jews'. He added, 'At Minsk, in the Opera House, we saw the piled-up effects of thousands and thousands of Jews killed, which will, it seems, be distributed to the population.' A 4 November 1942 memo from the Foreign Ministry to Mussolini, annotated with the words 'seen by the Duce', said that according to an Italian general on the spot, deported Jewish Croats from the German sector of Yugoslavia had been killed 'by the use of toxic gas'. In early 1943 the Foreign Ministry compiled a dossier of evidence on the German extermination of the Jews in Poland, which it sent to Mussolini.[167]

But everywhere, Italian government officials and senior army officers saved Jews from the Germans and others. Mussolini did nothing to stop them; indeed, he encouraged them. There were good political reasons for this, apart from humanitarian ones, which echoed Mussolini's ill-fated attempt to fight his own parallel war. By defending Jews, Mussolini hoped to undermine the reputation of Germany in the occupied territories. But in any case, as with German brutality generally, the deportation of Jews, even if their fate remained unclear, was suicidal from a propaganda point of view. As Franco, who never introduced anti-Semitic laws, told the Italian ambassador in Spain, Baron Giacomo Paolucci di Calboli, on 28 June 1943, 'How is it possible that the German government does not realise that the more it insists on such a course of action the more the Jews ... will react by creating abroad every type of hatred and obstacle to Nazi politics and the German people?'[168] Franco, like Mussolini by now, was also of the view that only Russia would benefit from a continuation of the war and that the only way to stop Russia was for the Allies to make peace with the Axis. Paolucci di Calboli added, 'The Caudillo is convinced that if Stalin's troops should break through the barrier of the Axis forces, Europe will be irremediably submerged under the Slav terrorist horde, regardless of the good intentions of Signor Roosevelt and Signor Churchill to impede them.'[169]

The Germans put increasing pressure on Mussolini to round up and deport Jews but he did not comply. When pressed by, among others, Himmler who saw him in October 1942 and Ribbentrop who saw him in February 1943, Mussolini said that he would ensure compliance with their requests. But he did not. After Ribbentrop's visit, for example, which he said had 'bored him rigid in every sense',[170] he told his generals in Yugoslavia to round up Jews and send them to Trieste for deportation. But a few days later he telegraphed to say, 'It is true that I have been obliged to give my consent to the expulsion. But you can use all the excuses that you like, so as not to hand over a single Jew. Say that we don't have the means to transport them by sea to Trieste, and that transport by land is impossible.'[171] But another document makes it even clearer that Mussolini was behind the Italian effort to save Jews from deportation – nowhere more so than in France. On 21 March 1943, the Italian Supreme Command in Rome issued orders to its generals in the Italian-occupied south east of France which said: 'As regards the measure proposed by *Il Duce* in reference to the Jews: no.1 priority is to save Jews living in French territory occupied by our troops whatever their nationality, be they Italians, French or foreigners.'

Mussolini also saved many non-Jewish political enemies from the Germans, notably his old Socialist friend Pietro Nenni. The Gestapo had arrested Nenni in Paris and decided to deport him to the East.[172] Mussolini intervened and he was deported instead to the tranquil island of Ponza in the Bay of Naples where he had a balcony overlooking the sea. The late Bettino Craxi, the leading light of Italian Socialism in the 1970s and 1980s and the first Socialist Prime Minister in Italy (later disgraced as a result of his involvement in the big political corruption scandals of the 1990s), knew Nenni well. In 1998 Craxi told a newspaper, 'Mussolini always protected the anti-Fascists. In his heart he remained a Socialist. He saved the life of Nenni.' Craxi said that he had once asked Nenni about this. 'Yes, he did for me what he did for other anti-Fascists,' replied Nenni. 'He meant: it is not what you think, it is not because we were friends of old; the fact was, Mussolini was like that,' said Craxi.[173] By the time of his overthrow in July 1943, Mussolini had not deported a single Jew from Italian-occupied France, Yugoslavia and Greece – or Italy.[174] When the Germans installed their de facto occupation of Italy in September 1943 there were about 50,000 Jews in Italy. Around 8,000 would now be deported to the Nazi death camps[175] – of whom only 837 came back alive.[176]

In October 1943, however, the Allies were not so protective or even concerned about the fate of Italy's Jews as Mussolini had been. On 6 October MI6 intercepted a coded German radio message from Berlin to SS Major Herbert Kappler, head of the Gestapo in Rome, saying that the Germans were about to arrest and deport the Jews in the Italian capital. Furthermore, the message said that these Jews were to be 'liquidated'. The message was deciphered at Bletchley Park.[177] The deciphered message was one of a number in late September and early October concerning the Jews of Rome whom the Nazis had decided to exterminate. Many German diplomats and senior army officers in Rome, however, opposed their planned arrest and deportation. It would seem that the deciphered message was sent as a result of protests to Ribbentrop from Friedrich Moellhausen, German consul general in Rome, that unless Ribbentrop himself authorised the operation, General Rainer Stahel, German military commander in Rome, would not authorise it.[178] Ribbentrop's insistence that the operation go ahead caused Moellhausen to inform Ernst von Weizsäcker, German ambassador to the Holy See, who told the Pope. Though he did not protest publicly, Pius XII gave secret orders to open Vatican-owned religious houses in Rome outside the Holy See to the Jews. As a result, a total 477 Jews were given sanctuary inside the Vatican itself and 4238 in Vatican-owned monasteries and convents in Rome.[179] Nevertheless, on 16 October the Germans arrested 1259 Jews out of the total 7000 Jews in Rome and held them in the Collegio Militare near the Vatican. About 200 of those arrested managed to secure release. But on the 19th the rest – 1000 – were deported to Auschwitz-Birkenau. Fifteen came back alive after the war.

Despite the interception of the German message by MI6, neither Churchill nor Roosevelt intervened during the ten days between its despatch and the round-up of the Jews. At the very least they might have broadcast a cryptic warning on the radio about the fate in store for the Jews of Rome. No doubt they had their reasons. Perhaps they worried that by making public their knowledge of it they would alert the Germans that they could crack their codes. Perhaps they knew that the Vatican had already warned the Jews. But once the round-up had happened, they might also have thought it their duty to issue a public protest at this, the first deportation of Jews from Italian soil. They did not. They too chose silence.

Pius XII is often criticised for not speaking out in public against Hitler, especially over the treatment of the Jews on this and other occasions. Indeed, his critics see his silence as the main obstacle to his becoming a saint. John Cornwell, for example, the best-known of late, writes that 'plain speaking might have made a difference'.[180] For the October 1943 round-up of Jews, Cornwell writes that he relies on the account by American journalist, Robert Katz, *Black Sabbath: A Journey Through a Crime Against Humanity* (London, 1969), because it 'remains the most authoritative account'.[181] But Cornwell does not mention that Pius XII's niece sued Katz for defamation – and won – over his claims that Pius XII was guilty of culpable silence in regard to an earlier book on the subject by him called *Death in Rome* (New York, 1967). In Italy, unlike in Britain, you can libel the dead. The court gave Katz a thirteen-month suspended sentence.[182] Regardless of the fact that Pius XII's actions in private on this occasion alone saved the lives of thousands of Rome's Jews, his silence, say his many critics, was culpable. There was, in addition, a moral and spiritual duty to speak out, they say. But were not, then, Churchill and Roosevelt also guilty on this occasion and elsewhere – there were many other occasions – not just of culpable silence but of culpable inaction? If, instead, Pius XII had chosen the path of valiant public protest, what then? What practical result would that have achieved? As Stalin famously said of the Pope: how many divisions has he got? Though the level of knowledge remained confused and incomplete, everyone knew by late 1943 what fate awaited captured Jews. So what – unless you could do something about it? Certainly, the Pope could not. True, little could be expected of Stalin, who was as guilty as Hitler when it came to the extermination of his enemies. But did Churchill and Roosevelt, who knew as much as the Pope, actually do anything? No. Critics of Pius XII say that if he had made a public protest, this would have created public outrage because he was a man 'who commanded the allegiance of half a billion human beings and whose capacity to protest could have given even Hitler serious pause for thought.'[183] Such a view is very naive indeed. Can anyone seriously believe that Hitler, as a result of papal protest, would have cancelled or toned down the Holocaust?

The Pope's public silence on the Holocaust was, it is true, a renunciation of moral and spiritual leadership. But against that must be taken into consideration the practical results which the silence enabled Pius XII to achieve *dietro le quinte*. For what public protest by the Pope would also have done is put at risk the work he, the Vatican and the Catholic Church were doing and would continue to do in secret to save the lives of Jews. This is because it would probably have led to his imprisonment and the seizure of the Vatican and its property elsewhere by the Germans. Hitler's instinctive reaction to the overthrow of Mussolini in July 1943 was not just to invade Italy, which he did, but to seize the Vatican and kidnap the Pope. He was restrained with difficulty.[184] On 26 July 1943, the day after Mussolini's overthrow, he told his generals, 'Do you think the Vatican impresses me? I couldn't care less. We'll clear out that gang of swine.' In September 1943 he told SS General Karl Wolff, commander of the SS and German police in Italy, to draw up a plan to seize the Vatican. Eventually, Hitler dropped the idea – claimed Wolff – after Wolff advised him that it would cause an extreme negative reaction in predominantly Catholic Italy.[185]

Wolff's statement is periodically wheeled out by critics of Pius XII such as Cornwell to show that Hitler would never have seized the Vatican and, that being the case, Pius XII had no excuse for remaining silent. The first problem with this argument is that Wolff was a notoriously unreliable and devious witness. Second, how was the Pope to know what Hitler would do? But third, even supposing that what Wolff told the tribunal is true, if the Pope had now begun to protest publicly against Hitler, the Vatican seizure plan would no doubt have been revived. For as the noose tightened, Hitler became increasingly barbaric in Italy as elsewhere – as all tyrants are in such situations – regardless of negative reaction on the part of the populace. If Hitler had seized the Vatican, Pius XII would not have been able to do anything at all to help the Jews even in secret. Such an outcome would have harmed, not helped, the Jews – not to mention Catholics. Breach of silence would also have caused Hitler to step up persecution of Catholics in Germany and the occupied territories. But this did not happen and it has been estimated that the Catholic Church saved the lives of 860,000 Jews in all during the Second World War.[186] The critics of Pius XII, who tend to be Anglo-Saxon, see morality in black and white. Pius XII, on the other hand – like Italians, like Catholics – saw it in colour. To entitle a book, 'Hitler's Pope' is not just inaccurate – it is obscene. He was also, by the way, silent in July 1944 when the Stauffenberg bomb failed to kill Hitler. The Nazis said that this silence signified his tacit support for Stauffenberg![187]

The Plot Thickens

Mussolini had lost his parallel war as soon as he had started it and to stay in the war had been forced to fight Hitler's war. But Hitler had also been sucked into Mussolini's war. Now, partly as a result, Hitler was losing his war as well. But Hitler would lose his war in the end because it was the wrong war, Mussolini's the right war.

By now, Ciano had begun to put out tentative peace feelers to the British via neutral Lisbon. Eden, once more British Foreign Secretary after replacing Halifax in December 1940, quickly snuffed these out.[188]

Mussolini had begun the war refusing help from Hitler; by now he was begging him for it. And as defeat followed defeat, the cracks in the Home Front became even bigger. His reaction was to try to paper over the cracks by sacking those in the key positions within the regime.

First to go was Marshal Cavallero, Chief of the General Staff, at the end of January 1943, replaced by General Vittorio Ambrosio. But as Ciano noted, 'I don't believe even a Bonaparte could perform miracles.'[189] By now, the Allies were on the verge of invading Fortress Europe via Italy –

the soft underbelly of Europe, as Churchill called it. Cavallero's view was that Italy should fight Germany's war. Ambrosio's view was the opposite – but it was too late by now.

After Cavallero, it was the turn of the politicians – in total the heads of nine of the twelve ministries not held by Mussolini – most notably Ciano, Grandi and Bottai.[190] On 5 February Mussolini saw Ciano and told him that he had decided to take over the Foreign Ministry personally. Instead, he offered his son-in-law various alternatives such as the lieutenancy of Albania, the ambassadorship in Berlin or at the Holy See. Ciano chose the Holy See. Three days later Mussolini saw Ciano again at Palazzo Venezia and told him, 'Your future is in my hands and as a result you can remain calm.' In November 1942 he had asked Ciano if he still kept his diary adding, 'it will serve to document how the Germans in the military and political field have always acted behind his back'.[191] Now he asked Ciano if all his documents were in order. ' "Yes" – I reply – "I have them all in order and remember, when the hard times come and by now it is certain that the hard times will come, that I can document one after the other all the betrayals perpetrated by the Germans to our cost, from the preparation of the conflict to the war on Russia communicated to you when the troops had already crossed the frontier ..." He has invited me to visit him often. "Even every day." The meeting was cordial. Which I am happy about because *a Mussolini voglio bene, molto bene* and the thing that I will most miss is contact with him.'[192] These were the last words written by Ciano in his diary, which ceases at this date.

Mussolini went back to La Rocca delle Caminate on 13 February and remained there until the 24th. He was ill again. On the 25th he returned to Rome to meet Ribbentrop, who had a sixty-page letter from Hitler, drafted on the 16th. Hitler's number one obsession remained Russia and he filled many pages with his plans for a new offensive. Peace with Russia was out of the question wrote Hitler 'since of course the Russians cannot be trusted'. But in addition Hitler had now become obsessed with the idea that the Allies would attack Fortress Europe through the Balkans rather than Italy or France; and that to repulse the invasion the Axis forces there had to 'exterminate' internal resistance first, whether Tito's Communists or Mikhailovic's Nationalists. Italy may have suffered its severest defeats in Russia and North Africa but it had by far the greatest concentration of troops in the Balkans. In November 1942 Italy had a total of ninety divisions deployed as follows: nine in France, Corsica and Tunisia; ten in Russia; twelve in Libya; twenty-six in Italy and its islands; but thirty-three in the Balkans and the Dodecanese.[193]

Mussolini's reply to Hitler's letter illustrates the quite different priorities of the two dictators. Just as Hitler was obsessed with Russia, Mussolini was obsessed with North Africa. He wrote, 'We must remain, at whatever the cost, in Tunisia. ... To obtain all this, Führer, I shall never tire of repeating, requires that the Axis aviation in the Sardinia, Sicily, Tunisia zone is at least *equal* to the enemy aviation.' Furthermore, he added, 'I wonder if it is not too much of a risk to repeat the struggle against the infinite space of Russia which is practically impossible to reach and grasp, while in the West, the Anglo-Saxon peril increases.'[194] On the 26th Mussolini wrote again to urge a concentration of the Axis war effort in the Mediterranean and Tunisia. For the first time he was blunt about Russia. He said, 'We must then in one way or another liquidate the Russian chapter ...'[195] But Mussolini felt unable to make a separate peace with Russia. He told the Hungarian Prime Minister – who had come to Rome to convince Mussolini that Italy and the smaller Axis powers must make a separate peace with Russia – in early April, 'if autumn fails to bring victory [in Russia], then – and only then – your line of thought can be considered.'[196]

Hitler demanded another face to face at Schloss Klessheim, outside Salzburg, which duly took place between 7 and 10 April. En route by train, Mussolini's stomach pains returned. During the journey Bastianini suggested that peace feelers should be made via third parties to Russia and Britain. Mussolini agreed these could be considered.

On arrival, Hitler tried to persuade Mussolini to see his doctor, Professor Theo Morell, but he refused. His illness, he told Alfieri who was with him, was simple; it was called 'convoys'.[197] But one day was lost because Mussolini was too ill to take part.[198] General Ambrosio, who was there as well, had urged Mussolini to press Hitler on peace with Russia. But Mussolini, unable to contradict Hitler at the best of times, was hardly in good enough shape to do so now. 'When Mussolini got off the train, the Führer thought that he looked like an exhausted old man; when he departed he was once again in perfect order and ready for anything ... The Duce realises perfectly well that there can be no salvation for him, except to win or die with us,' Goebbels noted in his diary.[199] No decisions of substance were reached.

That month Mussolini had told Bastianini, 'That tragic buffoon stubbornly seeks a victory in Russia that is completely out of the question. I have told him this at least ten times but he does not want to know.'[200] In desperation, as the military situation in the Mediterranean went from bad to worse, he began to think about making a separate peace with the Allies – but only half-heartedly. For he knew that his fate was to 'win or die' with the Germans as Goebbels had noted. He admitted this at the monthly Council of Ministers meeting on 19 June: 'All discussion is useless. Italy has only one alternative: to conquer or fall at the side of Germany.[201] Apart from anything else the Allied line on Italian peace feelers from whichever quarter was 'absolute silence'.[202]

The *Popolo* Stirs

In the spring of 1943 the Italian people began to stir at last, not because they had become anti-Fascists but because they were hungry. The war had never been popular but so long as it was short, distant and victorious, the Italians did not mind especially. But the war had become long, there had not been a single significant Italian victory and it was getting very close. In Italy itself it had by 1943 begun to cause severe hardship. Food prices had risen by 70 per cent between 1939 and 1942.[203] Furthermore, just as Mussolini was angry that the war had quickly become Hitler's war, not his, so were they angry that it was not theirs. The Italian soldier had become cannon fodder in someone else's war. During the winter of 1942–3 the Allies heavily bombed Italian cities, especially in the north, killing tens of thousands of Italian civilians.[204] Mussolini had begun to send Italians to work for the war effort in Germany in 1940, as the quid pro quo for German raw materials, where they were treated increasingly shoddily and in the end little better than those in the concentration camps. At their peak the Italian workers in Germany numbered more than 200,000.[205] It was against the law for German women to have any contact with them, as with any foreigner, and those caught doing so were tarred and feathered.[206]

The corruption of many senior Fascists – in this they were no different from every governing elite in Italy both before and after them – had done serious damage to the image of Fascism among the Italian people. For a long time, however, as in every field, Mussolini had escaped being tarred with the same brush, mainly because he was not corrupt. But by now his affair with Petacci was an open secret and the corruption of Petacci's brother, Marcello, common knowledge. Marcello Petacci had become very rich smuggling gold on the back of his sister's name and connections, and did more harm to Mussolini's reputation than fifteen battles lost, according to an OVRA report.[207]

Nor did Ciano's corruption, especially in the field of property dealing, help. Unlike Mussolini, who lived frugally, the Cianos lived an enviably luxurious life. But Ciano's corruption did not stop Edda Ciano from going to her father and presenting him with a dossier on the corruption of the Petaccis, which Umberto Albini, who had replaced Guido Buffarini Guidi as Under-Secretary at Interior, had furnished her with. In the spring of 1943 she used it to demand he ditch his mistress. Mussolini told Edda that he would end the affair and he told Navarra, his faithful usher at Palazzo Venezia, to tell Petacci not to come any more. On 1 May Petacci arrived as usual at Palazzo Venezia and the police officers at the side entrance in Via degli Astalli told her they had orders from Mussolini not to let her in. She forced her way in and managed to corner him long enough to scream at him and burst into tears. A week later he relented. He tried to stop seeing her twice more, but without success. Only Mrs

Mussolini, it seemed, did not know about Mussolini's relationship with Petacci.

In early March 1943 there were serious strikes in the north, which began on the 5th at the Fiat Mirafiori works in Turin, and rapidly spread to Milan and elsewhere. Apart from minor exceptions these strikes, which involved 130,000 workers, were the first since Mussolini had come to power.[208] The motive behind them, however – despite the myth invented subsequently by the Italian Left – was not political. It was hunger. By now the Italian economy was in deep crisis. Since the end of 1941 cars had been banned from the roads; at the end of 1942 cafés and pasticcerie were closed; between 1939 and 1942 average prices rose by around 50 per cent (but that of potatoes, for example, had nearly tripled and food prices in general risen by 70 per cent during the same period). Between 1940 and 1943 industrial production declined by 35 per cent and agricultural production by 25 per cent. Steel production fell as well from 2.32 million metric tons per annum in 1938 to 1.93 million in 1942. Rationing, though late in starting, became draconian. The black market flourished. By 1943 the per capita food ration was roughly the same as that of the Poles under Nazi occupation.[209]

At the Fiat Mirafiori works in Turin, for example, out of 21,000 workers, there were 80 Communists.[210] Nor, as the mythology of the Italian Left would have it, was the action of the strikers in March 1943 especially heroic. For the Left the strikes came to be seen as an epic uprising of the proletariat against the Fascist oppressor. But there were no casualties and once the strikers had got a few modest concessions they went straight back to work after a couple of days. The political element of the strikes, such as it was, was a reflection of the widespread revulsion against the war – not even Fascism – which existed by now. It had nothing to do with support for anti-Fascism, let alone Communism.

Whatever their cause, however, the strikes had happened because the PNF was 'absent' and 'impotent'. Mussolini's reaction was to address this grave problem. On 14 April he sacked the Chief of Police, Carmine Senise, who had succeeded Bocchini on his death in November 1940 but who had never joined the PNF. Then, on 17 April, Mussolini sacked the PNF general secretary, Vidussoni and replaced him with Carlo Scorza. Scorza, from Calabria, was only forty-six but had been a volunteer in the First World War and was a seasoned *squadrista* of old with a bloody past from Lucca, Tuscany, where he had lived most of his adult life. His blackshirts had beaten up Amendola in 1926. Mussolini announced the decision in a speech on 17 April to the PNF directorate at Palazzo Venezia at which he said, 'The party, we must recognise, was not up to the situation . . .'

Unconditional Surrender

The Allies had been studying what to do in the event of an Italian collapse ever since the disastrous invasion of Greece in late 1940. A December 1940 Foreign Office memo had ruled 'out of the question' any suggestion that Mussolini would ever seek a separate peace with the Allies. It concluded that the best outcome from an Allied point of view would be his overthrow by Italian elements who then sought an armistice with the Allies and Allied help to hold the Germans at bay. The worst outcome, they decided, from an Allied point of view would be the acceptance by Italy of German control so as to avoid collapse.

By autumn 1942 the general Allied view, certainly towards Germany and Japan, was unconditional surrender. Churchill, however, was far more flexible in regard to Italy. He was prepared to consider a separate peace. But not Eden, who was vehemently opposed to such a course of action for two reasons mainly: in his view there was no viable alternative national leader to Mussolini, not even the King, and anyway a separate peace would be impossible because in such an event Germany would seize power in Italy. For as he said in a letter to American Secretary of State, Cordell Hull in January 1943 the Germans 'controlled events in Italy' and there was still no one of 'sufficient strength' to replace Mussolini. He added, 'The King is regarded as a willing tool of Fascism, and the people appear no longer to be looking to him as a leader. The view of His Majesty's Government is, therefore, that we should not count on the possibility of a separate peace but should aim at such disorder in Italy as would necessitate a German occupation. We suggest that the best means of achieving this aim is to intensify all forms of military operations against Italy, particularly aerial bombardment.'[211]

Eden was certainly correct in believing that the forces of anti-Fascism were too weak even to warrant consideration. But his conclusion that a German occupation of Italy was the best solution had disastrous consequences for the Allies and the Italians. It meant that the Allies and those who overthrew Mussolini lost vital time in signing an armistice and failed to coordinate a rapid military response to the Germans who were thus able to occupy most of Italy. In consequence it would take the Allies twenty months to liberate Italy, Mussolini would return at the head of a puppet republic in the north, there would be civil war, and tens of thousands of Allied soldiers and Italians would die.

Churchill had a powerful strategic reason for being flexible on unconditional surrender in regard to Italy: he needed to get to the Balkans before Stalin so as to stop him establishing Communism there. The sooner Italy was out of the war, the sooner he could achieve this objective. While Eden thought bombing Italy was the best way to defeat Germany, Churchill was prepared to contemplate a separate peace with Italy to defeat Germany.

Eden's uncompromising view, however, prevailed at the Casablanca conference between 14 and 26 January 1943 where Churchill and Roosevelt agreed that they would accept nothing less than unconditional surrender not just by Germany and Japan but also Italy.

Arrivederci Africa

Tripoli fell on 23 January 1943. Rommel's only objective now was to hold Tunisia. Strategically, it was more important than Libya. If the Allies took it they could launch an invasion of Italy much more easily. But Rommel's heart was no longer in what he realised was a hopeless cause. Tunisia could only be held if Hitler diverted massive support from Russia. This he would not do. On 9 March Rommel saw Mussolini in Rome and told him how desperate the situation was. Mussolini had planned to hand him the *medaglia d'oro* but did not. The next day Rommel flew to see Hitler at his advance headquarters in Russia. Hitler relieved him of his command, telling him to take a rest, and did not make public the news. Hitler informed Mussolini by letter and said that Rommel was 'among my bravest officers' but had 'failed in the problem of supplies'. It was not Rommel, of course, but Hitler who was to blame for Rommel's lack of supplies.[212] The Desert Fox had departed and Mussolini and his armed forces were in a sorry state.

On 8 May Tunis and Bizerta fell; on 13 May the whole of Tunisia. The last Axis forces in North Africa, about 250,000, surrendered. The Allies were ready to begin the assault on Fortress Europe. If Hitler had sent sufficient men and matériel to North Africa in the first place it could have led to the victory of the Axis. Failing that, if he and Mussolini had withdrawn their forces to Italy when they had the chance it would have made it very difficult indeed for the Allies to capture Italy. As it was, partly because of lack of imagination, partly the difficult terrain, the Allies would make extremely heavy weather of their war in Italy. Hitler had always regarded the Mediterranean and North Africa as the secondary front; but now, with the invasion of Fortress Europe imminent, it was about to become a second primary front.

On 5 May General Anton von Rintelen, Chief German liaison officer with the Italian command, had sent Berlin his analysis of the total failure of the Italian army almost everywhere it had engaged. He said,

> The main reasons for this are its completely inadequate armament and equipment, the faulty training of the officer corps, the insufficient psychological preparation of most of the other ranks and the lack of enthusiasm owing to doubts as to the favourable outcome of the war ... There was no question of any inner participation in the vital battle of our time. The mass of the Italian people, as well as the soldiers, had on average no

understanding of an 'Italian Great Power' or a *'Mare Nostrum'* ... In summary, it must be said that the Italian army is not in a position to ward off a major assault on its metropolitan territory. This can only be expected with strong German support...[213]

Ill with stomach trouble again, Mussolini spent much of June 1943 at La Rocca delle Caminate. Banned by his doctors from riding or playing tennis, he found some consolation in chopping wood.[214] He had armed the tiny island of Pantelleria, south-west of Sicily, to the teeth. It bristled with coastal guns and 11,000 soldiers, and was regarded as untakeable. But the Allies bombed it heavily for six days and on the eleventh invaded. Promptly its commanding officer, Admiral Pavesi, surrendered. Neither he nor his soldiers wanted to fight. The only casualties were two Allied soldiers shot in error and one Italian kicked by a mule.

On 24 June Mussolini gave a speech to the PNF directorate which soon became known derisively as the *Discorso della Bagnasciuga*. In it he said, 'There are doubters and there is no need to be surprised. Christ only had twelve disciples ...' He denied responsibility for the way the war had gone and said that the historical destiny of leaders was to be betrayed and misunderstood. He explained, 'One day I will demonstrate that we could not, must not have avoided this war, on pain of our suicide.' Taking a customary swipe at the bourgeoisie, he said, 'The other day ... I saw [in the press] that the evacuated ladies of Rapallo have organised a game of golf with as many as twenty-two holes. This is of enormous interest. Just think: twenty-two holes! These are cases in which the whip is called for ... it's opportune to remember that the whip is rather fashionable in England. ... Now, the ladies who delight in golf with twenty-two holes deserve to be sent and will be sent to work in the factories or the fields. [According to the original uncensored text, Mussolini said 'deserve to be whipped in the parts where *"non e che luca"*, as citizen Dante would say'.] Such things are truly classic examples of what I call cretinous confusion, of those people who are not happy unless they can play at *pinnacolo*. Here as ever we are back with the bourgeoisie ...' He concluded, 'It is necessary that as soon as the enemy lands he is frozen on that line which sailors call the *bagnasciuga*, the line on the sand where the water ends and land begins.' *Bagnasciuga*, it was widely noted, means the waterline on a ship, not the tidemark on a beach.[215]

Actually, to defend Sicily Mussolini could count on 300,000 badly armed, badly equipped Italian troops, most of whom were Sicilians whose morale was rock bottom not least because their loyalty to Italy, let alone Mussolini, had always been in serious doubt (after the war, Sicily nearly became independent and there was much violence in the process). But even if the Italian soldiers in Sicily had wanted to fight it would not have made much difference. They hardly had any motorised transport, let alone tanks or armoured cars. There was only one artillery battery, for example, every five miles along the coast. There were, however, two German divisions – the Hermann Göring armoured division and the 15th Sizilien motorised division – some 30,000 men. The Italians had 100 tanks; the Germans 165. Between them, they had 500 planes of various types about half of which worked. The Italian navy was nowhere to be seen because, apart from anything else, it had no fuel and orders not to defend Sicily.

The Allied invasion force consisted of 150,000 troops – one-fifth of the total they had by now in Algeria, Tunisia and Libya – 600 tanks and 1000 pieces of artillery. They had command of the sea and the air. The invasion took place on the night of the 9–10 July. Montgomery, in command of the British 8th Army which had landed in the extreme south-east, had expected the gun battery at the naval base of Augusta, north of Siracusa, to be his most difficult obstacle. The admiral in charge blew up his guns and surrendered without firing a shot. On 12 July Mussolini telegraphed Hitler begging him to send planes. Conspicuously, he did not ask for troops.[216]

The American 7th Army, under General George Patton who landed further to the west, had to deal with the two German divisions and an Italian (non-Sicilian) division, the Livorno, and met stiff resistance. There was talk of Mussolini going in person to rally the troops. The King had told General Paolo Puntoni, his *aide-de-camp*, in his best ham Shakespeare, 'It would be grave if for a move of this kind the Duce should lose his life or be captured: though the thing would facilitate the solution of many important questions.'[217] But Mussolini did not go.

The Germans quickly decided that there was no hope of saving Sicily and the best they could achieve was a fighting retreat to the mainland. Patton, after his initial hitch on landing, moved quickly north and west. But Montgomery, cautious and unimaginative as ever, got bogged down at Catania under Mount Etna. His slowness meant the chance of trapping the two German divisions in Sicily was lost. Their escape would have serious consequences for the fate of Italy in the months to come. By 17 August, the Allies had occupied the whole of Sicily. Large numbers of Italian troops had surrendered or deserted without a fight. Consequently their casualties were far fewer proportionately than those of the Germans – 4178 dead compared with 5000 dead. The Allies had sustained casualties of 22,000 dead or wounded. They had taken 150,000 prisoners.[218] In the First World War Italy had stared defeat in the face at Caporetto but held at the Piave and bounced back to triumph at Vittorio Veneto. In the Second World War Sicily was Italy's Caporetto. This time, there would be no Vittorio Veneto. Many say this is because the Second World War was not popular with the Italian people – not *'sentità'*. But the First World War was even more unpopular. Nor had the Italian people wanted, or participated in the Risorgimento either. Indeed, the only war popular with the Italian people in modern history had been the conquest of Ethiopia.

15

JULY 1943: THE BETRAYAL OF MUSSOLINI AND THE DEATH OF THE FASCIST REGIME

Cloaks and Daggers

In 1923 Bottai, the thinking man's Fascist, had said, 'Heresies are born when religions decay, when they do not persuade any more, when their symbols are no longer evocative, when mysteries are no longer mysterious, when the dignity and power to fascinate of their priests decay.' Bottai was referring to the decadence of Italy's pre-Fascist democratic politicians. He might have been speaking in 1943 and referring to the decadence of Fascism.[1]

By the autumn of 1942 the Italian establishment – both inside and outside Fascism – began to wonder about how to get Italy out of the war. For a few this even meant the overthrow of Mussolini. In 1943, as the military situation went from bad to worse, the few increased in number. The ideal solution would be for Italy to secure Hitler's consent for a separate Italian peace with the Allies. The trouble was that all knew that Mussolini stood the best chance of getting such consent. Yet at the same time all knew, as did Mussolini, that Hitler was most unlikely to give his consent even to Mussolini and that if Italy made such a peace without it Hitler would promptly invade Italy. Nevertheless, an increasing number of people decided that Italy should be removed from the war regardless.

Yet the overthrow of Mussolini would do nothing to reduce the threat of invasion by Hitler. In fact, it would increase it. Nor would it hasten peace. Those who toppled Mussolini did not even try to make proper contact with the Allies to talk about peace. It was as if they thought that peace would somehow happen on its own as a result of Mussolini's departure. Naturally, it did not. In other words, they failed in their aim, which was not the removal of Mussolini but peace. The result of all this was not just the collapse of Mussolini and Fascism but nearly two years of bloody war in Italy.

By the spring of 1943 the numerous plots which had hatched as a result of military humiliation thickened with each move closer to Italy by the Allied armies. Sometimes the aims of these plots coincided, sometimes they did not. Sometimes, the plotters were aware of the plots of the other plotters, sometimes they were not. Very few plots had any chance of success, the plots of the anti-Fascist political groups, for example, such as the non-democratic Communists or the various democratic groups, had no chance. Such groups were too small and ineffectual. But everyone, it seemed, including the naive and somewhat silly Princess Maria Jose, married to the heir to the throne, Crown Prince Umberto, was desperate to get in on the plotting. Later, many of these plotters believed that they had had a hand in the downfall of Mussolini – or else boasted that they did so as to try to prove their anti-Fascist credentials once such credentials had become fashionable. But the truth is that virtually none of them did. Their secret prattle, however, did create, it has to be said, a mood of conspiracy – a 'conspiratorial yeast' as Luca Pietromarchi, senior Foreign Office official, defined it[2] – which provided a certain impetus for the very few plotters who counted – i.e. those with the power actually to do something except prattle.

Mussolini was aware, more or less, of what was going on. But, strangely, he seemed to care less and less, as if he knew that his good star had finally deserted him; as if he felt that the Goddess of Destiny had made up her mind; that destiny had trapped him at last. His stomach illness, which had dogged him since his return from Libya in July 1942, had anyway focused attention on an Italy without him – regardless of how well or badly the war was going. The illness also ate away at his resolve. At a Council of Ministers' meeting on 21 November 'he looked like a dying man who might faint at any minute', recorded one of those present.[3] Later, in captivity, Mussolini would write, 'From October 1942 [El Alamein] onwards I had a constant and growing presentiment of the crisis which was to overwhelm me. My illness greatly affected this.'[4]

There were also fears for Mussolini's sanity. In June 1943 Carlo Pareschi, the Agriculture Minister, told a meeting at which Mussolini was present that the harvest had not yielded as much as expected. 'Do you know what the birds get up to?' Mussolini interrupted. 'A few days ago I was in the countryside and I saw what the birds get up to. They land on the stem, and their weight bends the ear of the wheat so that they remain hidden. Then they eat the grain. ... Kill the birds! ... Kill them all!'[5] But what could Mussolini have done about the plots against him? His fate, as Goebbels had noted, was to 'win or die' with the Germans.

Mussolini had never revered Hitler, as Hitler still revered him, and had always found him irritating. Worse, however, he believed that Hitler had betrayed Italy ever since the Pact of Steel was signed and dragged Italy into a war it was not ready for and that Hitler's continued obsession with Russia at the expense of the Mediterranean was a fatal error. From late 1942 on he had regarded peace with Russia, not with Britain and America, as the only hope. But Hitler would not listen, possessed as he was by a fanatical desire to defeat Russia.

Italy was thick with portentous omens that spring of 1943 as well. Easter fell very late indeed, which worried magicians and prophets, but worse, a nineteenth-century visionary, someone recalled, had warned that during Easter 1943 'the atmosphere would be plagued by the visible presence of demons who would show themselves in a thousand different guises'.[6]

The King

The King, feeble but crucial as is the king in chess, was the key to it all. Without him no plot could succeed. He was, after all, the Head of State, even though this was often forgotten, not least, it seemed, by himself. He still had the constitutional power, despite twenty years of Fascism, to appoint the government and to declare war and make peace. But as he was incapable of talking except cryptically – perhaps because like everyone else he was scared that anything he said would be repeated – those who came to him seeking his support for a plot came away not knowing for sure if he had agreed to support them or not. What we do know, however, as Ciano told a friend, is that the King was 'more Hamlet-like than Hamlet'.[7] He was also as concerned about the fate of the monarchy as of the country. And the complicity of the monarchy in both Fascism and the war had placed it at serious risk. For the same reason he feared an Allied victory and had little enthusiasm for a separate peace with the Allies. But like everyone else, he also feared a German invasion.

Subsequently, the King would tell the Duke of Acquarone, the Minister of the Royal Household since 1939, in an undated letter, 'Dear Acquarone, I authorise you to declare that as from January 1943, I took the definite decision to put an end to the Fascist regime and to dismiss the head of the government, Mussolini. ... You were informed of my decisions and my personal directives, and you know that only these from January 1943 on caused the 25th July.'[8] But what the King said in this letter is misleading. Perhaps he began to consider the removal of Mussolini in January 1943. But he did not make up his mind actually to do anything about it until the second half of July. Yes, he listened to the conspirators when they came to see him between January and July but he did not take the initiative. Only at the very last moment did he act.

On 15 May 1943 – two days after the fall of Tunisia and the end of the Axis military presence in Africa – the King wrote a lengthy note – a rare document indeed, given that hardly any have reached the public domain – about the general war situation in which he spoke of the 'possible need' for a separate Italian peace. He thought – like Hitler – that an Allied invasion of Europe via Italy or its islands 'can be ruled out' but that an invasion via Greece 'would be easy and the most profitable for the Allies' as it 'would strike Romania from behind and would prevent Russian intervention in the Balkans'. Mussolini had thought the same. 'It would be more appropriate for the enemy to land in Greece where the population is starving,' he had told General Ambrosio on 28 January 1943.[9]

The King's note ended with these words: 'One must think seriously of the possible need to detach Italy's armed forces from those of Germany, whose internal collapse might come without warning, as happened to Imperial Germany in 1918.'[10] This last sentence of the King's May 1943 war note – assuming it is genuine – is evidence, therefore, that by the middle of May the King was thinking about the 'possible need' – a typical Vittorio Emanuele phrase – for Italy to detach itself from its alliance with Germany. This hardly tallies with his statement to Acquarone after the event that he had decided to remove Mussolini in January 1943.

Such a detachment, however, would not necessarily mean that Italy in addition would make a separate peace with the Allies, though that was the most likely outcome. It could also mean, for example, that Italy would bring home all its troops for its defence against the Allies. For what is striking about the note is the reason given by the King for this possible detachment from Germany: he wanted it not because Italy's armed forces were on the verge of defeat and Italy on the verge of invasion, nor because he wanted peace, but because Germany might make a separate peace herself and leave Italy high and dry. It implies that had the King been certain that Germany would carry on fighting he would have wanted Italy to carry on as well. And he was thinking these thoughts and writing them down as late as the middle of May 1943. We know in addition that four days later he made clear to General Paolo Puntoni, his aide-de-camp, that a separate peace remained no more than a 'possible need' and that if the Allies approached him on the matter he would have to 'speak to the Duce and agree with him a line of action'.[11]

The Two Plots that Counted

By June there were so many plots and sub-plots that Anfuso could not work out 'who was in what conspiracy'.[12] But only two plots mattered: one within the army; the other within the regime. The ringleaders were General Ambrosio, Chief of the General Staff, and Grandi, President of the *Camera dei fasci* and Fascist of the first hour. These two plots were quite separate. Neither Ambrosio nor Grandi was in touch with the other (apart from one inconsequential meeting in mid-June). But both were in touch with the King. Both wanted Mussolini removed and Italy out of the war. Ambrosio wanted a military dictatorship to replace Mussolini, while Grandi wanted some form of parliamentary government headed by a military dictator. Ambrosio planned the arrest of Mussolini; Grandi planned his replacement. But for both Grandi and Ambrosio the removal of Mussolini was only the first step to getting Italy out of the war. Stage two for Grandi was a separate peace with the Allies, combined with a declaration of war on the Germans. Stage two for Ambrosio – as it was for the King – was to make a separate peace with the Allies and a declaration of Italian neutrality. Yet neither Grandi nor Ambrosio made any provision whatsoever for the achievement of stage two. Grandi can be excused on the grounds that he formed no part of the new government. Ambrosio and the King cannot. Clearly, they were so afraid of a rapid German invasion as a result of the removal of Mussolini that they dared not make a separate peace once they had removed him. This, of course, defeated the object of the exercise. Furthermore, until the very last moment, Ambrosio and the King, though not Grandi, were against the removal of Mussolini because they still believed he might secure Hitler's approval for a separate peace. They feared occupation by the Allies; they feared occupation by the Germans. So, they hedged their bets – with disastrous consequences.

There was a third significant plot: a pro-German counter-plot led by Farinacci, which aimed for Mussolini to hand over control of the Italian armed forces to the Germans and for a dictatorship of the PNF. Ciano, though aware of most of the plots, did not identify himself with a particular one until the last minute. But given his family connection to Mussolini, his deep unpopularity in the country at large and his loose tongue, his role could not be a central one anyway. He remained at home 'with a political illness, hanging on to the various strings of the numerous plots'.[13]

Grandi wrote in his diary, 'This detachment [from Fascism] must be by us and not the inevitable effect of military defeat. It is we who, independently of the enemy, must show ourselves capable of reconquering our lost liberties. Mussolini, the dictatorship, Fascism, must sacrifice themselves, make way for a new governing class. They must "commit suicide" demonstrating with this sacrifice their love for the Nation ...' Marshal Caviglia, the only one of the famous First World War generals left who had not 'fornicated with Fascism', should head the new government, wrote Grandi, which should exclude all members of Mussolini's government including himself. He wrote,

Caviglia is the only one who perhaps could, even in the desperate conditions in which Italy finds itself, negotiate with the enemy an honourable peace which did not humiliate Italy, avoiding the unconditional surrender decided on by the Anglo-Americans at the Casablanca conference ... it is indispensable, and inevitable that it is we who will seize the initiative of war against Nazi Germany, against our potent ... ally ... There are in Italy thirty-five–forty of our divisions against four–five German divisions. ... We must ask nothing of the Anglo-Americans, but only confront them suddenly with the spectacle of an Italy which defends itself with arms in its fists against that which will be the inevitable revenge of Nazi Germany. How could the Allies continue to fight on against a nation that already on its own has decided to fight against the common enemy?[14]

Later, Ambrosio would recall, 'I certainly knew the military situation well: I realised it was desperate. But my initial hope was to be able to succeed in persuading Mussolini to make a rapid disengagement from the Germans.'[15] Until very late in the day Ambrosio, like so many, felt that only Mussolini could extract Italy from the war without catastrophic consequences. General Giuseppe Castellano, Ambrosio's *aide-de-camp*, was the other key plotter within the army High Command. At some point in April – when exactly remains unclear – Ambrosio asked Castellano to draw up a contingency plan for the arrest of Mussolini and related measures. These did not include making contact with the Allies. Ambrosio had not sought the permission of the King to do this. He had acted entirely on his own initiative. But he would need an order from the King to execute his plan. He did not seek this until 5 July.[16] Prior to then, however, he and Castellano did show the plan to the Duke of Acquarone, the Minister of the Royal Household. Castellano also showed it to Ciano. Ciano, one might think, given his loose tongue, was the last person on earth who should be shown it. But Ciano knew both Ambrosio and Castellano well. Apparently Castellano showed it to him in order to find out if Ciano and other senior Fascists were conspiring against Mussolini. Castellano, who met Ciano several times during this period, decided that they were not.[17] We do not know if Ciano told any of the other Fascist conspirators such as Grandi or Bottai of Ambrosio's plan to arrest Mussolini. From what Grandi said and wrote after the war, it seems that Ciano did not tell Grandi.[18] For once, perhaps, Ciano kept his mouth shut.

In early March (probably the 6th but the precise date is not known), the King saw Badoglio, who had not been involved in the running of the war since his sacking as Chief of the General Staff in December 1940. Badoglio, in civilian clothes, told the King that the war was lost and the country was against it.[19] But the King dithered on. In April, for example, when he saw Admiral Thaon di Revel, commander of the Italian navy in the First World War, he told him that 'only the Chamber and the Senate could provoke his intervention'.[20] And in early June Paolo Puntoni, the King's *aide-de-camp* noted, 'I think that, at least for the present, he is still decided to support Mussolini's action. The plan that His Majesty is elaborating in his head is a mystery to everybody ...'[21]

On 4 June the King saw Grandi in the latter's capacity as a member of the government.[22] Grandi had lost his job as Justice Minister in the February purge but was still President of the *Camera dei fasci*. In addition, on 25 March the King had awarded him the highest honour in his gift, the *Collare dell'Annunziata*, which made him a cousin of the King and gave him unlimited access to him. 'Was the conferring of the Collar a part of the conspiracy, by any chance?' Mussolini would write.[23] But 4 June was the only time, it seems, when Grandi saw the King during these crucial weeks. Grandi's version is that he urged the King to remove Mussolini and declare war on the Germans. The King replied, 'The moment is about to arrive. I know that I can count on you. Leave your king to choose the opportune moment, and meanwhile help me to procure the constitutional means.'[24] The King, of course, already had the constitutional means: the power to appoint and dismiss prime ministers by royal decree. Though strictly speaking he had to have the approval of parliament to replace a prime minister, this had not been the case in 1922, for example, when he appointed Mussolini Prime Minister after the March on Rome. The King had always stuck to the line that things be done constitutionally even though he had spent twenty years nodding through each erosion of the constitution perpetrated by Mussolini. What he meant in this context was that some government organ or other would have to make a decision before he could make a decision. But which government organ was capable of such a decision?

There remained the Grand Council. Mussolini had set up the Grand Council in 1923 as a means to bring the PNF under central control. It began life, therefore, essentially as a party institution controlled by the state. But in 1932, with the aim of destroying once and for all the threat the PNF posed to the Fascist state Mussolini made the Grand Council the highest governing authority in the Fascist state – separate from and higher than the Council of Ministers or the two Houses of Parliament. The theory was that as a result in the body of the Grand Council the PNF and the Fascist state were fused as one. The Grand Council's functions included the regulation of the PNF hierarchy, the Fascist militia and the right to be consulted over the succession to both Mussolini and the King. But its powers were ill-defined. Mussolini was its chairman, appointed its members, who numbered between twenty and thirty, and decided when and if it should meet. It did not reach decisions by vote but by consensus. In practice this meant Mussolini, having listened, decided. 'The Grand Council is not a small parliament: never, I repeat never, is there any question of voting in it,' Mussolini had said in 1925. But nevertheless it was defined under a 1928 law as the supreme organ of the state.[25] Yet Mussolini had not called it since 1939.

Having seen the King, Grandi went back to Bologna. From now on he was noticeably absent from Rome – as if waiting – though at some point in mid-June he saw General Ambrosio. But Ambrosio told Grandi, as he told everyone else, to talk to the King not him. Ambrosio had the impression that Grandi saw himself as a successor to Mussolini. Grandi always denied this. But given his serpentine ways and that he did not succeed Mussolini he would deny it, wouldn't he?[26]

The worse his military situation got, the less Mussolini wanted military help from Hitler inside Italy. In early May, though desperate for troops, he had turned down an offer of five more German divisions to defend Italy. He did, however, accept German assistance to set up an armoured unit of blackshirts – the 'M' Division – to be stationed just outside Rome. The task of the 'M' Division was the defence of Fascism and its Duce against those who might try to topple them within Italy. At the end of May the Germans supplied it with thirty-six Tiger tanks, artillery and machine-guns. Mussolini accepted this German weaponry for the 'M' Division but refused Himmler's offer of German SS personnel to train it. He wanted German weapons; but not Germans. On 20 May he gave an evasive reply to an invitation from Hitler to yet another summit. He was frequently ill. On the 26th he went to La Rocca delle Caminate for a week.

On 5 July Ambrosio, who had just met Badoglio, Bonomi and Acquarone at Badoglio's villa in Rome, saw the King to tell him of his plan to arrest Mussolini. This was the first time that the King spoke to Puntoni, he recorded, of 'the action that the *Capo di Stato Maggiore* is developing to arrive at the substitution of Mussolini'. But the King still thought the plan 'premature and dangerous' wherever the arrest was to take place. Quite apart from the Germans, what would the Fascists do?[27] But so too did Ambrosio regard the plan as premature. He still hoped that Mussolini would detach Italy from the alliance with Germany himself. The Allied invasion of Sicily on 9–10 July cleared heads considerably. On 14 July Ambrosio went to see the King again to persuade him to agree to the arrest of Mussolini. This time, the King agreed in principle though not on a date.

Grandi soon had his chance to provide the King with the constitutional means he sought. Scorza, the new PNF Secretary, had decided that senior Fascists should tour Italy to make rallying speeches. Grandi and Federzoni refused and remained in Bologna. On 16 July, led by Scorza the senior Fascists, who included Farinacci and Bottai, went to see Mussolini in his office at the Palazzo Venezia. Their pretext was that they wanted to know how they might rally the Italian people now that Sicily had been invaded. Instead, they urged Mussolini to share responsibility for the fate of Italy with them and to govern by means of all the organs of government, especially the Grand Council.

Bottai had always been in awe of Mussolini, who exercised a mystical influence over him. He had also had faith in Fascism as a revolutionary force for the good. He had, as he himself would write, the 'great unpardonable fault of having believed to the limits of the believable'.[28] Somehow Bottai forced himself to hold Mussolini's gaze during the fifteen minutes in which he said his piece. He told him, 'We ask that the revolution reconstitute its organs, so as to act as the hour demands. We are not here to ask to diminish your powers, or rather your power; nor to divide, that is dissect, fragment, your responsibility. We are here … to ask to share your responsibility. To make of it, that is, a co-responsibility, that binds us to you, but also you to us, in ready, absolute and declared solidarity ...' The bluntness of Bottai and the others persuaded Mussolini to agree to call the Grand Council in the 'secondo quindicina' of the month but add that the enemy would say that the meeting had been called 'to discuss the capitulation'. He said nothing more and the gerarchs left. That evening, Bottai went to see Ciano, who remained deeply sceptical. News that the Grand Council was to meet travelled quickly.[29] Ciano sent a message to Mussolini to say that he had 'never felt so close to the Duce'.[30]

The next day – the 17th – Mussolini wrote to Hitler seeking an urgent meeting. He said, 'I believe, Führer, that the time has come to examine closely together the situation, so as to reach conclusions conforming to the common interests of each country.'[31] That day Hitler had asked if there were any capable Italian officers and Rommel, who was there, had replied, 'There is no such person.'[32] On the 18th – a Sunday – the Russians began a major offensive in the East along the entire front.

Feltre

The two dictators agreed to meet for the thirteenth time.[33] Regardless of what Mussolini wanted, Hitler wanted him to agree that German generals, under the Duce, be in charge of all Axis forces in Italy. He was prepared even to come to Italy for a change. Mussolini suggested Feltre, near Treviso, not far from the Italian border with Austria. The date was fixed for the next day – the 19th – at the sumptuous seventeenth-century villa of an Italian senator – described by Mussolini as 'a crossword-puzzle frozen into a house' and 'a labyrinth' which reminded him of 'a nightmare.'[34] During the two-hour morning session Hitler spoke continuously, interrupted only by the sound of peacocks screeching in the garden. For the first time he displayed his anger to the Italians at Italian ineptitude, which he blamed for the failure of the Axis in North Africa and the Mediterranean. His torrential flow was interrupted only when a note was passed to Mussolini which said that the Allies were bombing Rome for the first time.[35] The raid, it later emerged, had killed 1500 Romans.[36] Mussolini read out the contents of the note, translating it into German. These were practically the only words he spoke that morning. Hitler, impatient at the interruption, carried on talking. During the break for lunch Ambrosio bluntly warned Mussolini that unless he told Hitler that Italy had to make peace, he would order the armed forces to cease fire within fifteen days. Mussolini replied, 'Do you believe perhaps that I have not felt this problem agitate my troubled spirit for some time? Behind the mask of my apparent impassiveness is a profound, harassing torment. I admit the hypothesis ... disengage from Germany. It appears so simple ... Are we prepared to cancel out all of a sudden twenty years of the regime? It's easy to say it:

disengage from Germany. What reaction would Hitler have? Do you believe perhaps that he would permit us freedom of action?'[37] Hitler and Mussolini ate lunch alone during which, according to Mussolini, Hitler said that he was about to recommence the submarine war with new submarines and attack London with new secret weapons which would destroy it within a matter of weeks.[38] Mussolini would speak of secret Hitler weapons with mounting frequency as defeat crept closer. On this occasion, what Hitler presumably meant were the V1 and V2 rockets, though he was also trying, as were the Allies, to develop the atom bomb. Only during lunch and going to and from Feltre by train was Mussolini alone with Hitler. We do not know if he raised the issue of a separate Italian peace during these occasions. Later, Mussolini would recall, 'I repeated my old theme; peace with Russia.'[39] This rings true. While Hitler might agree to an Axis peace with Russia he would never agree to a separate Italian peace with Britain and America. There was no point in Mussolini even raising the matter of a separate peace with the Allies, as he knew. If he were to make a separate peace, it had to be done separately and in secret.

After lunch, the summit broke up and the two dictators travelled together by train back to Treviso. Mussolini told Hitler that if the Axis had had air parity in Africa it would have won; Hitler told Mussolini that the defence of Italy was of maximum importance to Germany.[40] 'Ours is a common cause, Führer,' Mussolini said as Hitler boarded his plane.[41] As it took off, Mussolini told those around him that in the end there had been no need to tell Hitler that Italy could not go on with the war. 'This time he promised sincerely to send the help which we need,' said Mussolini.[42] Later Mussolini would recall that Hitler had told him that he was 'mystically and scientifically convinced of being possessed not by a demon, but by a spirit from Aryan mythological pre-history', which caused Mussolini to feel 'completely disorientated'.[43] Mussolini's personal rapport with Hitler had been the best chance of securing Hitler's consent to a separate Italian peace. But there had never been any chance of Hitler giving his consent even to Mussolini. Feltre proved this – not that proof was needed. For the conspirators, Ambrosio in particular, Mussolini no longer had a role.

The Daggers Are Drawn

Following Feltre, 'the conspiracy took definite shape: each character put on his mask and came on to the stage', as Anfuso put it.[44] Both the King and Ambrosio had hoped until the last that Mussolini would convince Hitler to agree that Italy withdraw from the war. Feltre shattered this hope. It had been a vain and ludicrous hope anyway, but it had provided the King and Ambrosio with an excuse to procrastinate. To be fair to them, of course, Italy was in a nightmare situation. While Mussolini was at Feltre the King had watched by telescope the Allied planes bombing Rome and then been to see the bomb damage. He had handed out money but the people had shouted, 'We don't want your dirty money, we want peace!'[45]

The day after Feltre, 20 July, Ambrosio saw Mussolini and asked to resign on the grounds that Mussolini had failed to tackle Hitler about a separate peace. But Mussolini would not let him. That same day Mussolini told Scorza to call the Grand Council for Saturday, 24 July. On that day Mussolini's wife, like the witch who warned Julius Caesar to beware the Ides of March, told him to arrest the traitors including their son-in-law. He told her that he was more worried about American tanks than traitors.[46] Mrs Mussolini would give many such warnings in the course of the next few days.

That day, too, Grandi arrived in Rome from Bologna. Before he knew that the Grand Council was to be called, he had prepared letters for both Mussolini and the King to alert them that he planned to put a motion either to the Chamber or the Grand Council as soon as the opportunity arose.[47] This motion called on Mussolini to share government with the various organs of the state and hand back command of the armed forces to the King. His arrival in Rome neatly coincided with Mussolini's decision to call the Grand Council. It was also on the 20th that the King made up his mind to set a date of sorts – 'within six or seven days' – to remove Mussolini and bring in Badoglio.[48]

On the 21st Scorza, PNF Secretary, issued the invitations for the Grand Council meeting to take place at Palazzo Venezia on Saturday, 24 July at 5 p.m. The news that the Grand Council had been called came as a complete surprise to the King and Ambrosio, and caused them to panic. This was not the constitutional means the King had had in mind. They feared a Fascist manoeuvre to remove Mussolini and replace him with a government of Fascists. Mussolini had written into the constitution, it should be remembered, that the Grand Council was the supreme organ of the state and had the constitutional right to name his successor. If it named a successor now the King, who had always tried to insist that everything be done according to the constitution, would find it difficult not to accept the nominee.

The King might have told Grandi at the start of June to find him the constitutional means to remove Mussolini, but there had been no direct contact between the two since; though there had been some indirect contact. Certainly, Grandi had no idea of Ambrosio's plan to arrest Mussolini. So, as far as the King was concerned, Grandi had failed until now to provide him with the constitutional means he sought. Indeed, Grandi, as far as we know, had played no role in the move to persuade Mussolini to call the Grand Council. But anyway, even before the meeting had been called – probably on the evening of the 19th or the morning of the 20th – the King had decided to arrest Mussolini at the weekly audience on

Monday, 26 July. Then came news of the Grand Council meeting. As a result the King decided that if the Grand Council expressed a hostile view to Mussolini, he could use that as the constitutional justification for Mussolini's arrest. If it did not, he would arrest Mussolini anyway. There remained only the problem of the Grand Council deciding to remove Mussolini but replace him with a government of Fascists.

The same day as the invitations went out for the Grand Council meeting[49] Acquarone told Ambrosio that the King had at long last decided to get rid of Mussolini and he should now prepare the operation to arrest him. Among other things, Ambrosio appointed General Giacomo Carboni commander of a new Motorised Corps (three divisions) being formed outside Rome. Its secret mission was to defend the capital from the Germans and/or Fascists in the wake of Mussolini's arrest.[50]

Grandi, meanwhile, once he had heard that the Grand Council was to be called, had one aim in mind: to put his motion to it and to get as much support for it as possible beforehand from members by whatever means. This meant, above all, being 'open' with everyone, even Scorza, even Farinacci, even Mussolini, about the purpose of the motion in an attempt to get their support for it. In other words it meant saying that the motion was for the good of Mussolini and Fascism not just Italy.

On the 22nd Mussolini had his usual Thursday morning audience with the King at which he reported on the Feltre meeting. Afterwards the King told Puntoni: 'I tried to make the Duce understand that by now only his persona ... stood in the way of internal revival ... He did not understand, or he did not want to understand. It was as if I had spoken to the wind.'[51] According to Mussolini the King said, 'A tense situation ... It can't go on much longer ... The Germans will double-cross us. The discipline of the troops has broken down ... We must tell the Germans our dilemma.'[52] In October 1943, Badoglio would tell a group of officers that Mussolini told the King that 'in any case we would have disengaged from Germany by 15 September.'[53] Churchill would write, 'Mussolini replied, so it seems, that he hoped to liberate Italy from the Axis alliance by 15 September.'[54] If it is true, as seems likely, that during the audience Mussolini did indeed tell the King that he would disengage from Germany by 15 September, then his version of the meeting rings more true than that of Puntoni.

Later that day, Farinacci saw Mussolini and showed him a message he had received from Cavallero, Ambrosio's immediate predecessor as Chief of the General Staff, who was pro-German. This said that Grandi and others were plotting Mussolini's downfall. It warned, 'Be extremely careful.'[55] But Mussolini said he had nothing to fear because only that morning the King had told him, 'These are bad times for you, but know that you have a friend in me. And if, to use an absurd hypothesis, everyone should abandon you, I should be the last to do so. I know how much Italy and the dynasty owe you.'[56] But how close was 'everyone' to abandoning Mussolini? How close the King?

Grandi had secured a meeting with Mussolini for the late afternoon, ostensibly to give him a book on the Spanish Civil War. Grandi, the traitor, had come to see Mussolini as a device to disguise his treachery. The meeting took place at 5.30 p.m. and had been allotted fifteen minutes. It went on until 6.45 p.m. Field Marshal Albert Kesselring (C.-in-C. German Forces South [Mediterranean]), due in at 6 p.m., had to wait.[57] Grandi showed Mussolini his motion and said he should accept what it proposed because it would be to his advantage – not disadvantage: namely, that the King be forced to share responsibility for the war. He wanted to convince him that the motion concealed nothing; that there was nothing trea-sonable going on *dietro le quinte* as the Italians say – nothing to worry about. The day before, Grandi had given Scorza his motion – again in the interests of openness – and Scorza had shown it to Mussolini who said that it was 'vile and inadmissible'.[58] Mussolini knew Grandi as well as Grandi knew him. Grandi had lied to Mussolini. Or had he? Did Grandi's visit plant a seed of doubt in Mussolini's mind as to the real aim of the motion? Perhaps the aim really was to advantage Mussolini. Or, perhaps, the veiled purpose of coming to him now was another one, a loyal one even: that for his own sake, Mussolini should fall on his sword before the meeting of the Grand Council. But Mussolini told Grandi, 'I will not cede the reins of command to anyone. The people is with me.'[59] And apart from the *popolo*, so too, Mussolini was convinced, was the King.

Grandi's version was that he wanted to secure Mussolini's permission to allow his motion to be put[60] and that Mussolini's reaction was to say that what the motion proposed would be fine if the war was lost but the war was not lost because 'within a few days' the Germans would launch a new weapon which would change the course of the war.[61] This is different from Mussolini's version. He left two brief written accounts of his meeting with Grandi. In *Storia di un anno*, written for propaganda purposes in 1944, he said, 'Grandi touched on various points but said nothing of what was to come.' Grandi then tried via Scorza, wrote Mussolini, to postpone the meeting – 'a clever move to look like an alibi'.[62] In *Pensieri pontini e sardi*, a diary of random thoughts written in captivity in August 1943, Mussolini wrote that Grandi had 'begged' him not to call the Grand Council, adding, 'Alibi? Manoeuvre?'[63] He repeated this to Admiral Franco Maugeri, com-mander of the corvette which had ferried him to Ponza and then to Mad-dalena, adding that he had refused to cancel the meeting because 'by then it was essential to make an end of such a critical situation.'[64]

The next day – the 23rd – Bottai met Grandi at PNF headquarters. Also there were Scorza, Federzoni and Ciano. Ciano now agreed to support the motion against Mussolini. Bottai convinced a reluctant Grandi, who had always disliked Ciano, to agree. The final wording of Grandi's motion stated that in addition to handing back military command to the King, the King should also 'assume ... that supreme initiative of decision which our institutions attribute to him and which, in all our national history, has always been the glorious heritage of our august dynasty of Savoy'.[65]

Farinacci was present for part of the time. Grandi told him that his motion was a means of going on with the war. He pointed out that it proclaimed 'the duty of all Italians to defend at all costs the unity, independence and liberty of the Motherland'.[66] Naturally, Farinacci had no idea that the King and Ambrosio planned to use it as the pretext for the arrest of Mussolini. But then nor did Grandi, Bottai, Ciano or anyone else. Grandi alone, however, knew that the King sought a constitutional pretext to replace Mussolini.

Farinacci, meanwhile, in liaison with General Cavallero and the Germans, had contrived his own plan. He would propose a second motion which was similar to Grandi's in calling on the King to assume nominal command of the armed forces and in stating that the duty of Italians was to fight but added crucially the words 'in observance of alliances concluded'.[67] Farinacci's aim was for Cavallero to replace Ambrosio as Chief of the General Staff and for the Germans to take command of all Axis forces in Italy. So unaware were the Germans of how close Mussolini was to being deposed that after the Feltre summit General Jodl had stood down Alaric and Konstantin – the codenames of the plans to invade Italy and Yugoslavia in the event of just such an eventuality. Scorza said that it would be 'useful', however, if he himself did not 'attack' at the Grand Council. He too had a hidden agenda. In secret, he prepared his own motion which called for 'new methods and means' so that the war could continue.[68] He wanted to replace Ambrosio as Chief of the General Staff not with Cavallero, as Farinacci and the Germans wanted, but with Graziani.

On the morning of the 24th, Grandi and Federzoni canvassed support among Grand Council members for the Grandi motion. Alfieri, Italian ambassador to Berlin, summoned to Rome by Scorza for the meeting, agreed, as did Tullio Cianetti, Corporations Minister, De Vecchi, with De Bono the only surviving Quadrumvir, and Alberto De Stefani. Grandi repeated his constant refrain – the motion did not propose to take away from Mussolini responsibility for the conduct of the war but merely to force the King to shoulder that responsibility – to share the blame. If he had said: my motion means that Mussolini and Fascism will be deposed and Italy declare war on Germany, few, apart from Federzoni and Bottai, would have agreed to support him. Grandi's openness with everyone was a trick to conceal his true intent.

Before the meeting of the Grand Council, Bottai noted in his diary,

Our duty has placed us at a crossroads, between country and party, between Italy and regime, between King and Duce … I am only, my persona is only, one of the actors of the drama. Which is, however, at its end.

My Fascism, embraced after four years of war, as a sublimation of the Italian cause in an experience capable of enriching it with new values, social ones above all, my corporative and free Fascism, self-critical and open to the discussion of ideas, had to conduct me to this dilemma.

It is no longer a question of 'betraying' or 'not betraying', but of having the courage to confess the betrayal done by him, consummated by him day by day, from the first disappointment to this moral collapse. Not one idea, one agreement, one institution, one law, to which he has remained faithful. Everything was broken, distorted, corrupted by him, in the wake of a conceited yet cunning empiricism, founded on a contempt for men and their ideals.

My, our resolution, in our realising it will become pure and clear and directed by fact [*nel suo attuarsi resa pura e diritta dal fatto*] because as a result of it we place ourselves at stake: it is a game without alternatives, that will end in renunciation, in sacrifice…[69]

That morning Acquarone, Ambrosio and Castellano went to Badoglio's splendid villa in Rome – the one he had received from Mussolini for gassing his way to glory in Ethiopia – to tell him that the King had decided to replace Mussolini with him. Badoglio accepted. He spent the afternoon playing bridge as usual. Castellano then went to see Senise, the ousted Chief of Police, to tell him that he should be ready to take back his old job. Together they drew up a list of those to be arrested. Ambrosio called in two battalions of Sardinian grenadiers from coastal defence duties to defend the *Quirinale*, the Royal Palace, and the *Viminale*, the Ministry of the Interior. But Carboni's Motorised Corps still existed only on paper and there were precious few troops in Rome. During the afternoon, Grandi dispatched a letter to the King with which he enclosed a copy of his motion.

The members of the Grand Council set off for the meeting due to start at Palazzo Venezia at 5 p.m. Rachele Mussolini told Mussolini, once again, to arrest the traitors. He did not reply and left Villa Torlonia for Palazzo Venezia by car as usual. Grandi, he himself would boast, went to the meeting with two grenades in his briefcase, one of which he handed to De Vecchi under the table; Bottai, his family would say, with one grenade in his pocket.[70] Others went with revolvers hidden about their person. Grandi, having written his will and letters to his wife and son, went to confession in the small church of San Bartolomeo in Piazza Colonna near the Palazzo Chigi.[71] He had had no contact this past month or two with the King and his aides. He was completely in the dark as to what the King planned to do if his motion should be passed. He knew nothing of the plan for a military coup. But he was terrified nevertheless. He did not trust those with whom he had conspired except Federzoni who was a close friend – let alone anyone else. His assumption was that the King would replace Mussolini with a government containing Fascists and non-Fascists in favour of a political solution to the war. He would recall, 'I did not want a *coup de main* ... That would have distorted entirely the character of our action ... The armed forces who arrived unexpectedly afterwards – and only after the sovereign had decided – set about transforming what in our intention had to be the constitutional development of the situation into a Balkan or Mexican-style *coup d'état*.'[72]

Looking back, Grandi would describe Mussolini thus:

> For many centuries there had not appeared in the life of the nation a personality of so much strength and so much fascination, of so much charismatic power, capable of inebriating men and crowds ... the problem was not to combat him, but rather to render this force fecund in the interests of the nation. Mussolini was like a raging flood that one had to canalise, a live flame that one needed to transform into heat so that it did not burn ... To collaborate with his greatness not by means of a dull and inert obedience, but by means of a conscious and constant fidelity, to be faithful to him even in disobedience and in being so in such a way as not to diminish but to enlarge his merit: thus I always intended my fidelity to be, convinced that fidelity and obedience are not synonymous.[73]

Bottai, however, said Grandi was so duplicitous that he somehow managed to be the most pro-Mussolini and the most anti-Mussolini of the gerarchs for twenty years. He 'learned English and foreign snobbisms ... he had himself made count. ... His was a revolution *da salotto*.'[74]

Montanelli wrote, 'It must be admitted: during the historic turning point of 25 July, the best among the Fascist gerarchs displayed moral strength and genuine anguish for the fate of the nation. Their *pronunciamento* had a patina of disinterested nobility. The royal and military conspiracy emerged, by comparison, narrow-minded, short-sighted and egotistical.[75] Mussolini had told the German journalist, Emil Ludwig that Julius Caesar was 'the greatest man that ever lived'. But then he had asked Ludwig, 'Why did he not look at the list of conspirators when it was thrust in his hand? Maybe he allowed himself to be killed, feeling that he had reached the end of his tether.'[76]

Saturday, 24 July: The Duce's 'Last Supper'

The twenty-eight members of the Grand Council made their way to the Palazzo Venezia wearing the summer uniform of the militia: black safari jackets and black breeches. The twenty-ninth member, the Duce del Fascismo, was already there. He was wearing his all-grey-green uniform of Corporal of Honour of the Militia. That day Palermo had fallen to the Allies. Mussolini would recall: 'On the afternoon of 24 July, Rome turned pale. Cities, as well as men have a face. And the emotions of the soul are reflected on that face. Rome felt that some grave matter was in the air.'[77] The weather was torrid and stiflingly hot. Mussolini had given orders for the Moschettieri del Duce, his personal bodyguard at Palazzo Venezia, not to be present to stand ceremonial guard and despatched them to do relief work in the badly bombed San Lorenzo area of the city.[78] There were, nevertheless, 200 or so police officers in the building and in the internal courtyard, where the cars of the gerarchs pulled up to park, a militia battalion.

The meeting took place in the Sala del Pappagallo (Parrot Room) which was on the piano nobile. The seats were arranged in a triangle at whose apex on a raised dais was Mussolini's seat. On his immediate left would sit Scorza, the PNF Secretary; on his immediate right De Bono, the senior surviving Quadrumvir. The members gathered in the Sala del Pappagallo to await Mussolini. Grandi scurried about soliciting last-minute support for his motion. At 5.14 p.m. Mussolini strode in.[79] Apart from the Enzo Galbiati, Commander of the Militia, and De Bono, wearing the uniform of an army marshal, he was the only one wearing grey.[80] Scorza called out the *Saluto al Duce*, to which the members, standing, raised their right arms in the Roman salute and shouted, as was the custom, '*A Noi!*' The meeting began. No minutes were taken.

Mussolini spoke first – for about two hours. He conceded that the war was in an 'extremely critical' phase and added, 'At the moment, I am the most detested, in fact hated, man in Italy, which is perfectly logical ... The truth is no war is popular at the beginning: it becomes so if it goes well, and if it goes badly it becomes *impopolarissima*.'[81] He now played the role of the 'military chief betrayed', noted Bottai. He insisted that he had never wanted supreme command of the armed forces but that in any case he had never assumed direct command. He turned to the future. The Allies would not invade Italy, he said, and Italy must fight on at the side of its ally Germany. The war must go on. To counter the argument that Germany had failed to provide Italy with sufficient military support, he recited detail after detail of support given. He compared the situation now with that of Caporetto in 1917. 'In 1917 the provinces of the Veneto were lost, but no one spoke of surrender, then they spoke of moving the government to Sicily. Today, if it were inevitable, I would move it to the Po Valley. ... War or peace?' asked Mussolini. That was the question. But the trouble with peace, he warned, was that the Allies were not at war with Fascism, they were at war with Italy. Remove Fascism and there would still be war. This was proof, if it were needed, that Mussolini knew precisely the true purpose of Grandi's motion.

Bottai had studied Mussolini's face carefully throughout. He noted, 'Up till then he had spoken with his head bent over his papers; and its features, in the harsh glare of the cold transversal light of the overhead lighting, appeared dehumanised, in a Caravaggioesque scene of violent brightness and threatening shadows ... Now, he lifted up his head in the strong light which shone down on all of us from above; the mask fell and the real face appeared, on which I read the signs of a will by now resigned to the great day of reckoning.'[82]

Mussolini went on, 'Another point of the capitulationists is that "the people's heart is not in the war". Now the people's heart is never in any war. ... Was the people's heart in the 1915–18 war, by any chance? Not in the least. The people were dragged into a war by a minority.'[83] He turned, at last, to Grandi's motion. He said it was nothing less than an appeal to the King for him either to let Mussolini carry on or to take over himself. 'Signori, attenzione! Grandi's motion may place the existence of the regime in jeopardy.' He ended with these words in Latin: 'Pacta sunt servanda.'[84]

De Bono and De Vecchi, the two surviving Quadrumvirs, spoke next but said nothing of importance. It was the turn of Bottai. The Italian mainland was on the verge of invasion, he said. Was Italy prepared for this? He asked, did Italy want war or peace? Italy was on the verge of catastrophe. Everyone had come to the meeting 'committed to the necessity of resistance', he said, but 'we must confess, or at least I must, that it is your account which has given us the feeling that a technically efficient defence of the peninsula is not possible ... Your account has been a sledgehammer blow to our last illusions and hopes.' He said that for the supreme commander to blame military errors on the refusal by the generals to obey his orders was an admission of failure on his part. 'And thus a worm is boring at the very fibres of our system of command,' said Bottai.[85]

Now Grandi rose and read out his motion. He spoke for about an hour. He must have been terrified. In serpentine fashion he tried to disguise his motion as an attack not on Mussolini, but on the monarchy and as in the interests not just of Italy and Fascism but Mussolini as well. His speech was full, too, of fawning praise for Mussolini. It was in Mussolini's interests, he said, that he be freed of a part of the enormous burden he had shouldered up to now – and part of the enormous responsibility. Mussolini's war should become Italy's war and the parasitism of the monarchy should be brought to an end. 'It is absolutely unjust that the monarchy, having accepted from the regime all that the regime had to offer it ... holds itself aloof now that the situation in the war is not favourable.'[86] When at last he did attack Mussolini it was to attack not Mussolini but the dictatorship. The crisis of Fascism had begun with its Germanisation by the dictatorship, he said. The dictatorship had 'destroyed and killed Fascism. The real enemy of Fascism was the dictatorship,' he added. From the day when the old motto 'Libertà e Patria' inscribed on the banners of the *squadristi* was replaced by '*Credere, Obedire, Combattere*', Fascism was finished. The responsibility for the disastrous war lay not with Fascism, or the army, but with the dictatorship. 'It is the latter which has lost the war ...' His motion, he said, aimed to create an 'internal national front which until today has not existed in Italy because the Crown has taken up an attitude of prudent reserve'. In the end, he did criticise Mussolini directly but only to beg him to change. 'Tear off those ridiculous Maresciallo's stripes and go back to what you were: our Mussolini, the Mussolini we obeyed and followed!' This prompted Mussolini to snap, 'The people is with me!' These were his first words since Grandi had begun to speak an hour beforehand. Grandi concluded, 'Listen to this cry of anguish which comes from the hearts of your faithful. Duce, let us share all responsibilities.'[87]

Smoking was banned at the meeting but nevertheless the stifling heat and the smell of human sweat had made the air in the Sala del Pappagallo unbearable. The black riding boots of the Fascists made their feet feel as if they were inside ovens. Briefly, Carlo Pareschi, the Agriculture Minister, lost consciousness and had to be helped out.[88]

Now Ciano spoke. Nor did he attack Mussolini directly. He attacked the Germans. He said that the Axis must hold out against the enemy. But he then detailed the history of the alliance with Germany and the German breaches of the alliance, in particular the promise not to do anything that might cause war 'until 1942'. 'The Germans set fire to the fuse ahead of time, against every pact and understanding with us.' It seemed as if Ciano was giving a speech in favour of Mussolini not against him, for these had so often been Mussolini's own arguments. But Mussolini knew exactly where such an argument would lead in the context of this meeting. Ciano came to the point: 'We will not have to fear any negative judgement of history as far as the correctness of our international relations are concerned if we should decide to separate our decisions from those of our ally.' He concluded, 'We were not ... traitors, but the betrayed.'[89]

Now Farinacci spoke. He read out his motion. Its aim was to achieve precisely what Grandi had tried to persuade members his motion aimed to do: to force the King to share the burden of responsibility for the war and hence the blame, 'to show the entire world that the whole population is fighting, united under his orders' – not to take away command from Mussolini. Like Grandi's, his motion proposed that all government organs shoulder the responsibility of government but including – unlike Grandi's - the PNF. And unlike Grandi's, it did not propose handing political power back to the King. Farinacci's aim – though his motion did not spell this out – was to give the Germans command of Axis forces in Italy. Just as Grandi had tried to conceal his main purpose behind another, so too did Farinacci. He also called for the dismissal of Ambrosio. He said, 'In this war our enemies, first the Anglo-French and then the Anglo-Americans, have set up a unified command and politico-military direction of the war. The Axis has reached this position in the political field, thanks to the Duce and the Führer, but in the military sphere we are completely sovereign and independent, and with the results which we see. I also ask, as comrade Grandi has rightly requested, that the King and the royal household be brought on to the stage, and called upon to share the honour and the burden of the war ...' Farinacci now turned on Grandi and accused him of conducting 'an underground and cannibal war' against Fascism.

After Farinacci, several others spoke.

It was getting on for midnight. Mussolini, after whispered consultation with Scorza, proposed that the meeting be adjourned until the next day, given the lateness of the hour. Such an adjournment would probably have meant that Grandi's motion would fail as Mussolini would have been able to bring pressure to bear on waverers overnight or worse. The air in the Sala del Pappagallo was fetid and he was in severe pain. But Grandi retorted, 'On the *Carta del Lavoro* you kept us here for seven hours. Today, when it is a question of the life of the *patria* we can, if necessary, go on discussing for a week.' So Mussolini proposed a short break instead. This lasted about half an hour.[90] Mussolini retired to his office – the Sala del Mappamondo – where he drank a glass of warm sugared milk and called for a number of members including Alfieri, Buffarini Guidi and Scorza to see him. 'What is happening in Germany?' Mussolini asked Alfieri. Outside, Grandi moved about seeking more signatures for his motion. Before it, he had managed to secure only ten.[91] During the break he increased the number to 20. These included Pareschi, now recovered, who was from Balbo's Ferrara and said, 'I sign for Balbo.'[92]

Ciano came up and said that he wanted to sign. Grandi, though he disliked him, told Ciano, 'We are all grateful for your support ... Now don't put yourself in too serious a position. No one will mind if you abstain.' But Ciano insisted. 'I have made the sign of the cross before the Madonna as a promise not to change course. I want to sign and I shall sign,' he said.[93]

When Alfieri emerged from Mussolini's office, Grandi came up to him to urge him to sign. He did. The twenty signatories included the deaf Marinelli.[94] Buffarini Guidi, meanwhile, urged Mussolini to arrest Grandi and his supporters. Mussolini told him to calm down.

The meeting resumed. Bastianini spoke and said that the PNF had lost touch with the nation, which prompted Mussolini to snap, 'The origin of this fracture can perhaps be found in certain rapid enrichments.' Cryptically, towards the end, he said, 'And then I have in hand a key to resolve the war situation.' This was probably a reference to the often talked about secret weapons. Galbiati, Commander of the Militia, was heard to mutter to himself, 'I don't see clearly what this resolution contains, but I don't like it, I don't like it.' He then spoke against the motion and defended

Mussolini against the charge that Italy had not prepared for the war and had fought it badly. 'Why did we enter the war? Let us consider this. We entered the war, at the side of Germany, confident of winning . . .'

Mussolini intervened a second time. He addressed in particular the charge that a rupture had developed between Fascism and the nation. He blamed this, however, not on the disastrous course of the war, but on the corruption of senior Fascists. This, of course, was designed to scare them. 'If there was a schism, it should be said that it was caused by the financial situation of many party bosses, whose economic standard is too high in relation to their political activity.' Mussolini ended by saying, 'Let us admit that he [the King] accepts the restitution of the delegated military powers. It is then a question of knowing whether I accept to be beheaded. I am sixty years old; and I know what certain things mean . . .' And he warned, 'If I am to be constrained to cede to the King the military command, that fracture between country and party of which you speak will swallow you all up.'

His remarks had caused many to waver. Later Grandi would recall, 'He had won back at a stroke all that which he seemed to have earlier lost. He had known how to press all the right buttons at the right moment and with his consummate wisdom, he had spoken to all and each, directly; he had threatened, flattered, proposed to each their individual dilemma, replied for each to their own secret question, obligations of fidelity, love of *patria*, responsibility, honour, doubt, self-interest. He was still, despite everything, the magician and the boss.'[95]

Now spoke Scorza, the PNF Secretary, and out of the blue announced his own motion. Having been a party to the plot, he had suddenly now 'sensed the wind' and 'changed tack', noted Bottai.[96] Grandi and the other conspirators were amazed.[97] Scorza had obviously been 'navigating', as the Italians say, in many waters. His motion made no mention of handing back military command to the King. It merely stressed the need for 'new methods and means' and the PNF to take the initiative but was unspecific. Prior to the meeting Scorza had been on the side of Grandi, it had seemed. Now he had done a volte-face. Bottai described his speech as a '*coup de théâtre*' which was 'unexpectedly' against Grandi and '*ultra-mussoliniano*'.[98] For Scorza the problem was that Mussolini had not been enough of a dictator. 'You have been . . . the most disobeyed man of the century,' said Scorza.[99] Scorza's speech also caused many to waver. It was 1 a.m. Others spoke, or spoke again, most significantly Bottai and Alfieri. Bottai said that neither Farinacci's nor Scorza's motion proposed what Italy needed most at this grave hour: 'that unity of instruction between King and Duce, which is the guarantee of the linked salvation of the nation and the regime.[100] Ciano back-tracked by suggesting some kind of compromise amalgamation of the motions.[101]

Giacomo Suardo, President of the Senate, stood up and withdrew his signature from Grandi's motion – sobbing. So too did Gaetano Polverelli. Tullio Cianetti, who would write a letter of apology to Mussolini the next day, said that he was perplexed. Some, such as Bottai, thought the motion was a call for a return to Fascism's revolutionary roots, others a means to strengthen not weaken Mussolini, others a call for harmony. Grandi stood up and placed the motion with the signatures attached in front of Mussolini. Mussolini looked at it, recalled Alfieri, with 'ostentatious indifference'.[102] He then called on Scorza to put Grandi's motion – the first of the three – to a vote. Scorza stood up. He was the first to vote. Despite his cosiness with the conspirators before the meeting he voted 'no'. De Bono voted 'yes'. Suardo abstained. Ciano's turn came. Mussolini half shut his eyes. He and his son-in-law looked at each other for what seemed like a long time, recalled Alfieri. 'Yes,' said Ciano in a clear voice.

The vote – which did not include that of Farinacci who insisted that he vote only on his own motion – was nineteen in favour, seven against, with one abstention – that of Suardo.[103] Like many of those present, Luciano Gottardi had never attended a meeting of the Grand Council. He had voted in favour of the motion because he had assumed that if Mussolini had given his permission for a vote on a motion the duty of all was to vote in favour of it! Marinelli, who had ordered the kidnapping of Matteotti in 1925, now aged sixty-six and deaf, voted 'yes' as well. Many who had voted 'yes' did not understand the implications of Grandi's motion. Certainly, they did not think it would lead to the fall of Mussolini. No vote was taken on either Farinacci's or Scorza's motion. De Bono would write in his diary, 'Mussolini knows that in the minds of the great majority of the signatories there was not the least intention of removing him from power. Yes, among them there were traitors, Grandi positively, but who could have imagined it?'[104] It was not until the following month that Bottai would find out about the plot by the King and the generals when he saw Federzoni. He would write, 'And the military plot? Federzoni confirms its existence, beyond all doubt; and he names Ambrosio as the one who led it ... So it is confirmed, then: the concomitance, reciprocally ignorant, of the two revolts, the political and the military; the first of which ... directed at, not against Mussolini, to reconnect him constitutionally to the King; the second directed at the King against Mussolini ...'

Mussolini asked, 'Who will take this motion to the King?' 'You,' replied Grandi. '*Signori*, you have provoked the crisis of the regime. The session is closed,' said Mussolini.[105]

Mussolini at least understood the significance of the motion but knew nothing of what the King and generals were up to. Scorza called the ritual salute to the Duce. But Mussolini motioned him to stop and strode out. One or two of the Fascist gerarchs still replied regardless with the ritual '*A noi!*'. It was 2.40 a.m. The meeting had lasted nearly ten hours. On the way out the deaf Marinelli asked, 'Was the Grandi motion approved?'[106]

Mussolini spent some time in the Sala del Mappamondo before leaving Palazzo Venezia. Scorza and others who had voted against the Grandi motion joined him. They urged him to arrest Grandi and those who had supported him. He replied, 'Arrest them? Occupy Rome with the 'M' Division and eventually with the help of the Germans? . . . And how would the King react? And the army? The possibility of a civil war at the backs of the troops lined up against the enemy?'[107] He telephoned Petacci. The call was tapped. He said, 'There's little to be afraid of. We have arrived at the epilogue … at the greatest turning point in history.' There was a silence. Then Mussolini added, 'My star has grown dim.'[108]

Mussolini and Scorza left Palazzo Venezia together by car for Villa Torlonia, from where Scorza went on to PNF headquarters. Scorza said he felt confident that the vote had no legal status as the Grand Council was merely a consultative body. Mussolini knew this, of course, but all he said during the journey was, 'Even Ciano.' Later he recalled, 'The streets were deserted. But one seemed to feel in the air, now almost clear in the morning twilight, that sense of the inevitable which comes from the wheel of destiny when it moves, and of which men are often the unconscious instruments.[109]

He would tell Marinetti, the Futurist and founder of the first hour who also suffered from a stomach illness, that he had been in severe pain. 'You alone can understand me, you who know the effects of our illness. The night of 24 July I was very ill. Two hours before the wretched meeting of the Grand Council I had had a violent attack …'[110] Mussolini drove home where his wife demanded, 'Well, you arrested them at least?' 'No, I'll do it tomorrow,' he replied. 'Tomorrow will be too late,' she said.[111] Mussolini agreed with Grandi that the only solution was for Italy to abandon the Axis and seek peace. But he knew that he, Mussolini, could not pursue that course. Regardless, he still believed that the King would stand by him. The King always had.

Grandi had gone to the apartment he had at Montecitorio as President of the *Camera dei Fasci*, where he was met by Acquarone at about 3.30 a.m. Together they went to the house of a friend of Grandi's and were in conclave for about two hours. Grandi said that the King should appoint Marshal Caviglia head of a new government not Badoglio as he was too tainted by Fascism. Caviglia – as Grandi had written in his diary – was the only general from the First World War left who had not 'fornicated with Fascism'.[112] He also warned Acquarone that Mussolini might use the Grand Council vote as an excuse with Hitler to disengage from the alliance with Germany and thus regain the initiative. He told Acquarone further that the coup against Mussolini must dovetail simultaneously with an 'immediate and direct' request to the Allies for an armistice and the preparation of the Italian armed forces to combat the Germans. 'There is no other solution possible. It is a question of defending ourselves from the inevitable Nazi vendetta ... Italy cannot exit the war. Neutrality is an illusion,' wrote Grandi.[113]

Following his meeting with Grandi, Acquarone went to see the King at 7 a.m. on Sunday, 25 July, who authorised him to tell Ambrosio to prepare to arrest Mussolini after the usual Monday royal audience. Though the King shared Grandi's reservations about Badoglio, he nevertheless now signed a decree appointing the Marshal, who had fornicated with Fascism, head of the new government. Those few Fascists who had pressed hardest on behalf of Grandi's motion, therefore, the few who understood where it would lead, were the first Italians to commit a revolutionary act against Fascism. Naturally, the Italian Left will not accept this. The Left is somehow able to see the coup against Mussolini as the result of mass protest against Fascism – as an attempt by the establishment to forestall left-wing revolution.[114] For the Left, the first revolutionary acts would be by the Italian resistance. Given that a resistance did not even exist in mid-1943, such acts were anyway still a long way off and even when they did come they were not exactly successful. It was the Allies, after all, not the resistance, who liberated Italy. Furthermore, unlike the resistance – which was never more than an irritant to the Germans – the coup which deposed Mussolini succeeded. There was no mass protest against Fascism anyway before the coup, unless you count the very short-lived March 1943 strikes.

The motive of those who conspired against Mussolini was not the desire to stop left-wing revolution, but to stop the war. For some, such as Bottai, it was a revolutionary act, not against Fascism but against what Fascism had become. As Bottai, who like Grandi had opposed Italian entry into the war in 1940, noted, 'The dictatorship had wanted the war: there was a need, therefore, to strike at the dictatorship, so as to be able to revise our entire politics in regard to the war and to impose on them the course most appropriate to the interests of the nation. It [the Grand Council meeting] was not the last attempt to save Fascism; it was the first step towards the new situation.'[115] Bottai was the most Fascist of Fascists. This made him, therefore, the most left-wing of Fascists. But his explanation of why the majority voted for Grandi's motion seems to misunderstand completely what Grandi was up to. This means that Grandi could never have spelled out to Bottai, virtually his closest ally in the conspiracy, what his motion meant to him. Bottai may have had in mind a return to the revolutionary origins of Fascism as the result of the Grand Council meeting. But Grandi – if we are to believe what he wrote – most certainly did not. Nor did others, many of whom failed to understand the motion. For Grandi, Fascism was finished. But then, unlike Bottai, he had never been a true believer. For Bottai, to vote against Mussolini was to reject his faith; Grandi had long ago lost whatever faith he had in Fascism. As for Ciano, he had never had faith.

Sunday, 25 July

Despite having had very little sleep, Mussolini got up as usual at about 7 a.m. on Sunday, 25 July and as he usually did, even on Sundays, went to the Palazzo Venezia. The Agenzia Stefani had contacted his secretary, Nicolo De Cesare, about the outcome of the Grand Council meeting. De Cesare said that 'the meeting was long, but neither interesting nor important'.[116] During the morning Mussolini saw various ministers including Umberto Albini, Interior Under-Secretary, who had voted for Grandi's motion but who now assured Mussolini of his devotion to him. Mussolini told him, 'I have looked at the rules and the King will confirm to me that I have the right to ignore the vote.'[117] He tried to contact Grandi by telephone to arrange a meeting but could not find him as Grandi, who had sought advice from Acquarone; had gone to ground. Mussolini pardoned two Croat partisans who had been sentenced to death. He received a letter from Cianetti repenting his 'yes' vote. He saw Galbiati who urged him at the very least to arrest Grandi. But then, at about midday, he did something unusual: he telephoned Puntoni to bring forward the usual Monday morning audience with the King to 5 pm. that day. The King agreed.

At about the same time Mussolini saw the new Japanese ambassador, Shinrokuro Hidaka, accompanied by Bastianini. This was significant for two reasons: despite all that was going on, Mussolini found the time; and diplomats were not received on Sundays. According to Bastianini, Mussolini told Hidaka, 'The Duce had therefore decided that in the course of the coming week he would undertake an energetic approach to the Führer ... to induce the Führer himself, as he had already attempted on previous occasions, to cease hostilities on the Eastern Front, and thus arrive at a settlement with Russia. Once this had been obtained, the Reich would be able to bring the whole weight of its military potential to bear against the Anglo-Americans in the Mediterranean. ... Otherwise the conditions in which Italy was fighting were such that she would, and in a short space of time, find herself absolutely unable to continue hostilities, and would be obliged to examine a solution of a political character.' He urged Hidaka to persuade his government to put pressure on Stalin (Japan and Russia were not at war) to agree to such peace talks.[118] Hidaka, in a telegram intercepted by Allied code breakers, told the Japanese Foreign Minister that Mussolini had said, 'The next time I see Hitler I shall tell him clearly and categorically that he must conclude the struggle against Russia. And I beg you Japanese to do the same ... Perhaps together we can succeed in wrenching Hitler away from his obsession. If we are to have any hope of still winning this war, we must do it. .... As for Italy, time has nearly run out. Certainly we can no longer say "time is on our side".'[119] Bastianini recalled how Mussolini told him to prepare a telegram to Hitler after the meeting with Hidaka.[120] There is no trace, however, of this telegram in the State Archives. But it is probably the one which turned up recently in photocopy form in Italy. Apparently, the photocopy came from the archives of the Italian Communist party (PCI). The original was probably among the many documents Mussolini had with him when captured at Lake Como by PCI-controlled Italian partisans in 1945. It is certain that these documents ended up in the hands of the PCI. The photocopy of the telegram says that 'given the military situation it is better to make use of politics. ... I have once again begged the [Japanese] ambassador to inform President Tojo that it is my firm desire that he supports my move towards you, Führer, with all his power so as to achieve as quickly as possible the cessation of hostilities against Russia.'[121] This was the first time that Mussolini had threatened to withdraw from the war unless peace with Russia was achieved (he had urged such a course of action many times before but not accompanied by a threat). It is clear that he planned to use such a threat as a means of regaining the political initiative.

Naturally he was aware, as he had told the Grand Council, that he and the regime were in crisis. But he had no idea that the King and the generals planned to arrest him as a result of the Grand Council vote. As Grandi had told Acquarone, and as the Hidaka meeting and telegram testify, Mussolini now had in mind using the Grand Council vote to give Hitler an ultimatum: unless Germany made peace with Russia Italy would have to withdraw from the war. He had told Bastianini to bring forward a planned visit by Göring to Rome for the 29th – Mussolini's sixtieth birthday – by two days. He may have had in mind using Göring, the least enthusiastic for the continuation of the war in Russia, to put pressure on Hitler. Conspicuously, neither Mussolini nor Scorza nor Galbiati gave orders for any precautionary measures of a military kind to be taken. Why did he not arrest anyone? Why did he continue to have confidence in the King?

At about 2 p.m. Mussolini left Palazzo Venezia with Galbiati by car to visit San Lorenzo, which had been the worst hit part of Rome during the devastating Allied bombing raid of 19 July, which had left so many dead, and many more injured.[122] Though his visit was somewhat tardy – nearly a week after the bombing (previously the King, Queen and Pope had been and he had visited other bombed zones) – there was even some applause for Mussolini. But when Pius XII had paid his visit, kneeling down in the rubble and soiling his white vestments with blood, the crowd had shouted, 'Viva il papa! Viva la pace!'[123] Galbiati asked Mussolini what his relations with the King were like. 'He has always been solidly behind me,' replied Mussolini.[124]

He then went to Villa Torlonia just after 3 p.m. for a late lunch. 'Arrest those who voted against you last night first and then go to the King,' his wife told him once again. At a quarter to five he set off for Villa Savoia, the royal residence in Rome, in his Alfa Romeo, accompanied by De Cesare, and driven as usual by his chauffeur, Ercole Boratto, a former racing driver who had twice won the Tobruk–Tripoli – the African Mille Miglia. He always wore civilian clothes for his meetings with the King.[125] This time he was wearing a blue suit and brown felt hat.

Acquarone and the generals had had to move fast. They had planned to arrest Mussolini at the usual Monday audience with the King. But this had now been brought forward. Furthermore the King, though he had decided to remove Mussolini, had not yet given the actual order for the arrest. The *carabinieri* would occupy government ministries and centres of communication. In addition, fifty of them under the command of Lieutenant-Colonel Giovanni Frignani, whose loyalty to the King was in no doubt, would be on stand-by at Villa Savoia, hidden in the bushes. An ambulance would be used to ferry Mussolini off to captivity.

But Carboni's Motorised Corps, whose task was to defend Rome, still only existed on paper.[126] This left Rome prone to the militia's new armoured 'M' division and its thirty-six German Tiger tanks, stationed sixteen miles outside the capital – if it chose to move. Whether it would or not was complicated by the fact that Ambrosio had convinced Mussolini to place it under the command of the army on 14 July.[127] Badoglio spent the afternoon at his sumptuous villa playing bridge.

Mussolini's Alfa Romeo drew up inside the grounds of the Villa Savoia five minutes early. Three escort cars containing his personal detectives remained parked outside the gate. The fifty *carabinieri* and the ambulance were hidden out of sight. The King, in his uniform of First Marshal of the Empire, met Mussolini and De Cesare on the steps leading up to the main entrance. They went inside to the drawing room. Boratto, the chauffeur, meanwhile, was called to the porter's lodge on the pretext that he was wanted on the telephone and locked inside. He was not let out until midnight. 'I entered Villa Savoia with a mind completely free from any forebodings,' Mussolini later wrote.

Mussolini and the King were together for approximately twenty minutes. The King had asked Puntoni to stand behind the open drawing-room door in case he was needed. After giving a résumé of the military situation, Mussolini turned to the Grand Council meeting. It was a purely consultative body, he said, whose vote carried no constitutional weight . . . The King interrupted him. According to Mussolini, he said, 'Things are no longer working . . . Italy is on its knees . . . the army's morale is rock bottom, the soldiers don't want to fight any more . . . the vote of the Grand Council is dreadful . . . At this moment you are the most hated man in Italy. You cannot count any more on more than one friend. Only one has remained with you, me. For this I tell you that you need not have any worries about your personal safety.' Even the Alpini had started singing a song, said the King, which called for the downfall of Mussolini, the assassin of the Alpini.[128]

Puntoni, listening from behind the open door, was the only witness. According to him the King told Mussolini, 'Io vi voglio bene, I have demonstrated it many times defending you from every attack, but this time I have to ask you to leave me free to leave the government to others. You can be sure that I will vouch for your personal safety. I have thought that the man for the situation is Marshal Badoglio. We will know within six months.'[129] The word 'Badoglio' prompted Mussolini to ask, 'Then, everything is finished?' 'I am sorry, I am sorry,' said the King, 'but there was no other solution.' The King accompanied Mussolini to the steps of the main entrance where he then did something which he had never done. He shook Mussolini's hand and that of De Cesare 'with great warmth', Mussolini recalled.[130]

Only the sound of the bees buzzing in the lavender could be heard. Mussolini turned to go towards his Alfa Romeo at which point Captain Paolo Vigneri of the carabinieri came up to him and aid, 'His Majesty the King has given me orders to accompany you to protect you from the crowd.' His orders were to arrest Mussolini dead or alive. Mussolini, who did not realise what was happening, said, 'I don't see the need for it. But do so anyway.' Mussolini moved closer to his Alfa Romeo at which point Vigneri stood in front of it and, motioning towards the ambulance, said, 'Not in this one, in that one . . .'[131] Vigneri then escorted Mussolini, holding him by the elbow, and De Cesare to the ambulance in which were several carabinieri and plain-clothes police officers. Mussolini was ushered inside the ambulance which, after sitting parked for two hours in the sun, was baking hot and it set off at speed for the Podgora carabinieri barracks in Trastevere. There, Mussolini was held for three-quarters of an hour before being transferred to the carabinieri cadet training school barracks in Via Legnano on the west bank of the Tiber, which were deemed more secure.[132] Still, apparently, Mussolini did not understand that he was under arrest, thinking, as he would later recall, that all this was being done to 'ensure, as the King had said, his "personal safety".'[133] That the King had in mind simply the withdrawal from circulation of Mussolini for his own safety as much as for that of the country rather than his arrest is the truth anyway. The King had been so badly affected by the whole affair that he was unable to hold back tears.[134] But Ambrosio had decided otherwise.

Shortly after 5 p.m. Acquarone telephoned Badoglio to invite him to Villa Savoia to see the King. Badoglio donned his army marshal's uniform and departed, leaving instructions at his home for a bottle of Veuve Clicquot to be put on ice – one of 5000 bottles he had in his wine cellar.[135]

Scorza, at PNF headquarters, soon became worried when Mussolini did not telephone him as agreed after the royal audience. He telephoned Palazzo Venezia but could not get through. He then drove off to carabinieri headquarters to see General Angelo Cerica, Commander of the *carabinieri*, to enlist his help in finding Mussolini, after leaving orders to mobilise the Rome PNF if he did not return. Cerica promptly placed Scorza under arrest but then let him go after Scorza told him that otherwise there would be civil war. But instead of doing anything, Scorza went into hiding. The PNF officials at headquarters did nothing either. Galbiati, meanwhile, at militia headquarters, dithered. It was a Sunday after all. When eventually he thought to contact the 'M' Division he could not do so because the telephone lines had been cut on the orders of the Interior Ministry. There were no other militia units on alert stand-by in Rome. Ambrosio meanwhile moved motorised army units into Rome to guard key buildings. Galbiati, having heard that Mussolini was under arrest and Badoglio now head of the government, resigned. News of Mussolini's arrest had spread fast via the bush telegraph. At 10.45 p.m. three radio messages were broadcast to say that the King had accepted Mussolini's resignation, that Badoglio was the new head of government and that the King was now commander-in-chief of the armed forces – but that *the war continued* nevertheless. No news was given of Mussolini's whereabouts or whether he was alive or dead. Either the King was too afraid of the Germans to sue for peace; or he did not want peace. Nevertheless, many Italians took to the streets to celebrate and destroy the emblems of Fascism. There were lightning strikes in the big northern cities and much singing of the '*bandiera rossa*'. The Italians thought that whatever the broadcasts said the war could not possibly continue now. Could it?

That Sunday Manlio Morgagni, director of the Agenzia Stefani, who had worked with Mussolini on *Il Popolo d'Italia* and known him for years, shot himself dead. He was the only casualty in the *coup d'état* of 24–25 July 1943. He left a note which said, 'The Duce has resigned. My life is finished. *Viva Mussolini!*'[136] That Sunday, too, Ciano tried to use the telephone at his home. The line had been cut. He knew nothing of what had happened until Sunday evening and still feared arrest by Mussolini. He went to Anfuso's house on the outskirts of Rome as a precaution. But at 3 a.m. in the small hours of Monday morning he decided it was safe to go home by car. The streets were still full of people celebrating the fall of Fascism. '*Che pizza!*' [How boring],' said Ciano to Anfuso who was in the car with him.[137] Earlier on Sunday evening, at around 9.30 p.m., Farinacci had arrived at the German embassy seeking refuge. 'His face was pallid and he trembled with fear,' recalled SS Colonel Dollmann.[138] He remained in the embassy overnight and the next day, disguised as an SS officer, fled by German plane to Munich.[139] Vittorio Mussolini also fled to Germany by car and plane.[140]

Meanwhile Carlo Mazzantini, a young Fascist, felt, he wrote, 'the physical sensation of the collapse of a universe, that in which you were born, and outside of which there was nothing ... The death of the planet.[141] On

Sunday afternoon von Mackensen, the German ambassador in Rome, had telegraphed Berlin to say that the situation was 'serious, but not alarming' and that Mussolini *'noch fest im sattel sitzte'* (still sits firmly in the saddle).[142] When finally informed of the coup by an aide he was in the embassy pool. *'Der Badoglio ist ein Schwein!'* he erupted.[143] At Villa Torlonia the telephone rang. Rachele Mussolini picked it up. A voice said, 'They have just arrested the Duce!' and hung up. One of her servants said that perhaps Mussolini did not deserve such devotion on account of his affair with Petacci. It was the first Rachele Mussolini knew of it.[144] Petacci, meanwhile, waited for her lover in the Sala dello Zodiaco at Palazzo Venezia – in vain.

It was not until Sunday evening that Hitler heard the news. He threw a tantrum. His generals had never seen him so distressed. He wanted the immediate occupation of Rome. They pointed out that the nearest troops, the 3rd Panzergrenadieren, were sixty miles away. Behind Hitler's outburst lay his belief that his destiny and that of Mussolini were inextricably linked and his genuine affection for Mussolini. Following Mussolini's overthrow, Albert Speer wrote of Hitler, 'He said he was oppressed day and night with anguish.'[145] So too were the Allies taken by surprise. On 24 July Francis d'Arcy Obsorne, British ambassador to the Holy See, telegraphed the Foreign Office to say, 'I do not expect any serious or successful movement from any quarter against the Fascist government ... typhus and famine are more probable.'[146] Harold Macmillan, British Minister Resident in North Africa responsible for British policy in the Mediterranean, heard at about 11.30 p.m. that Mussolini had resigned. It was 'only later' that the Allied leaders heard that he had been deposed.[147]

Late that night, Mussolini received a reptilian letter from Badoglio which assured him that his detention was 'uniquely devoted to Your personal interests, having arrived from more than one source precise indications of a serious plot against Your Person'. The letter also said that Mussolini could choose where he wanted to be held.[148] Badoglio was trying to do two things here: discourage a Fascist–Nazi backlash; but at the same time protect his back in the event of such a backlash. Mussolini replied saying that he wanted to go to La Rocca delle Caminate, promising Badoglio 'every possible collaboration' and expressing his support for Badoglio's decision to continue the war on the side of the Germans.[149]

Nobody had obeyed the Fascist oath to defend the Fascist revolution with their blood. The bloodless *coup d'état* by the head of the *état* was over. The first act of the Badoglio government was to impose martial law. During the course of the next week the Army shot dead 81 people and wounded 320. Nearly all were anti-Fascist strikers – not Fascists. There were about 850 arrests.[150] These included Starace who since his demise had had little to do with Fascism. Mussolini's wife was driven to La Rocca delle Caminate where she was held under house arrest. Badoglio ordered the press to disclose Mussolini's relationship with Petacci. Then, on 12 August, he ordered the arrest of Petacci and her family, and imprisoned them in Novara in the north. Marcello Petacci, her corrupt brother, was imprisoned at Forte Boccea near Rome.[151]

The new government also disbanded the PNF and the GIL, dissolved the *Camera dei fasci*, the Grand Council and the Special Tribunal, and placed the militia under the command of the army. It also seized the assets of the ex-gerarchs and launched a judicial inquiry into the origins of their wealth. Conspicuously, the immense wealth Badoglio had acquired under Fascism did not come under scrutiny. Among Fascist laws abolished was the bachelor tax.[152] Ciano lost his job as ambassador to the Holy See and was a major target of the investigations into ill-gotten gains but otherwise left alone.

But *the war continued*. The new government was more dictatorial than Mussolini had ever been and much blood would now flow as a result of its ineptitude. As Mussolini had told his entourage at Feltre, if Italy made a separate peace, Hitler would sweep into Italy. Italy, as Mussolini realised, had no choice with Mussolini still in power. With Mussolini gone, Hitler soon occupied Italy anyway. But there was a difference: whereas Mussolini could never have obtained military assistance from the Allies against Hitler, the Badoglio government might. If the King and Badoglio had possessed metal and flair they would have been able, in conjunction with the Allies, to have repulsed the Germans. Instead, as a result of their ineptitude Italy became a bloody battlefield for the next twenty months.

Bottai, like everyone else, had no idea that the King and the generals had planned to arrest Mussolini and replace him with Badoglio. On 2 August he saw Grandi, who was 'embittered' by the King's *coup d'état*.[153] Grandi gave him his word of honour that he had had no contact at all with the King before the Grand Council meeting. This was not strictly true. There had been the 4th June meeting and there were indirect contacts. But Grandi had not known that the King planned to arrest Mussolini. This, at any rate, is what he would always claim. Anfuso, Ciano's friend, was not so sure. He and Ciano had gone to Grandi's apartment at Montecitorio in the early evening of 25 July. News of Mussolini's arrest reached them there. Ciano was amazed, wrote Anfuso, but not Grandi, 'who, it is very probable, already knew the fate which lay in store for Mussolini ... It was clear that Grandi hid much from Ciano (the hoped-for succession to Mussolini and the passport for Portugal).'[154]

On 18 August Grandi left for Spain and Portugal – having been given a passport by the Badoglio government – in search of Sir Samuel Hoare, British ambassador in Madrid, and other Allied diplomats to talk about peace.[155] The trip had the added attraction of enabling him to escape the risk of arrest and death if the Germans occupied Italy and Mussolini returned to power. Having failed to make any headway with his unofficial peace feelers, he remained in Lisbon where he shaved off his beard, changed his name and gave Latin lessons. In 1948 he went to Brazil and did not return to Italy until the 1960s.[156]

From Rome, where he spent one night at the *carabinieri* barracks sleeping on a sofa, Mussolini was taken first on the evening of 27 July to the island of Ponza, in the Bay of Naples, then the island of Maddalena, between Sardinia and Corsica. He was still wearing the blue suit in which he had gone to see the King. At Ponza, where he remained confined in a house overlooking the sea until 8 August,[157] Mussolini received a telegram from Göring on 29 July, his sixtieth birthday. He also received letters and money from his wife and daughter, and clothes including a white yachting suit. At Ponza, he reread *Vita di Gesù Cristo*, by Padre Giuseppe Ricciotti whom he had commissioned to write for *Il Popolo d'Italia* in 1942. He gave the book to Don Luigi Dies, the parish priest on Ponza, along with a note describing it as 'an uplifting book which one really has to read at a sitting' and requesting that the priest say a mass for his dead son, Bruno, on 7 August – the second anniversary of his death.[158] Ironically, his old Socialist friend, Nenni, whom he had shared a prison cell with in Forlì in 1911, then saved from the Nazis, was still confined on Ponza – though they did not meet.[159] Badoglio was in the process of freeing Mussolini's political prisoners such as Nenni – though not the Communist ones. Nenni would play a significant role in the resistance.

On Maddalena Mussolini was confined in a villa which had been 'built by an Englishman called Webber', he wrote, which prompted him to wonder, 'The Secret Service? Possibly.'[160] There, on 19 August, he received the twenty-four-volume complete works of Nietzsche from Hitler as a belated birthday present.

During the month he was confined on these islands he kept a kind of diary which began, 'All that has happened had to happen, because if it did not have to happen it would not have happened.' Of the fall of Fascism, he said, 'Twenty years of work were destroyed in a few hours. I refuse to believe that there are no more Fascists in Italy ... Have I perhaps been dreaming? Was it all an illusion? Was it all just superficial? Was there nothing of depth to it?' Of himself, he said, 'My blood, the infallible voice of my blood, tells me that my star has set for ever.'[161] On Ponza, he asked one of his guards, 'Tell me, Sergeant, didn't the *squadristi*, my followers of '21, do anything?' 'No, Excellency,' the sergeant replied.[162] On Maddalena, he asked the parish priest if he could see him regularly to help overcome his 'grave moral crisis provoked by isolation rather than all the rest'. Mussolini promised the priest he would do nothing in the future 'that might wound Catholic religious principles.'[163]

On 28 August he was transferred yet again, this time to a hotel in the Apennines at the base of the 10,000 feet high Gran Sasso mountain in the Abruzzi.[164] On the 6th he was moved up the mountain to another hotel, the Campo Imperatore, at 6000 feet and accessible only by cable car. There, he was given a luxurious suite on the second floor and was able to listen to the radio and play cards with his guards. Often, he was seen at the window of his suite, studying the mountains with binoculars or sitting on a wall in front of the hotel staring at the horizon. 'One of his favourite subjects was that of betrayal.'[165] It was obvious that the King and Badoglio did not intend to kill Mussolini but protect him from those who had other plans for him, such as the Allies who wanted to put him on trial and the Germans who wanted to restore him to power.

24–25 July: Conclusion

Mussolini divided the members of the Grand Council who had voted against him into three distinct types: the traitors; the accomplices; the ignorant.[166] He regarded only Grandi, Bottai, Ciano, Federzoni and De Marsico as traitors. In captivity he would write, 'Three or four people knew what they wanted ... The others understood *nulla* and did not think that with that motion they would put in play the existence of the regime.'[167]

But the Grand Council meeting of 24–25 July did not oust Mussolini. The King did. Without his intervention Mussolini would have remained in power. The Grand Council meeting has gone down in history as the reason why Mussolini lost power. Without the vote in favour of Grandi's motion, so the story goes, the King would not have arrested Mussolini. This is false. If there had been no Grand Council meeting the King would still have arrested Mussolini. But Grandi did not know this. The significance of the motion was that it gave the King a more or less (less rather than more) constitutional justification at the eleventh hour to sack Mussolini. What the motion did not do, was give the King a constitutional justification to arrest Mussolini. And it was the arrest which made all the difference.

The consequence of the overthrow of Mussolini was the collapse not just of Fascism but of Italy itself. Perhaps Grandi had wanted the collapse of Fascism but few if any of those who had voted with him did – let alone the collapse of Italy. The King's arrest of Mussolini took them all by surprise – including Grandi.

The explanation for the myth of the Grand Council meeting is fourfold: the desire of Grandi and his fellow conspirators to atone for their Fascist past and carve out a place in history as heroes; the expertise, in particular of Grandi, as a self-publicist; the dramatic nature of the meeting itself; and not least the belief of Fascists that Grandi and his fellow conspirators were the ones responsible for the downfall of Mussolini. Mussolini, after all, would have four of those who voted against him, including his son-in-law, executed within a year. Certainly, if he had not fled Italy, Grandi, condemned to death *in absentia*, would have been shot as well. It does not help either that Churchill would describe Grandi as 'the principal actor in the final drama'.[168] But the principal actor was not Grandi; it was the King – however reluctantly. Grandi's aim was indeed to provide the King with a constitutional means to remove Mussolini. But the King had already decided to make do without such a means. The truth, as General Castellano told Pietromarchi at the time, was that the Grand Council vote merely 'accelerated' and 'orientated ... the unfolding of events' towards a 'more correct constitutional solution'.[169] Grandi and those who had voted with him were, to use Mussolini's phrase, the 'unconscious instruments' not so much as he had said of 'the wheel of destiny', but of the King.

Churchill's epitaph on Mussolini was as follows:

So ended the twenty-one years of the dictatorship of Mussolini in Italy, during which he had saved the Italian people from Bolshevism, into which it could have sunk in 1919, to carry it to a position in Europe which Italy had never had before. A new impulse was given to national life. The Italian Empire in North Africa was founded. Many important public works were completed in Italy ... His regime was too expensive, without doubt, for the Italian people, but it is undeniable that it attracted, in its period of success, a very large number of Italians ... The fatal error of Mussolini was the declaration of war against France and Great Britain after the victories of Hitler in June 1940. If he had not done it, he could have easily kept Italy in a position of equilibrium, courted and recompensed by both sides, gaining unaccustomed wealth and prosperity from the struggle of other countries. Even when the outcome of the war appeared clear, Mussolini would have been well received by the Allies. He had much to give to shorten the length of the conflict. He could have chosen with ability and intelligence the right moment in which to declare war on Hitler. Instead, he took the wrong road.[170]

Goebbels would write, 'The Duce will enter history as the last Roman, but behind his massive figure a gypsy people has gone to rot. We should have realised that sooner ... All this must teach us a great deal. National Socialism must undergo a renovation ... The National Socialist leadership must have no ties whatever with the aristocracy or with so-called society.'[171] Hitler would say that Mussolini was Italy's 'greatest son ... since the fall of the ancient world', adding, 'I have been and am glad to regard as my friend this great and loyal man.'[172]

Grandi's claim was that following the overthrow of Mussolini his aim was immediate peace with the Allies combined with a declaration of war against Germany. But he was not part of the new government and had soon fled Italy. Naturally, when neither peace with the Allies nor war with Germany happened but disaster struck instead, he did his best to tell the world, 'Told you so.' As part of these efforts he would write twice to Churchill – on 26 October 1943 and 18 August 1944, playing up his hostility to Mussolini over the years and his role in Mussolini's overthrow, and his despair that the King did not at once after Mussolini's arrest seek an armistice with the Allies and declare war on Germany. In the first letter, he wrote, 'I was firmly convinced that any delay would obviously strengthen the German hold on Italy and by diminishing our national possibilities of resistance to the Germans make more difficult our subsequent siding with the Allies.' In the second, 'I urged ... the King not to lose a single hour in putting the war to an end and in asking the Allies for an armistice ... I am still sorry that my advice was not followed, and that consequently a good part of the benefit which we expected from what had been done on 25 July was lost.'[173] Given that he did not see the King after the Grand Council meeting, his claim that he urged the King to end the war is untruthful.

Churchill did not reply to either letter. But in 1950 he would write to Grandi, 'Your plan directed at annulling the conditions of unconditional surrender established in January 1943 at Casablanca, involving Italy going to war with Germany, was a reckless plan, but the only one which in the conditions in which Italy found herself could have been attempted. It would have seriously embarrassed us Allies, because it is clear that we could not have continued to consider as an enemy a country which was fighting the common enemy ...'[174]

But on 22 September 1943 Churchill had given a more realistic assessment of the tragic situation in which Italy found itself after the overthrow of Mussolini when he told the House of Commons, 'So the Italian position had to be that although an internal revolution had taken place in Italy, they were still the allies of Germany and were carrying on common cause with them. This was a very difficult position to maintain day after day with the pistol of the Gestapo pointing at the nape of so many necks.'[175] The decision to continue with the war on the side of the Germans was based on an assessment of how the Germans would now react. This assessment depended not least on the strength of German forces in Italy. In truth, they were vastly out-numbered by the Italians. In July 1943 there were four German divisions on Sicily, two armoured divisions in Calabria, one division in Sardinia, and in central Italy the 3rd Motorised (Panzergrenadier) Division, which had no tanks, plus part of a parachute division. These two units in central Italy were the only ones that could strike at Rome immediately.[176] Including the two in Calabria, there were therefore just three and a bit German divisions on the mainland. The Italians had sixteen divisions in Italy and the islands (and thirty-four abroad).[177] But while the King, Badoglio and the generals dithered, more and more German troops arrived in Italy.

The King had tearfully and reluctantly got rid of Mussolini in order to get Italy out of the war. Yet Italy was still Germany's ally and the war continued. To 8 September 1943, Italy's military casualties had been 132,912 dead, 129,675 missing, and 115,000 injured.[178] The real slaughter was about to begin.

Mussolini would write, 'Meanwhile, the order was given to ignore my existence – the silence of the tomb must surround my name. I was a corpse whose death they hesitated to announce. Thus began the month of August, 1943, the month of infamy, of betrayal and of capitulation.'[179]

The Allies, meanwhile, at British insistence, especially Eden's, stepped up the bombing of Italian cities in August, in particular of Turin and Milan, with 'devastating' effect. The great Italian journalist Indro Montanelli – an Anglophile – found the 'rationality' for the bombing 'difficult to understand'. It was, he wrote, 'a blind bureaucratic crime'.[180]

16

SEPTEMBER 1943:
'UNA TRAGEDIA ALL'ITALIANA'

Byzantinely, Badoglio began secret peace talks with the Allies. The process degenerated first into farce then tragedy. Naturally, the Allies did not trust him. He had, after all, fornicated with Fascism for as long as anyone could remember. At the same time Badoglio swiftly assured the Germans that Italy would fight on by their side. Naturally, the Germans did not trust him either. Badoglio, in short, was your typical two-faced Italian. He even inspired a new word in an English dictionary of neologisms: the verb *'to badogliate'*.[1]

It did not help that Badoglio was an Italian. This made it unlikely that the British and the Germans would trust him whatever he said. As far as they were concerned, the Italian nation could not be trusted. It was not just that they were Italian. The Italians too had fornicated with Fascism for as long as anyone could remember. And when the time came to take tough decisions Badoglio behaved exactly how they expected an Italian to behave – dishonestly, weakly and selfishly. Badoglio badogliated.

But the real problem, perhaps, was not that Badoglio was an Italian. It was that he did not know what he wanted. He did not want to carry on fighting by the side of the Germans. But nor did he want to surrender. He would far rather have taken no decision at all and waited on events. The same was true of the King. But in defence of these two old men it has to be said that their dilemma was the same dilemma which faced the Italian people. In 2000, Roberto Vivarelli, now an old man, who volunteered to fight for Mussolini between 1943 and 1945, wrote a book about his experiences: 'I wish it were taken more into account how few Italians in 1943 had their papers in order to present themselves as enemies of Mussolini.'[2] Merely for saying that he had volunteered to fight for Mussolini from after the collapse of Fascism and tried to explain why, he was howled down. He was accused of having political ends by Italy's chattering classes. The behaviour of the Italian people was little different from that of the King and Badoglio. They had backed Fascism. They too waited upon events. They waited for other people to act.

The Allies, however, played a supporting role in the tragedy that was now to unfold in Italy. The decision by Churchill and Roosevelt to insist on unconditional surrender made it even more difficult for the reluctant Badoglio to surrender. But they also refused Badoglio military help which made it easier for the Germans to seize Italy once he had surrendered. Consequently, once Badoglio did surrender the Germans only had him and the shaky Italians to deal with. So the tragedy was not just the fault of the Latin temperament; it was also the fault of the Anglo-Saxon one. Above and around all this hovered the spectre of the absent Mussolini. What he had warned would happen if he tried to make a separate peace with the Allies did happen: the occupation of Italy by two invading armies.

By the end of the first week of August, and without the permission of the Italian General Staff, eight new German divisions had arrived in Italy – sent from France, Germany and Austria – in addition to the three and a bit divisions already in mainland Italy.[3] Ostensibly, the excuse for their presence was the defence of Italy against the Allies; but if necessary, the defence of Italy against the Italians. In addition, Hitler began the search for Mussolini in earnest, which included, on Himmler's orders, the consulting of clairvoyants and astrologists.[4]

Byzantinely, too, both the King and Badoglio insisted on avoiding the word arrest in their dealings with the Germans.[5] On 29 July von Mackensen saw the King who said that Mussolini was in a place of safety to protect him from 'party extremists'. Badoglio, meanwhile, had another expression for Mussolini's current status. He told Field Marshal Kesselring that he was in the private custody of the King.

According to Badoglio the decision to make contact with the Allies was taken at a meeting with the King on 28 July. But Harold Macmillan, British Resident Minister in North Africa, wrote, 'Marshal Badoglio did not, during the first three weeks of his Government, make any direct approach to the Allied Governments for an armistice.' Prior to that Badoglio did, however, 'put out a number of feelers', said Macmillan, but added, 'Their purpose seems to have been partly to gain time by explaining the difficulties of the Italian position and thus to obtain a mitigation of the force of Allied air attacks, and partly to confirm that the Allied intention to extract an unconditional surrender was not to be moved.'[6]

Finally Badoglio sent General Castellano, *aide-de-camp* to the Chief of the General Staff, General Ambrosio who had been instrumental in the overthrow of Mussolini, to Madrid and Lisbon to make contact with the Allies. Castellano left Rome on 12 August. But he insisted on going by train and did not arrive in Madrid until the 15th.[7] Physically, Castellano, who was in civilian clothes, had the air of classic Mediterranean deviousness about him; he smiled all the time. Furthermore, he spoke no English whatsoever. Worse, his instructions were to tell the Allies that Italy could not make peace without Allied military help and the Allies should invade Italy north of Rome and on the Adriatic coast around Rimini. Even worse, he had no instructions to agree to let alone sign, anything.

Castellano's first meeting, on 15 August, was with Sir Samuel Hoare, British Foreign Secretary at the time of the Ethiopian crisis and now British ambassador in Madrid. He then went on to Lisbon with his diplomatic delegation where he met Sir Ronald Campbell, British ambassador there. At the time Churchill, Roosevelt and the Chiefs of Staff were in Canada for the Quebec conference. They had not had time to agree detailed surrender terms, so instead decided that Castellano should be presented with a document called the 'Short Military Armistice'. While insisting on Italy's surrender, this did not mention the word 'unconditional' or spell out anything in detail. The detail, Churchill and Roosevelt decided, would be in the 'Long Armistice' to be agreed later.

Eisenhower sent General Walter Bedell Smith, his Chief of Staff, and Brigadier Kenneth Strong, the British head of his Intelligence Unit, to Lisbon in civilian clothes with false passports to hand Castellano the 'short' surrender terms. The two sides met in Lisbon on 19 August. Castellano amazed the Allies when he asked when and where the Allied invasion of Italy would take place. He amazed them more when he wondered if his government might have fifteen days' notice so as to ensure the protection of the Italian royal family and itself. All that Bedell Smith was prepared to concede was that the announcement of the armistice would signal that the main invasion was to take place within a few hours. He also disclosed the Allied position on military help to Italy: the more the Italians impeded the Germans, the more this 'would be put to their credit in the future'.[8] He gave Castellano a radio receiver/transmitter with which the Italian government must send a coded message by midnight on 30 August to say whether or not it accepted the surrender terms. The signing ceremony would then take place the next day in Sicily.

But it was not until 24 August that Castellano's diplomatic delegation left Lisbon by train and not until 27 August that Castellano arrived back in Rome.[9] He had been away more than two weeks. During his absence he had been incommunicado. Consequently Badoglio had become impatient and despatched another negotiator, General Giacomo Zanussi, assistant to General Mario Roatta, Army Chief of Staff, to Lisbon on 24 August. So on the same day as Castellano left Lisbon by train, Zanussi arrived by plane. To add a touch of the truly bizarre, Zanussi was accompanied by a captured British lieutenant-general, Adrian Carton de Wiart, who was well over six feet tall, blind in one eye, which he covered with a black patch, and had no left hand. The arrival of a second Italian and this dangerously conspicuous British general flabbergasted Campbell, but the invasion of mainland Italy was on for 8–9 September at Salerno south of Naples. If possible, the Allies wanted Italy out of the war by then – if not on their side. So despite fears that Zanussi was working for the Germans or involved in some other complicated piece of Italian trickery, they authorised Campbell to hand him the long surrender terms, which consisted of forty-two clauses, on 27 August.[10] These spelled out that the surrender was to be 'unconditional'. There were now two armistice documents, one moderate, one harsh, in the possession of two different Italian generals both of whom were unaware of the fact. The conditions were perfect for a classic Italian imbroglio – a combination of cock-up and conspiracy.

To encourage Badoglio to sign the armistice, the Allies offered to make a parachute drop on the airfields around Rome and capture the capital – as long as the Italians gave a guarantee that their forces would protect the airfields from the Germans and would supply the parachutists with transport. This would 'hearten the Italians' and encourage them to sign the armistice, and it would also 'bolster up the morale' of the Italian troops around Rome. The offer was sent to Rome via the special radio link.[11]

General Castellano returned to Allied headquarters near Syracuse in Sicily on 2 September. But he insisted he still had no authority to sign an armistice. His mission as ever, he explained, was to find out what military help the Allies would give Italy first.

By now the Allies were furious. The invasion of mainland Italy was only six days off. Bedell Smith erupted. He told Castellano to contact Badoglio and get authority, otherwise Rome would be razed to the ground. Badoglio replied in a weasel-like way to say that the Italian government had already 'implicitly' accepted the armistice terms in its previous message. This was untrue: Badoglio had merely agreed to a Rome drop. Back went another message. Finally Badoglio spelled out in black and white for the first time that Castellano had authority to sign. The Allies carefully filmed the signing ceremony in one of the tents at 5 p.m. on 3 September, not just for media purposes but also as evidence if the Badoglio government subsequently tried to slither out of the armistice – as indeed it would. Bedell Smith now produced the long terms for Castellano. Castellano, who had never seen them, said that he was unsure his government would have signed the short terms, had it known what was in the long terms. The Allies did not insist on signature, however, of the long terms at this stage.

But they did not help matters either. They had nit-picked from the word go about the details and, apart from the Rome drop idea, had not mentioned military co-operation with the Italians or military help for them.

The same day that the smiling Castellano signed the armistice in Sicily – 3 September – Rudolf Rahn saw Badoglio in Rome. Italy stood firmly with Germany, the reptilian Marshal told the icy Gauleiter. That day two British divisions under Montgomery invaded Calabria – the main invasion was imminent.

Badoglio therefore had two military tasks: to save the Italian armed forces at home and abroad from death and capture by the Germans, and to defend Rome. He had one political task: to safeguard the King, the royal family, himself and the government.

The armistice terms did not require Italy to declare war on Germany, only to give passive support to the Allies, but they did say that the harshness of Italy's treatment would depend on how firmly Italy opposed the Germans.[12] There were about 1 million Italian troops in Italy and her islands – compared with 400,000 Germans.[13] Abroad, there were a similar number: 230,000 in south-east France and Corsica, 300,000 in Yugoslavia, 300,000 in Albania and Greece, and 53,000 in the Greek islands.[14]

This being so, one might have thought that Badoglio would do something to prepare Italy's armed forces for this dramatic moment; at the very least issue secret and precise instructions to his generals as to what to do. But he did no such thing. On the day the armistice was signed he issued an order to senior military staff, breathtaking in its vagueness, which told them 'to provide for the broadcasting of instructions so that all dependent commanders can be kept informed about the possible future events and how to react'.[15] This was his only written order. He would claim that Ambrosio, the Chief of the General Staff, had assured him that the task was already in hand. 'My mind was tranquil,' he would write.[16] On 5 September Ambrosio drew up an order – *promemoria* 1 – which stated that the Italian armed forces should only fight if attacked by the Germans. In relation to the planned parachute drop on Rome the order said that the Italian forces should hold the airfields in Italian possession.[17] Then, on the 6th, Ambrosio followed this up with *promemoria* 2, sent by word of mouth for security reasons, to Italian commanders in Greece and Yugoslavia. This said that if the Germans did not commit acts of violence against the Italians, then the Italians would 'not make common cause' with either partisans or the Allies.[18] To irritate the Allies still further, Badoglio sent a message to Castellano, by now at Allied headquarters in North Africa, to urge the Allies to give twenty-four hours' notice of the invasion so that the King could flee Italy in good time and to provide air cover! Castellano managed to secure a meeting with Eisenhower at 7 p.m. to put Badoglio's request to him. Eisenhower, a taciturn man, laughed.[19]

The Italian forces in and around Rome should have been more than a match for the Germans. Carboni's Motorised Corps alone consisted of 50,000 men and had 200 armoured vehicles. Kesselring's Chief of Staff, General Siegfried Westphal, would say that the Italians had a total of six divisions compared with their two and that in total the Germans had about 30,000 men.[20]

The parachute drop on Rome – codenamed GIANT TWO – was to be the task of the American 82nd airborne division. In the early evening of 7 September General Maxwell Taylor, its Commanding Officer[21] and Colonel William Gardner, his aide-de-camp, arrived in Rome by ambulance. Disguised as civilians they had arrived in Italy at Gaeta, between Naples and Rome, by Italian corvette, which had picked them up off the island of Ustica. Their aim was talks with Badoglio and the Italian High Command about the Rome drop – principally to reassure themselves that the Italians would play the crucial part assigned to them: defend Rome's airfields for four days and provide transport. On the 4th Castellano had sent Badoglio a detailed report on the drop but Badoglio had done nothing about it. Incredibly, now neither Badoglio, Ambrosio, his number two Ricci, nor Roatta, nor Carboni was available.

Ambrosio, who knew that two American officers were on their way – though not that one was Taylor – chose this moment to leave Rome by train for his home in Turin to deal with family matters. Carboni materialised first but not until 9.30 p.m. that evening. Taylor told him that the drop and the invasion would take place the following evening. Carboni professed astonishment. He said that Castellano had assured Rome that the invasion would not happen until the 12th. The Germans were now too strong anyway around Rome, he claimed untruthfully, adding that not just the Rome drop but the invasion itself would have to be called off. Taylor insisted on seeing Badoglio who was in bed. So Carboni drove the two Americans through the centre of Rome to Badoglio's sumptuous villa in Via Bruxelles. Badoglio, who like Ambrosio had known that two American officers were on their way to Rome, merely repeated what Carboni had said. The invasion force, however, was already at sea. Given the hopelessness of the situation, Taylor agreed that Badoglio send a radio message to Eisenhower requesting that the invasion be postponed and the Rome drop be cancelled. Furious, Eisenhower cancelled the Rome drop and so the opportunity of a swift victory in Italy was lost.

That day Rahn saw the King who 'stressed the decision to continue the struggle, to the end, at the side of Germany, with whom Italy is bound in life and death', said Rahn.[22] For some time the King had been planning his escape. He had given the crown jewels to a trusted aide and sent to Switzerland forty freight cars of royal possessions.[23]

At 6.30 p.m. on 8 September Eisenhower broadcast the news of the Italian surrender on the radio, which was also confirmation to the Italians that the main invasion of Italy would be under way within a few hours. He said, 'The armed forces of the Italian government have surrendered unconditionally . . . all Italians who now act to contribute to the expulsion of the German aggressor from Italy will have the assistance and the help of the United Nations.' Fifteen minutes later Badoglio, the King, Ambrosio and all the rest of that sorry crew met at the *Quirinale* to decide what to do. The Allies had betrayed them, they all agreed, by invading four days too early and speaking of unconditional surrender. There was talk of denying the existence of the armistice. Why not tell the Germans that Italy continued to fight by their side, said Carboni, and tell the Allies that this was just a ruse to gain time until the opportune moment arose to switch sides? There was much support for Carboni's proposal until someone reminded those assembled that the Allies could simply make public the details of the secret negotiations, which included film footage of Castellano signing the armistice. Reluctantly Badoglio made his own broadcast. It was 7.45 p.m. when he spoke to the nation: 'The Italian government, recognising the impossibility of continuing the unequal struggle against the crushing power of the opponent, with the intention of avoiding more and more serious damage to the nation, has asked General Eisenhower for an armistice ... Consequently, any act of hostility against the Anglo-American forces must cease on the part of the Italian forces in every place. They, however, will respond to any subsequent attacks from whichever other source.'[24] The Allied camp, well versed by now in Italian trickery, felt 'considerable relief', wrote Macmillan.[25] The Allied invasion at Salerno began that night of 8–9 September. The switch-board at the Ministry of War in Rome was busy all night with calls from anxious commanders in the field seeking clarification – in vain.

It was now that the King and Badoglio decided to run away. Ambrosio, the armed forces Chief of Staff, and Roatta, army Commander-in-Chief, decided to do the same. Two pieces of news had reached them: firstly, the Allies had invaded in the 'wrong' place. Salerno was much too far from Rome for Rome to be saved by the Allies; secondly, two German divisions, the 3rd Panzer Grenadieren, fifty miles away at Viterbo, and the 2nd Parachute, on the coast at Ostia, were on the move towards Rome. Just after 5 a.m. on the 9th the King and his family, Badoglio and Acquarone, numerous generals and a couple of Cabinet ministers, set off from Rome by car for Pescara on the Adriatic coast across the Apennines. From there they embarked on the *Baionetta*, a navy corvette, for Brindisi on the heel of Italy. They went by boat because the Queen was afraid of flying, and arrived at their destination without incident just after lunch on the 10th. There were fifty-seven of them in all on the *Baionetta*.[26] Several hundred other politicians, bureaucrats and officers, their wives, lovers and prized possessions, were left behind on the quayside where there had been ugly scenes. Brindisi was ideal because it was not yet in Allied hands but the Germans had gone. Badoglio's luggage had gone missing. He had to write a cheque for the first time in his life.

The decision to abandon Rome for the south was not taken out of the blue. In early September, for example, Badoglio had sent very large sums of money to a bank in Bari, near Brindisi.[27] Furthermore, he had asked the Allies for twenty-four hours' notice of the armistice precisely so that the King could flee.

In Rome, Carboni, in command of the Motorised Corps on which the defence of Rome depended, had mysteriously donned civilian clothes and gone missing. Raffaele Guariglia, the Foreign Minister, was the only senior member of the government who continued to show his face in Rome. The justification for this mass desertion by Italy's political and military leaders was that it was not a desertion at all. Quite the contrary. By leaving Rome, they would be able to preserve the government, they said, and so deal with the military crisis more effectively. The opposite, however, was the case. The crucial periods when strong government mattered were the days immediately before and after the announcement of their armistice. They failed in both those periods.

Nor did the Germans act all that quickly. Within range of Rome, for example, they had only two divisions compared with the eight Carboni had.[28] But once it was clear that the Allied invasion was well to the south of Rome and that the Italians had no intention of attacking them they moved to disarm them. By 10 September, apart from isolated examples, all Italian forces everywhere – in Italy, France, the Balkans, Greece – had surrendered to the Germans. The same day Kesselring negotiated the surrender of the Italian troops in and around Rome and the next day declared Italy a theatre of war under German control[29] Within a fortnight the Germans had disarmed – according to their own estimates – fifty-one Italian divisions definitely but probably a further twenty-nine – eighty divisions in all – out of a total eighty-three and captured an enormous quantity of weaponry. They had taken 547,000 Italian soldiers prisoner.[30] It is impossible to be sure what those troops and their commanders would have done if the King and Badoglio had issued clear orders, ideally declared war on the Germans, and if the Allies had not been so short-sighted in their refusal to include them properly in their invasion plans or come to their aid.

Had the Allies gone ahead with the Rome drop and had the Italian forces protected Rome's airfields then, as SS Colonel Dollman would write, 'in my opinion and also in the opinion of the Field Marshal [Kesselring] the defeat of the Germans would have been inevitable'.[31] If the Allies had taken Rome, the Germans would have had to deploy their relatively small force in Italy in two places, Salerno and Rome, which would have meant its defeat. Or else they would have had to withdraw the entire force to the north of Italy. But instead, two wars lasting nearly two years would now take place in Italy: the war between the Allies and the Germans; and a civil war between the Italians themselves.

The King would not agree to declare war on the Germans until 13 October. But by then he had lost his army. A declaration of war would have only had genuine value immediately after the armistice announcement. The 450,000 Italian prisoners of war already held by the Allies remained PoWs because under the Geneva Convention, the Allies explained, although Italy was now a co-belligerent, it was not an ally.[32]

The Germans, on the other hand, played legalistic games to say precisely the opposite in regard to the half million Italian soldiers they had now captured. Under the Geneva Convention, these were not prisoners of war at all but *francs-tireurs*, they explained, because Italy had not declared war on Germany. So the Germans shipped them off in cattle trucks to labour or concentration camps mainly in Germany where conditions were appalling. As they were not prisoners of war but military internees, they could not have the same rights as prisoners of war such as International Red Cross visits, said the Germans. But most of them had fought neither with nor against the Germans on 8 September. They had simply surrendered. They were 'prisoners of war and citizens of an allied Power; that is, half Badoglio and half Mussolini'.[33]

But the worst fate was reserved for those few Italian divisions who had resisted the Germans and then surrendered. This too had a legal justification – the same one that said the Italians were not prisoners of war. Italy had not declared war on Germany so those Italians who fought Germans were *francs-tireurs*. On Cos in the Dodecanese, for example, where briefly the British and Italians did fight side by side before surrendering on 4 October, the Germans treated the British as prisoners of war but shot eighty-seven Italian officers.[34] The Germans felt that such atrocities were perfectly acceptable from a moral point of view. How else should desertion to the enemy in battle be dealt with?

The Island of Death

The worst atrocity inflicted on the Italians by the Germans occurred on the Greek island of Cephalonia, the largest of the Ionian Islands, south of Corfu and next to Ithaca where Ulysses is said to have been born. Similar atrocities happened throughout the Greek islands but nowhere on such a scale. Cephalonia encapsulated the full drama of the tragedy which befell Italy on 8 September 1943. The Italian soldier was now forced to ask himself wherever he was a series of very difficult questions, which began with a very simple question soldiers everywhere face to which the answer is usually fairly simple: Who is my enemy? But in the case of the Italian soldier in September 1943 the answer was far from simple.

Cephalonia was occupied by the 11,700-strong Italian Acqui division and 2000 German (mainly Austrian) troops. The Italians had vast superiority in numbers but if need be the *Luftwaffe*, based in mainland Greece where there were also 300,000 German troops, had control of the sky.[35] When Badoglio announced on the radio the armistice and immediate ceasefire against the Allies there was general rejoicing on Cephalonia among the Italians. Relations between the two occupying forces on the island had been very friendly. For eighteen months there had been no enemy to fight except for largely ineffectual partisans. Now the war, thought the Italians, was over. They could go home. But on Cephalonia it was peace, not war, that had ended.

That evening at 9.30 p.m. General Antonio Gandin, the Acqui's commanding officer, received a telegrammed order from the commanding officer of the 170,000 Italian troops in Greece, General Carlo Vecchiarelli. This was Ambrosio's *promemoria 2*. The order said that if the Germans did not attack the Italians the Italians should not attack them; but nor should the Italians 'make common cause' with the Greek partisans or, if they should arrive, the Allies.[36] Vechiarelli sent the same order to all troops under his command. He also sent a copy of it to the Germans. But what if, on the other hand, the Germans should attack the Italians? What then? Vecchiarelli only implied that the Italians should attack back; he did not spell it out. There was a further complication: to placate the Germans after the overthrow of Mussolini, Badoglio had agreed that the Italian and German armies in Greece become one army under German command. Therefore Vecchiarelli and Gandin were technically under German command even though the legal Italian government had signed an armistice with the Allies.[37]

Just after 10.30 p.m. Gandin received another order, this one from Ambrosio, which told him to send a large part of the group of naval and merchant vessels he had to Brindisi immediately.[38] Under the terms of the armistice all Italian naval vessels had to be handed over to the Allies. Gandin complied; the vessels left. He thus lost a possible escape route.

At 9 a.m. on the 9th Lieutenant-Colonel Hans Barge, who commanded the German forces on the island, saw Gandin. The two men liked each other. Gandin was not just from the Veneto but he was pro-German, spoke German well and loved Goethe. The Germans had awarded him the Iron Cross. He had only taken command of the Acqui on 18 June. Ambrosio had deliberately wanted him out of Italy as the plot against Mussolini thickened because he was pro-German. Barge told Gandin untruthfully that he had not yet received any orders. Gandin said they should await further orders from Vecchiarelli or Ambrosio. The meeting ended amicably with both agreeing that a solution could be found.[39] But during the night Vecchiarelli, under German pressure in Athens, sent out a new order to his troops which completely changed things: the Italian forces should stand by to be transferred to Italy and hand over their arms 'on request by the German command as of midday today' (the 10th). The order implied, but did not spell out, that the Germans had guaranteed safe passage home for the Italians. This order was a complete contradiction of the previous one and of what Badoglio had said in his broadcast. Nearly all Italian units in Greece, however, obeyed it.

Gandin sought the advice of his staff officers and the majority said that they should comply with the order.[39]

On the morning of 11 September Barge gave Gandin a written ultimatum. Gandin consulted his staff officers again and the seven divisional chaplains. He told the chaplains, 'The German ultimatum orders us to decide clearly on one of the following points: (1) continue the fight on their side; (2) fight against them; (3) hand over arms peacefully.' He said the Acqui could not continue to fight with the Germans because that was contrary to the King's orders via Badoglio. It could not fight against the Germans either because until the armistice they had 'fought with us and for us, side by side, for a common cause'. But nor could it hand over its arms because that would violate 'the spirit of the armistice'. 'As you see, for me, for my conscience as a man and soldier, none of the three points proposed by the German command is acceptable. Yet on one of them I must decide absolutely within a few hours ...' Even if the Acqui fought the Germans it could not expect any help from the Allies, he went on, whereas the Germans had 300,000 troops on mainland Greece as well as Stukas against which the Acqui would be powerless.

Six chaplains said that Gandin should comply with the ultimatum; the seventh that he should surrender outright.[40] As for the senior officers, a clear majority were also in favour of compliance with the ultimatum. In return for the Germans agreeing not to bring in reinforcements from the mainland, Gandin agreed to withdraw his troops from Mount Kardakata, the strategic nerve centre of Cephalonia. Then, early on the 12th, Gandin sent a message to Barge agreeing to hand over the Acqui's weapons.

But then Gandin changed his mind. By now the discontent of the junior officers had turned to talk of mutiny. Two other factors influenced Gandin: at about midnight on the 12–13th the Acqui regiment on nearby Corfu, which was not under Gandin's command, radioed to say that it had rejected the ultimatum and was determined to fight; and he had also heard reliable reports that Italian soldiers who had surrendered were being deported not repatriated. In addition, on the 11th Ambrosio had at last issued an order from Brindisi to all Italian forces in the field, signed by his number two, General Francesco Rossi, which said, 'Consider the German troops enemies.' Unknown to Gandin, Ambrosio had also tried to get the Allies to help in Cephalonia. But they would not supply a single ship or plane.[41]

On the morning of the 13th Italian artillery officers, on no authority but their own, ordered their batteries to open fire on two German landing craft full of troops approaching the harbour at Argostoli killing five Germans. This increased tension considerably and there were scores of minor contretemps. Gandin took the unprecedented step of conducting a poll of his men. A large majority – we are told this but there are no figures on how large the majority was – voted to keep their arms. Gandin now decided to fight. This, after all, was the order which General Ambrosio, his Commander-in-Chief, had now sent him. If, as seems probable, it was this order that decided it for Gandin, then it suggests that had such an order been issued immediately, Italian forces everywhere would have fought. Gandin had vast numerical superiority but no air cover, no escape route and he had forfeited the strategically crucial Mount Kardakata before the battle had even begun. On the 14th he sent a message to the Germans refusing to hand over the arms, telling them to leave the island and demanding a reply by 9 a.m. the next day. He also ripped off his Iron Cross ribbon which he had worn with pride. On the 15th the battle began. The Germans quickly sent reinforcements and deployed their Stukas from the mainland. Repeatedly, Gandin requested air and naval support from the Ministry of War, now sitting in Brindisi, but got no reply. This was available: on 9 September, 300 Italian air force planes loyal to Badoglio had flown to Lecce in the heel of Italy easily within range. But the Allies would not let the planes go for various reasons which included their fear that they would transfer to the Germans. Furthermore, the Allies ordered two Italian torpedo boats, which had put to sea to intervene, to return to port. Sorry, old boy.

The *Luftwaffe* dropped leaflets on the Italian lines which said, '*Camerati Italiani, ufficiali e soldati*! Why fight against the Germans? You have been betrayed by your leaders! ... LAY DOWN YOUR ARMS!! THE ROAD HOME TO YOUR *PATRIA* WILL BE OPENED UP FOR YOU BY YOUR GERMAN *CAMERATI*.'[42] The Acqui, though it did not know it for sure, was virtually the only Italian force still fighting the Germans. On the night of the 18th, in desperation, Gandin sent a lieutenant on a Red Cross launch to Brindisi over 200 miles away to beg for help. It broke down off the coast of Puglia after a three-day journey but made it to shore at Gallipoli, near Brindisi, with a makeshift sail. By the time the lieutenant got to see the Italian High Command in Brindisi it was too late. The Acqui, never a crack division, was no match for the now well-reinforced Germans and the Stukas. At 11 a.m. on 22 September Gandin ordered his men to surrender.

In the fighting, 1300 Italians had died and a far smaller number of Germans (German estimates say 300, Italian 1200). It was now time for the atrocities. The Germans, on the express orders of Hitler, massacred 5000 Italians as they surrendered. One group of captured Italians included a soldier whose singing voice was famous on the island. He had often sung arias for the Germans in the tavernas. Now the Germans made him sing arias as they shot his comrades. 'Then he was taken away, I can't say if his life was spared or if he too was shot,' recalled Alfred Richter, one of the German soldiers (like most, an Austrian, actually) recently. He and his colleagues felt 'a delirium of omnipotence', he added.[43] The Germans quickly burned those bodies lying in conspicuous places. This caused the air on Cephalonia to be thick with the smell and smoke of burning flesh. Others they threw down wells or into hastily dug pits, or if in secluded spots, simply left. Others they threw into the sea with rocks roped to them.

They took another 5000 Italians prisoner. But the killing was not over yet. Gandin was whisked off alone and shot soon after 7 a.m. on the 24th. That same day, just after breakfast, his officers were taken by truck to the narrow point just outside Argostoli jutting out into the sea, on which stood an isolated villa which would become known subsequently as the Casetta Rossa (little red house). The exact number of officers involved remains unclear. Figures vary between 166 and 400.[44] The Germans ordered them to come forward in groups of 'four, eight, twelve'.[45] Each then had to march the 300 metres from the trucks to the villa. There, three firing squads awaited them. Each squad consisted of eight men wearing white gloves who took it in turns to carry out the executions. They shot them four at a time. A sergeant informed each officer that he was being shot for treason, which, given that the Germans were technically in command of the Italians in Greece, was technically true. After the firing squad had opened fire, the sergeant then methodically delivered the *coup de grâce* with a pistol regardless of whether they were dead or alive.

Padre Romualdo Formato, one of the seven Acqui chaplains, was present. All kneeled as he delivered absolution. *'Ego vos absolvo a peccatis vestris in nomine Patris et Filius et Spiritus Sanctus.'* Before marching the 300 metres to the villa, each gave him their wallets, addresses, notes and personal effects such as wedding rings, pipes and watches to give to their families (these were later confiscated by the Germans, which made it impossible for Padre Formato to be precise about how many officers had perished). Some wanted to give confession and receive individual absolution. Some insisted on marching the 300 metres together arm in arm, others sang, one smoked his pipe. The killing process had been going on for about two hours when a German officer, wearing sunglasses, arrived. He decided to reprieve Italians who could prove that they were from the Trento and Trieste (annexed by Hitler after 8 September as German provinces). A handful survived as a result. At about 1 p.m. Padre Formato, in desperation, begged the German officer to stop the killings. He had seen, he recalled, emotion on the face of the officer. He shouted, 'I beg you, save for me this last group. You've been shooting for four hours. *Basta. Basta. Basta ...'*[46] Then he burst out crying and could not stop. The officer said that he would go and talk to his commanding officer. While he was gone, Padre Formato and the remaining officers sank to their knees to recite the *'Ave Maria'* over and over again. *'Santa Maria, Madre di Dio, prega per noi peccatori, adesso ed all'ora della nostra morte. Amen.'*[47] Half an hour later the German officer returned to say that the killings could stop. The survivors, including Padre Formato, totalled thirty-seven.[48] He wrote that 'even the Germans exulted, they congratulated us sincerely, they shook us warmly by the hand and fraternally offered us cigarettes.'[49] Later the Germans ordered twenty or so captured Italians to put the bodies of the dead officers on trucks, load them on a barge, then take them out to sea. The Germans then blew up the barge along with the living Italians.[50]

But the deaths continued. Of the remaining 5000 captured Italians about 3000 died when three ships ferrying them to mainland Greece for deportation to labour and concentration camps struck mines and sank. In all 9406 members of the Acqui division out of its complement of 11,700 died on Cephalonia. When the British captured the island in November 1944, they found 1200 Italian soldiers – some from other islands – who had deserted before or during the battle, or had managed to escape afterwards.

The Germans had refused to allow the Acqui to bury its dead. But subsequently, when things had – as it were – quietened down, another of the Acqui's chaplains searched the island high and low for the dead. Many had been burned or dumped at sea. But still the chaplain found bones all over the place. The prostitutes from the Italian army brothel on the island – now frequented only by the Germans – gave him all their money to help him buy coffins and crosses for the dead. The prostitutes had fond memories of the Acqui.[51]

In October 1943, when Mussolini set up the new Fascist republic in the north of Italy, the Germans gave the Italian prisoners on Cephalonia a choice: fight with the Germans, forced labour on the island, or concentration camps in Germany. Most opted to stay on the island. In January 1944 Mussolini saw a report on the German massacre of the Acqui division. Though he regarded the Acqui's officers, if not its men, as traitors, Mussolini was incensed at what the Germans had done. Aurelio Garobbio, a Swiss Fascist from the Italian-speaking canton of Ticino, who had thirteen lengthy conversations with Mussolini between 1943 and 1945 which he recorded in a diary, reported what Mussolini told him on 9 January 1944 at Lake Garda. 'I have here a report on the massacre on Cephalonia. A chaplain who managed to escape brought it me. They killed them all,' he said, banging his hand on the memoir. 'All of them! They were merciless!' Silence. Mussolini leaned back in his armchair, stiffening: 'But our men defended themselves well, you know. They hit several German landing craft, sinking them. They fought how Italians know how to fight.'[52]

In 1947 Major-General Lanz, German commanding officer in western Greece, and eleven other German officers were prosecuted for war crimes at Nuremberg. Padre Formato's book, which revealed to the world at large what had happened, had been published the previous year. But due to lack of evidence – as always in such trials on who gave what order – Lanz was charged 'only' with ordering the death of Gandin and his staff officers. His sentence was nevertheless remarkably light: twelve years in prison of which he served five. The other eleven received lesser sentences.

Even today, the tragedy of the Acqui division is not well known in Italy. True, a Hollywood film in 2000 of a novel, *Captain Corelli's Mandolin*, by

Louis de Bernières, an Englishman, did provoke a ripple of interest in the Italian press (the book was a flop when first sold in Italian translation in 1996). But as the Italian author Alfio Caruso wrote as recently as 2000 in his study of the tragedy, 'there does not exist a textbook that mentions it, there does not exist a schoolteacher who recalls it, there does not exist a student who knows about it. Cephalonia is an uncomfortable memory because it does not belong to anti-Fascism nor, still less, to the Left, for decades the distributor of licences on what was to be honoured and what was to be forgotten about the Second World War.[53]

Until 1980 there was not even an Italian war memorial on Cephalonia. No Italian president visited Cephalonia until 1980 when Sandro Pertini, the former (Socialist) partisan leader, unveiled the memorial. No other president went, however, until March 2001 when the current president, Carlo Azeglio Ciampi, a former (non-Communist) partisan, influenced no doubt by the Hollywood film, paid a visit. Those Italians who fought the Germans on Cephalonia were fighting to save their lives not for the cause of Communism or Fascism. Their cause, such as it was, was freedom – their own – not Freedom. But their resistance to the Germans, whatever its motive, is proof that the first page of the story of armed Italian resistance to the Germans was written not by the Italian Communists and their satellites in 1945 in the name of Moscow but by the army in 1943 in the name of the *patria*. It is the Fascists, however, who are keenest to forget Cephalonia. For them what the Acqui did there was a betrayal not just of Fascism but of the *patria*. But the Acqui were all that remained of the *patria* in September 1943.

Mussolini Escapes: The 600 Days of the Repubblica Sociale Italiana of Salò

Under the terms of the armistice Badoglio had agreed to hand over Mussolini to the Allies. But in their haste to abandon Rome Badoglio and the King had failed to leave instructions on what to do with the prisoner. It was yet another dereliction of duty by Badoglio. But the SS quickly found out where Mussolini was being held. They had deciphered a message to Badoglio's Interior Ministry.[54]

At lunchtime on the 12th – four days after the armistice announcement – twelve German gliders, with a hundred commandos on board, and a single engine Stork two-seater reconnaissance plane took off from Rome for the Gran Sasso a hundred miles away. Their commander was Captain Otto Skorzeny who was Austrian. Only nine of the gliders and the Stork made it to the Apennine meadow in front of the Campo Imperatore Hotel on Gran Sasso. The presence with the Germans of an Italian general, Fernando Soleti, confused Mussolini's 250 *carabiniere* guards. 'Don't shoot!' he shouted. Mussolini, who watched the scene from his hotel room, asked a guard, 'Are they English?' 'No, *eccellenza*, they are Germans,' the guard replied. 'That's all we need,' said Mussolini.[55] But the rescue, like all the best rescues, nearly came to grief. The plan was to take Mussolini down the mountain. But this was now impossible as the *carabiniere* battalion at the bottom had been alerted. The only possibility was the Stork. But with Mussolini and Skorzeny on board the Stork was very heavy and the Apennine meadow worse than an aircraft carrier as a take-off platform. It was short and full of rocks. Mussolini helped the Germans remove some of the rocks. Then he climbed aboard with Skorzeny. A dozen Germans had to grab the wings of the Stork to hold it back as the pilot throttled up for take-off and so give it maximum forward thrust. It then took off, plunging down into the abyss before gradually managing to straighten out.[56]

So happy was he when he heard the news in the Wolf's Lair that Hitler stamped and danced up and down on the spot as he had done after the fall of France in June 1940.[57] Goebbels wrote in his diary, 'I have the feeling that fortune smiles on us once again. The liberation of the Duce has created an enormous sensation in the fatherland and abroad. . . . One can say that virtually no other military event in the entire war has so profoundly shaken people's minds . . . We can celebrate a moral victory of the first order.'[58] But the reality was that Hitler had not liberated Mussolini, he had captured him.

In Rome, Mussolini told the Germans that he had no wish to return to politics. But Hitler had other ideas. He insisted that Mussolini be flown immediately to Vienna and from there the next day to Munich, where he was met by his wife and two youngest children who had been flown in the previous day. Ciano and Edda had already been there for about a fortnight. Ciano, who had wanted to go to Spain, decided instead to allow the Germans to fly him to Germany on 27 August with Edda and their children. It remains unclear why he made this fatal move. Edda later said the Germans had promised the Cianos that they would go on from Germany to Spain. But German accounts deny this.[59]

Ciano met Mussolini on the 13th.[60] He welcomed him 'a little sulkily, but paternally', Edda would recall.[61] Quite apart from the family tie, at this stage Mussolini had not yet had a proper chance to establish who precisely were the guilty parties on 24–25 July. He never really would. Mussolini's wife, however, who had always disliked Ciano, not least because she was a Romagnol peasant and he a Tuscan bourgeois par excellence, reacted 'with fury'.[62] Ciano, in her eyes, had always been a parasite and now he was a traitor.

Hitler insisted on seeing Mussolini in person and the next day – the 14th – flew him to the Wolf's Lair. Mussolini also met diehard, pro-German Fascists who had fled to Germany such as Farinacci, Renato Ricci, the former Fascist youth leader, and Giovanni Preziosi, a defrocked Catholic priest and rabid anti-Semite, defined by Mussolini as 'a repulsive human being'. His eldest son, Vittorio, was also there. Hitler was determined – despite the advice of his generals who felt a proper occupation of Italy was the only answer – to restore Mussolini to power. This was partly for the propaganda impact and partly because of Hitler's deep emotional attachment to Mussolini. But Goebbels wrote, 'In any case, we must begin to cancel out the Duce politically ... we cannot count any more on him with certainty, above all because he no longer has any power.'[63] But so too was Mussolini reluctant.

The alternative, however, was obvious: if he refused, Italy would become yet another German-occupied territory. Hitler would not allow anyone else to head a puppet regime. Mussolini would tell Carlo Silvestri, the Socialist journalist who interviewed him fifty times at Salò[64] between December 1943 and April 1945 and became a rare confidant, 'I had by then renounced all personal ambition; in addition, I did not believe in a possible resurrection of Fascism ... But Hitler replied to reservations in the following way: "I must be very clear. The Italian betrayal, if the Allies had known how to exploit it, could have provoked the swift collapse of Germany. Northern Italy will be forced to envy the fate of Poland if you do not accept to give renewed vigour to the alliance between Germany and Italy, by becoming head of the state and of the new government".'[65] But what were the alternatives if he refused? Perhaps Hitler would have kept him in Germany as his 'house guest' but even if he allowed him to retire to Italy, there was the threat of capture by the Allies or the partisans.

The next day – the 15th – Mussolini bowed to Hitler's will. The Germans broadcast the news by radio in Rome. Mussolini told Anfuso that 'the principal issue was not to win the war but to end it without losing everything ... If we want to survive, we must fight: it is the only way to arrive at the end of the war, saving the nation. I can also fold my arms and say to the Italians and the Germans that I don't want to know any more. That is not the way to end the war! The Germans will find a way to administer Italy according to their habits ... and the only result will be to lose that little respect which remains for Italy as a nation.'[66] He then returned to Munich, where he and his family were given a large house at Hirschberg to the south of the city and where he began, however reluctantly, to work on the creation of the new Fascist state.

Mussolini had two aims: first, to convince Hitler once and for all to abandon the hopeless war in Russia and concentrate instead on the war in the Mediterranean; but second, to save something of the nation, to shield it from the worst excesses of the Germans in a way that full-blooded German occupation would not. This was why Pétain had agreed to collaborate with the Germans. If he had been unable to be their sword, Pétain would tell the French in an attempt to justify himself, he had tried to be their shield. Salò would be 'the buffer between the vendetta of the betrayed Germans and the Italian population', Mussolini told Pavolini.[67]

Mussolini wanted to set up his new government in Rome or Milan. But Hitler refused to let him. So he chose Salò on Lake Garda near Gardone where d'Annunzio, the poet-warrior and spiritual father of Fascism, had lived and was buried. That it was to be a government in exile in the country it governed weakened its appeal to the Italian people from the start. Furthermore, Hitler insisted on full-blooded German rule by gauleiter of the extreme north – roughly the area which Italy had got from the Austro-Hungarian Empire as a result of the First World War. Hitler wanted the new Fascist state to be called the *Repubblica Fascista Italiana*. But Mussolini was able to override him on the name if little else. He decided to call it the *Repubblica Sociale Italiana* (RSI) which was officially born on 1 December. Significantly the word 'sociale' appeared in the title but the word 'Fascista' did not.

Back in Munich Mussolini broadcast a message to Italy via Radio Munich on 18 September announcing the creation of the new republic. '*Camicie nere! Italiani e Italiane!* After a long silence, once again my voice reaches you and I am sure that you recognise it; it is the voice which has summoned you in difficult moments and has celebrated with you the triumphal days of the *patria*.' But the voice, that voice, this time, was hesitant and lacked passion. Anfuso wrote that 'many Fascists could not recognise his voice and, when they were forced to recognise it, they repudiated it as his own.'[68] But Petacci, recently freed as well from prison in Novara, fell to her knees and hugged the radio when she heard the voice of Mussolini.[69]

On the 23rd Rahn broadcast the names of the members of the new government. These were unknown mediocrities except for Buffarini Guidi, the Interior Minister, and Marshal Graziani, who became Minister of War. Though also mediocrities, they were at least famous. Graziani, like Badoglio, had gassed his way to glory in Ethiopia but resigned his command in Libya after his dismal failure in North Africa against the British. As usual, Mussolini refused to give Farinacci a post. It was also announced that Pavolini, a forty-year-old charismatic Tuscan poet but a cruel and fanatical man, was to be the Secretary General of the new PNF – the *Partito Repubblicano Fascista* (PRF). Mussolini flew back to Italy on the 25th, landing at Forlì in the Romagna, from where he went to La Rocca delle Caminate. There, on the 27th, the new government met for the first time. In the second week of October[70] Mussolini took up residence at the Villa Feltrinelli in the small town of Gargnano on Lake Garda, ten miles from Salò and near Gardone where d'Annunzio had lived. He set up his *Capo dello Stato's* offices in the Villa delle Orsoline half a mile away.[71] Hitler insisted that a team of SS minders, neatly called liaison officers, take over a nearby villa and that one of them, twenty-two-year-old SS Lieutenant Hans Dyckerhoff, actually live in the Villa Feltrinelli. The telephone exchange, manned and tapped by the Germans, worked badly. Calls sometimes took a day to be put through. Once a call was through the line was so bad that it was necessary to shout. The ministries were dotted about all over the north: the Foreign Ministry, for example, was at Salò, Finance at Verona, Agriculture at Treviso. For a minister to see Mussolini at Gargnano often involved a two-day trip. Giovanni Dolfin, a former militia consul and prefect, became his official private secretary. His eldest son, Vittorio – 'one of the biggest boors that exist on the face of the earth' forever surrounded by athletes and sportsmen – became a sort of personal secretary and envoy.[72] SS General Wolff neatly summed up Mussolini's predicament at Salò: 'I did not give him orders ... but in practice he could not decide anything against my will and my advice.'[73]

Lake Garda's resort towns teemed with diehard Fascists, parasites, the grotesque and the absurd. The ghost of d'Annunzio hovered. This may have given some comfort to Mussolini. But he had never liked lakes, which in his view were a weak compromise between the sea and rivers; their water was still; it did not march. The diehard Mussolini women completed the *fin de régime* atmosphere. His wife and two youngest children, Romano and Anna-Maria, lived with him at Villa Feltrinelli. While Mussolini received political and military visitors, Rachele would shuffle about in silence wearing an apron.[74]

Petacci, meanwhile, freed from prison on Wolff's orders, took up residence in Gardone, eventually in Villa Mirabella situated within the grounds of d'Annunzio's Vittoriale estate. A favourite mistress of old, Angela Curti Cucciati, and her twenty-one-year-old daughter Elena Curti came to live in Gargnano. Mussolini was Elena's father and very fond of her.[75] He invited her to see him once a week to read the newspapers to him. Petacci, who knew about Curti Cucciati because Mussolini still used to receive her at the Palazzo Venezia, found out and insisted Mussolini banish mother and illegitimate daughter to Milan.[76] But Mussolini's wife, who now knew about her, was equally furious at the proximity of Petacci. For the first time in her life Rachele Mussolini could keep a close eye on her husband who had to invent all sorts of tricks to deceive her when he wanted to see his mistress. Finally, on 24 October 1944, she turned up at Petacci's villa for a showdown. She had insisted the rotund sycophant Buffarini Guidi, the Interior Minister, come with her. Mussolini had telephoned Petacci to warn her. 'She's coming round to you ... Don't let her in. She is out of her mind and I fear she is armed.' Petacci telephoned her handsome young blue-eyed SS minder, Lieutenant Franz Spoegler, to come at once. Each woman, therefore, had a champion of sorts.

It was raining heavily. The wrought-iron entrance gate was locked. But Mrs Mussolini kept her finger pressed on the doorbell until Petacci sent Spoegler out to tell her to go away. Mrs Mussolini started shouting and then attempted to climb over the gate. Petacci succumbed. Spoegler, after asking her if she were armed, let her in. It was the first time wife and mistress had met. Mrs Mussolini had come to tell La Petacci to depart from Lake Garda and leave her poor husband alone in these difficult times. A violent row ensued with Mussolini required to try to keep the peace by means of the faulty telephone in his office at the Villa delle Orsoline. 'What are you? *Signora* or *signorina*?' sneered Mrs Mussolini. 'What elegance! She dresses really well *la mantenuta*! This is how *la mantenuta* of a Capo di Stato dresses! And look at me, me who married him!' Everyone knew that they had a submarine on stand-by at La Spezia to run away in, she went on. 'She is a dangerous madwoman, take her away!' shouted Petacci at Spoegler with whom she liked to go fishing on the lake. She then fainted under the ferocity of the onslaught of the Romagnol vixen. But she soon recovered and it was then that Mussolini, worried, telephoned. Petacci told him, 'Do you know what she called me? She called me *mantenuta*!' 'What!?' said Mussolini. 'Hand me Spoegler.' Petacci passed him Spoegler. 'Spoegler, try to keep the encounter within the limits of the reasonable,' said Mussolini. 'Duce,' said Spoegler, emphasising each word slowly. 'The situation is difficult.' Petacci took back the telephone and asked Mussolini for permission to show his wife his letters to her. 'Is it really necessary?' asked Mussolini. 'Indispensable,' said Petacci.

Petacci put down the telephone and went to get the letters, then began to read them out loud. Mrs Mussolini snatched them from Petacci. Spoegler intervened and sustained scratch wounds. 'Are you or are you not the Minister of the Interior? Well, use your authority!' Mrs Mussolini snapped at Buffarini Guidi. She then lunged for Petacci and had to be restrained by both Spoegler and Buffarini Guidi. Mussolini remained at his office that night at the Villa delle Orsoline in order to avoid his wife. Petacci did not leave Lake Garda but she did, on Spoegler's advice, move house.[77]

But at least Mussolini's stomach trouble was alleviated by the stern attentions of his new German army doctor, Dr Georg Zachariae, despatched by Hitler, like the SS minders, to look after him. Zachariae decided that the stomach problem was largely psychosomatic, though he did discover that Mussolini had a disordered abdomen, dry skin and an enlarged liver. He banned milk, which Mussolini had drunk copiously for years, and grapes, which Mussolini adored.[78]

Italy was a country occupied by two invading armies at war, 'ruled' by two puppet governments neither of which had the consent of the people. Just as the King and Badoglio were head of a puppet regime of the Allies in the south up to Naples – the Kingdom of the South – so now did Mussolini become head of a puppet regime of the Germans in the rest of Italy – the RSI. Economically Italians under Mussolini's puppet regime, however, were much better off than Italians under the King's. In the south Italians suffered terrible deprivation and rampant inflation after liberation by the

Allies, which the Allies did little about. In cities such as Naples there were epidemics of typhus, lice, nits, crabs and gonorrhea. The arrival of the Allies was like the arrival of the plague.

But the existence of Mussolini's puppet regime ensured that tragedy would pile up on tragedy for the Italian people. First, it would buttress the German attempt to rebuff the Allied invasion. But, perhaps worse, it would cause civil war between those Italians who for whatever reason still stood by Fascism and those who did not. The declaration of war against Germany by the King's puppet regime in October 1943 compounded the problem. But for the two puppet regimes, the only targets left for the discontented Italian people would have been either the Germans or the Allies, not each other.

Among those trapped in the moral maze and the physical danger was the poet Ezra Pound. Pound was a passionate supporter of Mussolini – he met him briefly in 1933 – and had lived in Italy for many years. Since 1941 he had delivered regular seven-minute propaganda broadcasts on the radio from Rome aimed at America. Each broadcast began, 'Europe calling, Pound speaking.' Since December 1942 the FBI had had him under investigation for treason, incitement and mutiny, and in July 1943 charged him with treason. The broadcasts were 'a masterly performance', according to one of his biographers, Humphrey Carpenter, who wrote, 'Certainly there were Americans who, in 1941, would have agreed with virtually every word Ezra said at the microphone about the United States Government, the European conflict, and the power of the Jews.'[79] Pound, who also admired Lenin and wrote for Communist publications, was, if he had to be labelled something, very left-wing – he described himself as a 'Fascist of the left'. But he despised Communism because of its obsession with materialism – with money. As he said in a June 1942 broadcast, 'Every man of common sense, including the odd British MP, knows that every man of common sense prefers Fascism to Communism, from the moment that he learns a few concrete facts about both of them.'[80] But when he spoke of Jews what he really meant was bankers. Money was the root of all evil; money caused wars; money was unproductive and parasitical. Pound despised usury and as a result was anti-Semitic – but in the abstract. He was against materialism and for spiritualism. Instead of a monetary economy he wanted a natural economy. He made his last radio broadcast from Rome on 25 July – the day that Mussolini was arrested by the King. He checked out of his hotel and decided to set off on foot from Rome for his Italian home in Rapallo near Genoa in the north-west. He was fifty-seven. During the two-month odyssey, sometimes he hitch-hiked and sometimes he slept out in the open.[81] He continued to be a passionate supporter of Mussolini after his return to power at the head of the RSI. 'A thousand candles shine,' he wrote in 1942, 'The light of no one candle damages the light of another. That is the freedom of the individual in the ideal and Fascist state.'[82] In April 1945 two Communist partisans arrested him at his home in Rapallo and handed him over to the Americans. He took with him into captivity a copy of the writings of Confucius. The American military authorities held him in an open-air cage in a prison camp in Pisa for three weeks, only transferring him to the prison hospital when he was near death. It was here that he wrote the *Pisan Cantos*. He was then transferred to America where a judge declared him insane and mentally unfit for trial, and confined him to a psychiatric hospital in Washington. In a written statement he had made in May 1945 for his American interrogators – but which did not reach the public domain until 1997 – he comes across as entirely sane, did not retract his support for Fascism and ironically said that Roosevelt was a suitable case for psychiatric treatment.[83] In 1958, after an international campaign, he was released. He returned to Italy and died in Venice in 1972. His support for Fascism had not been the product of insanity at all.

Mussolini *Socialista*

Mussolini had appointed Renato Ricci to reconstitute and command the Fascist militia, which was now called the *Guardia nazionale repubblicana* (GNR). As before, it would not be under army command. But it was in the creation of a new army that Mussolini placed what little faith he had left.

As ever, he was exasperated with the Germans. On 9 November he had told his new private secretary, Giovanni Dolfin, 'It is absurd for those people to pretend to call us Allies. I would rather they took off their masks and said that we are an occupied territory and a subject people like all others. That would put an end to the farce and simplify our problems.' Godolfin suggested a meeting with Hitler. But from bitter experience Mussolini knew there was no point. 'A meeting would solve nothing,' he said.[84] But Mussolini could not bring himself to say to Hitler, that's it, I've had enough of you. If he could not do it in 1939, he could not possibly do it in 1943. He was, even if the word was never mentioned, Hitler's prisoner now. Yet he was hugely energetic at Gargnano. He rarely appeared formally in public but he returned to journalism with a vengeance. Badoglio had closed down his newspaper *Il Popolo d'Italia* and he did not relaunch it. But he started a press agency, *Corrispondenza repubblicana*, for which he wrote unsigned articles. He also wrote anonymous articles for other publications such as the Fascist youth publication, *Libro e Moschetto*, which he signed not as in his own youth, *L'Homme qui cherche*, but Fabrizio del Dongo, the anti-hero of Stendhal's *La Chartreuse de Parme*. It was in 1944 that he wrote *Storia di un anno: il tempo del bastone e della carota* – his account of his overthrow and imprisonment. His journalistic output was enormous in the last year and a half of his life and bristled with passion.

This can only mean that even now he had not given up hope that somehow the tables could still be turned.

Bottai had voted for the Grandi motion at the Grand Council because he wanted Fascism to return to its revolutionary roots. He had not had in mind the fall of Fascism. He was now regarded as a traitor of Fascism. But it was at Salò that Mussolini attempted to do with Fascism precisely what Bottai had wanted. The moment of defeat for Fascism was the moment of triumph for the Fascist left wing. At long last the Fascist state had rid itself of the monarchy. But also, as the title of the new republic shows, it aspired to be 'social'.

The first congress of the new Fascist party took place at Verona on 14 November where it agreed the so-called Verono Manifesto – a kind of constitution for the new republic – largely based on the Socialist ideas of Nicola Bombacci. Mussolini gave his full backing to the manifesto. Bombacci, who had gone to the same school as Mussolini in Forlimpopoli in the Romagna and like him become a Socialist, had then co-founded the Italian Communist party in 1921 with Bordiga, Togliatti and Gramsci. Bombacci was the only Italian to have been made an honorary colonel in the Red Army and, like Togliatti, had been a member of the Comintern.[85] After the March on Rome, Lenin had told Bombacci that Mussolini was the only Socialist capable of leading the Italian people to revolution. In 1927 the PCI had expelled Bombacci, and in 1933 he broke with Communism and became a supporter of Fascism. He never joined either the PNF or its reincarnation after 1943, the PFR. But he supported Fascism, he said, because it was more Socialist than Socialism. His dream was to fuse the Bolshevik and Fascist revolutions and he saw Mussolini as the man to do it.[86] Bombacci was tall (for an Italian) and thin and had an immense white (by now) beard and startling china-blue eyes. Along with Silvestri, the Socialist journalist, he was one of the few confidants Mussolini had at Gargnano. He continued to describe himself as a Socialist and believed that Fascism offered the best chance of establishing Socialism in Italy.

During the war, as military defeat followed defeat, Mussolini's age-old hostility to the bourgeoisie had grown in intensity and his real anima – Socialism – began to dominate his thinking once again. Lieutenant-Colonel Wilhelm Hottl, head of the German Secret Service for southern Europe, who spoke with Ciano several times in Munich, recalled, 'Ciano and his wife repeatedly asserted that with the increasing deterioration of the war situation, Mussolini's Socialist views became more and more apparent.' The Cianos feared that after the war he would set up in Italy 'a system little different from that in Russia'.[87] At Gargnano, he said that whoever won the war, Italy would be crushed. But he added, 'Soon, the Italians will have to choose a *padrone*. In that case, which seems by now certain, I, as an Italian citizen, would not hesitate to choose Stalin.'[88]

Mussolini had always realised that to win the war military conquest alone was not enough. The Axis also had to conquer minds by winning the war of ideas. This had been yet another source of tension with Hitler. Hitler was content to bleed conquered countries dry and keep them conquered by military might and atrocities, not the might of ideas. Ideas could wait until after the war was won. Hitler's National Socialism had tarred Fascism with the same brush. So Mussolini's *socializzazione*, as he called it, was his attempt at the eleventh hour to resurrect Fascism as the winning ideology it had for so long been before the Pact of Steel – regardless of German objections. His aim was to get the support of those Italians who despised both Communism and the bourgeoisie who, though class enemies, had become temporary allies on the side of America, Britain and Russia, until hostilities could be resumed after the war. He wanted to build a bridge between Fascism and Socialism. 'Fascism has by now had its day,' he had told Hitler at the Wolf's Lair. 'To reconquer the Italians, it needs to return to its origins.'[89] The RSI was against the following: Communism; Capitalism; Russian imperialism; Anglo-American imperialism; Italian cowardice; counter-revolution. It was for: *Socializzazione*; Europe; Civilisation; Italian bravery; revolution. Mussolini knew that the differences between the Fascists and the anti-Fascists were not black and white as the propaganda made them out to be. Within every Italian the *rosso* battled with the *nero*, as they did within Mussolini. He now tried once again to blend the *rosso* and the *nero* together. Despite their heated objections, Hitler told Rahn and others on the ground in Italy not to interfere.

Mussolini told Anfuso, his new ambassador in Berlin, 'Fascism aimed to spare the Italians the class struggle. For this, everyone believed that it wanted to defend the bourgeoisie ... They say that I am doing this socialisation out of disrespect! I am doing it because this is the only possible moment and because now, and in this piece of Italy which remains, are the only people who can put it into effect, maybe out of desperation, but certainly not disrespect! If the workers do not want it, it is because they do not want to continue fighting the war together with the Germans.'[90]

The Verona Manifesto took as its guiding principle 'the struggle against the world plutocracies'. It guaranteed private property as long as it did not harm 'the physical and moral personality of other men through the exploitation of their work'.[91] Already, under Fascism, via IRI, three-quarters of Italian industry was nationalised – in terms of management if not in terms of ownership. The manifesto proposed the full-scale nationalisation of public services. It also proposed the joint management of enterprise by workers and bosses who would all be required to join trade unions.[92] The representatives of the workers on the management boards would be elected by the workforce. The phrase *socializzazione* described Mussolini's Fascist brand of Socialism. In October 1944 he would define *socializzazione* as 'the Italian, human, our, workable, realisation of *socialismo*.' He would add, 'I say "our" insofar as it makes work the only concern of the economy, but rejects the mechanical levelling of everything and everyone, a levelling inexistent in nature and impossible in history.'[93] This, then, was what set *socializzazione* apart from *socialismo*. It recognised that individuals were not equal.

Mussolini did not attend the Verona congress. In an unsigned article of 13 November, however, he wrote, 'Fascism, liberated from all those frills which slowed down its march and from the too many compromises which circumstances obliged it to accept, has returned to its revolutionary origins in all sectors, and particularly in the social one.'[94] On 12 February 1944 Mussolini's Cabinet would issue a decree law to put into effect *socializzazzione*. This stated that in all private companies with a capital of 1 million lire or more, or a hundred employees or more, management would be by an equal number of representatives of labour and capital. Similar arrangements would apply in companies already owned by the state.

Garobbio reported his conversation with Mussolini on 16 February 1944 as follows: ' "*Socializzazione*", said the Duce, "has got on the nerves of the Germans tremendously, it is a toad they have had to swallow. They are not revolutionaries, they do not understand the needs of peoples. We have our pockets full of their New Order! Tell me: what does New Order mean? Unless they mean Europe as a German protectorate! ... We do not want a state Socialism, the worst of the tyrannies which Capitalism can invent. We want to continue the revolution, to reach out to the people with real facts and not idle chat, for a higher social justice. We have already lost too much time ... The anti-Fascists fear *socializzazione*. I hear that their propaganda is intensifying in this area ..." ... I tell him, "You have placed a time bomb under Europe, and it is called: *socializzazione*." The expression pleases him.'[95] If Fascism should be defeated, *socializzazione* would remain.

But hostility from people like Pavolini and Farinacci within Fascism, the major industrialists, the Germans and the clandestine parties of the Left, ensured that it was inoperable.[96] The Left, especially the Communists, were, however, very worried that the policy would pull the rug from under their feet. The Communists themselves had once tried similar tactics towards Fascism. In 1936, at the height of Mussolini's prestige and popularity, the Comintern had published an important article, probably written by Togliatti, addressed to 'the blackshirt brothers' in Italy. It was an appeal for unity between Communists and Fascists. It said, 'We Communists have made ours the Fascist programme of 1919, which is a programme of peace, liberty and defence of the interests of the workers ... The Fascist programme of 1919 has not been realised! Let's struggle united for the realisation of this programme.'[97] The Spanish Civil War put a stop to the attempt at rapprochement. But in March 1941 – when the Axis powers were still allied to Russia – Togliatti had told the Comintern that it had to be conceded that Fascism had done much good for the Italian working class. He said, 'We must accept that the elements of strength in Fascism do not lie only in violence and in the apparat. This dictatorship has done something – not just by means of violence ... It has done something even for the workers and the young. We cannot deny that the introduction of social security is a fact.'[98] The same fears resurfaced now.

But the workers – the urban workers, that is – were hostile anyway to *socializzazione*, not because it was Socialist – but because it was proposed by Mussolini. Yet Mussolini still had much support, all things considered. In 1943 and 1944, 300,000 young men responded to the introduction of conscription by the RSI and 50,000 joined the new Fascist Party, the PFR, in Milan alone.[99]

That Mussolini was head of a republic alienated many other Italians who remained royalists. The programme of *socializzazione* never became operative except in one or two places, most notably in the newspaper industry. That he could ever imagine that it could reincarnate popular support for him is a sign of how he had lost touch with the reality of the situation. Only military triumphs could restore the support he had once enjoyed. Certainly, Mussolini spoke at Salò with gathering intensity of Hitler's secret weapons, which would snatch victory from the jaws of defeat.

To make things worse, Fascism was riven by discord. The Verona congress, chaired by the new party secretary Pavolini, was turbulent, chaotic. It drowned in a mass of competing ideas. Those present were more interested in recrimination and revenge than reconstruction and it decided to set up an Extraordinary Special Tribunal to try the traitors of 25 July. It was pressure from the party, not Hitler, which ensured they be put on trial. Ribbentrop wrote to Rahn, 'The Führer has decided that the trial of Ciano should be exclusively a matter of concern for the Duce and that from our side there should be no pressure in favour of a conviction.'[100] All but six of the traitors had gone to ground. But the six included his son-in-law Ciano. The others were the now very old Quadrumvir, Marshal Emilio De Bono, the deaf Giovanni Marinelli, who had ordered the kidnap of Matteotti, Carlo Pareschi, Luciano Gottardi and Tullio Cianetti who had written on 25 July to Mussolini to retract his vote in favour of the Grandi motion.

Mussolini Executes his Son-in-Law

The Germans had allowed Edda to come back to Italy on 27 September by train and on 19 October they allowed Ciano to return. Pavolini, the secretary of the PFR, had asked Hitler to extradite him for trial. Hitler had agreed. It was because of Ciano that Pavolini had flourished under Fascism. They had even been friends. Despite this the fanatical Pavolini was determined to punish any traitor he could get his hands on. Rachele Mussolini remained in Munich alone with her two youngest children and those of Ciano. Ciano was accompanied on the flight from Munich to Verona by a striking SS minder, Major Felicitas Beetz.[101] The role of SS Major Beetz, who was fluent in Italian, was among other things to try to locate Ciano's diaries, which Hitler was worried would prove damaging if handed to the Allies. As soon as Ciano arrived in Verona the Fascists arrested and imprisoned him. SS Major Beetz saw him every day in his prison cell.

Initially the Justice Minister, Piero Pisenti, opposed putting Ciano and the other traitors on trial. Mussolini procrastinated. Pisenti told Mussolini, 'Duce, I have analysed the documents, and the charge is not valid; there is not the slightest proof of conspiracy by those who signed the resolution by Grandi and the Royal House. Voting was carried out in the correct manner and it was you, Duce, who asked for a vote. I assure you that the charge of betrayal can in no way be substantiated in court.'[102] But on 24 November, Pavolini successfully convinced the Cabinet to hold the trial.

SS Major Beetz, who was married to a *Luftwaffe* pilot serving on the Russian Front, soon developed an emotional attachment to Ciano. 'Frau Beetz, a capable and even cynical spy, but even so always a woman, a nordic woman, and sensitive to the *fascino latino*, fell for Ciano,' wrote Montenelli.[103] In 1996 she would deny to an Italian magazine that she 'fell in love with him' but admitted, 'I loved him, certainly, but it is not true that I made love to him.'[104] At Ciano's request, SS Major Beetz went to meet Edda who had checked into a clinic in Ramiola, near Parma, after retrieving Ciano's diaries from a secret hiding place. Ciano's wife and his SS minder now tried to save his life. Their efforts included SS Major Beetz, in agreement with Edda, proposing to her SS superiors that in return for Ciano's diaries the SS would spirit him out of Italy to a neutral country. Himmler agreed. But Hitler refused. Edda saw Mussolini on 26 December to try to persuade him to intervene. It was the last time she ever saw her father.[105]

Ciano wrote letters, smuggled out of prison by SS Major Beetz, to the King and Churchill. In his letter to Churchill he blamed Mussolini alone – 'that tragic and vile puppet' – for Italy's entry into the war. In addition he wrote an introduction to his diary, likewise smuggled out, in which he said, 'Only the base cowardice of Mussolini could tolerate this without protest, and pretend not to see it.' Not forgetting the base cowardice of

Ciano, one might add. But in neither of the letters, nor the introduction, does Ciano either deny or admit the charge against him at Verona: treason. Churchill described Ciano's letter to him as 'pathetic'.

The trial before the nine judges of the Extraordinary Special Tribunal began on 8 January and lasted two days. Edda, meanwhile, once among the most zealous supporters of Fascist Italy's alliance with Nazi Germany, who had left for Switzerland, wrote to Hitler, Mussolini and General Harster, German military commander at Salò, threatening to do everything in her power to bring ruin on them, including the handover of Ciano's diaries to the Allies, unless Ciano were released within three days of the end of the trial. She wrote the letters on the night of 8–9th but dated them the 10th.[106] To her father she wrote, 'If Galeazzo is not in Switzerland in three days ... I shall make merciless use of all I know.'

On 10 January the judges found all six defendants guilty of treason and sentenced all but one, Cianetti, to death. Cianetti, on account of his letter of apology, was sentenced to thirty years in prison. In addition they found Grandi and the other thirteen guilty of the same charge and sentenced them to death *in absentia*. Bottai was still in Rome in hiding. In June 1944, when the Allies liberated Rome, he joined the French Foreign Legion aged forty-nine and fought the Germans until the end of the war.

The prosecution case was that the accused knew precisely what the consequences of voting for Grandi's motion would be because they were involved in a conspiracy with the King to overthrow Mussolini. This was untrue. The Grand Council meeting, which came out of the blue, provided the King with a timely excuse. That is all. Historians argue to this day about why Mussolini was overthrown in the July 1943 coup. The prosecution case – or lack of it – makes it clear that it did not know the answer either, which means that at this stage nor did Mussolini. The closest thing to evidence the prosecution had of any plot by anyone to overthrow Mussolini was the so-called confession[107] by Marshal Ugo Cavallero, Chief of the General Staff between Badoglio and Ambrosio. In it, Cavallero had said that the plot involved various military figures including himself. But Cavallero was pro-German and Badoglio had arrested him after the July 1943 coup. He was not involved in the plot which overthrew Mussolini. He was part of Farinacci's pro-German plot. He made his confession in prison to gain release. It was useful to Badoglio as an insurance policy because it would mean that Cavallero was in deep trouble with the Germans if they should get to hear about it. Indeed, when Badoglio fled Rome in September 1943, he left a copy of it on his desk for the Germans to find. Shortly afterwards Cavallero died in mysterious circumstances at Kesselring's residence in Frascati outside Rome. The Germans had handed the confession to Mussolini.

There were, however, three facts which made it look as if the defendants were involved in a plot against Mussolini. First, Mussolini had warned the

Grand Council that the motion, if approved, would cause the crisis of the regime. That being so, all who voted for the motion knew what its consequences would be. Second, if the nineteen who had voted for the motion had not been party to a plot, why then had thirteen of them fled? Third, if those who had voted for the motion did not know what its result would be, why then did Cianetti write immediately afterwards to Mussolini to apologise and retract his vote?

To the first point the defendants said that they did not agree with Mussolini's view that the motion would place the regime in crisis 'not thinking that the position of the Duce himself was being called into doubt', as Ciano put it according to a report of the trial in *La Stampa*. The answer to the second point was obvious: the others had fled because they knew there would be no chance of a fair trial. To the third point Cianetti's answer was that he had not realised that Grandi aimed to use the motion to overthrow Mussolini until too late. He had not realised that Grandi was a traitor until he began to 'reflect' on it afterwards, he said. Other members who voted against the motion, such as Suardo and Scorza, were called as prosecution witnesses. But all had to concede that the true implications of the motion were far from clear. They had voted against it, however, because during the meeting they had 'the impression' that 'something was scheming against the Duce' (Suardo) or that 'something not perfectly orthodox was being prepared towards the Duce' (Scorza).[108]

But Fascism required a scapegoat and Mussolini now behaved like Pontius Pilate. The five defendants condemned to death wrote to Mussolini seeking clemency. Pavolini and Pietro Cosmin, the *ras* of Verona, did not pass on the appeal, fearing that Mussolini would grant it. Pavolini, anxious to deprive Mussolini of the chance to intervene, ordered the execution to take place the next day at dawn. He and Cosmin spent all night trying to get the death sentence confirmed by someone with the authority to do so – in vain. In the end, they browbeat General Italo Vianini, local commander of the GNR – the Fascist Militia, to do so.

That night Mussolini had not gone to bed. He had retired to his bedroom but could be heard pacing up and down all night. At 3 a.m. he had telephoned General Wolff, the SS commander in Italy, to ask him if he should intervene. Wolff said that he could not respond officially but his personal view was that he should not.

At 9 a.m. on 11 January, the five condemned men were taken in a bus to Forte San Procolo. There a firing squad, comprising thirty militiamen from the new Fascist militia, the GNR, awaited them.[109] They were tied to chairs with their backs to the firing squad. (That they were all tied is visible from the photographs of the execution.) Marinelli had become hysterical. Gottardi shouted, '*Viva il Duce! Viva L'Italia!*' Ciano was silent but at the last moment looked back over his shoulder. The firing squad opened fire at 9.20 a.m. It failed to kill them outright. They writhed and groaned on the ground. An officer gave each one the *coup de grâce* with his pistol. There was silence except for the sound of the jackdaws which inhabited the battlements of the fortress. The radio announced the news of the execution of the five traitors preceded by the jaunty, jovial strains of '*Giovinezza*'. Later that day SS Major Beetz laid a bunch of red roses beside Ciano's coffin at the Verona mortuary. He was still only forty.

At 10 a.m. Mussolini was informed. He told his secretary Dolfin that Ciano had deliberately provoked the crisis but that De Bono and Gottardi had probably not understood what was happening at the Grand Council meeting. He said, 'If I had not had Ciano shot, they would have said without doubt that I wanted to save my son-in-law. Today they will say I have had the father of my grandchildren shot.'[110]

In his 3 a.m. telephone call to Wolff, Mussolini had asked, 'What does the Führer think?' Wolff: 'The Führer does not think the sentence will be carried out.' Mussolini: 'A failure to execute could harm me in the consideration of the Führer?' Wolff: 'Yes, and very much so.'[111] Mussolini's wife had urged him to have Ciano shot, whom she regarded as a second Brutus.[112] Whether her opinion counted we do not know. What we do know is that as time passed, invariably Mussolini blamed the King alone for his overthrow in everything he said and wrote on the matter. The view was, after all, the correct interpretation of the events of 24–25 July.

Edda, who had crossed the Swiss border in secret on 9 January in a perilous journey with her husband's diaries, only heard about his death on 14 January. 'It was a brusque shock,' she remarked. She told the children that their father was dead. 'Which papa?' asked the youngest.[113] Mussolini found out where she was and via a priest, Don Giusto Pancino, sent her money and wrote her letters. Pancino, who had been a friend of Edda's in their youth, saw her three times: on 5 March and 15 May 1944 and 9 March 1945.[114] She had last seen Mussolini on 26 December.[115] She would never speak to him or see him again. But she replied to one of his letters in July 1944, 'All is so black, but everyone must pay.' By then she was in a psychiatric clinic in Monthey. André Repond, her psychiatrist, diagnosed serious physical and moral depression.[116] In January 1945 she gave a copy of the Ciano diaries to the American OSS. In April 1945 – the month her father died – she sold the newspaper rights to the *Chicago Daily News* for $25,000 and retained the book rights.[117] The diaries did not contain damning evidence of anything much – except the anger and despair of both Mussolini and Ciano as they allowed themselves to be dragged ever deeper into the mire by Hitler.

There were many other arrests of Fascists who had either co-operated with Badoglio's government or been guilty of dereliction of duty. There was talk of executing them as well. But Mussolini intervened to put a stop to it. Meanwhile, he began to have regular talks with Don Pancino about religion. 'I am a Catholic out of conviction,' he told a delegation of priests from a Catholic newspaper.[118] Other priests have testified that at Gargnano Mussolini made confession and took mass in private. 'As a young man I was a heretic, with the Conciliation I became religious politically, now I feel religious also in my intimate life,' Mussolini told Padre Ginepro da Pompeiana at Villa Feltrinelli on 14 December 1943.[119]

The Allied advance had got stuck. They were unable to break through the Gustav Line – which ran (roughly) from the mouth of the River Garigliano on the west coast north of Naples, to the mouth of the River Sangro on the east coast, to Rome. So on 22 January 1944 they decided on an outflanking invasion behind enemy lines on the west coast at Anzio, south of Rome, on the famous Pontine Marshes. It was not a success. They would remain stuck there until May. In March they made a massive effort to break through the Gustav Line at Montecassino, a Benedictine monastery perched on a mountain north of Naples, a place of quite exceptional ethereal beauty in peacetime. Montecassino was held only by a small number of Germans, but the Allies mistakenly thought it was bristling with them. So they pulverised it from the air, completely destroying it. But still they failed to take it. They stepped up aerial bombardment of Italy's major cities. In the month to 10 May 1944 they carried out 3807 missions – Operation Strangle – causing huge destruction and loss of life. Each Italian city was graded according to how much architectural and artistic value it had.[120] It has been calculated that between the overthrow of Mussolini in July 1943 and the end of the war in Italy in April 1945, the Allied bombing of Italy killed 64,000 Italian civilians. The *Luftwaffe*, by comparison, killed 54,000 British civilians with its bombing of Britain between 1940 and 1945.[121] Finally, on 18 May the Allies took Montecassino and on the 23rd they broke out from the Anzio beachhead. The road to Rome was open.

On 22–23 April Mussolini met Hitler – yet again at Klessheim, near Salzburg. Once more Mussolini tried to persuade Hitler to make peace with Russia. But Hitler chewed little pills and spoke of secret weapons. From Klessheim Mussolini went on to Grafenwohr in Bavaria where one of the four new divisions being trained in Germany was headquartered. For perhaps the first time since his overthrow he regained real passion. He gave his first speech in public since his overthrow and it was proof that he had not lost his touch. He said, 'The shame of our betrayal will not be expunged unless we fight the invader who contaminates our soil ... You have the privilege of fighting this witches' cauldron of bastard nations who respect nothing and nobody as they invade Italy.'[122] The troops responded to Mussolini's speech with wild applause and he then insisted on going among them and they regaled him.

In July 1944 Mussolini decided to visit all four divisions in Germany, then Hitler at the Wolf's Lair to demand that he allow them to leave for Italy and fight to save the *patria*. Frequent Allied air raid warnings forced the train to stop repeatedly and those on board to rush out into the countryside. As it went through Munich, the Germans smothered it in thick black smoke to hide it from Allied aircraft. Mussolini arrived at the Wolf's Lair on the 20th to confront Hitler, the day von Stauffenberg's bomb had nearly killed him. Keitel told Graziani he needed three of the four Italian divisions for the Russian Front, which caused a violent argument. But for the first time, certainly since the Pact of Steel, Mussolini felt confident in Hitler's presence and for once, Hitler actually agreed to a request from Mussolini. The first two divisions arrived in Italy almost immediately. Hitler also agreed to improve the terrible conditions of the captured Italians in the German camps – though he would renege completely on this. Bidding Mussolini farewell at the station, he said, 'I know I can count on you. I beg you to believe me when I say that I consider you as my best, and perhaps the only friend I have in the world.' Hitler looked at Mussolini like a woman in love, recalled Rahn.[123] The two dictators had met sixteen times in all. They would never meet again. But they would speak frequently on the very bad telephone line between the Wolf's Lair in the forests of East Prussia and the Villa Feltrinelli on Lake Garda haunted by the ghost of d'Annunzio.

By the beginning of 1944 Mussolini had an army of about 200,000, though in practice it was under German command. In addition Ricci's new Fascist militia, the *Guardia nazionale repubblicana* (GNR), was about 140,000 strong.[124] In June 1944 Pavolini decided to arm the party by creating the *Brigate Nere*, a volunteer force similar to the Fascist *squadre* of old, which at its peak had 110,000 men in thirty-nine brigades. Its role was to combat the partisans.[125] This was a serious error. Mussolini should, as he had done in the 1920s, have used the state not the party to combat the partisans. The creation of the black brigades, many of which were a rule unto themselves and gratuitously violent, increased hatred for Fascism. But Mussolini bowed to the fanaticism of Pavolini.

The army included the four German-trained and equipped divisions, which totalled some 57,000 men – in the end Hitler had allowed Mussolini to recruit 14,000 of them from the captured Italians in his camps, the rest were either conscripts or volunteers.[126] But up to 10,000 of these had deserted within the first few weeks of their return to Italy at the end of 1943 in part because Kesselring did not want to use them in the front line and they got bored.[127] Those that remained were hardly the crack disciplined troops that Mussolini had hoped for. There were frequent reports of them looting and cropping the hair of Italian women who had German boyfriends. (In Germany they had been banned from dating German women and understandably they were angry.) An October 1944 report to Mussolini on the antics of one division – the San Marco – noted, 'A musical instrument shop in Savona was sacked, and a concert was given by the Regimental Band in a villa near the city two days later using the stolen instruments.' In addition they were short of good equipment and weaponry, and assailed on all sides by competing propaganda. Many deserted to the partisans – on one occasion an entire battalion and its commanding officer.[128]

On 4 June 1944 Rome had fallen to the Allies. Mussolini ordered the closure of all public places of entertainment for three days.

On the 6th the Allies invaded Normandy. Once Rome fell, Kesselring decided on a fighting retreat north to a line which had good man-made and natural defences running (roughly) from Viareggio in Tuscany on the west coast to Rimini in the Romagna on the east – the so-called Gothic Line. Among the cites now liberated was Florence where the retreating Germans destroyed every bridge over the Arno except the Ponte Vecchio. There, Italian women had armed themselves and fiercely resisted the Allies. Twenty-five were taken prisoner and the international press paid tribute to the courage of the Italian women of Florence. The *Daily Mirror* noted with amazement that many were well dressed and therefore must have been the daughters of Fascist fanatics. Mussolini wrote,

In the Florentine *francs-tireurs* is the newest essence of the Italian woman ... a simple, modest woman, apparently closed within the small circle of her family ... whose femininity has never been called into question by anyone. And yet at the decisive moment, when the supreme values in which she believes are in danger, this Italian woman, who is not used to political life like the French woman, or passionate about sport like the English woman, or an adventurer like the American woman, this simple woman knows how to take the place of the men and reach their level. She thinks virilely and she acts virilely ... as always happens with the women of Italy, they let their instinct speak, which is perhaps the safest guide ... an instinct which caused them to rise up in a supreme and desperate attempt to save the sacred things in which they believed: *idee, terra, casa, famiglia* ... Our hearts as Italians swell with pride and emotion at the thought of these creatures who know how to fight in the name of an idea truly felt, who, regardless of their twenty years and their fragile flesh, knew how to grab hold of a weapon and shoot straight against the enemy barbarian who arrived to bring terror into their world. *Fanciulle d'Italia*, they felt the weight and shame of an inertia which perhaps could be justified in their own sex. It is a lacerating lesson for those men who do not want to feel it and faced with action place all the subterfuges that cowardice can teach in the way.[129]

The Allies could now see the Lombard plain stretch before them towards the great cities of the north and victory. But they failed to break through despite a concerted effort in the autumn, which only managed to push the Gothic Line back slightly north above La Spezia at its western end. Winter set in.

Civil War: Dad's Army versus the Duce

The first significant act of resistance by Italians against the Germans was on Cephalonia in September 1943. The first significant act of resistance against Fascism by Italians was the overthrow of Mussolini by the King and the generals on 25 July 1943 – and to a lesser extent by the Fascists who had voted for Grandi's motion at the Grand Council meeting on the night of 24–25 July. The first significant act of resistance against either the Germans or Fascism by Italian anti-Fascism was still some way off.

On 9 September a group of anti-Fascists founded in secret the first serious resistance organisation, the *Comitato di liberazione nazionale* (CLN) in Rome. They agreed to form a coalition whose task would be to persuade the Italian *popolo* to rise up against the Germans and the Fascists. Most of them were determined to get rid of the monarchy as well but that problem was put on hold for the moment. Present were the leading figures of the main political currents which opposed Fascism. They soon began to squabble among themselves over means and ends. Indeed, for many the abolition of the monarchy was a bigger priority than the defeat of the Germans and the Fascists. Macmillan, who had to speak to these Italian politicians regularly, soon became exasperated. Croce, the Neapolitan philosopher, who was very active at this time, saw him in October 1943. 'The Senator-philosopher talked to us for one hour and thirty minutes without drawing breath. He did not say very much ...' Of Bonomi, he wrote, 'but [oh my!] he is wet as the ocean.'[130]

The first act of resistance against the Germans by the Italian people came in late September 1943 in Naples as the Germans abandoned the city to the Allies. A few hundred Neapolitans rioted for four days against the few Germans left. The Germans killed sixty-seven rioters but in order to leave Naples unmolested were forced to free forty-seven prisoners.[131] Then in November 1943 there was a second general strike in the north which swiftly fizzled out as had the one in March.

Partisan groups meanwhile began to spring up spontaneously in the area of Italy still controlled by the Germans. But by the end of 1943 there were no more than 4000 partisans in total in the whole of Italy.[132] The numerous political currents that existed meant the partisans, like the politicians, soon began to squabble over means and ends as well. To give one example, it was difficult for a former soldier whose loyalty was to the crown to fight alongside a Communist whose loyalty was to Moscow and whose ambition was not just the defeat of the Germans and the Fascists but the abolition of the monarchy and Capitalism. Such squabbles inevitably meant that many who would otherwise have become partisans decided instead to wait for the Allies to liberate Italy. But to the Communists armed resistance was not just a war to defeat the Germans and the Fascists but a revolutionary war to defeat Capitalism. The Communists, led in the north by the Spanish Civil War veteran Luigi Longo, had the clearest vision and were the most ruthless. Each of their armed units, the *Brigate Garibaldine*, had a political commissar, little different from a Nazi Gestapo officer, as well as a military commander.

The CLN in Rome, meanwhile, expended most of its energy trying to abolish the monarchy and replace Badoglio. In October 1943 it issued a proclamation which stated that until the monarchy was abolished the Italian people could not achieve the unity of spirit necessary to carry the struggle to the Germans and the Fascists! But in January 1944 the Allies handed sovereignty over much of the liberated south away from the front line to the Badoglio movement. Despite a growing clamour for his abdication, the King refused. Then, in March 1944, out of the blue, Stalin recognised the Badoglio government as the legitimate government. This completely foxed the Italian Communists, not to mention the CLN and the Allies who were reluctantly forced to follow suit. The move was the signal for the return to Italy after eighteen years of exile in Russia of Stalin's Italian – Ercole Ercoli, né Palmiro Togliatti, co-founder with Gramsci and Bombacci, Mussolini's Communist, of the Italian Communist party (PCI) in 1921. Togliatti had been a member of the Comintern which directed International Communism. On 27 March Stalin's Italian arrived by ship in Naples. His first move, on Stalin's orders, was to direct his Italian comrades, for the sake of national unity, to withdraw their objections to the abolition of the monarchy until after the liberation. His aim – and that of Stalin – was cynically simple: to ensure that the Communists formed part of whichever government replaced Badoglio. He did not interest himself in the partisan struggle, which he rightly regarded as of minor importance. The Allies would liberate Italy, not the partisans. Togliatti and Stalin were thinking from the start of after the Liberation when the Allies had gone home. So he stood back as the clamour from other quarters for the King to abdicate and Badoglio to resign grew ever louder. On 12 April the King relented to a formula which did not deprive him of his precious crown or abolish the monarchy. Instead, for the sake of national unity, he announced that he would retire and that his son, Crown Prince Umberto, would become Lieutenant-General of the kingdom on the day the Allies entered Rome. The decision signalled the end for the Badoglio government and on 22 April a new government of national unity – headed by Bonomi – took over in the liberated south though

Badoglio remained as Foreign Minister. Togliatti, naturally, entered the government as one of several ministers without portfolio. Among its actions the Bonomi government purged the civil service of Fascists and put on trial any of the Fascist gerarchs it could get its hands on. But the trial of Giacomo Acerbo illustrated how complex the issue of guilt had become in Italy. Acerbo, one of the nineteen members of the Grand Council who had voted for Grandi's motion, had sought refuge in the south after the overthrow of Mussolini. At the Verona trial in January 1944 he had been condemned to death *in absentia*. Now he went on trial for crimes related to his Fascism and a court sentenced him to forty-eight years in prison.[133]

The partisans only started to become a problem for the Germans in April 1944, according to Kesselring, when they began to be active in the Apennines in the north.[134] But there were still no more than 12,000 in total – and nearly half of them were in the Garibaldi brigades under the sole command of the Communists.[135] Their terrorist attacks on Germans and Fascists led to brutal reprisals, which were directed against political prisoners, and against the civilian population. Such attacks, therefore, were counter-productive. '*Spararono e poi sparirono* [they shoot and then they disappear],' said many civilians. The attacks included the assassination by Communist partisans of Gentile, the philosopher, who had continued to support Fascism, at his home in Florence on 15 April 1944. One of the killers allegedly shouted at Gentile, 'I am not killing the man but the idea.' Mussolini, in an unsigned article for the RSI's *Corrispondenza repubblicana* press agency, wrote, 'Giovanni Gentile was not killed just because he was a Fascist; he was killed because he was an Italian, and his assassin is not an Italian patriot ... Italy already suffers the pain of hell without the need of Italians to butcher each other, especially when the fight is not to their advantage but to that of the foreigner ... *Italiani, basta*. He who kills a Fascist, kills an Italian, and so is an enemy of Italy.'[136] On 18 April, at a Council of Ministers meeting, Mussolini reported that, to date, the partisans had killed 1023 members of the party and 535 members of the GNR.[137]

The worst partisan attack to date had been the killing in March 1944 by Communist partisans of thirty-three German soldiers on patrol in Via Rasella, in the centre of Rome, and seven civilians, one of whom was a child, with two home-made bombs ignited by a fuse. This prompted the worst reprisals by the Germans, whose policy was to kill ten Italians for every German killed in such attacks. They drew up a list of 335 people – mainly political prisoners, including Lieutenant-Colonel Frignani, commanding officer of the *carabiniere* who had arrested Mussolini at the Villa Savoia on 25 July 1943, for execution. To make up the numbers seventy-two Jews, who had been rounded up and were awaiting deportation, were added to the list. On 24 March the Germans shot them dead in a series of caves in Rome called the Fosse Ardeatine. They then blew up the entrance to the caves to seal them off.

If the Communist partisans had given themselves up those lives would have been saved. But Giorgio Amendola, a Communist leader in Rome, said, 'The duty of us fighting partisans was not to give ourselves up, even if our sacrifice could have stopped the deaths of many innocent people ... We had only one duty: to continue the fight.'[138] Two Fascists were directly involved in the slaughter: Pietro Caruso, the Questore of Rome, who provided the names of fifty civilians, and Lieutenant Pietro Koch, in command of an Italian SS squad, which helped round up the prisoners. But Mussolini, when he heard, though powerless in the north, was furious and ordered all political prisoners in the RSI not charged with murder to be freed immediately.[139]

The attitude of the Allies to the activities of the partisans was equivocal because they did not regard them as a relevant military force and they feared that the predominance of the Communists created a threat of a Communist takeover of Italy once the war was won. Nor did they agree that partisan actions such as the bombs in Via Rasella achieved anything positive, only brutal reprisals. They tried unsuccessfully to persuade the partisans to concentrate on sabotage and intelligence instead. Nevertheless, they agreed to supply the partisans with weapons, though only in return for a signed declaration that these would be returned at the end of hostilities. Wherever possible, they tried to avoid supplying weapons to Communist partisan brigades.

By the late summer of 1944 the partisans numbered around 80,000.[140]

On 9 August Communist partisans in Milan had killed nine German soldiers as well as eight passers-by. Kesselring had wanted to apply the ten for one rule, but relented after an appeal by the Archbishop of Milan, Ildefonso Schuster. A Fascist firing squad executed fifteen political prisoners the next day in Piazzale Loreto. (That they were Fascists needs explaining. The firing squad was from the Ettore Muti legion – the Milan-based paramilitary police force. The Muti was under German command. The Germans ordered it to provide the firing squad. The Fascist prefect of Milan resigned in protest afterwards. In 2000 an Italian court was near to bringing charges against the former German officer considered responsible for the killings.)[141] Mussolini, who was at La Rocca delle Caminate, protested in writing to Rahn on his return to Gargnano: 'According to an official report, the execution in Piazzale Loreto took place in circumstances of extreme violence, without any respect for normal procedure ... We must not give the minimum justification to those who, insofar as we are your allies, consider us traitors.'[142] When he saw Rahn, he complained that such reprisals were 'inflaming' the Italian civil war.[143] According to Moellhausen, Mussolini always protested to the Germans when he heard news of German atrocities 'with insistence, anger and bitterness'.[144] Of course Mussolini could have resigned in protest. But, rightly, his answer would have been that it would have made the situation worse for the Italian people.

Mussolini also objected to atrocities by Fascist *Brigate Nere* which, though reprehensible, were nowhere near as bad as those of the Germans. On 24 September 1944 he ordered the abolition of the infamous *Banda Koch*, led by Pietro Koch, but under German command, and the imprisonment of Koch and his key personnel. His paramilitary police force had been responsible for torturing prisoners in Milan. The Germans then freed some of Koch's men. But Koch remained in jail.[145]

The Allied assault on the Gothic Line in the autumn of 1944 had failed. The Allies knew that they could not launch any more attempts on it until the spring. So on 19 November 1944 Field Marshal Harold Alexander, Commander-in-Chief of the Allied forces in Italy, issued a proclamation to the partisans to cease all large-scale operations for the duration of the winter and hide their weapons. Though the decision was taken for purely military reasons, the partisans were disillusioned.[146]

As a result, the number of partisans decreased from about 80,000 to about 50,000.[147] But the Allies did sign an important agreement with the *Comitato di liberazione nazionale dell' alt' Italia* (CLNAI), the partisan resistance leadership in the occupied north, and the Bonomi government in December 1944. The CLNAI recognised the Bonomi government as the legitimate government of Italy. In return the Bonomi government agreed that the CLNAI represent it in the north. All three parties agreed that in the brief period between the evacuation of the north by the Germans and the arrival of the Allies the CLNAI would form a provisional government in the north. But as soon as the Allies had liberated the north, it would hand over power to the Allied military government, disband all partisan units and surrender their weapons to the Allies. The CLNAI also agreed that it would obey orders from the Allies. In return, the Allies agreed to finance and arm the CLNAI.[148] But the Allies, especially the British, less so the Americans, were rightly deeply suspicious of the Communist partisans who made up about 40 per cent of the partisan forces. They feared that they would use Allied money and weaponry to seize power and that this in turn would cause the civil war to escalate by sucking in the Bonomi government as well. They feared another 'Greek situation'.[149] But their attempts to ensure that the *materiél* they sent did not reach the Communist partisan brigades were largely in vain.

Partisan terrorist attacks on German and Fascist targets, which led to brutal reprisals on the populace, alienated support, as did the widespread practice of stealing or demanding – at gun point – money and food from the populace. For many Italians the partisans were not freedom fighters but criminals. The numbers of Italians who chose to become partisans was much smaller than the number of Italians who chose to fight for Mussolini's republic even taking into account conscription. Figures for the RSI's armed forces are easier to establish from those for the partisans – though not with total precision. They totalled, according to a reliable estimate, a minimum 573,000 (of whom 239,000 were volunteers): 254,000 were in the army; 20,000 in the navy; 28,000 in the air force; 50,000 in the anti-aircraft service; 140,000 in the GNR; 49,300 in the *Ispetterato del lavoro*; and 25,000 in the *Wehrmacht*.[150] The vast majority of the Italian *popolo*, meanwhile, did its best to keep its head down. The truth, however unpalatable to the mythologists of the Italian Left, is that the partisan resistance only became a populist movement at the very last moment. Miraculously, by April 1945, with the Allied victory over the Germans in Italy days away, the number of partisans would shoot up to about 200,000.[151]

17

THE END

During the winter of 1944–5 Mussolini retreated ever further into himself in the dense fog at Gargnano on Lake Garda. He prepared for military defeat. He put out feelers in Berne to try to get permission for his family to be granted asylum in Switzerland. On 1 December he sold his cherished newspaper, *Il Popolo d'Italia* (it had not been published since July 1943). The terms remain murky but the purchaser, a perfume manufacturer, Gian Riccardo Cella, got the newspaper free, it seems, in return for paying off its 35 million lire debts.[1] Mussolini thought about posterity and death.

On 16 December, cajoled by diehard Fascists such as Pavolini, Mussolini made his last important speech in Milan. He travelled there with Bombacci.[2] He spoke at 11 a.m. at the Teatro Lirico. The only pre-publicity for the speech was a message on the radio informing listeners that an event of 'exceptional importance' was about to happen. The theatre was packed nevertheless. 'Who betrayed?' he asked his audience. Yet his answer was not the Fascists who had voted for Grandi's motion. He did not mention them. His answer was the King, the court, defeatist generals, certain clerics, freemasons and the bourgeoisie. This was a clear sign that in the end he had understood the true mechanism of his downfall. He deplored too the brutal reprisals on Italians from whichever quarter they came which, he said 'repel me profoundly'.

But the speech is important for another reason. In it Mussolini spelled out at length his vision of *socializzazione* and said that its aim was to create the 'largest possible national concord'. Britain would live to regret its alliance with Bolshevik Russia, he said, adding,

One day a Soviet ambassador in Rome, Potemkin, told me, 'The First World War Bolshevised Russia, the second will Bolshevise Europe.' ... Politically Albion is already defeated. The Russian armies are on the Vistola and the Danube, that is halfway across Europe. The Communist parties, that is the parties which act in the pay of and according to the orders of Marshal Stalin, are partially in power in the western countries. ... The 'liberated' Greeks who fire on the English 'liberators' are merely Russian Communists who fire on British Conservatives ... Churchill must, to use an English expression, be eating his hat and, thinking about the entry of Russia in the Mediterranean and Russian pressure on Iran, must be asking himself if the politics of Casablanca [where the unconditional surrender formula was agreed for all three Axis powers] was not truly for 'poor old England' a politics of failure.[3]

When Mussolini finished, the applause was spontaneous and deafening. Outside, he toured areas of Milan badly hit by Allied bombs. Enormous crowds gave him a hero's welcome. The Germans were amazed. He remained in Milan for three days. But then, all too soon, he was back in the silence of Gargnano on the melancholy fogbound lake. Five months later another crowd in Milan would cheer as his corpse was strung up before it.

In February 1945 Zachariae, his German army doctor, decided that he was the 'victim of a serious physical and moral collapse'.[4] In March, Mussolini gave a frank interview to Maddalena Mollier, photographer, nurse and wife of the press officer at the German embassy at Salò, full of foreboding. He helped Mollier set up her camera and plugged in her flash lamps to a lamp socket.[5] He said,

Why do you come to interview me, *signora*? I am dead. Look at what remains of me ... Go for a swim in the lake, sunbathe, enjoy your liberty and all the beautiful things that life reserves for you; don't concern yourself with a ghost ... This morning in my room a little swallow got trapped. It flew about, it flew desperately, until it fell exhausted on my bed; I picked it up in my hands; a little trembling creature. I caressed it and, gradually, it calmed down; and in the end it dared to look at me. I went to the window, I opened my hand. It, still stunned, did not understand immediately ... then it opened its wings and, with a cry of joy, it flew to liberty ... I will never forget that cry of joy. The only doors that will open for me are those of death. And it is also just. I have erred and I shall pay ... I have never made a mistake following my instinct, but always when I obeyed reason ... I do not blame anyone, I do not reproach anyone apart from myself. I am responsible, just as much for the things that I did well, that the world can never deny me, as for my weaknesses and my decline ... My star has set. I work and make an effort, even though knowing that everything is a farce. ... My star has set, but I did not have the strength or the courage to retire in time ... Have you ever seen a prudent, calculating dictator? They all become mad, they lose their equilibrium in the clouds, in quivering ambitions and obsessions. And it is actually that mad passion which brought them to where they are. A *bravo borghese* would never discomfort himself so much ... There is no doubt that we are heading towards, in short, a Socialist epoque ... I see the salvation of Europe only in a Socialist union of European states. A formidable block that will defend our civilisation and existence against the red materialism of the Bolsheviks and for us more or less damaging experiments of the American type. Soon the German, French, Spanish, Italian etc. question will be of no interest; only Europe will be of interest. Everyone will realise it. If in time or not, who knows.[6]

One evening he gave another interview to the journalist, Ivanoe Fossani, which took place on a starry night on a small island in Lake Garda. He returned to a favourite theme: the short-sightedness of Britain which would now, as a result of its declaration of war on Germany, lose its empire. Britain had gone to war to save Poland. It had failed. The Russians had Poland now. Britain's number one enemy was Communism not Fascism, not even National Socialism. Churchill, no less, had supported Mussolini and Fascism to stop Communism. Yet Churchill had made a military alliance with Communism to stop National Socialism and Fascism. He would live to regret it. He said, 'If England, instead of sending the knights of St George to create discord and unquenchable hatreds, had fused Europe in a block of ideals and interests, our position would be unassailable ... Before entering into the Pact of Steel I tried everything to reach an understanding with the other side ... England didn't want it. It wanted our neutrality and our ports at its disposal ...' But Italy's geography meant it had to choose war, 'Either with one side or with the other ... Our geographical position is outside the orbit of neutrality. Either accept war or become an encampment of enemy armies.' He also said, 'The only socialism workable socialistically is corporativism, the point of confluence, equilibrium and justice for private interests in respect of the collective interest ...'[7]

By September 1944 Mussolini had begun to accumulate documents which would serve to defend him before a war crimes court and before history. According to German intercepts of his letters and phone calls, he spoke often of a correspondence and secret agreements with Churchill. On 9 January 1945 he wrote to Graziani, 'At the moment I regard as of great importance to place in safety these documents, above all the exchange of letters and the accords with Churchill. These will be the witnesses of the English *malafede*. These documents are worth more than a war won, because they will explain to the world the real, the only reasons for our intervention at the side of Germany ...'[8] Like so many documents to do with Mussolini these intercepts, given to an Italian historian by SS General Karl Wolff, have the whiff of forgery about them. Examples include, 'My relations with Churchill are still today such as to exclude a priori any difficulties';[9] 'Churchill knows I have got the correspondence ready and waiting ... He is biting his fingernails for the letter he wrote me in October 1940.'[10] Apart from anything else, Mussolini knew that his phones were tapped and his letters intercepted, and Wolff was notoriously devious and unreliable.

The only genuine Churchill–Mussolini letters ever to come to light, however, are those exchanged in May 1940 which do not mention accords of any kind – though numerous forgeries have surfaced over the years which do. Despite the absence of actual letters, most Italian historians have an unshakeable belief that Churchill and Mussolini did conduct a secret compromising correspondence both before and during the war – compromising to Churchill, that is. In it Churchill is said to have made all sorts of attempts to bribe Mussolini with territory to stay out of the war or, once it had started, to withdraw from it or at the end of it to let Mussolini off the hook so that he could concentrate on stopping Stalin in the Balkans. Churchill is also said to have written to Mussolini in June 1940 to say that he understood why Mussolini had declared war on Britain and France, and that this was a good thing because if Hitler won, Mussolini could moderate Hitler's demands on Britain and France at the peace table! Yet the Italian historians are unable to produce any evidence whatsoever – let alone an actual letter – to back their unshakeable belief apart from hearsay evidence such as Mussolini's letters to Graziani and Hitler quoted above. But anyway it would not be especially embarrassing if Churchill did write to Mussolini other letters in 1939 and 1940 to try to keep Italy out of the war. We already know (see relevant earlier section on Italian entry into the war) that both the British and the French made concerted attempts to stop Italy declaring war on them. These included the French offering territory to Mussolini. What we also know is that Halifax in particular was keen to appease Mussolini but Churchill lukewarm on the grounds that such offers would probably be counter-productive.

But it is obvious why, as the noose tightened, Mussolini would want to let it be known that such a correspondence with Churchill existed and it was entirely in character for him to make such false claims. Furthermore, especially just after the war, the forging of documents in Italy reached industrial proportions. Nor is it beyond the realms of possibility either that Mussolini himself forged such letters. He was, after all, an Italian.

But what is true is that Mussolini still thought he had a role to play. He thought he had something concrete to offer Churchill: assistance in the fight against Communism. The threat of a Communist takeover of much of Europe loomed large. Tito's Communists had occupied the north-east of Italy bordering Yugoslavia. The Greek Communists had begun civil war. Stalin had 'liberated' much of central Europe. Mussolini thought that Churchill might agree to a soft surrender so as to be free to try to stop Stalin 'liberating' any more of it. He even thought that Churchill might use him as a mediator or allow him to fight alongside the Allies against Stalin. So in early 1945 Mussolini put out secret peace feelers to the Allies behind the backs of the Germans (so too did the Germans in Italy behind Mussolini's back – and Hitler's). Mussolini also thought that he might still be able to reach an agreement with Italy's Socialists by playing on their hostility to the capitalism of the Allies and the Communism of Stalin. But the peace feelers, notably via Cardinal Schuster the archbishop of Milan and the Vatican, went nowhere.

The Germans were on the run everywhere. On 12 April the Allies crossed the Elbe, sixty miles west of Berlin – the same day that Roosevelt died. The Russians had reached the Oder thirty miles east of Berlin. In Italy the Allies at long last broke through the Gothic Line on 10 and 11 April.[11] They were at last able to move north across the Lombard plain to the great cities of Bologna, Milan, Turin and Venice.

On 16 April Mussolini announced to his ministers that he had decided to transfer the government of the RSI to the *Prefettura* in Milan. On the 18th all set off by car, complete with SS minders. Mussolini left his wife and the two youngest children, and his sister Edvige behind. He told his sister that if she needed protection she should make contact with Churchill because only he had the gift of historical objectivity. Doggedly, Petacci persuaded her SS minder, Lieutenant Spoegler, to take her to Milan[12] to be with her Duce.

Petacci and Mussolini had ten days left to live. Apart from Vittorio, who went with him, Mussolini would never see his family again. He had two aims: to negotiate peace with the partisans before the Allied troops arrived, and if that failed, which it would, to leave Milan and go north into the Alps, and from there …? There was talk of Switzerland; there was talk of Spain. There was talk about setting up the Alpine redoubt in the Valtellina, in the Alto Adige (South Tyrol), where Fascism would make its last stand. Those gathered around Mussolini in the Milan *Prefettura* in these last frenetic days included the Socialist journalist Silvestri, and the ex-Communist Bombacci – his only confidants.

In Berlin, on the 20th, Hitler celebrated his fiftieth birthday in the bunker, emerging briefly to make his last public appearance and review a guard of honour of Hitler Jugend aged fourteen–sixteen. In Milan Mussolini gave a last interview to a journalist, Gian Gaetano Cabella, former editor of *Il Popolo di Alessandria*, and diehard Fascist. 'Do you desire anything from me?' Mussolini began. Cabella produced a photograph of Mussolini and asked him to autograph it, which he did. Timidly, he then asked Mussolini if he might ask him some questions. 'Mussolini got up. He came close to me. Looking at me in the eyes, with an emphasis and expression which I shall never forget, he asked me, all of a sudden, "Interview or testament"?' It was the signal for a lengthy discourse by Mussolini on his political record. In particular, he defended his declaration of war against Britain and France in June 1940. Germany had won by then, he said, and if he had not declared war Italy would have been 'invaded and crushed' by Germany. 'The truth is simple: I had no pressure from Hitler. Hitler had already won the continental game. He did not need us. But we could not remain neutral if we wanted to maintain that position of parity with Germany which until then we had had ...' And he spoke, as so often nowadays, of secret weapons. 'But is there any hope? Are there secret weapons?' asked Cabella. 'There are. It would be ridiculous and unforgivable to bluff. If there hadn't been the attempt on Hitler's life last summer, there would have been the time necessary to put into action these weapons ... The famous destructive bombs are nearly ready. Just a few days ago, I received very precise news. Perhaps Hitler only wants to *vibrare il colpo* in the absolute certainty that it will be decisive.'[13]

On the 21st Bologna fell to the Allies and the partisans there indulged in an orgy of violence against Fascists. In Germany the Russians were about to enter Berlin. On the 22nd Mussolini asked Silvestri to write to the leaders of the Republican and Socialist partisans 'since the succession is open he desires to consign the *Repubblica Sociale* (RSI) to the Republicans and not the monarchists, and *socializzazione* to the Socialists and not the bourgeoisie'.[14] The letter said that Mussolini would surrender to the Socialists and hand over Milan to them. They rejected the offer.[15] His main effort, however, at a surrender which salvaged something from the catastrophe was done via the Archbishop of Milan, Cardinal Schuster.

On the 23rd Mussolini saw Petacci, whose parents had left on the 22nd by plane for Spain. Previously he had urged her to go; they had urged her to go. But she had insisted on remaining behind in Milan with her Duce. Mussolini also telephoned his wife to tell her and the two youngest children to leave Gargnano and go to Monza just north of Milan. They arrived there at dawn the next day. Incredibly, the Fascists in the *Prefettura* in Milan still kept up the pretence of government. On the 22nd, for example, Carlo Alberto Biggini, the Minister for National Education, saw Mussolini to speak about 'most pressing matters', namely, the new law on teachers and a radio broadcast on the completion of Turin University.[16]

On the 24th Hitler sent his last message to Mussolini. He said that the German people 'in its spirit of tenacious disregard for death' fought on and that their 'unequalled heroism' would change the course of the war 'in this historic moment in which the fate of Europe for future centuries is decided'.[17]

But in Italy the Germans, who had been treating secretly with the Allies to surrender in Italy since February, had more or less given up. In Milan there was an uneasy stand-off between the partisans and the Fascists as the city awaited the arrival of the Allies who were just hours away.

Their Finest Hour

There is much nonsense talked in Italy about the partisan movement and its role in the liberation of Italy. In April 2001, for example, in an episode of the daily press round-up programme on RAI 1, the main state television channel, Paolo Flores d'Accais the editor of *Micromega*, the influential high-brow left-wing periodical, said, 'When the partisans liberated Italy ...' Such a view is so ingrained in the psyche not just of the Italian Left but of Italy's chattering classes (politicians, journalists etc.) that it is allowed to pass without comment. Yet it is nonsense. The significance of the partisan movement was not military. It could not and did not liberate Italy from the Germans. The Allies did. It was a small, badly armed, disorganised, badly trained, disunited, Dad's Army. In June 1944 the CLNAI agreed that the partisan brigades of the five (there were six in the south) political parties should unite under one command with the creation of the *Corpo volontari della libertà* (CVL). The CVL was incorporated in the Allied army; it was therefore – in theory at least – under Allied command. The British, however, fearful as ever of the Communists, insisted that on the ground the CVL be under the command of someone they trusted. They despatched General Raffaele Cadorna, who was a conservative and anti-Fascist, to be the CVL's Commander-in-Chief. The Communists had pressed hardest for this unification of partisan forces because they had the most partisans and therefore the best chance of extending their control over the other partisan groups as a result.[18] They would not accept Cadorna as Commander-in-Chief and treated him merely as a military adviser or chairman of a committee. He soon became exasperated.

The Communists, in order to deflect attention from their divided loyalties between Italy and Russia, insisted on calling their partisans 'patriots'. The aim was to convince Italians that they were fighting for both the nation and democracy. This was not true, of course. They were fighting for Moscow and Communism not Italy and democracy. They aimed to use the chaos of liberation to launch an insurrection which would cause a revolution. As in the Spanish Civil War, their political commissars all too often meted out summary justice on their own men as well as the enemy. An OSS field agent reported, for example, that each of the Modena division's unit military commanders 'was flanked by a Communist commissar' and one of these, known for 'various cruelties', 'was able to eliminate [i.e. kill] personalities who had influence on the partisans because of their gallantry but had cast aspersions on his character.'[19]

The significance of the partisan movement was political not military. By 1945 both its political leadership – the CLNAI – and its military forces – the CVL – were dominated by the parties of the Left: the Communists, the Socialists, and the *Partito d'azione*, but especially the Communists. Just as Mussolini had appreciated the revolutionary potential of war, so did they. For the Communists the partisan movement was the vanguard of the revolution.

On 13 April Togliatti wrote to Longo, 'Take all the measures necessary ... Choose the moment of the insurrection yourself.'[20] Such an insurrection was the precise opposite of what the legitimate Italian government, that of Bonomi of which Togliatti was a minister, and the Allies wanted. They wanted the partisans simply to maintain law and order until the arrival of the Allied troops.

The CLNAI, meanwhile, had proclaimed that Mussolini and the gerarchs were war criminals who would be condemned to death. On the 20th it had announced the formation of people's courts to try and punish the guilty. Exasperated, General Cadorna told the CLNAI that he would obey its directives only 'provided that these concord with those of the Allies and the Italian government'.[21] But the reality was that Cadorna, despite his title, was not in command of the partisans. If anyone was, the Communist and other left-wing partisan leaders were.

On the 25th the CLNAI called a general strike in Milan to begin that afternoon. This was the signal for the insurrection to start. The Germans were pulling out of Milan. The CLNAI declared itself the provisional government. But in Milan the only insurrection of any significance to occur was by the *Guardia di finanza*, the finance police, who seized the *Prefettura* and other important buildings – not the partisans.[22]

According to Indro Montanelli, who was there, the first partisan units did not enter Milan until 7.30 a.m. on 28 April – three days after the call for a general insurrection. There were 600 of them. Whatever the true date, the partisans sustained hardly any casualties in their liberation of Milan between 25 and 28 April 1945. On the morning of the 26th Lieutenant-Colonel Max Salvadori, the senior SOE (Special Operations Executive) man in Milan, whose task was liaison between the CLNAI and the Allies, saw a minor skirmish between 'a few Fascists' and partisans. 'The bullets whistling past my ears were the last I was to hear,' he wrote.[23] As Montanelli wrote, 'The general insurrection flared up, in practice, when there was no longer anything to rise up against.[24] The first Allied troops arrived in Milan on the 29th and the official Allied entry into the city took place the next day.

On the afternoon of the 25th Mussolini saw Cardinal Schuster at the Curia to meet representatives of the CLNAI – the partisan leadership.[25] The cardinal was also mediating between the Germans in Italy and the partisans, and expected the Germans to be present as well. He hoped to broker a deal between all three. But the Germans, by this time, were on the verge of their secret surrender to the Allies via Switzerland. Despite the cardinal's optimism, SS General Wolff cancelled coming at the last minute. There had been contact between the cardinal and Mussolini on and off since February. Once Mussolini had arrived in Milan this contact, via intermediaries, became intense. The meeting on the 25th was the result. The cardinal who, like the Catholic Church as a whole, had once been so keen on collaboration with Fascism, received Mussolini at the Curia. In February 1937 he had described Mussolini in a speech to the School of Mystical

Fascism as 'the providential man of genius who saved the state, founded the empire and gave to the consciences of Italians the most perfect national unity by virtue of the *Pace Religiosa* [Lateran Pact].'[26]

The cardinal would recall the Mussolini he saw that day as 'a man without will ... who moves towards his fate without reaction'. Mussolini proposed conditional surrender: his army and militia would surrender the next day but among his conditions was that he could then withdraw to the Valtellina with 3000 blackshirts. After an hour the partisan delegation arrived: General Cadorna, the CVL's commanding officer, and two moderate representatives of the CLNAI, one a Christian Democrat, the other a liberal. The partisan leaders demanded the unconditional surrender of the Fascist forces. Outside the cardinal's *sala delle udienze* the Fascist gerarchs who had come with Mussolini to the Curia, who included Paolo Zerbino, Interior Minister, Francesco Barracù, Under-Secretary to Mussolini, and Marshal Graziani, heard from one of the Archbishop's aides that the Germans in Italy were about to surrender to the Allies. One of them – it is not clear who – interrupted the meeting to inform Mussolini of the secret German surrender talks. The Cardinal was forced to admit that he too knew about these talks and had been involved. This seriously weakened Mussolini's already weak negotiating hand. He erupted, 'They have always treated us like slaves, and now at the end they have betrayed me!'[27] Mussolini walked out of the talks. 'Your General Wolff has betrayed us!' he shouted at Lieutenant Fritz Birzer, the commanding officer of his SS minders. Yet it is likely that both he and Graziani were already aware of the separate German peace initiative, though not how close it was to being signed.[28]

By the afternoon the partisans had begun the first reprisal killings of Fascists and associated atrocities in Milan. Fascists melted away as best they could. The partisans, as agreed with the Allies, had orders to hand over Mussolini alive to the Allies, but believed, especially the Communists among them, that their revolutionary moment had come. Nevertheless, Mussolini might have sought refuge at the Curia. The Cardinal had even prepared a room for him in case he should ask. He might also have barricaded himself inside the *Prefettura*, just as he had barricaded himself inside his newspaper office in 1922 on the eve of coming to power, until the Allies arrived. Instead, he decided to leave Milan. Vittorio suggested staying in Milan until the Allies arrived but he exploded, 'If they think I can be put in the stocks in the Tower of London like a wild beast or in a cage in Madison Square Garden, they deceive themselves.'[29]

At about 8 p.m. he and his entourage hastily organised a convoy of cars and a few armoured vehicles, and left the *Prefettura* along with his SS escort and a small number of armed blackshirts. In the convoy were, among others, Graziani, his eldest son Vittorio, his brother Arnaldo's son, Vito, Barracù, *medaglia d'oro*, black patch over one eye, Paolo Zerbino and Bombacci. Bombacci, the honorary Red Army colonel, travelled in Mussolini's car. Mussolini's chauffeur, however, the former racing car champion, had disappeared, like so many others.[30] Those in the convoy took with them whatever money, gold and jewellery they could lay their hands on and any documents useful either to defend themselves from, or use as blackmail against, their accusors. Mussolini was wearing his usual grey-green militia uniform and had with him two leather briefcases containing his most important documents: in one the 'proof' that Germany had betrayed its ally Italy; in the other documents relating to Britain including, it is insisted, the so-called Churchill–Mussolini correspondence. There was also a Fiat *Balilla* van in the convoy, which contained other documents, valuables and personal effects – most belonging to Mussolini. The van was said to contain a white wooden box, lined with zinc, with the words '*Documenti Personali del Duce*' written on it.[31] There were about thirty vehicles in total in the convoy.[32] Pavolini remained behind to raise a Fascist force to protect Mussolini. There was talk of rallying 5000.

Like the King and his court before him, Mussolini now fled with his. Indeed, the casual observer would have been hard pressed to tell the difference. Each would have seemed like a group of important people in a hurry – running away from something. Petacci and her corrupt brother, Marcello, his female companion and his two children, complete with false Spanish diplomatic passports, followed a little later. Petacci had large sums of money and jewellery hidden about her person. The convoy reached Como, where Mussolini decided to stop for the night in the *Prefettura* – the Fiat *Balilla* van, driven by the husband of Mussolini's housemaid with her as passenger, failed to show. It had broken down on the way and the wife had hitch-hiked a lift on to Como to tell Mussolini. The husband, meanwhile, had hidden the van as best he could, then left the scene because he was scared of being captured by the partisans. Mussolini was angry, understandably, and ordered various people to search for the van. But they failed to find it.

Subsequently, soon after the liberation, two local partisans who were brothers – Carlo and Arturo Allievi – handed over the documents from the van to the Allies at their headquarters which had remained at Caserta in the south. It is impossible to say if these documents constituted all the documents in the van. (They are now in the Public Record Office at Kew and contain no Churchill–Mussolini letters.)

That night, Mussolini's wife and the two children also reached Como from Monza. They stayed in a villa not far from the *Prefettura*. During the night those Fascist forces still loyal to Mussolini and within striking distance arrived at Como. News reached Mussolini that the Swiss government would not grant him entry. He now wrote his wife – she would allege – a letter of farewell. 'Dear Rachele, I have reached the ultimate phase of my life, the ultimate page of my book. Perhaps we two will never see each other again, therefore I write to you and I send you this letter. I ask you to forgive all the bad things that I have involuntarily done to you. But you know that you have been for me the only woman that I have truly loved. I swear to you in front of God and our Bruno in this supreme moment. We have to go to the Valtellina. You, with the children, try to get to the Swiss frontier. Up there you can make a new life. All my affection to you and the children. Your Benito. Como, 27 April 1945, *Anno XXIII Era Fascista*.[33] The letter is said to have been delivered to Rachele Mussolini at the villa where she was staying that same night. Eventually, she managed to speak to her husband on the telephone. He did not seek to see her. The letter casts Mussolini in a favourable light for two reasons: it shows that despite all his affairs and the fact that he would die with his mistress, his wife was the woman he 'truly loved'; and secondly, it shows that his intention was not to run away to Switzerland but to make a last stand in the Valtellina. Conveniently, Rachele Mussolini – everything she wrote about her husband must be taken with a pinch of salt – said that she subsequently destroyed the letter but had memorised its contents! In addition, the date on the letter is wrong. The letter, if genuine, was written in Como on the night of 25–26 April.[34]

Before dawn on the 26th Mussolini's convoy set off once more, going north along the road which hugs the western edge of Lake Como. Bombacci travelled in Mussolini's car. The convoy stopped at Menaggio seven miles further on to wait for Pavolini. Another convoy carrying Graziani and other gerarchs arrived; soon afterwards so did Petacci and her brother. Graziani had come only to tell Mussolini that he had to return to Como because he felt that it was his duty to be with his troops. In fact, he went to Wolff's headquarters at Fasano, near Como, where he wrote out an authority for the Germans to surrender the Fascist forces on the same terms as the Germans (he had no right to as Mussolini was Commander-in-Chief). He then surrendered to the American OSS agent, Captain Emilio Daddario, who had only just entered Italy from Switzerland. Daddario had received information that Graziani was at Cernobbio, near Como, and gone there to get him.

Graziani had saved his life but not his honour. But then he had never been an honourable man. On the evening of the 26th Daddario drove, via Como, with Graziani and an armed escort to Milan, arriving at about 11 p.m.[35] Graziani knew more or less where Mussolini was. But he did not, it seems tell his captor Daddario.

In Milan, Pavolini had rallied a reasonable number of Fascist *Brigate Nere* and GNR militiamen and he and they had set off for Como at dawn on the 26th. But by the time the column of about 200 military vehicles, including some artillery pieces and armoured cars, arrived in Como, Mussolini had left. Pavolini decided to head on alone to find him. Elena Curti,

Mussolini's illegitimate daughter, who was determined to join her father, gave him a lift in her car. They met up with Mussolini's convoy near Menaggio. After talking to Mussolini, Pavolini returned to Como to get his forces. He and Mussolini had agreed that the convoy would wait for him at Grandola. Quite why Mussolini went to Grandola in the mountains above Lake Como remains unclear. From Grandola – ten miles from the Swiss frontier – the only place to go was Switzerland. Certainly Grandola was west – the opposite direction to the Valtellina – where the famous last stand was due to happen.

Diehard Fascists claim that Mussolini went to Grandola either because it was safer to wait there for Pavolini than down by Lake Como or to make contact with the British or Americans in Switzerland. But what was the point of trying to make contact with them now? Like the partisans, they had insisted on unconditional surrender. Ah yes, but Mussolini had an ace in the hole, say the Fascists: his threat to reveal the famous Churchill–Mussolini correspondence. Let us suppose for a minute that the correspondence did exist. What use was it now? Was Churchill, on the brink of total victory in Europe, going to offer Mussolini favourable surrender terms to stop him revealing its contents? The only point in Mussolini trying to contact the Allies via Switzerland now was to give himself up. That at least would protect him from the revolutionary fury of the partisans leaders, especially the Communists, who wanted to execute him summarily. But he did not need a correspondence with Churchill to give himself up – and the Alps on the Swiss border were not exactly the best place to try to surrender to the British in April 1945. In any case, there is no evidence of any contact in Grandola with Allied representatives from Switzerland or anywhere else.

While waiting for Pavolini at Grandola Mussolini listened to the radio which, among other things, announced that the CLNAI had repealed all his *socializzazione* laws – a sign of how worried the Italian Left was about them – and said that people's tribunals would punish Fascists for their crimes. Members of the Fascist government guilty of suppressing constitutional guarantees, destroying popular liberty, creating the Fascist regime etc., said the announcement, would be condemned to death or 'in less serious cases' life in prison. This did not, however, mean that they would be shot on sight.[36] The hours ticked by. There was no sign of Pavolini and his force of loyalists. Mussolini decided to go back down the mountains to Menaggio on Lake Como with his convoy. It was raining heavily.

Pavolini's problem was that while he had been away his forces had decided not to fight on after all but to surrender to the partisans. The last stand in the Valtellina, whether seriously meant or not, was no longer possible. Nor was the armed defence of Mussolini from partisans if the need should arise. Desperately, Pavolini had tried to raise forces – in vain. The best he could do was three armoured trucks. Humiliated, he set off once again from Como with the trucks to find Mussolini, which he did at 4 a.m. on the 27th in Menaggio. Mussolini's situation was now desperate but then a retreating *Luftwaffe* anti-aircraft column arrived in Menaggio. It was heading in the direction of the Valtellina and its commanding officer, Lieutenant Hans Fallmeyer, agreed to escort Mussolini's convoy north. The arrival of the anti-aircraft unit and its 200 soldiers[37] decided Mussolini's destination once and for all. At least the Germans knew where they were going and had the weapons to get there.

At about 6 a.m. on the 27th the convoy and its German escort provided by destiny set off from Menaggio, led by one of the armoured trucks, snaking their way north along the narrow road beside Lake Como. Mussolini travelled in the armoured truck along with Pavolini, Barracù and Bombacci. Petacci who travelled with her brother, was wearing blue overalls and leather flying hat.[38] At about 7.30 a.m. in the hamlet of Musso their path was obstructed by a rudimentary roadblock manned by a handful of partisans. The partisans had decided to come down from the mountains that day because they were desperate for cigarettes but had then heard that a large column was heading up the road towards them. So they decided to set up a roadblock. They fired their weapons in the air in warning; Pavolini's armoured truck, which had a heavy machine-gun on top, fired back. A peasant walking in the fields nearby fell dead.[39] Talks ensued. Fallmeyer told the partisans that he and his men did not want to fight them but were determined to return to Germany. The partisans said they would have to speak with their superiors and that Fallmeyer should come with them. Fallmeyer agreed. In reality, there were no superiors; only colleagues. It was a ruse to gain time so as, among other things, to mine a bridge further along the road and call for reinforcements.[40] The clock ticked. News of the arrival of the column spread. Local people milled about it. More partisans – many as everywhere, of the eleventh hour – materialised. Finally, at about 2.30 p.m. Fallmeyer returned. The partisan commanding officer would allow only the Germans in the convoy to proceed, Fallmeyer told Mussolini and he insisted on searching the German vehicles for hidden Italians. Fallmeyer had agreed, he said. The Italians were on their own. Had Fallmeyer decided to fight, the handful of partisans in Dongo would have been no match for him. But he did not know how many other partisans there were in the vicinity and his men were homesick. It was yet another German betrayal – the last. It would cause Mussolini's death.

The Germans did agree, however, to take Mussolini with them but only Mussolini. They suggested that he disguise himself as a German and hide in one of their trucks. He agreed. He donned a *Luftwaffe* corporal's greatcoat and helmet, and took his place in the back of a truck just behind the driver's cabin. He put on sunglasses and held a submachine-gun between his knees. The convoy moved off slowly from Musso at about 3 p.m. to the small lakeside town of Dongo, less than a mile away, where the partisans had decided to conduct the agreed search for Italians.

During the search of the German troop trucks a partisan, the Dongo clog-maker, noticed something strange about one of the soldiers. He was wearing sunglasses, but the sun was not shining.The soldier's chin was resting on the tip of his submachine-gun barrel and the lapels of his greatcoat were turned up. The partisan then noticed something familiar about the helmeted face of the soldier. He decided to take a closer look. The soldier's comrades said in Italian, 'Camerata ubriaco, camerata ubriaco [comrade drunk, comrade drunk].' Despite the turned-up lapels and the sunglasses, the profile was unmistakable: it was that of the Duce; a profile depicted everywhere, often helmeted, on postcards, posters, walls, in photographs, the subject of statues and busts, a profile chiselled in the sides of mountains, a profile presente! in the lives of the Italian people for more than twenty years. The partisan went off to tell Urbano Lazzaro, nom de guerre 'Bill', a name inspired by Wild Bill Hicock, a twenty-year-old Guardia di finanza deserter, who was in charge of the search. 'Oh! Bill, ghe chi el "Crapun" [It's the bald big head]!' he told him in dialect. Bill went to take a look. He got up into the truck and tapped the soldier on the shoulder. 'Camerata!' he said in Italian (camerata was the Fascist word for comrade, compagno the Communist word). Silence. 'Eccellenza!' he said ironically. Silence. 'Camerata Benito Mussolini!'he shouted. A flicker of a response on the face. It was enough. Bill took off the sunglasses and removed the submachine-gun. Mussolini did not resist, nor did he speak. He asked Mussolini if he had any other weapons. Mussolini handed over a small pistol. Bill and another partisan then escorted him to the town hall. By now the piazza in Dongo and the waterfront road along which the convoy stretched back towards Musso was packed. Dongo was in the grip of a lynch mob atmosphere.

The partisans had also been checking the papers of the Italians. Gradually it became clear that not only had they got the 'crapun' but also what was left of his government. Those arrested included Bombacci, Barracù, Zerbini, Pavolini and la Petacci. Initially the partisans had no idea who Petacci was. There had been no pictures or busts of her down the years. Pavolini had made a run for it, dived into the lake and disappeared. He was found some time afterwards hiding behind some rocks with only his head above water.

Lieutenant Fallmeyer and his anti-aircraft unit started up their engines and proceeded on their journey home to the fatherland.

The partisans who arrested Mussolini described themselves as a detachment (distaccamento) of one of the Communist Garibaldi Brigades: the 52a Brigata Garibaldina. Officially – in other words for the purposes of history and propaganda – such brigades consisted of three battalions and each battalion of three detachments. Brigades varied in size between 300 and

1000.[41] There is much confusion, however, about the status of this particular detachment and its size. Most Italian authors simply describe it not merely as a detachment of the 52nd Garibaldi Brigade but as the 52nd Garibaldi Brigade itself. That would mean that if the Communist propaganda were true, there were between 300 and 1000 partisans at Dongo that day. The truth, however, seems to be that the detachment of the 52nd Garibaldi Brigade was in fact the entire 52nd Garibaldi Brigade and that this brigade or detachment, or whatever it was, consisted of just nineteen partisans. The figure of nineteen is the verdict of one of the most authoritative authors on the subject of Mussolini's death.[42] In other words, despite the relentless desire to over-inflate the importance of the resistance, a Garibaldi Brigade did not always have a minimum of 300 men, let alone 1000. Indeed, sometimes, as in this case, it only had nineteen. Of the 52nd's total complement of nineteen it is not clear how many were in Dongo on the day in question looking for cigarettes. But it is certain that there were far fewer than nineteen. The brigade's twenty-five-year-old commanding officer, Count Pier Luigi Bellini delle Stelle, *nom de guerre* 'Pedro', was not a Communist; he was a lawyer and a weak man, as events were now to prove. Nor was Bill, the brigade's vice-political commissar, a Communist. But he was a naive and emotional man.

The situation at Dongo on 27 April 1945 was chaotic. Looting of the abandoned Italian vehicles in the column began immediately. The partisans recovered a large amount of gold bullion, cash, documents and personal effects, which they took to the town hall, but in the days to come it all disappeared – as did the vehicles.

Pedro had sent word by messenger to the partisan leadership in Milan of the capture of Mussolini. He could not telephone the information, he said, because the Dongo telephone exchange was not working properly. He moved Mussolini twice that night, first at about 7 p.m. to the barracks of the *Guardia di finanza* at Germasino in the mountains above Dongo. Mussolini asked Pedro to do him a favour: could he pass on his regards to *la* Petacci? This was the first the partisans knew of her presence in the column. Pedro agreed. He drove back down to Dongo.[43] 'In your opinion what will they do with me?' Mussolini asked a guard. 'They will put you on trial,' the guard replied. 'For what?' Mussolini enquired. It was a good question.[44]

Pedro spent about an hour with Petacci. At first, she denied that she knew Mussolini but then came clean. She said, 'To become the lover of the Duce, of the man who was then at the apogee of power, had become the secret or confessed ambition of nearly all *le signore* of high society ... I did not want this, I did not look for this ... I followed him to Milan, to Como, to Menaggio ... I want to die with him. My life would have no point after his death.' She begged Pedro to let her see Mussolini. Moved, Pedro agreed.[45]

It was past midnight when Pedro returned to Germasino and it was raining hard and there were flashes of lightning which lit up the mountains around the narrow lake. Later, he wrote, 'On two fundamental points I had already made a decision, with the full agreement of my comrades: we would avoid summary executions and we would not consign Mussolini to the Allies, but only to our command.'[46] By now, too many people knew where Mussolini was, therefore in the middle of the night Pedro moved him again. His intention was to take him and Petacci to a safer hiding place, an Alpine hut, in the mountains above Como. He bandaged up Mussolini's face to make him look like a wounded partisan so that only his eyes and mouth were visible, and he drove him back down the mountain to Dongo. There, he allowed him to speak briefly to Petacci who had been put in another car which was parked outside the town hall. '*Buona sera, Eccellenza,*' Petacci said. 'Why did you want to follow me?' Mussolini enquired. 'I prefer it that way,' she replied.[47]

The two cars, each with several partisans in it, set off. It was still raining heavily and it was cold. They passed through a number of partisan roadblocks without serious incident but at Moltrasio, just outside Como, there was the sound of heavy gunfire. The Allies had arrived in Como, it seemed. Pedro wanted Mussolini to be put on trial but not by them. So he decided to turn back and he took the prisoners instead to a house in Mezzegra – a small town above the lake halfway between Como and Dongo – whose occupants he trusted. He and his comrades had to leave the two cars some distance from the house as it was off the road and down a track. They and the prisoners walked to the house in the pouring rain. Mussolini's face was still bandaged and Petacci wore a fur coat and high-heeled shoes, and she had difficulty walking. Pedro took one arm, Mussolini the other. 'Certainly we formed a somewhat unusual trio, in which one would perhaps have been able to find some strange symbolic meaning,' Pedro recalled.[48] Pedro left two of his comrades to stand guard and departed. Mussolini and his mistress went to bed in an upstairs room.[49] It was gone 5 a.m. The rain continued. There was thunder and the lightning flickered about the mountains and the lake. The rain stopped with the new day but the sky remained menacing. Mussolini had just two guards. But he did not try to escape.

The partisan leadership in Milan received news of Mussolini's capture at some point on the evening of the 27th – the day of his capture – probably from different sources. But it was not the combined leadership who issued the order to execute him and the other prisoners without trial. We now know that the order came from those of its members who were revolutionaries – notably the Communists – acting entirely on their own initiative. The only unanswered question is which Communist or Communists pulled the trigger?

By the December 1944 agreement between the Allies and the CLNAI –

the partisan political leadership in the occupied north – the CLNAI would form the government in the brief period between the departure of the Germans and the arrival of the Allies, and in the interim maintain law and order. The CLNAI agreed that in the event of the capture of Mussolini by partisans it would hand him over to the Allies alive.

The CLNAI was also answerable to the Italian government in the liberated south, which was committed, under Article 29 of the September 1943 armistice, to hand Mussolini over alive. On 6 March 1945 the Allies had issued orders that all Fascist forces, including the GNR and the *Brigate Nere*, be treated as prisoners of war not *francs-tireurs*.[50] The order extended to any civilian who could prove armed service or wore a distinctive emblem. In any case, the partisans were under the command of the Allies whose orders were clear. In early 1945, the Allies repeatedly reminded the CLNAI of these orders in radio messages.[51]

Initially, in the euphoria of the moment, the CLNAI – which represented the five political parties in the north – claimed collective responsibility for the decision to execute Mussolini without trial. But outrage at the manner of the killing, not to mention the killing of an innocent woman, soon gathered momentum and this caused the CLNAI to attempt to distance itself from the crime.

Leo Valiani, acting leader of the left-wing *Partito d'azione*, was a member of the CLNAI and the only member of it in a position to know ever to speak out in detail about the matter. He gave several versions of what happened. In one version, he said that the CLNAI took the decision to execute Mussolini at a meeting on 25 April. But this meeting also decided, he said, that if Mussolini surrendered he would not be executed. 'If Mussolini had surrendered, the death sentence would have been suspended and he would have been handed over to the Americans. But he did not surrender: in fact, he fled, and this way, he put himself outside the law,' Valiani explained.[52] Yet Mussolini did surrender. And what law, exactly, had Mussolini put himself outside of except the gun law of the partisans? So much for what the CLNAI had decided before the capture of Mussolini. What about after his capture? Valiani said that the decision actually to execute Mussolini once captured was taken not by the CLNAI but by the *comitato insurrezionale* – the insurrectional committee – on the night of the 27th.

The *comitato insurrezionale*? The members of this committee were Sandro Pertini (Socialist, later President of Italy), Emilio Sereni (Communist) and Valiani. Its role was to exploit the chaos and euphoria of the liberation of Italy to stir up revolution. Its members were also members of the CLNAI but in theory it was entirely independent. Luigi Longo, the Communist leader in the north, was a 'co-opted' member of the committee, said Valiani. It was this committee, with Longo co-opted, which took the decision to execute Mussolini without trial 'telephonically' on the 27th, he added. In another interview, Valiani spelled it out. 'We four [Longo is now not simply co-opted but a full-blooded member] of the *comitato insurrezionale* consulted each other, without even meeting, by telephone. Pertini, Sereni, Longo and me made the decision in the night to execute Mussolini without trial, given the urgency of the matter. In fact, the Americans were asking, on the radio, for Mussolini to be handed over.'[53] In 1980, Valiani was created a life senator by his old CLNAI comrade, Pertini, who was then President.

There is one other crucial witness whose testimony seems to have escaped the notice of Italian historians and journalists: Lieutenant-Colonel Max Salvadori, the SOE's senior man behind enemy lines, who was present at the CLNAI meeting at which the capture of Mussolini was announced. Unfortunately, Salvadori did not give a date for the meeting. But he did write two versions of what happened at it. In 1958 he wrote, 'Orders were given to bring the prisoners to Milan for trial.'[54] In 1990 he wrote, 'Orders were given to bring the prisoners to Milan where they would be tried immediately by the [people's] tribunals.'[55]

In the later version Salvadori wrote, 'I spoke (this was the only occasion on which, not invited to do so, I intervened in a discussion of the CLNAI) in order to avoid misunderstandings which had created on several occasions a state of tension between the Allies and the CLN [the name of the liberation committee in the south] after the liberation of zones to the south of the Gothic Line: I made it clear that ... during the interim period the governing authority was delegated to the CLNAI; that the power of government naturally included the administration of justice; that in such an exceptional moment it was up to the CLNAI to decide which laws to apply; I emphasised above all that with the arrival of the Allied troops, the governing authority passed automatically to the Allies and with it control over the prisoners ... I also reminded members of the CLNAI that in regard to the enforcement of justice it was impossible to expect that the Allies would behave as the Italians would have done.'[56]

It is clear from his account that Salvadori, an Anglo-Italian, had great sympathy for the partisan cause. But his very carefully worded memoir cannot hide the thrust of his message to the partisan leadership: if you want to top him, get on with it. Indeed, he took great pains to try to justify the executions in the book. 'For many in Italy and outside it was an act of war or – worse – civil war. They were wrong; it was something quite different. The Dongo execution was the punishment for crimes which until then had remained unpunished.'[57] What Salvadori had told the CLNAI was quite contrary to his orders, let alone the law, which were to ensure that Mussolini was handed over alive. Nor did he disclose in his books – presumably deliberately – what punishment the CLNAI meeting had decided to mete out once the people's kangaroo court in Milan had tried him and the other Fascists. But he added, 'The execution of the gerarchs did not take place in Milan but in Dongo.'[58] Salvadori's testimony – though deliberately vague – does at least make one thing clear: it was not the CLNAI who ordered the execution of Mussolini and the others at Dongo.

Initially, however, all the partisan leaders rushed to claim responsibility for the execution of Mussolini. Indeed, on the 29th, the day afterwards, the CLNAI issued a joint communiqué which said, 'The CLNAI declares that the shooting of Mussolini and his accomplices, ordered by it, is the necessary conclusion of a historical phase ... The Italian people could not initiate a new life, which for twenty years Fascism denied it, if the CLNAI had not at the right time demonstrated the firm decision to make its own a judgement already pronounced by history.'[59] But this is not how it happened. It was the *comitato insurrezionale*, controlled by Longo – co-opted or not – which took the decision to execute Mussolini. As to who actually pulled the trigger, that is quite another matter.

It was not until 1947 that the Communist party wheeled out the partisan said to be responsible: Walter Audisio, a book-keeper, *nom de guerre* 'Colonel Valerio', who would become a Communist MP in 1948. The party also revealed that with him at the time was Aldo Lampredi, a carpenter, *Vice-comandante* of the Garibaldi Brigades, *nom de guerre* 'Guido' and Longo's right-hand man. On the morning of the 28th these two assembled a group of partisans to act as the firing squad and set off from Milan by car and truck for Dongo. They arrived at the town hall at about 2 p.m. where Colonel Valerio (Audisio) told Pedro that his mission was to execute Mussolini and the gerarchs, and he ordered Pedro to hand them over. Those were his orders from the general command of the CVL, he lied. He had no orders from the CVL, let alone its political master, the CLNAI. His orders were from the Communist-controlled *comitato insurrezionale*. Naturally, he had no orders in writing but he did have an identity card signed by Cadorna, which made Pedro begin to believe him. But surely Petacci did not deserve to die, said Pedro. 'She has been his *consigliere* all these years and inspired his politics ... she is as responsible as him ... It is not I who have condemned her. She has already been condemned,' Valerio replied. But not even Longo's revolutionary committee had issued orders to kill Petacci – at least, not according to Valiani.

Pedro now displayed the stuff of which he was made and caved in. Later, he would attempt a justification: 'We are soldiers, regularly organised in the army of liberation and therefore subordinate to a hierarchical order and constrained to be obedient to orders from above.' What orders from above? Pedro was under the command of the Allies and their orders were crystal clear: hand over Mussolini alive. Pedro bottled out. He disobeyed orders.[60] He had about fifty prisoners in his charge including the women and children, and the majority were still in the town hall apart from the most important gerarchs, who had been taken to the *Guardia di finanza* barracks at Germasino, and Mussolini and Petacci. He now agreed to deliver up Mussolini and Petacci and the gerarchs to their assassins. First, he told Valerio and Guido (Lampredi) where Mussolini and Petacci were being held. He even sent Michele Moretti, the 52nd's political commissar, along with them so that they would not get lost. Moretti, *nom de guerre* 'Pietro Gatti', was a fanatical Communist but in real life a plumber. Then Pedro agreed to go in person to the barracks in the mountains and bring the gerarchs back down to Dongo for execution.

The assassins set off for Mezzegra, leaving behind their firing squad. Once there, they parked their car, walked the 200 yards to the house and went inside past the two guards. They told Mussolini and Petacci that they had come to take them to safety. Petacci was in bed; Mussolini was up. She could not find her underwear. No time for that now, Valerio said. The assassins and their victims then left the house, walked to the car and got in. The car moved off. After a short distance it stopped in front of a house called the Villa Belmonte. Valerio told Mussolini and Petacci to get out, then he opened fire on them at point-blank range with his sub-machine-gun. According to some reports the gun jammed and he had to borrow Moretti's. According to others, Moretti did the deed. It was ten minutes past four on 28 April. From the spot where Mussolini and his mistress fell you can see the lake below and the mountains beyond.

Audisio, though probably there, did not pull the trigger. You only have to look at the photographs of his startled rabbit's face to realise that. His various written accounts before his death in 1973 of how he, as Colonel Valerio, had heroically executed Mussolini in the name of the Italian people are riddled with inconsistency. In these accounts, however, he could never bring himself to put down in black and white the words 'I Audisio', shot an innocent woman in cold blood. In his last account, for example, he wrote that Petacci 'was hit as well'. By whom?[61]

Tellingly – no one seems to have spotted – Audisio did not speak Spanish either. Yet according to Pedro, when Colonel Valerio interrogated Petacci's brother, Marcello, who was pretending to be a Spanish diplomat, at the town hall in Dongo he did so in Spanish to catch him out. Both Lampredi and Longo, however, were Spanish Civil War veterans and spoke Spanish well.[62]

Millions of words have been written on the death of Mussolini in books with ominous titles such as *The Last Five Seconds of Mussolini*. Yet none of these books manages to mount a serious challenge to the essential truth. The Communist party always refused to allow access to its archives on the matter, as do its heirs. The truth about the identity of the assassin(s) no doubt lies within them. Some say Longo did it,[63] some Lampredi, many Moretti. Certainly, the party could not wheel out Moretti as its heroic killer because by then he was one of fifty defendants on trial for the theft of the considerable amount of money and property the gerarchs had with them at the time of their capture. It would have been a trifle embarrassing.

Longo, a Stalinist *à outrance*, would have had no qualms whatsoever but to disclose that he was the killer would have been even more embarrassing. In 1945 he was both Communist party leader in the north and Commander-in-Chief of the Garibaldi Brigades, the Communist-controlled partisan units which accounted for 40 per cent of the entire partisan force. He was also one of two deputies to Cadorna, Commander-in-Chief of the CVL, the partisans as a whole and, according to Salvadori, 'ready to make any sacrifice if it served the party'.[64] In 1964 he would become leader of the Communist Party on the death of Togliatti who was still in the liberated south in 1945. He remained silent on the events of Dongo until 1979, the year before his death, when he said, 'Italy had to and wanted to ensure justice for itself. The Resistance could not renounce this final act, to delegate it to the Allied troops and their courts. Apart from anything else I have many doubts as to whether in this case Mussolini would have been condemned to death.'[65]

In 1956 the Petacci family tried in vain to get Audisio, who died in 1973, charged with murder. The case, had it been brought, would have been fascinating. Audisio would either have had to insist that he did it for the sake of the cause or come clean to save his skin. But the 1946 government amnesty for crimes committed during the civil war ensured that the case went nowhere.

When the Communist party ordered Audisio to reveal himself as the killer in March 1947 he did so, protected by 'elaborate police precautions' and 'several hundred Communists' before a crowd of 10,000 people in Rome. Mussolini had died 'not like a man, but like an inferior being', he told the crowd.[66] But in 1996, the heirs of the Communist party allowed publication in *Unità*, the party newspaper, of Lampredi's written testimony which until then had been locked away in their archives. Lampredi, who had died in 1973, had written that Mussolini had died with dignity and that his last words were, 'Aim for the heart.'[67]

One of the most popular conspiracy theories, however, has nothing to do with the Communists. It points the finger at – yes – the British. So desperate was Churchill to destroy that compromising correspondence of his with Mussolini – so the conspiracy theory goes – that he would stop at nothing to get his hands on it. Here we enter the realms of the truly Italian. Such a theory tells us more about the psyche of Italian historians and the Italian people than about the truth. The Italians are a nation of conspiracy theorists. This is because Italy is a country where the conspiracy theorist is sometimes right. No matter that not one letter has ever come to light. For just as Italian historians cannot prove that there was a Churchill–Mussolini correspondence, nor can anyone else prove that there was not. You cannot prove that there was not a correspondence. The conspiracy theory lives on.

The official historian of the SOE in Italy, however, Christopher Woods, who was an SOE officer in Italy at the time and has access to all the documents, including those held under the secrecy rules, has found nothing to suggest that Churchill or any other Briton was involved in any way in the execution of Mussolini. There were no British agents north of Milan, he says.[68] Perhaps it was some organisation so secret that not even Mr Woods is aware of its existence. Perhaps Churchill commissioned private assassins to do his dirty work. Perhaps. But why bother? The Communists could not wait to get their hands on Mussolini in order to liquidate him.

Or perhaps the American OSS agent, Captain Daddario, who had crossed into Italy from Switzerland on the morning of the 26th, did it. But his orders, 'chief among which was the capture of Mussolini', were to protect not execute prisoners.[69] At Cernobbio, near Como, as we have seen, he got sidetracked from his main objective when Graziani surrendered to him. He went out of his way to protect Graziani from the partisans.

The trouble is that the great Renzo De Felice, of all people, started saying before his death in 1996 that he too believed in the conspiracy theory![70] He pointed the finger at Salvadori, the senior SOE man in Milan. But like everyone else who believes in the conspiracy, he could not provide one scrap of evidence. Much remains unclear about what happened between the point at which Pedro left Mussolini and Petacci at the safe house in Mezzegra at 5 a.m. and ten past four that afternoon when their execution took place – but not the essential truth.

Colonel Valerio left the corpses of Mussolini and Petacci lying in the road outside the Villa Belmonte guarded by the two partisans who had stood guard on them during the night. He returned to Dongo, arriving just before 5 p.m. Pedro was angry that he had not brought them to the town hall as agreed but had already shot them. Not that he did anything to try to stop Audisio now dispensing summary justice in the name of the Italian people to the gerarchs. Audisio organised a firing squad and lined them up on the pavement alongside Lake Como, and ordered them to face the lake so that they could be shot in the back. It is most unlikely that any of those now looking out over Lake Como and the snow-capped mountains beyond as they awaited death would have been imprisoned, let alone condemned to death, if they had gone on trial – except Pavolini, the Party Secretary.

There were sixteen altogether. Not all were even gerarchs. They included Bombacci, the co-founder of the Italian Communist party with Gramsci and Togliatti, latterly Mussolini's Rasputin, and Petacci's brother, Marcello, who, though a criminal, was not a war criminal and had never been involved in politics. A large crowd had gathered in the town square to watch. Petacci managed to make a run for it and dived into Lake Como. He was recaptured and brought back. Pertinently, the gerarchs refused to die with him. Audisio granted them their last wish. A priest was allowed to deliver swift absolution. The firing squad opened fire. The gerarchs fell to the ground where their bodies lay quivering. The firing squad then despatched Petacci.

Audisio arranged for the corpses of the sixteen dead Fascists to be piled on to the truck with which he had arrived earlier that day. He set off with it back to Milan, stopping at Mezzegra to pick up the corpses of Mussolini and Petacci. They had lain in the road outside Villa Belmonte for about two hours by now. In Milan, in the middle of the night, he deliberately dumped the eighteen bodies in Piazzale Loreto where, to the fury of Mussolini, fifteen partisans had been executed by a Fascist firing squad in August 1944.[71]

The next morning – a Sunday – a crowd came to Piazzale Loreto. The crowd grew as the hours passed and the news travelled. People kicked, spat at and urinated on the corpses. Someone had the idea of hanging them upside down from the girders of the roof over the petrol station with rope attached to their feet. They hauled up Mussolini first. His head hideously battered and swollen. There was an immense cheer. Then it was the turn of Petacci. Her dress fell down exposing her suspenders and stockings. She had no underwear on. The crowd fell silent. The women in the crowd noticed the quality of the stockings. 'There's not a single ladder in them,' said one.[72] But someone had tied another rope to the skirt which was now hauled up. It was strange that those who strung up Petacci as a macabre trophy should feel that was all right but that it was necessary to hide her nakedness. They strung up seven corpses in all.[73] The corpses swayed in the breeze, their arms stuck out, made rigid by death, in different positions. They included that of Bombacci – the honorary Red Army colonel. The crowd danced and skipped around them.[74]

The seventh corpse was that of Achille Starace – the longest-serving general secretary of the PNF. Starace had held no post under Fascism since being sacked as commander of the militia in 1941. He had lived in poverty, separated from his wife, in Milan and had had nothing to do with the RSI. Each day he went for a run in his blue tracksuit. On the 28th – the day that Mussolini was shot – he had gone running as usual. Some partisans recognised him and took him to a lecture room at the Politecnico, where they put him on trial and sentenced him to death. The next day they paraded him through the streets of Milan before taking him to Piazzale Loreto where they shot him. He died doing the Roman salute and shouting, 'Viva il Duce!'

The journalist, Montanelli, who was in Piazzale Loreto that day, wrote that the scene 'dishonoured those who wanted it, those who consented to it, and the crowd which indecently attacked the wretched corpses, insulted them, spat on them, and soiled them in even worse ways. It raged exultantly, the *"popolo"*, against him whom it had acclaimed until not many months beforehand.'[75] An American army camera crew filmed the sickening scene. The footage quite clearly shows that the partisans responsible were laughing and joking as they strung up the bodies.

The first American troops entered Milan on the next day, 30 April. During the first few days of the liberation it is estimated that the partisans' people's tribunals executed about 2000 people in the city.[76] It is impossible to quantify the orgy of blood unleashed by the partisans in the days and weeks that followed. The Fascists claimed that in the two years that followed the liberation, the partisans slaughtered 50,000 to 70,000 people. Giorgio Bocca, the pro-partisan journalist and historian, put the figure at 3000 in Milan and between 12,000 and 15,000 in the rest of northern Italy.[77] The figure seems to have been in the region of 35,000.[78]

Like their Italian comrades, Tito's Communist partisans, who had seized Istria from Italy, indulged in terrible atrocities against Italians, whose crime was not that they were Fascists but because they were Italians who wanted to remain so. They disposed of the bodies of their victims by throwing them down *foibe* – natural deep holes in the mountains of the Carso where Mussolini had served in the First World War. Once again precise figures are not available but is is said that 15,000 Italians died as a result. From one of these *foibe* alone, between July and August 1945, the Allies extracted 450 cubic metres of human remains.[79] In January 1945 the Italian Communist Garibaldi Brigades in north-east Italy – despite Cadorna's fierce resistance – had placed themselves under Tito's command.[80] The Communists had always insisted that their partisans be called patriots. So much for the patriotism of their forces in the north-east.

On 30 April Hitler committed suicide in his Berlin bunker. Unlike Mussolini, he had taken the Roman option. But was Hitler's suicide the way out of the brave man or of the coward? Was it an admission of guilt by Hitler and a self-imposed sentence of death? Or was it a last act of defiance to deprive the victors of the chance to impose the sentence of death? Was Mussolini a lesser man than Hitler for refusing to take the Roman option?

During the autopsy on Mussolini a piece of his brain was sliced off so that Italian and American scientists could study it in order to understand the science of dictatorship. He was then buried in an unmarked grave in Milan. But word soon got out. There were fears that those who hated him would defile the grave and that those who loved him would transform it into a shrine. In 1946 the new Italian government therefore exhumed his mortal remains in secret and transferred them to a monastery near Milan where they were kept in a wooden box.[81] They remained at the monastery until 1957 when the then Prime Minister Adone Zoli – the second citizen of Predappio after Mussolini to become Prime Minister – agreed that they could be returned to Mussolini's birthplace Predappio. The widow Mussolini, Donna Rachele, as she was known, presided over their final burial inside a stone tomb in the Mussolini family crypt at the cemetery. There the remains of Mussolini lie to this day, as if in state, visited by tens of thousands of people each year. A young man, swathed in a floor-length black cloak, stands guard in front of the tomb. He stares straight ahead and will not speak.

They used to say that the Fascists had defeated the other parties of the Left not because they were more violent but because they had the best songs. The irresistible *'Giovinezza'* was their best song; a song of hope and promise, and better times ahead. No one sang it any more. Yet just as the dead *camarata* is always *presente*, so too is 'Giovinezza' as a reminder of how different Fascism once was before the fatal alliance with Hitler: *'Salve, o Popolo d'Eroi, / Salve, o Patria immortale! / Sono rinati i figli tuoi / con la fe nell'ideale. / Il valor de' tuoi guerrieri, / la virtù dei pionieri / la vision dell 'Alighieri / oggi brilla in tutti i cuor. / Giovinezza, giovinezza / Primavera di bellezza / della vita nell'asprezza / il tuo canto squilla e va.'*[82]

Edda Ciano heard about the death of her father on the radio in Switzerland. Later, she would write, 'I hated him. I really hated him. I believe you can really hate only a person you have loved. And when I saw him, my father and all the others hanging in that barbarous way at the petrol station in the Piazzale Loreto in Milan, I said to myself, "It was the final act of love of the Italians for him".'[83]

SOURCE NOTES

SOURCES

The monumental biography of Mussolini by the Italian historian Renzo De Felice is the starting point for any biographer seeking factual source material.

De Felice's oeuvre consists of eight books, the first published in 1965, the last in 1997 (posthumously), and runs in total to just over 7,000 pages. The books are labyrinthine and impossible going for all but the very committed. Understandably, they have never been published in English. Yet they contain what far too many books on Mussolini in any language lack: facts – thousands of them.

I list them below with in brackets the date of first publication. I have used the Einaudi paperback edition published between 1995 and 1998.

Mussolini il rivoluzionario 1883–1920 (1965)

Mussolini il fascista

I . La conquista del potere 1921–1925 (1966)

II. L'organizzazione dello Stato fascista (1968)

Mussolini il duce

I . Gli anni del consenso 1929–1936 (1974)

II. Lo Stato totalitario 1936–1940 (1981)

Mussolini l'alleato

I . L'Italia in guerra 1940–1943

  1. Dalla guerra 'breve' alla guerra lunga (1990)

  2. Crisi e agonia del regime (1990)

II. La guerra civile 1943–1945 (1997)

In addition the eighteen volumes of Benito Mussolini, *Scritti e discorsi* are a source throughout the text. Whenever a new volume appears it is quoted as, for example, *Scritti e discorsi, 3* [being the volume number], *La mia vita (Con il Diario di guerra)* [being the volume title], p. 11. Thereafter subsequent references to the volume are referred to as, for example, *Scritti e discorsi, 3*, p. 11.

CHAPTER NOTES

Where an author has written more than one book referred to in the notes that follow the device 'op. cit.' usually refers to the title most recently referred to.

1 The Land of the Duce [pp. 1–7]

1 Edvige Mussolini, *Mio fratello Benito: memorie raccolte e trascritte da Rosetta Ricci Crisolini*, La Fenice, Florence, 1957, p. 12.

2 Anita Pensotti, *Rachele e Benito, Biografia di Rachele Mussolini*, Mondadori, Milan, 1993, p. 10.

3 Mussolini, *La mia vita dal 29 luglio 1883*

al 23 novembre 1911, in Benito Mussolini, *Scritti e discorsi, 3, La mia vita (Con il Diario di guerra)*, 18 vols, La Fenice, Florence, 1983–84), p. 11 (*La mia vita*, written in 1911–12 when Mussolini was in prison in Forli, was first published by Editrice Faro, Rome, in 1947).

4 Margherita Sarfatti, *Dux*, Mondadori, Milan, 1926, p. 30 (but published first in Britain in 1925 as *The Life of Benito Mussolini* where it was the publishing event of the year and reviewed 150 times according to the frontispiece of the first Italian edition).

2 The Youth of the Duce [pp. 8–20]

1 Mussolini, op. cit., p. 12.

2 Mussolini, *My Autobiography*, Hutchinson, London, 1928, p. 18 sg (published only in English, written largely by his brother, Arnaldo, and translated by the American Ambassador from May 1921 to February 1924 to Italy, Richard Washburn Child).

3 Raffaello De Rensis, *Mussolini musicista*, in the periodical *Mussolinia*, Edizioni Paladino, Mantua, August 1927, p. 13 sg.

4 Emil Ludwig, *Talks With Mussolini*, AMS Press, New York, 1982 (first published in 1932), p. 217.

5 Vittorio Emiliani, *I tre Mussolini: Luigi Alessandro Benito*, Baldini & Castoldi, Milan, 1997, p. 93.

6 Obituary in *La Lotta di classe*, 26 November 1910, quoted in Sarfatti, op. cit., p. 19.

7 Mussolini, *Vita di Arnaldo* (first published 1932), in *Scritti e discorsi, 12, Fascismo e religione* p. 77.

8 Sarfatti, op. cit., pp. 38, 304–5.

9 *Scritti e discorsi, 3*, pp. 12–13.

10 Ibid., p. 14.

11 Ibid., p. 14.

12 Ibid., pp. 16–17.

13 Ibid., p. 21.

14 Ibid., p. 21.

15 Ibid., p. 23.

16 Ibid., p. 26.

17 Ludwig, *Talks*, op. cit., pp. 35–6.

18 *Scritti e discorsi, 3*, p. 31.

19 Rino Alessi, *Il giovane Mussolini rievocato da un suo compagno di scuola*, Edizioni del Borghese, Milan, 1970, p. 39.

20 Bedeschi quoted in Fabrizio Castellini, *Il ribelle di Predappio Amori e giovinezza di Mussolini*, Mursia, Milan, 1996, p. 10.

21 Ludwig, *Talks*, op. cit., p. 215.

22 Mussolini on Gustave Le Bon in Mussolini, *Opera Omnia, vol. XXII*, ed. Edoardo e Duilio Susmel, 36 vols, La Fenice, Florence, 1951–63, p. 156 (hereafter, *O.O.*).

23 Speech, *Al popolo di Mantova*, 25 October 1925.

24 Speech, *Il caso Ludlow*, 28 December 1937.

25 Emiliani, op. cit., p. 38.

26 Song quoted in Paolo Monelli, *Mussolini piccolo borghese*, Garzanti, Milan, 1954 (fourth edition), p. 20.

27 Paolo Monelli, op. cit., p. 23. Duilio Susmel, a major post-war biographer, estimated that Mussolini had 169 lovers in all, see Philip V. Cannistraro and Brian R. Sullivan, *Il Duce's Other Woman*, William Morrow, New York, 1993, p. 602; Roberto Gervaso, a biographer of the most famous mistress, Claretta Petacci, put the figure even higher at 'about four hundred', see Roberto Gervaso, *Claretta la donna che morì per Mussolini*, Bompiani, Milan, 1995, p. 54:

28 Ludwig, *Talks*, op. cit., pp. 187, 170, 62.

3 The Duce as Tramp and Teacher [pp. 21–33]

1 Mussolini letters in *O.O. XXXIII*, pp. 206–8.

2 Castellini, op. cit., p. 27.

3 Monelli, op. cit., pp. 23–4.

4 *Scritti e discorsi, 3*, p. 38.

5 Castellini, op. cit., p. 40.

6 *Scritti e discorsi, 3*, p. 38.

7 Castellini, op. cit., p. 41.

8 *Scritti e discorsi, 3*, p. 39.

9 Ibid., p. 39.

10 Ludwig, *Talks*, op. cit., p. 37.

11 *Scritti e discorsi, 3*, pp. 40-l.

12 Mussolini letter to Sante Bedeschi in Alessi, op. cit., pp. 73–8.

13 Sarfatti, op. cit., pp. 65–6.

14 *Scritti e discorsi, 3*, p. 41.

15 Sarfatti, op. cit., p. 76–9.

16 Angelica Balabanoff, *My Life as a Rebel*, Hamish Hamilton, London, 1938.

17 *Scritti e discorsi, 3*, p. 44.

18 Ibid., p. 45.

19 Renzo De Felice, *Mussolini il rivoluzionario 1883–1920*, Einaudi, Turin, 1995 (first published 1965), p. 35.

20 Angelica Balabanoff, *Il Traditore Mussolini*, Napoleone, Rome, 1945.

21 B. Mussolini, *Giovanni Huss il Veridico*, Bonanno Editore, Arcireale, 1988 (first published by Podrecca & Galantara, Rome, 1913), pp. 40, 99–100, 5.
22 Monelli, op. cit., p. 20.
23 The security report – compiled by Inspector Giovanni Gasti – is reproduced in full in De Felice, op. cit., at appendix 18, pp. 725–37.
24 Castellini, op. cit., pp. 94–5.
25 Arnaldo Pozzi, *Come li ho visti io*, Mondadori, Milan, 1947.
26 The autopsy on Mussolini was done by Prof. Mario Cattabeni, of the University of Milan's legal medical department, on 30 April 1945. A copy is in the papers of Valerian Lada-Mocarski, then American Vice-Consul in Lugano, which are held at Yale University.
27 *Scritti e discorsi, 3*, p. 48.
28 *New York Times* article quoted in De Felice, op. cit., p. 59.
29 *Scritti e discorsi, 3*, p. 50.
30 Ibid., p. 51.
31 Ibid., p. 52.
32 Ibid., p. 53.
33 Ibid., p. 53.
34 Ibid., p. 54.
35 Ibid., p. 54.
36 Castellini, op. cit., p. 104.
37 *Scritti e discorsi, 3*, p. 56.

4 The Duce as Journalist [pp. 34–46]

1 *Scritti e discorsi, 3*, p. 57.
2 Pensotti, op. cit., p. 20.
3 B. Mussolini, *La filosofia della forza*, in *Scritti e discorsi, 1, Il mio socialismo*, pp. 32–42 (first published in *Il Pensiero romagnolo*, 29 November, 6 & 13 December 1908).
4 Sarfatti, op. cit., p. 43.
5 *Scritti e discorsi, 1*, p. 38.
6 Pensotti, op. cit., p. 22.
7 Speech, Udine, 20 September 1922, *Scritti e discorsi, 5, La marcia su Roma*, pp. 93–103.
8 Speech to the party congress, 22 June 1925, *Scritti e discorsi, 6, Cos'è il fascismo*, pp. 75–85.
9 B. Mussolini, *Claudia Particella l'amante del cardinale*, Luigi Reverdito editore, Trent, 1986 (first published in serialisation form in *Il Popolo* of Trent 20 January–11 May 1910 and first published in English as *The Cardinal's Mistress* by Cassell, London, 1929).

10 *Scritti e discorsi, 3*, p. 59.
11 Rachele Mussolini, *La mia vita con Benito*, op. cit., quoted in Castellini, op. cit., p. 151.
12 Rachele Mussolini, *La mia vita con Benito*, Mondadori, Milan, 1948, quoted in Castellini, op. cit., p. 152.
13 Ibid., p. 152.
14 *Scritti e discorsi, 3*, p. 60.
15 Pensotti, op. cit., p. 26.
16 Article quoted in De Felice, op. cit., p. 103.
17 Pensotti, op. cit., p. 31.
18 Article in *O.O. IV*, pp. 147 sg.
19 Speech quoted in Monelli, op. cit., p. 72.
20 Article in *O.O. IV*, pp. 173 sg.
21 *Scritti e discorsi, 3*, p. 61.

5 *Avanti!* [pp. 47–65]

1 Balabanoff, *Il traditore*, op. cit., pp. 34 sg.
2 Ibid., pp. 41, 54 sg.
3 E. Mussolini, op. cit., pp. 32 sg.
4 Balabanoff, *Il traditore*, op. cit., pp. 54 sg.
5 Leda Rafanelli, *Una donna e Mussolini*, Rizzoli, Milan, 1946, pp. 8–10, 14 sg, 51.
6 Castellini, op. cit., pp. 173 sg.
7 Cannistraro and Sullivan, op. cit., p. 59.
8 Sarfatti, op. cit., p. 153.
9 *Scritti e discorsi, 2, Dal socialismo alla nazione*, pp. 35–6.
10 *Mussolini giornalista*, ed. Renzo De Felice, Rizzoli, Milan, 1995, pp. 62 sg.
11 Quoted in De Felice, *Mussolini il rivoluzionario*, op. cit., p. 247.
12 Sarfatti, op. cit., p. 159.
13 *Mussolini giornalista*, op. cit., p. 57 sg.
14 Sarfatti, op. cit., p. 159.
15 *Mussolini giornalista*, op. cit., p. 70 sg.
16 Quoted in De Felice, op. cit., pp. 266–8.
17 De Felice, op. cit., p. 278.
18 Viscount Templewood (Sir Samuel Hoare), *Nine Troubled Years*, Macmillan, London, 1954, p. 154.
19 *Chips: The Diaries of Sir Henry Channon*, ed. Robert Rhodes James, Weidenfeld & Nicolson, London, 1967, entry for 2 January 1939.
20 George Seldes, *Sawdust Caesar*, AMS Press, New York, 1978 (first published in 1935), pp. 51–2.
21 Milan police intelligence report, April 1915, in De Felice, op. cit., p. 301.
22 Pierre Milza, *Mussolini*, Fayard, Paris, 1999, pp. 176–81.
23 Gaetano Salvemini, *Mussolini Diplomatico*, Laterza, Bari, 1952, pp.

420–8 (first published as *Mussolini Diplomate*, Paris, 1932).
24 Seldes, op. cit., pp. 391–2.
25 A. Rosmer, *Le mouvement ouvrier pendant la guerre, I*, Paris, 1936.
26 Seldes, op. cit., p. 391.
27 De Felice, op. cit., see the Gasti report in appendix 18, p. 731–32.
28 Ibid., p. 735.
29 Monelli, op. cit., p. 86.
30 Figures in De Felice, op. cit., p. 283.
31 Sarfatti, op. cit., p. 163.
32 *Mussolini giornalista*, op. cit., pp. 91–94.
33 Freya Stark, *Traveller's Prelude*, London, 1950, ch. 13.
34 Quoted in De Felice, op. cit., p. 279.
35 Monelli, op. cit., p. 88.
36 Pensotti, op. cit., pp. 42–3.
37 *Mussolini giornalista*, op. cit., pp. 120–2.
38 Quoted in Sarfatti, op. cit., pp. 167–8.
39 Quoted in Fabio Andriola, *Mussolini segreto nemico di Hitler*, Edizioni Piemme, Turin, 1997, pp. 40, 50.
40 Seldes, op. cit., p. 58.

6 Trench War in the Alps [pp. 66–74]

1 Duilio Susmel, 'I cinque duelli di Mussolini', in *Il Meridiano*, 6 March 1960, quoted in De Felice, op. cit., p. 311.
2 All Italian casualty figures from Cannistraro and Sullivan, op. cit., chapter 11.
3 Cannistraro and Sullivan, op. cit., p. 138–9.
4 Rachele Mussolini's recollections are from Pensotti, op. cit.
5 Castellini, op. cit., p. 173.
6 All war diary entries in *Scritti e discorsi, 3*.
7 Sarfatti, op. cit., p. 185.
8 See Mussolini's service record in De Felice, op. cit., appendix 1, pp. 665–7.
9 See De Felice, op. cit., p. 353.
10 Pensotti, op. cit., p. 38–9.
11 Cannistraro and Sullivan, op. cit., pp. 180–1.
12 Sarfatti, op. cit., p. 202.
13 Sarfatti, op. cit., pp. 211–12.
14 E. Mussolini, op. cit., pp. 163–4.

7 The Birth of Fascism [pp. 75–109]

1 De Felice, op. cit., see appendix 18, p. 734.
2 Figure in De Felice, op. cit., pp. 443–5.
3 See, for example, Milza, op. cit., p. 218.
4 Article in *O.O. XI*, p. 485.

5 Adolf Hitler, *Conversazioni segrete*, Napoli, 1954, p. 286.
6 De Felice, op. cit., see appendix 18, p. 735.
7 Born 26 November 1871.
8 Seldes, op. cit., p. 106.
9 Ferruccio Vecchi, *La Tragedia del mio ardore*, Milan, 1923.
10 De Felice, op. cit., see appendix 18, p. 730
11 Sarfatti, op. cit., p. 221.
12 *Scritti e discorsi, 4, Come nacque Il fascismo*, pp. 50–2.
13 Ibid., pp. 58–60.
14 Monelli, op. cit.
15 Arturo Rossato, *Mussolini, colloquio intimo*, Modernissima Casa Editrice Italiana, Milan, 1923.
16 *Scritti e discorsi, 2*, pp. 83–5.
17 *Scritti e discorsi, 4*, p. 102.
18 De Felice, op. cit., p. 627.
19 Ludwig, *Talks*, op. cit., pp. 191–2.
20 Michael L. Ledeen, *The First Duce – D'Annunzio at Fiume*, Baltimore, 1977.
21 Nino Daniele, *D'Annunzio politico*, Sao Paolo, 1928.
22 De Felice, op. cit., pp. 560, 562.
23 De Felice, op. cit., p. 572.
24 Complete table of election results in Ivone Kirkpatrick, *Mussolini Una biografia*, TEA Storica, Milan, 1997, p. 81 (first published as *Mussolini: Study of a Demagogue*, Odhams Books, London, 1964).
25 Vittorio Mussolini, *Vita con mio padre*, Mondadori, Milan, 1957, p. 22.
26 Monelli, op. cit., p. 109
27 Quoted in De Felice, op. cit., p. 577.
28 Cannistraro and Sullivan, op. cit., p. 219.
29 *Scritti e discorsi, 4*, p. 111–13.
30 Figures in De Felice, op. cit., p. 511.
31 Quoted in De Felice, op. cit., p. 578.
32 Mussolini frequently referred to the Socialist party – the PSI – as the 'PUS', pun intended. The word means the same in Italian as English. The PSI was often called the PSU or PUS – the 'U' standing for 'Ufficiale'.
33 Giulietti, newspaper interview, 8 August, 1920, in De Felice, op. cit., p. 556.
34 *Scritti e discorsi, 4*, pp. 116–17.
35 Speech quoted in De Felice, op. cit., pp. 595–7.
36 Charles H. Sherrill, *Bismarck and*

Mussolini, New York, 1932, p. 188.

37 Seldes, op. cit., pp. 88–9.

38 *Il Popolo d'Italia*, 22 January, 1921, in *Mussolini giornalista*, op. cit., p. 318.

39 R. Bachi, *L'Italia economica nel 1919*, Città di Castello, 1920, pp. 274 sg; in De Felice, op. cit., p. 611.

40 Quotes from Luigi Preti, *Le lotte agrarie nella valle padana*, Torino, 1955, p. 422, in De Felice, op. cit., p. 612.

41 Angelo Tasca, *Nascita e avvento del fascismo*, Florence, 1950, pp. 147, 150 sg, in De Felice, op. cit., p. 612.

42 Quoted in De Felice, op. cit., p. 55.

43 Quoted in De Felice, op. cit., p. 625.

44 Figures in De Felice, op. cit., p. 608.

45 *Mussolini giornalista*, op. cit., p. 305.

46 *La Stampa*, 10–11 May, 1921.

47 *Il Popolo d'Italia*, 8 November 1921. Quoted in De Felice, *Mussolini il fascista*, vol. I, *La conquista del potere 1921–1925*, Einaudi, Turin, 1995 (first published 1966), p. 7. Hereafter, De Felice, op. cit., unless otherwise stated.

48 Agostino Lanzillo, *Lo stato e la crisi sociale e monetaria*, Città di Castello, 1920.

49 Italo Balbo, *Diario 1922*, Mondadori, Milan, 1932.

50 *Il Popolo d'Italia*, 25 March, 1921, *Mussolini giornalista*, op. cit., pp. 318–21.

51 *Il Popolo d'Italia*, 25 March, 1921, quoted in De Felice, op. cit., p. 60.

52 Quoted in De Felice, op. cit., p. 28.

53 Figures in De Felice, op. cit., p. 35.

54 *Il Popolo d'Italia*, 28 April, 1921, quoted in De Felice, op. cit., p. 90.

55 Adrian Lyttelton, *The Seizure of Power: Fascism in Italy 1919–1929*, Charles Scribner, New York and London, 1973.

56 *Il Popolo d'Italia*, in *Mussolini giornalista*, op. cit., p. 294.

57 *Scritti e discorsi*, 4, p. 122–3.

58 *Scritti e discorsi*, 5, pp. 11 seg.

59 Ivanoe Bonomi had become leader of the *Partito socialista riformista italiano* (PSRI) on the death of Bissolati in 1920. The PSRI, formed after their expulsion from the Socialist party at the 1912 Reggio Emilia congress, was the first reformist Socialist party. It would become the Social Democratic (PDS) party.

60 *Il Popolo d'Italia*, 24 July, 1921, *Scritti e discorsi*, 5, p. 27–8.

61 *Il Popolo d Italia*, 27 July, 1921, *Mussolini giornalista*, op. cit., pp. 327–8.

62 *Il Popolo d'Italia*, 3 August, 1921, *Scritti e discorsi*, 5, pp. 29–32.

63 De Felice, op. cit., p. 249.

64 *Il Popolo d'Italia*, 18 August, 1921, *Mussolini giornalista*, op. cit., pp. 335–7.

65 De Felice, op. cit., p. 151.

66 Quoted in ibid., pp. 178–9.

67 Ibid. p. 182.

68 *Il Popolo d'Italia*, 12 November, 1921, *Scritti e discorsi*, 5, pp. 33–5.

69 Ibid., 28 December 1921, pp. 58–60.

8 The March on Rome [pp. 110–123]

1 Filippo Turati – Anna Kuliscioff, *Carteggio, V: Dopoguerra, e fascismo (1919–1922)*, ed. by Alessandro A. Schiavi, Turin, 1953, p. 542.

2 De Felice, op. cit., p. 203 fn.

3 *L'Assalto*, 29 July, 1922.

4 Pietro Nenni, *Vent' anni di fascismo*, Milan, 1964, pp. 11 sg.

5 Kirkpatrick, op. cit., p. 112.

6 *Gerarchia*, March, 1922, quoted in De Felice, op. cit. p. 237.

7 *Scritti e discorsi*, 5, pp. 109–10.

8 *Il Popolo d'Italia*, 12 February, 1922, in De Felice, op. cit., p. 246.

9 Quoted in Giordano Bruno Guerri *Fascisti – gli italiani di Mussolini, il regime degli italiani*, Mondadori, Milan, 1996 (first published Mondadori, Milan, 1995), pp. 76–7.

10 Figures in De Felice, op. cit., appendix 6, p. 765.

11 *Il Popolo d'Italia*, 10 May, 1922, quoted in De Felice, op. cit., p. 257.

12 Giuseppe Bottai, *Vent' anni e un giorno*, Garzanti, Milan, 1949.

13 Cannistraro and Sullivan, op. cit., p. 256.

14 *Scritti e discorsi*, 5, pp. 93–104.

15 Cesare Rossi, *Mussolini com 'era*, Ruffolo editore, Rome, 1947, p. 113.

16 Italo Balbo, account published in 1938, reprinted in *O.O. XVIII*, pp. 581 sg.

17 Attilio Tamaro, *Vent' Anni di Storia 1922–1943*, Editrice Tiber, Rome, 1953–4.

18 Cesare Maria De Vecchi, 'Mussolini vero, III', in *Tempo illustrato*, 24 November, 1959.

19 Speech in *Popolo d'Italia*, 25 October, 1922, *Scritti e discorsi*, 5, pp. 118–124.

20 Balbo, *Diario 1922*, op. cit., p. 195.

21 Cesare Rossi, *Trentatre vicende*

mussoliniane, Casa Editrice Ceschina, Milan, 1958, pp. 141. sg.

22 For Rachele Mussolini's version see Pensotti, op. cit., pp. 45–6; for Sarfatti's version, Sarfatti, op. cit., p. 275.

23 Francobaldo Chiocci, *Donna Rachele*, Ciarrapico editore, Rome, 1983, p. 119.

24 Figures in De Felice, op. cit., p. 358.

25 Monelli, op. cit., pp. 121–2.

26 Efrem E. Ferraris, *La Marcia su Roma veduta dal Viminale*, Edizioni Leonardo, Roma, 1946, p. 95.

27 Figures in De Felice, op. cit., p. 324.

28 Luca Goldoni and Enzo Sermasi, *Benito contro Mussolini*, Rizzoli, Milan, 1995, p. 47.

29 De Felice, op. cit., p. 322.

30 Ibid., p. 325.

31 Paolo Puntoni, *Parla Vittorio Emanuele III*, Palazzi, Milan, 1958, pp. 40, 286 sg.

32 *Il Popolo d'Italia*, 29 October, 1922, *Scritti e discorsi*, 5, p. 125.

33 Galeazzo Ciano, *Diario, 1939–1943*, vol. 1, Rizzoli, Milan, 1947 (4th edition), 2 vols (first published in 1946), entry for 12 June, 1939.

34 Silvio Bertoldi, *Camicia nera*, Rizzoli, Milan, 1998, p. 60.

35 Mussolini, *O.O. XVIII*, p. 492.

36 De Felice, op. cit., p. 348.

37 Cannistraro and Sullivan, op. cit., p. 261.

38 Chiocci, op. cit., p. 127.

39 Cannistraro and Sullivan, op. cit., p. 263.

40 Graham to Curzon, Public Record Office, FO 371/7659/C 14926, 15130/366/22, in Jasper Ridley, *Mussolini*, Constable, London, 1997, p. 137.

41 Ludwig, *Talks*, op. cit., p. 92.

42 Denis Mack Smith, *Mussolini*, Weidenfeld & Nicolson, London, 1981, p. 56.

43 Speech, Milan, 28 October, 1922, *Scritti e discorsi*, 6, *Cos'è il fascismo?*, p. 57.

44 Quoted in Richard Lamb, *Mussolini and the British*, John Murray, London, 1997, p. 27.

9 Power: Year One of the Fascist Era [pp. 124–160]

1 *Gerarchia*, February, 1922, *Scritti e discorsi*, 11, *Fascismo e democrazia*, pp. 14–20.

2 Speech, 18 October 1925, *Scritti e discorsi*, 11, pp. 45–6.

3 *Gerarchia*, February 1922, *Scritti e discorsi*, 11, pp. 14–20.

4 Ibid.

5 *Luce Sulla Storia D'Italia*, Istituto Luce, Rome, 1999, series of 30 pamphlets and videos, no. 5, essay by Renzo De Felice.

6 See for example, De Felice, op. cit., p. 399 sg.

7 Lyttelton, op. cit., p. 149.

8 Monelli, op. cit., p. 124.

9 For full list see De Felice, op. cit., appendix, pp. 775; Kirkpatrick, op. cit., p. 138.

10 Quoted in De Felice, op. cit., p. 483.

11 Benedetto Croce, *Nuove pagine sparse*, Napoli, 1959, vol. 1, p. 6.

12 Mack Smith, op. cit., p. 58.

13 Clare Sheridan, *To the Four Winds*, André Deutsch, London, 1957, p. 194. Clare Sheridan (1885–1970), neé Frewin, was a cousin of Winston Churchill through her American mother but lived mainly in Ireland. She was a sculptress, intrepid traveller and journalist, and Communist sympathiser. She did busts of among others Trotsky, Gandhi and Churchill and was an early advocate of 'free love'. In 2002, MI5 files were released which reveal that the British security services strongly suspected her of being a Soviet spy and informed Churchill of their suspicions in 1925 (*Daily Telegraph*, 28 November 2002).

14 Harold Nicolson, *Curzon: the Last Phase*, London, 1934, p. 290.

15 Ernest Hemingway, *By-Line: selected articles and despatches of four decades*, ed. W. White, New York, 1967, 27 January, 1923.

16 Sheridan, op. cit., p. 194 sg.

17 De Felice, op. cit., p. 481.

18 Arrigo Petacco, *L'Archivio segreto di Mussolini*, Mondadori, Milan, 1998, p. 10.

19 Clare Sheridan, *In Many Places*, Jonathan Cape, London, 1923, p. 268.

20 Quoted in Bertoldi, op. cit., p. 113.

21 Sheridan, *In Many Places*, pp. 257. sg.

22 Ibid., p. 266.

23 Sheridan, *To the Four Winds*, pp. 201–3.

24 Ridley, op. cit., p. 142.

25 Lamb, op. cit., p. 32.

26 Kirkpatrick, op. cit., p. 10.
27 Lamb, op. cit., p. 36.
28 De Felice, op. cit., p. 417.
29 Lyttelton, op. cit., p. 104.
30 De Felice, op. cit., p. 432.
31 Mack Smith, op. cit., p. 62.
32 *Gerarchia*, June 1925, *Scritti e discorsi, 6*, p. 85.
33 *Gerarchia*, October, 1925, *Scritti e discorsi, 9, Andare verso il popolo*, p. 29.
34 De Felice, op. cit., p. 396.
35 Ibid., p. 440.
36 Mack Smith, op. cit., p. 64.
37 Bertoldi, op. cit., p. 145.
38 Lamb, op. cit., p. 39.
39 De Felice, op. cit., p. 572.
40 Literally 'flanker', comes to mean 'supporter', but cf. 'fellow traveller'.
41 Lyttelton, op. cit., p. 176.
42 Ibid., p. 171.
43 Petacco, op. cit., p. 39.
44 Indro Montanelli, *L'Italia in camicia nera*, Rizzoli, Milan, 1999 (first published in 1976), p. 160.
45 Quoted in De Felice, op. cit., p. 463.
46 Guerri, op. cit., *Fascisti*, p. 97.
47 Ibid., p. 98.
48 Montanelli, op. cit., p. 149.
49 *Luce Sulla Storia D'Italia*, op. cit., no. 5, essay by Renzo De Felice.
50 Quoted in Kirkpatrick, op. cit., p. 191, author's translation from the Italian.
51 Mack Smith, op. cit., p. 72.
52 Monelli, op. cit., p. 136.
53 Speech, *Scritti e discorsi, 10, L'Italia fascista davanti al mondo*, p. 31.
54 De Felice, op. cit., p. 577.
55 Ibid., p. 573.
56 Ibid., p. 582.
57 Ibid., p. 583.
58 Guerri, op. cit., p. 104.
59 Election figures in De Felice, op. cit., p. 585.
60 24 May, 1922
61 *Gerarchia*, March 1923, in *Scritti e discorsi, 6*, pp. 52–3.
61a *Gerarchia*, April 1924, *Scritti e discorsi, 6*, pp. 71–4.
62 Quoted in De Felice, op. cit., p. 600.
63 Montanelli, op. cit., p. 167.
64 Kirkpatrick, op. cit., p. 223.
65 Rossi's testimony in Cesare Rossi, *Il delitto Matteotti nei procedimenti guidiziari e nelle polemiche giornalistiche*, Ceschina, Milan, 1965.
66 Quoted in Kirkpatrick, op. cit., p. 223.
67 Lyttelton, op. cit., p. 242.
68 De Felice, op. cit., p. 687.
69 *Scritti e discorsi, 7, Lo Stato fascista*, pp. 17–18.
70 Lyttelton, op. cit., p. 248.
71 Monelli, op. cit., p. 378.
72 Quinto Navarra, *Memorie del cameriere di Mussolini*, Longanesi, Milan, 1946.
73 Monelli, op. cit., p. 147.
74 Lada-Mocarski papers, op. cit.
75 Navarra, op. cit.
76 Ludwig, *Talks*, op. cit., p. 223.
77 Ibid., p. 222.
78 Ibid., p. 224.
79 *Pensieri pontini e sardi*, August 1943, in *Scritti e discorsi, 18, Testamento politico*, p. 120.
80 Ludwig, *Talks*, op. cit., p. 196.
81 Cannistraro and Sullivan, op. cit., p. 271.
82 Ibid., p. 272.
83 Ibid., p. 275.
84 Ibid., p. 273–4; Monelli, op. cit., p. 134.
85 Monelli, op. cit., p. 134.
86 Ludwig, *Talks*, op. cit., p. 218.
87 Monelli, op. cit., p. 134.
88 Ludwig, *Talks*, op. cit., p. 226.
89 *Pensieri pontini e sardi*, in *Scritti e discorsi, 18*, p. 103.
90 Chiocci, op. cit., p. 142.
91 Pensotti, op. cit., p. 52.
92 Ludwig, *Talks*, op. cit., p. 56.
93 Pensotti, op. cit., p. 53.
94 Milza, op. cit., p. 350.
95 Kirkpatrick, op. cit., p. 206.
96 De Felice, op. cit., p. 687.
97 See De Felice, op. cit., pp. 718, 720 for details on the decree, electoral reform etc.
98 De Felice, op. cit., p. 719.
99 Ludwig, *Talks*, op. cit., p. 189.
100 Navarra, op. cit., p. 71.
101 Rossi, *Mussolini com'era*, op. cit., p. 260.
102 *Scritti e discorsi, 7*, pp. 83–8.
103 *Luce Sulla Storia D'Italia*, op. cit., no. 6, essay by Renzo De Felice.
104 De Felice, op. cit., p. 722.
105 15 May 1925, quoted in De Felice, op. cit., p. 726.
106 Ludwig, *Talks*, op. cit., p. 209.
107 All Shaw references in George Bernard Shaw, *Bernard Shaw & Fascism*, Favil Press, London, 1927.
108 Chiocci, op. cit., p. 167.
109 Pensotti, op. cit., p. 52.
110 Chiocci, op. cit., p. 166.

10 Dux [pp. 161–213]

[nb: except where mentioned the Renzo De Felice volume used by the author in this chapter is *Mussolini il fascista*, vol. II, *L'organizzazione dello Stato fascista 1925–1929*, Einaudi, Turin, 1995 (first published 1968).]

1 Monelli, op. cit., p. 156. Lady Chamberlain is Lady Ivy, wife of Sir Austen.

2 Monelli, op. cit., p. 171.

3 Ascension Day speech, 26 May 1927, *Scritti e discorsi*, 7, pp. 97–126.

4 From 1925 Grand Council motion, quoted in De Felice, op. cit., p. 134.

5 Speech in Milan, 28 October 1925, *Scritti e discorsi*, 11, p. 46.

6 Lyttelton, op. cit., p. 269.

7 Giuseppe Bottai, *Diario 1935–1944*, ed. Giordano Bruno Guerri, Rizzoli, Milan, 4th edition, 1997, entry for 29 July 1940.

8 Quoted in Kirkpatrick, op. cit., p. 155.

9 Quoted in Aurelio Lepre, *Mussolini l'italiano Il Duce nel mito e nella realtà*, Mondadori, Milan, 1996, p. 138.

10 Quoted in Lyttelton, op. cit., p. 333.

11 *Scritti e discorsi*, 9, p. 24.

12 Giorgio Pini and Duilio Susmel, *Mussolini: l'uomo e l'opera*, vol. IV, p. 486, 4 vols, La Fenice, Florence, 1953–55.

13 Cannistraro and Sullivan, op. cit., p. 271; Milza, op. cit., p. 379.

14 Ibid.

15 Count Vicenzo Fani Ciotti, known as 'Volt', in *Critica Fascista*, February 1925.

16 Ibid.

17 Quoted in De Felice, op. cit., p. 11.

18 Ibid., p. 25.

19 Ibid., p. 26

20 Aldo Castellani, *Microbes, Men and Monarchs*, Victor Gollancz, London, 1960.

21 A. Pensotti, op. cit., p. 51; Cannistraro and Sullivan, op. cit., p. 274.

22 See André Repond, La 'famiglia Mussolini', *I Colloqui di Edda Ciano con lo psichiatra svizzero, 1944–45*, ed. Renata Broggini, in *Italia contemporanea*, June 1966.

23 Ridley, op. cit., p. 170.

24 Lepre, op. cit., p. 175.

25 *Gerarchia*, August 1925, Gioacchino Volpe.

26 Roberto Farinacci, *Un Periodo aureo del Partito Nazionale Fascista*, Franco Campitelli editore, Foligno, 1927, p. 367.

27 De Felice, op. cit., p. 105.

28 Census figures, De Felice, op. cit., p. 66.

29 Lyttelton, op. cit., p. 287.

30 Luigi Federzoni, *Italia di ieri per la storia di domani*, Mondadori, Milan, 1967, p. 110.

31 Quoted in De Felice, op. cit., pp. 70, 73.

32 Seldes, op. cit., p. 232.

33 Ibid., p. 192.

34 Ibid., p. 193.

35 Ibid., p. 194.

36 Quoted in De Felice, op. cit., p. 151.

37 Ibid., p. 203.

38 Ascension Day speech, 26 May 1927, *Scritti e discorsi*, 7, p. 118.

39 Speech notes.

40 Kirkpatrick, op. cit., p. 159.

41 Mussolini, *Corrispondenza inedita*, ed. Duilio Susmel, Edizioni del Borghese, Milan, 1972, p. 62.

42 De Felice, op. cit., p. 134.

43 Lyttelton, op. cit., p. 286.

44 Quoted in De Felice, op. cit., p. 65.

45 *Corrispondenza inedita*, op. cit., p. 103.

46 Mussolini notes for Turati, February 1927, quoted in De Felice, op. cit., p. 178.

47 See the Gibson file at the Public Record Office, Kew, HO 144/7950 99809, 492147.

48 Letters quoted in Petacco, op. cit., pp. 127–132.

49 *Speaking for Themselves, The Personal Letters of Winston and Clementine Churchill*, ed. Mary Soames, Doubleday, London, 1998.

50 Winston S. Churchill, *The Second World War*, vol. II, *Their Finest Hour*, Cassell, London, 1949. Churchill's *The Second World War* consisted of six volumes published between 1948 and 1954.

51 *The Times*, 17 January 1927.

52 Quoted in Martin Gilbert, *Winston S. Churchill, The Prophet of Truth, vol. V, 1922–1939*, Heinemann, London, 1977, pp. 222–6.

53 Navarra, op. cit.

54 See De Felice, op. cit., p. 158 for comprehensive details of the literature on the Duce's illness.

55 Ridley, op. cit., p. 183.
56 Ibid.
57 Seldes, op. cit., p. 229.
58 Ibid., p. 228.
59 Ibid., p. 229.
60 Ibid., p. 223 – see also Monelli, op. cit., pp. 380–2n on the Arpinati connection.
61 Montanelli, op. cit., p. 42.
62 Letter to *Manchester Guardian*, 11 August 1927.
63 Ascension Day speech, 26 May 1927, *Scritti e discorsi, 7*, p. 117.
64 Milza, op. cit., p. 382, says this happened in 1928.
65 Montanelli, op. cit., p. 57.
66 *Corrispondenza inedita*, op. cit., p. 93.
67 Ridley, op. cit., p. 192.
68 Montanelli, op. cit., p. 39.
69 De Felice, op. cit., p. 466.
70 Montanelli, op. cit., p. 41.
71 Figures from Montanelli, op. cit., p. 43 and De Felice, op. cit., pp. 83–4.
72 Guerri, *Fascisti*, op. cit., p. 94.
73 De Felice, op. cit., p. 396.
74 Ibid., p. 397.
75 *O.O. XXII*, p. 196.
76 See De Felice, op. cit., p. 236 for details.
77 Ibid., p. 242; see also reference in p. 257n about the gold standard.
78 See Ascension Day speech, 26 May 1927, *Scritti e discorsi, 7*, p. 123.
79 De Felice, op. cit., p. 80.
80 Ibid., p. 238.
81 Quoted, Ibid., p. 241.
82 *Scritti e discorsi, 9*, p. 24.
83 Milza, op. cit., p. 389.
84 Alan Cassels, *Fascist Italy*, Harlan Davidson, Illinois, 2nd edition, 1985, p. 61.
85 Lepre, op. cit., p. 172.
86 Guerri, *Fascisti*, op. cit., p. 94; see also *Scritti e discorsi, 7*, p. 100.
87 *Scritti e discorsi, 7*, p. 100.
88 Ascension Day speech, 26 May 1927, *Scritti e discorsi, 7*, pp. 97–126.
89 Ibid.
90 De Felice, op. cit., p. 379.
91 Milza, op. cit., p. 390.
92 Cannistraro and Sullivan, op. cit., p. 316.
93 Quoted in Seldes, op. cit., p. 317.
94 Giordano Bruno Guerri, *Giuseppe Bottai Fascista*, Mondadori, Milan, 1998 (first published 1996), p. 72.
95 Quoted in ibid., p. 74.

96 See De Felice, op. cit., pp. 474 and 321.
97 *Scritti e discorsi, 7*, p. 121.
98 Lyttelton, op. cit., p. 331.
99 Quoted in Guerri, *Fascisti*, op. cit., p. 141.
100 Quoted in Seldes, op. cit., p. 284.
101 Ibid., p. 289.
102 Quoted in Guerri, *Fascisti*, op. cit., p. 142.
103 Ibid.
104 Quoted in Lyttelton, op. cit., p. 310.
105 Ibid., p. 315.
106 Ibid., p. 316.
107 De Felice, op. cit., p. 101.
108 Giolitti would not die until 1928, aged eighty-six.
109 De Felice, op. cit., p. 325.
110 Ibid., p. 476.
111 Romano Mussolini, *La Repubblica*, 1 November 1997.
112 Ibid.
113 Testimony of Prince Torlonia's governess's children, *La Stampa*, 2 November 1997.
114 Kirkpatrick, op. cit., p. 160.
115 *Corrispondenza inedita*, op. cit., p. 84.
116 Chiocci, op. cit., p. 159.
117 Navarra, op. cit.
118 See Repond, *La 'famiglia Mussolini'*, op. cit.
119 Giovanni Ansaldo, *Diario*, 20 June 1935, quoted in Cannistraro and Sullivan, op. cit., p. 335.
120 Ibid., p. 340.
121 Harold Nicolson, *Diaries and Letters, 1930–1964*, ed. Stanley Olson, Collins, London, 1980, pp. 35–6.
122 Cannistraro and Sullivan, op. cit., p. 357.
123 Ibid., p. 344.
124 Quoted in Rino Camilleri, *Sherlock Holmes e il misterioso caso di Ippolito Nievo, Il Giornale*, 14 December 2000.
125 Carlo Galeotti, *Mussolini ha sempre ragione*, Garzanti, Milan, 2000, p. 101.
126 *Evening Standard*, 13 December 1927.
127 Marco Innocenti, *Parlami d'amore Mariù*, Mariu, Mursia, Milan, 1998, p. 19.
128 See *Scritti e discorsi, 12, Fascismo e religione*, p. 9, for another Mussolini statement on God made at the time of the Salò Republic 1943–5, this one reportedly to a Catholic priest.
129 Emil Ludwig, *Colloqui con Mussolini*, Mondadori, Milan, 2000, p. 180. This

edition, hereafter referred to as 'Ludwig, *Colloqui*', is a reprint of the uncensored version of Ludwig's 1932 interviews with Mussolini first published by Mondadori in 1950. The 1932 English version used by the author up till now remains 'Ludwig, *Talks*'.

130 Quoted in Armando Carlini, *Filosofia e religione nel pensiero di Mussolini*, Istituto di Cultura Fascista, Rome, 1934, p. 15.

131 *Scritti e discorsi, 12*, pp. 77–126.

132 Ibid., p. 12.

133 Kirkpatrick, op. cit., p. 242.

134 Montanelli, op. cit., p. 68.

135 Quoted in De Felice, op. cit., p. 401.

136 Ibid., p. 406

137 Lyttelton, op. cit., p. 418.

138 Kirkpatrick, op. cit., p. 240.

139 Galeotti, op. cit., p. 161.

140 The correct figures are in *Atleti in Camicia nera, Lo sport nell'Italia di Mussolini*, Volpe, Rome, 1983, p. 87.

141 Giorgio Galli, *Il Fascismo*, Teti editore, Bussolengo, 1995, p. 39.

142 Pini and Susmel, vol. III, op. cit., pp. 151–4.

143 De Felice, *Mussolini il duce*, vol. I, *Gli anni di consenso 1929–1936*, Einaudi, Turin, 1996 (first published 1974), p. 219.

144 Stanley G. Payne, *Il Fascismo*, Newton & Compton editori, Rome, 1999 (first published as *A History of Fascism, 1914–1945*, University of Wisconsin, 1995), p. 229.

145 *Il primo libro del fascista*, quoted in Galeotti, op. cit., p. 87.

146 Figures in Guerri, *Fascisti*, op. cit., p. 149.

147 Quoted in De Felice, *Mussolini il Fascista*, vol. II, op. cit., p. 401.

148 Kirkpatrick, op. cit., p. 248.

149 Montanelli, op. cit., p. 71.

150 Kirkpatrick, op. cit., p. 248.

151 De Felice, *Mussolini il fascista*, vol. II, op. cit., p. 428.

152 Ibid., p. 415; see also Mussolini's speech to the Chamber, May 1929 for more details, quoted in *Scritti e discorsi, 12*, p. 47.

153 Guerri, *Fascisti*, p. 148.

154 Quoted in Lyttelton, op. cit., p. 419.

155 Galeotti, op. cit., p. 90.

156 Quoted in Max Gallo, *L'Italie de Mussolini*, Librairie Académique Perrin, Paris, 1964, p. 292.

157 Milza, op. cit., p. 400.

158 *Scritti e discorsi, 12*, p. 98.

159 Lepre op. cit., p. 165.

160 Quoted in De Felice, *Mussolini il Fascista*, vol. II, op. cit., p. 430.

161 Ibid., p. 431; see also Seldes, op. cit., p. 252.

162 E. Mussolini, op. cit., pp. 131–5.

163 *Scritti e discorsi, 12*, p. 50.

164 Francesco Pacelli, *Diario*, p. 150, quoted in De Felice, *Mussolini il fascista*, vol. II, op. cit., p. 435.

165 Pacelli, *Diario*, op. cit., quoted in Antonio Spinosa, *Mussolini, Il fascino del dittatore*, Mondadori, Milan, 2000 (first published 1989), p. 226.

166 Monelli, op. cit., p. 187.

167 Quoted in Seldes, op. cit., p. 253.

168 *Scritti e discorsi, 12*, p. 67.

169 *Mielosi globale leucemica, Scritti e discorsi, 12*, p. 87.

170 Galeotti, op. cit., p. 71.

171 Quoted in Guerri, *Giuseppe Bottai Fascista*, op. cit., p. 13.

172 Quoted in Montanelli, op. cit., p. 79.

173 Figures in Guerri, *Fascisti*, pp. 149–150.

174 See also Guerri, *Fascisti*, p. 150.

175 Quoted in Montanelli, op. cit., p. 80.

176 Quoted in Seldes, op. cit., p. 255.

177 Ibid., p. 256.

178 Paul Guichonnet, *Mussolini e il fascismo*, Xenia Edizioni, Milan, 1994 (first published in Paris in 1993) p. 61.

179 Date in Galeotti, op. cit., p. 59.

180 Quoted in Guerri, *Giuseppe Bottai Fascista*, op. cit., p. 134.

181 Ibid., p. 134. Note: exact figures are impossible to establish, but the number who refused is usually put at twelve.

182 Spinosa, op. cit., p. 247.

183 Renzo De Felice, *Storia degli ebrei italiani sotto il fascismo*, Einaudi, Turin, 1993, p. 295 (first published 1961).

184 Guerri, *Giuseppe Bottai Fascista*, op. cit., p. 150.

185 Ibid., p. 151.

186 Mussolini's summary of visit to Pius XI in A. Corsetti, *Dalla preconciliazione ai Patti del Laterano. Note e documenti*, in Annuario 1968 della Biblioteca Civica di Massa, Lucca, 1969, pp. 222 sg.

187 *Scritti e discorsi, 12*, p. 7.

188 Seldes, op. cit., p. 259.

189 Ludwig, *Talks*, op. cit., pp. 177–8.
190 Ludwig, *Colloqui*, p. 137.

11 The Fascist Faithful and the Cult of the Duce [pp. 214–251]

[nb: except where mentioned the Renzo De Felice volume used by the author in this chapter is *Mussolini il duce*, vol. I, *Gli anni del consenso 1929–1936*. Einaudi, Turin, 1996 (first published 1974).]

1 Emilio Gentile, *Le origine dell'ideologia fascista (1918–1925)*, Bologna, Il Mulino, 1996, pp. 11–12.
2 *Scritti e discorsi, 9*, pp. 112–13.
3 In the *Enciclopedia Italiana*, vol. XIV, Rome, 1932, pp. 847–51. The entry in the encyclopaedia for Fascism was written by Mussolini and the philosopher Giovanni Gentile. In 1933, it was published as a book entitled *La Dottrina del fascismo*.
4 Lepre, op. cit., p. 186.
5 *Scritti e discorsi, 18*, p. 53, interview with Maddalena Mollier.
6 Ibid., p. 70, interview with Ivanoe Fossani.
7 *La Dottrina del fascismo*, op. cit.
8 Quoted in Lyttelton, op. cit., p. 365.
9 Innocenti, op. cit., p. 105.
10 Milza, op. cit., p. 585.
11 Quoted in De Felice, op. cit., p. 55.
12 Luigi Barzini, *The Italians*, Penguin, London, 1968, p. 169.
13 Quoted in Guerri, *Fascisti*, op. cit., p. 172.
14 Roger Griffin, *The Nature of Fascism*, London, 1991, p. 44.
15 Payne, op. cit., p. 11.
16 Quoted in Guerri, *Fascisti*, op. cit., p. 171.
17 Ibid., p. 117.
18 Giordano Bruno Guerri, *L'Arcitaliano. Vita di Curzio Malaparte*, Bompiani, Milan, 1981, quoted in Milza, pp. 585, 587.
19 Quoted in Cannistraro and Sullivan, op. cit., p. 379.
20 Lyttelton, op. cit., p. 390.
21 Ludwig, *Colloqui*, op. cit. pp. 71–2.
22 Yvon De Begnac, *Palazzo Venezia. Storia di un regime*, La Rocca, Rome, 1950.
23 Renzo De Felice, *Intervista sul fascismo*, ed. Michael A. Ledeen, Mondadori, Milan, 1975, p. 12.
24 *La Dottrina del fascismo*, op. cit.

25 *Scritti e discorsi, 8*, p. 117.
26 Milza, op. cit., p. 583.
27 *La Dottrina del fascismo*, op. cit.
28 *Scritti e discorsi, 8*, p. 111.
29 Jacob L. Talmon, *The Rise of Totalitarian Democracy*, Boston, 1952.
30 Quoted in Cannistraro and Sullivan, op. cit., p. 425.
31 *Scritti e discorsi, 11*, p. 6.
32 Ludwig, *Talks*, op. cit., p. 172.
33 Payne, op. cit., p. 76.
34 Quoted in Galeotti, op. cit., p. 166.
35 Ibid., p. 164.
36 Quoted in *Italian Fascism from Pareto to Gentile*, ed. Adrian Lyttelton, London, 1973, pp. 211–12.
37 De Felice, op. cit., p. 86.
38 Milza, op. cit., p. 568.
39 Montanelli, op. cit., p. 124.
40 Milza, op. cit., p. 569.
41 Quoted in Carlini, op. cit., pp. 50–6.
42 Quoted in Emilio Gentile, *Il culto del littorio*, Laterza, Bari, 1994, pp. 137–8.
43 Ibid., p. 138.
44 *Scritti e discorsi, 11*.
45 Quoted in Galeotti, op. cit., p. 212.
46 *Mostra della Rivoluzione Fascista*, exhibition catalogue, p. 30, reprinted by Edizione del Candido Nuovo, Milan, 1982 (first published 1932).
47 Montanelli, op. cit. p. 125.
48 Cannistraro and Sullivan, op. cit., p. 391.
49 De Felice, op. cit., p. 43 says 6 July 1933, however.
50 Details and quotations from the catalogue, op. cit.
51 B. Mussolini, *Parlo con Bruno*, Ultima Crociata Editrice, Rimini, 1996 (first published 1941), p. 166.
52 Montanelli, op. cit., p. 91.
53 Ibid., p. 127.
54 Ibid.
55 *Scritti e discorsi, 16, Storia di un anno: il tempo del bastone e della carota*, p. 110.
56 Channon, op. cit., entry for 6 July 1935.
57 Cannistraro and Sullivan, op. cit., pp. 455–8.
58 Gilbert, op. cit., pp. 456–7.
59 Seldes, op. cit., p. 369.
60 Foreword to *My Autobiography*, op. cit.
61 *Vita di Arnaldo, Scritti e discorsi, 12*, pp. 77–126.
62 Roger Eatwell, *Fascism, A History*, Chatto & Windus, London, 1995, p. 61.

63 Quoted in De Felice, op. cit., p. 543.
64 Ibid., p. 34.
65 George Ward Price, *I Know These Dictators*, Harrap, London, 1937, pp. 7, 161.
66 *Caro Duce, Lettere di donne italiane a Mussolini 1922–43*, ed. Giorgio Boatti, Rizzoli, Milan, 1989, p. 6.
67 Petacco, op. cit., p. 10.
68 First published by Duckworth, London, 1916.
69 'Twilight in Italy' in *D. H. Lawrence in Italy*, Penguin, London, 1997, pp. 44, 136.
70 Carlo Emilio Gadda, *Eros e Priapo*, Garzanti, Milan, 1967, pp. 59, 63–4.
71 Angela Curti Cucciati, *Un'amica di Mussolini racconta*, in *Oggi*, Milan, 10 November–29 December 1950.
72 Milza, op. cit., pp. 478–9.
73 Navarra, op. cit., pp. 216–7.
74 Petacco, op. cit., p. 3.
75 Navarra, op. cit., p. 220.
76 Gervaso, op. cit., p. 23.
77 Ibid., p. 24.
78 Ibid., p. 25.
79 Ibid., p. 31.
80 Ibid., p. 59.
81 Petacco, op. cit., pp. 150–1.
82 Quoted in Gervaso, op. cit., p. 68.
83 Ibid., p. 87.
84 Innocenti, op. cit., p. 40.
85 Giordano Bruno Guerri, *Italo Balbo*, Mondadori, Milan, 1983, p. 255.
86 Quoted in Lepre, op. cit., p. 184.
87 Quoted in *Atleti in Camicia nera*, op. cit., p. 87.
88 Ibid., p. 89.
89 Ibid., p. 95.
90 Ibid., p. 115.
91 Ibid., p. 159.
92 Payne, op. cit., p. 230.
93 De Felice, op. cit., p. 57.
94 Payne, op. cit., p. 235.
95 De Felice, op. cit., p. 63.
96 Ridley, op. cit., p. 226.
97 Milza, op. cit., p. 606.
98 Ibid., p. 600.
99 The figures quoted, apart from the ones from Payne, Milza and Ridley are from Montanelli, op. cit., pp. 97–8.
100 *Il Popolo d'Italia*, 17 October 1932.
101 *Capitalism and the Corporate State*, quoted in Seldes, op. cit., p. 423.
102 Ludwig, *Talks*, op. cit., pp. 153–4.
103 De Felice, op. cit., p. 175.
104 Ibid., p. 139.
105 Montanelli, op. cit., p. 102.
106 Payne, op. cit., p. 234.
107 Gallo, op. cit., p. 297.
108 Figures in *Luce Sulla Storia D'Italia*, op. cit., no. 8, essay by Valerio Castronovo.
109 Payne, op. cit., p. 236.
110 Milza, op. cit., p. 605.
111 Ibid., p. 604.
112 Eatwell, op. cit., p. 39.
113 Ibid., p. 56.
114 Galeotti, op. cit., pp. 95–6.
115 1979 interview in J. A. Gili, *Le Cinema Italien à l'ombre des Faisceaux (1922–1945)*, 1990.
116 Milza, op. cit., p. 577.
117 Aurelio Lepre, *Mussolini*, Laterza, Bari, 1998, p. 68.
118 Giuseppe Spina, *Per una nuova anima italiana*, Casa Editrice Avanguardia, Cassino, 1927.
119 Lyttelton, op. cit., pp. 410–11
120 Seldes, op. cit., p. 348.
121 Galeotti, op. cit., p. 107.
122 Figures in Guerri, *Fascisti*, op. cit., p. 157.
123 Eatwell, op. cit., p. 56.
124 Guerri, *Fascisti*, op. cit., p. 198.
125 Guerri, *Guiseppe Bottai Fascista*, op. cit., p. 136.
126 Guerri, *Fascisti*, op. cit., p. 178.
127 Quoted in Galli, op. cit., pp. 51–2.
128 *La Dottrina del fascismo*, op. cit.
129 Petacco, op. cit., p. 60.
130 Galeotti, op. cit., p. 50.
131 See Gentile, *Il culto del littorio*, op. cit.
132 Ludwig, *Talks*, op. cit., p. 218.
133 Carlo Galeotti, *Achille Starace e il vademecum dello stile fascista*, Rubbettino, Catanzaro, 2000, p. 134n.
134 De Felice, op. cit., p. 223.
135 Eatwell, op. cit., p. 56.
136 Milza, op. cit., p. 521.
137 Petacco, op. cit., p. 59.
138 Galeotti, *Achille Starace*, op. cit., p. 51.
139 4 September 1933.
140 25 May 1934.
141 Guerri, *Fascisti*, op. cit., p. 191.
142 Figures in Guerri, *Fascisti*, op. cit., p. 198.
143 Galeotti, *Mussolini ha sempre ragione*, op. cit., p. 30.
144 Monelli, op. cit., p. 374.
145 De Felice, op. cit., p. 591.
146 Quoted in Seldes, op. cit., p. 422.
147 Ludwig, *Talks*, op. cit., p. 145.

148 Ibid., p. 57.
149 *Il Popolo d'Italia*, 1 January, 1919.
150 Ludwig, *Colloqui*, op. cit., p. XLV.
151 Milza, op. cit., p. 643.
152 Quoted in De Felice, *Storia degli ebrei*, op. cit., pp. 512–14.
153 Ludwig, *Colloqui*, op. cit., p. XXXVII.
154 *Scritti e discorsi, 8*, p. 114.
155 FO 371/10784, quoted in Lamb, op. cit., p. 80.
156 Montanelli, op. cit., p. 135.
157 Ibid., p. 139.
158 Petacco, op. cit., p. 137.
159 Andriola, op. cit., p. 105.
160 Petacco, op. cit., p. 146.
161 Quoted in Lamb, op. cit., p. 85.
162 Ibid., p. 89.
163 FO 371/49934.
164 Ibid.
165 Oswald Mosley, *Il Fascismo inglese*, Edizioni del Borghese, Milan, 1973 (first published in English as *My Life*, London, 1968), pp. 130, 135, 139.
166 FO 371/49934.
167 Mosley, op. cit., pp. 157, 358–60, 167.
168 Cannistraro and Sullivan, op. cit., p. 397.
169 *Scritti e discorsi, 16, Storia di un anno*, pp. 152–2.
170 Gilbert, op. cit., pp. 456–7.
171 Montanelli, op. cit., p. 144.
172 De Felice, op. cit., p. 464.
173 Quoted in Lamb, op. cit., p. 98.
174 Ibid., p. 99.
175 Petacco, op. cit., p. 134.
176 Milza, op. cit., p. 643.
177 Kirkpatrick, op. cit., p. 275.
178 Lamb, op. cit., p. 104.
179 Milza, op. cit., p. 642.
180 Kirkpatrick, op. cit., p. 274.
181 Andriola, op. cit., p. 127.
182 Monelli, op. cit., p. 182.
183 Quoted in ibid., p. 185.
184 Quoted in Kirkpatrick, op. cit., p. 273.
185 Milza, op. cit., p. 645.
186 *Archivio storico degli affari esteri*, Rome, report of Major Renzetti, 19 June 1934, *Fondo Lancellotti*, p. 234.
187 E. Mussolini, op. cit., p. 147.
188 Monelli, op. cit., p. 185.
189 Lamb, op. cit., p. 106.
190 Ibid.
191 *Il Popolo d'Italia*, 3 December 1917, quoted in Andriola, op. cit., p. 59.
192 Andriola, op. cit., p. 107.
193 Ludwig, *Colloqui*, op. cit., pp. LXIX–L.
194 Prince Ernst Rudiger von Starhemberg, *Between Hitler and Mussolini*, London, 1942, pp. 168–71.
195 Denis Mack Smith, *Le Guerre del Duce*, Mondadori, Milan, 1976 (first published in London as *Mussolini's Roman Empire*, 1976), quoted in Payne, op. cit., p. 243.
196 De Felice, op. cit., p. 554.

12 Ethiopia 1935–6: Mad Dogs and Englishmen [pp. 252–280]

1 Quoted in Ray Moseley, *Mussolini's Shadow, The Double Life of Count Galeazzo Ciano*, Yale UP, New Haven and London, 1999, p. 11.
2 Repond, *La 'famiglia Mussolini'*, op. cit., p. 354.
3 Gaetano Afeltra, *La spia che amò Ciano*, Rizzoli, Milan, 1993, p. 137.
4 Pensotti, op. cit., p. 61.
5 Antonio Spinosa, *Edda, una tragedia italiana*, Mondadori, Milan, 1993, pp. 108–15.
6 Ibid., pp. 130–2; Moseley, op. cit., p. 10.
7 Repond, op. cit., pp. 350, 353, 354, 358, 359.
8 Norman Stone, *Hitler*, Hodder & Stoughton, London, 1980, p. 97.
9 Cassels, op. cit., p. 84.
10 Figures in Renzo De Felice, *Mussolini il duce*, vol. II, *Lo Stato totalitario 1936–1940*, Einaudi, Turin, 1996 (first published 1981), p. 181. [Unless otherwise stated this is the volume referred to hereafter.]
11 Monelli, op. cit., p. 190.
12 *The Times*, 19 May 1936.
13 Montanelli, op. cit., p. 155.
14 Quoted in Lamb, op. cit., pp. 53, 56.
15 Ward Price, op. cit., p. 231.
16 De Felice, *Mussolini il duce*, vol. 1, op. cit., p. 608.
17 Milza, op. cit., p. 648.
18 Pierre Laval, *Laval Parle . . .*, Les Editions du Cheval Ailé, Paris, 1948, pp. 27, 244.
19 Quoted in Milza, op. cit., p. 654, but see Mack Smith, *Mussolini*, op. cit., p. 191 and note *O.O. XXVII*, p. 287, 19 February, 1936.
20 Milza, op. cit., p. 652.
21 Quoted in Lamb, op. cit., p. 115.
22 Stone, op. cit., pp. 94, 101.
23 Kirkpatrick, op. cit., p. 280.
24 Leon Noël, *Les illusions de Stresa*,

Source Notes

Editions France-Empire, Paris, 1975, p. 63.

25 Montanelli, op. cit., p. 164.
26 Bottai, *Diario 1935–1944*, op. cit., 21 March 1939.
27 James Barros, *Betrayal from Within. Joseph Avenol, Secretary-General of the League of Nations 1933–1940*, Yale UP, New Haven and London, 1963, p. 63.
28 Quoted in Montanelli, op. cit., p. 164.
29 Stephen W. Roskill, *Hankey, Man of Secrets, vol. III*, Collins, London, 1974, p. 191.
30 Interview with Grandi in Kirkpatrick, op. cit., p. 282.
31 Laval, op. cit., p. 28.
32 Jens Petersen, *Hitler e Mussolini, la difficile alleanza*, Laterza, Bari, 1975, p. 13.
33 Quoted in Lamb, op. cit., p. 121.
34 Stone, op. cit., p. 94.
35 Robert Rhodes James, *Anthony Eden*, London, 1986, p. 135.
36 *English History 1914–1945*, Oxford, 1965, p. 754.
37 See *I Documenti diplomatici italiani, ottava serie: 1935–1939, vol. 1 [15 aprile–31 agosto 1935]* – abbrev: *DDI VIII* – Libreria dello Stato, Rome, MCMXCI, p. 457 – this date, as do many, varies.
38 Mario Toscano, *Eden a Roma alla vigilia del conflitto Italo-Ethiopico* in *Nuova Antologia*, January 1960, pp. 21–4.
39 Quoted in Montanelli, op. cit., p. 172.
40 *DDI, VIII, 1935–1939, vol. 1 [15 aprile–31 agosto 1935]*, p. 457.
41 Quoted in Montanelli, op. cit., p. 173.
42 Quoted in Lamb, op. cit., p. 125.
43 David Dutton, *Anthony Eden, A Life and Reputation*, Arnold, London, 1997, p. 36.
44 Victor H. Rothwell, *Anthony Eden: A Political Biography 1931–57*, Manchester, 1992, p. 21.
45 Quoted in Dutton, op. cit., pp. 67, 72.
46 Quoted in Lamb, op. cit., p. 125.
47 Figures from Montanelli, op. cit., p. 166; Lamb op. cit., p. 125. But see Ridley, op. cit., p. 251, who says 94 per cent and 74 per cent.
48 Quoted in Lamb, op. cit., p. 130.
49 Hoare to the Cabinet 29 November 1935, quoted in Lamb, op. cit., p. 142.
50 Montanelli, op. cit., p. 169; Channon, *Diaries*, op. cit., entry for 2 January

1939 and Templewood (Hoare), op. cit., p. 154.
51 Quoted in Kirkpatrick, op. cit., p. 296.
52 Quoted in *The Essays, Articles and Reviews of Evelyn Waugh*, ed. Donat Gallagher, Methuen, London, 1984, p. 180.
53 Quoted in Montanelli, op. cit., p. 173.
54 Ward Price, op. cit., pp. 240–1.
55 Milza, op. cit., p. 671.
56 Quoted in Waugh, op. cit., p. 182.
57 Milza, op. cit., p. 672; Mack Smith, op. cit., p. 192.
58 Quoted in Montanelli, op. cit., p. 190.
59 Kirkpatrick, op. cit., p. 303.
60 British Ambassador in Rome, quoted in Lamb, op. cit., p. 141.
61 Kirkpatrick, op. cit., p. 303.
62 Richard Collier, *Duce! Duce! Ascesa e caduta di Benito Mussolini*, Mursia, Milan, 1971 (first published in English as *Duce! The Rise and Fall of Benito Mussolini*, Collins, London, 1971), p. 154.
63 Cannistraro and Sullivan, op. cit., p. 479.
64 Quoted in Guerri, *Fascisti*, p. 209.
65 Quoted in Lamb, op. cit., p. 141.
66 Quoted in Lepre, *Mussolini l'italiano*, op. cit., p. 209.
67 Montanelli, op. cit., p. 124.
68 Pensotti, op. cit., p. 80.
69 Montanelli, op. cit., p. 197.
70 Grandi letter to Mussolini, 18 October 1935 in FO 371/49934.
71 Quoted in Lamb, op. cit., p. 137.
72 Laval, op. cit., p. 213.
73 Ibid., pp. 245–6.
74 Ridley, op. cit., p. 267.
75 Kirkpatrick, op. cit., p. 301.
76 See e.g., Montanelli, op. cit., p. 204.
77 Laval, op. cit., p. 245.
78 Kirkpatrick, op. cit., p. 307.
79 Milza, op. cit., p. 678.
80 Dutton, op. cit., p. 52.
81 Earl of Avon, Anthony Eden, *Memoirs – Facing the Dictators*, London, 1962, p. 301.
82 *English Historical Review*, vol. 89, 1972.
83 Quoted in Eden, *Memoirs*, op. cit., p. 335.
84 Quoted in Dutton, op. cit., p. 67.
85 Quoted in Hugh Thomas, *The Spanish Civil War*, 3rd edition, Penguin, London, 1977, p. 154.
86 *DDI, VIII, 1935–1939, vol. IV [10 maggio–31 agosto 1936]*, p. 305.

87 Quoted in De Felice, *Mussolini il duce*, vol. 1, op. cit., p. 726.
88 *Documents on British Foreign Policy 1919–39* (DBFP), 2nd series, vol. 16, no. 246, HMSO, London.·
89 Vittorio Mussolini, *Voli sulle Ambe*, Sansoni, Florence, 1937, pp. 48, 78–9, 141.
90 *Corrispondenza inedita*, op. cit., pp 156–7.
91 Ward Price, op. cit., p. 239.
92 *I gas di Mussolini, Il Fascismo e la guerra d'Ethiopia*, ed. Giorgio Del Boca, Editori Riuniti, Rome, 1996; see also *L'Espresso*, 26 April 1996.
93 Lepre, *Mussolini l'italiano*, op. cit., p. 209.
94 Quoted in ibid., p. 206.
95 Collier, op. cit., p. 155.
96 Ibid., p. 156.
97 Ibid., p. 175.
98 Chiocci, op. cit. p. 217.
99 Guerri, *Balbo*, op. cit., p. 299; Ridley, op. cit., p. 284.
100 De Felice, *Mussolini il duce*, vol. II, op. cit., p. 336.
101 Ridley, op. cit., p. 284.
102 *DDI, VIII, 1935–1939, vol. III [1 gennaio–9 maggio 1936]*, p. 864.
103 Kirkpatrick, op. cit., p. 311.
104 *DDI, VIII, 1935–1939, vol. IV [10 maggio–31 agosto 1936]*, p. 293.
105 Lamb says he announced that Britain was ending sanctions, op. cit., p. 168.
106 Quoted in Dutton, op. cit., p. 74.
107 A. J. P. Taylor, *The Origins of the Second World War*, London, 2nd ed. 1965.
108 Laval, op. cit., p. 245.
109 Book review in *London Mercury and Bookmen*, June 1937, in Waugh, op. cit., pp. 192–3.
110 De Felice, *Mussolini il duce*, vol. 1, op. cit., pp. 749–50.
111 Quoted in Montanelli, op. cit., pp. 252–63.
112 Bottai, *Diario 1935–1944*, op. cit., 27 August 1936.
113 Pensotti, op. cit., p. 70.

13 The Spanish Civil War (1936–9): The Blurring of Good and Evil and the Taking of Sides [pp. 281–329]

1 Rachele Mussolini, *My Life with Mussolini*, Robert Hale, London, 1959, p. 91.
2 De Felice, *Mussolini il duce*, vol. II, op. cit., p. 379.
3 Quoted in Thomas, op. cit., p. 398.
4 Ibid., pp. 270, 272.
5 Carlos Baker, *Hemingway: The Writer as an Artist*, Princeton, 1952, p. 401.
6 *Spain Betrayed: The Soviet Union in the Spanish Civil War*, ed. Ronald Radosh, Mary R. Habeck and Grigory Sevastianov, Yale UP, 2001.
7 Thomas, op. cit., p. 353.
8 Bottai, *Vent'anni*, op. cit., p. 81.
9 Joachim C. Fest, *Hitler*, Rizzoli, Milan, 1991, p. 618.
10 Thomas, op. cit., pp. 977–8, says 50,000; De Felice, *Mussolini il duce*, vol. II, op. cit., p. 465, says 80,000.
11 German Foreign Policy Documents (GFP), London, HMSO, 1951, vol. III, p. 172, quoted in Kirkpatrick, op. cit., p. 314.
12 Figures in De Felice, *Mussolini il duce*, vol. II, op. cit., p. 390–1.
13 B. Mussolini, *Parlo con Bruno*, op. cit., p. 40.
14 Montanelli, op. cit., p. 233.
15 Thomas, op. cit., p. 455.
16 Ibid., pp. 340, 709.
17 Indro Montanelli, *L'Italia dell'Asse*, Rizzoli, Milan, 1999 (first published in 1989), p. 67.
18 George Orwell, *Spilling the Spanish Beans*, New English Weekly, 29 July 1937.
19 Thomas, op. cit., p. 625.
20 Ibid., p. 807.
21 Galeazo Ciano, *Diary 1937–1938*, Methuen, London, 1952, pp. 91–2.
22 Giordano Bruno Guerri, *Galeazzo Ciano: una vita, 1903–1944*, Bompiani, Milan, 1979, pp. 246–7.
23 Moseley, op. cit., p. 27.
24 Quoted in Milza, op. cit., p. 695.
25 Figures in Thomas, appendix seven, op. cit., pp. 977–86.
26 Alfred Cobban, *A History of Modern France*, vol. III: *1871–1962*, Penguin, London, 1965, p. 168.
27 Moseley, op. cit., p. 40.
28 Thomas, op. cit., p. 396.
29 Kirkpatrick, op. cit., p. 320.
30 Duilio Susmel, *Vita sbagliata di Galeazzo Ciano*, Aldo Palazzi, Milan, 1962, pp. 64–6.
31 Spinosa, *Edda*, op. cit., p. 187.
32 Quotations from De Felice, *Mussolini il duce*, vol. II, op. cit., p. 354.
33 P. Schmidt, *Der Statist auf*

Diplomatischer Bühne, Bonn, 1950, p. 347, trans as *Hitler's Interpreter*, London, 1950, in Kirkpatrick, op. cit., p. 329; see also Andriola, op. cit., p. 154.

34 Thomas, op. cit., p. 602.
35 Hemingway, 'The Spanish War', in *Fact*, June 1937.
36 Thomas, op. cit., pp. 717–18.
37 Quoted in Montanelli, op. cit., p. 59.
38 See Milza, op. cit., p. 694, for correct name – some say Bagnoles; Milza, who is French, Bagnoles-de-l'Orne.
39 Montanelli, op. cit., p. 71.
40 Quoted in Lamb, op. cit., p. 177.
41 Keith Feiling, *The Life of Neville Chamberlain*, Macmillan, London, 1946, p. 330; Eden, *Memoirs*, op. cit., p. 445; De Felice, *Mussolini il duce*, vol. II, op. cit., pp. 425–6.
42 Andriola, op. cit., p. 155.
43 Filippo Anfuso, *Da Palazzo Venezia al Lago di Garda* (1936–1945), Settimo Sigillo, 1996 (first published in 1957), Rome, p. 36.
44 Monelli, op. cit., p. 233.
45 Ibid.
46 In *O.O. XXVIII*, pp. 248–53; Anfuso, op. cit., p. 46.
47 Monelli, op. cit., p. 233.
48 In *O.O. XLII*, p. 194.
49 GFP, vol. I, pp. 1–2, quoted in Kirkpatrick, op. cit., pp. 326–7.
50 Anfuso, op. cit., p. 52.
51 Ciano, *Diary 1937–1938*, op. cit., 31 January, 1938.
52 Anfuso, op. cit., p. 22.
53 Churchill, 'The Great Dictators', *News of the World*, 10 October 1937, Churchill Archives, CHAR 8/566, in Ridley, op. cit., p. 281.
54 Ciano, *Diary 1937–1938*, op. cit., 6 November 1937.
55 DBFP, op. cit., 2nd series, vol. XIX, pp. 590–623.
56 De Felice, *Mussolini il duce*, vol. II, op. cit., pp. 452–3.
57 Eden to Chamberlain 9 January 1938, PREM 1/276.
58 Quoted in Dutton, op. cit., p. 78.
59 *The Diplomatic Diaries of Oliver Harvey 1937–1940*, ed. John Harvey, Collins, London, 1970, p. 65.
60 L. R. Pratt, *East of Malta, West of Suez*, Cambridge UP, 1975, p. 70.
61 Quoted in Lamb, op. cit., p. 197.
62 *Archivio D. Grandi*, b. 55, fasc. 144, in

De Felice, *Mussolini il duce*, vol. II, op. cit., p. 455.
63 Quoted in Dutton, op. cit., p. 107.
64 Hitler letter to Mussolini, 11 March 1938, quoted in De Felice, *Mussolini il duce*, vol. II, op. cit., p. 471.
65 Quoted in Andriola, op. cit., p. 200.
66 Keith Feiling, op. cit., p. 348.
67 Cabinet 16 February 1938, CC[38]5, CAB 23/92, in Dutton, op. cit., p. 102.
68 *O.O. XXIX*, pp. 67–71.
69 Ciano, *Diary 1937–1938*, op. cit., 10 April 1938.
70 DBFP, 3rd series, vol. III, No. 285.
71 Monelli, op. cit., p. 243.
72 Ranuccio Bianchi Bandinelli, *Dal Diario di un borghese*, Editori Riuniti, Milan, 1948, p. 123.
73 Anfuso, op. cit., p. 63.
74 Quoted in Bandinelli, op. cit., pp. 132–4.
75 Anfuso, op. cit., p. 65.
76 Ciano, *Diary 1937–1938*, op. cit., 9 May 1938.
77 Schmidt, op. cit., p. 387.
78 Ibid., p. 83.
79 Rosaria Quartararo, 'Inghilterra e Italia dal Patto di Pasqua a Monaco' [con un appendice sul canale segreto italo-inglese], *Storia Contemporanea*, October–December 1976, p. 619.
80 Ciano, *Diary 1937–1938*, op. cit., pp. 150, 145.
81 Kirkpatrick, op. cit., p. 348.
82 Anfuso, op. cit., pp. 68–9.
83 Kirkpatrick, op. cit., p. 352.
84 Quoted in Lamb, op. cit., pp. 225–7; De Felice, *Mussolini il duce*, vol. II, op. cit., pp. 526–7.
85 Ciano, *Diary 1937–1938*, op. cit., 28–9 September 1938.
86 Contemporary newsreel commentary in the video accompanying *Luce Sulla Storia*, op. cit.
87 Monelli, op. cit., p. 239.
88 Ibid., p. 164.
89 Moseley, op. cit., p. 46.
90 Stone, op. cit., p. 112.
91 Bottai, *Diario 1935–1944*, op. cit., 30 September 1938.
92 DBFP, op. cit., 3rd series, vol. III, No. 285, pp. 319–20.
93 Montanelli, op. cit., p. 203.
94 Ibid., p. 202.
95 Luigi Gasparotto, *Diario di un deputato*, Milan, 1945, p. 286.

96 DBFP, op. cit., 3rd series, vol. III, No. 285, pp. 525–34; FO 371/32793; Cab 23/97.
97 Anfuso, op. cit., p. 93.
98 Galeazzo Ciano, *Diario 1939–1943, vol. 1 (1939–1940)*, Rizzoli, Milan, 4th edition 1947, two vols, (first published Rizzoli 1946), 11 January 1939.
99 Alexander Stille, *Benevolence and Betrayal*, Vintage, London, 1993, p. 22.
100 Churchill, 'Zionism versus Bolshevism', Churchill Archives, CHAR/8/36, pp. 90–7.
101 'La razza bianca muore?' *New York American*, 26 August 1934.
102 Cannistraro and Sullivan, op. cit., p. 529.
103 'Il Lavoro fascista', 4 September 1938 in De Felice, *Mussolini il duce*, vol. II, op. cit., p. 250.
104 De Felice, *Storia degli ebrei*, op. cit., p. 257.
105 Ibid.
106 Guerri, *Fascisti*, op. cit., p. 222.
107 *O.O. XXIX*, pp. 185–96.
108 De Felice, *Mussolini il duce*, vol. II, op. cit., p. 118.
109 *Critica Fascista*, 1 August 1938.
110 De Begnac, op. cit., p. 642.
111 Ludwig, *Colloqui*, pp. 54–5.
112 *La Dottrina del fascismo*, op. cit.
113 Quoted in Antonio Spinosa, *Mussolini razzista riluttante*, Mondadori, Milan, 2000, p. 29 (first published 1952–3 in *Il Ponte*).
114 *La Stampa*, 12 September 1945.
115 Ciano, *Diary 1937–1938*, op. cit., 3 December 1937.
116 See Spinosa, *Razzista riluttante*, op. cit., p. 82. Several estimates exist, including government figures, but all give much the same total.
117 Andriola, op. cit., p. 170.
118 *Il Giornale d'Italia*, 19 March 1937.
119 Ciano, *Diary 1937–1938*, op. cit., 6 September 1937.
120 Petacco, op. cit., p. 32.
121 Ciano, *Diary 1937–1938*, op. cit., 4 June 1938.
122 See Spinosa, op. cit., p. 42 and appendix, p. 105.
123 The *Manifesto della Razza*, first published in *Il Giornale d'Italia* on 14 July 1938, unsigned, is reproduced in De Felice, *Mussolini il duce*, vol. II, op. cit., as appendix 5, pp. 866–77.

124 Quoted in Stille, op. cit., p. 73.
125 *Carta della razza*, published in *Il Giornale d'Italia*, 8 October 1938; see also De Felice, *Storia degli ebrei*, op. cit., pp. 573–4.
126 Ciano, *Diary 1937–1938*, op. cit., 10 November 1938.
127 Quoted in Spinosa, op. cit., p. 45.
128 'La questione giudaica' in *La Civiltà cattolica*, 25 September 1936.
129 *La Civiltà cattolica*, 5 June 1937.
130 *La Civiltà cattolica*, 10 August 1938.
131 *L'Osservatore romano*, 30 July 1938.
132 De Felice, *Mussolini il Duce*, vol. II, op. cit., p. 150.
133 Reported in *Il Giornale d'Italia*, 20 September 1938.
134 Spinosa, *Razzista riluttante*, op. cit., pp. 51, 53, 93.
135 *Il Giornale d'Italia*, 6 August 1938.
136 *Provvedimenti per la difesa della razza italiana*, 17 November 1938, in De Felice, *Storia degli ebrei*, op. cit., pp. 577.
137 Spinosa, *Razzista riluttante*, op. cit., pp. 97, 100.
138 Letter quoted in *Il Giornale d'Italia*, 21 February 2001.
139 De Felice, *Storia degli ebrei*, op. cit., pp. 337.
140 Bottai, *Diario 1935–1944*, op. cit., 30 November 1938.
141 Details quoted ibid., 4 February 1939, p. 141; De Felice, *Mussolini il duce*, vol. II, op. cit., pp. 321–5.
142 Ciano, *Diary 1937–1938*, op. cit., 28 October 1938.
143 De Felice, *Mussolini il duce*, vol. II, op. cit., pp. 351–2.
144 Quoted in Andriola, op. cit., p. 199.
145 Guerri, *Fascisti*, p. 230.
146 Ciano, *Diario 1939–1943*, op. cit., 19 March 1939.
147 Ibid., 17 March 1939.
148 Anfuso, op. cit., p. 95.
149 Bottai, *Diario 1935–1944*, op. cit., 21 March 1939.
150 Lamb, op. cit., p. 242.
151 Quoted in De Felice, *Mussolini il duce*, vol. II, op. cit., pp. 602–5.
152 Bottai, *Diario 1935–1944*, op. cit., 24 November 1938.
153 Mack Smith, *Le Guerre*, op. cit., p. 182.
154 Quoted in Lamb, op. cit., p. 246.
155 Quoted in Montanelli, op. cit., p. 252.
156 Ibid., p. 254.
157 Anfuso, op. cit., p. 115.

158 Quoted in Collier, op. cit., p. 191.
159 Ciano, *Diario 1939–1943*, op. cit., 13 May 1939.
160 Repond, op. cit., p. 356.
161 Quoted in De Felice, *Mussolini il duce*, vol. II, op. cit., p. 255.
162 Anfuso, op. cit., pp. 12–13.
163 DBFP, 3rd series, vol. III, pp. 473 sg and 654ff; De Felice, *Mussolini il duce*, vol. II, op. cit., p. 631.
164 Quoted in Kirkpatrick, op. cit., p. 372.
165 Moseley, op. cit., p. 68.
166 Mack Smith, *Le Guerre*, op. cit., p. 204.
167 *DDI, VIII*, 12, op. cit., pp. 49–50.
168 Mack Smith, *Le Guerre*, op. cit., p. 206.
169 Quoted in Kirkpatrick, op. cit., p. 375.
170 De Begnac, op. cit., p. 618.
171 Archivio D. Grandi, b. 64, fasc. 157, sott. 2 in De Felice, *Mussolini il duce*, vol. II, op. cit., p. 642.
172 Ciano, *Diario 1939–1943*, op. cit., 9 and 10 August, 1939.
173 Ibid., quoted in Montanelli, op. cit., p. 259.
174 Ibid., pp. 132–3; Anfuso, op. cit., p. 102.
175 Anfuso, op. cit., p. 105.
176 Enrico Caviglia, *Diario*, Gherardo Vassini, Rome, 1952, p. 225.
177 Kirkpatrick, op. cit., p. 382; Moseley, op. cit., p. 76.
178 Ciano, *Diario 1939–1943*, op. cit., 13–14 August 1939.
179 Anfuso, op. cit., pp. 105–6.
180 Ciano, *Diario 1939–1943*, op. cit., 21 August 1939.
181 Bottai, *Diario 1935–1944*, op. cit., 31 August 1939.
182 Stone, op. cit., p. 115; Mack Smith, *Le Guerre*, op. cit., p. 241.
183 Bottai, *Diario 1935–1944*, op. cit., 1 September 1939.
184 Ibid., 4 September 1939.
185 Ibid., 2 September 1939.
186 Quoted in Montanelli, op. cit., p. 266; Milza, op. cit., p. 764; Lamb, op. cit., p. 256.
187 Kirkpatrick, op. cit., p. 391.
188 Mack Smith, *Le Guerre*, op. cit., p. 248; De Felice, *Mussolini il duce*, vol. II, op. cit., p. 655.
189 Mack Smith, *Le Guerre*, op. cit., pp. 207, 214, 227, 230, 234.
190 Quoted in Montanelli, op. cit., p. 269; Kirkpatrick, op. cit., p. 394.
191 Ciano, *Diario 1939–1943*, op. cit., 23 August 1939.
192 Bottai, *Diario 1935–1944*, op. cit., 31 August 1939.
193 Prince Marcello del Drago, unpublished memoirs, quoted in Moseley, op. cit., p. 83.
194 Bottai, *Diario 1935–1944*, op. cit., 7 September 1939.
195 Ibid., 23 January 1939.
196 De Felice, *Mussolini il duce*, vol. II, op. cit., p. 270.
197 Kirkpatrick, op. cit., p. 396.
198 Bottai, *Diario 1935–1944*, op. cit., 1 September 1939.
199 Ciano, *Diario 1939–1943*, op. cit., 1–2 October 1939.
200 Anfuso, op. cit., p. 116.
201 Guerri, *Galeazzo Ciano*, op. cit., p. 123.
202 Susanna Agnelli, *We All Wore Sailor Suits*, Weidenfeld & Nicolson, London, 1976, pp. 70–71.
203 Michael Sheridan, *Romans – Their Lives and Times*, Weidenfeld & Nicolson, London, 1976, p. 103.
204 Curzio Malaparte, *Kaputt*, Daria Guarnati, Milan, 1948, p. 331.
205 Roberto Ducci, *La bella gioventù*, Il Mulino, Bologna, 1996, p. 135.
206 Chiocci, op. cit., p. 250.
207 DDF, s, II, XIII, p. 147 in De Felice, *Mussolini il duce*, vol. II, op. cit., p. 256.
208 Bottai, *Diario 1935–1944*, op. cit., 4 November 1939.
209 Ibid., 8 December 1939.
210 Quoted in Andriola, op. cit., p. 236.
211 De Felice, *Mussolini il duce*, vol. II, op. cit., pp. 738, 758.
212 Quoted in ibid., p. 656.
213 Collier, op. cit., pp. 198–9.
214 Ciano, *Diario 1939–1943*, op. cit., 4 September and 26 December 1939.
215 Anfuso, op. cit., p. 107.
216 Ciano, *Diario 1939–1943*, op. cit., 20 November 1939.
217 Mack Smith, *Le Guerre*, op. cit., p. 176.
218 Quoted in De Felice, *Mussolini il Duce*, vol. II, op. cit., p. 309.
219 John Colville, *The Fringes of Power*, Hodder & Stoughton, London, 1985, p. 61.
220 Ciano, *Diario 1939–1943*, op. cit., 18 August 1939.
221 Andriola, op. cit., p. 233.
222 Guerri, *Italo Balbo*, op. cit., p. 369.
223 Anfuso, op. cit., p. 114.

224 Gaetano Salvemini, *Opere: Scritti sul fascismo*, vol. II, ed. N. Valerie and A. Merola, Feltrinelli, Milan, 1966, p. 281.
225 Mack Smith, *Le Guerre*, op. cit., p. 181.
226 Bottai, *Diario 1935–1944*, op. cit., 15 April 1940.
227 Monelli, op. cit., p. 258.
228 Ciano, *Diario 1939–1943*, op. cit., 11 April 1940.
229 Monelli, op. cit., p. 258; Duilio Susmel says Mussolini decided on war, though not the date, on 10/11 March, during Ribbentrop's Rome visit, *Corrispondenza Inedita*, p. 244, see p. 244 as well for more detail on chronology leading up to declaration of war.
230 Quoted in De Felice, *Mussolini il Duce*, vol. II, op. cit., pp. 772–4.
231 Ibid., pp. 780–1, 682.
232 Quoted in Bruno Gatta, *Si firmava Mussolini*, Settimo Sigillo, Rome, 1998, p. 294.
233 Renzo De Felice, *Intervista sul Fascismo*, op. cit.
234 Tommaso Senise, *Mussolini e Hitler dal punto di vista psichiatrico*, Biblioteca di 'Il Cervello', Naples, 1947.
235 *Gazette de Lausanne*, 19 September 1939.
236 *Daily Telegraph*, London, 28 April 1941.
237 Quoted in De Felice, *Mussolini il Duce*, vol. II, op. cit., pp. 265–6.
238 Ottavio Dinale, *Quarant'anni di colloqui ... con lui*, Edizioni Ciarroca, Milan, 1962, p. 158.
239 *The Spectator*, 2 June 1939.

14 1940–3: Defeat [pp. 330–377]
1 Quoted in Monelli, op. cit., p. 258.
2 Quoted in De Felice, *Mussolini il duce*, vol. II, op. cit., p. 793.
3 B.Mussolini, 'Storia di un anno: il tempo del bastone e della carota', English translation in *Memoirs 1942–1943*, Weidenfeld & Nicolson, London, 1949 (first published in Italy in serialisation form in the *Corriere della Sera* June 25–July 18 1944), p. 192.
4 *Scritti e discorsi, 18*, interview with Ivanoe Fossani, p. 67,
5 Ciano, *Diario 1939–1943*, op. cit., 10 May 1940.
6 Figures in Stone, op. cit., p. 126.
7 Ciano, *Diario 1939–1943*, op. cit., 13 May 1940.
8 Ibid., 14 May 1940.
9 Figures, Payne, op. cit., p. 387.
10 F. W. Deakin, *The Brutal Friendship*, Weidenfeld & Nicolson, I.ondon, 1962, p. 12.
11 Admiral Franco Maugeri, 'Mussolini mi ha detto' in *Politica Estera*, Rome, 1944; in English 'What Mussolini Told Me' in B. Mussolini, *Memoirs 1942–1943*, op. cit., p. 221.
12 Moseley, op. cit., pp. 100–1.
13 Ninety per cent of Italy's coal came from Britain and Germany, see Andriola, op. cit., p. 237.
14 Winston S. Churchill, *The Second World War*, vol. I, *The Gathering Storm*, Cassell, London, quoted in Andriola, op. cit., p. 232.
15 For Churchill's letter and Mussolini's reply see Churchill, *The Second World War*, vol. II, op. cit., pp 121–2.
16 Ibid., pp. 107–8.
17 Quoted in Lamb, op. cit., p. 281.
18 Anfuso, op. cit., pp. 127–9; Andriola, op. cit., p. 241.
19 Ciano, *Diario 1939–1943*, op. cit., 27 May 1940.
20 Lamb, op. cit., p. 285.
21 Harold Macmillan, *War Diaries, The Mediterranean 1943–1945*, Macmillan, London, 1984, 12 January 1945, pp. 646–7.
22 Vanna Vailati, *Badoglio racconta*, Turin, 1955; Monelli, op. cit., pp. 262–3.
23 *O.O. XXIX*, p. 403; film footage from the Archivio Istituto Luce in the *Il Borghese* video series, 2000, no. 4, *I Discorsi de Benito Mussolini*.
24 Milza, op. cit., p. 777.
25 Quoted in Lamb, op. cit., p. 286.
26 Renzo De Felice, *Rosso e Nero*, ed. Pasquale Chessa, Baldini & Castoldi, Milan 1995, p. 35.
27 Quoted in ibid., p. 83.
28 Marco Innocenti, *L'Italia del 1940*, Mursia, Milan, 1990.
29 Bottai, *Diario 1935–1944*, op. cit., 22 October 1943.
30 Indro Montanelli and Mario Cervi, *L'Italia della disfatta*, Rizzoli, Milan, 2000 (first published Rizzoli 1979), p. 510.
31 Ibid.
32 B. Cruccu, 'Gli studi sulla presenza italiana nel secondo conflitto mondiale sotto il profile tecnica' in *La*

Source Notes

Seconda guerra mondiale nelle prospettiva storica a trent'anni dall'epilogo, Como, 1975; J. J. Sweet, *Iron Arm. The mechanization of Mussolini's Army (1920–1940)*, ed. Renzo De Felice, Westport and London, 1980, both quoted in De Felice, *Mussolini il duce*, vol. II, op. cit.

33 Taped telephone call in Susmel, *Vita sbagliata*, op. cit., pp. 215–16.

34 Luigi Barzini, *The Italians*, op. cit., p. 207.

35 Milza op. cit., p. 782.

36 Ciano, *Diario 1939–1943*, op. cit., 5 July 1940.

37 Victor Barthélemy, *Du Communisme au Fascisme L'histoire d'un engagement politique*, Paris, 1978, p. 478.

38 Figures in Montanelli, op. cit., pp. 12, 18.

39 Official report for Mussolini on the incident quoted in Petacco, op. cit., pp. 51–3.

40 Monelli, op. cit., p. 278; Collier, op. cit., p. 219.

41 Milza, op. cit., p. 796.

42 *Parla Boratto, l'autista di Mussolini*, in *Il Giornale del mattino*, 24 March 1946.

43 Monelli, op. cit., p. 395.

44 Quoted in ibid., p. 284; Navarra, quoted in ibid., p. 217.

45 Channon, *Diaries*, op. cit., 2 May 1939.

46 Renzo De Felice, *Mussolini l'alleato*, vol. 1, *L'Italia in guerra 1940–1943, book i, Dalla guerra 'breve' alla guerra lunga*, Einaudi, Turin, 1996 (first published 1990), p. 303. [Hereafter, *Mussolini l'alleato*, vol. I (i).]

47 Interview with Göring, in Kirkpatrick, op. cit., p. 450.

48 See De Felice, *Mussolini il duce*, vol. II, op. cit., pp. 715–16.

49 Mack Smith, *Le Guerre*, op. cit., pp. 298–300.

50 Paolo Monelli, *Roma 1943*, Einaudi, Turin, 1993 (first published in 1945), p. 67.

51 Figure in Milza, op. cit., p. 790.

52 Mack Smith, *Mussolini*, op. cit., p. 257.

53 Stone, op. cit., p. 135.

54 Caviglia, op. cit., quoted in De Felice, *Mussolini l'alleato*, vol. I (i), op. cit., p. 303.

55 Ciano, *Diario 1939–1943*, op. cit., 12 October 1940.

56 *DDI, IX*, V, p. 452.

57 *O.O. XLIII*, p. 37.

58 Minutes of the meeting in B. Mussolini, *Memoirs 1942–1943*, op. cit., p. 269.

59 Minutes of the 15 October 1940 meeting, in Mario Cervi, *Storia della guerra di Grecia*, Mondadori, Milan, 1976, 3rd edition, pp. 358–66.

60 Mack Smith, *Le Guerre*, op. cit., p. 288.

61 Montanelli, op. cit., p. 37.

62 Mussolini to Hitler, *DDI, IX*, V, p. 720.

63 Collier, op. cit., p. 214.

64 *The Testament of Adolf Hitler: The Hitler–Bormann documents February–April 1945*, ed. François Genoud, London, 1959, see entry 17 March 1945.

65 Captured documents, FO 371/49936.

66 Obituary of Michael Torrens-Spence, *Daily Telegraph*, 9 November 2001.

67 Montanelli, op. cit., pp. 70–1; see also Ridley, op. cit., p. 317.

68 Ciano, *Diario 1939–1943*, op. cit., 6 December 1940.

69 Ibid., 27 September 1941.

70 Montanelli, op. cit., p. 59.

71 Winston S. Churchill, *In guerra. Discorsi pubblici e segreti*, I, 1938–1942, Milan, 1948, p. 106.

72 Josef Goebbels, *The Goebbels Diaries 1939–1941*, Sphere, London, p. 214.

73 Figures in Montanelli, op. cit., p. 78.

74 Quoted in ibid., p. 80.

75 Milza, op. cit., p. 790.

76 Ciano, *Diario 1939–1943*, op. cit., 17 September 1940.

77 Mack Smith, *Le Guerre*, op. cit., p. 291.

78 Montanelli, op. cit., p. 64. Milza, op. cit., p. 786.

79 Quoted in Montanelli, op. cit., p. 100.

80 Ciano, *Diario 1939–1943*, op. cit., 7 December 1941.

81 Dino Alfieri, *Due dittatori di fronte*, Rizzoli, Milan, 1948, p. 115.

82 Payne, op. cit., p. 390.

83 Ciano, *Diario 1939–1943*, op. cit., 25 January 1941.

84 Ibid., 16 May 1941 and 4 June 1941.

85 De Felice, *Mussolini l'alleato*, vol. I (i), op. cit., p. 314; Moseley, op. cit., p. 123.

86 Quoted in Montanelli, op. cit., p. 85.

87 Gaetano Afeltra, *La spia che amò Ciano*, op. cit., p. 150.

88 Spinosa, *Edda*, op. cit., p. 250.

89 Quoted in Moseley, op. cit., p. 143.

90 Bottai, *Diario 1935–1944*, op. cit., 18 September 1942.
91 Quoted in Cervi, *Storia della guerra in Grecia*, op. cit., p. 341.
92 Figures in Montanelli, op. cit., p. 92.
93 In *Scritti e discorsi*, 15, *La difesa armata della nazione*, pp. 75–86.
94 Ciano, *Diario 1939–1943*, op. cit., 10 June 1941.
95 Ibid., 10 July 1941.
96 Stone, op. cit., p. 141, says 3 million Germans and their allies.
97 Ciano, *Diario 1939–1943*, 2 June 1941.
98 Nino D'Aroma, *Mussolini segreto*, Cappelli, Rocca S. Casciano, 1958, in Andriola, op. cit., p. 254.
99 Ciano, *Diario 1939–1943*, 6 July 1941.
100 Figures in Montanelli, op. cit., pp. 131–2.
101 Ciano, *Diario 1939–1943*, op. cit., 1 July 1940.
102 Ibid., 20 December 1941.
103 Stone, op. cit., p. 138.
104 Born 22 April 1918; see *Parlo con Bruno*, op. cit., p. 10.
105 Collier, op. cit., p. 220.
106 B. Mussolini, *Parlo con Bruno*, op. cit., pp. 10, 11, 33, 45.
107 Ciano, *Diario 1939–1943*, op. cit., 22 September 1941.
108 Ibid., 8 December 1941.
109 Ibid., 11 December 1941.
110 Fidia Gambetti, *Controveleno*, Osimo, 1942, pp. 141 sg.
111 Ciano, *Diario 1939–1943*, op. cit., 13 October 1941.
112 Ibid., 22 December 1941.
113 At their peak in March 1943, there were only 101 U-boats operational in total in all theatres, see Stone, op. cit., p. 167.
114 Figures in Stone, op. cit., p. 170.
115 Erwin Rommel, *The Rommel Papers*, ed. Basil H. Liddell-Hart, Collins, London, 1953, p. 203.
116 Guichonnet, op. cit., p. 96.
117 Date in Stone, op. cit., p. 170.
118 Montanelli, op. cit., pp. 171–2.
119 Quoted in ibid., p. 174.
120 Ibid.; Deakin, op. cit., p. 19.
121 B. Mussolini, *Memoirs 1942–1943*, op. cit., p. 2.
122 De Felice, *Mussolini l'alleato*, vol. I (i), op. cit., p. 650.
123 Maugeri, in B. Mussolini, *Memoirs 1942–1943*, op. cit., p. 220.

124 Ciano, *Diario 1939–1943*, op. cit., 8 October 1942.
125 Kirkpatrick, p. 475.
126 Pietro Carradori with Luciano Garibaldi, *Vita col Duce*, Effedieffe Edizioni, Milan, 2001, pp. 8–9.
127 Renzo De Felice, *Mussolini l'alleato*, vol. I, *L'Italia in guerra 1940–1943*, book ii, *Crisi e agonia del regime*, Einaudi, Turin, 1996 (first published 1990), pp. 1081–3. Hereafter, *Mussolini l'alleato*, vol. I.
128 Ciano, *Diario 1939–1943*, op. cit., 26 September 1942.
129 De Felice, *Mussolini l'alleato*, vol. I (ii), op. cit., p. 1079.
130 Ibid., p. 1085.
131 Collier, op. cit., pp. 234, 269.
132 Figure in De Felice, *Mussolini l'alleato*, vol. I (ii), op. cit., p. 1084.
133 Bottai, *Diario 1935–1944*, op. cit., 7 October 1942.
134 Quoted in Deakin, op. cit., pp. 39–40.
135 Monelli, *Roma 1943*, op. cit., p. 49.
136 Quoted in Montanelli, op. cit., p. 185.
137 Figures in Stone, op. cit., pp. 186–7.
138 Montanelli says the 8th (op. cit., p. 333), Kirkpatrick, the 7th (op. cit., p. 477).
139 Cobban, op. cit., p. 192.
140 *Scritti e discorsi*, 15, pp. 103–13; O.O. XXXI, p. 136.
141 B. Mussolini, *Memoirs 1942–1943*, op. cit., p. 1.
142 Deakin, op. cit., p. 83.
143 Figures in Montanelli, op. cit., p. 180–1; De Felice, *Mussolini l'alleato*, vol. I (i), op. cit., p. 605.
144 Stone, op. cit., p. 172.
145 Ibid., pp. 177, 179.
146 B. Mussolini, *Memoirs 1942–1943*, op. cit., p. 148.
147 *Scritti e discorsi*, 15, pp. 88–102.
148 Quoted in Andriola, op. cit. p. 255.
149 Bottai, *Diario 1935–1944*, op. cit., 15 December 1942.
150 Leonardo Simoni, *Berlino, ambasciata d'Italia 1939–1943*, Rome, 1946. Simoni was the pseudonym of Barone Michele Lanza, Italian Minister in Berlin – the number two position – who was there with Italian Ambassador to Berlin, Alfieri.
151 Teresa Giusti, 'Dalle marce del 'davaj' at campi di prigionia', *Nuova storia contemporanea* November–December 2000.

152 Letter quoted in ibid.; *Panorama*, 9 February 1992; *La Stampa*, 15 February 1992.

153 Kirkpatrick, op. cit., p. 482.

154 Pozzi, op. cit., pp. 122–8.

155 Stone, op. cit., pp. 159, 162–3.

156 Jonathan Steinberg, *All or Nothing: The Axis and the Holocaust*, Routledge, London and New York, 1990, p. 106.

157 Ibid., p. 131.

158 John Bierman, article in *The Italian Refuge*, ed. Ivo Herzer, Washington DC, 1989, p. 219, quoted in Moseley, op. cit., pp. 152–3.

159 Robert O. Paxton, *Vichy 1940–1944: Il regime del disonore*, Il Saggiatore, Milan, 1999, pp. 171–2 (first published as *Vichy France: Old Guard and New Order 1940–1944*, 1972).

160 Milza, op. cit., p. 810.

161 De Felice, *Mussolini l'alleato*, vol. I (i), op. cit., p. 453.

162 Ibid., p. 455.

163 Steinberg, op. cit., pp. 52–3, 58.

164 De Felice, *Mussolini l'alleato*, vol. I (i), op. cit., p. 456.

165 Steinberg, op. cit., p. 133.

166 Luca Pietromarchi, *Diario*, 26 July 1942, quoted in De Felice, *Mussolini l'alleato*, vol. I (i), op. cit., p. 450.

167 Vidussoni to Mussolini, 21 June 1942, Archivio Centrale dello Stato, Segretaria personale del Duce, Carteggio riservato, busta 50. Office note, 4 November 1942, Ministero degli esteri, Rome, in Milza, op. cit., pp. 809–11.

168 Report to Mussolini by G. Paolucci di Calboli on conversation with Franco 28 June 1943, see Giovanni Tassani, in *Madrid 1943; tre colloqui col Caudillo*, *Nuova storia contemporanea* January–February 2002, p. 122.

169 Ibid., p. 123.

170 Quoted in De Felice, *Storia degli ebrei*, op. cit., p. 457.

171 Ibid., pp. 413–16.

172 Monelli, *Mussolini piccolo borghese*, op. cit., p. 312.

173 *Il Giornale*, 25 April 1998.

174 Steinberg, op. cit.

175 Meir Michaelis, *Mussolini and the Jews*, Clarendon Press, Oxford, 1978, pp. 392, 405.

176 *Libro della memoria*, Mursia, Milan, 2002.

177 Report in the *Daily Telegraph*, 27 June 2000, on release of US Office of Strategic Services (OSS) documents.

178 Richard Lamb, *The War in Italy 1943–1945, A Brutal Story*, Penguin, London, 1995, p. 41.

179 Michaelis, op. cit., pp. 352–91.

180 John Cornwell, *Hitler's Pope*, Penguin, London, 2000 (first published 1999), p. 268.

181 Ibid., p. 406.

182 Giorgio Gariboldi, *Pio XII, Hitler e Mussolini, Il Vaticano fra le dittature*, Milan, 1988, p. 270; Lamb, *The War in Italy*, op. cit., p. 58.

183 Cornwell, op. cit., p. 304.

184 Gariboldi, op. cit., pp. 206–7.

185 Oral evidence from Wolff in 1972 to the tribunal for the beatification of Pius XII, quoted in Gariboldi, op. cit., p. 217, certainly not unpublished, until Cornwell's 1999 book, *Hitler's Pope*, as Cornwell states.

186 See Pinchas Lapide (former Israeli consul in Milan), *Roma e gli ebrei*, Mondadori, Milan, 1967.

187 Guenter Lewy, *Catholic Church and Nazi Germany*, Weidenfeld & Nicolson, London, 1964, quoted in the *Corriere della Sera*, 26 April 2002.

188 Lamb, *Mussolini and the British*, op. cit., pp. 304–5.

189 Ciano, *Diario 1939–1943*, op. cit., 30 January 1943.

190 De Felice, *Mussolini l'alleato*, vol. I (ii), op. cit., p. 1047.

191 Ciano, *Diario 1939–1943*, op. cit., 6 November 1942.

192 Ibid., 8 February 1943.

193 Report by General Enno von Rintelen, Chief German liaison officer with the Italian Command, Rome, 18 November 1942, to Berlin, in Deakin, op. cit., p. 161.

194 Quoted in Kirkpatrick, op. cit., pp. 485–6.

195 Ibid., p. 486; Deakin, op. cit., p. 217.

196 Quoted in Ibid., p. 257.

197 Simoni, op. cit., entry for 11 April 1943.

198 Deakin, op. cit., p. 275.

199 Josef Goebbels, *Diaries*, ed. L. P. Lochner, Hamish Hamilton, London, 1948, entry for 6 May 1943.

200 Giuseppe Bastianini, *Uomini, cose, fatti: memorie di un ambasciatore*, Vitagliano, Milan, 1959, p. 92.

201 Deakin, op. cit., p. 331.
202 Quoted in Lamb, *Mussolini and the British*, op. cit., p. 314.
203 Deakin, op. cit., p. 223.
204 Milza, op. cit., p. 806.
205 Figures in De Felice, *Mussolini l'alleato*, vol. I (i), op. cit., p. 547.
206 Ibid., p. 577.
207 Milza, op. cit., p. 807.
208 A Communist estimate, but other sources put the figure at 40–50,000, see Deakin, op. cit., p. 223. Mussolini himself said the total was about 100,000, see De Felice, *Mussolini l'alleato*, vol. I (ii), op. cit., p. 953.
209 Figures in Guerri, *Fascisti*, p. 240; Cassels, op. cit., p. 104; De Felice, *Mussolini l'alleato*, vol. I (i), p. 539 and *Mussolini l'alleato*, vol. I (ii), p. 701.
210 The Communists' own figures, see Deakin, op. cit., p. 224.
211 Foreign Relations of the United States Diplomatic Papers, vol. II, pp. 318–22, in 371/33240 in Lamb, *Mussolini and the British*, op. cit., p. 307.
212 Deakin, op. cit., p. 211.
213 Rintelen report, 5 May 1943 in Deakin, op. cit., pp. 284–5.
214 Monelli, *piccolo borghese*, op. cit., p. 293.
215 Monelli, *Roma 1943*, op. cit., p. 64.; the published text of the 'bagnasciuga' speech and the original uncensored text are in De Felice, *Mussolini l'alleato*, vol. I (ii), appendix 11, op. cit., pp. 1466–9.
216 Deakin, op. cit., p. 372.
217 Montanelli, op. cit., p. 223.
218 All Sicily figures in Montanelli, pp. 217–23, except last, in Lamb, *Mussolini and the British*, op. cit., p. 309.

15 July 1943: The Betrayal of Mussolini and the Death of the Fascist Regime [pp. 378–413]

1 '*Il Fascismo, principio di sintesi nazionale*', speech 19 March 1923, in Giuseppe Bottai, *Fascismo e Italia nuova*, Berlutti, Rome, 1923, p. 251.
2 Quoted in De Felice, *Mussolini l'alleato*, vol. I (ii), op. cit., p. 1227.
3 Quoted in Deakin, op. cit., p. 124.
4 *Pensieri pontini e sardi, Scritti e discorsi, 16*, p. 105.
5 Interview with Professor Giovanni Balella, former Fascist President of the National Confederation of Industrialists and member of the Grand Council, quoted in Collier, op. cit., p. 235.
6 Monelli, *Roma 1943*, op. cit., p. 50.
7 Melton S. Davies, *Who Defends Rome?* Allen & Unwin, London, 1972, p. 40.
8 This undated letter to the Duke of Acquarone, Minister of the Royal Household since January 1939, was written after 25 July 1943, probably on 1 June 1944 and is quoted in pro-monarchist works and in Monelli, *Rome 1944*, op. cit., pp. 76–7; see also Deakin, op. cit., p. 232; Montanelli, *L'Italia della Disfatta*, op. cit., p. 229; Indro Montanelli Mario Cervi, *L'Italia della Guerra civile*, Rizzoli, Milan, 2000 (first published 1983), p. 158.
9 Quoted in Deakin, op. cit., p. 160.
10 This note was apparently found on the King's desk at the *Quirinale* in August 1943 and first published as pro-Fascist propaganda in the review, *La Voce Italiana*, 15 April 1945, as evidence of his betrayal of Fascism and reprinted in Deakin, op. cit., p. 337–40.
11 Puntoni, op. cit., p. 132.
12 Anfuso quoted in Davies, op. cit., p. 23.
13 Quoted in Anfuso, op. cit., p. 283.
14 Dino Grandi, *Il mio paese: ricordi autobiografici*, ed. Renzo De Felice, Il Mulino, Bologna, 1985, p. 624.
15 Ambrosio interview in the *Corriere della Sera*, 11 March 1955.
16 Puntoni, op. cit., p. 136.
17 Monelli, *Roma 1943*, op. cit., p. 84; Davies, op. cit., p. 52.
18 See Collier, op. cit., p. 253.
19 Monelli, *Roma 1943*, op. cit., p. 89.
20 Ivanoe Bonomi, *Diario di un anno*, Garzanti, Milan, 1947, p. xxxvii.
21 Puntoni, op. cit., 1–3 June 1943.
22 For date see De Felice, *Mussolini l'alleato*, vol. I (ii), op. cit., p. 1236.
23 B. Mussolini, *Memoirs 1942–1943*, op. cit., p. 142.
24 Indro Montanelli interview with Grandi, *Corriere della Sera*, 9 February 1955, quoted in Monelli, *Roma 1943*, op. cit., p. 323; see also Deakin, op. cit., p. 341; Montanelli, *L'Italia della disfatta*, op. cit., p. 234; Dino Grandi, op. cit., p. 627.
25 Deakin, op. cit., pp. 29, 36 and quoted on p. 457.
26 Monelli, *Roma 1943*, op. cit., p. 84.

27 Puntoni, op. cit., p. 133.
28 Guerri, *Giuseppe Bottai Fascista*, op. cit., p. 203.
29 Bottai, *Diario 1935–1944*, op. cit., 16 and 17 July 1943.
30 Quoted in Deakin, op. cit., p. 393.
31 *Corrispondenza inedita*, op. cit., pp. 187–9.
32 Hitler Naval Conferences 1943, op. cit., pp. 59–62, in Deakin, op. cit., p. 381–2.
33 Montanelli, op. cit., p. 237.
34 B. Mussolini, *Memoirs 1942–1943*, op. cit., p. 50; *Scritti e discorsi, 16, Pensieri pontini e sardi*, p. 123.
35 Andriola, op. cit., p. 262.
36 Luce Sulla Storia D'Italia, op. cit., no. 13, essay by Valerio Castronovo.
37 Alfieri, *Due dittatori di fronte*, op. cit., p. 315.
38 *Pensieri pontini e sardi, Scritti e discorsi, 16*, p. 123.
39 Maugeri, op. cit., in B. Mussolini, *Memoirs 1942–1943*, op. cit., p. 221.
40 Deakin, op. cit., p. 408.
41 B.Mussolini, *Memoirs 1942–1943*, op. cit., p. 51.
42 Alfieri, op. cit., p. 317.
43 Ottavio Dinale, op. cit., pp. 246–7.
44 Anfuso, op. cit., p. 282.
45 Collier, op. cit., p. 246; Davies, op. cit., p. 41.
46 R. Mussolini, op. cit., p. 188.
47 De Felice, *Mussolini l'alleato*, vol. I (ii), op. cit., p. 1248.
48 Testimony of Acquarone to Castellano, according to Castellano, 20 July 1943, Deakin, op. cit., p. 436.
49 Moseley op. cit., p. 169.
50 Deakin, op. cit., p. 437.
51 Puntoni, op. cit., p. 141.
52 B. Mussolini, *Memoirs 1942–1943*, op. cit., p. 52.
53 Andriola, op. cit., p. 262.
54 Winston S. Churchill, *The Second World War*, vol. V, *Closing the Ring*, p. 62.
55 Quoted in Moseley, op. cit., p. 169.
56 Susmel, *Vita sbagliata*, op. cit., p. 281–2. The date is given as 21 July for Farinacci's meeting with Mussolini, but as Mussolini refers to his meeting with the King only that morning it must be the 22nd – unless Mussolini saw the King on the 21st, as most state.
57 De Felice, *Mussolini l'alleato*, vol. I (ii), op. cit., p. 1251.
58 Collier, op. cit., p. 254.
59 Quoted in Monelli, *Roma 1943*, op. cit., p. 101.
60 Guerri, *Giuseppe Bottai Fascista*, op. cit., p. 203.
61 Grandi, *Corriere della Sera*, 9 February 1955 and *Milano-Sera*, 16 January 1946.
62 B. Mussolini, *Memoirs 1942–1943*, op. cit., p. 53.
63 *Pensieri pontini e sardi, Scritti e discorsi, 16*, p. 100.
64 B. Mussolini, *Memoirs 1942–1943*, op. cit., p. 236.
65 Motion quoted in full, Deakin, op. cit., p. 455.
66 Ibid.
67 Farinacci's motion in full quoted in ibid., pp. 455–6.
68 Scorza's motion in full quoted in ibid., p. 456.
69 Bottai, *Diario*, op. cit., 24 July 1943.
70 Guerri, *Giuseppe Bottai Fascista*, op. cit., p. 208. Gianfranco Bianchi, *Perché e come cadde il fascismo*, Mursia, Milan, 1970, p. 449.
71 Davies, op. cit., p. 14.
72 Quoted in Montanelli, op. cit., p. 239.
73 Grandi, *Il mio paese*, quoted in Guerri, *Fascisti*, op. cit., p. 249.
74 Bottai, *Diario 1935–1944*, op. cit., 22 October 1947.
75 Montanelli, op. cit., p. 242.
76 Ludwig, *Talks*, p. 197.
77 *Storia di un anno, Scritti e discorsi, 16*, p. 56.
78 Collier, op. cit., p. 277.
79 Montanelli, op. cit., p. 243.
80 Kirkpatrick, op. cit., p. 506; Davies, op. cit., p. 101.
81 *Storia di un anno, Scritti e discorsi, 16*, p. 60.
82 Bottai, *Diario 1935–1944*, op. cit., 24 July 1943.
83 B. Mussolini, *Memoirs 1942–1944*, op. cit., p. 59. Quoted in *Storia di un anno*, English edition, p. 59.
84 Ibid., p. 61. Bottai, 'Pro Memoria 1944', in *Vent'anni*, op. cit., pp. 319–23. Kirkpatrick, op. cit., p. 508; Monelli, *Roma 1943*, op. cit., p. 115.
85 Bottai, *Vent'anni e un giorno*, op. cit., pp. 304–6.
86 Quoted in Montanelli, op. cit., p. 246.
87 Quoted in Davies, op. cit., p. 114.
88 Collier, op. cit., p. 260.

89 Quoted in Susmel, *Vita sbagliata*, op. cit., pp. 284–5; Davies op. cit., p. 116.
90 Collier, op. cit., p. 262.
91 Ibid., p. 255.
92 Ibid., p. 262.
93 Susmel, *Vita sbagliata*, op. cit., p. 285.
94 Bottai, *Diario 1935–1944*, op. cit., 24 July 1943.
95 *Il mio paese*, op. cit., quoted in Guerri, *Fascisti*, op. cit., p. 253.
96 Bottai, *Diario 1935–1944*, op. cit., 24 July 1943.
97 Monelli, *Roma 1943*, op. cit., p. 123.
98 Bottai, '*Pro Memoria 1944*', in *Vent'anni*, op. cit., pp. 319–23.
99 Bottai, *Diario 1935–1944*, op. cit., 24 July 1943.
100 Bottai, *Vent'anni*, op. cit., pp. 316–17.
101 Dino Grandi, *25 luglio. Quarant' anni dopo*, Il Mulino, Bologna, 1983, p. 265.
102 Collier, op. cit., p. 265.
103 See Bottai, *Diario 1935–1944*, op. cit., 24 July 1943, pp. 420–1, i.e. only twenty-seven of the twenty-eight gerarchs voted; also Milza, op. cit., p. 824; Guerri, *Fascisti*, p. 254.
104 Emilio De Bono, unpublished diary, Archivio dello Stato, Fondo De Bono, entry for 28 September 1943.
105 *Storia di un anno, Scritti e discorsi, 16*, p. 63.
106 Quoted in Collier, op. cit., p. 266.
107 Carlo Scorza, *La notte del Gran Consiglio*, Palazzo editore, Milan, p. 163.
108 Renzo Trionfera, *L'Orecchio del Duce*, in *L'Europeo*, 29 April–27 May 1956.
109 *Storia di un anno, Scritti e discorsi, 16*, p. 63.
110 Pini and Susmel, op. cit., vol. IV, p. 254.
111 Pensotti, op. cit., p. 92.
112 Grandi, *Il Mio Paese*, op. cit., p. 627.
113 Grandi, *25 luglio*, op. cit., p. 269.
114 See, for example Roberto Battaglia, '*Il Contemporaneo*', Anno II, no. 5, 29 January 1955.
115 Bottai, '*Pro Memoria 1944*', in *Vent'anni*, op. cit., pp. 319–23.
116 Quoted in Montanelli, op. cit., p. 251.
117 Interview with Albini, 15 October 1968, Rome, in Collier, op. cit., p. 268.
118 Bastianini, op. cit., p. 132; Monelli, *Roma 1943*, op. cit., p. 128; De Felice, *Mussolini l'alleato*, vol. I (ii), op. cit., p. 1387.
119 NAW, War Department, Office of Assistant Chief of Staff, G-2, in *Magic Summary*, 492n and 496.
120 Bastianini, op. cit., p. 132.
121 Fulvio and Gianfranco Bellini, *Storia segreta del 25 luglio '43*, Mursia, Milan, see *Il Giornale*, 30 July 2001.
122 Collier, op. cit., p. 244.
123 See photograph of Pope in Davies, op. cit., p. 18.
124 Galbiati, op. cit., in Deakin, op. cit., p. 465; Kirkpatrick, op. cit., p. 518.
125 Monelli, *Roma 1943*, op. cit., p. 130.
126 Ibid., p. 82.
127 Davies, op. cit., p. 136.
128 *Storia di un anno, Scritti e discorsi, 16*, p. 80; pp. 68–9.
129 Puntoni quoted in Monelli, *Roma 1943*, op. cit., p. 329.
130 *Pensieri pontini e sardi, Scritti e discorsi, 18*, p. 101.
131 Monelli, *Roma 1943*, op. cit., pp. 296–7.
132 Bottai, *Diario*, op. cit., 4 August 1943.
133 *Storia di un anno, Scritti e discorsi, 16*, p. 82.
134 See De Felice, *Mussolini l'alleato*, vol. I (ii), op. cit., pp. 1393–5.
135 Vanna Vailati, *Badoglio risponde*, Rizzoli, Milan, 1958, p. 86.
136 Barzini, op. cit., p. 159.
137 Anfuso, op. cit., p. 296.
138 Eugen Dollmann, *Roma Nazista*, Longanesi, Milan, 1951.
139 Monelli, *Roma 1943*, op. cit., p. 331.
140 Montanelli, op. cit., p. 258; Milza, op. cit., pp. 830–1.
141 C. Mazzantini, *I Balilla andarano a Salò. L'Armata degli adolescenti che pagò il conto della Storia*, Venice, 1995, p. 59.
142 Quoted in Davies, p. 136.
143 Interview with Gumpert in Collier, op. cit., p. 278.
144 R. Mussolini, op. cit., p. 132.
145 Albert Speer, *Memorie del Terzo Reich*, Mondadori, Milan, 1995, p. 403.
146 FO 371/37289, in Lamb, *Mussolini and the British*, op. cit., p. 313.
147 Macmillan, op. cit., entry for 25 July 1943, p. 163.
148 Archivio dello Stato, Mussolini, *Valigia*, b. 3, fasc. 18.
149 Quoted in De Felice, *Mussolini l'alleato*, vol. I (ii), op. cit., p. 1404.
150 Deakin, op. cit., p. 475.
151 Milza, op. cit., pp. 830–1.
152 Monelli, *Roma 1943*, op. cit., p. 153.

153 Bottai, *Diario 1935–1944*, op. cit., 2 August 1943.
154 Anfuso, op. cit., p. 291.
155 Monelli, *Roma 1943*, op. cit., p. 148.
156 Ibid., p. 333.
157 B. Mussolini, *Memoirs 1942–1943*, op. cit. p. 90.
158 Maugeri, op. cit., in ibid., pp. 228–9.
159 Montanelli, op. cit., p. 275; Milza, op. cit., p. 829.
160 B. Mussolini, *Memoirs 1942–1943*, op. cit., p. 91.
161 *Pensieri pontini e sardi, Scritti e discorsi, 16*, p. 104.
162 Maugeri in B. Mussolini, *Memoirs 1942–1943*, op. cit., p. 235.
163 *Pensieri pontini e sardi, Scritti e discorsi, 16*, pp. 116–17.
164 B. Mussolini, *Memoirs 1942–1943*, op. cit., p. 115.
165 Account of hotel manager in ibid., p. 246.
166 B. Mussolini, *Memoirs 1942–1943*, op. cit., p. 64.
167 *Pensieri pontini e sardi, Scritti e discorsi, 16*, p. 114.
168 Churchill, vol.V, op. cit., p. 57.
169 Pietromarchi, *Diario*, op. cit., 26 July 1943.
170 Churchill, *The Second World War*, vol. V, op. cit., p. 66.
171 Quoted in Deakin, op. cit., p. 531.
172 Ibid., p. 532.
173 Ibid., pp. 522–7.
174 Quoted in De Felice, *Mussolini l'alleato*, vol. I (ii), op. cit., p. 1203.
175 Quoted in B. Mussolini, *Memoirs 1942–1943*, op. cit., p. 105.
176 Deakin, op. cit., p. 483.
177 Garibaldi in Carradori, op. cit., p. 112.
178 Figures in Guerri, *Fascisti*, op. cit., p. 240.
179 B. Mussolini, *Memoirs 1942–1943*, op. cit., p. 98.
180 Montanelli, op. cit., p. 261.

16 September 1943: *'Una Tragedia all'Italiana'* [pp. 414–452]

1 Goldoni and Sermasi, op. cit., p. 176.
2 Roberto Vivarelli, *La Fine di una stagione: memoria 1943–1945*, Il Mulino, Bologna, 2000; this quote is from an interview with the author in *La Stampa*, 11 November 2000.
3 Garibaldi in Carradoni, op. cit., p. 113.
4 Ibid., Montanelli, op. cit., p. 278;

Charles Foley, *Teste Calde*, Longanesi, Milan, 1955 (first published as *Commando Extraordinary* in 1954), p. 82.
5 Quoted in Deakin, op. cit., p. 493.
6 Macmillan, op. cit., 8 August 1943, p. 179.
7 Montanelli, op. cit., p. 266.
8 Macmillan, op. cit., 20 August 1943, p. 186.
9 Montanelli, op. cit., p. 269.
10 Macmillan, op. cit., 29 August 1943, p. 196.
11 Ibid., 3 September 1943, p. 202.
12 Macmillan, op. cit., ibid., p. 205.
13 Ibid., p. 310.
14 Figures in ibid, op. cit., p. 311.
15 Quoted in ibid., p. 288.
16 Ibid., p. 289.
17 Ibid., p. 294.
18 Quoted in Lamb, *The War in Italy*, op. cit., p. 127.
19 Montanelli, op. cit., p. 300.
20 Montanelli, op. cit., p. 298.
21 See Macmillan, op. cit., p. 208. Taylor was Chief of Staff to Artillery Commander, US 82nd Airborne Division.
22 Deakin, op. cit., p. 529.
23 Montanelli, op. cit., p. 304.
24 Quoted in ibid., p. 309.
25 Macmillan, op. cit., 8 September 1943, p. 210. Date in ibid., p. 210.
26 Montanelli, op. cit., p. 317.
27 Montanelli, *L'Italia della Guerra Civile*, op. cit., p. 12.
28 Garibaldi in Carradoni, op. cit., p. 117.
29 Deakin, op. cit., pp. 530–1.
30 German estimates in Montanelli, op. cit., p. 33.
31 Quoted in ibid., p. 319.
32 See Macmillan, op. cit., p. 233. It was not until 27 September 1943 that the Allies presented a copy of the 'long terms' to Badoglio in Brindisi which he signed in Malta on 29 September 1943.
33 Anfuso, op. cit., p. 376.
34 Lamb, op. cit., p. 145.
35 Figures in Alfio Caruso, *Italiani dovete morire*, Longanesi, Milan, 2000, p. 26.
36 Ibid., p. 26.
37 See table of command structure in Father Romualdo Formato, *L'Eccidio di Cefalonia*, Mursia, Milan, 1996 (first published 1968).

38 Caruso, op. cit., p. 28.
39 Ibid., pp. 37, 41, 48.
40 Formato, op. cit., pp. 33–7; Caruso, op. cit., pp. 66–8.
41 Caruso, op. cit., p. 113.
42 Ibid., p. 161.
43 Interview in *Il Giornale*, 5 March 2001.
44 See Caruso, op. cit., p. 241.
45 Formato, op. cit., p. 102.
46 Ibid., p. 142.
47 Ibid., p. 143.
48 Ibid., p. 144.
49 Ibid., p. 197.
50 Ibid., p. 240.
51 Caruso, op. cit., p. 242.
52 Aurelio Garobbio, *A colloquio con il Duce*, Mursia, Milan, 1998 (first published, 1948), p. 70.
53 Caruso, op. cit., p. 289.
54 Quoted in Foley, op. cit., p. 88.
55 Quoted in Montanelli, op. cit., p. 37.
56 Foley, op. cit., pp. 102–3.
57 Ibid., p. 107.
58 Goebbels, *Diaries*, op. cit., September 1943.
59 Moseley, op. cit., pp. 185–6.
60 Ibid., p. 188.
61 'La Stanza di Montanelli', *Corriere della Sera*, 3 April 2001.
62 Quoted in ibid.
63 Goebbels, *Diaries*, op. cit., 28 September 1943.
64 Figure in *Scritti e discorsi, 18*, p. 10.
65 Interviews with Carlo Silvestri in Susmel archives, ACS, b. 8, fasc. I.
66 Anfuso, op. cit., pp. 343–44. Anfuso had been ambassador in Hungary and was now in Germany, soon to become Mussolini's ambassador in Berlin.
67 Quoted in Marco Innocenti, *Mussolini a Salò*, Mursia, Milan, 1996, p. 51.
68 Anfuso, op. cit., p. 319.
69 Miriam Petacci, *Dopo sedici anni una testimonianza definitiva*, *Oggi*, 2 March to 18 May 1961.
70 Sources vary as to the precise date.
71 Montanelli, *Guerra Civile*, op. cit., p. 48.
72 Quoted in ibid., p. 49.
73 Ibid., p. 130.
74 Garobbio, op. cit., p. 29.
75 It has never been proved that Mussolini was Elena Curti's father. However, in 2001, Pietro Carradori, Mussolini's personal bodyguard (*attendente*), admitted 'we all knew it'; see Carradori, op. cit., p. 12.
76 Monelli, *piccolo borghese*, op. cit., p. 280.
77 Montanelli, *Guerra Civile*, op. cit., p. 225; R. Mussolini, op. cit., p. 252; Duilio Susmel, '*Un uomo ebbe le confessioni di Claretta Petacci'* in *Visto*, 20 October 1956; Collier, op. cit., pp. 363–5; Gervaso, op. cit., pp. 167–73.
78 Pini and Susmel, op. cit., vol. IV. p. 345; Milza, op. cit., p. 862; Carradori, op. cit., p. 49.
79 Humphrey Carpenter, *A Serious Character: the Life of Ezra Pound*, Faber, London, pp. 589, 597.
80 Quoted in *Pound Radiodiscorsi*, Edizione del Girasole, Ravenna, 1998, p. 159.
81 *Ezra Pound 1972–1992*, ed. by Luca Gallesi, Greco & Greco, Milan, 1992, pp. 315–19.
82 'A Visiting Card' quoted in Peter Ackroyd, *Pound*, Leonardi, Milan, 1989, p. 80.
83 *The Times*, 4 December 1997.
84 Giovanni Dolfin, *Con Mussolini nella tragedia*, Garzanti, Milan, 1949, pp. 71, 86–91.
85 Innocenti, *Salò*, op. cit., p. 42.
86 Arrigo Petacco, *Il comunista in camicia nera*, Mondadori, Milan, 1997, p. 112.
87 Wilhelm Hottl, *The Secret Front*, Weidenfeld & Nicolson, London, 1953.
88 Attilio Tamaro, *Due anni di storia 1943–1945*, II, Giovanni Volpe editore, Rome. 1948–50, p. 425.
89 Quoted in Petacco, *Il comunista*, op. cit., p. 142.
90 Anfuso, op. cit., p. 468.
91 See text in De Felice, *Mussolini l'alleato*, vol. II, *La guerra civile 1943–1945*, Einaudi, Turin, 1998 (first published posthumously in 1997), pp. 610–13.
92 Innocenti, *Salò*, p. 42; Garibaldi in Carradoni, op. cit., p. 127.
93 Speech to the Brigata nera 'Aldo Resega', *Scritti e Discorsi, 18*, p. 37.
94 *Corrispondenza repubblicana*, 13 November 1943, *Scritti e Discorsi, 17*, *La Repubblica sociale italiana*, p. 34.
95 Garobbio, op. cit., pp. 94–5.
96 Tamaro, op. cit., pp. 419, 442–4; Garibaldi in Carradoni, op. cit., p. 127.
97 Quoted in Petacco, *Il comunista*, op. cit., pp. 132–3.
98 Speech of Comrade Ercole Ercoli, alias Palmiro Togliatti, to the secretariat of

the Comintern, March 1941, quoted in Aldo Agosti, *Togliatti negli anni del Comintern*, Fondazione Istituto Gramsci, Carocci, Rome, 2000.

99 Roberto Chiarini, *'Guareschi, la destra e l'antimito della Resistenza'*, *Nuovo storia contemporanea*, March–April 2000.

100 Quoted in Montanelli, *Guerra Civile*, op. cit., p. 93.

101 Felicitas was a nickname, her maiden name was Hildegard Burkhardt – see Howard McGraw Smyth, *Secrets of the Fascist Era*, Southern Illinois University Press, 1995, p. 31.

102 Piero Pisenti, *Una repubblica necessaria (RSI)*, Giovanni Volpe editore, Rome, 1977, pp. 92–8.

103 Montanelli, *Guerra Civile*, op. cit., p. 98.

104 *Gente*, nos 4–5, 1996, quoted in Moseley, op. cit., p. 205.

105 De Felice, *Mussolini l'alleato*, vol. II, op. cit., pp. 527–8.

106 McGraw Smyth, op. cit., p. 44.

107 The Cavallero confession is reprinted in Deakin, op. cit., appendix to part 3, book 1, pp. 647–53.

108 Press coverage of the trial, *La Stampa*, 12 January 1944.

109 Montanelli, *Guerra Civile*, op. cit, pp. 103–5.

110 Dolfin, op. cit., pp. 197, 201–2.

111 Susmel, *Vita sbagliata*, op. cit., pp. 352 seg.

112 Montanelli, *Guerra Civile*, op. cit., p. 96.

113 Fabrizio Ciano, *Quando il nonno fece fucilare papa*, Mondadori, Milan, 1993, pp. 96–8.

114 Garobbio, op. cit., p. 101.

115 Innocenti, *Salò*, op. cit., p. 116.

116 Repond, op. cit.

117 Moseley, op. cit., p. 252.

118 Pini and Susmel, op. cit., vol. IV, p. 407.

119 See Don Ennio Innocenti, *Disputa sulla conversione di Benito Mussolini*, Rome, 1995, quoted in Carradori, op. cit., pp. 138–9.

120 Montanelli, *Guerra Civile*, op. cit., pp. 121–2.

121 Eric Morris, *La guerra inutile. La campagna d'Italia 1943–45*, Milan, 1993 (first published as *The Useless War: the Italian Campaign 1943–45*).

122 Italian Documents, 049851, quoted in Lamb, op. cit., p. 100.

123 Eitel. F. Moellhausen, *La Carta perdente*, Sestante, Rome, 1947, p. 450, quoted

in Monelli, *piccolo borghese*, op. cit., p. 322.

124 Milza, op. cit., p. 844.

125 Innocenti, *Salò*, op. cit., p. 58.

126 Montanelli, *Guerra Civile*, op. cit., p. 134.

127 Lamb, op. cit., p. 115.

128 Italian Documents, 044541–56, quoted in Lamb, op. cit., pp. 116, 117–18.

129 *Scritti e discorsi*, 17, pp. 95–6.

130 Macmillan, op. cit., 29 October 1943, p. 270 and 26 March 1945, p. 724.

131 Montanelli, *Guerra Civile*, op. cit., p. 55.

132 Ibid., p. 58.

133 Ibid., p. 210.

134 Ibid., p. 135.

135 Ibid., p. 136.

136 *Scritti e discorsi*, 17, p. 72.

137 Garobbio, op. cit., p. 118.

138 Montanelli, *Guerra Civile*, op. cit., p. 148.

139 Gariboldi, *Pio XII, Hitler e Mussolini*, op. cit., pp. 205–45.

140 Montanelli, *Guerra Civile*, op. cit., pp. 185, 198; De Felice, *Rosso e Nero*, op. cit., p. 49.

141 See Lamb, op. cit., pp. 70–1; Monelli, *piccolo borghese*, op. cit., p. 414; Sergio Romano, *'La guerra delle memorie,'* in *Nuova storia contemporanea*, November–December 2000; Milza, op. cit., pp. 862–3.

142 Letter quoted in Kirkpatrick, op. cit., p. 584.

143 Lamb, op. cit., p. 71.

144 Monelli, *piccolo borghese*, op. cit., pp. 414–15.

145 Montanelli, *Guerra Civile*, op. cit., p. 194; Lamb, op. cit., pp. 275–7.

146 *Luce Sulla Storia D'Italia*, op. cit., no. 15, essay by Valerio Castronovo.

147 Montanelli, *Guerra Civile*, op. cit., p. 198.

148 Antonella Ercolani, *Gli ultimi giorni di Mussolini nei documenti inglesi e francesi*, Editrice Apes, Rome, 1998, pp. 12–13.

149 Lamb, op. cit., p. 232.

150 De Felice, *Rosso e Nero*, op. cit., p. 49.

151 De Felice, *Mussolini l'alleato*, vol. II, op. cit., p. 308.

17 The End [pp. 453–477]

1 Montanelli, *Guerra Civile*, op. cit., p. 98; Garobbio, op. cit., p. 262.

2 Petacco, *Il comunista*, op. cit., p. 200.

3 *Scritti e discorsi*, 18, pp. 39–52.

4 Innocenti, *Salò*, op. cit., p. 131.
5 Garobbio, op. cit., p. 54.
6 *Scritti e discorsi, 18*, pp. 53–57.
7 Ibid., pp. 63–79.
8 Letters in Ricciotti Lazzero, *Il sacco d'Italia*, Milan, 1994. Lazzero writes that he was handed these German intercepts of phone calls and letters by SS General Karl Wolff on 28 March 1973 in Munich.
9 Ibid., to Hitler, 28 February 1945.
10 Ibid., to Graziani, 7 March 1945.
11 Montanelli, op. cit., p. 207.
12 E. Mussolini, op. cit., pp. 225–7; Carradori, op. cit., p. 153.
13 *Scritti e discorsi, 18*, pp. 84–95.
14 Quoted in Monelli, *piccolo borghese*, p. 326.
15 Kirkpatrick, op. cit., pp. 598, 600.
16 Biggini diary quoted in Luciano Garibaldi, *Mussolini e il professore, Vita e diari di Carlo*, Mursia, Milan, 1983, pp. 321–2.
17 Tamaro, Due anni di storia, op. cit., p. 514.
18 See also Montanelli, *guerra civile*, p. 231.
19 W0204/11415, in Lamb, op. cit., p. 222.
20 Ercolani, op. cit., p. 10.
21 Quoted in Montanelli, op. cit., p. 232.
22 See Ercolani, op. cit., p. 36–7.
23 Massimo Salvadori, *The Labour and the Wounds, a personal chronicle of one man's fight for freedom*, Pall Mall Press, London, 1958, p. 226.
24 Montanelli, op. cit., p. 240.
25 Kirkpatrick, op. cit., p. 600.
26 Quoted in Garobbio, op. cit., p. 134.
27 Carradori, op. cit., p. 148.
28 See Ercolani, op. cit., pp. 34–5.
29 V. Mussolini, op. cit., p. 223.
30 Carradori, op. cit., p. 69.
31 Urbano Lazzaro, *L'oro di Dongo*, Mondadori, Milan, 1966, p. 16.
32 Monelli, *piccolo borghese*, op. cit., p. 331.
33 R. Mussolini, op. cit., p. 260.
34 See Ercolani, op. cit., p. 50. Chiocci, op. cit., p. 308.
35 Max Corvo [head of OSS/SI Italy 1943–5], *The OSS in Italy 1942–1945: a Personal Memoir*, Praeger, New York, 1990, pp. 250, 251–2.
36 For the relevant part of the text see Ercolani, op. cit., p. 34.
37 Figures in Milza, op. cit., p. 874.
38 Monelli, *piccolo borghese*, p. 335.
39 Pier Luigi Bellini delle Stelle (Pedro) and Urbano Lazzaro (Bill), *Dongo, La fine di Mussolini*, Mondadori, Milan, 1975, pp. 83, 96.
40 Ibid., p. 100.
41 Ibid., p. 160 and subsequent references, pp. 117–19, 131, 133.
42 Franco Bandini, author of *le ultime 95 ore di Mussolini*, Milan, 1968, writing in *Il Giornale* on 16 April 1996.
43 Bellini & Lazzaro, op. cit., pp. 149–50.
44 Marino Vigano, *Arresto e esecuzione di Mussolini nei rapporti della Guardia di finanza, Italia contemporanea*, March 1966, pp. 202, 117.
45 Bellini & Lazzaro, op. cit., pp. 154–6.
46 Ibid., p. 166.
47 Ibid., pp. 174–5.
48 Ibid., p. 181.
49 Monelli, *piccolo borghese*, op. cit., p. 281. Though they had hardly ever spent a night together this was not the first time.
50 Lamb, op. cit., p. 235.
51 Ercolani, op. cit., pp. 27, 46.
52 Interview in *Corriere della Sera's* magazine *Sette*, 11 July 1996.
53 Interview with Massimo Pini in *Sessant' anni di avventure e battaglie*, quoted in Montanelli, *Guerra Civile*, op. cit., pp. 246–7.
54 Salvadori, *The Labour and the Wounds*, op. cit., p. 227.
55 Salvadori, *Resistenza e azione: ricordi di un liberale*, Bastogi, Foggia, 1990, p. 239.
56 Ibid., pp. 239–40.
57 Ibid., pp. 239–40.
58 Ibid., p. 239.
59 Quoted in Bellini & Lazzaro, op. cit., p. 194.
60 Ibid., pp. 184–92.
61 Walter Audisio, *In nome del popolo italiano*, quoted in Montanelli, op. cit., p. 249.
62 Bellini & Lazzaro, op. cit., p. 195.
63 Author's interview with Urbano Lazzaro, 'Bill' April 1995.
64 Salvadori, *Labour and the Wounds*, op. cit., pp. 217–18.
65 *Panorama*, 3 December 1979.
66 *New York Times*, 31 March 1947.
67 *Corriere della Sera*, quoted in Giorgio Pisanò, *Le ultime cinque secondi di Mussolini*, Il Saggiatore, Milan, 1996, p. 170.
68 Author's interview, 1996.
69 Daddario's official report, quoted in Corvo, op. cit., p. 350.
70 De Felice, *Rosso e Nero*, op. cit., p. 145.

71 The eighteen corpses comprised the fifteen Fascist gerarchs executed at Dongo, plus Marcello Petacci, plus Mussolini and Claretta Petacci, see Monelli, *piccolo borghese*, op. cit. p. 414.

72 Eye witness account by the journalist, Gaetano Afeltra, in the *Corriere della Sera*, 8 April 1994.

73 Pisanò, op. cit., p. 185, Monelli, *piccolo borghese*, op. cit., p. 350.

74 Collier, op. cit., p. 437.

75 Montanelli, op. cit., p. 252.

76 Lamb, op. cit., p. 238.

77 Montanelli, op. cit., p. 255.

78 Lamb, op. cit., p. 236; Garobbio, op. cit., p. 82.

79 Diego de Castro, *Il problema di Trieste*, quoted in Montanelli, op. cit., p. 257.

80 Lamb, op. cit., p. 233.

81 Chiocci, op. cit., pp. 332–3.

82 Bertoldi, op. cit., p. 19.

83 Edda Ciano, *Il testamento di mio padre Benito*, Dino, 1990, p. 32.

INDEX

Index

Index

Index

Index

Index

Index

Index

Index

Index

Index

Index

GUILDFORD **college**

Learning Resource Centre

Please return on or before the last date shown.
No further issues or renewals if any items are overdue.

2 3 JUN 2008

- 3 MAR 2011

Class: 945.091 FAR

Title: Mussolini, A New Life

Author: Farrell, Nicholas

151737